ROSES

'Magnifica'

Peter Beales

ROSES

*An Illustrated Encyclopaedia and Grower's Handbook
of Species Roses, Old Roses and Modern Roses,
Shrub Roses and Climbers*

A John Macrae Book
HENRY HOLT AND COMPANY
NEW YORK

By the same author

CLASSIC ROSES
TWENTIETH-CENTURY ROSES

First published in the United States in 1992 by Henry Holt
and Company, Inc., 115 West 18th Street, New York,
New York 10011.

First published in Great Britain in 1992 by Harvill,
an imprint of HarperCollins Publishers.

Library of Congress Catalog Card Number: 91–58153

ISBN 0–8050–2053–5

Henry Holt books are available at special discounts
for bulk purchases for sales promotions, premiums,
fund-raising, or educational use. Special editions
or book excerpts can also be created to specification.

For details contact:
Special Sales Director
Henry Holt and Company, Inc.
115 West 18th Street
New York, New York 10011

First American Edition—1992

Recognizing the importance of preserving the written
word, Henry Holt and Company, Inc., by policy, prints
all its first editions on acid-free paper. ∞

Printed in Hong Kong
by Dai Nippon Printing Co.
Hong Kong Ltd.

1 3 5 7 9 10 8 6 4 2

Preface

Between them Classic Roses, published in 1985, and *Twentieth-Century Roses*, which followed some three years later, cover fairly comprehensively the *genus rosa*. So initially, when the idea to combine them into one volume was conceived, I thought that the merger would be relatively simple. Not so, for as I progressed, I found myself not only revising and rewriting considerable sections of the first parts of each book, but updating, restructuring descriptions, and adding over three hundred additional species and hybrids to the combined Dictionary, thus bringing the total number of roses to 1900, no less than 140 of which are wild roses or species.

Fascinating to prepare were the height and colour charts for Appendix B. These, I hope, will make the choosing of roses for specific purposes a little easier, whether for the amateur selecting just one or two varieties or the professional planning a complete new garden.

Although some illustrations from the two previous books have been used, albeit in different format, by far the majority are new and, except for a few which were kindly loaned, were photographed as I came upon their subjects, at various times of the day in nature's own light and in an assortment of weathers, either in my own garden or in various gardens around the world.

Some readers who know that my first love is for the older roses may well raise their eyebrows at the comprehensive nature of this book; but those who know me better and have seen my garden will be aware of my roving eye and of the fact that, in the height of the rose season, whilst captivated by the grace, charm and beauty of the old, I frequently fall for modern varieties and grow them side by side in close embrace.

Leaving aside matters of taste, I believe some modern varieties will in time be treasured as beauties from the past; never again should so many good, contemporary varieties be allowed to fall by the wayside as has happened since about 1930; varieties now sought after by breeders and gardeners alike.

In my researches for this and my other books I have inevitably learned a great deal more about my subject than I knew when I started to write. Furthermore, there is no better way to get to know roses intimately than through a camera lens, and as a result I have come to enjoy them just a little more, and so I hope, as you read on, will you. Then publication will have been worthwhile and my purpose will have been fulfilled.

PETER BEALES
Attleborough, Norfolk
August 1991

Acknowledgements

Without numerous contributions from others I fear this book would be somewhat sterile. In fact it would have been much more difficult to write, if not impossible, had it not been for the generosity of many friends and colleagues. It is impossible to mention them all by name but I wish to express my warmest thanks and appreciation to all the following.

For their individual, direct contributions – Jack Harkness for his chapter on Classifications, Lorna Mercer for her descriptions of the Bermudian mystery roses, Malcolm Manners for his essay on Mosaic Virus and Malcolm Lowe for his piece on the Japanese Beetle and other American pests and diseases.

For allowing me to take photographs of, or to include pictures of their gardens, J. P. Agawal, Sally and Bey Allison, Richard Balfour, Natalie Brooke, David and Shirley Cargill, Henry Cecil, Donna Fuss, Trevor and Dixie Griffiths, Malcolm and Irene Lowe, Clair Martin III, Bill and Lorna Mercer, Keith Money, Trevor Nottle, John Ottaway, Lord and Lady Prior, William and Meredyth Proby, Nigel and Judy Pratt, Raymond J. Rogers, Deane and Maureen Ross, David Ruston, James Russell, Lady Salisbury, Stephen Scanniello, Elizabeth Schultz, Mike and Jean Shupe, David Steen, David Stone, Toni Sylvester, Graham Stuart Thomas, Lord and Lady Tollemache, Lord and Lady Walpole, Miriam Wilkins, Pat Wiley and Barbara Worl, and those listed elsewhere who kindly loaned me photographs.

The owners, administrators and head gardeners of the following historic or public gardens: Blickling Hall, Birmingham University, Brooklyn Botanic Gardens New York, Cambridge Botanic Gardens, Camden House Bermuda, Edinburgh Botanic Garden, Harlow Carr, Hidcote Manor, Kiftsgate Court, Kew Gardens, Leeds Castle, Mottisfont Abbey, the Parnell Rose Gardens Auckland, Sissinghurst Castle, the Royal National Rose Society, Syon Park, the Royal Horticultural Society, the Royal Hospital Chelsea, Saville Gardens, Queen Mary's Rose Garden, the Institute of Floriculture New Delhi, the National Arboretum Washington DC and the American Rose Society.

My thanks are also extended to many members of rose societies who freely gave their time to chauffeur me around to gardens during my visits to their countries. They are too many to mention individually, but the societies to which they belong are – the Heritage Rose Society of South Australia, the Bermuda Rose Society, the Canadian Rose Society, the Indian Rose Society, Heritage Roses New Zealand, the Northern Ireland Rose Society and the South-West Regional Heritage Rose Society, USA.

I owe special thanks to the following members of the Harvill team who have produced this book from what, to me, seemed just a muddle of papers and photographs: Christopher MacLehose who has supported me through thick and thin – not always in publishing matters – thanks Christopher; Bill Swainson, my editor, who was a constant inspiration; Jane Powell for her help in botanic matters; Vera Brice whose artistry has brought forth this design; and Lucy Rutherford who dealt with the printers and kept us all on target.

I must thank two other teams for their help: my staff, for running the nursery during my frequent absences, especially managers Heather Friend and Ian Limmer; and my family, Joan, my wife, and Amanda and Richard, who were not only of immense help in so many material ways but were, and always are, an inspiration.

The Photographs

The author and publishers wish to thank the following people and companies for contributing the photographs listed below. All other photographs are by Peter Beales.

David Austin: Brother Cadfael, Chianti, Country Living, The Countryman, Evelyn, Fair Bianca, Gertrude Jekyll, Graham Thomas, L. D. Braithwaite, The Pilgrim, The Prince, Sharifa Asma, Wife of Bath, Winchester Cathedral.

Richard Balfour: Gardens: Deutsches Rosarium, Westfalenpark, Dortmund; Municipal Rose Gardens, Genoa; Palmengarten, Frankfurt; Parque de Oeste, Madrid; Roseraie de l'Hay-les-Roses, Paris; Roseraie du Parc de Bagatelle, Paris; Roseraie du Parc de la Tête d'Or, Lyon.
Roses: Anisley Dickson, Anna Ford, Anne Harkness, Baby Masquerade, Blue Moon, Champneys' Pink Cluster, Cinderella, Clarissa, Dresden Doll, Easlea's Golden Rambler, Eden Rose, Eleanor, Geranium, Honorine de Brabant, King's Ransom, Lavender Jewel, Masquerade, Nozomi, Orange Sunblaze, Peek-a-boo, Penelope Keith, Pink Favourite, Red Ace, Regensberg, Robin Redbreast, *R. davidii, R. fargesii, R. macrophylla, R. moyesii, R. primula, R. rugosa rubra,* Scarlet Gem, Sutters Gold, Tricolore de Flandre, Wedding Day, Wee Jock.

John Beales: Reformat of pictures previous published in *Classic Roses* (1985): Eugénie Guinoisseau, Henri Fouquier, Omar Khayyam, Président de Sèze, Ritter von Barmstede, *R. gallica officinalis,* Sanders White.

Cants Roses: Buck's Fizz, Dame Wendy, Ingrid Bergman.

Dickson Nurseries: Harvest Fayre, Melody Maker, New Horizon, Painted Moon, Pink Chimio, Red Trail, Tequila Sunrise, Valentine Heart.

Fryer's Roses: Reformat of pictures previously published in *Twentieth Century Roses* (1988): Mini Metro, Sweet Dream.

Betty Harkness: Armada, By Appointment, Euphrates, Golden Years, Harold Macmillan, Jacqueline du Pré, Nigel Hawthorne, Pandora, Phoebe, Radox Bouquet, Savoy Hotel, Tigris.

W. Kordes Sönne: Anna Livia, City of Birmingham, Congratulations, Mary Hayley-Bell, Partridge, Perestroika, Suffolk, Surrey.

Hazel le Rougetel: Previously published in *Twentieth-Century Roses* (1988): Corylus.

Mattocks Roses via Poulsens, Denmark: Essex, Kent, Norfolk, Northamptonshire, Queen Mother, Sussex, Warwickshire.

Bill Mercer: Baronne Henriette de Snoy, Brightside Cream, Duchesse de Brabant, Emily Gray, Général Schablikine, Homère, Maitland White, Mme Berkeley, Maman Cochet, Miss Attwood, Mrs Dudley Cross, Smith's Parish, Trinity, Vincent Godsiff, White Maman Cochet.

Keith Money: Albertine, *R. californica plena:* H.T. roses with sundial.

New Rose Marketing: Penthouse, Regensberg, Sexy Rexy, Tango.

Vincent Page: Reformat of pictures previously published in *Classic Roses* (1985) and *Twentieth Century Roses* (1988): Clarissa, Cosimo Ridolfi, Frühlingsmorgen, Mme Grégoire Staechelin, Master Hugh, Petite Lisette, Petite Orléonaise, Pink Perpétue, *R. kochiana, R. luciae, R. pisocarpa, R. setipoda.*

Thomas Robinson: Guernsey Love, Jenny Robinson, Joan Ball.

Warner Roses: Laura Ashley, Laura Ford, Warm Welcome.

Whartons Nurseries: Hotline.

Trevor White: Cécile Brünner, Scotch Double White, Louis XIV, *R. nitida.*

Contents

Preface   v
Acknowledgements   vi
The Photographs   vi

PART I
THE CLASSICS FROM THE PAST   1

The First Roses: an Introduction   3
Wild Roses and their Distribution   4
The Old Garden Roses and their Origins   8

PART II
THE DEVELOPMENT OF MODERN ROSES   27

Classification Systems   63
Some Thoughts on Rose Classification (by Jack Harkness, OBE)   66

PART III
ROSES IN THE LANDSCAPE   71

Choosing Roses for Poorer Soils   72
Old Roses in the Landscape   73
Modern Roses in the Landscape   101

PART IV
THE DICTIONARY   111

Genus ROSA

Subgenus HULTHEMIA (Simplicifoliae)   117
H. persica, × *Hulthemosa hardii*   118

Subgenus HESPERHODOS   121
R. stellata; *R. stellata mirifica*

Subgenus PLATYRHODON   123
R. roxburghii

Subgenus EUROSA (Rosa)

Section BANKSIANAE   125
R. banksiae, forms and hybrids   126
R. cymosa
R. × *fortuniana*

Section LAEVIGATAE   127
R. laevigata, forms and hybrids

Section BRACTEATAE   129
R. bracteata and hybrid

Section PIMPINELLIFOLIAE   133
R. ecae, forms and hybrids   133
R. foetida (Austrian Briars), forms and hybrids   134
R. × *hemisphaerica*   135
R. hugonis, forms and hybrids; *R.* × *involuta*; *R. koreana*   136
R. pimpinellifolia (Scotch Roses), forms and hybrids   137
R. × *hibernica*   140
R. primula; *R.* × *pteragonis*; *R.* × *reversa*; *R.* × *sabinii*;   141
    R. sericea, forms and hybrids
R. xanthina and hybrids   142

Section GALLICANAE   143
R. gallica (Gallicas), forms and hybrids   143
R. × *centifolia* (Cabbage or Provence Roses), forms and hybrids   153
R. × *centifolia muscosa* (Mosses), forms and hybrids   156
Damasks   164
Portlands   169
R. macrantha, forms and hybrids   172
R. × *richardii*   172

Section CANINAE   173
R. agrestis   173
R. × *alba* (Albas), forms and hybrids   175
R. biebersteinii; *R. britzensis*   177
R. canina (Dog Rose), forms and hybrids   177
R. × *collina*; *R. corymbifera*; *R. dumales*   179
R. eglanteria (Sweet Briar), forms and hybrids   179
R. glauca, forms and hybrids   182
R. inodora; *R. jundzillii*; *R. micrantha*; *R. mollis*; *R. orientalis*;   183
    R. pulverulenta; *R. serafinii*; *R. sherardii*; *R. sicula*; *R. stylosa*
    R. tomentosa; *R. villosa*; *R. villosa duplex*; *R. waitziana*

Section CAROLINAE   185
R. carolina, forms and hybrids   187
R. foliosa; *R.* × *kochiana*; *R.* × *mariae-graebnerae*; *R. nitida*;   187
    R. palustris
R. virginiana, forms and hybrids   188

Section CASSIORHODON (CINNAMOMEAE)   189
R. acicularis; *R. acicularis nipponensis*; *R. amblyotis*; *R. arkansana*;   191
    R. banksiopsis; *R. beggeriana*; *R. bella*; *R. blanda*; *R. californica*;
    R. californica plena; *R. caudata*; *R. coriifolia froebelii*; *R.* × *coryana*;
    R. corymbulosa; *R. davidii*; *R. davurica*; *R. farreri persetosa*;
    R. fedtschenkoana; *R. forrestiana*; *R. gymnocarpa*; *R. hemsleyana*;
    R. kamtchatica
R. × *kordesii*, forms and hybrids   193
R. latibracteata   194
R. × *l'heritieriana* (Boursaults)   196
R. macrophylla, forms and hybrids   197
R. majalis; *R. marretii*; *R. maximowicziana*; *R. melina*;   198
    R. × *micrugosa*; *R. mohavensis*
R. moyesii, forms and hybrids   199
R. fargesii; *R. holodonta*   201
R. multibracteata, forms and hybrids   201

R. murielae; R. nanothamnus   202
R. nutkana, forms and hybrids   202
R. × paulii; R. pendulina; R. pisocarpa; R. prattii; R. pyrifera   202
R. rugosa (Rugosas), forms and hybrids   203
R. sertata; R. setipoda; R. spaldingii; R. suffulta; R. sweginzowii   213
    macrocarpa; R. ultramontana; R. wardii; R. webbiana;
    R. willmottiae; R. woodsii; R. woodsii fendleri; R. yainacensis

Section   SYNSTYLAE   215
R. anemoneflora   215
R. arvensis (Ayrshires), forms and hybrids   216
R. brunonii and hybrid   217
R. × dupontii   217
R. filipes and hybrids   219
R. gentiliana   219
R. helenae and hybrid   219
R. henryi; R. longicuspis; R. luciae   219
R. moschata (Musks), forms and hybrids   220
R. mulliganii   222
R. multiflora, forms and hybrids   222
Hybrid Musks   223
Multiflora Ramblers   230
Modern Climbing Roses   236
Modern Shrub Roses   245
Polyanthas   257
Floribundas   259
Climbing Floribundas   286
Procumbents (Ground-Cover Roses)   288
Miniatures and Patios (Compact Floribundas)   298
R. phoenicia; R. polliniana; R. rubus   310
R. sempervirens, forms and hybrids   310
R. setigera and hybrids   311
R. sinowilsonii and hybrid   312
R. soulieana and hybrids   312
R. wichuraiana and hybrids   313

Section   CHINENSIS   321
R. gigantea and hybrids   321
R. chinensis (Chinas), forms and hybrids   323
Bourbons   329
Climbing Bourbons, forms and hybrids   337
Noisettes   338
Teas   342
Bermuda Roses   351
Hybrid Perpetuals   352
English Roses   365
Hybrid Teas   373
Climbing Hybrid Teas   411

PART V

THE CULTIVATION OF ROSES   419

Choosing and Buying Roses   421
Planting   423

Pruning   425
Weed Control   429
Propagation of Roses   430
Pests and Diseases   435
Malformation of Flowers   440
Other Ailments   441
Commercial Production   441
Breeding New Varieties   442

APPENDICES

A. World Climatic Map   444
B. Height and Colour Charts   445
C. Rose Societies of the World   458
D. Rose Gardens of the World   459
E. Rose Producers and Suppliers of the World   461

Glossary   462
Further Reading   462
General Index   464
Index of Roses   465

PART I
The Classics from the Past

R. alba 'Semi-plena'

'Duchess of Portland'

The First Roses

Introduction

Privileged, I was, to be born and brought up in the countryside, and although I did not become a rose grower until the age of sixteen, I was well aware of nature's wild roses long before that age; the roses of slow meanderings through country lanes returning from school on hot, balmy days in June. It was wartime and hedges were thriving in glorious neglect, so between daydreams I espied Dog Roses at their very best, for where hedges grow so Dog Roses flourish. Later, when hips were ripe and orange in the autumn, I collected them at half-a-crown a stone for the war effort. I learned to notice subtle variations in the colour, shape and growth habits of those wild species and, from time to time, came upon a white one, different not only in colour of flower but in colour of stem, shape of leaf and habit of growth. Later I learned that this was the Field Rose, *Rosa arvensis*, and that the Dog Rose was *Rosa canina*. Those hedges have long since gone but a lonely plant or *R. arvensis* and a few *R. canina* still live on in a small stretch so far saved from the plough. A simple childhood memory, but the beginning of a lifetime's fascination with roses and the on-going desire to learn all I can about them.

The two species I encountered as a child do not, in themselves, form the ancestral beginnings of any particular modern rose, although *R. canina* can stake a claim as progenitor of that beautiful group, the Albas, and *R. arvensis* was responsible for starting off those interesting ramblers, the Ayrshires.

The genesis of roses and their subsequent early evolution must inevitably be a matter for conjecture, but there is good reason to suppose, from fossilized evidence and the rose's present-day distribution, that it has flourished in some form since remote prehistoric times. It is likely that the garden cultivation of roses began only some 5000 years ago, probably in China. It is tempting to believe – romantic fancy though it may be – that the practical uses and attractions of the rose were recognized by early man, perhaps widely separated on different continents long before, possibly in Neolithic times.

Indeed, it seems likely that the edible properties of the rose would have been appreciated even before it became prized for its

R. canina hips

aesthetic qualities. The nutty, sweet, succulent tips of the shoots of such species as the common Dog Rose, of my childhood memory, are quite tasty; and later in the year much nourishment and, as we now know, vitamin C supplement could have been extracted from the fleshy skin of the fruit of this and similar species. We would be arrogant indeed if we assumed that our primitive ancestors were not capable of deriving pleasure from the scent, form and colour of what, even in its simplest form, is an incomparably beautiful flower.

During this long period of evolution, of course, any changes which have occurred in the genus *Rosa* have been subtle and brought about by nature. Less subtle, though, has been man's intervention, especially that which has taken place over the last few centuries, for in seeking his ideal of perfection he has brought about immense changes in the shape, form, colour, floriferousness and growth habits of nature's original pure roses to provide us with a vast and unrivalled family of garden plants.

Some may argue that we humans have now, as so often, gone too far and that the genus has been a victim rather than a triumph of progress, and it is true that some of the haphazard creations of the early breeders have the most graceful forms, and wear the most compelling perfumes. Comparisons, though, are odious for, as in all things, tastes vary. Judgement as to the merits of one rose over another can only be made against very arbitrary criteria.

Much of the detail of man's early work in manipulating nature has to be conjecture, but surely all was not left to the bees? Haphazard though it must have been, there can be little doubt that during those early days of civilization, both in the Mediterranean and in the Far East, deliberate hybrids were raised. It was not until horizons were broadened, with travel becoming more commonplace, that it became possible for makers of roses to mix and match species from different parts of the world to release the potential of the genus.

Wild Roses and their Distribution

The species of the genus *Rosa* can be conveniently divided into four groups, each from geographically defined areas of the northern hemisphere where they are to be found growing wild. These areas are Europe, Asia, the Middle East and America. There is no evidence that any species evolved naturally south of the Equator.

Except for a few which are double or semi-double and are, therefore, the result of natural hybridity or mutation and not true species, all wild roses have single flowers comprised of five petals;

Top: R. arvensis and above left: R. sericea pteracantha and right, R. pimpinellifolia

R. virginiana

R. villosa

R. multiflora

R. gymnocarpa

European Wild Roses

The European wild roses include the Dog Rose, *R. canina*, and two similar species which are, perhaps, related to it: *R. eglanteria*, the Eglantine Rose or Sweet Briar, and *R. villosa*, the Apple Rose. All of them may be found in a variety of habitats, especially in central areas and the north of the continent. *R. arvensis*, the Field Rose, on the other hand, is a natural climber and can be found in the same latitudes but mostly in hedgerows, scrambling through and being supported by a variety of other flora. *R. pimpinellifolia*, until recently better known as *R. spinosissima* or the Scotch Rose, inhabits coastal regions and less fertile areas, especially colder areas. It is notable for its prickly nature and bushy growth.

Further south, although less commonly now since the increase in the human population and all the problems this brings to nature, *R. gallica* can be found; its origins are perhaps more widely distributed than those of the other European species, since this rose can also be found, from time to time, growing wild further east. Another species occasionally found wild in southern regions but with a preference for the warmer climate of the Mediterranean shores is *R. moschata*. This rose, too, may well have been introduced from further east.

All of these species have, throughout the ages, played their part, as will be seen later, in the book, to a greater or lesser extent as studs in the development of the modern rose.

The American Wild Roses

Two of the most important wild roses native to the North American continent are *R. virginiana* and *R. carolina*. Important not because they have played any part in the development of modern rose, but because, with the shorter-growing *R. nitida*, they have become valuable garden plants in their own right and, as such, useful in fulfilling a variety of roles from hedgerow to ground-cover plants; likewise, *R. palustris*, the Swamp Rose, but to a lesser extent. *R. blanda* and *R. gymnocarpa* are perhaps the American continent's nearest equivalents to Europe's Dog Rose, at least in appearance and habit, and *R. foliolosa*, preferring the more temperate zones, is the most distinctive in that it is free of thorns and has almost grass-like foliage.

One important native of this region, though, has played its part

except one, *R. sericea*, which has just four. All, in their natural habitat, will reproduce true-to-type from seeds when pollinated by themselves or others of the same species; earlier evolution having guaranteed survival in hostile conditions and against predators by furnishing most of them with thorns, and giving most of them scent and colour to attract insects, vital for the reproductive process.

Whilst writing of American native roses it is worth mentioning at this point that several other species now grow wild all over America, having escaped from gardens at some time since their introduction during the last 200 years; and some of them enjoy their new-found habitats so much that they are seen far more commonly than their native counterparts. *R. multiflora* in particular, originally from Asia, is now considered a weed, and in the warmer areas *R. laevigata* has become so much at home as to be known as the 'Cherokee Rose'. *R. gigantea* also flourishes in the lower-rainfall areas of the south and west.

Oriental and Asian Wild Roses

The most important of the numerous species from Asia and the Orient is *R. indica*, now more correctly *R. chinensis*, which undoubtedly existed during the early Chinese dynasties although it now seems to be extinct, at least in the wild. What is certain is that it was once alive and well and this, or forms of this recurrent rose, could well have been cultivated by gardeners in China around 3000 BC. Much later, genes from this species, introduced by others by breeding, laid the foundations for our familiar modern recurrent roses. It is a sad paradox that such an important stud rose should, in its true form, have become extinct even in its native land, and its demise was probably the sin of nurserymen the whole world over, the arrogant assumption that new strains are essentially better than old.

Other fascinating species growing wild in the Far East are *R. laevigata* and *R. bracteata*, distinct but with similar characteristics. Both are climbers and have very large, single, white flowers with pronounced stamens, glossy foliage and large, cruel barbs. As already stated, these both now grow wild in America. Quite the opposite is *R. banksiae* with its smooth, light-green foliage, long, pliable, thornless shoots and large clusters of flowers.

The huge and abundant trusses of *R. multiflora* make a superb display in the wild, its generous nature now forming the basis of many modern cluster-flowered roses from Floribundas to shrub roses and ramblers. Another cluster-flowererd species with climbing instincts is *R. wichuraiana*. This species, when used as a seed parent by breeders at the turn of this century, yielded some of our best-loved ramblers, notably 'Albertine', 'Albéric Barbier', 'Emily Gray' and 'New Dawn'. Many other less well-known, ancient species flourished in various parts of Asia and the Orient, amongst them *R. brunonii* and *R. filipes*, and in the same area can be found several of the species which bear elongated or flagon-shaped hips,

as a parent to modern roses: *R. setigera*, from which has come the ubiquitous rambler 'Baltimore Belle', amongst several others. A distinguishing feature of all America's wild roses is colourful autumn foliage and, while their flowers may all lack any strength of fragrance, they make up for this with an extra intensity of colour.

Thumbing through the 1917 edition of the *American Rose Annual* I came upon an interesting article by Wilhelm Miller, a landscape architect from Chicago. In it, he wrote: 'About ninety per cent of the commonest landscape problems can be solved with the aid of nine species of wild roses.' Six of these were the American species already mentioned; the other three were *R. rugosa*, *R. multiflora* and *R. wichuraiana*, all from Asia. I am heavily biased of course but, even allowing for a change in 'commonest problems' since 1917, if ten per cent were solved by roses these days, some unimaginative so-called 'landscape schemes' I know of could be, if not solved, made more interesting.

Top: R. wichuraiana at Mannington Hall
Above left: 'Fru. Dagmar Hartopp' and *right, R. moyesii* hips

such as *R. moyesii*. Southern Asia and Japan are the homes of *R. rugosa* where it grows so freely from seed. Its promiscuity has resulted in many and varied offspring since it came west, notably the hybrids 'Roseraie de l'Hay', 'Blanc Double de Coubert' and 'Fru Dagmar Hartopp'.

R. multiflora

R. brunonii

The Wild Roses of the Middle East

This area is best seen in our minds as covering both eastern Europe and western Asia, as well as the piece in between. It is here that we can find the only true yellow species, in the form of *R. foetida*, and nowadays yellow rose species are few and far between. Closely related are two forms, probably garden hybrids or natural mutations that occurred in the distant past – *R. foetida bicolor*, although this could have occurred anywhere at any time, and *R. foetida persiana*, the double form. The strangely shaped, very double *R. hemisphaerica* is obviously closely related to *R. foetida* but has never been seen in the wild, nor apparently has the almost extinct single form of this species. Both are rather tender in Europe so they must have come from the warmer parts of the region. *R. foetida* is, more often than not, sterile, so one wonders if this too is not a hybrid of some yellow species now extinct.

Two other roses, both hybrids, have their origins shrouded in mystery, but the probably now extinct species that sired them

R. foetida

R. banksiae lutea

undoubtedly lived in this part of the world; they are *R.* × *damascena* and *R.* × *centifolia*, both in their forms very double and therefore incapable of perpetuating themselves except by vegetative propagation. *R.* × *damascena*, of course, and some of its forms have been very important in parts of this region for centuries as the source of attar of roses, so it is not difficult to understand that a rose grown in such vast quantities would, from time to time, yield mutations or, indeed, new chance hybrids. However, the origins of *R.* × *centifolia* are extremely obscure; we can surmise that it simply developed naturally from a single fertile form which once existed in the wild, but more likely it is a hybrid prized for its beauty and important as another commercial high yielder of attar, brought to Europe by traders and developed in its present-day form by the Dutch, who are said to have bred many varieties in the seventeenth and eighteenth centuries.

R. × *centifolia*

The Old Garden Roses and their Origins

Centifolias (Provence Roses)

It was in the fifteenth and sixteenth centuries that man began to interfere with the progeny of the rose to much effect. The Dutch, in particular, did pioneering work, especially in selected improved strains of *R.* × *centifolia* and its hybrids. Proof of this comes from the frequent appearance of these blowsy, many-petalled roses in the works of the Old Masters, captured in perpetuity, sometimes with equally well-proportioned ladies of the era.

Examination by plant cytologists in recent years of the chromosomes of *R.* × *centifolia* prove beyond doubt that it is a complex hybrid and not, as previously thought, a true species. Apparently the Centifolias are made up of genes from *R. gallica*, *R. phoenicia*, *R. moschata*, *R. canina* and *R. damascena*. The late Dr C. V. Hurst* declared that they were one of the youngest groups, developed in Holland some 300 years ago, contradicting the belief, based on references to 'hundred-petalled roses' as early as 300 BC, that they were among the oldest. When and how such a complex line of hybridity occurred is open to speculation. If, as is said, the Dutch introduced over 200 variations or varieties of Centifolias between 1580 and 1710, this is a tremendous quantity of roses, suggesting a very fertile parent stock. One wonders how much of the work done by the Dutch was wholly original. Might they have used single or semi-double clones from warmer climates, thus building on work done by earlier civilizations? And did they perhaps witness the gradual extinction of originals in favour of over 200 novelties? There are no records to determine the origins of *R.* × *centifolia*, which is likely to remain yet another fascinating horticultural mystery.

As garden plants, it must be said, they leave something to be desired, being awkward and ungainly in growth and rather prone to mildew. However, with support, they are easily manageable and, in good weather, rewarding, with very beautiful, superbly scented, cabbage-like flowers. Their foliage is coarse and darkish-green and their shoots are very thorny.

* Dr Hurst's work is collated and documented in Graham Stuart Thomas's book *The Old Shrub Roses*.

Damasks

With the decline of the Roman Empire, roses lost much of their importance, and it was not until the Crusaders of the twelfth and thirteenth centuries brought back specimens of Damask roses from their travels to the Middle East that they once more became popular in Europe. When they proved sufficiently hardy to withstand the rigours of a more northerly latitude, they soon found their way into the gardens of noblemen and rich merchants, some of whom turned them to profit. The petals were used for making perfume and for their tenuous medical properties exploited by the apothecaries of the day. The 'Autumn Damask' known as 'Quatre Saisons' in France would have been particularly valuable as the first rose in Europe to produce two crops of flowers every summer. There may have been more varieties in those days but there are fewer Damasks to choose from today than any other group. To the experienced eye they are distinctive in that they have grey downy soft-textured foliage and their shoots are almost always very thorny, with the flowers borne on rather short, flexible stalks.

'Quatre Saisons'

Mosses

The first Moss rose apparently emerged as a sport from a Centifolia prior to the mid-eighteenth century. In the early nineteenth century a few single-flowered forms appeared in their ranks, enabling a few hybridists to cross them with hybrids from other groups in an attempt to prolong their flowering period, but this was soon discontinued.

Rivers', Woods' and Hooker's catalogues listed some thirty between them and Paul listed thirty-two Moss roses in *The Rose Garden* (10th ed., 1903). Many of these probably came about by seedlings raised haphazardly and in large numbers, yielding a small proportion of moss-bearing offspring which, in turn, were selected for this propensity – rather than for the high quality of their flowers. Nowadays many of us still appreciate the Moss rose but we are more selective when it comes to quality.

Top left: 'Common Moss', and *right,* Laneii.
Below: 'William Lobb'

Gallicas ('Roses of Provins')

Before the introduction of the Damasks the major source of medicine and rose oil in Europe was presumably the 'Apothecary's Rose' or 'Red Damask', *R. gallica officinalis*, later to become the emblem of the Lancastrians. This was the rose which 'sported' to produce the legendary striped rose *R. gallica versicolor*, better known perhaps as 'Rosa Mundi', named, it is said, after 'Fair Rosamund', mistress of King Henry II. If this romantic legend has

any validity – and it seems plausible that such a striking sport would have created quite a sensation at that time – this would date it from the mid-twelfth century; but it could well have been brought back to England as a novelty by some crusading knight, implying an earlier origin. Whatever the origin of 'Rosa Mundi', I have no doubt that a striped rose of some variety existed at the time of Henry II, for the Gallicas are a very old race indeed. They also figure to some extent in the ancestry of many other roses, including some of our present-day modern hybrids. As garden plants they are most amenable with no variety exceeding 4′ in height. When in flower in midsummer no other group of old roses can challenge them for quantity and, more often than not, quality. What is more they are easy to grow and will tolerate even the poorest soil. Their foliage is variable but, in most varieties, it is darkish green and their shoots have few thorns of consequence.

R. gallica officinalis

'Semi-plena'

R. gallica versicolor 'Rosa Mundi'

'Maiden's Blush'

Albas (White Roses)

Although normally I dislike putting roses into any sort of pecking order, since they all have their attributes, faults and appeal according to taste, the Albas occupy a high position in my league table.

They are a beautiful and intrepid group, going far back in time, and although there is some uncertainty about their origins and the early parentage of the original form, a few varieties certainly existed in medieval times. Their foliage, fruit and stems are rather similar to, if more refined than *R. canina*, supporting the belief that they are all derived from this species, the other parent being either *R.* × *damascena* or *R. gallica*. All of the dozen or so varieties of this group grown today are blessed with a strong constitution and start to flower in mid- to late June. Few other types of rose can match their refinement of texture and quality of perfume. All are of pastel shades from pure white through to clear deep pink.

The Flower Garden, an old gardening book of 1840, lists forty-two distinct varieties, quite a few of whose names I have not seen recorded elsewhere and which are probably simply variations of *R.* × *alba* 'Maxima' or 'Maiden's Blush', varieties I frequently get asked to identify each year. These two varieties between them have more alternative names than any others I know. 'Maiden's Blush' has been known over the years as 'La Royale', 'La Séduisante', 'La Virginale', 'Incarnata' and 'Cuisse de Nymphe', a slightly deeper form having the name 'Cuisse de Nymphe Emue'. It was this rose, growing in the garden of my birthplace in north Norfolk and affectionately known as 'Grandad's Rose', which first excited my curiosity and led to my lifelong affinity with roses. I have a vivid childhood memory of enjoying this rose, drawn to her no doubt by her 'expensive' perfume which seemed to pervade the entire garden each June. Despite years of neglect, this old plant is still growing exactly where I remember it, and will certainly out-live me. It gives me pleasure to know that her offspring are now growing in many places around the world since it was from this very plant that I obtained my first budding eyes of this old variety when starting my nursery twenty-three years ago.

The several names for *R. alba* 'Maxima' indicate an auspicious rose, for they include 'Bonnie Prince Charlie's Rose', 'Jacobite Rose', 'Cheshire Rose' and White Rose of York'. The true 'White Rose of York', however, was probably a specific single form of *R.* × *alba*, though I wonder sometimes if it might have been the white form of the common Dog Rose?

Chinas

From paintings and other artefacts depicting roses there is ample evidence that the Chinese were growing roses of considerable hybridity as early as the tenth century and probably long before. Certainly, during the sixteenth century, occasional visitors to China and other parts of the Far East reported sightings of roses which bloomed for a very long season. Later, in the eighteenth century, as travels from Europe to the East steadily increased, plant material was collected in great quantities; it is therefore not surprising that some of the old Chinese garden varieties should find their way to Europe.

In 1781 a pink form of *R. chinensis*, now known as 'Old Blush', was planted in Holland and soon reached England. Some eight years later a red form was found growing in Calcutta and brought to England by a captain of the British East India Company. It soon found favour and was variously named *R. semperflorens*, the 'Bengal Rose' and 'Slater's Crimson China'. This rose and 'Old Blush',

R. chinensis (an unnamed form, see p. 12)

then called 'Parson's Pink China', were between them responsible for the remontancy factors in most of our modern roses. Although 'Slater's Crimson China' is now seldom seen, having been superseded by such excellent red Chinas as 'Gloire de Rosomanes' in 1825 and 'Cramoisi Superieur' in 1832, 'Old Blush' is quite common, blessed as it is with considerable longevity and a fond liking, it seems, for neglect.

As mentioned earlier, *R. chinensis* is now thought to be extinct in the wild and I became excited in 1983 when I received a batch of cuttings and some seed from China labelled *R. chinensis*. These came at quite the wrong time of year for ideal propagation but some of the staff of the John Innes Institute in Norwich and Jim Russell of Castle Howard quickly agreed to help me spread the risk and consequently, between us, we have raised several plants, both from the seeds and some of the cuttings and although these all came from the same parent plant the number of petals (which are reddish pink) varies from five on some plants to as many as eighteen on others.

This rose and one or two other garden hybrids from China came

Top: 'Old Blush'; *below:* 'Sanguinea'

'Tipsy Imperial Concubine'

to me via Mrs Hazel le Rougetel, who visited China in 1982. One in particular is a charming Tea with shapely flowers of sulphur-yellow flushed pinkish-red. Hazel tells me that its name translated from the Chinese is 'The Tipsy Imperial Concubine'!

Portlands

Towards the end of the eighteenth century a rose of much significance appeared in France. Its origins were obscure, as is so often the case, but its habit of flowering almost continuously throughout the season won it instant favour. It arrived there by way of England with the name *R. portlandica* but later became known as 'Duchess of Portland', after the 3rd Duchess of Portland,* who is reputed to have brought it to England from Italy. It is said to have originated from a cross between a Damask × Gallica seedling and an unknown China rose, probably 'Slater's Crimson', a mating which is thought to have established, at least in part, the invaluable remontancy habit of many of our present-day roses.

Having observed the 'Portland Rose', as it has become known, for many years, I am of the opinion that no China rose was in any way involved in this scattering of pollen, although Damask and Gallica certainly played their part: Damask in the form of *R. × damascena bifera* ('Quatre Saisons') from which it inherits its remontancy and Gallica in the form of *R. gallica officinalis* (the 'Apothecary Rose') from which it inherits its tidy, compact habit. Whatever its parentage this rose was immediately put to stud by the perceptive French hybridists, amongst whom was Comte Lelieur who was in charge of the Imperial Gardens in France at that time. It was he who raised 'Rose Lelieur', later renamed by request of Louis XVIII 'Rose du Roi'. To produce this rose it is said that Lelieur crossed the Portland Rose with *R. gallica officinalis*. This is another curious fact since such a cross brought more Gallica genes into the little dynasty of Portlands and even more curious when one observes 'Rose du Roi' and its descendants closely. One would suspect a pollen parent or ancestor with a higher petal count. I don't doubt the use of a Gallica but why a

common rose such as *R. gallica officinalis* when apparently the Empress Josephine had over 150 different varieties of Gallicas in her collection at the time the cross was made?

In my small way I have dabbled with other Gallicas as both seed and pollen parents and, with few exceptions, their offspring have tended to be of shortish growth. Some years ago I crossed various named Gallicas with 'Scharlachglut', a very vigorous Gallica hybrid which seemed to contradict my theory. These yielded a number of seedlings, all of similar short to medium height; one of the taller of these has now been introduced and given the name of 'James Mason'. Judging from this and other crosses made, I cannot help feeling either that 'Scharlachglut' has somehow been wrongly classified or that its Gallica 'blood' is several times removed. Interestingly, the late Edward LeGrice used pollen from various purple Gallicas to breed his unusually coloured Floribundas. Most of these, many of which were never introduced, tended to a shortish habit with their remontancy not influenced by the introduction of Gallica genes.

Coming back to the little dynasty of Portlands raised during the nineteenth century, these are amongst the best and the most useful of all the old roses in that not only are they remontant but they are of accommodating size and ideal therefore for smaller gardens. My favourites are 'Comte de Chabord' and 'Jacques Cartier'.*

* 'Jacques Cartier' is distributed in America as 'Marquise Boccella'.

'Rose du Roi'

---

* Recent correspondence with Sally Festing, who has written a biography of the 2nd Duchess of Portland (1715–85), reveals that the rose was named after her and not the 3rd Duchess. Not only was the 2nd Duchess of Portland a keen rosarian but she never left England in her lifetime. Mr John C. MacGregor IV, formerly of the US Huntington Botanic Garden, brought this fact to Sally Festing's attention, pointing out that the rose was listed in an old nursery catalogue of 1782 and appeared in France three years later. This must cast doubt on Italy as its country of origin.

'Bourbon Queen'

Bourbon Roses

Soon after the Portlands appeared, another new race of roses came about, again by chance. It was the promiscuous old China rose 'Parson's Pink', now better known as 'Old Blush', which played its part by cohabiting, it is said, with the Damask 'Quatre Saisons' on the Ile de Bourbon, an island in the southern Indian Ocean, now renamed Réunion, where roses were used as partition hedges. The results of this union were localized plants of a rose commonly called by the islanders 'Rose Edouard'. M. Bréon, director of the island's small botanic gardens, collected seeds from this rose and sent them to his friends in France among whom was M. Jacques, head gardener to the Duc d'Orléans, who recognized the resulting seedlings to be the forerunners of a new race, naming the first one 'Bourbon Rose'. Although this is generally accepted as the means by which the first Bourbon rose was born, there is reason to believe that another 'Rose Edward' had been growing in the Botanical Garden, Calcutta, for some years before M. Bréon collected his seed. Perhaps the Réunion rose had first found its way to India,

maybe as seeds which could easily produce variable offspring. Since 1984 I have grown a 'Rose Edward' from Trevor Griffiths of New Zealand, originally obtained by Nancy Steen from a grower in New Delhi as the genuine Calcutta form. It is very Portland-like with high-centred flowers of reddish pink.

Whatever its origins, several French nurserymen recognized its potential and it was used extensively for crossing and recrossing, so giving rise to a range of mostly continuously flowering shrub roses which were to adorn gardens worldwide, with very little competition, well into the nineteenth century. Some of these remain favourites to this day. Notable Bourbons which still give excellent value as shrub roses are 'Bourbon Queen', 'Souvenir de la Malmaison', 'Louise Odier', 'Mme Isaac Pereire' and, of course, the thornless 'Zépherine Drouhin'. In the main Bourbons are fairly vigorous shrub roses but some make excellent climbers and should be used more widely for this purpose. Bourbons fall roughly into two types: those which have inherited the flower forms of the Chinas, the best examples being 'La Reine Victoria' and its paler sport 'Mme Pierre Oger', and those that follow the form of their Damask ancestors such as 'Bourbon Queen' and 'Souvenir de la Malmaison'. Conspicuous differences also appear in their growth habits and in the form and texture of foliage and thorn patterns. This suggests that, through the years, other 'blood' has been introduced from time to time. As a rule, however, there is a correlation between flower style and growth habit which helps to identify their respective ancestral types, those with few thorns and twiggy, pliable wood leaning to the Chinas and those with thorny, stiffer growth, to the Damasks. Victorian writers, in particular William Paul, divided Bourbons into classes based on their predominant ancestral likenesses.

'La Reine Victoria'

'Souvenir de la Malmaison'

Noisettes

Another family of roses to emerge at about the same time as the Portlands and Bourbons was that of the Noisettes. These had their beginnings in America. Here again the China rose was involved, this time mating with the Musk Rose, *R. moschata*.

'Parson's Pink China' or 'Old Blush' was crossed with *R. moschata* by a rice grower from Charleston, South Carolina, one John Champneys, who, in return for the original gift of 'Parson's Pink', passed on the seedlings to his friend and neighbour Philippe Noisette, a French emigrant. Philippe then made more crosses, sending both seeds and plants to his brother Louis in Paris. The latter, seeing them flower, and doubtless realizing the importance of his brother's gift, named the first seedling 'Rosier de Philippe Noisette', subsequently shortened to 'Noisette'. The original 'Champneys' Pink Cluster' and one of its first seedlings 'Blush Noisette' are still widely grown today and well worth garden space.

William Paul writes of his introduction to the Noisette group: 'The peculiar features recommended to notice were its hard nature, free growth, and a large cluster of flowers, produced very late in the year, which were indeed recommendations of no common order.'

Descendants from the first Noisette rose vary both in stature and floriferousness. Most start their flowering rather later than, for example, the Bourbons, and many repeat or flower virtually continuously throughout the summer. Later in their history they were heavily interbred with other groups, especially the Teas, and some of their distinctive Noisette characteristics were lost, not least their hardiness. Important varieties in the group include 'Blush Noisette', 'Aimée Vibert', 'Bouquet d'Or', 'Céline Forestier' and 'Mme Alfred Carrière' to name but a few. They are still available and doing stalwart service in many gardens here in the UK today.

There is no doubt, though, that many of this group are far happier in less harsh climates than this one. During a recent trip to New Zealand I could not help feeling envious. Of their Noisettes, 'Lamarque' flourished, but outstanding in my memory is a superb example of 'Alister Stella Gray'. I saw it at the home of Sally and Bey Allison of Fernside, near Christchurch, but then theirs is a wonderful garden and they know just how to get the best from their roses, as indeed do most New Zealand rose lovers.

Top: 'Céline Forestier'. *Above left:* 'Mme Alfred Carrière', and *right* 'Blush Noisette'

Teas

At the time the somewhat haphazard and largely undocumented scattering of pollen was taking place to bring forth the Bourbons, Noisettes, Portlands and early Hybrid Perpetuals, a few new and hitherto unknown hybrids were finding their way into the hands of rose breeders. These, like their very close relations the Chinas, had originated in the Orient and were probably the result of a much earlier programme of hybridizing by the Chinese, which

started from a chance cross between *R. gigantea* and *R. chinensis*. Like the Chinas, they had the desired characteristic of remontancy. The first of these to arrive in Europe was *R. indica odorata*, soon to become known as 'Hume's Blush' after Sir Abraham Hume to whom it was sent from the Fa Tee Nurseries of Canton in 1810. The second came in 1824, found during an expedition to China to collect plants for the Royal Horticultural Society. This was later classified as *R. odorata ochroleuca*, but its original name of 'Parks' Yellow Tea-scented China' after its collector, John Parks, has been used ever since. Yellow clouded sulphur and scented, it was this rose, in 1830, which brought forth the first of several yellow or near-yellow Noisettes, beginning with 'Lamarque' and tapering off to the last important introduction, 'William Allen Richardson', in 1878. It was Parks' rose and 'Fortune's Double Yellow', found by Robert Fortune in a Chinese mandarin's garden in 1845, which brought the valuable yellow colouring into some of the many Tea roses bred and introduced during the early twentieth century. Although the above roses were thought to be extinct for many years, thanks to the kindness of various donors I believe that I now have plants of all three. I only hope they can endure our chilly Norfolk climate.

It seems that the early Tea roses as well as the Chinas arrived in ships of the East India Company, which were of course primarily concerned with the transporting of tea, but since a small part of their cargo yielded another new race of roses, it is possible that this, coupled with their unusual scent, led to the term 'Tea-scented rose' as a nickname coined perhaps by the sailors whose job it was to tend them. I grow several varieties of 'Teas' and have yet to detect any real resemblance to the scent of tea in any of them.

Whatever the origins of the name, Tea roses soon became quite fashionable, especially in the warmer parts of Europe. Many were not totally hardy, but this fact, coupled with their beauty, simply made them more sought after, and the Victorians proceeded to grow them in abundance, the hardiest outdoors, and the tender ones in conservatories and stove-houses. The blooms were borne on rather slender, weak stalks and most had high, pointed centres when in bud, which distinguished them from other roses of the day. The Victorians loved to wear roses in their buttonholes and many were grown specifically for this purpose.

Top left: 'Hume's Blush' growing in a courtyard in India, and *right,* 'Perle des Jardins'. *Above:* 'Fortune's Double Yellow'

The Mystery Roses of Bermuda

Members of the Bermuda Rose Society since its formation in 1954 have preserved all the many naturalized and garden roses they can find.

For those who do not know of the Bermuda mystery roses, the following account of my first visit to this lovely island will serve as an introduction.

'Mme Lombard'

'Rosette Delizy'

'Miss Atwood'

'Parks Yellow'

'Smith's Parish'

'Agrippina' (Cramoisi Supérieur)

I went to attend a conference and had very little time for rose-hunting, but those I found or was shown were fascinating, and there were many I had never seen before. For a week, the island was teeming with rose people and there was much discussion. Who knows what subtle variations occur in roses that grow and flower all the year round and have never experienced frost? Can we compare such roses to those that take a rest for six months each winter in less temperate climates? Of the roses I recognized, their 'Cramoisi Supérieur', known in Bermuda as 'Agrippina', is certainly the same as the European although more vigorous. I noticed subtle differences in 'Archduke Charles', the European having fewer petals, but our 'Safrano' has more than theirs. 'Slater's Crimson', which, sadly, I have now lost, I recall having more petals than the one I saw on Bermuda. The flowers of my 'Sanguinea' are identical to those of their plant, but whereas their form grows to more than 5' (1.5 m) mine struggles to attain even 2' (60 cm). Their 'Anna Olivier' is exactly the same as mine, but I believe we both have it wrongly identifed. With the help of Bill and Lorna Mercer I was able to sort out a mix-up in my nursery between 'Maman Cochet' and 'White Maman Cochet'. Also, thanks to the Mercers, I came back very confused as to the true identities of 'Homère' and 'Mme de Tartas'.

By way of a positive identification of a mystery rose, the nearest I dare go is to say that the Bermudan 'Miss Atwood', although taller, closely resembles my 'Arethusa'. Interesting though a correct identification would be, I suspect that many Bermuda roses will remain mysteries, and anyone who dares name them on the evidence of roses currently available for comparison would be very brave indeed. And, until positive proof is found, they should certainly retain their charming Bermudan names – 'Smith's Parish', 'Trinity', 'St Davids' or 'Brightside Cream' – and be known under those names not just in Bermuda but throughout the world. Furthermore, any suggestion as to probable names should be based on good, sound evidence, not on tenuous descriptions from books and catalogues except where such evidence forms part of more positive proof in the form of a proven, authenticated rose.*

If I could be sure that all the names by which we now know our old roses are those designated by their raisers then I would, perhaps, take a different view. I concluded several years ago that it is impossible to be sure whether or not every rose in present-day catalogues which pre-dates 1920 is true to the raiser's name; and this bothered me. Now I ask myself; providing it has been proved

* A special section by Lorna Mercer on the mystery roses of Bermuda can be found in the Dictionary.

'Brightside Cream'

The formal rose garden at Camden House, Bermuda

to be a garden variety, does the name matter? Roses are not signed like works of art, so surely what matters most is that we have the rose, by whatever name, interesting though speculation and research might be.

Naturally I am fully conscious of the importance of correct names, but for want of a name too many good roses from the past have now been lost to our gardens for ever. For the sake of our roses, let us not get bogged down by nomenclature and authenticity. I have several good but so far nameless roses sent to me over the years by keen rosarians which are probably destined never to go beyond our nursery gates. I call them 'was-not' roses – 'wait and see – name official tomorrow'.

Cogratulations, Bermuda Rose Society, for naming your 'was-nots': the rose world is the richer for your doing so.

Hybrid Perpetuals

As a result of a fusion between the Bourbons and, it would seem, any other parent that came along, a race of roses appeared which, following initial confusion, became known as Hybrid Perpetuals. They were accepted as a new group sometime in the 1820s and many varieties were later to fill catalogues. Their sheer numbers and very hybridity, however, proved to be the downfall of many, and only the best survived. Those that are still with us today are well worth a place as shrubs in the modern garden. Some, indeed, are truly beautiful, and most have a powerful scent. I like, in particular, 'Reine des Violettes', 'Baroness Rothschild', 'Baronne Prévost', 'Dupuy Jamain', 'Paul Neyron' and 'Ulrich Brunner Fils'. One of the latest to be raised and introduced, in 1901, was the indefatigable 'Frau Karl Druschki', later renamed 'Snow Queen' in the UK because it had reached the height of its popularity at about the time of the outbreak of World War I when anything with a Teutonic connection was frowned upon. This rose, out of character with others of its group, had no scent but no rose has everything and 'Druschki', as it became affectionately called by nurserymen, amply makes up for this little foible in all other respects.

As stated earlier, most Hybrid Perpetuals make useful shrubs and although 'pegging-down' is not common practice today, some of the taller varieties lend themselves ideally to this technique of training roses. In fact it was probably invented specifically for them by head gardeners of large estates at a time in history when labour saving was not a priority.

'Dupuy Jamain'

A few have 'sported' into climbers over the years, with 'Frau Karl Druschki' amongst them. In climbing form they are usually very vigorous and need plenty of space but if this is a problem then several of the bush forms will grow happily as wall plants.

Pimpinellifolias (Scotch Roses)

I have already made a brief reference to the Pimpinellifolias. These charming little roses were much sought after at the beginning of the nineteenth century, only declining in popularity when superseded by longer-flowering types. Although only a few varieties now remain, I find them delightful to grow. They are not fussy about soil and can be reproduced easily from cuttings. When grown on their own roots, they sucker freely, but in so doing never outgrow their welcome. The so-called Scotch or Burnet roses were almost as preponderant in 1824 as the Floribunda rose is today.

Although there is little doubt that the 'double' Pimpinellifolias flourished long before 1800, it is worth recalling Joseph Sabine's

Top: 'Paul Neyron'   *Above:* 'Baronne Prévost'

account of their introduction , which was published while he was Secretary of the Royal Horticultural Society in 1822. Two brothers named Brown, one of whom was a partner in a nursery trading as 'Dickson & Brown' of Perth, were apparently the first to realize the potential of these roses when one of them, Robert, found a malformed, wild 'Scotch Rose on the hill of Kinnoul' near Perth, in 1793. From this one rose, which they planted in the nursery, they collected seed. These seeds produced plants with semi-double flowers. Eventually, by continuous seed-sowing and selection, they assembled some good, double forms which included a

Top: 'Scotch Double Pink', and *above, R. × harisonii*

marbled pink-and-white variety. From these they increased stock and supplied nurseries on both sides of the border. In Scotland, Robert Austin of Glasgow had, by 1814, 'upwards of 100 varieties of new and undescribed sorts'. In England, William Malcolm of Kensington and Messrs Lee & Kennedy of Hammersmith had, between them, purchased most of Dickson & Brown's stock, and as a result these roses soon won deserved popularity in the south and subsequently spread far and wide. I have collected about ten varieties at present but, apart from a few, I fear most, while a pleasure to grow, will be impossible to name.

The Scotch roses were formerly known as 'Spinosissimas' from *R. spinosissima*, which has recently been changed to *R. pimpinellifolia*.

In the 1830s a Mr Lee of Bedfont succeeded in crossing one of these varieties with the 'Autumn Damask' to produce 'Stanwell Perpetual'. This rose bears a close resemblance to the Scotch roses in foliage and thorns but is taller and more straggly. Flowering almost continuously and superbly scented, it is still a favourite today.

With the notable exception of Wilhelm Kordes in Germany, who used forms of *R. pimpinellifolia* in the 1930s and 1940s to give us 'Frühlingsgold' and 'Frühlingsmorgen' among others, few other breeders have used them, at least not successfully, since their heyday, although Roy Shepherd of America produced a very worthwhile hybrid Pimpinellifolia shrub, 'Golden Wings', in 1956. Another American rose which belongs in this group is *R. harisonii* or 'Harison's Yellow', also known as 'The Yellow Rose of Texas'. This is probably the outcome of the chance mating of *R. pimpinellifolia* and *R. foetida*. It is perhaps the most intense yellow of the group. I had always thought this rose had originated in Texas and never bothered to look deeply into its origins but, reading *Roses of America* by Stephen Scanniello and Tania Bayard recently, I discovered it was found on a farm in Manhattan in the 1830s and became so popular that it was taken west by homesteaders who planted it wherever they decided to settle.

Sweet Briars

A native of Europe, *R. eglanteria*, the wild Sweet Briar, has, over a fairly long period, it would seem, since we have one, 'Manning's Blush', which dates back to 1799, produced some excellent and useful garden hybrids, all or most of which have inherited its distinctive apple-scented foliage. It is primarily this scented foliage which gives them their place in most gardens but many are worth-

R. eglanteria hips

'Pax'

'Felicia'

'Prosperity'

'Cornelia'

while for their flowers alone. Apart from being colourful and freely produced they usually carry the apple aroma and are followed by attractive, oval, bright orangey-red hips in late summer and autumn. Particularly interesting in this group are the Penzance Briars produced during the 1890s. More about these later in the section on shrub roses.

A favourite of mine is the beautiful single 'Meg Merrilies'. Until recently I had assumed that this rose carried the name of Keats' 'Old Meg' but a customer friend has now told me of a lady named Meg Merrilies who spent much of her time and money attending to 'down and outs' in the Soho district of London in the 1890s, when this rose was introduced. It is most likely therefore that it was named for her, especially as Lord Penzance, its raiser, was a Judge and would have known about her good deeds.

Hybrid Musks

Strictly speaking, if age alone is the criterion for qualification, then this group should not be in this section of the book, but since I always think of them as 'classics' I cannot bring myself to place them elsewhere. They were an important development in shrub roses and emerged as a group during the first quarter or so of the twentieth century.

Tucked away in rural Essex, a clergyman, Joseph Pemberton, worked at rose-breeding and came up with a complete breakthrough. It was obvious from the start that Pemberton's roses were different, but for want of another classification they were introduced to begin with as Hybrid Teas. His first roses came on the market in 1913; they were 'Moonlight' with semi-double white flowers and 'Danaë' with smallish flowers of soft primrose-yellow. Both had flowers borne in clusters on long branches from shrubby plants. What is more, they both flowered throughout the summer and were scented. To create these and many of his subsequent introductions, Pemberton used a bushy, long-stemmed cluster rose called 'Trier', bred and introduced by Lambert of Germany in 1904. He could see at a glance that the habits of this variety were not too far removed from the Polyanthus, although much taller. He probably knew that 'Trier' was a seedling from a French rose called 'Aglaia', a climbing Polyantha of 1896, the parents of

'Ballerina'

which were *R. multiflora* and 'Rêve d'Or', a Noisette from as far back as 1869. There is no reason to doubt this pedigree, for at certain times of the year considerable family resemblances, especially in foliage, can be seen between great-grandparent 'Rêve d'Or' and some of Pemberton's Musks. Obviously, too, it was from this lineage that his roses inherited their musk-like scent. Whoever christened Pemberton's roses could well have called them Hybrid Multifloras, but since they and their scent can be traced directly back through the Noisettes to *R. moschata*. Hybrid Musk is quite a suitable and appropriate collective name. Most of the shrub roses to come from the Pemberton stud between 1913 and his death in 1926 still adorn our gardens unsurpassed today. In chronological order, the best are 'Pax' (1918), 'Prosperity' (1919), 'Vanity' (1920), much taller and more angular in growth than the rest, 'Francesca' (1922), 'Penelope' (1924) and the versatile 'Cornelia' (1925). Some authorities attribute 'Buff Beauty', introduced thirteen years after his death, to Pemberton. I have faded recollections of a conversation with Edward LeGrice about this rose; it took place many years ago and had I realized its importance I would have listened more closely. I feel sure it affirmed Pemberton as the raiser of 'Buff Beauty', but I cannot be certain. LeGrice, of course, would have known Pemberton well.

After Pemberton's death, one of his gardeners by the name of J. A. Bentall started growing and breeding roses on his own account, and very successfully, for in 1932 he introduced 'The Fairy' and five years later, in 1937, 'Ballerina', both invaluable and, in many

ways, ahead of their time. It would seem that Joseph Pemberton had been not just an accomplished rose breeder but a first class tutor.

As garden subjects the Hybrid Musks are invaluable today, making fine specimen plants, subjects for shrubberies or excellent ornamental informal hedges.

Multiflora Ramblers

R. multiflora has been mentioned several times in relation to its influence on other roses or strains of roses, but is included here for its own sake. It first came to the West from China towards the end of the nineteenth century and it did not take long after its arrival for breeders to realize its potential as a parent and put it to stud with other diverse types. It is largely this species which is responsible for almost all the cluster-flowered characteristics in modern roses; but the Multiflora ramblers were the first to emerge.

William Paul listed twenty-seven varieties, many of which are still available today. Most of these have their place as camouflage for unsightly buildings or decrepit trees; others would be well placed both on pergolas and on walls. Most Multifloras root readily from cuttings and because of this, some varieties were used extensively as understocks for other roses, especially during World War I and the 1920s. A variety particularly favoured for this purpose was 'de la Grifferaie', a persistent rose which is often sent to me for identification, for having shed its more delicate enforced charge of the budded rose, it seems to thrive on neglect.

'Veilchenblau'

'Janet B. Wood'

Ayrshires

I make no apology for devoting some space to another interesting diversion from the main line of rose development, *R. arvensis*. I have always been interested in this rose and its few offspring, and since other authors have tended to neglect it, this is an opportunity to redress the balance slightly.

In its wild habitat it has great charm and is the only native climbing rose in Britain, and climb it will, to the top of the tallest thicket or hedge. No matter how coarse its competition or support, it remains graceful by cascading its long, thin, dark-coloured shoots back towards the ground. It is equally at home scrambling through undergrowth or simply creeping along the ground or banks. Of its hybrids, Ayrshire 'Splendens' is now the most common; and an excellent example of this, some 10′ (3 m) tall and 10′ (3 m) wide can be seen at Castle Howard in Yorkshire, where it is grown as a specimen shrub with support. Most of the other members of this race of superb climbers, known collectively as Ayrshires, are rather overwhelmed in popularity by the Wichuraiana hybrids with their stronger colouring.

Good climbers were, of course, very scarce before the mid-nineteenth century, but when they became more plentiful the Victorians used them extensively, as is evident from some of the monochrome photographs in Jekyll and Mawley's *Roses for English Gardens*, published in 1902.

Lack of authentic records prevents us from tracing the first double 'Ayshire' back to its precise source. Various stories connect the rose with places as far apart as Germany, Canada and Yorkshire; but if not actually bred in Scotland, it certainly started its career there. I am inclined to feel, however, in spite of the work done on these roses by Mr Martin of Dundee, that had it originated there local pride would have prohibited the name 'Ayrshire', as it seems to have been called from its beginning. Of all the stories surrounding this rose, I think the following is the most plausible. It was first seen in 1776 by a Mr J. Smith of Monksgrove Nurseries, Ayrshire, growing in the garden of a Mr Dalrymple of Orangefield, near Ayr. It had been planted there by Mr John Penn, a huntsman who was a keen gardener. Penn told Smith that he had brought the rose from his native Yorkshire where he had found it growing in a garden, having supposedly been introduced there from Germany. The 'Orangefield Rose' attracted much local attention and found its way to Loudon Castle, from where it was eventually widely distributed. I believe I now have this rose, a happy rediscovery by Mrs

Janet McQueen of Dunfermline, Scotland, named at her request 'Janet B. Wood' for its re-introduction in 1991.

Some of the other stories about the origin of the Ayrshires only make sense if one recognizes an understandable confusion with other climbers of this period, namely the evergreen roses.

Ayrshires are supposed to prefer a colder climate, so imagine my surprise and delight in finding an aged and struggling plant growing, tucked away from general view, I admit, in the gardens of the Getty Museum and Art Gallery, California, in 1988.

Sempervirens Roses
(the Evergreens)

The 'Evergreen Roses', as they were known by the Victorians, are hybrids of *R. sempervirens*, bred in France in the first half of the nineteenth century. They are less vigorous and have fewer thorns

'Adélaide d'Orléans'

than the Ayrshires, although the latter are not themselves over-thorny. Furthermore, the Ayrshires produce their flowers singly, or in small clusters, while the Evergreens produce theirs in large trusses some two weeks later. Varieties worth special mention in this group are 'Félicité et Perpétue' and 'Adélaide d'Orléans'. I love these roses and am heartened by the fact that we are growing and selling more and more each year.

Wichuraianas

If I were just embarking upon a career of breeding roses I would pursue the development of *R. wichuraiana*, and of *R. luciae*, parents of many of our garden ramblers. Most of the impressive results achieved by Barbier (in France), by Jackson & Perkins, and by Brownell (both in the USA), came to a dead end over sixty years ago. Apart from nature herself giving us 'New Dawn', a sport from 'Dr Van Fleet', in 1930, the work initiated by these hybridists was, until recently, largely neglected. It is a testimony to their work that

ramblers such as 'Albéric Barbier', 'Albertine', 'Sanders White' and 'Excelsa', raised in the early years of the present century, are still widely grown and still listed in most rose catalogues.

The chance birth of 'New Dawn' was indeed a happy event, for not only did it provide us with perhaps the best-ever remontant climbing or rambler rose but, when used as a parent by modern hybridists, it has also given us several very good modern long-flowering climbers such as 'Bantry Bay', 'Coral Dawn', 'Pink Perpétue', 'Rosy Mantle' and 'White Cockade'. More recently *R. wichuraiana* has also become the foundation of the modern procumbent varieties.

'New Dawn'

'Albertine'

'Sander's White'

'Excelsa'

The Influence of Empress Josephine

By the end of the eighteenth century, the foundation for our present-day roses was well and truly established. The French, in particular, played an important role and an array of diverse varieties emerged, inspired by the Empress Josephine, who not only filled her garden at the Château de Malmaison with a collection of her favourites, but by her patronage encouraged Pierre Joseph Redouté to make his masterly paintings of them. Redouté published his work in conjunction with Claude Antoine Thory, a botanist, who made the first serious attempt to sift the tangled genealogy of roses. Much of his work has been proved accurate and stands up, when tested, against the much more scientific methods employed today.

This period of rose history holds much fascination for me. To have been a French nurseryman at that time would have been fulfilling, both in job satisfaction and financial reward. How I would have survived in the Revolution I dare not speculate, but Redouté somehow managed to sit on the fence, working for both factions at various times throughout his career. I know nothing of his personality but his talents somehow isolated him from the politics, intrigue and bitterness of that turbulent period of French history. Or was it his subject? Roses, at least in Europe, have somehow always emerged from troubles and strife with enhanced values, notably the Holy Wars, with the introduction of several new species to the West, the Wars of the Roses, with the birth of an emblem, and the Napoleonic Wars and the French Revolution with a new-found respectability brought about by Josephine, Thory and Redouté.

Josephine's garden at Malmaison brought together the biggest collection of roses ever assembled, and it continued to expand until her death in 1814, when it quickly fell into neglect. It seems that in spite of the strife, roses still managed to pass from Britain to France, and a recently discovered irony is that one of the original designs of the rose garden at Malmaison (although I think never used) is very close to that of the Union Jack. A touch of sarcasm? A gesture of goodwill? Or patriotism from an Englishman named Kennedy employed by the Empress to help her lay out her rose garden? None of these, I suspect – merely coincidence – a rose garden can hardly be based on the design of the Tricolore.

Top: 'Duchesse d'Angoulême', and *below*, 'Empress Josephine'

'Hermosa'

PART II
The Development of Modern Roses

'Anna Pavlova'

'Buff Beauty'

Hybrid Teas

The first Hybrid Tea was launched upon the world amid controversy. It was found by Jean-Baptiste Guillot among a patch of seedlings in his nursery at Lyon, France. Immediately he recognized it as 'something different'. Its flowers, held on a strong neck, were freely produced and rather portly in shape, at least until they were fully open; they were also high-centred in the fashion of the Teas of the day and filled out with lots of petals. Its habit of growth was upright and altogether more tidy than the rather sprawling Hybrid Perpetuals. Guillot had no idea of its true parentage but concluded that it was the result of a secret liaison between one of his 'upper class' Hybrid Perpetuals and a Tea rose with a roving eye.

Although clearly seen as 'different' by its raiser and by many of the experts in France, it took several years to convince the Rose Society there that M. Guillot had stumbled upon a rose worthy of distinction as being the first Hybrid Tea. It was named 'La France' in 1867. It took even longer to convince the British National Rose Society. It was Henry Bennett, a prominent English raiser, who forced them eventually to accept the new classification. Between 1879 and 1890, Bennett succeeded in raising several distinct varieties from a deliberate programme of crossing Teas with Hybrid Perpetuals and, in his lifetime, raised well over thirty new roses. Several, such as 'Mrs John Laing' and 'Captain Hayward', were clearly Hybrid Perpetuals but most had the characteristics of the new class. He believed and proved that all that was new and good did not necessarily have to come from France. Some of Bennett's roses won major awards, others fell by the wayside; but one in particular, 'Lady Mary Fitzwilliam', when put to stud – unlike her French counterpart, 'La France', which was virtually sterile – proved very fertile and was used extensively by both French and British breeders to produce many more good roses. Credit must go to Henry Bennett for his all-round work on the rose, but it was 'Lady Mary Fitzwilliam' above any other that established his reputation as, beyond doubt, 'Lord of the Hybrid Teas'.

I cannot exclude a personal anecdote at this juncture. It is about an illustration which appeared in a small book entitled *Late Victorian Roses*, written by myself, with photographs by Keith Money. This picture was of an unidentified variety discovered by Keith at Caston in 1975. We did not state dogmatically that it was 'Lady Mary Fitzwilliam', but it was hoped it might create some interest, either confirming that it was 'Lady Mary', or suggesting a suitable name. Two letters came from Australia, both expressing the opinion that the rose was indeed 'Lady Mary Fitzwilliam'. One was from Deane Ross, a professional rose grower whose father had started their business in 1906, and who, when shown the photograph, was an alert gentleman of eighty-seven years. Deane wrote: 'When I showed him your book he said, "Now that is Lady Mary Fitzwilliam."' Deane then went on to say that his father had grown this variety extensively in his early years as a nurseryman, and remembered it well. This does not necessarily authenticate the rose – photographs are not the easiest means of identification – but it is particularly interesting, since later I acquired a colour print of 'Lady Mary Fitzwilliam' which strengthens my belief that the rose could well have been rediscovered. It came from Mrs Margaret Meier, a niece of Henry Bennett's great-granddaughter, Mrs Ruth Burdett; and Mrs Burdett herself added support to this belief by informing me that Henry Bennett's son Charles emigrated to Australia and started commercial rose-growing there at the turn of the century, doubtless taking with him ample stocks of his father's roses.

Prior to Bennett's day, most of the best British roses had been Hybrid Perpetuals and had come from either William Paul of

'La France'

Cheshunt or Rivers of Sawbridgeworth. Between them, they raised some excellet roses, and although many of their varieties only appeared fleetingly in their catalogues they must receive credit for stalwart work in helping Bennett with the initial material.

Despite Bennett, however, French breeders were still ahead of the field. In 1890 Joseph Pernet-Ducher raised what must still rank as one of the world's favourite roses, 'Mme Caroline Testout'. Today this rose is better known in its climbing form. Then, as a bush rose, it had no rivals, producing an abundance of large, blowsy, scented, satin-pink flowers on a sturdy, accommodating plant. Few gardens would have been without at least one specimen of 'Mme Caroline'. Pernet-Ducher was a discerning man and selected his introductions carefully, introducing only those which showed improvement of class or were a clear breakthrough in colour. As testimony to this he was also responsible for raising two excellent forcing roses of the era, 'Mme Abel Chatenay' and 'Antoine Rivoire'. With 'Mme Caroline Testout' flaunting herself in gardens everywhere and his florist's roses adorning many a

'Lady Mary Fitzwilliam'

bridal bouquet, his Hybrid Teas had certainly made their mark. Pernet-Ducher's most important introduction, however, was 'Soleil d'Or'. It was this rose, a cross between the clear yellow *Rosa foetida persiana* and the red Hybrid Perpetual 'Antoine Ducher', which brought the first hint of yellow ever to be seen in the Hybrid Perpetuals, thus making possible the many beautiful yellow Hybrid Teas of today. Initially, 'Soleil d'or' and its descendants were grouped together as a separate class. To honour their raiser they were called Pernetianas. Sadly, they did not make good garden plants for they were very susceptible to black spot, an affliction inherited from the yellow side of their ancestry. By the early 1930s most Pernetianas had disappeared or, for reasons of convenience in commercial catalogues, had been merged with the Hybrid Teas.

The warm and sunny climate of southern France was the main reason for the French breeders' dominance during the nineteenth century, but roses were becoming big business and the British – fed up with the many French names in their catalogues – started to raise their own new varieties by hybridizing under glass. Henry Bennett had proved that such methods worked and they were soon adopted by others, among them the firm of Alexander Dickson of Newtownards, Northern Ireland. After several false starts, Dickson's were on the trail of some excellent Hybrid Teas and won the first ever gold medal to be given to a Hybrid Tea with a pink rose named 'Mrs W. J. Grant' (1892). One of the oldest of their varieties still available today is the beautiful single 'Irish Elegance', raised in 1905. Since then, the Dickson family have been responsible for some very auspicious Hybrid Teas, outstanding

'Mme Caroline Testout'

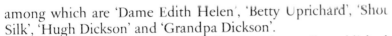

among which are 'Dame Edith Helen', 'Betty Uprichard', 'Shot Silk', 'Hugh Dickson' and 'Grandpa Dickson'.

Soon after Dickson's began breeding, another well-established Irish nursery, Samuel McGredy of Portadown, started with their pollen brush and it was not long before they, like Dickson's, were winning high awards for beautiful roses such as 'Mrs Herbert Stevens', 'Mrs Henry Morse', 'McGredy's Yellow', 'Picture' and 'Piccadilly'. Not so famous as a garden rose but a name that will live forever is 'Margaret McGredy', raised in 1927 and pollen parent to 'Peace', the most famous rose of all. Both Pat Dickson and Sam McGredy are perpetuating the family tradition by breeding some excellent roses today, although McGredy has moved to the more reliable climate of New Zealand to pursue his quest.

Although these two firms led the way until the beginning of World War I, other breeders were busy scattering pollen in search of Hybrid Teas both east and west of Ireland. By the time the war was over and things had returned to normal in Britain, competition for the coveted Gold Medal of the National Rose Society was intense. While it may be unfair to make such a judgement, there were too many winners by far: performance on the show bench rather than garden worthiness had become the criterion of success.

During the early 1940s, the rose growers of Britain were mindful of other things. Partly by choice and partly by government decree, they devoted most of their time and land resources to growing vegetables and their greenhouses to such things as tomatoes. The

'Dame Edith Helen'

Top left: 'Antoine Rivoire', and *right,* 'McGredy's Yellow'   *Above:* 'Piccadilly'

gardening public, too, were preoccupied with similar enterprises for the war effort, so selling roses would have been difficult. Once the war was over, however, raisers quickly resurrected their breeding programmes by planting up hybridizing houses and introducing the seedlings which had been lovingly nurtured in some corner plot through those five long years.

In the 1950s and '60s, demand for novelty was insatiable and the Hybrid Tea hit a high point of popularity. To satisfy demand some breeders, it seemed, introduced everything and anything – some not sufficiently tried and tested – that could be remotely called new. Sadly, this disenchanted customers who rightly became fed up with so many Hybrid Teas failing to live up to raisers' promises and turned either to other types such as Floribundas or away from roses altogether. Fortunately, some excellent varieties emerged from the more responsible raisers during that period of plenty and these have proved themselves by the test of time.

Ironically, considering how fervently professionals had sought the perfect red rose, one of the best came from an amateur, Albert Norman, who raised 'Ena Harkness' for posterity in 1946. This rose was introduced to the world by the famous firm of R. Harkness & Co. of Hitchin at about the time that Jack Harkness was beginning his own illustrious rose-breeding career. Jack's hybridizing followed several different lines, but two excellent Hybrid Teas of his are the shapely 'Elizabeth Harkness' (1969) and the outstanding Hybrid Tea-like shrub rose 'Alexander' (1972); and even more recently, 'Savoy Hotel', introduced in 1989.

Further north near Aberdeen another conspicuous career was getting under way. Aberdeen, now rich as the headquarters of the North Sea oilfields, geographically awkward and climatically inclement, always seemed to me an unlikely place to grow roses, and in those days its economy was based on the fishing industry. In my young days, exhibiting at rose shows, I was always envious of the high quality and size of Cocker's roses; no doubt fish manure helped. Aberdeen is built on land of good heart, and an enlightened city council – inspired partly no doubt by the success of Alex Cocker – has made it a city of roses. 'Alec's Red' (1970) was Alex Cocker's first successful Hybrid Tea, its name chosen by his friends in the trade who tried and tested the rose before its intro-

'Ena Harkness'

'Savoy Hotel'

duction. Disease resistance had always been a high priority for this breeder and his efforts were rewarded in 1978 when 'Silver Jubilee' was launched; no better rose could possibly commemorate Her Majesty Queen Elizabeth II's first twenty-five years on the throne.

Since the Second World War, Dickson, McGredy, Harkness and Cocker have each made their own indelible mark on the Hybrid Teas, but they have not had it all to themselves. Other British breeders have been busy too, notable among them Edward B. LeGrice of North Walsham with the still widely grown 'My Choice' (1958), Bees of Chester with the much-loved 'Josephine Bruce' (1949), Gregorys of Nottingham with 'Blessings' (1967) and Cants of Colchester with 'Just Joey' (1972).

In their wisdom and after much lobbying from plant breeders, the British Government introduced an Act of Parliament that was to have far-reaching consequences for the British rose industry. This was the Plant Varieties and Seeds Act 1964. It brought Britain into line with other European countries and with the United States, by allowing breeders to patent new varieties and receive a just return for their efforts, a return directly linked to the virtues or otherwise of their chosen introductions. It was a complex act and received a mixed reception – so mixed that, for a time, harmony within the industry was, to put it lightly, disturbed. After a short while breeders organized themselves into an association with the apt – it seemed to growers at the time – acronym BARB, standing for British Association of Rose Breeders. When it was realized that patenting was here to stay, relations between breeders and growers became friendly again. New varieties are the lifeblood of the industry and no grower should begrudge the breeder of any successful rose a fair return for his work. With several hundred varieties already patented in Britain since 1964, however, and more and more joining their ranks each year, it is becoming increasingly difficult to sort the wheat from the chaff, especially as royalties are levied on plants produced and not on the numbers sold.

'Silver Jubilee'

Top: 'My Choice' *Below left:* 'Alexander', and *right,* 'Josephine Bruce'

often as a climber. A fact from my 1917 *American Rose Society Annual* which indicates the popularity of Hybrid Teas in America at the time is that, of 349 roses listed as raised by American nurserymen, no fewer than 114 were Hybrid Teas, twenty-seven of which were accredited to E. Gurney Hill. some, of course, would have been sports. Hill continued to raise roses until well into the 1930s, and since we mention sports his firm was responsible for introducing in 1918 one of the great favourites of the 1920s and '30s, the beautiful pink 'Mme Butterfly', a deeper sport of William Paul's soft pink 'Ophelia' (1912). Millions of these two roses were produced and sold between the wars and they still enjoy nostalgic popularity to this day, despite, I suspect, some loss of vigour from constant propagation. Both roses are excellent forcers and acres were grown under glass for the cut-flower market of the period.

My favourite American rose by far is the superbly scented, shapely, deep silvery-pink 'The Doctor' (1936) raised by F. H. Howard and named in honour of Jean Nicolas, a hybridizer for the firm of Jackson & Perkins, which at that time was probably the biggest and wealthiest rose company in the world. Interestingly, the pollen parent of 'The Doctor' was 'Los Angeles'.

The early 1940s were lean years for European breeders and with the notable exception of 'Peace' the flow of new seedlings westwards across the Atlantic virtually dried up. Shortage quickly created demand and soon many American rose nurseries were busy cross-pollinating with vigour. In the 1940s, '50s and '60s they introduced some vintage Hybrid Teas. The superb 'Diamond Jubilee' (1947) by Eugene Boerner of Jackson & Perkins was one of the best and is still worthy of a place in any modern garden, as is Herbert Swim's shapely 'Helen Traubel' introduced by Armstrongs in 1951. I fell heavily for this rose soon after it came to England and will always forgive her when she pouts and hangs her head. Nothing, it seems, condemns a rose to the sidelines more than a weak neck, but I have never quite understood why so mild an affliction should be considered so serious a fault. Deportment, however, is never a problem for the long-necked 'Mojave' (1954), the free-flowering 'Sutter's Gold' (1950) or the sophisticated 'Royal Highness' (1962), all American roses of distinction, and all from Herbert Swim. Patent rights, fluctuating currency, improvements in introductions from elsewhere and changing demand for other types of roses help to explain why very few newer Hybrid Teas from America are listed in British catalogues today, but many good oldies still flourish in Britain, where they are much cherished by discerning rosarians.

As with perfumes and wines, not to mention language, the

Westwards from Ireland, in North America the rose had long been very popular and in 1899 the American Rose Society was founded. It would be discourteous of me to presume too much about American rose history, but rose breeders there have been increasingly active since John Champneys raised the famous Noisette 'Champneys' Pink Cluster' at Charleston in *c.* 1811.

At the beginning of this century, the first all-American Hybrid Teas started to emerge. Two in particular are worth special mention since they soon established themselves as favourites on both sides of the Atlantic: 'Los Angeles' was raised by Fred H. Howard and named after his home town; the other, 'General MacArthur', was raised in 1905 by a very active breeder of the early 1900s, E. Gurney Hill of Richmond, Indiana. Both varieties can be found growing in Britain today, although the latter is now seen more

Top left: 'Ophelia', and *right,* 'The Doctor'
Below left: 'Mme Butterfly', and *right,* 'Angèle Pernet'

'Mme Edouard Herriot'

'Peace'

world would be a duller place without French roses, for it was the French who not only gave us some of the best old-fashioned roses but also laid the foundations for Hybrid Teas as we know them today. The debt owed to men like Guillot has already been acknowledged, but other Frenchmen of similar mould have not been idle in more recent times. Although his most famous achievements were his pioneering yellow varieties, 'Rayon d'Or' and 'Soleil d'Or', Joseph Pernet-Ducher continued to breed excellent roses until the early 1920s. In 1913, amid controversy, he won £1000 from the *Daily Mail* newspaper for his rich coral 'Mme Edouard Herriot'; and in 1924, just before retiring, he gave us the shapely 'Angèle Pernet', to this day worth a place in any garden.

Space does not permit me to cover much of the detail of the prodigious rose fraternity in France during the first forty years of this century, though men like Frances Dubreuil, Charles and Antoine Meilland and others all made significant contributions to Hybrid Tea roses. They all knew one another and, no doubt, had their disagreements, but like rose people the world over each respected the other's work and they were the greatest of friends. Even marriages

between families ensued from time to time.

To select one family of French rose growers and breeders from the twentieth century is almost as unfair as choosing a raiser from the nineteenth century and informing the world that he was the best. I would do no injustice in isolating the Meillands for special mention, however, for while there may have been elements of good fortune involved in the raising of 'Peace', there was no such luck in the way they used the wealth this one rose created.

'Peace', without doubt, is the finest Hybrid Tea ever raised and it will remain a standard variety for ever. Roses have never made anyone wealthy, they are a vocation and few vocations make men rich – except in spirit. Those rose growers I know who have become rich have done so by other means than in the pursuit of their profession. Having said this, had Antoine Meilland and his son Francis thought this way in late 1945 they would never have invested the proceeds of 'Peace' in more land, more greenhouses and more staff to breed yet more roses. We must be grateful for 'Peace' and thankful for their investments. Without either, the modern roses would be the poorer. In their time, they have also given us such beautiful Hybrid Teas as 'Michèle Meilland' (1945), 'Grandmère Jenny' (1950), 'Charles Mallerin' (1951) and 'Bettina' (1953), not to mention the long-stemmed 'Baccara' (1954), a red florist's rose which has saved more marriages than all the guidance counsellors of the world put together.

Sadly, Francis died prematurely in 1958 but in his short life had been the driving force behind the building of the biggest and probably the best rose-breeding establishment in the world at Cap d'Antibes. The business is now in the capable hands of the third-generation Meilland, Alain, who introduced 'Papa Meilland', a beautiful dark red, in honour of his grandfather in 1963 and 'Sonia' ('Sweet Promise'), named after his daughter in 1974. The Meilland name will crop up often in these pages, for not only have they created some excellent Hybrid Teas but they have also been world leaders in several other types of roses.

German rosarians were not particularly active in the early stages of the development of the rose, and although men like Peter Lambert, who bred the famous 'Frau Karl Druschki', were hybridizing before 1900, it was not until after World War I that German breeders stamped their mark and began to influence the pedigree of the modern rose. The first of these was Wilhelm Kordes. His work spanned a wide range of types and, in his time, he introduced some very important roses indeed. He is best known for his hardy, shrubby varieties developed from *R. kordesii* and for his foundation work in extending the colour range of modern roses through 'Independence' (1951), a rose I could never really take to but whose issue brought forth a multitude of vivid flame and orange colours.

My bias towards Wilhelm Kordes as the world's greatest hybridizer is well substantiated by the roses to his credit, but as a young apprentice, before I had even heard of him, I knew that the raiser of 'Crimson Glory' had to be someone special. Not only was I first taught to cut roses for shows among rows and rows of this variety, but I was also almost intoxicated by its perfume while being shown how to arrange my first-ever bowl of roses at a flower show. Each bloom had to be wired to support a very weak neck, but the raiser himself could not have been more proud of the result. 'Crimson Glory' had been introduced in 1935 and remained popular as the best red until superseded in the 1950s by one of its descendants, 'Ena Harkness'. Floppiness of bloom had been the recurring habit of most red Hybrid Teas, and indeed of Hybrid Perpetuals, since the days of 'Général Jacqueminot', but by 1950 Kordes had solved the problem with 'Karl Herbst' and later in 1964, his retirement year, with the even better 'Ernest H. Morse'. In between these two in 1957 had come the superb 'Perfecta', a

lovely mixture of pinks and cream. Wilhelm died in 1976, leaving a wealth of unique rose progeny for his son Reimer to continue the tradition of the Kordes line with excellent Hybrid Teas such as 'Colour Wonder' (1964), 'Congratulations' (1978) and 'Royal William' ('Korzaun') (1984).

Not far from Kordes' establishment another German breeder was busy pollinating, one Mathias Tantau. His early work was largely with Polyanthas and Hybrid Polyanthas, and although he

Top left: 'Michèle Meilland', and *right*, 'Papa Meilland'   *Below:* 'Perfecta'

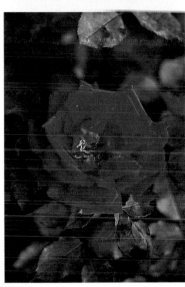

Sheer weight of numbers prohibits mention of all but a few of the great Hybrid Teas raised during this century, and I have given no more than a cursory glance at the work of some of the people behind them, but it would be wrong to assume that only those so far mentioned have created the world's best and wrong also to ignore altogether other parts of the world. Modern roses would be much the poorer without significant contributions from such men as Pedro Dot of Spain with 'Condesa de Sastago' (1932) and 'Angels Mateu' (1934), Louis Lens of Belgium with, among others, 'Pascali' (1963), Verschuren of Holland who gave us the beautiful and well-loved 'Etoile de Hollande' in 1919 and Jan Spek, also of Holland, with 'Spek's Yellow' ('Golden Sceptre', 1948). For some years the Japanese have been working with roses and although their Hybrid Teas are seldom seen in our Western gardens, this is not through lack of fine varieties but simply, I think, that we have many good ones of our own. I could go on, for wherever roses grow the Hybrid Tea is revered and breeders, both famous and unknown, will forever continue to hone it to perfection.

Population density and climatic differences influence where roses are bred as well as the distribution of new species. Parts of Australia, for example, have an ideal climate for hybridizing. I know some first-class rosarians and nurserymen there, but it is not surprising that in such a large country with a relatively small market they have never considered breeding roses to be a viable proposition – although I can think of no better place for someone to start.

Looking back over those so far mentioned, my own contribution to Hybrid Teas is insignificant. My first was 'Pinta' in 1973, a shapely, smallish-flowered creamy-white with Sweet Briar perfume. It came as a big surprise since, at the time, I was seeking a red. 'Royal Smile', named for one of the world's most famous smiles, that of Queen Elizabeth the Queen Mother, on her eightieth birthday, and introduced in 1980, is a blush-white, also with a very strong scent. Over recent winters this rose has not proved as hardy as I would like, but it is beautiful and does well in warmer climates.

I declare, somewhat immodestly, 'Anna Pavlova' (1981) to be my favourite Hybrid Tea, even if it is my own. Knowing this rose was shy in producing flowers, I had left it growing in my trial beds for several years, unintroduced, never having the heart to cast it aside. It was spotted one day by my good friend Keith Money, who was then working on his biography of Pavlova. Keith fell for the rose, and, by sheer persistence over several months, persuaded me to name it 'Anna Pavlova'. As Keith had christened the rose, I asked him to write a piece about it in our catalogue. He wrote:

introduced a few Hybrid Teas between the wars, none became very well known. It was not until his son, also Mathias, got to work that quality Hybrid Teas started to emerge from the Tantau nurseries. The first of these was 'Prima Ballerina' in 1957, then in rapid succession such eminent roses as 'Super Star' ('Tropicana') (1960), 'Blue Moon' (1964), 'Whisky Mac' (1967) and 'Duke of Windsor' (1969). Need I say more, for these roses speak for themselves? One of his latest roses, the excellent white 'Polar Star', was voted 'Rose of the Year' by British nurserymen in 1985.

The agent for all Tantau roses in Britain during the 1960s was Harry Wheatcroft. There was no better showman than this flamboyant man, whose personality alone sold millions of roses. He attracted publicity wherever he went and succeeded in becoming a household name synonymous with roses.

Top left: 'Blue Moon', and *right,* 'Crimson Glory'
Below left: 'Etoile de Hollande', and *right,* 'Pinta'

'Royal Smile'

Polyanthas and Floribundas

It is difficult to imagine a world without roses, but even with them it would be a much duller place without Floribundas, which are now taken for granted. Imagine our parks without them. Some Hybrid Teas, I suppose, could play their part and act as bedding plants, but few could emulate the summer-long colour and floriferousness of well-grown Floribundas.

The early development of the cluster-flowered rose has been briefly mentioned already and need not be repeated here, especially as it is doubtful if the early raisers of these roses had any notion of just how far-reaching and significant their haphazard experiments would prove to be. Suffice to say that however little the preconception – from the moment that genes of *R. moschata* and *R. multiflora* were linked to those of *R. chinensis* – the progress of this type of rose was assured. What has evolved, given the curiosity of rose people, was inevitable, for no raiser, however committed to the cabbage-shaped rose, could resist crossing it with a cluster-flowered rose in the hope of getting even more, if smaller, cabbage-shaped roses together on the same plant.

The early Polypompons, as they were delightfully called, were rather awkwardly grouped together for they were a mixed bag; distinct in having clusters of blooms in one inflorescence, but diverse and varied in size, shape of bloom and habit of growth. It was, therefore, not until the early 1900s that enough uniformly distinct characteristics came forth from among them to form a splinter group, the Dwarf Polyanthas. I adore this little group of roses, or at least those still with us today. They have such cheerful dispositions, are very adaptable and never any trouble, except for occasional bouts of mildew for which I can readily forgive them. They enjoyed deserved popularity in the period between the wars when lots and lots were introduced.

Hardiness is an attribute of the Dwarf Polyanthas which is especially useful in northern Europe and Scandinavia where the winters are too cold for many large-flowered roses to flourish without mollycoddling. It was therefore appropriate and predictable that a Danish nurserymen should be the first to cross such roses with other types. His name was Dines Poulsen, one of a family of rose growers with a nursery at Kvistgarrd. He used as his seed parent a red Polyantha called 'Mme Norbert Levavasseur' and, for his first pollen parent, the rambler 'Dorothy Perkins'. The result was a rosy-pink which he called 'Ellen Poulsen'. This was shortish in growth after its Polyantha parent and cluster-flowered but not too different from the existing range of Polyanthas; nevertheless it

There is a real period charm about the full, slightly frilled petals with their shades of face-powder pink, all set off with the darkest possible leaves, strangely circular. It is quite haunting: the nearest I can get to describing it would be to imagine a picnic of fresh fruit salad with Turkish Delight and served under a flowering May tree.

I know that without his persistence this rose would still be unnamed.

Here, in England, it never produces any great quantity of flowers but to my incredulity and delight a telegram fell on my desk one day in 1985 saying that 'Anna Pavlova' had been awarded a silver medal by the judges at the Genoa Rose Trials in Italy, primarily for freedom of flower. Despite this award it was not until I saw her in full flush at Deane Ross's nursery in South Australia that it dawned on me that this lady dances much better in warmer climates than she does in chilly Norfolk.

was worthy of introduction and proved, as he suspected, very hardy. Dines Poulsen then produced a rose called 'Red Riding Hood' using the same seed parent but this time crossing it with the Hybrid Tea 'Richmond'. This too proved very hardy, but unlike 'Ellen Poulsen', its half-sister, its habit of growth was much less like a Polyantha.

After this foundation work, Dines' brother, Svend, took responsibility for hybridizing and soon after, using the Dwarf Polyantha 'Orléans Rose' as 'mum' and the Hybrid Tea 'Red Star' as 'dad', raised two outstanding seedlings. These were introduced in 1924; one was 'Else Poulsen', a pink semi-double, and the other was 'Kirsten Poulsen', a red single. Each had largeish flowers compared to the Polyanthas and was taller in growth; the flowers, however, unlike those of their seed parent, were produced in large clusters. They also continued flowering throughout the summer, whereas most of the Hybrid Teas of the day took a rest between their first flush in June/July and their second in September. It turned out – for genetic reasons that we need not go into here – that these exciting new roses were almost sterile and not easy to breed from, but persistence paid off and more of a similar type followed from the Poulsen stable. The most famous is probably the lovely red 'Karen Poulsen' (1932). The Poulsen roses, as they became known, proved very popular and were soon widely grown throughout the world. Although not as well known as some of the others, 'Poulsen's Yellow' (1939) was of even greater significance, for it brought yellow into the colour range of the dwarf cluster flowered roses for the first time. Talking of yellows, I rate the shrubby, well-foliated 'Chinatown' (1963) the best rose ever to come from the family Poulsen, this time from Svend's son Niels, who in the family tradition started to breed roses in the mid-1950s.

Nothing succeeds like success, and soon other breeders were following the 'Poulsen School' by working with roses of this kind. Obviously, when others started, such roses could hardly be classified as 'Poulsens'; so, after some debate, the powers-that-be grouped them together and reclassified them as Hybrid Polyanthas. They remained thus known for about two decades, but such was their advance, and for very good reasons relating to size of flower, improved colour range and growth habits, they were reclassified in the early 1950s as Floribundas. I well recall this change of name, for it was in 1951 that I first joined the firm of E. B. LeGrice as a new apprentice. Two other Peters were already working there and, on my first day, to help him differentiate when issuing orders, the foreman, cruelly and to my horror, decided that I should be known as 'Floribunda'. Fortunately, this name did not

stick; otherwise, being a sensitive lad, I might have turned away from roses forever.

As it turned out, however, Floribundas were to play an important part in my career, for by then my boss, Edward LeGrice, had been breeding these roses with considerable success for several years. 'Dainty Maid', a lovely single pink, was his first in 1940 with 'Dusky Maiden', of which he was particularly proud, following in

Top: 'Chinatown'. *Below left:* 'Dusky Maiden', and *right,* 'Lilac Charm'

Top: 'News', and *below*, 'Ripples'

1947. A pride not misplaced, for not only is 'Dusky', as he called it, a beautiful rose but it is also scented, proof that the elusive attribute of fragrance would eventually come to Floribundas. Edward Burton LeGrice was a fine man and I was privileged to spend some of the most rewarding days of my life fetching and carrying for him as he lovingly hybridized his roses, all the time quietly talking and unselfishly imparting to my eager ear what I now know to be his own, unique knowledge of roses.

After two seasons of writing the labels for each cross he made, I was taught to emasculate the flowers of his seed parents for him. He would give me a list at the beginning of each day of all those he wanted to hybridize and, a little later, humming a hymn tune, would apply the pollen to make carefully thought-out crosses. It was while I was his label boy in the early 1950s that he laid the foundations for some of the unusually coloured roses he raised and introduced from the 1950s to the early '70s. To get some of these colours, he used, as I can confirm from the bitter experience of having to spell the awkward long names, the whole range of purple and dark red Gallicas, especially those that were generous with their pollen, such as 'Tuscany Superb' from which came some very strangely coloured seedlings and, indeed, some very beautiful ones, for example 'Lilac Charm' (1952), 'News' (1968) and 'Ripples' (1971).

Only a few plants of his masterpiece, 'Allgold', were growing at the North Walsham nursery when I arrived. It had flowered for the first time as a seedling some two years before. He knew then that, if the rose stood up to its proving trials, it would be a winner and I recall the many hours I spent cutting budwood of this variety for distribution around the world. 'Allgold' was a few years ahead of its time. It is a sad irony that the man who first mooted the idea of plant breeders' rights in Britain received such small financial returns for his work in producing the first deep yellow Floribunda. I have always felt very proud of 'Allgold', partly I suppose for the very small part I played in its beginnings, but more, I hope, because it is an ever-present memorial to a man who taught me a lot about life and shared with me his deep love of roses. In 1961 my wife Joan, to my great delight, chose buds of 'Allgold' for her wedding bouquet. One year after 'Allgold's' introduction in 1956 I was compelled to leave LeGrice's establishment for compulsory National Service. At the end of two years as a soldier I could have gone back, but instead, inspired by Edward LeGrice, I chose to go it alone. Had I returned to work for him, I know I would have learned much more about roses than I will ever now know. 'Father', as he was affectionately known by his staff, died in 1977, leaving my world and the world of many others the poorer for his

'Allgold'

loss, but the world as a whole much the richer for his roses.

Another memory of my days at North Walsham is of the frequent visits Edward LeGrice received from eminent rose people from around the world. One such person was a big man from the United States named Eugene Boerner, hybridizer for Jackson & Perkins. He, too, worked with Floribundas with considerable success. Jackson & Perkins had large investments in the breeding of roses and, while anyone with limited resources can cross two roses, there is no doubt that the more crosses one can make the greater the likelihood of breeding a winner. If this sounds cynical it is not meant to sound that way, for without the extensive breeding programme of Eugene Boerner and Jackson & Perkins the world would never have enjoyed such superb Floribundas as 'Goldilocks' (1945), 'Lavender Pinocchio' (1948), 'Fashion' and 'Masquerade' (1949), 'Ma Perkins' (1952) and 'Jiminy Cricket' (1954).

Jackson & Perkins led the way, but some very good Floribundas came from other American breeders during the 1950s and '60s.

Herbert Swim raised the excellent and colourful 'Circus' (1956) and followed this with, among others, a rose that must rate as one of the best Floribundas ever raised, 'Pink Parfait' (1960). Both were introduced by the Armstrong Nursery, California.

Gordon Von Abrams gave us the lovely 'Golden Slippers' through Peterson & Dering in 1961. Another of the best cluster-flowered roses ever to be raised came from Dr E. Lammerts of California in 1954. 'Queen Elizabeth' (strictly, 'The Queen Elizabeth Rose') was introduced to Britain by Harry Wheatcroft and immediately took the country by storm. In the United States it is classified as a Grandiflora, a term used there to separate the large-flowered, taller cluster roses from the general run of short varieties. This classification has never been accepted in Britain because its botanical connotations are thought to be misleading,

Top: 'Fashion'. *Below left:* 'Jiminy Cricket', and *right*, 'Ma Perkins'

'Pink Parfait'

'Frensham'

so, although obviously different from most Floribundas, it never-theless comes into that category here. Endowed with healthy foliage and blooms of superb quality, impervious to all weather and good for cutting, such a rose had to win many friends.

In order to link the two Floribunda specialists, LeGrice and Boerner, I digressed geographically to America. To return to Brit-ain for a while, men other than LeGrice have bred some outstand-ing Floribundas. The notable amateur, Albert Norman, gave us the prickly but stalwart 'Frensham' in 1946. He also bred 'Red Dandy' (1959), a rose I always liked but which, sadly, seems now to have disappeared forever. Interestingly, all Norman's red roses that I know of came directly or indirectly from the famous Kordes Hybrid Tea 'Crimson Glory'. Less prodigious in output than some modern breeders but nonetheless successful · was Herbert Robinson, who raised, among other good varieties, a rose called 'Highlight' from Kordes' 'Independence' in 1957. 'Highlight' never really caught on but deserves a mention for its role as a pollen parent to McGredy's famous 'Elizabeth of Glamis'.

In 1967 Jack Harkness sent out his first Floribunda, 'Escapade'. Perhaps because of my preference for quiet colours I consider 'Escapade' and the highly scented 'Margaret Merril' (1977) to be the best of his cluster-flowered varieties. Of his brighter coloured, 'Mountbatten' (1982), better qualified as a shrub, and 'Amber Queen' (1984) are two fine roses that are obviously here to stay.

Alec Cocker's time was not totally taken up with Hybrid Teas. Some very good Floribundas have come from his work, the best known of which are probably 'Anne Cocker' (1970) and 'Glenfiddich' (1976). Another very good Floribunda which I rate very highly is 'English Miss' (1977) from Cants of Colchester.

Before World War II, Dickson's of Northern Ireland had built their reputation on Hybrid Teas, but after the war was over they did not take long to get back into the swing of things with some notable Floribundas. Their first were two richly coloured roses, 'Shepherd's Delight' (1956) and 'Dickson's Flame' (1958), fol-lowed soon after by the outstanding 'Dearest' (1960). Of the 135 Floribundas listed in the Royal National Rose Society's current Rose Directory, no fewer than seventeen are accredited to Pat Dickson. They include such well-known varieties as 'Scarlet Queen Elizabeth' (1963) and 'Sea Pearl' (1964). Dickson's roses have been chosen as 'Rose of the Year' by the British Rose Trades Association on three occasions in the 1980s: 'Beautiful Britain' in '83, 'Gentle Touch' in '86 and 'Sweet Magic' in '88, although the last two fall more readily into the newly evolved group of 'Patio' roses. That other famous Ulsterman, Sam McGredy, has twenty-

four Floribundas to his credit in the RNRS Directory. The quiet 'Chanelle' is one of his best, another is the louder and robust 'Orangeade' (both 1959). His best known, though, is probably 'Elizabeth of Glamis', named for Her Majesty Queen Elizabeth the Queen Mother in 1964, a beautiful rose which does well when mild winters allow it to make some older wood. The first of his

Left: Top: 'Queen Elizabeth', and *below*, 'Scarlet Queen Elizabeth' *(left)* and 'English Miss' *(right)*
Above: Top: 'Escapade', and *below*, 'Elizabeth of Glamis' *(left)* and 'Beautiful Britain' *(right)*

'hand-painted' roses, the well-named 'Picasso' (1971), was introduced by McGredy just before he moved to New Zealand. His breeding stock obviously did not suffer from the move and a steady flow of worthy varieties has been raised by him, including 'Old Master' (1974) and 'Sue Lawley' (1980).

After their initial work with the Polypompons and Polyanthas, and a little flurry of activity at the turn of the century with varieties such as Guillot's beautiful 'Irène Watts' (1896) and Turbat's 'Yvonne Rabier' in 1910, nothing of any real significance came from French breeders until after World War II. Since then, however, they have certainly not been idle, and as with Hybrid Teas, it has been the family Meilland who have led the way. This nursery is now concentrating more and more on raising fashionable procumbent roses, but of the Floribundas they have introduced over the years I particularly admire 'Zambra' (1961), 'Frenzy' (1970) and 'Poppy Flash' ('Rusticana', 1971). Another very beautiful French rose I like, not from Meilland but from Delbard-Chabert, is 'Centenaire de Lourdes' (1958). It is a seedling from 'Frau Karl Druschki' but, sadly, it has inherited none of its parent's hardiness.

De Ruiters of Holland introduced quite a number of Dwarf Polyanthas during the early part of this century and followed these much later with some very good Floribundas. Of their roses I am particularly fond of the beautifully shaped 'Rosemary Rose' (1954). I also like 'Sweet Repose' ('The Optimist', 1955), but this is seldom seen today. Of de Ruiter's roses 'Orange Sensation' (1961) is probably the best known and has stood the test of time with distinction. Another first-class rose from Holland which has lasted well is 'Mevrouw Nathalie Nypels' (1919); it was raised by Leenders and is now better known simply as 'Nathalie Nypels'. A German named Geduldig raised the beautiful, free-flowering 'Grüss an Aachen' in 1909, way ahead of its time. Originally it was classified as a Polypompon but it fits in happily with the modern Floribundas and in my opinion is one of the best ever introduced.

With Denmark just across the border, Wilhelm Kordes was well aware of the work of the Poulsens in the 1920s and '30s, so anything they could do he knew he could do too – not that he was a pirate; rose breeders the world over use the results of one another's ideas. After all, Poulsen himself had had to make use of other breeders' roses to start his own initial strains. Even before the war, Kordes had raised one or two very good Hybrid Polyanthas and one in particular, 'Rosenelfe' (1939), clearly indicated the way ahead. It had been bred from 'Else Poulsen', which, considering that it was not very fertile, was an achievement in itself. Its pollen parent was a colourful, fully double, lesser-known McGredy Hybrid Tea called 'Sir Basil McFarland' and with it Kordes proved that the petal numbers of the Hybrid Polyanthas could be

'Irène Watts'

'Centenaire de Lourdes'

already done and lots of breeding stock available, Kordes was thus well placed to help satisfy a craving for Floribundas which were tailor-made for colouring the new industrial and commercial landscape of Germany, not to mention the gardens, parks and open spaces that were part of the scheme of things there. 'Korona' (1955) was just one exciting, colourful Floribunda that seemed to symbolize the bright new future ahead for its raiser and its Fatherland. When Reimer Kordes took over from his father in 1956 he excelled in Floribundas with 'Iceberg' (1958), surely the best of its type ever introduced, followed by 'Lilli Marlene' (1958), 'Honeymoon' (1960), 'Marlena' (1964) and his most recent, the blood-red 'The Times Rose' (1984). I find this rose a little disappointing and still prefer 'Lilli Marlene'.

increased without the loss of the larger flower clusters. His other outstanding introductions were 'Pinocchio' (1940) with its mixed ancestry of Hybrid Musk, Hybrid Tea and Dwarf Polyantha – later to prove invaluable in the progeny of many a future Floribunda – and 'Orange Triumph' (1937), more red than orange but with an unrivalled constitution and the longevity of an oak.

With so many successful Hybrid Teas coming out of their nurseries one wonders how the two Mathias Tantau managed to find time for anything else. Judging by the conspicuous succession of Floribundas created by them since the late 1940s, however, they fully realized that time working with such roses was time well spent. Having said this, some Hybrid Teas and Floribundas are

The rebuilding of Germany after World War II brought roses for landscaping into much demand. With a great deal of work

'Rosemary Rose'

'Grüss an Aachen'

'Lilli Marlene', and *below*, 'Iceberg'

crossed a seedling from these two with a red rose of his own breeding called 'Heros' which had the famous Dutch rose 'Etoile de Hollande' as one of its parents. The result in 1951 was a rose he called 'Garnette'. Together with its several sports and close hybrids, it is still to this day a major florist's rose throughout the world on account of its hard-wearing and long-lasting qualities. I may be wrong, but I cannot really believe that in making such a cross Tantau was actually aiming for a forcing rose. With foresight or not, he must have been fortunate to observe its qualities while it was growing under glass, for this rose is hardly worth a second glace when grown out of doors. Later, in 1971, Mathias Tantau junior introduced another successful forcing rose, the orange 'Belinda'. From the early 1950s onwards this firm bred and introduced a succession of successful Floribundas. I well remember the excellent 'Red Favourite' (1954), which seems to be lost now, and 'Anna Wheatcroft' (1958), a lovely, bright salmon single which I used without much success in my own first attempts at breeding, although it did yield for me a pleasant little salmon rose, the first I ever introduced, called 'Penelope Plummer' (1970), which never caught on as I had dreamed but is still cherished by me. Other excellent Floribundas from the Tantau stable are the vigorous 'Paprika' (1958) and two very useful shorter roses, 'Tip Top' (1963) and 'Topsi' (1971).

Well aware as I am that my achievements as a rose breeder will never put me anywhere but near the bottom of any league table of breeders, I hesitantly mention my own small contributions to the vast array of Floribundas available today. Now and then, sandwiched in between the preoccupation of building a collection of historical and classical roses, running a business and, I suppose, in deference to my learning the trade with Edward LeGrice, I have, from time to time, dabbled in the fascinating, time-consuming pastime of hybridizing. I still do occasionally, but now as tutor to my children, who – who knows? – may one day do better than Dad. We have abandoned any search for Floribundas or indeed Hybrid Teas to explore other avenues, but in days now past I concentrated especially on the cluster-flowered varieties.

I confess that 'Penelope Plummer' should never have been introduced. I had tested it well, I thought, but it developed a mild proneness to black spot which had not been noticed in its trials. Not having been in business long, I suppose I was anxious to make my mark. I shudder now at my naïvety for I named it after the then reigning Miss World, thinking that such a name would bring stardom to the rose and recognition to its breeder. Sadly, no, the most I got was a picture of Miss World and myself together in our local weekly newspaper and a teasing from my friends.

now so interbred that it is almost pot luck as to what comes forth when crossing them with one another.

Like Kordes, Mathias Tantau the first was well aware of Poulsen's work in Denmark; although without any conspicuous success, he had been dabbling in Floribundas since the 1920s and '30s. This continued into the '40s for, ironically, Germans were not forced by government decree to stop breeding roses as the British were. It was Tantau's use of two Kordes roses, 'Rosenelfe' and 'Eva', that gave him his first big break with Floribundas. He

The launch in 1975 of my next Floribunda was stage-managed much more efficiently, for it was sponsored by the insurance company Norwich Union. Colin Page, the company's publicity manager, and his colleagues were very good to me, for I was hard up at the time and without their sponsorship it would not have been easy to carry on in business, let alone continue the expensive luxury of breeding roses. For the rose this may not have been quite so good, for excellent and well-intentioned though the company was, its name did not lend itself well to a rose. 'Norwich Union' is an excellent, short-growing yellow bedding rose with a good scent. It has never been widely grown in Britain and – except for Australia and New Zealand, where I understand it is quite popular – is probably unheard of elsewhere. Other Floribundas of mine are 'Norwich Castle' (1979), which has been likened to the colour of best bitter beer, and the tall 'Everest Double Fragrance' (1979). This rose has one of the strongest scents of any Floribunda I know, though its colour, which changes from coral to soft blush-pink as it ages, does not endear it to some but pleases me enormously. My latest two are 'Lady Romsey' (1985), a short creamy-white with a pink blush and fine dark green foliage, and 'Great Ormond Street',

'Lady Romsey'

Left: 'Norwich Castle', and *below*, shrub roses in the author's garden

a lemon-yellow introduced for the famous children's hospital. I am fond of both these little roses but others, unbiased, will decide their destiny.

Modern Shrub Roses

Although differences in dimension are built into most plant families, few have such wide diversity of size as the genus *Rosa*. By providing variation within a species, nature dictates just how far man can go in capturing advantage from any given attribute. As the majority of species within the genus are tallish and shrubby and the majority of colourful hybrids are short and shrubby, there can be no more lucrative area for a hybridizer to explore in order, perhaps, to break new ground than among the middle size-ranges; that is to say shrub roses, broad or tall or both. Of course, the laws of heredity are such that dominant and recessive factors will frequently intervene, but this only adds variety and interest to the job and will keep the hybridizer's feet firmly on the greenhouse floor.

Present-day landscaping trends and those for the foreseeable future demand the use of easily maintained shrubby plants. No other group or family of plants can possibly fulfil this role more successfully than roses – more specifically, shrub roses – while, at the same time, providing a succession of flowers. Several modern rose breeders saw this trend long before me and already there is a wide range of roses for this purpose. I suspect several more exciting new ones are on the way.

Hybrid musks at Helmingham Hall

As with some other groups, the early development of hybrid shrub roses was more by chance than design, so I will not dwell on those from the nineteenth century except to say that before the introduction of the Tea-Scented and Chinese hybrids from the East, most of the European and Middle Eastern hybrids were, by today's criteria, shrub roses. There were one or two exceptions, such as the Dwarf Centifolias for example, but by and large the old Centifolias Damasks and Albas were tall, lax and shrubby. The Gallicas, generally speaking, were shorter but still could only be classified as shrubs in today's sense.

How is a shrub rose defined? These days, it is more a case of definition by usage rather than by description for, of course, all roses are shrubs; some of the larger ones, admittedly, could be called trees but most of us think of trees, even small trees, as being much bigger than roses. In the past – and even now from time to time – roses were regularly referred to as trees. This is a hark back to the days when the average garden variety was far bigger than it is today. My own definition is very much in usage terms: bush roses are those that should not normally reach more than 4′ (1.2 m) high when fully grown and which, by their tidy habit of growth, are generally used for bedding, group planting or as border plants. Such roses invariably have a long flowering season. Shrub roses are those that are as a rule taller than 4′ (1.2 m) when mature and which can be used individually for specimen planting or grown as shrubs in a shrubbery. Shrubs can flower once, can repeat or be continuous.

Most rose breeders of this century have concentrated on working with Hybrid Teas and Floribundas. Although several good shrubs emerged from their work from time to time, any deliberate and planned breeding has been left to no more than a handful of dedicated men. One such man was Lord Penzance, who worked with Sweet Briars and bred no fewer than sixteen of these in the 1890s. Another was Joseph Pemberton, a clergyman turned nurseryman, whom by the time he introduced his first roses in 1913, was sixty-one years of age and well respected as an authority on his subject. The work of both these breeders has already been discussed in the sections on Sweet Briars (page 21) and Hybrid Musks (pages 21–2).

Another Briton to work primarily with shrub roses is David Austin, but his work has all been done during the last thirty years. Nevertheless, the first of Austin's roses has made a real impact on the rose world. It is the tall, sprawly, almost climbing rose called 'Constance Spry' (1961), the first rose raised in modern times with enough charm, personality and fragrance to compete on almost

level terms with the old classic roses from the past. But Austin was not satisfied. Although 'Constance Spry' showed him and, indeed, the rest of the world that a market existed for what might loosely be called reproduction roses, it flowers for only a short season and therefore is of limited appeal. After this rose, he set about a planned programme of crossing and recrossing old roses such as Damasks and Gallicas with modern Hybrid Teas and Floribundas.

Top: 'Charles Austin'. *Below left:* 'Evelyn', and *right*, 'The Pilgrim'

Progress was slow at first, but gradually he realized that his theories were beginning to yield results. Although 'Chianti' (1967) was not remontant, most of those which have followed in steadily increasing numbers are, if not fully continuous, certainly repeat-flowering. He calls his creations as a group 'English roses' and there is little doubt that many are here to stay. Most are scented and of accommodating size, hence their popularity for smaller gardens where long flowering is an important factor. Of those introduced in the 1970s, I very much like the tall 'Charles Austin'

'Chianti'

scarlet 'Geranium' (1938), a *R. moyesii* seedling from the Royal Horticultural Society, Wisley Gardens, and 'Helen Knight' (1964), a *R. ecae* seedling from Frank Knight of the same gardens. Another interesting *R. ecae* hybrid is 'Golden Chersonese' (1967), raised by E. F. Allen; both are spring-flowering, deep yellow singles. Another good yellow single of this type is 'Cantabrigiensis', which came forth as a chance seedling, probably from *R. hugonis*, at Cambridge University Botanic Gardens in 1931.

Although the Americans have quite a lot of their own, not many shrub roses have come to Europe from across the Atlantic. Of those that have, only a few are widely grown. Excellent among them is the *R. pimpinellifolia* hybrid 'Golden Wings' (1956) from Roy Shepherd, which has enjoyed ever-increasing popularity over the years. One I like is 'Lafter' (1948), this time from Brownell, which should be much more widely used. Another shrub rose from the United States which ought to get more attention is 'Eos' (1950) from Ruys. A sumptuous rose which cannot decide whether or not to be a climber but nevertheless makes an excellent shrub is 'Aloha' (1949) from Boerner, and a hybrid Rugosa rose from Canada, 'Agnes', is exceptionally hardy; it was raised in 1900 but not introduced until 1922. It is one of the few yellow Rugosas and for this reason will always be in demand. Two other Canadian varieties that do well in Britain are 'Eddie's Crimson' (1956) and 'Eddie's Jewel' (1962). Both are hybrids of *R. moyesii*.

(1973) and 'Chaucer' (1970). So many have been produced in the 1980s that it is quite impossible for me to pass judgement on the merits of all of them. Two in particular, however, 'Mary Rose' and 'Graham Thomas', both brought out in 1983, have taken my eye as being both beautiful and healthy. For more on the English roses, see the Dictionary section (pages 365–73).

A few very good shrub roses have come from other British breeders this century. Two of real merit and note are the bright

'Cantabrigiensis'

Left: 'Lafter', and *right*, 'Eddie's Jewel'

There can be no doubt that one of the most important roses ever sent to Europe from America is the trailing shrub 'Max Graf' (1919), discovered and named by James H. Bowditch of Connecticut. As it was a foundling some disagreement initially arose over its parentage, but now it is generally accepted to be a cross between *R. wichuraiana* and *R. rugosa* or perhaps the other way round. 'Max Graf' seldom sets any seed, but there could be no better place for a pod to form than in Germany under the eyes of Herr Wilhelm Kordes. Lesser rosemen might have raised their eyebrows at such a sight but no more than that. Kordes, of course, raised the seed and produced a seedling which was later named *R. kordesii*. The flowers of his new species were of no great significance; its main attribute was hardiness and again a less interested person might have ignored it as a fluke – but not Wilhelm. He found it to be

quite fertile and eventually bred some very hardy and useful climbing roses from it. In pursuit of hardiness for German winters, other interesting lines of breeding were followed by Kordes which threw up some very good shrub roses: 'Fritz Nobis' (1940), for example, came from the hybrid Sweet Briar 'Magnifica'; his 'Spring' or 'Frühling' roses came from *R. pimpinellifolia* and 'Scarlet Fire' ('Scharlachglut') from (1984), are excellent. Two other shrub roses of note from Germany are Peter Lambert's Rugosa 'Schneezwerg' (1912) and 'Mozart' (1937), a 'Ballerina'-like rose that deserves to be better known.

A shrub rose that cannot go unmentioned is 'Nevada' (1927) from Pedro Dot of Spain. It makes a superb flowering shrub and is probably a *R. pimpinellifolia* hybrid. A pink form was discovered by Graham Thomas at Hillings Nurseries in 1959 and named 'Marguerite Hilling'. An omission so far is mention of the delightful 'Omar Khayyam', a Damask seedling from Edward Fitzgerald's grave in Suffolk, having been grown there from a seed collected from the great poet's tomb in Nashipur. The seed was sown in 1893 but the rose was not propagated and offered for sale till several years later.

Although most of nature's own roses found their way into our gardens in the last century, a few excellent species or near species have been discovered or raised during the past eighty years or so. These are too numerous to discuss in any great detail, but one or two must receive at least a small mention. *R. farreri persetosa*, for example – dubbed the 'Threepenny Bit Rose' – makes a fascinating and most useful shrub. It came from seeds sent from China by the plant-hunter Farrer in 1914. Another, *R. stellata mirifica* or the 'Sacramento Rose', is not easy to grow but well worth a try; it comes from northern Mexico and was introduced in 1916. One of the loveliest of species is *R. primula* or the 'Incense Rose', a

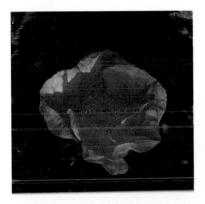

Top left: 'Max Graf', and *right*, 'Schneezwerg'
Below: 'Scharlachglut'

Above left: 'Fritz Nobis', and *right*, 'Geranium'

medium-sized shrub with a large density of thorns; its waxy foliage, especially when crushed, gives off a strong aroma reminiscent of incense. The delicate single flowers are soft primrose-yellow. 'Micrugosa (*R. × micrugosa*) is a very hardy and little-used shrub with a long flowering season; its soft pink flowers are single, of a satiny texture and sweetly scented. There is also a white form which I like even better.

While talking of first crosses, I must mention a very fine recent addition to these roses sent to me in 1984 by Mrs Hazel Le Rougetel of Liphook, Hampshire. It is a cross between *R. rugosa* and *R. nitida*; not only does it have a long season but its flowers are

followed by a good crop of attractive hips. A special feature is its rich and colourful autumn foliage. It was introduced in 1988 with the name 'Corylus'. Most of the best Rugosa hybrids were raised towards the end of the nineteenth century, but a few excellent ones have emerged spasmodically since. The most notable are the spreading 'Fru Dagmar Hartopp' (1914), 'Hansa' (1905) and 'Scabrosa', a foundling of the 1950s.

So far, I have introduced three shrub roses of my own: 'James

Top left: R. primula, and *right*, 'Corylus' foliage and hips. *Below:* 'Marguerite Hilling'

Top left: 'Sadler's Wells', and *right*, 'William and Mary'. *Below:* 'James Mason'

Mason' (1982), 'Sadler's Wells' (1983) and 'William and Mary' (1988). The first is a dark red, summer-flowering hybrid Gallica named after the late actor of that name. I had mentioned to his wife Clarissa at a rose show that her husband really should have a rose named after him since she already had one from Harkness named after her. I sent them a photograph, they liked it, and I duly went ahead with registration and despatched several plants to their home in Switzerland. They flowered in June the following year and James wrote to me saying how much he had enjoyed its first flowering. One month later he died, very suddenly. James Mason loved roses, as does his widow. He was a fine actor with a fine, out of the ordinary voice, so it is fitting that he should have chosen an out of the ordinary rose to be named after him. Sadly, so out of the ordinary that it will never be as widely grown as it should be.

I well recall the launching of my second shrub rose. It was named to commemorate the tercentenary of the Sadler's Wells ballet company in 1983 and their publicity department had arranged for Lesley Collier, the ballerina, to visit our stand at the Chelsea Flower Show for a presentation of a bouquet. It was planned that I should meet her outside the main gate of the show on Chelsea Embankment to escort her to the rose. Having never met before, neither of us would recognize the other, but I felt sure that even in a crowd I would know a ballerina when I saw one. Just in case, we were each to wear a rose. I turned up at the Embankment gate in good time and waited. The pavement was crowded but not so much as to prevent recognition – or so I thought. Then came an announcement over the public address system: 'Would all members and visitors kindly leave the showground in an orderly way immediately.' The announcer did not say why such an evacuation was necessary, but in fact a terrorist organization had warned the police that a bomb was concealed somewhere among the flowers. Within minutes the whole of Chelsea Embankment was crowded with thousands of people standing shoulder to shoulder and, worse – many wearing roses as buttonholes. My chances of spotting a ballerina were nil.

Eventually, after about an hour, the all clear came. As expected, it had been a hoax. The crowds jostled back in through the gates, and I embarrassedly accosted several likely-looking ballerinas but none was Miss Collier. At last, feeling very confused, I followed the last line of stragglers into the showground and made my way back to our stand where I was met by a agitated reporter asking where I had been. Miss Collier, one of the first through the gate at the all clear, had done her stuff, posed for her picture with the rose and was then happily looking round the rest of the show. I never did meet her.

My third shrub rose in 1988 was also to commemorate a tercentenary. The years 1688 and 1689 are important years in British history, for it was then that William of Orange, and Mary, his Queen, arrived from Holland to supplant Mary's father, the unpleasant James II. To great public rejoicing, they became joint monarchs and ushered in a period of peace and prosperity throughout the kingdom. To commemorate this event and as a small part of the celebrations, I was invited to name a rose 'William and Mary'. To do justice to such an important historical event it was felt that the rose selected should not only be a reliable garden plant but should also reflect the type of rose that could well have been growing in the gardens of England and Holland at that time. Thus we chose a blowsy, pinkish-crimson seedling, reminiscent of the roses to be seen in many an old master of the Baroque period. Its size restricts its use in smaller gardens, except as a pot plant or small climber, and its weakness by today's standards is a short flowering season. I wish it was slightly less vigorous, but I have never considered that length of flowering should necessarily rank higher than beauty in one's judgement of a rose, and with such a name, true historical reflections are not such a bad thing.

Procumbents (Ground-Cover Roses)

A most recent development, obviously through demand, has been the steady increase in the number of spreading or prostrate roses which have been bred to cover the ground. They are usually termed 'ground-cover roses', a term I dislike because I believe it

'Red Blanket'

exaggerates their potential and implies that all of them can be used as dense, spreading shrubs to suppress weeds or take the backache out of gardening. Only a few of them will do this. Perhaps one day many more such roses will be bred, but until then I propose to call them 'procumbents'. After all, many much older roses can be used to cover ground and only their voracious nature has prevented their widespread usage for this purpose. I am thinking, in particular, of the Wichuraiana climbers and ramblers. Nevertheless, the recent procumbent roses are excellent garden plants, when massed in groups, not requiring too much labour to keep tidy. Several of the more recent introductions have the advantage of a much longer flowering season than those bred hitherto. Notable among these are the delightful 'Snow Carpet', with tiny leaves and dense growth, 'Smarty', a more vigorous, spreading variety of soft

Top: 'Nozomi'. *Above:* 'Surrey'

pink, and 'Red Blanket', again vigorous but rosy-red and with persistent foliage.

Over the past ten years or so, several British breeders have had a measure of success with the introduction of some very useful procumbent roses. Jack Harkness, for example, has bred a number from 'The Fairy', giving them rather pretty names like 'Fairyland' (1980) and 'Fairy Damsel' (1981). An out of the ordinary, offbeat colour from Harkness is the bluish-maroon semi-procumbent 'Cardinal Hume' (1984).

The founders of the Floribunda roses, Poulsen's of Denmark, have also been working on procumbent varieties in recent years. Notable among their newer introductions are 'Pink Bells', 'Red Bells' and 'White Bells', all in 1983 and all ground-hugging varieties with healthy, dense foliage; and even more recently some superb little spreaders in 'Kent' – white, 'Norfolk' – yellow, and 'Rutland – pink (all 1988). These are part of what are termed the County series.

Pat Dickson has produced, among others, a very good yellow spreader called 'Tall Story' (1984) which is, apparently, excellent for cutting. Using *R. wichuraiana* as a parent, Dennison Morey of the United States has added to the procumbents with 'Temple Bells' (1971), sometimes described as a climbing miniature. Contributions to shrub roses from Meilland's of France have been more recent, most notably the introduction of some very good spreaders, outstanding among which are 'Swany' (1977), 'Bonica '82' (1981) and 'Fiona' (1982). Throughout the 1980s this firm has made a speciality of what they now call their 'Landscape Varieties' with the trade name 'Meidiland'. They are particularly aimed at the municipal market since they need very little maintenance, but most make excellent garden plants in their own right.

Kordes of Germany, too, have now set about developing a range of procumbents and, in the mid-1980s, these were introduced with the names of game birds, 'Grouse' – soft pink, 'Partridge' – white, and 'Pheasant' – pink. All have a spreading growth and are the nearest to ground-cover that I know. More of the 'County' series are coming along, of which 'Surrey' – pink, and 'Suffolk' – scarlet, are the most recent to come to the UK.

The Japanese may not have made too many inroads into the ranks of Hybrid Teas and Floribundas west or, indeed, east of Tokyo, but the same cannot be said of their shrubby spreading varieties. Notable is the pinkish-white 'Nozomi', a rose from Toru Onodera which came to Britain in 1968 and is now seen almost everywhere where a dense, shrubby, ground-cover variety is called for; its many plum-coloured shoots and density of foliage compensating for its limited flowering season. Another densely foliated, shrubby spreader from Japan, this time with light green foliage, is 'Ferdy' (1984), raised by Suzuki. This too is non-recurrent. The latest from Onodera is 'Suma', a fully double, rosy-red form of 'Nozomi', which is very promising.

It is important, I think, to point out here that several of the roses mentioned in this group and, to a lesser extent, in others may well be introduced to other parts of the world under different names. Although the patent or trade name helps, it is impossible for an author to keep up with such practices which are becoming more and more prevalent.

Miniatures

Throughout my horticultural career and often to my regret, I have found myself avoiding plants that appear to be at all fiddly to handle; and shying away, too, from any form of gardening that is not compatible with the wielding of a spade. Since, by definition, only roses that are smaller than others in every respect can qualify for classification as Miniatures, it would be wrong of me to pretend to know everything about this group. This is not to say that over the years I have not come to know quite a few of these little charmers, nor that these particular roses have always escaped my bedtime reading. Like all other types of small things, plants or otherwise, the more one gets to know them the more fascinating they become.

No one is quite sure from where the first true Miniature came. Several theories exist, some with credibility and considerable circumstantial evidence, but like so much of the scantily documented history of the rose one has to suspect a certain amount of factual licence. That so many hybrids, especially the early ones, have close *R. chinensis* characteristics makes the supposition that it came from China the most plausible.

R. chinensis is a far from stable species, and even within its several garden types considerable variation in growth is not uncommon. Seeds sent to me from China some years ago as the long-lost *R. chinensis* and still not authenticated, all from the same plant, have yielded offspring of considerable variation. Of course, reproduction from seed, even of a species, does not take into account the activities of some Chinese-speaking bee. It may be a whimsical thought, but could it have been an early ancestor of that self-same bee that, perchance, way back in time, pollinated *R. chinensis* to spark a fusion of genes that led to a dwarf clone of this species? A clone which was eventually to find its way, by who knows what circuitous route, into the hands of breeders to become the progenitor of the Miniatures. Even though as far as I know it does not exist today, *R. chinensis minima* would have been the obvious name and, therefore, we can accept that it came via Mauritius, having been found there by one Robert Sweet in about 1810, as was reported by the well-known and highly respected botanist Lindsey in 1920.

During my two visits to Bermuda, knowing the chameleon-like growth habits of Chinas, I have kept my eyes open for any sign of a dwarf China among their 'mystery' roses. Bermuda has the perfect climate for rose longevity and I knew that many Chinas and Teas had found their way to the island at a time when *R. chinensis minima* would have been around, so why should it not still be there – but so far it has not shown up.

Little roses known as Miniatures enjoyed a longish spell of popularity as pot plants during the first part of the nineteenth century. In Victorian times other types became popular at their expense, and this, coupled with a rise in demand for other kinds of pot plants, caused Miniatures virtually to disappear from catalogues and florists. In 1918, however, so the story goes, a Swiss army officer named Roulet found in Switzerland a dwarf rose that he had never set eyes on before. A few years later, his discovery was introduced to the world as *R. rouletii*. Although designated a species it was really a hybrid, and after a short spell of popularity as a pot plant in its own right it inevitably fell into the hands of a hybridizer who put it to work as breeding stock. Others may have used it too, but the distinction of breeding the first popular hybrid Miniature goes to the Dutchman de Vink. He crossed 'Rouletii' with the Dwarf Polyantha 'Gloria Mundi' to bring forth 'Peon', a small Miniature whose red flowers each have a white eye. The polka-dot effect of each cluster was eye-catching and sales of the little rose in Holland, as a pot plant, soon proved its worth. De Vink then went on to produce a succession of other good Miniatures.

Just before World War II a few examples of 'Peon' found their way to North America. When it arrived a man named Robert Pyle of Pennsylvania obtained permission to change its name to 'Tom Thumb', whereupon it found a ready sale. Furthermore, no doubt to Tom Thumb's great delight, he was put to stud and admirably proved his worth by producing a succession of colourful progeny. After the war Miniatures, as pot plants, caught on in a big way, first in America and then throughout the world. Names were no small factor in this success story, for such roses lent themselves admirably to pretty names like de Vink's 'Cinderella' (1953) and 'Humpty Dumpty' (1952). The lovely 'Cinderella' is still popular to this day, its charm inbred, for although 'Peon', its pollen parent, is hardly beautiful in the refined sense, its seed parent, 'Cécile Brünner', most certainly is.

While de Vink and Pyle were taking advantage of the consumer boom of the 1950s by breeding, promoting and selling their varieties, other breeders had not been idle; in fact, as time was to prove, others had not only been working with 'Rouletii' since the 1930s but were having even greater success. One of these men was an American, the other a Spaniard. The American was Ralph Moore from the state where so many good roses have been bred, California. Moore, it seems, found 'Rouletii' a reluctant parent, skipped the first generation and worked initially with 'Peon', crossing and recrossing it with other roses and, in particular, with seedlings of his own, many of complex genealogy. Moore has found Miniatures fascinating to work with and has devoted a

Top: 'Little Flirt' and *right*, 'Dresden Doll'. *Above:* 'Gentle Touch'

distinguished career to breeding them in profusion; he is still very active and I had the great pleasure of meeting him in 1989. So far, he has given us such excellent varieties as 'Easter Morning' (1960), 'Baby Darling' (1964) and 'Rise 'n' Shine' (1977). He has also introduced several unusual ones, for by going back in time with his breeding stock he has found that he can induce some of the older roses to release some of their personality into the constitution of his Miniatures. 'Dresden Doll' (1975) and 'Mood Music' (1977), for example, are two Miniatures with flowers in the old-fashioned style and with as much moss on their buds and stems as the old Moss roses have themselves.

The Spaniard, Pedro Dot, has been mentioned elsewhere in connection with his Hybrid Teas, and like Ralph Moore he soon came to realize that breeding Miniatures could be rewarding. He too discovered that, since the dwarfing characteristic of Miniatures was inbuilt and dominant, he could cross them with almost any type of rose and still retain the dwarfing habit. He used Hybrid Teas, in particular, to very good effect. It was Dot who first introduced yellow into Miniatures with 'Baby Gold Star' (1940). Whether 'Baby Gold Star' was responsible I do not know, but, like the early yellow Hybrid Teas, the first few yellow Miniatures were dogged with that horrible affliction, black spot. Another good yellow Miniature from Dot is the shapely 'Rosina' (1951), still a firm favourite today, but my favourite of all is his 'Perla de Montserrat' (1945), a soft pinkish colour with superbly shaped flowers in the mould of one of its parents, 'Cécile Brünner'.

Although the breeders so far mentioned have made by far the biggest contribution to the development of Miniature and shorter-growing roses, their range has been extended from time to time by several worthy contributions from others, among them de Ruiter, McGredy, Paolino, Harkness, Kordes, Saville and Laver. As we would expect, Meilland's of France have not been slow in their appreciation and exploitation of dwarfing genes and, as a result, have bred and introduced some outstanding varieties. Two I particularly like are 'Darling Flame' (1971) and 'Colibri' (1979), both bright in colour and rather taller than average Miniatures.

As garden plants Miniatures have a variety of uses, and are commanding an ever-growing slice of the overall market for roses. Their main advantage is that they provide the opportunity for gardeners with the tiniest of plots, or even just a window box, to grow roses. Furthermore, providing they can get plenty of light, they are reasonably happy as pot plants; although, as such, they need plenty of loving care and attention. Out of doors I have seen them used for a variety of purposes from massed bedding to small group planting, and in rockeries and mixed borders.

Patios

We now come to another new range of roses finding its way into most catalogues – Patio roses. 'Patio' as applied to roses is not a term that endears itself to a grower of old-fashioned roses such as myself. Its merit as a name is that it describes usage, but while a real patio may well be the thing to have in certain sections of society, such a name for a group of roses implies restrictions of use quite out of proportion to the not inconsiderable merits of these roses. I would much prefer the collective name 'Compact Floribundas'. At present 'Patio' is a term not in use in America. Perhaps I am just a 'rose snob' for, if I am honest, had I been around in the nineteenth century I would probably have objected to such group names as 'Bourbons' derived from their origins, 'Noisettes' from their introducers, and even 'Teas' from their scent, or mode of arrival, or whatever prompted the collective name of the group.

I have digressed yet again, so now back to the 'Patios'. They are taller than the Miniatures but not necessarily shorter than the short Floribundas; it is their denser habit and more numerous, smaller leaves that isolate them. They can be slightly spreading but not too much so, otherwise they become procumbent roses. Their flowers are always smaller than those of the shorter Floribundas; and in spite of what I have said about their group name, I can see why they are considered different from other roses and why they are here to stay. The trouble is that as they become more numerous, as they surely will to judge from the number of breeders now sending them into the marketplace, it will become more difficult to define a borderline between these and other roses.

Meilland's have been notably active in this field and those of their free-flowering, bright and colourful 'Sunblaze' or 'Meillandii' range are outstanding. Following a similar line to Meilland's, both McGredy and Dickson have brought out some delightful Patios. I like McGredy's 'Regensberg' (1980), perhaps nearer to a procumbent, and 'Penelope Keith' ('Freegold') (1984).

'Clarissa'

'Regensberg'

Of Dickson's varieties both 'Gentle Touch', which speaks for itself as 'Rose of the Year' in Britain in 1986, and the charmingly named 'Peek-a-Boo' (1981) have made many friends since their introduction. Harkness has contributed two very good varieties in 'Anna Ford', and what he calls his 'China' rose, 'Clarissa' (1983), named for Mrs James Mason.

In recent years others have come from all parts of the globe, but I have not seen them all and where raisers have not defined them as Patio roses it is probably safer to confine my observations to those already mentioned. Their place in the garden and their care and cultivation are much the same as for Miniatures – in the Dictionary section of this book I have grouped the Patios and Miniatures together.

Climbers

The history and evolution of this wide-ranging group of roses is, to some extent, covered in Part I of this book but in order to give this chapter some semblance of continuity I will have to repeat some of it again.

Although climbers have been used in our gardens ever since roses have been grown, it was not until the close of the last century and the early years of this one – when a wider colour range was introduced – that their true value was appreciated. The difference between climbers and ramblers is considerable. The obvious common factor between the two groups is, of course, their vigour. The less obvious is their ancestry. Most of our present-day garden hybrids owe their genealogy to just a handful of the many wild climbing species so far discovered growing in various parts of the world, mostly China. Just as with our bush and shrub roses, the biggest single influence on their development has been R. chinensis: each time a new cross is made, it is the inherent dominance of the genes of this species that dictates the result. The other wild roses to play their part are R. moschata, R. multiflora, R. gigantea and, to a lesser extent though no less important, R. wichuraiana. Here and there another gene or two, from brief encounters with other types, show their influence, but until some enlightened young hybridizer sets about exploiting the vast range of possibilities within the ranks of climbers and ramblers only those few species will dictate their future.

Once again, it was John Champneys' seedlings from his cross of 'Old Blush' with R. moschata that led the way. For it was the Noisettes, when fused with R. gigantea through the Teas, that

dued performance in the autumn. For those with more modern tastes, however, several very good climbers have been introduced in recent years which can be relied upon to flower from June to October. To call them climbers is perhaps misleading, for they do not send up climbing shoots in the way of the once-flowering varieties but produce flowers on the end of each vigorous shoot instead. They are best supported in some way, perhaps on walls, trellises or pillars. It was Wilhelm Kordes who first got to work on this type of rose by breeding 'Hamburger Phoenix' (1954), 'Leverkusen' (1954) and 'Parkdirektor Riggers' (1957) from his *R. kordesii* (see page 193). Some excellent long-flowering climbers came from France in the 1950s and '60s. I consider the splendid 'Clair Matin' (1960) from Meilland to be one of the finest, but perhaps the most familiar is the bright red 'Danse de Feu' (1953) sent out by Mallerin, better known in America as 'Spectacular'. Mentioning America, no one can fail to notice Lammert's 'Golden Showers' (1956), for it is perhaps the most widely grown of all yellow climbers. Boerner's climbers are not so well known in Britain, but of those that are, 'Parade' is superb.

Of British raisers, McGredy has been by far the most productive, although he is now in New Zealand. Among his varieties are 'Handel' (1956), 'Casino' (1963), 'Schoolgirl' (1964) and 'Bantry Bay' (1967). One of the best of the whites is the free-flowerer 'White Cockade' (1969) from Cocker, but without doubt the two best sellers today are Harkness's shapely 'Compassion' (1973) and Gregory's prolific 'Pink Perpétue' (1965). Apart from those from Kordes, it is interesting that by far the majority of this type of

brought forth many of the lovely old climbers of the nineteenth century. As the century progressed, more and more appeared and by 1900 the choice of varieties was extensive. By then two clearly distinct types had evolved, one with largish flowers produced on laterals from sturdy, upright growth, known as climbers, and another with clusters of smaller flowers with a more relaxed growing behaviour, generally called ramblers.

I have already expressed the opinion that a short flowering season too often comes between a rose and success, but I fully realize that continuity of flower is of considerable importance in a small garden. There are one or two excellent varieties from the past quite capable of flowering all summer, among them the lovely 'Zéphirine Drouhin' (1868). Others, such as 'Gloire de Dijon', produce their first flush and take a rest, giving a repeat, if slightly sub-

Top: Ann Endt's garden in Auckland, New Zealand
Below left: 'Gloire de Dijon', and *right,* 'Golden Showers'

'Parkdirektor Riggers'

climber raised around the world since World War II have come, directly or indirectly, from that superb rose for all seasons, 'New Dawn'.

Other important groups of modern climbers are the Climbing Hybrid Teas and Climbing Floribundas. These have mostly come about by chance in that a bush of the same variety has, unprompted, turned itself into a climber. See pages 411–18 and page 386 of the Dictionary section.

Ramblers

Ramblers were undoubtedly the result of planned breeding by a few very worthy hybridists, most important of whom were Manda of America and Barbier of France. It was Manda, just before the turn of the century, who first crossed R. wichuraiana, or possibly *R. luciae* (see Graham Stuart Thomas, *Climbing Roses Old and New*), with a large-flowered hybrid to produce the first of what are now loosely termed Wichuraiana ramblers. Those were the days of Gertrude Jekyll and it was largely from her flair and imagination that gardeners of the day learned how to get the best from them.

'May Queen'

Indeed, her appreciation of the value of climbers and ramblers still has a great influence on the way we grow and use them today.

Manda's first introduction was 'May Queen' in 1898. Barbier, pursuing similar lines of breeding, gave us the lovely 'Albéric Barbier' in 1900 followed by a succession of other equally good ramblers. His last of significance was 'Albertine' in 1921. A few other breeders followed the lead given by those two men and ramblers have now become commonplace in most gardens as a result.

Another breeder to have success with ramblers was the American Van Fleet, his major contribution coming in the form of 'Dr W. Van Fleet' (1910). It was this rose that sported in 1930 to become continuous-flowering and give us the lovely 'New Dawn'.

The other types of ramblers are those that owe much of their pedigree, or at least that part which provides the cluster flowers, to *R. multiflora*. Again, breeders crossed this species with large-flowered types to good avail and several are still quite widely grown today. Although *R. multiflora* was tried as a parent as early as 1835 by a man named Wills to produce 'Mme d'Arblay', it was Schmitt of France who introduced the first two varieties of signifi-

'Alexander Girault'

cance in 'Thalia' (1895) and 'Aglaia' (1896). As already mentioned elsewhere, the latter was used to good effect by Pemberton in breeding the first of his Hybrid Musks. Numerous breeders worked with *R. multiflora* from the late nineteenth century to the 1930s, their efforts being helped considerably when 'Crimson Rambler', of unknown parentage but with obvious Multiflora leanings, arrived from Japan in 1893. This rose was also known as 'Turner's Crimson' and 'The Engineer's Rose'. The first to use it successfully was B. R. Cant of England who produced 'Blush Rambler' in 1903; Walsh of America bred 'Hiawatha' from it in 1904 and Paul of England 'Tea Rambler' in the same year; but most importantly of all Schmidt of Germany used it as a parent for the bluest of all ramblers, 'Veilchenblau', in 1909. Although almost all of the early Multiflora ramblers had quite a short flowering season, one or two eventually came along that flowered all summer through. Outstanding among these are 'Ghislaine de Féligonde', raised by Turbat of France in 1916, and 'Phyllis Bide' by Bide in 1923, both well ahead of their time and fitting comfortably into gardens today.

'Tea Rambler'

Top: 'Ghislaine de Féligonde'. *Above:* 'Phyllis Bide'

Scramblers

This is not a group recognized by any of the nomenclature organizations. It is a term which I consider aptly describes the most vigorous and adventurous of both climbers and ramblers, and amongst them are several hybrids from species previously not mentioned, as well as Moschatas and Multifloras.

It is from among these that we can find some of our best and most stunning tree climbers. Top of my list for this job is 'Rambling Rector'; it is far older than any of the others and its parentage is unknown, but there can be little doubt that its origins are rooted in *R. multiflora*. It is a popular rose, because of its name, and so it should be, for it is, without doubt in my eyes, the best of the middle-sized scramblers for festooning trees and covering eyesores. 'Rambling Rector's' main rival for excellence as a tree climber is 'Seagull' (1907) with 'The Garland' a very close third although, unlike the other two, the latter probably has *R. moschata* in its make-up. A very vigorous tree scrambler is the more recent 'Bobbie James' (1961) from Sunningdale Nurseries, which, although of unknown parentage, also probably owes something to *R. multiflora*. This rose is capable of reaching the top of the tallest tree.

These roses perform a valuable service in modern garden landscapes. The most vigorous of all is, of course, that incredible hulk 'Kiftsgate', a refined – if that is the word – form of *R. filipes* discovered at Kiftsgate Court and introduced in 1954 by the late Hilda Murrell of Shrewsbury, a dedicated rosarian.

Other climbers and ramblers from the past, but pertinent in the context of modern gardening, are numerous and amongst these are several species such as *R. gentileana*, *R. helenae* and *R. arvensis*, and the 'Evergreens' or hybrids of *R. sempervirens*, which although not as vigorous as those so far mentioned, make very useful scramblers for smaller trees.

While writing of Evergreens, I must at this point bring in 'Mermaid' (1918) from William Paul, a rose with vicious thorns, shiny foliage and beautiful single primrose-yellow flowers. It is not really a scrambler in this country but each time I admire a well-grown plant of this rose here in England and sing its praises to its owner, I do so with tongue in cheek for it brings back memories of a 'Mermaid' encountered in Australia in 1986. It was not only the biggest plant of this variety I had ever seen but probably the biggest ever rose tree. To tell you of this I must again digress. I was taken to see it by its owner, David Ruston, to conclude a tour of what must rank as, if not the best, then by far the most interesting

rose garden I have ever visited. I had not realized the importance of this garden until my arrival in Adelaide, and since it was at Renmark over 200 miles to the northeast I had thought that a visit would be far too time-consuming to fit in during a stay of only two weeks. When I saw some of David Ruston's roses decorating the conference hall, however, I knew I would have to find the time to go. We left for Renmark in the Ruston van immediately after the conference. I shall be forever grateful to David – tired though he was after his heavy stint at the conference – for taking me by the

Top: 'Seagull'. *Above:* David Ruston with 'Mermaid' in South Australia

scenic route, fifty or so miles further through South Australia than he need have done.

At Mount Pleasant we came, by chance, upon a small overgrown garden full of huge, unpruned roses. As rosemen often do when they find a rose garden, we stopped, knocked on the door and asked the surprised owner if we could look around. Permission granted, David was saddened by so many 'Indica Major' suckers. but not I, for although this rose is commonly used as an under-stock in Australia it is seldom seen in England. Among the suckers, and rising above them, was the biggest plant of 'Sutter's Gold' either of us had ever seen. I lost count at seventy blooms on one side of the plant only. Its owner was a young lady, who, after getting over the shock of two grown men drooling over her roses, explained apologetically that her roses had not been pruned since the death of her father ten years earlier. Before leaving, we extracted a promise from her that she would never, ever, buy seca-teurs.

I had seen some very good roses around Adelaide, in particular a 'Mutabilis' some 8′ (2.5 m) high and 10′ (3 m) wide and a wealth of superb specimens of a variety of roses at Deane Ross's display gar-den at Willunga, but I was quite unprepared for what I was to see in the Ruston gardens. Long before I awoke the next day, David had been out to turn on the irrigation, for without water from the Murray River Renmark's fertile soil would be far too dry and parched to grow anything but native scrub. He makes his living from roses, but he is also a superb gardener and an avid collector. His display gardens extend over several acres and include a wide variety of plants other than roses, including many interesting

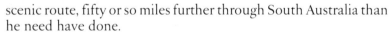

Deane Ross's display gardens at Willunga, South Australia

Top: Seedling *multiflora* grown as a pillar rose and *below*, Roses growing with citrus, the Ruston Gardens, South Australia

natives. I will forever remember that hot day in November when I found myself let loose among one of the biggest informal collections in the world. I came upon 'Maman Cochet' roses growing 10′ (3 m) into a citrus and 'Devoniensis' 20′ (6 m) up a gum tree. I found myself reacquainted with roses that were no more than memories from a far-off youth, for this garden is rich in roses from the 1950s. I must have missed dozens, but I came upon such Hybrid Teas as 'Charlotte Armstrong', 'Monique', 'Dr Debat' and 'Symphony', and upon the Floribundas 'Fashion', 'Donald Prior' and 'Goldilocks'. It was here that I met, for the first time, some of Thomas's Bloomfield roses of the 1920s. These are not hardy enough for England, so I was pleased to find them, in particular several fine specimens of 'Bloomfield Courage' and a superb 'Bloomfield Dainty' on a pillar. The gardens are surrounded by a tall, wire-mesh, kangaroo- and stock-proof fence which is festooned with climbers and it was among these that I found that huge plant of 'Mermaid'.

Roses growing around David Ruston's lily pool in South Australia

Classification Systems

As stated elsewhere, the genus *Rosa* is, botanically, very complex, and its many thousands of hybrids are visually diverse. Botanical complexity, however, need not concern us here (see page 113) except inasmuch as it provides the ground rules for helping to segregate the vast range of hybrids into classes, with each class made up of members with sufficient common characteristics to be meaningfully different from the others.

In modern times three important organizations have concerned themselves with the formulation and the nomenclature of classes:

1. the American Rose Society through their publications *Modern Roses*, of which *Modern Roses 9* is the latest;

2. the World Federation of Rose Societies;

3. the British Association of Rose Breeders.

At present, therefore, and probably for the foreseeable future, there are three different lists of classes, not one of which is universally adopted, and this is how it should be at least until there is sufficient consensus for the world to agree on one system. This state of affairs, though very interesting to the expert, is confusing to the layman, although it should not be difficult for any of us to appreciate the dilemmas and challenges these organizations have faced in arriving at their separate conclusions. There is no difficulty with species, nor is there a problem with the old garden roses; all the organizations are agreed on the classification of these since they were largely formed before the rose reached its present-day complexity and are unlikely to be added to very much in the future. It is in the moderns that their lists differ and the reasons for these differences in the end come down to –

1. Which criteria dictate the class into which a variety is placed. Is it botanical relationship, visual similarity, usage, habit or behaviour, flower form, flower quantity, geography, tradition, sentiment, something else, or a combination of two or more of these?

2. What name is used for a class, given that there ought to be a correlation between the class name and the criteria or criterion used in formulating the group. Or should it be some other adjectival or meaningful name?

Actually, what it comes down to is that all three organizations simply use different class names for what amount in the end to very similarly comprised groups. The three separate lists follow.

AMERICAN ROSE SOCIETY
Modern Roses 9
(Rose Classes)

1 Alba	30 Hybrid Laevigata
2 Ayrshire	31 Hybrid Macounii
3 Bourbon	32 Hybrid Macrantha
4 Boursault	33 Hybrid Moyesii
5 Centifolia	34 Hybrid Musk
6 China	35 Hybrid Multiflora
7 Climbing Bourbon	36 Hybrid Nitida
8 Climbing China	37 Hybrid Nutkana
9 Climbing Floribunda	38 Hybrid Perpetual
10 Climbing Grandiflora	39 Hybrid Rugosa
11 Climbing Hybrid Perpetual	40 Hybrid Sempervirens
12 Climbing Hybrid Tea	41 Hybrid Setigera
13 Climbing Moss	42 Hybrid Spinosissima
14 Climbing Miniature	43 Hybrid Suffulta
15 Climbing Polyantha	44 Hybrid Tea
16 Climbing Tea	45 Kordesii
17 Damask	46 Large-Flowered Climber
18 Eglanteria	47 Moss
19 Floribunda	48 Miniature
20 Gallica	49 Miscellaneous Old Garden
21 Grandiflora	Rose
22 Hybrid Alba	50 Noisette
23 Hybrid Bracteata	51 Portland
24 Hybrid Blanda	52 Polyantha
25 Hybrid Bourbon	53 Rambler
26 Hybrid Canina	54 Shrub
27 Hybrid China	55 Species
28 Hybrid Foetida	56 Tea
29 Hybrid Hugonis	

WORLD FEDERATION OF ROSE SOCIETIES
(Rose Classes)

Modern garden roses	*Old garden roses*
1 Modern Shrub Recurrent Large-Flowered	20 Alba
2 Modern Shrub Recurrent Cluster-Flowered	21 Bourbon
	22 Boursault
3 Ground-Cover Recurrent	23 China
4 Large-Flowered	24 Damask
5 Cluster-Flowered	25 Gallica
6 Dwarf Cluster-Flowered	26 Hybrid Perpetual
7 Polyantha	27 Moss
8 Miniature	28 Portland
9 Modern Shrub Non-Recurrent Large-Flowered	29 Provence (Centifolia)
	30 Sweet Briar
10 Modern Shrub Non-Recurrent Cluster-Flowered	31 Tea
	32 Ayrshire
11 Ground-Cover Non-Recurrent	33 Climbing Bourbon
12 Rambler Recurrent	34 Climbing Boursault
13 Large-Flowered Climber Recurrent	35 Climbing Tea
	36 Noisette
14 Cluster-Flowered Climber Recurrent	37 Sempervirens
15 Climbing Miniature Recurrent	*Wild roses*
16 Rambler Non-Recurrent	38 Wild Roses Non-Climbing
17 Large-Flowered Climber Non-Recurrent	39 Wild Roses Climbing
18 Cluster-Flowered Climber Non-Recurrent	
19 Climbing Miniature Non-Recurrent	

This is the system now adopted by the British Royal National Rose Society.

Briefly analysing these lists in turn, *Modern Roses 9* is the most comprehensive and, in many ways, the most accurate except that while a layman will readily understand the term 'hybrid', he is less likely to know the difference between one species and another. This may be good in that it stimulates interest or bad in that it can be off-putting, especially in the case of some classes.

The World Federation of Rose Societies divide their classification into three. In their modern roses they link flower form and floriferousness to the behaviour of the plant. The old roses are much the same as the others' lists although I am baffled as to why there is a class for Sweet Briars and not one for Rugosas. With their system the layman knows immediately how a particular modern rose will perform, but from a rather complex set of class names. They basically divide the species into two groups, climbing and non-climbing.

The British Association of Rose Breeders, largely through Mr Jack Harkness, have worked out a set of classes based on a combination of simplicity and almost all the criteria mentioned earlier but with emphasis on habit and behaviour. Of the three systems theirs is the shortest list and by far the easiest to understand. Having said this, when I used their system for preparing the Dictionary for this book, I found it difficult to place several of their

BRITISH ASSOCIATION OF ROSE BREEDERS
(Rose Classes)

1 Species and Groups	16 Wichuraiana Rambler
2 China	17 Wichuraiana Carpet
3 Noisette	18 Wichuraiana Shrub
4 Tea	19 Gallica
5 Hybrid Tea	20 Damask
6 Floribunda	21 Centifolia
7 Florishrub	22 Moss
8 Miniature	23 Portland
9 Patio	24 Bourbon
10 Climbing Hybrid Tea	25 Hybrid Perpetual
11 Climbing Floribunda	26 English
12 Climbing Miniature	27 Scotch
13 Polyantha	28 Alba
14 Climbing Polyantha	29 Sweet Briar
15 Hybrid Musk	30 Rugosa

'Floribunda' would stay but would embrace all cluster-flowered roses of all types. Thus, having divided all hybrid roses into two groups, the rest of classification could be based on stature as follows. Miniatures could stay as they are, and the Patios would be named 'Compact'. All roses above 1′ (33 cm) and below 3′ (100 cm) would be termed 'Bush', all those over 3′ (100 cm), 'Shrub'. A new class, 'Procumbent', could absorb the ground-coverers and wide-growing Patios. Climbers could stay as they are now. Ramblers could be placed in the old rose section. As is invariably the case in books on the subject and in nurserymen's catalogues nowadays, all other behavioural factors could be taken into account in the written descriptions of varieties including the critical one of height, which is always stated in the descriptions of any given variety anyway. So my list of classifications for modern roses would be just eleven in number, as follows –

1 Grandiflora Bush	7 Floribunda Shrub
2 Grandiflora Shrub	8 Floribunda Climber
3 Grandiflora Climber	9 Floribunda Procumbent
4 Grandiflora Procumbent	10 Miniature
5 Floribunda Compact	11 Miniature Climber
6 Floribunda Bush	

classes and yet still follow the ground rules of botanical accuracy, which would not have been the case, for different reasons, with either of the other lists. Notwithstanding this, I believe that with more and more diversity appearing within classes, and new types of roses emerging all the time, we have to find a system which is easy to follow, allows for expansion without having to add new classes and, above all, is based on the average person's perception of the different types of roses available to him or her; to me at least, while I do not like some of their class names, the BARB system comes closest at present to this ideal. Others will disagree, and as a lover of roses I can fully appreciate that point of view, but as a nurseryman in daily contact with the average gardener I believe the aim should be for simplicity.

At this point, I intend to indulge myself, 'tongue in cheek', by putting forward an even more simple formula. It is based on the premise that the average person grows the rose for its flower and that all other considerations are supplementary. Therefore size and quantity of flower could be the basis for classification irrespective of pedigree and since non-recurrent roses are now a thing of the past and few will be raised in the future, these could be placed into the most appropriate group of old roses which would stay classified as they are now. To achieve this the term used in America for large-flowered, taller Floribundas could be adopted, namely 'Grandiflora'. This would replace 'Hybrid Tea'. The term

Throughout the Dictionary section of this book I have indicated, usually after each group heading, the appropriate classification of that group according to each of the organizations. However, since here and there, in passing, I have questioned – I hope respectfully – some of the BARB classes and class names, I am delighted that Jack Harkness has agreed to do me the honour of writing the following essay to explain his views on this fascinating subject and outlining the thinking behind the BARB classification.

Some Thoughts on Rose Classification

By Jack Harkness, OBE

The classification of roses is not an exact science, but rather a matter of convenience whereby we may obtain an approximate picture of whatever relativity we require between members of the genus. I am grateful to Peter Beales for the generous hospitality of his pages in which to insert my experiences of the matter.

To take classification to its extreme, it can be argued that as every species and variety is unique, each one could be in a class of its own; but that would not help our understanding unless we had minds like computers. My brain, and no doubt yours, needs some common agreement in apportioning the thousands of rosy individuals into a few more or less definable groups.

Classification is pliable; it can be adapted to various purposes. My own purpose may not be yours, for what suits my taste and my rose breeding instincts is to express relationship. Others may prefer to express garden purposes, or history, or colour, or commerce, or stature, or scent or botany or anything else they may devise. Classification can express all these things, but usually only one at a time, or it becomes muddled; it is interesting, useful, amusing, adaptable. It rests on the general consent of the rose world, expressed by the use or neglect of what has been proposed.

It is a surprising thing that a subject so reasonable and elastic brings out in its proponents the most intolerant and dictatorial instincts. One finds unholy wishes to impose systems upon the rose world regardless of expressed wishes; and to defend theories, fancies and names as if they were immutable tenets of prejudiced religion.

Let me show that the names, to take an instance, are not and never have been unchangeable. Henry Bennett introduced his Pedigree Hybrids of the Tea Rose in 1879. In 1880, the Horticultural Society of Lyon coined for them the name 'Hybrides de Thé'. This was adopted in France, with British firms using 'Hybrid Teas' (Paul & Son in 1883, and Dickson in 1884). After objections on the way, the National Rose Society followed suit in 1893. Nowadays the Society calls these roses Large Flowered.

In 1913, two roses were introduced as Hybrid Teas by their breeder, the Rev. J. H. Pemberton. They were 'Danaë' and 'Moonlight', which looked nothing like Hybrid Teas. The Secretary of the National Rose Society, Courtney Page, is reported to have said:

'They smell like Musk Roses, why don't you call them Hybrid Musks?'

In 1917, Courtney Page used this class name for 'Pax'. Pemberton adopted it in 1919. Hybrid Musk has therefore been in use for more than seventy years, but still today purists chide it for inaccuracy. Consent is what matters, with a spice of tradition or romance, and blow the purism.

When a class arises out of two different parents, it can reasonably take its name from either of them. 'Else Poulsen' and 'Kirsten Poulsen' were children in 1924 of a Polyantha and a Hybrid Tea. They were called Hybrid Teas, although they were as strange to that class as Pemberton's roses had been eleven years earlier.

In 1932, the National Rose Society tried to put this right by putting them in a class Hybrid Polyantha. Some people called them Poulsen Roses. The flowers of this class became more and more double, and so arose the class Hybrid Polyantha Hybrid Tea type. These roses are now Cluster Flowered, in spite of the fact that the great majority of roses flower in clusters.

The Americans had an answer to the Hybrid Polyantha problem through Jean Henri Nicolas, a Frenchman living there. In 1934 he suggested the name Floribunda, destined to win general consent. This name aroused the fury of the purists, who declared it ineligible and a target for scorn. It was 1951 before the National Rose Society bowed to popular consent and accepted it for a time, but only for twenty years.

Floribunda was called into being for the rose 'Rochester'; but as these notes may suggest, it can be a mistake to rush into classes at the first acquaintance of a new variety. Candidates need time to settle. They start as proposals, and only belong to a class when general consent welcomes them to it. 'Rochester' wore its class name well, but 'Queen Elizabeth' was less successful.

Those who first saw that remarkable variety assumed that it would shortly be one of a great number of similar, wonderful roses. Without waiting to see them, the Americans established the class Grandiflora for them on Herb Swim's suggestion. But alas! 'Queen Elizabeth's' counterparts never showed up. The Grandifloras became an indefinite class of small Hybrid Teas or large Floribundas, some of which shuffled from class to class and back again over the years. A little decisiveness could have parked them in Hybrid Tea or Floribunda; but in a lively hope that roses like 'Queen Elizabeth' could unleash a torrent of sales, the American growers clung to Grandiflora. There has recently been a proposal in America to give it a decent burial, and about time. The Royal National Rose Society was consistently against Grandiflora; quite right too.

These notes illustrate the imprecision and elasticity of classification, and its gentle handhold with history. Are these not pleasant English qualities? Class names will change with fashion and familiarity. It is entirely likely that bright sparks might strike better names than those we have, and that general consent will hug them to its bosom.

A meeting of the British Association of Rose Breeders (BARB) in 1987 began to discuss classification, a subject guaranteed to keep any British rose meeting talking into extra time. In short, BARB said that the systems in current use were not helpful in the breeders' work. Needed was a simple system which gave an approximate picture of the relationship between members of the genus.

As current systems were not helpful, it was a short step to the proposition that we devise our own system. I was asked to do it.

It was done by preparing a draft, which was put up as a cockshy for members and friends. They helpfully shied at it, leading to second, third and fourth drafts, until with thanks to the contributions of our well-wishers, we were able to publish BARB's *Rose Classes* in 1989.

The system was based on the botanic classification of Rehder, set out by E. F. Allen in *The Rose Annual 1973*. We heeded Allen's warning that if a classification reflected the course of evolution, it is termed 'natural'; and that 'it is self-evident that the more natural any system of classification may be, the more useful it will be to rose breeders and to ordinary rosarians'.

We therefore took Rehder's four subgenera, although we did not need to name them in the classification; they were, so to speak, the invisible framework. They are *Simplicifoliae*, which we put back, for it had been omitted; *Hesperhodos, Platyrhodon* and *Eurosa*. We then inserted the various classes where we thought they belonged in that framework, for example the Polyantha Roses in *Eurosa – Synstylae*; the Moss Roses in *Eurosa – Gallicanae*; and the Scotch roses in *Eurosa – Pimpinellifoliae*. This is a proceeding that would scarcely appeal to botanists, but we found it extremely helpful, and it is perhaps the most original contribution we made to the work.

We considered that many species had a group of varieties associated with them, indeed every species had that potential; for example, *R. bracteata* has 'Mermaid', *R. moyesii* has 'Geranium', *R. macrophylla* has 'Doncasteri'. We therefore named class 1 'Species and Groups' to cover all of these; but if there were enough varieties to form a class, as in China, Gallica, Rugosa, then a class was provided.

We saw that the World Federation of Rose Societies system allocated varieties to classes mainly by the habit of the plant, and the size or frequency of the flower. The American Rose Society relied mainly on parentage. We did not find either of these methods satisfactory on its own, but found ourselves combining four criteria: family likeness, breeding records, tradition and common sense. These are too simple to expound but perhaps I may expose the fallibility of breeding records.

My firm raised a pretty rose called 'Grace Abounding', and following the seedling number on the label, we introduced it as having been raised from 'Pink Parfait' × 'Circus'. I was in the habit of checking our breeding records, a regular audit they got, labels, record cards, seed pods, pollen, how did ten crosses come to give twelve seed pods? I found that 'Grace Abounding' was really from 'Pink Parfait' × 'Penelope'. I reckoned our work was fairly accurate, say to ninety per cent or so, but certainly not perfect.

A more obvious case which I have mentioned before is 'Nevada'. For over half a century wise men have protested that the given parentage, Hybrid Tea × *R. moyesii*, was a genetical impossibility. Brave fellows, I scarcely dare say anything is impossible! When it sets any, the hips of 'Nevada' are squat and black, nothing like the long red ones of *R. moyesii*, nothing like the fat brown or red ones of Hybrid Teas. The only roses with such black hips are some Scotch Roses of the Pimpinellifoliae. Add another point: in sporting to 'Marguerite Hilling', 'Nevada' displayed the marbled colouring typical of the sportive Scotch Roses. Therefore, breeding records and tradition take a back seat in this case. Family likeness and common sense step forward. We call 'Nevada' a Scotch Rose, supposing its parent may have been *R. spinosissima altaica* or *hispida* instead of *R. moyesii*. To this day it is immutably down in *Modern Roses 9* as Hybrid Moyesii, and seems likely to stay that way to the end of time.

Some of our classes have been criticized for the names of them, and we hope that better names will be proposed. One can feel irritation at critics who condemn the whole system because they don't like a name. It is more helpful to invent a better name.

Our class 26, English, has had some stick, on the grounds that the roses may not necessarily be bred in England. That is true; I would identify some German varieties as belonging to this class. We have had regional names in the past. Not all the Ayrshire Roses were bred in Ayrshire, nor the Chinas in China, nor the Bourbons in Réunion, and so we could continue through Scotch, Provence, Holland, Bengal and others. David Austin has been mainly responsible for many English Roses, which we describe as having affinity to an old garden rose on one side and to a modern rose on the other, but not fitting into one of the other classes. We think David Austin should rightly have his chosen name on the class.

We might mention in passing that this breeding is bound to yield in time not only English Roses, but also Modern Roses and Old Garden Roses. If breeders use Portlands and Albas and Gallicas, they will get Portlands and Albas and Gallicas in due time. No old class should be closed to modern varieties, because we can if we wish breed Chinas or Gallicas as they did centuries ago; but if we introduced, say, new Gallicas, then we would be under obligation to preserve the essential character of that class when adding to it.

Our class 9, Patio, is criticized because it appears to confine the roses to a small, un-English area; but there is a sense of matching between the compact, neat roses and the trim little area. Well, other suggestions are Dwarf Cluster Flowered, Floramin, Floratea, Baby This-or-That. I think Patio is the best so far, but let somebody give us a better one if they can.

Our class 17, Wichuraiana Carpet, was made as a sop to those who want Ground Cover classes. Many different roses can be used as ground cover: Species, Climbing Miniatures, Polyanthas, Wichuraianas both Ramblers and Shrubs, Scotch and Rugosas. To make a class 'Ground Cover' is to row across our tide of relativity. It is like making classes for Shrub Roses, Hedge Roses, Bush Roses, Climbers, Miscellaneous Old Garden Roses. We noticed, however, that Kordes and Poulsen in particular were introducing Wichuraianas which were markedly procumbent, and better so grown than on supports as ramblers; with some misgivings we separated them into class 17.

Class 7, Florishrub, is perhaps a cheeky one, needing a better name. We find a difference between bush roses that lend themselves to bedding, and shrub roses which have more spreading growth. Those shrubs whose flowers and leaves, if seen on bushes, would cause those bushes to be Floribundas, we call Florishrubs. Examples are 'Dorothy Wheatcroft', 'Chinatown', 'Westerland', 'Fountain' and 'Wilhelm'; we do not consider the latter a Hybrid Musk.

'Chaplin's Pink' growing at the Garden of the Rose, St Albans, Hertfordshire

PART III

Roses in the Landscape

*Some thoughts on where, why and how
to use them or not to use them*

The gardens at Mannington Hall, Norfolk

Roses growing with shrubs and herbaceous plants at Leeds Castle, Kent

For several centuries roses have enjoyed the dual role of the most popular and the most versatile of all outdoor garden plants. Rose breeders over the years have successfully produced not merely pretty faces but a range of plants which, used correctly and imaginatively, can meet almost any landscaping challenge. I doubt whether so many of the now-called old-fashioned roses would have survived had they not fulfilled both roles so effectively. Yet post-war trends in landscaping seem largely to have ignored shrub and old-fashioned roses. Only since Graham Thomas revived interest in them during the late 1950s and 1960s have they become increasingly popular. To some extent this has been a cult and they have been enjoyed for their intrinsic beauty as flowers rather than for their wider value as garden plants; but the reverse is true for, in particular, the Rugosas which are now almost 'stock in trade' for municipal landscapers, and more imaginatively, some of the more vigorous climbers which are now enjoying a popularity they have not experienced since Gertrude Jekyll used them so cleverly in many of her gardens.

Although there is usually a rose to fit any situation, be it old or modern, this is not to advocate roses for their own sake. Good landscaping should always take all possibilities into account. The best schemes are achieved by the harmonious use of a variety of subjects in sympathy with the buildings they serve, and the wider boundaries surrounding them. The role most often given to roses in smaller and medium-sized gardens is that of 'supporting' plants, i.e. to provide background to other plants, or as individual shrubs for additional height or colour. In larger gardens, on the other hand, they usually find themselves playing the entire cast, segregated from the landscape into separate communities to form the complete rose garden. Both roles are admirable and should be encouraged, but many landscape schemes would benefit considerably if roses were given the chance to prove themselves 'good mixers'. Presumably fashion plays its part in all this but one suspects that it goes deeper than simple vogue. Rather, it is a question of 'image'. All are inexorably linked by their given name, 'roses', and the long reign of modern Hybrid Teas and Floribundas has resulted in confusion of purpose between these and other types of

roses. If we bear in mind that Hybrid Teas and Floribundas, in their widest sense, are bedding plants and old-fashioned roses are shrubs, then their virtues would not be confused merely because of a generic name. Also, many beautiful old roses would not be rejected for the sin of having a short flowering season, and would, perhaps, receive the same consideration as other shrubs with equally short flowering seasons, instead of living a life of inferiority simply because their shorter-growing sister, with the same

Roses with perennials and eucalyptus tree in Sally and Bey Allison's garden at Fernside, nr. Christchurch, New Zealand

All roses are really equal, but some, for the wrong reasons, are more equal than others. Of course a long flowering season is important but is it as important as beauty, charm or fragrance? Some roses combine all these things but are difficult to grow. Others, with one or more of these virtues, perhaps, grow like weeds or may have other faults. It is this very unpredictability that makes them so fascinating both for their own sakes and as landscape subjects.

Another probable reason why they are used so sparsely in landscape schemes is, paradoxically, their sheer weight of numbers. With such a vast array of characteristics, the choice of roses for specific tasks is daunting both to the uninitiated and expert alike. This is further complicated by photographs of the same variety which look quite different and by descriptions in catalogues and books that often contradict one another. When choosing roses, bear in mind these small discrepancies and avoid, if possible, falling into the trap of choosing from photographs alone. Read about the ones you like, preferably from more than one book, and try to see them growing either at a nursery or in one of the many gardens that are open to the public. Advice, based on experience, from rose-growing friends is also invaluable. Do not be afraid of making mistakes; all the best gardens have developed by trial and error. So if a particular variety fails to come up to expectation, does not suit a particular spot or, equally important, does not fit into a preconceived colour scheme, find another home for it or just give it away and start again with another rose.

Choosing Roses for Poorer Soils

Roses, like most plants, will flourish or struggle in direct proportion to the quality, condition and type of soil into which they are planted and, if the soil should be poor, according to how much is put into its preparation and how much attention it receives after the roses are planted.

Roses have a distinct preference for clay-based, heavier soils and, in my experience, the more hybrid the variety the stronger that preference. This is not to say that there are not varieties and types that can be grown in lighter soils. All of the species are worth trying as are most of the members of the following Garden Groups – Albas, Gallicas, Damasks, Centifolias, Portlands and Mosses. The Bourbons and Hybrid Perpetuals will find life difficult but not impossible and the Teas, Hybrid Teas and Floribundas will really struggle without considerable extra nourishment. The

family name, can produce flowers all summer. I would never exchange one bloom of 'Mme Hardy' for an armful of 'Iceberg'. Nor would I plant a bed of 'Mme Hardy' in the middle of my lawn.

To a lesser extent, once-blooming, climbing roses suffer the same fate. With few exceptions, nature has decreed that her finest blooms come in small doses; consequently, some of her most beautiful climbers are overshadowed by more flamboyant subjects whose only claim to fame is remontancy.

Roses in the gardens of Hatfield House, Hertfordshire

Old Roses in the Landscape

'Paul's Himalayan Musk' in Miriam Wilkins' garden, California

Chinas will put up with some degree of hardship, as will both the Multiflora and Wichuraiana ramblers, but Standard or Tree roses will not tolerate stress of any kind.

A point worth bearing in mind is that no rose will achieve its full potential in the more difficult, lighter soils so allow for diminished ultimate sizes when making a selection.

The following types, over and above those already mentioned, are worth trying in poor soil conditions.

SHRUB ROSES

R. rugosa and hybrids, *R. pimpinellifolia* and hybrids, *R. eglanteria* and hybrids.

CLIMBING ROSES

Climbing 'Cécile Brünner', 'Leverkusen', 'Mme Alfred Carrière', 'Maigold', most Wichuraianas and Multiflora ramblers, 'Parkdirektor Riggers', 'Paul's Himalayan Musk', all the tree-climbing varieties listed elsewhere.

Quite a few of the more vigorous modern procumbent varieties are also worth trying.

Old and Shrub Roses for an Established Garden

Old roses can be mixed with most other garden subjects with comparative ease, although as a matter of personal taste, except for some of the short-growing or procumbent varieties, I do not consider that they mix well with heathers or conifers. They can, however, cohabit happily with herbaceous plants, especially grey foliage types. I will discuss the various plants to grow with roses later, but as a general rule, when mixing old roses with herbaceous perennials, the best effect is achieved if the rose selected blends with the border both in terms of form and colour. Often this is best achieved by planting in groups of three. One group of roses, strategically placed, can add strength and maturity to flimsy areas of the border, whereas another of graceful shape will reduce the coarse lines of the more robust border plants. Try, where possible, to use upright-growing roses in the taller, upright areas of the border, and more pendulous ones in the shorter zones. These are not golden rules but sensitivity in such matters can be most rewarding. Colour, too, is important. Soft pinks, purples and whites go very well with grey foliage plants, buffs, creams and magentas with dark green or purple foliage, and the stronger colours of red, yellow and flame with the brighter green and variegated foliage. Another important factor is the timing of flowers. Try, where possible, to achieve continuity in particular areas. Plan, too, for scent, placing a scented rose in an area where scent is absent in the other plants.

Standard roses are often difficult to position, especially in the more informal gardens, but the herbaceous border is an ideal place for them, since they can provide the extra height required to give the border better contours, without seeming to intrude, as might be the case with a shrub rose. Climbing roses on pillars are also excellent, though again care must be taken to choose colours sympathetic to the herbaceous plants.

Rustic trellis placed behind herbaceous borders to support climbers and ramblers can look effective. Remember, however, that throughout the winter most roses will lose their leaves, so care should be exercised in designing the trellis in order for it not to appear too unsightly and obtrusive when the roses are dormant.

In larger gardens very pleasant walkthroughs can be created by using a combination of old-fashioned roses, climbing roses and herbaceous plants. I am not too much in favour of walks that go

The late Nancy Steen's White Garden, Auckland, New Zealand

nowhere; it is better if they have a purpose, such as leading to another part of the garden or to a summerhouse or some such feature. Such walks can, of course, be created from old roses alone, but they are more interesting if compatible perennials and flowering and foliage shrubs are used in moderation. The climbers can be placed on rustic trellis at the back of the border.

Smaller gardens, especially those of modern style, are often surrounded by closeboard fencing or interwoven panels. These, often by necessity, form the background to mixed or herbaceous borders, and climbing roses, with the additional help of wire, can make an ideal backdrop and camouflage for the fence.

Old-fashioned Roses in Mixed Shrubberies

Species, old-fashioned and shrub roses fit perfectly into mixed shrub borders and, in my opinion, are very much under-used for this purpose. I would omit a few stalwarts such as 'Canary Bird', 'Frühlingsgold', 'Nevada', *R. moyesii* and some of the Rugosas – not that these are unsuited to shrubberies, but simply because there are so many other ideal varieties of diverse size and habit which are never given the chance, except occasionally by more adventurous landscape gardeners. The colour range of roses is vast when compared with that of flowering trees and shrubs. True, if left to their own devices, the more vigorous varieties can get out of hand, and some will take over if permitted to do so. Many, however, will fit comfortably amongst shrubs and provide a variety of attributes such as scent, autumn colour and hips. In the front of the shrubbery, too, numerous short-statured shrubs, both flowering and evergreen, have grey, purple or variegated foliage, and are primarily grown for this reason; short shrub roses, planted in groups of three, can enhance such shrubs by providing a much longer flowering season.

MODERN SHRUB ROSES WHICH MAKE GOOD MIXERS
Tall varieties (5' [1.5 m] and over)

'Copenhagen', 'Eddie's Jewel', 'Elmshorn', 'Erfurt', 'Fritz Nobis', 'Hamburger Phoenix', 'James Cabot', 'Nymphenburg', 'Scharlachglut', 'William Baffin'.

Part of the walled Rose Garden at Mannington Hall, Norfolk

'The Garland' in the late Humphrey Brooke's garden, Lime Kiln, Suffolk

Border of roses and other plants in Sally and Bey Allison's garden, New Zealand

Mixed planting, including shrub roses, at Leeds Castle, Kent

Shorter varieties (under 5' [1.5 m])

'Ballerina', 'Corylus', 'The Fairy', 'Fiona', 'Golden Wings', 'Graham Thomas', 'Kathleeen Ferrier', 'La Sevillana', 'Mary Rose', 'Westerland'.

In addition, almost all of the procumbent varieties are useful mixers.

Roses for Parks and Municipal Planting

A few parks departments, to their credit, already use shrubs and old-fashioned roses for municipal landscaping schemes; and more would perhaps follow suit if they could obtain them in sufficient numbers. By and large, however, with the exception of the traditional Rugosa varieties, they tend to be neglected in favour of the

modern bush roses. Admittedly, many local authorities grow their modern roses quite well, but others, where soil is less favourable, persist in growing these when common sense dictates they should be replaced with shrub and old-fashioned roses. Cost is doubtless a factor in such decisions, but surely most people would much prefer to see successful plantings of these types rather than some of the ailing apologies for rose beds so frequently encountered – probably due to an insistence on bright colour, often orange, to the exclusion of everything else. In any case, on the basis of cost-per-square-metre, shrub roses are probably less expensive, since their planting density is lower. I suspect, however, that the biggest responsibility for lack of imagination in rose planting schemes by local government rests with some nurserymen, who offer large numbers of modern roses at very low prices and fewer varieties of old-fashioned roses and shrub roses.

The Rugosas, of course, have their fair share of space in parks, municipal gardens and industrial planting schemes. These are often used as 'barrier plants' between dual carriageways and also to furnish roundabouts, providing greenery and flowers without the need for expensive maintenance. Yet there are several other species roses which would serve this purpose admirably, notably *R. virginiana*, *R. woodsii fendleri*, *R. pimpinellifolia* and *R. wichuraiana* to name but four. I accept that *R. rugosa* and its hybrids are excellent subjects for industrial and roadside planting, but to my mind they emit a somewhat urban aura and, perhaps because of their Japanese origin, look out of place in rural schemes

where European or American species roses would be more congruous.

There are some very good modern shrub roses which are already used in high-density planting, particularly the newer prostrate varieties, and obviously these, too, have considerable future potential. I can, nevertheless, think of several ramblers which would make admirable prostrate roses, especially for use on banks and mounds, both of which are now an almost compulsory part of the contour groundwork in modern industrial developments and roadworks. I wish, too, that climbing roses were used more freely to adorn public buildings. This is probably ruled out on grounds of cost and possibly on the basis of likely structural damage. This may have been true in the days of soft bricks and mortar, but I cannot really believe that modern building materials will come to much harm in the arms of a rose. Many new buildings cry out for greenery, if not for flowers, and it should not be too difficult to make provision for rose supports even at the design stage.

Roses for Woodland, the Wild Garden and Partial Shade

Most old roses are not too happy if planted in dense shade, but several species and varieties will tolerate partial or dappled shade. They usually look somewhat out of place in coniferous woodland,

Parnell Rose Gardens, Auckland, New Zealand

Assorted procumbent roses in the author's garden, Norfolk

Left: R. willmottiae growing in the Ruston Gardens, South Australia
Top: R. woodsii hips
Below: R. wichuraiana at Mannington Hall

but some species combine well with deciduous plantings or even mixed plantations where conifers are in the minority. This is not to advocate turning such areas into rose gardens, but a few groups planted here and there in glades, clearings and along paths can provide added interest to a woodland walk. Apart from the pleasure offered to the eye, they attract, in season, insects to their flowers, provide thickets for nesting birds, and, in due course,

yield edible fruit for a variety of wildlife. Many species also have attractive autumn foliage.

The wild garden is sometimes an area designated as such within the garden proper, and here the single-flowered wild species can be a considerable asset by providing added interest when the wild spring flowers are over.

In more open spaces such as parkland, groups of species roses, if not overdone, can be effective. On golf courses, too, they can provide interesting hazards, grouped here and there along the edge of the fairway.

It is important to use group planting in all these situations. By groups I mean a minimum of five plants, but often, depending on the space, considerably more than this number would be used in one area. If more than one variety is wanted, plant a single variety per group and allow ample space between each group. The density of planting within a group will depend upon the ultimate dimensions of each species, but they should be planted in such a way as to intermingle within two or three years. Soil condition is not normally a problem, but it may help to feed the soil well at the initial planting and, of course, to keep the roses free of competitors such as brambles and ivy, especially for the first year or two.

N.B. Roses suitable for woodland are marked (W) in the Dictionary section. Those suitable for partial shade are marked ●.

TEN GOOD MEDIUM GROWERS
FOR INFORMAL HEDGES

'Ballerina', 'Buff Beauty', 'Commandant Beaurepaire', 'Cornelia', 'Felicia', 'Félicité Parmentier', 'Königin von Dänemark', 'Louise Odier', Pink, Red and White 'Grootendorst', 'Prosperity'.

TEN SHORTER-GROWING OLD ROSES
FOR INFORMAL HEDGES

'Alfred de Dalmas', 'Comte de Chambord', 'Jacques Cartier', 'Duchess of Portland', 'Little White Pet', 'Rose de Meaux', *R.* × *centifolia* 'Parvifolia', *R. gallica officinalis*, 'Rosa Mundi', 'Rose de Rescht'.

'Clytemnestra' growing in the Brooklyn Botanic Garden

Shrub Roses and Old-fashioned Roses
with Water Features

If water is present in the garden, there are usually roses that can be planted by or near to it. Roses, however, should not be planted in boggy areas, so if there is danger of frequent flooding from a natu-

'Raubritter' growing against the central pool at Mottisfont Abbey, Hampshire

with the water and its surroundings. Where grassy banks or open spaces permit, a group of semi-pendulous species roses drooping towards the water can be quite enchanting when viewed from the opposite bank. Equally, if you can persuade a vigorous climber such as *R. helenae* or *R. filipes* 'Kiftsgate' to grow into overhanging trees and cascade, the effect can be very rewarding.

Man-made lakes, moats and lily ponds can all accommodate the quieter hybrids as well as species roses along their banks. Again, however, shape and ultimate dimensions of the bushes relative to other plants should provide the criteria rather than colour, important though this is. Paradoxically, the smaller the water feature, the longer the list of suitable roses. For stone or concrete ponds or small pools, perhaps with statuary, stronger colours and the more upright-growing roses may be used. In my opinion, though, any rose planted within 'reflection' distance of the water, no matter how small the pool, should at least have a semi-pendulous habit of growth; and any rose planted directly by the water's edge should be pendulous.

N.B. Roses likely to look attractive in proximity to natural water are marked with a ≈ in the Dictionary section.

TEN GOOD LANDSCAPING ROSES FOR GROWING ADJACENT TO WATER (NOT IN BOGS)

'Belle Amour', 'Canina Abbotswood', 'Cerise Bouquet', 'Fru Dagmar Hartopp', 'Frühlingsschnee', 'Lady Curzon', 'Pomifera Duplex', *R. farreri persetosa*, *R. wichuraiana*, *R. willmottiae*.

TEN GOOD SPECIES FOR WOODLAND

R. californica plena, *R. × coryana*, *R. × dupontii*, *R. eglanteria*, *R. gymnocarpa*, *R. macrantha*, *R. moyesii*, *R. nutkana*, *R. virginiana*, *R. woodsii fendleri*.

SIX GOOD CLIMBING SPECIES FOR WOODLAND

R. arvensis, *R. brunonii*, *R. filipes* 'Kiftsgate', *R. gentileana*, *R. helenae*, *R. mulliganii*.

TEN HYBRID SHRUB ROSES WHICH WILL TOLERATE THE DAPPLED SHADE OF WOODLAND

'Autumn Fire' (Eglanteria), 'Celestial' (Alba), 'Complicata' (Gallica), 'Greenmantle' (Sweet Briar), 'Karl Förster' (Hybrid Scotch), 'Lady Penzance' (Sweet Briar), 'Maiden's Blush' (Alba), 'Meg Merrilies' (Sweet Briar), 'Scharlachglut' (Hybrid Gallica), 'Semi Plena' (Alba).

ral water feature, they should be ruled out in favour of plants that enjoy higher water tables.

It is possible to select several species to grow on the banks of natural water features such as rivers, streams, ponds and lakes. I mention species deliberately, for with few exceptions it is better to use natural plants in natural landscapes. Where water exists naturally in a garden setting, its presence should be harnessed as a natural habitat for trees and shrubs which grow in sympathy both

R. gallica 'Complicata' growing up into a tree at Mottisfont Abbey, Hampshire

Roses for Hedges

In addition to the natural hedgerow roses, which are better grown in hedges rather than to form them, small roses for hedging fall roughly into two groups, formal and informal, the demarcation line being somewhat ill-defined, but with the majority belonging to the latter group.

'Roseraie de l'Hay' grown as a hedge: in flower *(above)*, with autumn foliage *(below)*

Formal Hedges

When planting a formal rose hedge, consideration should be given to any upright-growing variety capable of reaching the desired height. Bushes should be planted either in a single row, with 18″ (45 cm) between each plant or, for a really thick hedge, a double row of staggered bushes with 12″ (30 cm) between each row and 24″ (60 cm) between each plant. It is essential to prune the bushes very hard in the first year to encourage basal growth for later years, when such hard pruning will not be possible. If formality is desired from some of the old-fashioned and species roses, traditional methods of pruning have to be abandoned in favour of shears; and since not all types take kindly to such treatment, the choice of variety is particularly important. Clipped hedges can look very attractive, but these must be pruned very hard both their first and second year. Once the hedge is growing well, clipping can start, but if this is not timed correctly flowering may be affected. Clipping should be practised after flowering so that the hedge has time to make growth for the following year. Throughout the rest of the summer it should only be necessary to remove extra vigorous or 'awkward' shoots as they appear. Only the 'once-flowering' varieties are suitable for treatment in this way. So if you require more from your hedge, such as autumn flowers and/or hips, then informality must be accepted. Planting distances for old-fashioned and species roses will depend on the variety but few will need to be closer than 24″ (60 cm) and most make satisfactory hedges planted 36″ (90 cm) apart.

TEN GOOD SHRUB ROSES WHICH CAN BE KEPT TRIMMED FOR ORNAMENTAL HEDGES

'Maxima' (Alba), 'Semi Plena' (Alba), 'Anne of Geierstein' (Sweet Briar), 'Bourbon Queen', 'Double White' Scotch, 'Magnifica', 'Meg Merrilies' (Sweet Briar), *R.* × *dupontii*, *R. hibernica*, *R. rubrifolia*.

Informal Hedges

The scope of varieties of old roses for informal hedging is vast. In fact, almost any variety can be used for this purpose, depending upon the degree of informality required. Some of the Hybrid Musks, for example, make quite neat plants as hedgerows, whereas the Centifolias will form wide, impenetrable, untidy jungles. The secret of good informal rose hedges, no matter what the type, is, as already stressed, hard pruning in the first year and light clipping or tidying when the hedge is matured. Feeding, too, is important to keep them at their best.

Just a note of warning. Beware of misleading claims. All rose hedges need attention, perhaps more than some traditional hedging shrubs. Low-cost rose plants, advertised as unsurpassable, may prove a considerable disappointment. Some of those on offer are no more than simple understocks which, in spite of their apparent cheapness, are, in fact, sold at highly inflated prices.

N.B. Roses suitable for hedging are marked (H) in the Dictionary section.

TEN GOOD TALL, RECURRENT OLD AND SHRUB ROSES FOR USE AS INFORMAL HEDGES

'Agnes', 'Autumn Fire', 'Belle Poitevine', 'Blanc Double de Coubert', 'Marguerite Hilling', 'Nevada', 'Pax', *R. rugosa alba*, 'Roseraie de l'Hay', 'Scabrosa'.

Old Roses in Pots and Tubs for Terraces and Patios

Many gardens, especially those in towns, have paved areas suitable for pot-grown roses. Ideally, of course, roses are best grown directly into the ground, so it is a good idea, when designing such features, to make provision to accommodate the odd rose or two simply by leaving small, unpaved areas in strategic places, by surrounding a patch of soil with a low stone wall or even building double walls and filling the space between with soil. This last

option will provide an admirable opportunity for growing shorter or cascading varieties; and space can usually be left unpaved, too, at the base of these walls for growing suitably selected roses. Patios and terraces, especially those close to the house, often look incomplete simply as extensions to living-rooms. With a little care and thought they can also provide a 'lived in' part of the garden.

Roses are far happier in pots and tubs than many gardeners realize. Their cultivation is discussed in a later chapter but the choice

'Nyveldt's White' hips

Top: R. pimpinellifolia. Below: 'Swany' in a willow stump in the author's garden

'White Pet'

'Perle d'Or'

TEN GOOD OLDER ROSES FOR GROWING IN POTS

'Ballerina', 'Cécile Brünner', 'Comte de Chambord', 'The Fairy', 'Grüss an Aachen', 'Jacques Cartier', 'Little White Pet', 'Perle d'Or', 'Rose de Meaux', 'Yvonne Rabier'.

Note: This is only a selection. Many more will do well in pots, in particular the Teas and Dwarf Polyanthas.

of suitable varieties is almost as important as the choice of a receptacle in which they are to grow. Many garden centres offer a good choice of ornamental containers in all sizes. Rose bush and container should, however, be in sympathy with each other; thus, broad, dumpy roses are best accommodated in broad, dumpy pots, whereas slender, upright pots are best for taller, erect roses, or for pendulous, cascading varieties. Where space or walls permit, and a sufficiently large container can be provided, even climbing roses are feasible. These may never reach their full dimensions but, if properly looked after, can reach to the eaves of a two-storey house or be trained to cover adequately the side wall of an average-sized garage. Climbers, suitably staked, can also be grown in good-sized tubs as small pillar roses. Patios and terraces, especially in modern and town gardens, are often designed on fairly formal lines, as are rooftop gardens, and for these shrub roses grown as standards in square, wooden tubs are most effective.

N.B. Roses recommended for growing in pots are marked with ⊙ in the Dictionary section.

'Albéric Barbier'

Climbing Roses for Pergolas, Trellises, Pillars and Arches

Read any gardening book from the Victorian or Edwardian era and it will be noticed immediately that a variety of structures were used as props for their roses. These came in a wide range of building materials. Brick piers were highly favoured, elaborately designed wrought iron was popular for arches and railings, sophisticated timber structures were used as pergolas, gazebos and trellises. In those days, of course, labour was plentiful and materials relatively inexpensive. To indulge in such things today would be costly. Of course these are not always to our modern taste and structures of this nature are scarcely ever built today. Perhaps we have become frugal in our attitudes in this direction, open-plan gardens, lawns and the inevitable curved shrubbery being the vogue, with plants acting their part upon this stage without support or other props.

Leaving aside the capital and maintenance costs, all sorts of structures can be built quite easily with rustic poles, and provided the main posts are substantial, these can last for many years. Indeed, they can be designed and built to suit almost any type of garden. Most timber for this purpose comes from the thinning of plantations and woodlands. Spruce and larch are by far the most common. Birch can look attractive though it lasts less well than other species. Of the hardwoods, ash is particularly good. The cost of such posts and poles will depend on what is locally available, but in comparison with prepared timber, it is never expensive. It is best bought ready-treated under pressure with preservatives, thus giving it longer life.

For those seeking a more formal structure, rough-sawn timber is the least expensive of the prepared materials and should likewise be ready-treated with preservative. Upright poles or posts should be a minimum thickness of 4″ (10 cm) and should always be sunk at least 2′ (60 cm) into the ground. Rails and cross-members can be thinner than this but not less than 2″ (5 cm). Since the principal purpose of such structures is to provide support for climbing roses which will eventually cover them almost completely, the pattern created by the criss-crossing timber need not – unless so desired – be very elaborate. What is important, in order to ensure long life, is the quantity and quality of the upright poles placed in the ground. The spacing of these poles is therefore crucial. The best rustic trellis has uprights placed at about 6′ (1.8 m) intervals. Rustic arches should be well anchored in the soil at each corner.

A more simple form of support for climbers and ramblers is post and wire. Posts can be set, say, 10′ (3 m) apart, with straining wire stretched across at approximately 12″ (30 cm) vertical intervals. Remember that the roses, when fully grown, will be of considerable weight and the wire used must be of sufficient thickness to support them. All end or corner posts should have additional straining posts to enable the wire to be stretched tightly.

Although they will eventually hold one another upright, posts for pillar roses should be placed at least 2′ (60 cm) into the ground.

Above: Roses growing on arches in the Cranford Rose Garden, Brooklyn Botanic Garden
Below: Climbing roses in the Garden of the Rose, St Albans, Hertfordshire

Above: Ramblers at Hatfield House, Hertfordshire, and *below*, at Mannington Hall, Norfolk

'Cadenza' growing on an arch in the Cranford Rose Garden, Brooklyn Botanic Garden

Tripods are an excellent means of giving support to some of the more awkward old shrub roses, and make it possible to use climbers and ramblers within a shrubbery to good effect. Such tripods can be of any size, and indeed built with specific roses in mind; three posts of rustic timber are simply placed in 'wigwam' fashion and secured at the top with wire.

The possibilities using rustic timber are unending and, with a little time and thought, structures built from it can provide the opportunity to grow a range of climbers and ramblers which, in many gardens, would be impossible.

TEN GOOD OLD-FASHIONED RAMBLERS FOR TRELLIS AND ARCH

'Albéric Barbier', 'Albertine', 'Alister Stella Gray', 'Céline Forestier', 'Chaplin's Pink', 'Emily Grey', 'Excelsa', 'Félicité et Perpétue', 'New Dawn', 'Veilchenblau'.

TEN GOOD OLDER CLIMBERS FOR TRELLISES AND ARCHES

'Captain Christy', 'Crimson Conquest', 'Desprez à Fleurs Jaunes', 'Etoile de Hollande', 'Lady Waterlow', 'Mme Alfred Carrière', 'Mme Grégoire Staechelin', 'Mrs Sam McGredy', 'Paul's Lemon Pillar', 'Zéphirine Drouhin'.

Top: 'Bobbie James'. *Below left:* 'Mme Grégoire Staechelin', and *left*, 'Crimson Conquest'

Roses for Walls and Fencing Panels and for Northerly Aspects

Walls and fencing come in all shapes and sizes but the one thing they have have in common is the provision of an extra dimension to gardening. All the best gardens I know possess walls that are well clothed with a variety of climbing plants. Some walls may be worth admiring for their own sake, but many are not, and these could be considerably improved, even if only partially covered with plants. Builders and architects will throw up their hands in horror, but walls should be used for more purposes than that of 'retaining space'. We adorn interiors, why not exteriors? I agree that some of the most pernicious such as the more rampant species of ivy and Virginia creeper can play havoc with guttering, get under tiles and spoil the face of bricks. With few exceptions, however, no such charge can be levelled at the rose. In any case, modern building materials are far more impervious to damage from plants than were their older counterparts and few buildings less than a century old can be seriously damaged by climbing plants of any type. More care should be taken, of course, on older buildings of very soft brick, clay-lump, sandstone or timber. It boils down to common sense.

Climbing roses, if grown on walls, will need support. The commonest method is to use wire fixed to the wall by special nails with clips, or screws with eyes, which can be bought especially for this purpose. On soft walls, these are best held in with the aid of wooden plugs which, when placed into pre-drilled holes, expand when the nail or screw is driven in. Wires should be stretched parallel to the ground at 12″ (30 cm) intervals. Each wire should be held an inch or so (2.5 cm) from the wall by placing the special nails or screws approximately every 3′ (90 cm) along its length. As the climbers grow, the main shoots can be fixed to the wire, training some shoots along and others upwards; the more twists and turns the better. The shoots are usually quite pliable and a dense covering can be achieved by this means. A soft twine should be used for fixing the shoots, otherwise they can be strangled as they grow. Another method of training climbers to walls is to fix an adequately sized piece of trellis about an inch (2.5 cm) away from the wall and to train the rose as it grows, as already described. This method is probably more suitable for modern buildings since trellis can look rather out of place on an older house. Walls facing east and west, blessed with a minimum of four to six hours of sunshine daily, are probably the best for climbing roses. Roses can also be

'Paul's Lemon Pillar' in the Cranford Rose Garden, Brooklyn Botanic Garden
Below: 'Mme de Sancy de Parabère'

grown on south-facing walls but there temperatures can get extremely high and, unless they are well nourished and kept watered, they will have difficulty giving of their best in high summer.

The north wall is the problem wall and, I may add, not just for roses. Few worthwhile plants enjoy such a situation. Most roses will grow on such a wall but only a few will flower to their full potential. Because they show up better, Nature has decreed that the best of these will be white or cream in colour. The additional

problem with a north wall and, to a lesser extent, the east wall, is hardiness. So this restricts the choice even further.

Recent years have seen the rise to prominence of the fencing panel or close-board fence, which springs up everywhere when new developments take place. Before condemning this phenomenon, it is worth asking what could be used in its place at comparable cost. Hedges, perhaps, but that is another argument. At the cost of a few strands of wire and a few nails such panels can make admirable supports for the less vigorous climbers which, when fully grown, will themselves help support the fence.

N.B. Climbing roses for colder, northerly aspects are marked with an (N) in the Dictionary section. Those that are tolerant of shade are marked ●

TEN GOOD OLDER CLIMBERS AND RAMBLERS FOR NORTH WALLS

'Aimée Vibert', Albéric Barbier', 'Crimson Conquest', 'Emily Gray', 'Félicité et Perpétue', 'Mme Alfred Carrière', 'Mme Grégoire Staechelin', 'Mermaid', 'Paul's Scarlet', 'Rambling Rector'.

'Mermaid'

Climbing Roses for Trees

When I was a child, our garden was relatively devoid of roses, but being fairly old, it was well populated with ancient apple trees, none of which had any real character and all of which were rather out of condition. Their names were not known, except for one which my grandfather called a 'snout', I know not why, except that

'Souvenir de Mme Léonie Viennot' growing up into a tree in Ann Endt's garden, Auckland, New Zealand

when the tree deigned to produce apples, each had a nose-shaped projection at the stalk end. Year after year these trees produced varying quantities of fruit most of which was blown down by the wind to rot on the ground. Few were edible and, apart from making strong cider which I was never allowed to sample officially, they had little real use. The point of this somewhat sudden deviation is to contemplate how many such trees, of dubious purpose, exist throughout the world. All could be put to the admirable use of supporting a climbing rose. I am against growing roses up into trees which, in themselves, have character, but many country gardens have trees which could well be improved in partnership with a rose; and not just trees, some rather boring stretches of hedgerow, attractive only for their bird population, could well be enhanced by the addition of a few well-chosen vigorous climbing species.

Not all the vigorous climbing roses are suitable for this purpose, of course, but many are and many more could be. Nature has her own way, she does not provide for growing and flowering at the same time; thus, without exception, all the vigorous tree-climbing roses flower only once each season. Some, though, do have good autumn foliage and produce abundant hips to give colour later. As with the climbers for north walls, the most suitable, with one or two exceptions, are white, cream or yellow in colour. Size of tree should not present a problem since some of the very vigorous climbers can reach 30' (9 m) with ease, although it will take a number of years for these to flower very freely; probably because, until

Top left: 'Bleu Magenta', and *right,* 'Rambling Rector'

a helping hand initially with string or wire, until they can scramble their own way up through the branches. Bear in mind that, being vigorous, they need to make big roots. If soil is poor, as so often under trees, give them a good start by adding a pocket of good soil at planting time and apply plenty of water at the height of summer.

N.B. Roses suitable for tree-climbing are marked with a (T) in the Dictionary section.

TEN OLDER ROSES SUITABLE FOR GROWING UP INTO TREES AND HEDGEROWS

'Bobbie James', 'Chaplin's Pink', 'Kew Rambler', *R. filipes*, 'Kiftsgate', 'La Mortola', 'Rambling Rector', *R. helenae*, *R. mullig. anii*, 'Seagull', 'Wedding Day'.

'Rambling Rector'   'Paulii Rosea'

Procumbent and Semi-procumbent Roses

As already mentioned, I wish to avoid the term 'ground-cover roses'. This can be misleading and wrongly equates these roses with plants better described as such. Certainly there are several shrub roses and species roses which grow broader than tall and some which prefer simply to creep along the ground, but none, to my knowledge, that do ground-cover work by excluding light and suppressing weeds in the same manner as prostrate evergreen shrubs and conifers. Nevertheless, prostrate and semi-prostrate roses will, if planted fairly close together, form impenetrable mounds over large areas of ground, so reducing maintenance to the minimum, and provide an effective display in the process. Breeders now realize the potential of such roses and are working hard to enlarge the range.

A use can be found for these roses almost anywhere where spread rather than height is an advantage – among other shrubs, to hide a manhole cover, or to camouflage, if not conceal, unsightly

their heads appear above the branches, they are growing in relative shade.

Dead tree trunks, and trees which are past their best, can also make ideal supports for less vigorous ramblers and climbers. Even unsightly trees, perhaps awkward to remove, can become more congenial if supporting a rose.

It is best to plant these roses a little distance, about 2′ (60 cm), from the trunk on the side of the tree with most light, giving them

'Bobbie James' growing up into an apple tree

tree stumps. Some, if chosen with care and given space, can even be used effectively and attractively in large rockeries.

N.B. Procumbent roses suitable as ground-creepers are marked with a (G) in the Dictionary section.

TEN OLDER SPREADING VARIETIES

'Daisy Hill', 'Dunwich Rose', 'Fru Dagmar Hartopp', 'Harry Maaze', 'Lady Curzon', 'Macrantha Raubritter', 'Max Graf', *R. paulii*, *R. paulii rosea*, *R. wichuraiana*.

Old Roses for Flower Arranging

All the flower arrangers I know enjoy working with roses, though most will admit to a nervousness when using them because of their relatively short life when cut. I have never quite made up my mind whether or not I totally approve of cutting roses from the garden, a hark back, I think, to the days when it was quite in order for my grandmother to have flowers in the house, provided they came from someone else's garden. There are no such rules in our house, however, so I suppose I belong to the cutting brigade.

Flower arranging is an art, and is all about proportion and balance. In its simplest form, one bloom placed in a vase by one person can look elegant, but by another, ridiculous. In its complex form, like painting, the same dozen roses can look either a daub or a masterpiece. At flower shows I always visit the Floral Art section but so far have seldom agreed with a judge's verdict. This makes it all the more fascinating. The ladies of flower clubs must have temperaments of steel. Some years ago, a very persuasive lady telephoned me to ask for help. 'I need a thousand blooms,' she said, 'for a festival of Rossini Music and Song.' Until the day I arrived in Sunderland I cursed myself for not saying No; the logistics were ridiculous – cut 1000 blooms one day, up at the crack of dawn, travel for seven hours the next. But when I arrived at Bishopswearmouth church I knew it was all worthwhile. I was besieged, embraced and thoroughly spoilt by an army of 'Geordie' lady flower arrangers who produced some real works of art with my roses in that church. Later, when the soprano hit top C, petals fluttered to the floor to add an extra sense of unreality to my first encounter with the friendly Northeast. The lady's name who twisted my arm to do this is Marjorie Barton, who since has become a very good friend.

Selecting roses for cutting is an acquired skill. Cut them too tight and they never open, too open and they last only fleetingly.

The best stage is when the sepals have started to fold back and the furled petals are showing colour. Timing is important. Early morning or late evening is best, but at whatever time flowers are cut they should always be placed in water up to their necks and stood in a cool place for two or three hours before they are arranged. A couple of spoonfuls of sugar or even a pint of lemonade to about a gallon of water will help them to stay fresh for a few hours longer. Before placing the flowers in water it is best to remove the two bottom leaves – no more – and scrape the thorns from the bottom 3″ (7.5 cm). Some people crush the base of each stem but I usually make a cut about half-an-inch (1 cm) long upwards into it. This exposes a bigger area of inner tissue and enables the flower to take up more water. Cut roses will wilt in warm, dry conditions, and lightly syringing the leaves with cold water will help to revive them. I am told by the experts that plunging the bottom inch of stem into boiling water for about a minute and then placing them quickly back into cold water will sometimes revive wilting blooms.

Some people believe that harm can be done to rose bushes by the cutting of blooms, and certainly if too many are taken with long stems the plants do suffer slightly, but they should come to no real harm. Try to cut to an eye though, so as not to leave an unsightly stump to die back on the bush.

Old-fashioned roses, in almost any context, make ideal companions in the home, the range of their colours, shapes and flower formation being adaptable to vases of all types, from the single rose on the dressing table to the large pedestal in the hall. Two or three carefully chosen bushes, growing in even the smallest garden, can usually provide enough flowers for taking indoors without any detriment to the outdoor display; and their scent will pervade the entire house, rivalling both sweet peas and ten-week stocks.

Old roses are better displayed by themselves, but this is a matter of taste. Some species and varieties have very attractive foliage which can be used effectively with other flowers, as can their hips in the autumn.

N.B. It would be quite misleading to single out special varieties of old roses for cutting. Those particularly suitable are marked ✂ in the Dictionary section.

Old Shrub Roses under Glass

Although the very old roses such as Centifolias, Damasks and Gallicas can be grown under glass, it does not really make much sense to do this, except for exhibition purposes. In such conditions their flowering season is further shortened and their ungainly growth habit becomes difficult to tame. However, there are a number of interesting old varieties, originating in warmer climes, notably the Teas and the Chinas, which can be very rewarding when grown in this way. No extra heat is necessary. Roses are quite happy in cold greenhouses where they will flower from early May onwards. Those with larger greenhouses or conservatories can indulge themselves by growing one or two of the more tender but very beautiful climbing Teas and Noisettes, in the way of vines on wires, about 12″ (30 cm) inside the glass. This method was often used by Victorian gardeners, for in addition to providing early flowers, the foliage provided shade for other plants growing in the conservatory in high summer.

The older Tea roses, apart from those which grow happily out of doors, actually prefer the protected environment and can give much pleasure even in the smallest of greenhouses. They are best grown in 10″ (25 cm) pots which make them sufficiently portable

'Catherine Mermet'

to move around. In fact, they are probably better after flowering in the spring inside, spending the summer outside.

Treatment is much the same as for outdoor roses except that the demands of early flowering will need consideration when feeding, and watering will be necessary every day as they start to grow. Pruning, too – which in the case of Teas should be sparing – is essential, otherwise, in such an environment, they will soon become 'leggy'.

N.B. Roses which grow and flower particularly well under glass are marked (Gh) in the Dictionary section.

Top: 'Lady Hillingdon'. *Below left:* 'Lamarque', and *right*, 'Maréchal Niel'

TEN GOOD OLDER BUSH ROSES FOR GROWING UNDER GLASS

'Antoine Rivoire', 'Archiduc Joseph' ('Mons. Tillier' in America), 'Briarcliffe', 'Catherine Mermet', 'Dr Grill', 'Général Schablikine', 'Lady Hillingdon', 'Mme Bravy', 'Souvenir de la Malmaison', 'The Bride'.

TEN GOOD OLDER CLIMBERS AND CLIMBING SPECIES FOR GROWING UNDER GLASS IN COLDER CLIMATES

'Bouquet d'Or', 'Cloth of Gold', 'Devoniensis', 'Duchesse d'Auerstadt', 'Lamarque', 'Maréchal Niel', 'Niphetos', *R. banksiae lutea*, 'Sombreuil', 'William Allen Richardson'.

Old Roses for their Hips

Whatever may be said by the critics of old and shrub roses, the faculty of some to produce ornamental hips is one attribute which cannot be denied. Such is their attraction that several varieties are well worth growing for their hips alone. In some cases the fruits far excel the flowers. Most of the species bear some form of fruit, varying in shape from plump and round to long and slender, and ranging in colour from bright orange to deep purple and black. They may be highly polished, or bristly. Some are borne erect, others pendulously; and many – presumably those that taste bitter to birds – last well into winter to brighten an otherwise dull time of year.

Whilst species are the main fruit bearers, some hybrids better known for their flowers also bear hips. 'Scharlachglut', for example, produces huge, urn-shaped fruit of rich scarlet and 'Mme Gregoire Staechelin', a beautiful climbing rose, will produce a good crop of large hips in a good summer.

N.B. Roses which produce a good crop of ornamental fruit are marked (F) in the Dictionary section.

TEN ROSES AND SPECIES WORTH GROWING FOR THE VALUE OF THEIR ORNAMENTAL HIPS

'Eddie's Jewel', 'Highdownensis', 'Master Hugh', *R. altaica*, *R. davidii*, *R. moyesii* 'Geranium', *R. villosa*, *R. rugosa* 'Alba', *R. sweginzowii macrocarpa*, 'Scabrosa'.

R. woodsii fendlerii hips

'Master Hugh' hips

'Geranium' hips

R. villosa hips

R. glauca hips

R. sweginzowii macrocarpa hips

Above: Autumn foliage of *R.* × *kochiana*, and *below, R. virginia*

Roses for their Ornamental Foliage

Although autumn coloration is not, as a rule, a major feature of shrub and old-fashioned roses, it is sufficiently important to be taken into account when planning a garden. Several species, and indeed hybrids, display richly toned foliage which will harmonize pleasingly with other trees and shrubs at the end of summer. Amongst these are most of the better known varieties of the Rugosas whose leaves change with the shortening days to mustard tints deepening to russet before falling early in winter. 'Roseraie de l'Hay' is a particularly good example of these.

The small, almost fern-like foliage of the Burnet roses, *R. pimpinellifolia* and its hybrids, changes to russety-red which adds further to the attraction of their black hips. Outstanding, especially after a dry, hot summer with a display of rich coppery-red are the thornless Boursault climbing roses; of this group 'Morletti' is particularly striking. As mentioned earlier, most of the American native species are conspicuous for their autumn display. *R. virginiana* is perhaps the best example, its naturally shiny leaves changing to burnished gold before the early frosts of winter persuade them, inevitably, to fall.

Autumn colour in roses is, of course, a bonus yet a wide gamut of colours can be found both in foliage and stems throughout the flowering season. Variations, though often subtle, range from the bright rich green of *R. banksiae*, the greys of *R. brunonii* 'La Mortola' and the Albas such as 'Celestial' and 'Maiden's Blush' to the rich plum colouring of *R. glauca*, better known as *R. rubrifolia*, not to mention the Moss roses with their distinctive, variably toned, mossy stems and such hybrids as the lovely 'Albertine' with its rich bronzy-red young shoots and leaflets.

Many of the species have vicious thorns, a problem when attempting to prune, but even these can be an additionally attractive, ornamental feature. Such a useful species, often planted specifically for the ornamental value of its thorns, is *R. sericea pteracantha*, whose young stems, in common with others of its group, are covered with broad, wedge-shaped, cherry-red, translucent thorns which when mature become an almost impenetrable armour and give considerable character to what would otherwise be a rather dull shrub in winter. Another interesting shrub, this time for its dense population of tiny thorns, is *R. farreri persetosa*, the 'Threepenny-bit Rose'; after it drops its numerous small ferny leaves in winter, this semi-procumbent shrub becomes a tawny-coloured thicket of arching, hairy branches, enhanced even more by hoar frost on a winter's day.

N.B. Old-fashioned and shrub roses with colourful autumn foliage are marked with an (A) in the Dictionary section.

TEN SHRUB ROSES AND SPECIES WHICH GIVE GOOD AUTUMN COLOUR FROM THEIR FOLIAGE

'Corylus', *R. altaica*, *R. fedtschenkoana*, *R. × kochiana*, *R. micrugosa*, *R. nitida*, *R. glauca* (all-year colour), *R. rugosa* 'Alba', *R. virginiana*, 'Roseraie de l'Hay'.

Older Roses and their Perfume

The principal attribute that distinguishes the old roses from their modern counterparts is their fragrance. This is not to say that modern roses are not fragrant. In fact, more perfumed roses are probably being introduced than ever before; 'Anna Pavlova', for example, a recent introduction, has a stronger perfume than any other rose I know. However, scent, being intangible, can only be evaluated subjectively, and perfume manufacturers would be out of business if this were not so. I happen to think that quality is more important than quantity, and, for sheer beauty of fragrance, the old roses still have the edge.

The variations of scent are, of course, fascinating. The heady, all-pervading, almost intoxicating perfume of the Centifolias is in no way similar to the refined elegance of that of the Albas; the spicy, somewhat lingering perfume exuded by the Damasks differs completely from the softer, more delicate fragrance of the Gallicas. Fragrance is not confined to flowers; foliage too can be scented. *R. primula*, for example, has leaves that smell distinctly of incense and many of the Mosses exude the strong odour of balsam from their moss, especially when touched.

High on my list of favourite perfumes from roses is that of the Sweet Briar, *R. eglanteria*. The scent comes from the foliage, especially the young foliage, after rain. Of all our senses smell is probably the most evocative. My first job as an apprentice nurseryman was to weed a large patch of Sweet Briars and a whiff of its scent even now never fails to transport me back to that time.

N.B. A fragrance rating is given to each rose in the Dictionary section.

TWENTY OLD SHRUB ROSES WITH PERFUME OF EXCEPTIONAL REFINEMENT

'Belle de Crécy', 'Celestial', 'Charles de Mills', 'Conrad F. Meyer', 'Empress Josephine', 'Fantin Latour', 'Général Kléber', 'Gloire des Mousseux', 'Hugh Dickson', 'Kazanlik', 'Königin von Dänemark', 'Louise Odier', 'Mme Hardy', 'Mme Isaac Pereire', 'Maiden's Blush', 'Parfum de l'Hay', 'Reine des Violettes', *R. × centifolia*, 'Roseraie de l'Hay', 'Souvenir de la Malmaison'

TEN OLDER CLIMBERS WITH EXCEPTIONAL FRAGRANCE

'Etoile de Hollande', 'Gloire de Dijon', 'Guinée', 'Long John

'Fantin Latour'

Silver', 'Mme Caroline Testout', 'Mrs Herbert Stevens', 'Souvenir de la Malmaison', 'Souvenir du Docteur Jamain', 'Surpassing Beauty', 'Zéphirine Drouhin'.

Shrub and Climbing Roses as Standards

Roses have been grown in this somewhat contrived way for many years, and it seems they have been quite popular throughout that time. I came across a delightful little snippet in *A Shilling Book of Roses* by William Paul, published in the nineteenth century:

> The late Colonel Calvert once told me that he was present at an auction sale of standard roses in London when the 'Village Maid' Rose was first introduced. Twenty plants were sold at one Guinea each. When they came to be distributed only nineteen could be found. Two purchasers seized the nineteenth plant, fought over it and paid half a Guinea each to the Auctioneer as compensation for the mischief done.

If nothing else, this should put the cost of a present-day standard rose into perspective.

Except for a few varieties of weeping standards very few old-fashioned roses are grown in this way, for although such plants are technically feasible, demand is so low as to make them uneconomical for modern nurseries. A few shrub roses, however,

Left: 'Excelsa', and *right,* 'Ballerina' growing as standards

do make excellent standards and by searching around or ordering early, it is still possible to obtain stocks of these. Their greatest asset is that they enable other plants to be grown underneath. On my travels I have seen excellent standards, or tree roses as they are called in some parts of the world. Two, in particular, stand out in my memory, both in Australia at the Ruston rose garden; each had trunks thicker than we could ever expect in Europe and heads

Above: 'Buff Beauty', and *below,* 'Raubritter' growing as standards

large enough to conceal their upright disposition. One was 'Buff Beauty', the other 'Veilchenblau'.

Half standards I like, and it has always baffled me why these are not more popular. Their height relative to other plants makes them much less ungainly than full standards.

The cultivation and growing of weeping standard roses is discussed later in the book.

TEN SHRUB ROSES WHICH MAKE GOOD STANDARDS

'Ballerina', 'Buff Beauty', 'Canary Bird', 'The Fairy', 'Felicia', 'Marjory Fair', 'Nozomi', 'White Pet', 'Yvonne Rabier', 'Yesterday'.

TEN RAMBLING ROSES WHICH MAKE GOOD WEEPING STANDARDS

'Albéric Barbier', 'Albertine', 'Dorothy Perkins', 'Emily Grey', 'Excelsa', 'Félicité et Perpétue', 'François Juranville', 'Golden Glow', 'Minnehaha', 'Sanders White'.

Pegging Down

It is sad, though understandable, that the practice of 'pegging down' has now largely died out as a means of getting the best from roses, for it is a most effective and tidy way of persuading masses of flowers from otherwise ungainly and sometimes reluctant varieties. Nowadays however, the cost of this practice, where space might permit it, as in parks and large gardens, would be prohibitive; furthermore, with the advent of newer types of procumbent roses, such areas as lent themselves to pegged-down roses can now be furnished with relative ease. Nevertheless, there are still strong arguments for pegging, which comes into its own in herbaceous and mixed borders, especially near the front of such borders when one bush, if pegged down correctly, can cover quite a large area among other short-growing plants at very little extra cost and effort. The mechanics are quite simple. In the first year, having pruned the roses hard at planting time, the shoots should be allowed to grow up naturally. In the second year, instead of pruning, train these shoots as near to parallel to the ground as possible and also in as many directions as they will permit, holding each shoot in position some 12″ (30 cm) from the ground by wire pegs. The ends of the shoots should be pruned off to an eye. Such training will encourage each parallel shoot to send up numerous

vertical shoots, most of which will flower. At the end of each season, these shoots, having flowered, can be shortened and spurred, like fruit trees. In this way – especially if new, main shoots, as they appear, are trained into position to replace less productive older ones – the plants will go on flowering quite efficiently for many years.

The main problem encountered by this method of growing roses is weed control, but if the soil is initially clean and given a generous mulching of bark chippings, any weed growth should be manageable.

Some of the Bourbons and Hybrid Perpetuals are almost custom-built for this purpose. In the past 'Frau Karl Druschki' and 'Hugh Dickson' were two great favourites for pegging down, both fairly free-flowering and with long, strong shoots.

'Hugh Dickson'

Companion Plants for Old and Shrub Roses

Whether or not roses should be grown in association with other plants is a matter of some argument. As will by now be clear, my own opinion is that roses, admirable though they can be on their own in an enclosed area, should form part of the overall garden scheme. Sometimes roses should even play a minor role, enhancing rather than dominating the landscape. Conversely, where they are dominant, their presence can be enhanced by other plants in less commanding roles.

In the formal setting, old-fashioned roses are often grown in beds separated by paths and lined with edging plants; such edging should be quite formal in habit and not too tall. In the nineteenth century, clipped dwarf box, *Buxus sempervirens suffruticosa*, was used extensively for this purpose, and this can still be effective in re-creating the atmosphere from that period, especially in conjunction with crazy-paving paths. Dwarf lavender, *Lavendula*, especially cv. 'Munstead', also makes a good natural edging to borders, but careful pruning is necessary to keep it in good condition. Catmint, *Nepeta mussinii*, with its lavender-blue flowers and grey foliage is the least expensive edging plant but looks bedraggled and dead in winter, unless clipped back each year. If allowed to do so, it will also over-reach into the rose bed. Other small, shrubby plants suitable for edging are some of the varieties

Roses growing with nepeta

Roses with mixed foliage plants at Castle Howard, Yorkshire

of dwarf hebe, not all of which are fully hardy, and *Santolina*, with grey foliage but yellow flowers, which needs careful placing. One of my particular favourites is *Berberis thunbergii atropurpurea nana*, with bronzy-red foliage, which looks particularly good with roses of most shades of pink.

It is in the more informal areas where shrubby plants can be combined with shrub and old-fashioned roses with some measure of abandon. A few combinations for shrubberies, worth consideration, are as follows:

Roses growing with cacti and Mediterranean plants in Dott. Carmine Russo's garden, Capri

pendula rosea, Pyrus salicifolia 'Pendula' (willow-leaved pear), *Salix caprea* and *Salix caprea pendula* (pussy willows), *Sorbus aria lutescens, Sorbus aucuparia* (mountain ash) and *Stranvaesia davidiana.*

SHRUBS FOR USE WITH BRIGHT RED, ORANGE AND YELLOW ROSES

Berberis thunbergii, B. candidula and *B. × stenophylla, Chimonanthus fragrans* and *C. praecox, Choisya ternata, Cornus stolonifera*

SHRUBS FOR USE WITH WHITE, PINK AND DEEP RED ROSES

Berberis thunbergii atropurpurea and its various purple forms, *Buddleia* 'Royal Red', *Caryopteris × clandonensis, Ceanothus, Ceratostigma willmottianum, Cistus × crispus, Daphne, Deutzia, Escallonia* various, fuchsias, hebes – grey foliage varieties, *Hydrangea paniculata grandiflora, Kolkwitzia*, lavender, *Olearia haastii, Philadelphus, Pittosporum, Potentilla, Prunus cistina, Romneya coulteri*, rosemary, viburnum × *burkwoodii*, and *Weigela florida foliis purpureis.*

SOME PERENNIAL PLANTS IDEAL WITH WHITE, PINK AND DEEP RED ROSES

Aquilegia, Artemisia, Astilbe – soft colours, *Campanula* – all varieties, *Dianthus* (pinks) – most colours, *Geranium* – cranesbill types, *Gypsophila, Hosta fortunei, Paeonia* – especially the soft-coloured varieties, *Phlox* – soft colours, *Scabiosa, Sedum, Stachys.*

SMALLER TREES SUITABLE AS A BACKGROUND FOR WHITE, PINK AND DEEP RED ROSES

Amelianchier, Arbutus unedo, Betula purpurea, Cercis siliquastrum, Eucalyptus gunnii, Fagus purpurea pendula, Malus (crab apple) 'Golden Hornet', 'John Downie' and *M. tschonoskii, Morus niger* (Black Mulberry), *Populus alba, Prunus* 'Amanogawa', *Prunus*

Above: Shrub roses growing in an informal setting with foxgloves *(left)* and in a formal setting with water and a sundial *(right)*

Top: Roses as an important part of a fragrant garden. *Below:* the Rose Garden, Elton Hall, Peterborough

'Maigold' growing under the eaves of a house

'Buff Beauty' grown as a hedge

'Maigold'

'Flaviramea', *Corylopsis pauciflora*, *Cytisus* (broom) – bright-coloured varieties, *Euonymus* – variegated varieties, *Genista* – most varieties, *Hypericum* – most varieties, *Ilex* (holly) – variegated varieties, *Ligustrum* (privet) – variegated varieties, *Mahonia* – all varieties, *Potentilla* – most shrubby varieties, *Pyracantha*, *Sambucus nigra aurea* and *Weigela florida variegata*.

PERENNIALS FOR USE WITH BRIGHT RED, ORANGE AND YELLOW ROSES

Alchemilla mollis, *Alyssum saxatile*, *Euphorbia* – various, *Paeonia* – brighter colours, *Rudbeckia* and *Saxifraga* (London Pride).

SMALL TREES FOR USE WITH BRIGHT RED, ORANGE AND YELLOW ROSES

Acer negundo 'Variegatum', *Acer platanoides* 'Drummondii', *Acer pseudoplatanus* 'Brilliantissimum', *Cotoneaster* × *rothschildianus*, *Cytisus battandieri*, *Liquidambar*, *Parrotia persica*, *Populus candicans* 'Aurora', and *Salix alba* 'Chermesina'.

Mixed Climbing Roses

Many delightful combinations can be achieved by mixing climbing roses with other climbing plants. The scope for this is practically limitless and, provided care is taken to ensure that the

Modern climbers growing on a fence at the Royal Hospital, Chelsea

marriage will work, much pleasure can be derived from experimenting with various combinations. If an interesting colour effect is desired, it is obviously important that all the plants will flower at the same time. Clematis (except the *montana* types, which are too vigorous) and roses flowering together are a superb combination, particularly white clematis with purple or dark red roses and vice versa. Summer jasmine also combines well with purple roses.

Roses with Bulbs, Corms, etc.

Spring-flowering bulbs can always be used with shrub and old-fashioned roses, helping to give colour to rose borders at a time of year when roses are at their least interesting. Combining and blending colours is not so important with bulbs since they come into flower well before the roses. As a matter of personal taste, I prefer to keep tulips away from the old-fashioned roses, and to plant them in beds of cluster-flowered and large-flowered varieties; and even then I would only use the shorter-growing varieties and some of the species. Daffodils and narcissi are quite

at home among old roses, and clumps of these go well among, underneath and alongside them. However, despite their different flowering seasons, I feel that species roses are best paid the compliment of being grown with the less flamboyant bulbs.

Other bulbous plants which make good bedfellows for the older roses are *Allium*, *Camassia*, *Chionodoxa*, crocus, *Galtonia*, grape hyacinth, *Puschkinia*, *Scilla* and snowdrop. Most lilies are happy growing with roses, but I sometimes find their upright stance slightly incongruous among the taller shrub roses and therefore feel that they should be planted in fairly large groups for best effect. Most lilies also prefer to keep their heads in the sun and feet in the shade, so this is a good reason to plant them with the shorter-growing roses; and for the same reason I would exclude gladioli altogether, although the shorter-growing montbretia can be effective. The tuberous-rooted forms of anemone are happy growing in the partial or dappled shade of shrub roses, as are hardy cyclamen. Aconites, if naturalized, give a refreshing lift to a group of rather dull, dormant shrub roses in early spring. Both the bulbous and tuberous-rooted iris flourish in most soils, and groups of these will grow harmoniously with shrub roses. All the above-mentioned flowers are, of course, suitable for growing beneath climbers and ramblers.

Annuals and Biennials with Roses

Annual bedding plants conjure up pictures of massed beds of brightly coloured salvias and french marigolds, but this need not be the case, for several of the annuals can combine well with old-fashioned roses if planted in random groups among the bushes. Petunias, clarkias, ten-week-stocks and, among the taller roses, nicotiana, all blend quite well especially if you can obtain the seed in specific colours. Old-fashioned roses grown in pots, especially those of paler shades, will not object to a few plants of lobelia and alyssum shading their roots and falling gently over the edge of their containers, nor will they object to the company of such upright plants as petunias.

Biennials, too, can look quite at home with old-fashioned roses, especially in cottage gardens where such flowers as hollyhocks, foxgloves, brompton stocks, aubretia, forget-me-nots, violets and pansies, all help to evoke a feeling of Victoriana.

Old Roses with Herbs

Old-fashioned roses make superb companions for culinary herbs. When strategically placed in the herb garden such roses can add colour, height and scent to a visually rather drab area. Old roses have much in common with herbs, both historically and aesthetically, and a few well-chosen varieties will help capture an atmosphere from the past.

Conversely, herbs placed in groups among old roses can look most effective and, at the same time, keep the kitchen well supplied throughout the year.

TEN OLD ROSES WHICH FOR REASONS OF ANTIQUITY OR COMPATIBILITY MAKE GOOD COMPANIONS FOR HERBS

'Alain Blanchard', 'Chapeau de Napoléon', 'Comte de Chambord', 'Double White Scotch', 'Empress Josephine', *R.* × *centifolia* 'Parvifolia', *R. gallica officinalis*, 'Rosa Mundi', 'Rose de Meaux', 'Tuscany Superb'.

Fruit and Vegetables with Old Roses

To consider growing fruit and vegetables among roses may seem contrary to all the laws of gardening; but when ground space is limited, and with careful choice of subjects, there is no reason why they should not be grown together. Beetroot, for example, has lush dark red foliage, and a few plants, either in clumps or at random, cannot look out of place; nor do clumps of purple broccoli, spinach or parsley. Marrows and ridge cucumbers, provided the soil is good and fertile, will happily crawl about the shrub rose border without causing offence, least of all to the roses; and the same goes for the odd clump of rhubarb, or bush of whitecurrant, redcurrant and/or gooseberry. I would avoid blackcurrants because of their distinctive smell, but strawberries, especially the delicious alpine species, can make quite a cheerful and useful ground cover.

Wild Flowers with Old Roses

I have already mentioned the use of species roses in the wild garden; conversely, wild flowers can make a most effective ground cover through which to plant both species and many of the less hybrid varieties of old roses. Wild flowers or even weeds, provided they are not too pernicious, would certainly be welcomed by such types of roses as the Gallicas, Centifolias and Damasks, although the more modern hybrids might well resent too many intrusions of this kind. Wild flowers can arrive naturally and be encouraged to spread by the removal only of those weeds that offend the eye, or which, at a later date, may infest other parts of the garden by

their seeds or roots; in particular, couch grass, ground elder, bindweed, thistles, docks and fat hen. Alternatively, wild flowers can be introduced by the sowing of seed or, in some cases, planting; both may be obtained from specialist seedsmen or nurserymen. The list of suitable wild flowers is endless and, in any case, I do not know enough about them to be too specific. If you choose to introduce some wild flowers among your roses, do be sure to purchase your seed. It is not worth plundering our countryside for seed or plants. There are few enough left growing there now.

Modern Roses in the Landscape

Roses as Bedding Plants and for Massed Display

Apart from half-hardy annuals, there are few plants better suited to massed display than shorter-growing bush roses. They have a distinct advantage over annuals in that, once planted and with proper care and attention, they will remain *in situ* for many years. As I have mentioned, breeders of roses have not been slow to appreciate the value of massed bedding and any good modern catalogue will give a choice of almost any colour in almost any height.

By far and away the best roses for bedding are Floribundas. They start flowering in late June and continue in flower until the first frost of November. As they come in all sizes, however, they are most effective when only one variety is grown en masse; and this applies not just in parks and large gardens but in small gardens too. No matter how great the temptation to choose a wide variety of colours, mixed roses in beds, especially Floribundas, are never as effective as a single colour. This rule can perhaps be relaxed slightly if more than one variety of a particular colour range is used; but however hard one tries, it is very difficult to get an even height throughout any wide-ranging mixture. If a wide colour range is desired, the best effects are achieved by planting in groups of three or four of each variety.

The larger-flowered roses such as Hybrid teas are not grown for massed display very often now, though several varieties enjoy just as long a flowering season as any Floribunda and provide the extra advantage of scent, which is still barely perceptible in so many Floribundas. Recent developments in other types now widen the choice for massing in beds and borders. Although short and compact, Patio roses lend themselves perfectly to group planting, especially in paved areas and formal, modern settings. For very large plantings where big expanses of one colour are required, there can be no better choice than some of the newer Procumbent roses, for not only do they provide continuity of flower but their

planting density is also lower and their maintenance easier. To help promote their own roses of this type, Meillands advise local authorities and landscapers to use tractor-drawn flayers to prune them! Hardly advice to be heeded by experienced gardeners, but Meillands' recommendations are not given lightly and I understand they have used this method to prune the roses in their trial beds and display gardens for several years.

N.B. Roses suitable for bedding or for planting in groups are marked (B) in the Dictionary section.

Above: Hybrid Teas as massed bedding. *Below:* a bed of 'Lilli Marlene'

TWENTY WIDELY AVAILABLE HYBRID TEAS FOR BORDER BEDDING

'Alec's Red', 'Blessings', 'Colour Wonder', 'Double Delight', 'Ernest H. Morse', 'Grandpa Dickson', 'Just Joey', 'Mme Louis Laperrière', 'Meilland Jubilee' ('Electron' in America), 'Mischief', 'National Trust' ('Bad Nankeen' in America), 'Olympiad', 'Pascali', 'Paul Sherville', 'Peaudouce', 'Peer Gynt', 'Piccadilly', 'Royal William', 'Silver Jubilee', 'Whisky Mac'.

TWENTY FLORIBUNDAS FOR BEDDING

'Amber Queen', 'Anisley Dickson', 'Ann Harkness', 'Arthur Bell', 'Beautiful Britain', 'City of Belfast', 'City of Leeds', 'English Miss', 'Escapade', 'Europeana', 'Evelyn Fison', 'Fragrant Delight', 'Korresia', 'Lili Marlene', 'Margaret Merril', 'Matangi', 'Pink Parfait', 'Sexy Rexy', 'Southampton', 'The Times Rose'.

Modern Roses with Companion Plants

In Victorian times roses were seen as somehow different from other plants and were almost always grown in fairly formal gardens set aside especially for them. This was the practice not only in larger gardens; smaller gardens, too, had their own patch for roses, and these were seldom mixed with other types of plants. There is still no more pleasant sight than to see roses growing together, either in their own part of a garden or as a whole rose garden forming a collection. However, minds have broadened since the turn of the century and roses are now used far more often in conjunction with other plants, a practice I wholeheartedly support. I have dealt with the use of older roses as support plants in an earlier chapter.

By far and away the most common use of Floribundas and Hybrid Teas is for bedding, but both can happily fit into mixed planting schemes. As individuals they are excellent in herbaceous borders, simply dotted here and there among shorter perennials of sympathetic colours or, conversely, adding a bright splash of contrasting colour to a group of quieter foliage plants. Standards and half standards are, I think, more at home when used functionally as relief plants in herbaceous borders, where they rise above the foliage, than when standing like soldiers in ranks, alone with their own kind. Roses of all dimensions can be found that will fit into mixed shrubberies, although except for the very tallest, some Hybrid Teas can look incongruous. Floribundas, especially in groups of three, will admirably provide that little extra colour and length of season without looking out of place.

The best mixers of all, however, are modern shrub roses, including the English roses, for they not only have all the characteristics of Floribundas but some also have the added dimension of height. Some of the more bushy ones fit comfortably among shrubs as individual plants, but others give the best effect planted in groups. Of all the modern roses adaptable to mixed shrubberies, the Rugosa hybrids are the most widely used, for not only do they provide flowers but in many cases also autumn colour and hips – valuable assets to any modern landscape. It baffles me, though, why modern shrub roses are not used more extensively in mixed shrub plantings. Perhaps they are thought of too much as roses rather than as shrubs? Surely any shrub which flowers all summer through, as modern roses do, would be a natural choice if it were not a rose. When I talk to landscapers about this they usually cite high maintenance factors as the reason for their neglect – how do they know if they never try? My shrub roses need no more maintenance than most other shrubs; and even if it is true that such roses are more expensive to maintain, I can think of several dull shrubberies where it would have been cost-effective to have included them. Speaking of cost-effectiveness, most modern climbing roses are grown on walls, trellises or pillars, so what could be more efficient than to plant other climbers such as clematis, honeysuckle and jasmine to intermingle with them? Such mixtures take full advantage of their site and add extra colour and foliage to the roses.

To return to mixed borders. Procumbent roses are the modern landscaper's dream and, in fairness, gardeners have not been slow to appreciate their potential; even so, they are still too often segregated on plots of their own rather than integrated with the shrubbery. Groups of three or five, allowed to grow naturally into spreading clumps, are ideal among slightly taller shrubs, even conifers. Indeed, with their habit of growth, the quieter colours of such roses make them as compatible with conifers as heathers and spreading cotoneasters.

N.B. Wide-growing or ground-cover roses are marked (G) in the Dictionary section.

Pillar roses at the Roseraie de l'Hay – Les Roses, Paris

The Use of Modern Climbers

It is interesting, in view of the not inconsiderable number of modern climbers introduced over recent years, how many climbers and ramblers from earlier times are still used today. It prompts one to wonder what the great Gertrude Jekyll would have made of modern-day climbers, for she relied heavily on cascading, garlanding and festooning. Had she had the range of today's long-flowering climbers at her command, would she have ignored their existence? I doubt it. She would have realized, ahead of her time, that all that was new was not necessarily bad and would have harnessed the extensive capabilities of the modern climbing rose, painting it into her landscape just as she did delphiniums and fox-gloves.

Just as I feel sure Miss Jekyll would have enjoyed our modern varieties, I am equally sure that we should not let the utilitarian qualities of such plants dominate our thinking to the exclusion of her type of roses today. For there is a place for both in our late-twentieth-century gardens. Flipping through my old copy of Jekyll and Mawley's book *Roses for English Gardens* makes me realize just how underused climbing roses now are. Why? Is it that they need attention from time to time; that they need expensive supports, that they have thorns that might grab us as we pass, that they spoil our modern sandfaced bricks or, simply, that we do not know how to use them with no modern Gertrude Jekyll to show us how? It is likely a combination of all these things.

One reminder of bygone days which is certainly not out of fashion, to judge by the number sold, is the tree climber, but not many modern climbers are suitable for this. This subject was dealt with in an earlier section (see pages 87–8). Rustic timber and iron trellises and arches can support the heaviest of climbers with ease, each eventually holding up the other. The trouble is that many modern continuous-flowering climbers are upright in stance and not flexible enough to look comfortable on an arch in the way of the older varieties. This does not mean that modern roses fail to respond to a little persuasion. Given time and patience, 'New Dawn', for example (perhaps no longer thought of as a modern), and some of her offspring such as 'Pink Perpétue', can be bent and twisted to good effect. It is their upright stance that lends modern climbers so readily to walls and other solid structures like interwoven panels, for against such supports they need less attention than their more eager, older counterparts. Many of the modern climbing sports are also far too stiff and upright for use on anything other than a fairly strong structure; the more such roses can be bent, twisted and trained, the more productive they are.

N.B. Shrub roses suitable for use as climbing or pillar roses are marked (CL) in the Dictionary section; vigorous kinds suitable for growing up into trees are marked (T).

TEN PROVEN MODERN CLIMBING ROSES

'Aloha', 'Bantry Bay', 'Dublin Bay', 'Handel', 'Leverkusen', 'Maigold', 'New Dawn', 'Parkdirektor Riggers', 'Pink Perpétue', 'Swan Lake'.

Climbers at the Roseraie du Parc de Bagatelle, Paris

'Bantry Bay' at Tasman Bay Roses garden, Motueka, New Zealand

Modern Roses as Hedges

There are few natural hedging plants, but nature offers gardeners many subjects adaptable to this purpose. Roses fit comfortably among them.

Roses not only make good hedges by themselves but can also do wonders in softening the sometimes harsh outlines of modern man-made fences. No matter what size the fence or from what material it is made, there is always a rose that will willingly perform such a task without much effort. Some of the modern shrub roses are ideal, especially those of upright stance.

Obliging in hiding, disguising or adding colour to the shorter man-made fence are many of the taller, upright-growing Floribundas. Like the modern shrubs, they need pruning annually in spring and dead-heading and occasional spraying in summer; beyond that, they require little or no attention nor will they intrude too much into adjacent borders, drives or paths. If uniformity is required, plant all of the same variety. For informal, free-standing rose hedges some of the older once-flowering roses are worth consideration. Many thrive on neglect and form rugged, impenetrable screens; I have described some of these in an earlier section (see pages 80–1).

Modern roses usually flower throughout the summer. This necessitates pruning and, in consequence, they do not lend themselves too readily to informality. Some of the Hybrid Musks are quite relaxed in growth, however, and will provide some informality, particularly when different varieties are mixed and planted close enough to embrace. The Rugosa hybrids make some of the best hedges and they, too, can be informal when allowed to run free, especially those that bear hips. The double forms do not produce many hips and with a combination of dead-heading and pruning they can be formed into quite dense, formal hedges. Rugosas provide superb autumn colours as a bonus.

Although they are useful for concealing fences, many modern shrub roses make good hedgerows in their own right. This is not to say that such roses are suitable as boundary hedges on their own, but in conjunction with wire mesh they are superb. They also make excellent free-standing ornamental hedges within the garden. The list is almost endless. For the shorter hedge it is almost impossible to exclude any of the Floribundas. To a lesser extent some Hybrid Teas also make reliable, trouble-free hedges.

Dwarf Polyantha roses were used to great effect as dividing hedges during the 1920s and '30s, a fashion I would love to see resurrected. They have a good range of colour, are dense in habit, quite unobtrusive when not in flower and demand the minimum of attention.

As for the cultivation of a good rose hedge, this simply means plenty of organic material in the soil to start it off, pruning as and when appropriate to keep the hedge in shape, spraying and feeding as with other roses and the removal of unsightly dead-heads when necessary. The one golden rule is to prune hard in the first year of planting to encourage all the first year's growth to come from the base of the plant.

N.B. Roses that make fine hedging plants are marked (H) in the Dictionary section.

TEN PROVEN MODERN ROSES FOR HEDGING

'Alexander', 'Chinatown', 'Escapade', 'Iceberg', 'Margaret Merril', 'Mountbatten', 'Queen Elizabeth', 'Sally Holmes', 'Sexy Rexy', 'Southampton'.

TEN PROVEN SHRUB ROSES FOR HEDGING

'Ballerina', 'Bonn', 'Elmshorn', 'Fiona', 'Fountain', 'Fred Loads', 'Fritz Nobis', 'Joseph's Coat', 'Lavender Lassie', 'Nymphenburg'.

Modern Roses in Containers

Pots, urns, boxes and tubs come in a variety of shapes and sizes, and to avoid repeating myself too often I will refer to them all as containers. Since Victorian times this method of growing roses has gone slowly out of fashion. The decline is fairly predictable because until the turn of the century there were far more conservatories and far more Tea roses to grow in them. Terraces, too, were more common, especially in bigger gardens, and they made ideal standing areas in summer for container-grown roses after the first flush of flower under glass. Gardens are much smaller today, so in a way it is surprising that more roses are not grown in pots, particularly as the range of varieties suitable for the purpose is infinitely greater than it was a century ago. This is not to say that only certain roses can be grown this way, for given the right size of container almost any rose can be made to feel comfortable in one, even climbers 10' (3 m) tall – I know a superb seven-year-old 'Coral Dawn'. The secret, apart from size and capacity, is in the soil. If the right compost is used and good drainage provided, roses grown in containers will live and thrive for years. More details on soils and so forth will come later in the cultivation section (see page 419).

While all modern roses will grow in pots, some are better at it than others. Miniatures, for example, do well, especially those propagated by grafting, as such plants are bigger and more vigorous than those grown on their own roots. Dwarf Polyanthas also thrive and look quite at home, as do many Floribundas, particularly shorter ones like 'Lady Romsey', 'Meteor' and 'Amber

Queen'. Hybrid Teas will, of course, grow quite successfully but may not be such good value, for they tend to have fewer blooms. Of all the shorter-growing roses, though, the newer Patios lend themselves best to this purpose and the posture of such varieties as 'Sunblaze' and 'Gentle Touch' is well suited to modern stoneware. Of the larger roses, the taller Floribundas do well; 'Queen Elizabeth' and 'Iceberg', for example, make excellent container plants, as do some of the wide range of bushy shrubs – 'Ballerina' and 'Yesterday' spring readily to mind. Most suitable of all are some of the Procumbents, especially when they can be given their head in large containers and cascade over the edge. 'Nozomi' is ideal and enjoys the extra mollycoddling it gets by being grown in this way, but sadly its flowering season is rather short and others, such as 'Fairyland', 'Fairy Damsel' and 'Smarty' are better. In larger pots it is possible to use the very prostrate varieties such as 'Snow Carpet' as undergrowth to larger, more upright roses such as 'Iceberg'. Tall standards often look ridiculous in such situations, but half and quarter standards can be effective, particularly when underplanted with smaller roses.

For those who have never tried growing roses in this way, it is well worth the effort, indeed in small gardens roses may not be possible in any other way. I can vouch for the fact that it is not difficult, for we have several hundred at our nursery, some over ten years old. They almost thrive on neglect, and year after year find themselves on display at the Chelsea Flower Show.

N.B. Roses suitable for growing in containers are marked ⊙ in the Dictionary section.

TEN HYBRID TEA AND FLORIBUNDA ROSES FOR GROWING PERMANENTLY IN CONTAINERS

Hybrid Teas
'Alec's Red', 'Anna Pavlova', 'Grandpa Dickson', 'Royal William', 'Silver Jubilee'.

Floribundas
'Amber Queen', 'Escapade', 'Fragrant Delight', 'Iceberg', 'Sexy Rexy'.

Roses under Glass

Throughout the world many millions of roses are grown commercially under glass. Where climates are unpredictable this is the sure way of producing roses for the cut-flower market, at least in centres of high population where demand is high. To produce cut

'Lady Sylvia'

flowers on this scale, growers plant their roses direct into greenhouse soil. Such methods are not possible for most amateurs since they usually have to make do with far less space; so, the most common practice is to grow them in pots. To get roses very early in spring, heaters have to be used, but this is an expensive luxury and it is quite possible to bring roses into flower four to five weeks earlier than those outdoors by growing them in cold greenhouses or conservatories.

Forced roses can be very rewarding and, properly tended, can be equal to, if not better than, blooms grown outdoors. As mentioned elsewhere, many of the old Tea-Scented and China roses were grown in this way in days gone by. I have tried several such roses over the years and can well see why so many Victorian gentlemen sported roses as buttonholes out of season.

For those with more modern leanings, all the Hybrid Teas have Tea rose in their veins to some degree and will respond to the extra loving care they receive under glass with blooms of excellent quality. To get the best quality flowers, plants need to be disbudded so that only the blooms on the central apex are allowed to mature. I

seldom do this, however, preferring my roses to look natural. If the aim is to produce cut flowers, then it is better to use varieties that have been specifically bred for forcing. If quantity rather than quality of flowers is the target, then a variety named 'Garnette' is a must, for this red rose produces clusters that last for well over a week when cut. Some of the older Hybrid Teas make superb forcing roses too, and, unlike so many modern forcing varieties, quite a few are superbly scented.

From time to time under glass, shading is necessary to protect the blooms from intense sunlight. In larger greenhouses, it is nice to use a climbing rose to help provide this. Choose a variety with ample foliage, plant it at the edge of the greenhouse border nearest to the glass and train it to scramble up on the inside of the glass by stretching strands of wire 6″ (15 cm) from the glass at about 12″ (30 cm) apart along the length of the greenhouse. When the rose is fully grown it will provide dappled shade for the plants beneath. A rose ideal for this purpose is the vigorous, half-hardy, soft yellow *R. banksiae lutea*; under glass it will flower in early April and give little or no trouble with disease, and, being evergreen, although it sheds its leaves from time to time, these are never a problem.

N.B. Roses suitable for forcing or for growing under glass are marked (Gh) in the Dictionary section.

TEN ROSES FOR FORCING FOR CUT FLOWERS (NOT NECESSARILY FLORISTS' ROSES)

'Baccara', 'Carol', 'Ernest H. Morse', 'Garnette', 'King's Ransom', 'Lady Sylvia', 'Mme Butterfly', 'Mojave', 'Sonia' ('Sweet Promise'), 'Sutter's Gold'.

Note: Most Hybrid Tea and Floribunda roses can be grown under glass successfully.

Roses for Cutting and Arranging

Most modern roses can be cut and taken indoors for arranging, especially the Hybrid Teas and Floribundas. I have discussed the practicalities of cutting and arranging roses in the section on old roses. The following are roses of all types and are, from my experience, good yielders and last for a good time in water when cut.

N.B. Roses that make good cut flowers are marked ✄ in the Dictionary section.

TEN GOOD CUTTING VARIETIES

'Anna Pavlova', 'Anne Cocker', 'Bloomfield Abundance', 'Fountain', 'Fritz Nobis', 'Lady Sylvia', 'Magenta', 'Prosperity', 'Sadlers Wells', 'The Fairy'.

Roses for Exhibition

The first ever National Rose Show in Britain was staged in Piccadilly, London, in 1858. It heralded the beginning of an important aspect of rose growing which has been popular ever since, giving growers the opportunity to pit their skills against one another by producing the shapeliest and biggest possible blooms and staging them at their best. Exhibitors need an immense amount of expertise, a thorough understanding of the subject and the patience of Job. It also helps to be a good loser, for judges have a habit of awarding first prize to the other chap's rose, which in no way is ever as good as yours.

I should declare here that I have not entered roses for 'the best bloom in the show' for many years. At most shows, both national and provincial, nurserymen compete for the best overall display of roses, but the quality of their blooms, although very high on the judges' list, is just one criterion; the others are quantity, arrangement and educational interest. Nurserymen also compete for customers, which is a very good reason for beating the other chap at his own game.

Competitive exhibiting for the amateur is not without cost, so, having gone through catalogues and visited shows to select those varieties likely to win awards, the decision has to be made as to which ones to grow. Bear in mind that show schedules often have classes of from one to twelve blooms of the same variety, so purchases have to be made in sufficient quantity to allow for spares. Certain varieties constantly win prizes and they are the ones to choose; they will, almost certainly, be Hybrid Teas.

Having selected the varieties, it is then a case of getting down to growing them for this special purpose. First, you need a good, heavy loam with plenty of added organic matter, followed by regular feeding with rose fertilizers. Hard pruning is vital in the first year; remember, it is quality that counts, not quantity, so usually, depending upon the variety, only the best and strongest shoots should be allowed to develop. Healthy roses lead to big blooms, so spraying programmes must be religiously followed. Timing, too, is important and pruning dates should be adjusted to the date of the show. As the show gets nearer so the protection of blooms becomes necessary; small umbrellas and windbreaks then come into play – on or off – according to the weather. Most Hybrid Teas, as a matter of course, produce several buds around the central apex bud. To encourage the bush to put all its efforts into one good bloom, all the smaller buds should be removed.

Well before the show, exhibitors should familiarize themselves with the expectations of the particular society staging the show and carefully read the schedule. Disqualification will follow for even the slightest infringement of the rules. In Britain a set of standard rules, covering both exhibitors and judges, has been drawn up by the Royal National Rose Society. America has a different set of rules, but in most countries judges will have passed an examination in the subject. Judges are usually experienced growers themselves. The winning bloom of each class will be the one, or group, that displays the best form, size, substance, freshness, purity of colour, refinement and trueness to type at the exact time it is judged. Different criteria apply to other types but Hybrid Teas are at their best when, at the time the judge examines them, they display all these attributes and are at a stage where the outer rows of petals are unfurled and well spaced, and the centre ones are still holding a conical shape. Other factors come into the reckoning, too, depending upon the class and the type of rose. These include quality, cleanliness of foliage, length and condition of stem, balance between size of flower and thickness of stem, and so on.

Exhibitors are free to indulge in what is termed 'dressing'. This requires much skill and patience, and hours are spent preparing blooms with camelhair brushes, tweezers, bent wire, cottonwool buds, toothpicks, etc. With these instruments every petal and petal fold is preened to form the favoured shape of the particular variety. All beauty treatment is done during the last hours before the blooms are left alone on the bench and to the mercy of the judges. Prior to this, from the moment the roses are selected and cut, the utmost care is taken to ensure that no harm comes to them. Special travelling boxes are often used, with each rose segregated in its own compartment. While in transit blooms showing any signs of opening too much are held together with soft wool or raffia, and those of slightly uneven shape, or not yet sufficiently open, have little pellets inserted between the rows of petals to correct, if possible, these faults. The pellets are usually shaped to fit and can be made of polystyrene, cottonwool or tissue paper.

Most show schedules have dozens of classes for dozens of different types of roses. This necessarily brief account has not touched on such things as the spacing of blooms, the importance of correct length of stem, the different skills required in displaying cluster-flowered types and how the wiring of blooms is frowned upon by some but not others. Already I may have gone too far, for the skills of exhibiting are best explained by those who have proved themselves at the art. I can, perhaps, recommend a few roses that I have seen winning major prizes from time to time: they are 'Admiral Rodney', 'Amatsu-Otome', 'Big Chief', 'Lakeland', 'Montezuma', 'Perfecta', 'Red Devil' and 'Royal Highness'. There are lots of others, but attention must be paid to labelling. Judges like correct names, and if they fail to notice an incorrect one, a fellow exhibitor surely will.

N.B. Roses suitable for exhibiting are marked (E) in the Dictionary section.

Modern Roses as Standards (Tree Roses)

Growing roses as standards, or Tree Roses as they are called in America, is not a favourite pastime of mine. I find them contrived and too regimental for my taste. Nevertheless, in fairness, I accept that there is considerable scope for this type of rose in many modern gardens.

Standards are produced by the budding of named varieties at preselected heights on to specially grown stems (for the technique of budding, see pages 431–2). In Europe *R. rugosa* is by far the most popular for this purpose; another is a form of *R. canina* called 'Pfander'. In other parts of the world *R. multiflora* and climbing 'Dr Huey' are more widely used. Standards are usually 'worked' (that is, budded) at about 3′ 6″ (1.05 m), half standards at 2′ 9″ (82.5 cm) and weeping standards at 5′ (1.5 m). A fairly recent development is the quarter standard which is budded at about 18′ (45 cm) from the ground; Miniatures are often seen at this height and, as such, make good subjects for growing in pots. Another group now popular as standards are the long-flowering Procumbents. 'Nozomi', although once-flowering, is extremely good grown in this way, drooping, as it does, to the ground from at least 5′ (1.5 m). This variety seems to be incompatible with *R. rugosa* and, for no obvious reason, suddenly dies off. It is better on 'Pfander' stems, it would seem.

The weepers are my favourites, flexible ramblers that cascade to the ground without too much help. Special wire frames can be employed to assist their downward growth and add extra strength, but I prefer to grow them naturally. 'Albéric Barbier', 'Minnehaha' and 'Excelsa' are excellent. Some shrub roses also make good standards but these can easily get top-heavy as they grow, so staking is important. In particular I like 'Ballerina', 'Yesterday' and, of course, the lovely 'Canary Bird' which, when placed at the top of a stem, makes an elegant semi-weeper.

Floribundas such as 'Iceberg', 'Evelyn Fison' and 'Arthur Bell' make superb plants as either full or half standards. Of the Hybrid Teas, the best are those that grow bushily with good foliage such as 'Silver Jubilee', 'Alec's Red' and 'Grandpa Dickson'. Orange is a popular colour, but in colder areas roses of this shade are best avoided since they tend to be less hardy than those of other colours. Standards are vulnerable to wind damage, so they should be secured to an adequate stake by, at least, two strong straps; and all weepers should be pruned very hard in their first season, for nothing looks more ungainly than a leggy standard.

Fragrance in Modern Roses

Noses are instinctively drawn to roses and it is always a great disappointment to find a beautiful bloom without perfume. An unfair criticism levelled at modern roses is lack of fragrance. Certainly there was a period in the 1950s and '60s when many varieties were introduced without much scent, but breeders soon realized the error of their ways and things are different now. These days very few Hybrid Teas are introduced that are not worth a second sniff. Floribundas still have some way to go but there are several fine exceptions; no gardener should lack choice if perfume is his or her priority.

The famous 'Frau Karl Druschki' was the first white rose to be

Standard roses at the Roseraie du Parc de Bagatelle, Paris

condemned for lack of scent. Since then, several other white varieties have suffered the same fate, though two recent introductions, 'Margaret Merril' and 'Sir Frederick Ashton', are both well endowed. When talking of roses with perfume, it is impossible to exclude the sisters 'Ophelia', 'Mme Butterfly' and 'Lady Sylvia', for these three ladies owe much of their long-standing popularity to this virtue alone. And since the Second World War, 'Prima Ballerina', 'Fragrant Cloud' and 'Anna Pavlova' have won many friends as the result of that first sniff.

'Dusky Maiden' was the first Floribunda with perfume, and although still in a minority, several excellent and highly scented varieties have been raised since then; 'Arthur Bell', 'Fragrant Delight' and 'Margaret Merril', again, immediately spring to mind. Breeders are well aware that a good scented rose will always triumph over a good non-scented one of the same colour, so we need never fear that perfume will disappear from our favourite flower.

N.B. A fragrance rating is given to each rose in the Dictionary section.

TWENTY VERY FRAGRANT MODERN ROSES

'Admiral Rodney' (HT), 'Alec's Red' (HT), 'Anna Pavlova' (HT), 'Compassion' (Climber), 'Constance Spry' (Shrub or Climber), 'Crimson Glory' (HT), 'Fragrant Cloud' (HT or Climber), 'Josephine Bruce' (HT or Climber), 'Lady Sylvia' (HT or Climber), 'Mme Butterfly' (HT or Climber), 'Margaret Merril' (Floribunda), 'My Choice' (HT), 'Ophelia' (HT or Climber), 'Papa Meilland' (HT), 'Pink Peace' (HT), 'Prima Ballerina' (HT), 'Sir Frederick Ashton' (HT), 'Susan Hampshire' (HT), 'Wendy Cussons' (HT), 'Whisky Mac' (HT).

'Sir Frederick Ashton'

'Orange Sunblaze'

The Dictionary

'Alchemist'

'Petite de Hollande'

Introduction

SPECIES

Ever since that great Swedish botanist Carl von Linné (*Linnaeus* in the Latin) laid down the ground rules in the mid-eighteenth century, plant systematics have been in a constant state of change. Despite this, however, the basic structure he, with others, devised still remains as the order of things in the plant kingdom. This structure, in simple terms, places groups of plants with common characteristics (not always apparent to the layman such as myself) into divisions. These divisions are, in turn, put into subdivisions, each of which is then split up again into classes. After classes come subclasses which are then divided into orders, the orders into families, the families into tribes and the tribes into genera.

The genus *Rosa* is part of the tribe Roseae, itself part of the family Rosaceae which as well as roses embraces plants as diverse as Potentillas and Apples. It is, however, at the genus level that enough visual characteristics and likenesses emerge within a group for easy recognition of the relationship of one plant to another; and it is at this point in the structure that species emerge: each different but obviously related one to the other and each perpetuating its kind by breeding true to type when fertilized by itself.

In the case of roses, to complicate things just a little more the genus is split up into four subgenera, *Hulthemia*, *Hesperhodos*, *Platyrhodon* and *Eurosa (Rosa)*. In turn *Eurosa* is further subdivided into sections according to predominant characteristics and recognizable relationships.*

* Since the publication of *Classic Roses* in 1985, my attention has been drawn to an article by Mr E. F. Allen entitled 'A Simplified Rose Classification' which appeared in the Royal National Rose Society's *Rose Annual* 1973. In this article Mr Allen, following 'Rehder', divides the genus *Rosa* into just three subgenera and places these in natural evolutionary sequence as follows – *Hesperhodos*, *Platyrhodon* and *Eurosa (Rosa)*. It is this sequence which BARB follows; but with the addition of *Hulthemia (Simplicifolia)* as the first in line. Since in this dictionary I have included the BARB Classification System for Garden Groups, it is proper that I also follow this sequence of botanical division. Thus, the order in which the four subgenera are placed in this book is different to that of *Classic Roses*. This change in no way reflects any inaccuracy in that publication, merely an adaptation.

Following these rules, therefore, in this dictionary I have placed each species in alphabetical order into the section to which it belongs, under its appropriate subgenus heading.

HYBRIDS

Over the years, earlier by chance mutation or natural hybridity, and later by deliberate manipulation or by a combination of all these factors, hybrids occurred, or were developed, with the mixed genealogy of the various species. These lead us to what may be loosely termed the 'garden groups', viz. for the old roses, Albas, Gallicas, Damasks, Bourbons, Teas etc., and for the modern roses, Hybrid Teas, Floribundas etc. The garden groups are then placed in their rightful position under the species to which they most owe their lineage. Where lineage is obscure or for any reason impossible to determine, I have used either my instinct or observations to place them under a heading that seems appropriate for a particular rose.

The Selection of the Species and Hybrids

All but the most obscure species are included, the two main criteria for selection being significance in the genealogy of a particular garden group and garden-worthiness.

In choosing which hybrids to include I analysed the most recent catalogues of the specialist rose nurseries of Britain, America, the Antipodes and the rest of the world, and my final selection consists only of varieties that are currently available.

I confess to a degree of favouritism in my choice of several roses, but of those selected, by far the majority should remain obtainable for quite a few years to come.

In addition to trade catalogues, I have relied heavily on information gleaned from the following invaluable publications: *Find That Rose*, published annually by the British Rose Growers Association; *The Rose Directory*, published periodically by the Royal National Rose Society; *The Combined Rose List (Roses in Commerce and Cultivation)* compiled and published annually by Beverly R. Dobson, New York; *Modern Roses 7, 8 and 9*, published by McFarland in conjunction with the American Rose Society; Bean's *Trees and Shrubs hardy in the British Isles* (1984); *Roses* by Gerd Krüssman; and the works of Graham Thomas, Jack Harkness, David Austin and Trevor Griffiths.

The Descriptions

Most of the roses are described from personal experience and observation. For those outside my sphere of knowledge which deserved inclusion, I have used the raiser's description or obtained the information from the most reliable source I could find.

Honours and Awards

Many roses have won awards of excellence at various trial grounds and shows throughout the world. While I acknowledge such achievements as significant and fully accept that such awards generally indicate a good variety, I do not believe that they necessarily reflect superiority in a worldwide context, especially where awards are made on an annual basis or after a relatively short period of, say, three years of trial. No specific honours are therefore mentioned except where appropriate in passing.

Credits

Works with more emphasis on botanic systematics and taxonomy often credit those who work or have worked in these fields by placing their names against species which they have discovered, classified, identified or named. This is a gardening book and I have not done this, largely in the interests of simplicity, and not from any lack of respect for those whose names are omitted. In the case of hybrids the raiser's name and nationality, parentage and date of introduction are included where known.

Synonyms

Where a synonym is in brackets it indicates the registered name of the rose for trademark purposes. Unbracketed synonyms are the names by which they may well be otherwise known in other countries.

Dimensions

Dimensions are expressed in both imperial and metric terms and assume the variety to be growing in formal garden soil and pruned regularly according to need.

Presentation

Letters and symbols are used throughout to indicate the special usages, aptitudes and foibles of roses. These are intended only as a guide for those who are not familiar with a particular variety; they merely indicate my own experience or, in some cases, the raiser's comments. Colour and degree of fragrance are, for example, from personal observation, likewise susceptibility to disease, which can depend upon factors outisde the constitution of a particular variety, such as weather, soil conditions or, simply, bad husbandry.

Key to Letters and Symbols

(AW) Available widely.

(AL) Availability limited to specialist growers.

(A) Good autumn foliage.

(B) Good for bedding or planting in groups.

(C) More or less continuous flowering throughout summer.

(CL) Suitable also for use as a climber or pillar rose.

(E) Good for exhibition.

(F) Worth growing for the ornamental value of their fruit.

(G) Procumbent or wide-growing ground-cover varieties.

(Gh) Suitable for forcing or growing under glass.

(H) Suitable for hedging.

(MF) Moderately fragrant.

(N) Suitable for northerly aspect. (NB: Roses only tolerate such a situation, they don't necessarily enjoy it).

(P) Tolerant of poor soils.

(R) Recurrent or repeat flowering (not continuous).

(S) Summer flowering only. (Seldom if ever remontant.)

(SF) Slightly fragrant.

(SP) Spring flowering only.

(T) Suitable for growing up into trees.

(VF) Very Fragrant.

(W) Suitable for woodland and covert planting.

BS✿ Susceptible to Black Spot.

M✿ Susceptible to Mildew.

R✿ Susceptible to Rust.

● Tolerant of shade.

☼ Prefers a sunny position to thrive.

≈ Suggested for growing adjacent to water.

(WW) Hates wet weather when in flower.

✂ Good for cutting.

☉ Suitable for growing in pots.

Classification Abbreviations
(for more details see pages 63–8)
BARB = British Association of Rose Breeders.
MR9 = *Modern Roses 9*.
WFRS = World Federation of Rose Societies.

Table comparing Seasons in the Rose Cycle in the Northern and Southern Hemisphere

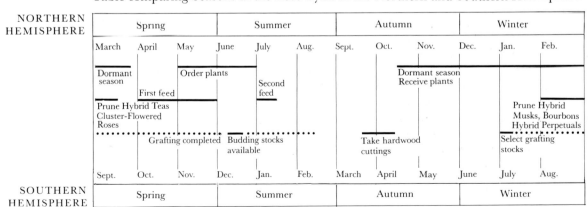

'Cooper's Burmese'

ROSA Subgenus *Hulthemia*

Simplicifoliae

In evolutionary terms this is the oldest of the four subgenera. It is classified outside the genus by some authorities.

Growth spreading, dense in *Hulthemia persica*,
tall and dense in ×*Hulthemosa hardii*.
Stems angular with many thorns.
Leaves entire, without stipules.
Flowers produced singly.
Fruit greenish, densely spiny, globose.
Sepals persist.

'Nigel Hawthorne'

SPECIES

Hulthemia persica
×*Hulthemosa hardii*

ORIGIN AND DISTRIBUTION

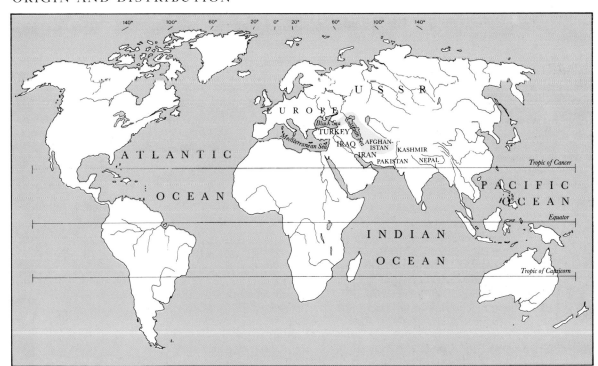

Hulthemia and ×*Hulthemosa*

FORMS AND HYBRIDS

Although included here, strictly speaking, this subgenus may not be part of the genus *Rosa*. However, except for the foliage which is made up of simple leaves without stipules, it grows, behaves and looks just like a rose; so much so that it would be quite wrong to discriminate against it and exclude it on grounds of race. For several years Jack Harkness has been working with this subgenus and has succeeded in raising a number of seedlings, four of which have been introduced. Like their parents, these are quite fascinating and clearly different to any other group of hybrids, making useful garden plants where something out of the ordinary is fancied.

'Euphrates'

CLASSIFICATION

BARB	Species: Class 1	Hybrids: Class 1
MR9	Species: Class 55	Hybrids: Class 55
WFRS	Species: Class 38	Hybrids: Class 38

Hulthemia persica,
R. persica, R. berberifolia

CENTRAL ASIA 1789
Difficult to grow but worth some perseverance. Leaves slender with no stipules. Small, single flowers of bright clear yellow with a browny-crimson splodge in the centre of each; usually borne at end of twiggy, downy, angular shoots with hooked thorns which are arranged in pairs below the leaves. Flowers produced spasmodically for a fairly long season.
(S) ☼ ☉ (AL)
2' × 2'   60 × 60 cm

×*Hulthemosa hardii,*
R. × hardii

Hardy FRANCE c. 1830
Hulthemia persica × R. clinophylla
A medium-growing rose, very unusual with small, single, butter-cup-size flowers of deep, golden yellow with a striking, bright, reddish-brown eye in its centre. Growth twiggy but dense with spiteful thorns and numerous pinnate leaves without stipules. Supposed not to be hardy.
(S) ☼ ☉ (SF) (AL)
6' × 4'   1.8 × 1.2 m

'Euphrates' (Harunique)

Harkness UK 1986
H. persica seedling
Small to medium, single flowers of rosy-salmon with a pronounced brownish-scarlet blotch in the centre, borne in small clusters. Small, light green foliage similar to that of its parent in shape and produced on a low, dense plant.
(S) (P) ● ☉ (AL)
1' 6" × 3'   45 × 90 cm

'Nigel Hawthorne' (Harquibbler)

Harkness UK 1989
H. persica × 'Harvest Home'
Single blooms of salmon-rose each with a pronounced red eye, produced plentifully on a dense, wiry, prickly, well foliated plant of moderately spreading habit.
(C) (P) (G) ☼ ☉ (AL)
3' × 4'   90 × 120 cm

'Tigris' (Harprier)

Harkness UK 1985
H. persica seedling
Flowers, described by its raiser as 'powder puff-like' are about 1" across, and produced in profusion, each with attractive scarlet markings on a canary-yellow background. Growth is low, slightly spreading and dense.
(C) (P) ☼ ☉ (AL)
1' 6" × 2'   45 × 60 cm

'Xerxes' (Harjames)

Harkness UK 1989
H. persica × 'Canary Bird'
By far the tallest of these fascinating hybrids. This rose produces considerable numbers of bright sulphur-yellow flowers each with a crimson eye. Growth upright.
(S) (P) (G) ☼ (AL)
5' × 3'   1.5 × 1 m

'Tigris'

R. stellata mirifica

ROSA Subgenus *Hesperhodos*

Hesperhodos

Very prickly with small leaves.

SPECIES
R. stellata
R. stellata mirifica

R. stellata mirifica hips

ORIGIN AND DISTRIBUTION

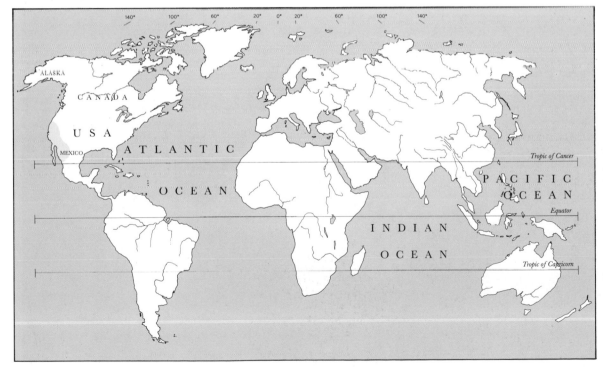

R. stellata

TWO FORMS

This species and its cultivars are both eccentrics of the rose world but this fact, in itself, makes them much more attractive. As plants, they each appear and behave very much like a gooseberry bush, except that neither of them is as tall. Their buds, before opening, and also their fruit, have an exaggerated gooseberry quality in that both are covered with soft spines. Their flowers are not conspicuous *en masse* but, individually, are worth closer inspection. Quite lovely.

CLASSIFICATION
BARB   Class 1
MR9   Class 55
WFRS   Class 38

R. stellata

S. USA 1902
An interesting species with dense, spiny wood and gooseberry-like, light green foliage. Not an easy rose to grow. Flowers rich pinkish-purple, produced solitarily among dense foliage.
(S)   (W)   ●   ☉   (AL)
3′ × 3′   90 × 90 cm

R. stellata 'Mirifica', 'The Sacramento Rose'

Greene S. USA 1916
Compact plant, slightly more vigorous than the other form, with many long spines and gooseberry-like foliage. Flowers single, lilac-pink, with prominent stamens. Bush dense and reasonably compact. Easier to grow in the garden than *stellata* but quite difficult for the nurseryman to produce.
(S)   (W)   (AL)
4′ × 4′   1.2 × 1.2 m

R. roxburghii

ROSA Subgenus *Platyrhodon*

Platyrhodon

Flaky bark and prickly hips.
Small leaves.

R. roxburghii plena

SPECIES

R. roxburghii
R. roxburghii normalis
R. roxburghii plena

CLASSIFICATION

BARB	Class 1
MR9	Class 55
WFRS	Class 38

ORIGIN AND DISTRIBUTION

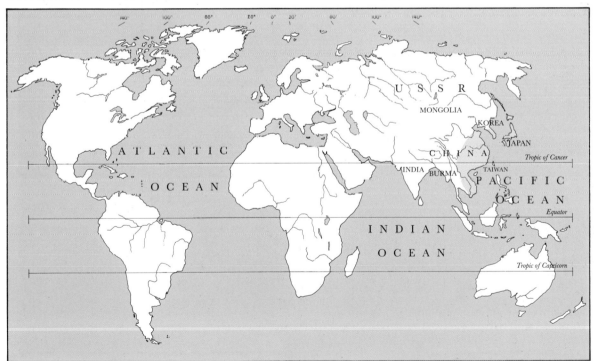

R. roxburghii

FORMS

This little group of fine shrubs deserves to be seen more often. Their weakness, I suppose, is that they are too discreet to draw attention to themselves for they never produce a large crop of flowers. Those they do bring forth are delightful in their simplicity, even the double form. Their foliage is quite refined and their general deportment places them amongst the tidier of the large shrub roses. Not to mention minor foibles such as peeling bark and spiny fruit which appears never to ripen.

R. roxburghii, 'Burr Rose', 'Chestnut Rose'
CHINA 1814
Quite distinct. This medium to tall shrub has leaves composed of up to 15 small, firmly textured, light green leaflets. Stems tawny-brown and slightly angular, both in structure and direction. Bark is flaky on the older wood. Thorns stout and quite long, often arranged in pairs. Flowers single, clear shell-pink. Fruit spherical, orange-yellow and covered in pronounced, stiff stubble, as are the bracts. The flowers are very much enjoyed by bees.
(S) (W) (P) (F) (A) ●
(MF) (AL) 8′ × 8′ 2.5 × 2.5 m

R. roxburghii normalis
CHINA 1908
A taller form of *roxburghii* with pure white, sometimes blush-white single flowers.
(S) (W) (P) (F) (A) ●
(SF) (AL) 10′ × 8′ 3 × 2.5 m

R. roxburghii plena
1824
Less vigorous than either of the other forms. Fully double flowers, not produced very freely in my experience.
(S) (W) (P) (F) (A) ●
(SF) (AL) 6′ × 5′ 1.8 × 1.5 m

R. banksiae alba plena

ROSA Subgenus *Eurosa (Rosa)*

SECTION : *Banksianae*

Growth vigorous, climbing to 20′, 7 m.
Thorns few or none.
Foliage smooth – 5 to 7 leaflets.
Flowers in clusters or singly.
Hips small.
Sepals drop before ripening.

R. banksiae lutea

ORIGIN AND DISTRIBUTION

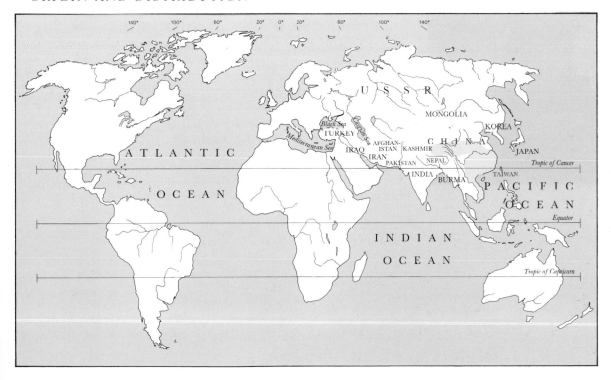

R. banksiae lutescens

SPECIES

R. banksiae normalis
R. banksiae alba plena
R. banksiae lutea
R. banksiae lutescens
R. cymosa
R. × fortuniana

R. banksiae

FORMS AND HYBRIDS

In some parts of the world where frosty winters are not in the normal course of events, 'Banks' roses flourish and are taken for granted, almost to the point of dismissal as weeds. In colder climates however they are cherished as rarities and treasured for the beautiful display of scented flowers they provide each spring.

CLASSIFICATION

BARB	Species: Class 1	Hybrids: Class 1
MR9	Species: Class 55	Hybrids: Class 55
WFRS	Species: Class 39	Hybrids: Class 16

R. × fortuniana

R. banksiae alba plena, R. banksiae banksiae

CHINA 1807
Small, rosette-like, double white flowers. Otherwise as *normalis*.
(S) ☼ (Gh) (SF) (AL)
20' × 8'   6 × 2.5 m

R. banksiae lutea, 'Yellow Banksia'

CHINA c. 1825
Needs a sheltered, sunny spot to flower but hardier than given credit for. Profuse foliage and growth produces large cascading trusses of small, pale yellow, double flowers in late spring. Slightly scented.
(S) ☼ (Gh) (SF) (AL)
20' × 10'   6 × 3 m

R. banksiae lutescens

CHINA 1870
Flower diameter rather larger than that of *R. banksiae lutea*, but single and more sweetly scented. Foliage and growth habit also similar but young shoots and leaves sometimes copper-tinted. A good example can be seen on the south wall of Mannington Hall, Norfolk, home of Lord and Lady Walpole.
(S) ☼ (Gh) (MF) (AL)
20' × 10'   6 × 3 cm

R. banksiae normalis

CHINA 1877
Although coming to Europe rather later than its offspring, this climber is probably the true species. Flowers white and single, foliage light green and plentiful, stems free of thorns. Not fully hardy.
(S) ☼ (Gh) (SF) (AL)
20' × 8'   6 × 2.5 m

R. cymosa, R. microcarpa, R. sorbiflora

CHINA c. 1904
A lovely but tender, vigorous climber or scrambler, amply clothed with light-greyish glabrous foliage. Flowers single, white with pronounced golden-yellow stamens, produced in corymbs. Too tender for all but the warmer parts of Britain.
(S) ☼ (Gh) (AL)
30' × 20'   10 × 7 m

R. × fortuniana

CHINA 1850
Thought to be *R. banksiae × R. laevigata* Not known in the wild Large, scented, double, white flowers, almost thornless, resembling *R. banksiae*, with slightly darker green leaves and stems. A most interesting rose but needs protection or a sheltered, warm position to flourish. From a nurseryman's viewpoint, much easier to propagate than *R. banksiae* and its other relatives. In fact in some parts of the world it is used as an understock. In its own right very beautiful.
(S) ☼ (Gh) (MF) (AL)
15' × 8'   4.5 × 2.5 m

ROSA Subgenus *Eurosa (Rosa)*

SECTION : *Laevigatae*

Growth sprawling or climbing with hooked, irregular thorns.
Leaves large, mostly of 3, rarely 5, leaflets.
Almost evergreen.
Flowers produced singly.
Hips when formed have persistent sepals.

SPECIES
R. laevigata

R. laevigata
FORMS AND HYBRIDS

This is another rose that is taken for granted in the more temperate parts of the world. Having struggled for years to keep mine alive and seldom having seen it flower, I recall the pleasure and excitement I felt when I first saw a plant, amongst a dozen neighbours, flowering in a roadside hedgerow in rural Texas where it was flourishing to its heart's content, quite oblivious to the fact that man had introduced it to such a friendly American habitat from its native China almost 200 years earlier.

CLASSIFICATION

BARB	Species: Class 1	Hybrids: Class 1
MR9	Species: Class 55	Hybrids: Class 30
WFRS	Species: Class 39	Hybrids: Class 16

ORIGIN AND DISTRIBUTION

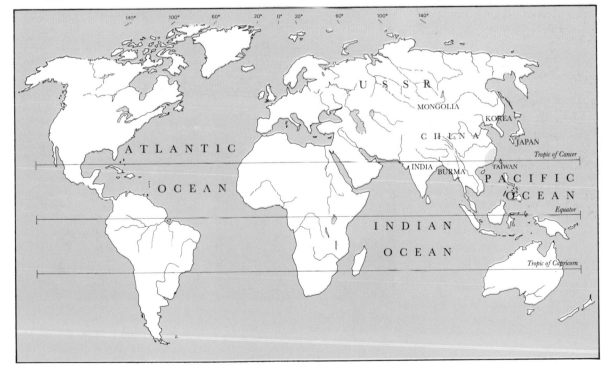

R. laevigata

**R. laevigata,
'Cherokee Rose'**

CHINA c. 1759 Later naturalized
N. AMERICA
Not hardy enough for colder climes. In southern USA, however, it grows wild, having become naturalized since arriving there from China, at the end of

the 18th century. Flowers single, very large, white with superb, golden-yellow stamens. Leaves crisp, polished and dark, as is the wood, which is armed with large hooked thorns. Fruit oval, with sparse bristles. I have an interesting and rare pale pink form kindly sent to me by Mr Trevor Griffiths of New Zealand, but after nearly 8 years I've yet to see it flower.

(SP) (F) ☼ (Gh) (SF) (AL)
15′ × 15′   4.5 × 4.5 m

'Anemone Rose',
'R. × anemonoides'

J. C. Schmidt GERMANY 1895
R. laevigata × a Tea Rose
Large, single, papery, pink flowers with a touch of mauve, giving this rose a vaguely oriental look. A vigorous climber with angular, branching shoots of darkish brown, liberally armed with hooked thorns. The foliage is dark green, glossy and healthy. Although it prefers a sunny position, it will tolerate sheltered shade.

(R) (P) (N) ☼ ● (SF)
(AL)   10′ × 8′   3 × 2.5 m

'Ramona'

'Cooper's Burmese',
R. cooperi

Introduced 1927
R. laevigata hybrid
An excellent, creamy-white rose which, if carefully placed in a warm, sheltered position, can be very rewarding. The dark, glossy foliage makes a superb foil for the large, single, scented flowers. The shoots are quite thorny, fawn-brown in colour, and produced in angular fashion. Until recently, this rose was thought to be a hybrid of *R. gigantea*.

(R) ☼ (P) (Gh) (MF) (AL)
15′ × 15′   4.5 × 4.5 m

'Ramona', 'Red Cherokee'

Dietrich and Turner USA 1913
'Anemone Rose' sport
This beautiful rose is of much deeper pink than its parent, almost red in fact. In other ways it is identical.

(R) (P) (N) ☼ ● (MF)
(AL)   10′ × 8′   3 × 2.5 m

'Silver Moon'

Van Fleet USA 1910
R. laevigata hybrid
An interesting rose. Large pure white, single flowers on a vigorous, well-foliated plant. Well scented. Inclined to be rather shy at times but well worth space, even for just a few of its very lovely flowers. Good in small trees or on trellis. Good examples can be seen in the Queen Mary Rose Garden, Regents Park, London.

(R) (T) (N) ● (SF) (AL)
15′ × 8′   4.5 × 2.5 m

R. laevigata hips

'Anemone Rose'

'Silver Moon'

ROSA Subgenus *Eurosa (Rosa)*

SECTION : *Bracteatae*

Growth climbing or angularly sprawling.
Thorns numerous, hooked and in pairs, smaller thorns scattered.
Leaves – 7 to 9 leaflets.
Hips with reflexed sepals which drop off when ripe.

SPECIES

R. bracteata

ORIGIN AND DISTRIBUTION

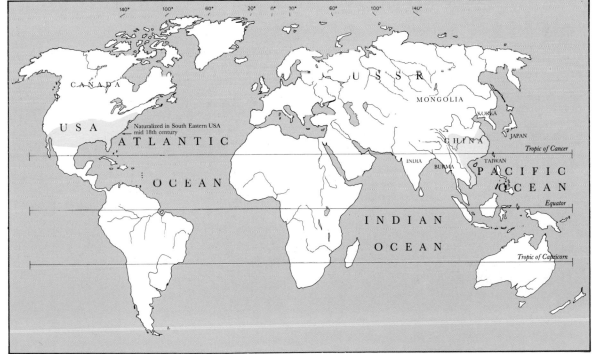

R. bracteata

AND HYBRID

In our climate these two roses can, at one and the same time, be both adorable and infuriating. For, at their best, their flowers are beautiful and, at their worst, they will get frostbite every so often and, just as they are recovering, another cold winter will set them back yet again. This is not to mention their vicious armoury of thorns which is designed to draw blood, it seems, without provocation! But do not be put off. They are both wonderful roses.

CLASSIFICATION

BARB	Class 1
MR9	Class 23
WFRS	Classes 12 and 13

R. bracteata,
'The Macartney Rose'

CHINA Introduced 1793
A rose of Chinese origin which is rather tender but, somewhat paradoxically, flowers happily on a north wall. Lord Macartney brought it back from China in the late 18th century. When introduced to America in the early 19th century, it found the climate in the south and east much to its liking and established itself in the wild. Despite its reputation for tenderness, I would like to see this species used more nowadays, even if only as an occasional change from 'Mermaid'. Single, pure white with pronounced golden stamens, the rose has much to offer, especially as it flowers intermittently from June until the November frosts. Well armed with vicious thorns, the stems are fawny-brown and the

R. bracteata

leaves dark green and slightly downy to touch. Best grown as a climber.

(C) (N) ● (MF) (AL)
8′ × 8′   2.5 × 2.5 m

'Mermaid'

W. Paul UK 1917
R. bracteata × double yellow Tea Rose

Undoubtedly, a most useful and beautiful climber. Almost evergreen, the foliage alone has much to commend it, being large and a rich dark green. It is vigorous and the dark brownish maroon wood is armed with cruel thorns. The rewards from the flowers, however, give ample compensation for scratches received whilst pruning, which should be done sparingly. Each flower is single, 3″–4″ (8–10 cm) across, lemon yellow with pronounced golden brown stamens. It is also fragrant. Furthermore, the flowers are produced throughout the summer, often improving in quality as the season progresses. Slightly more hardy than its parent, *R. bracteata*, from which it inherits tolerance of shade. Quite at home on most walls, including those facing north. In very severe winters it will die back badly from frost damage. During the winters of 1981 and 1985 many well-established plants were killed in the UK.

(C) (N) ● (MF) (AL)
30′ × 20′   9 × 6 m

'Mermaid'

'Golden Wings'

ROSA Subgenus *Eurosa (Rosa)*

SECTION : *Pimpinellifoliae*

Growth mostly upright, varying from 3' to 12', 1 m to 4 m.
Stems invariably very prickly with many thorns and spines.
Leaves small, some 7 to 9 leaflets, others 9 to 11.
R. sericea 13 to 17 leaflets.
Flowers mostly produced singly on short stems.
Sepals always persist on ripe hips, which are usually oval or
rounded, some smooth, others bristly. Colours varying from
bright red to black, according to species.

SPECIES

R. × cantabrigiensis
R. dunwichensis
R. ecae
R. foetida (R. lutea)
R. foetida bicolor
R. foetida persiana
R. × hemisphaerica
R. × hibernica
R. hugonis
R. × involuta (R. gracilis,
  R. rubella, R. wilsonii)
R. koreana
R. pimpinellifolia
  (R. spinosissima)
R. primula
R. × pteragonis
R. × reversa
R × sabinii
R. sericea
R. xanthina

GARDEN GROUPS

Austrian Briars
Scotch or Burnet Roses

R. ecae

FORMS AND HYBRIDS

Not many hybrids have been developed from *R. ecae*, probably
because this species is, perhaps, the least amenable of those in this
section. However, the two I have selected are excellent and far
more easy-going than the others, and can be relied upon for a veri-
table outburst of golden-yellow each spring.

CLASSIFICATION

BARB	Species: Class 1	Hybrids: Class 1
MR9	Species: Class 55	Hybrids: Class 54
WFRS	Species: Class 38	Hybrids: Class 10

ORIGIN AND DISTRIBUTION

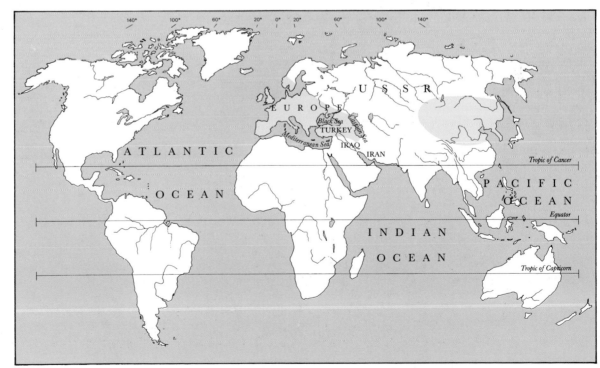

R. ecae

AFGHANISTAN 1880
A small, very prickly shrub with
reddish-brown twigs and small,
fern-like leaves. Numerous but-
tercup-size flowers of deep, rich
yellow with pronounced stamens.
Needs extra special care, when it
can be spectacular.
(SP) ⊙ (AL)
4' × 3' 120 × 90 cm

'Golden Chersonese'

E. F. Allen UK 1963
R. ecae × 'Canary Bird'
A fine shrub with single, rich
golden-yellow flowers produced
profusely early in the season.
Upright growth with dark
brownish wood and thorns. Foliage fern-like, individually small
but abundant.
(SP) (N) (P) ● (AL)
6' × 4' 1.8 × 1.2 m

'Helen Knight'

F. P. Knight UK 1966
R. ecae × R. pimpinellifolia altaica
A useful hybrid with large,
slightly cupped, single, deep
yellow flowers produced in late
spring amid fern-like foliage.
Vigorous shrub with darkish
stems and thorns. Should be
better known.
(SP) (P) ● (AL)
5' × 4' 1.5 × 1.2 m

R. ecae

'Golden Chersonese'

R. foetida

FORMS AND HYBRIDS

Quite apart from its great importance as an influence for yellow in
modern roses (see page 30) this Asian species has sired some
interesting close relatives in the form of vigorous shrubs and
accommodating climbers. Those described here are an important
group in that they can provide some of the few options where a
very vigorous, informal shrub of golden-yellow is called for.

CLASSIFICATION

BARB	Species: Class 1	Hybrids: Class 1
MR9	Species: Class 55	Hybrids: Class 28
WFRS	Species: Class 38	Hybrids: Class 10

R. foetida, R. lutea, 'Austrian Briar', 'Austrian Yellow'

ASIA 16th century or earlier
Large, single flowers of rich
golden-yellow with prominent
stamens produced in early June.
Erect growth with large, blackish
thorns. Wood chestnut brown.
Foliage bright green and firm in
texture. An important rose, being
largely responsible, with its cousin
R. foetida persiana, for the yellow
colour in our modern roses. The
rather unusual specific name
comes from the slightly
unpleasant smell of the flowers.
(S) ⊙ BS⚘ (AL)
8' × 5' 2.5 × 1.5 m

R. foetida bicolor, R. lutea punicea, 'Austrian Copper'

ASIA 16th century or earlier
A sport from R. foetida which
occurred at some time in the distant past. In this form the flowers
are rich copper-orange, dazzling
when at their best. The flower
occasionally reverts to the original
yellow and sometimes both
colours appear on the plant
simultaneously. Like its cousins,
rather prone to black spot.
(S) (P) ⊙ BS⚘ (AL)
8' × 5' 2.5 × 1.5 m

R. foetida persiana 'Persian Yellow'

S. W. ASIA 1837
Very double, globular flowers of
rich, golden-yellow. Has all the
attributes and faults of both previous species, except that I believe
it to be slightly less vigorous.
(S) (P) BS⚘ (AL)
6' × 4' 1.8 × 1.2 m

R. foetida

R. foetida bicolor

'Lawrence Johnston'

'Lawrence Johnston', 'Hidcote Yellow'

Pernet-Ducher FRANCE c. 1920
Introduced 1923
'Mme Eugène Verdier' × *R. foetida persiana*
An early flowering climber, with clusters of semi-double, yellow flowers with prominent stamens. Fragrant. Very vigorous with abundant, lush, light green foliage.
(R) (P) (N) ● (VF) (AL)
20' × 20'   6 × 6 m

'Le Rêve'

Pernet-Ducher FRANCE c. 1920
'Mme Eugène Verdier' × *R. foetida persiana*
Similar to 'Lawrence Johnston', in fact, from the same cross. Slightly less vigorous. Very fragrant. Both are excellent varieties which should be grown more often. Both will also make good free-standing large shrubs.
(R) (P) (N) ● (AL)
15' × 15'   4.5 × 4.5 m

'Star of Persia'

Pemberton UK 1919
R. foetida × 'Trier'
An interesting hybrid from Pemberton proving that he explored other avenues of breeding while working on his Hybrid Musks. Tall, vigorous bush, or small climber. Semi-double, bright yellow flowers which, when fully open, display deep golden stamens to effect. Its parent, *R. foetida*, shows through in its growth habit and foliage. Not often seen these days.
(R) ☼ ☉ BS❀ (SF) (AL)
10' × 4'   3 × 1.2 m

R. × hemisphaerica, 'The Sulphur Rose'

S. W. ASIA Pre-1625
The globular, fully-double, luminous, rich sulphur-yellow flowers nod amid plentiful, greyish-light green foliage. They seldom open properly in damp weather but are well worth perseverance, since when they do open the flowers are most attractive. Prefers a warm, sheltered position to thrive. Is 'smelly' rather than scented.
(S) ☼ ☉ (WW) (Gh)
(AL) 6' × 4'   1.8 × 1.2 m

R. foetida persiana

R. hugonis

FORMS AND HYBRIDS

The few *R. hugonis* hybrids are quite free-flowering, vigorous shrubs, noteworthy like their parent for favouring us with a profusion of fragrant, late spring flowers. They are trouble-free and will tolerate most soils.

CLASSIFICATION

BARB	Species: Class 1	Hybrids: Class 1
MR9	Species: Class 55	Hybrids: Class 29
WFRS	Species: Class 28	Hybrids: Class 10

Above and *right:* 'Cantabrigiensis'; *below: R. hugonis*

R. hugonis, 'Golden Rose of China'

CHINA 1899
Large quantities of medium-sized, primrose-yellow flowers, when open slightly cupped, on an upright-growing bush. Densely thorny, the stems are bronzy-brown in colour. Leaves plentiful with a fern-like quality both in appearance and to touch, turning bronzy-orange in autumn. This rose also bears small, dark red fruit in late summer.
(SP) (P) (W) (A) (F) ☼
(SF) (AW) 8' × 5' 2.5 × 1.5 cm

'Cantabrigiensis',
R. × cantabrigiensis,
R. pteragonis cantabrigiensis

Cambridge Botanic Gardens
UK c. 1931
R. hugonis × R. sericea
Less upright than *R. hugonis*. The flowers are larger and slightly paler. They also withstand the weather in a more determined fashion. The shoots are graceful, arching and of a fawny-brown colour as are the numerous thorns. Foliage is fern-like but not as colourful in autumn as its parents.
(SP) (P) (W) (F) ☼ (SF)
(AW) 7' × 5' 2 × 1.5 m

'Earldomensis',
R. earldomensis

Page UK 1934
R. hugonis × R. sericea
A spreading shrub, with flat reddish thorns which are translucent when young. Attractive fern-like foliage. Its flowers are rich yellow, single and produced from late May to early June. Difficult to propagate but easy to grow.
(SP) ☼ (P) (W) (A) (F)
● (AL) 7' × 5' 2 × 2.5 m

'Headleyensis', *R. headleyensis*

Warburg UK
R. hugonis × unknown, possibly R. pimpinellifolia altaica
A handsome shrub, more compact than *R. hugonis*. Foliage is particularly good, being rich clear green and produced in profusion from thorny, brownish stems.

Flowers soft primrose yellow with good perfume.
(SP) (P) (W) (A) ● ⊙
(MF) (AL) 7' × 4' 2 × 1.2 m

R. × involuta, R. gracilis, R. rubella, R. wilsonii

N. EUROPE c. 1820
Thought to be a natural hybrid between *R. pimpinellifolia* and *R. villosa*, but the pollen parent could possibly be another species of its habitat region, such as *R. tomentosa* or *R. sherardii*. Flowers of small to medium size, white on a spiny, free-suckering plant with smallish, grey-green leaves. Stems, especially the older ones, are fawnish-brown. Hips oval to round, slightly bristly. Frequently seen in the wild in parts of Scandinavia.
(S) (W) (P) ● (AL)
3' × 3' 90 × 90 cm

R. koreana

KOREA 1917
A shrubby, fairly dense, bristly plant with reddish wood. Single, white to blush-pink flowers followed by small, pendulous oval, orange hips. Leaves dark green and numerous, made up of 7 to 11 leaflets.
(S) (W) (P) ● ⊙ (AL)
3' × 3' 90 × 90 cm

R. pimpinellifolia (Scotch Roses)

FORMS AND HYBRIDS

A wealth of very garden-worthy shrub roses have been developed over the years by crossing all and sundry other types with the various forms of wild Scotch roses. In the last century the many and varied double forms were very popular, especially in cottage gardens. Today, they and the newer, taller shrubs developed by Kordes in the 1940s and 50s are still sought after, for they are not only trouble-free and easy to grow but early flowering; and amongst their ranks are several that provide us with the first roses of summer.

CLASSIFICATION

BARB	Species: Class 1	Hybrids: Class 27
MR9	Species: Class 55	Hybrids: Class 42
WFRS	Species: Class 28	Hybrids: Class 10

R. pimpinellifolia, R. spinosissima, 'Scotch Briar', 'Burnet Rose'

EUROPE Pre-1600
Charming, single flowers, creamy white, sometimes with subtle hints of pink, borne freely early in the season. Pronounced stamens. Foliage small and coarsely fern-like. Stems very densely populated with long, needle-like prickles. Globular, almost black, shiny fruit. Suckers freely when it is grown on its own roots. Happy in most soils, particularly sandy soil. This species has given rise to many and varied hybrids over the years.
(SP) (P) (W) (H) (A) ●
☺ (AW) 3' × 3' 90 × 90 cm

R. pimpinellifolia altaica, R. pimpinellifolia spinosissima 'Altaica'

ASIA c. 1818
Dark brownish wood with numerous spiny thorns and soft-textured, well-serrated, greyish-light green foliage. Flowers white, large and beautiful, single with pronounced golden-yellow stamens. A useful, healthy shrub with maroon-purple to black hips in the autumn.
(SP) (H) (W) (P) (A) (F) ● ☺ (AL)
5' × 3' 150 × 90 cm

R. pimpinellifolia hispida

N. E. ASIA, SIBERIA C. 1781
An upright growing shrub with slightly larger foliage than R. pimpinellifolia altaica. Flowers large and soft yellow to white with prominent stamens. Shoots darkish green to brown with numerous spiny thorns. Black hips. Very hardy.
(SP) (H) (W) (P) ● (AL)
6' × 4' 1.8 × 1.2 m

R. pimpinellifolia lutea, 'Lutea'

ASIA
Single deep yellow flowers on an upright bushy plant. Similar to R. pimpinellifolia altaica in growth habit but less vigorous and with smaller flowers.
(SP) (II) (W) (P) ● (AL)
4' × 3' 120 × 90 cm

R. pimpinellifolia 'Nana', R. spinosissima nana

Pre-1805
A delightful dwarf form of the Scotch rose. Semi-double to double flowers produced in great profusion in late spring to early summer on a dense mounded plant with fern-like foliage.
(SP) (G) (W) (P) (H) ●
☺ (AL) 12" × 12" 30 × 30 cm

SCOTCH OR BURNET ROSES

Many double forms of R. pimpinellifolia have existed over the years since the first were introduced around 1800. These came in many colours and all were named. Some of these charming little roses are still with us but their names have become lost in time.

The Royal National Rose Society has a good and varied representative collection of these which are well worth seeing in May and June, at St Albans. Only the most important are described here, otherwise the list could be endless.

'Double White', 'Double Pink', 'Double Marbled Pink', etc.

All these have globular flowers, produced in profusion on tidy, well-foliated, thorny plants. Most

R. pimpinellifolia hips

R. pimpinellifolia altaica

R. pimpinellifolia altaica hips

'Scotch Double White'

'Dunwich Rose'

'Frühlingsduft'

'Frühlingsgold'

produce globular, dark, almost black hips in late summer and all make useful, tidy, rounded shrubs or attractive, thick hedges.
(S) (G) (F) (P) (H) (A) ● ☉ (SP) (AL)
3′ × 3′   90 × 90 cm

Double Yellow Forms

Several exist with the yellow in their make-up obviously derived from *R. foetida*. The most important are:

R. × harisonii or 'Harison's Yellow' (Yellow Rose of Texas) – very double USA 1846
'Williams' Double Yellow' – semi-double UK 1828
I find both of these rather coarser in growth than the other colours and prefer an old, double form which I call, simply – 'Old Yellow Scotch'. This is more compact in growth, pleasingly scented and of very ancient origin.
(SP) (G) (P) (H) ● ☉ (AL)   4′ × 3′   120 × 90 cm

'Albert Edwards'

Hillier UK 1961
R. pimpinellifolia altaica × *R. hugonis*
A free-flowering shrub. Medium-sized, single, creamy to soft yellow flowers on a tall, vigorous, well foliated plant. One of its finest attributes is its scent. it would be a pleasure to see this rose more widely used as a specimen landscape plant.
(SP) (H) (P) ● (MF) (AL)
10′ × 4′   3 × 1.2 m

'Andrewsii'

R. pimpinellifolia andrewsii

c. 1806
Semi-double flowers of deep pinkish-red and cream, displaying yellow stamens when fully open. A dense, well-foliated and well-prickled plant. Sometimes repeating in the autumn, an occasional trait of quite a few of the Pimpinellifolia roses.
(SP) (G) (W) (P) ● ☉ (AL)   4′ × 3′   120 × 90 cm

'Dunwich Rose'

R. dunwichensis

Discovered growing on sand dunes at Dunwich, Suffolk UK 1956
A most useful rose, its medium-sized, soft yellow, single flowers have prominent stamens and are produced singly all along arching branches. Foliage light green and fern-like, with many spiky thorns. There is some evidence that this rose could have been growing as a garden variety in the late nineteenth century.
(S) (P) (G) (SF) ● (AL)
2′ × 4′   60 × 120 cm

'Falkland'

UK
Lovely, semi-double, cupped flowers of soft lilac-pink, paling with age to blush white. Compact growth. Typical Pimpinellifolia foliage. Good-sized, deep maroon hips in late summer and autumn.
(SP) (H) (W) (P) (F) ● ☉ (AL)   3′ × 3′   90 × 90 cm

'Frühlingsanfang'

Kordes GERMANY 1950
'Joanna Hill' × *R. pimpinellifolia altaica*
Superb, medium-sized, pure white flowers with prominent stamens and a strong scent. Dark green foliage on an upright yet arching, healthy plant. Large maroon hips in the autumn.
(S) (P) (W) (H) (F) ● (VF) (AL)   10′ × 6′   3 × 1.8 m

'Frühlingsduft'

Kordes GERMANY 1949
'Joanna Hill' × *R. pimpinellifolia altaica*
A vigorous, healthy plant with rather crinkled, dark green, glossy foliage. Flowers large, fully double, soft lemon-yellow, heavily flushed with pink and highly scented.
(S) (P) (W) (H) ● (VF) (AL)   10′ × 6′   3 × 1.8 m

'Frühlingsgold'

Kordes GERMANY 1937
'Joanna Hill' × *R. pimpinellifolia* hybrid
Large, almost single flowers of rich golden-yellow paling to primrose. Very profuse blooms on a vigorous, upright plant with dark green foliage. Stems also darkish green and rather thorny. This is the best known of the

'Frühlings' roses, and deservedly so, for it makes a fine flowering shrub.
(SP) (P) (W) (H) ● (VF) (AW)   7' × 5'   2 × 1.5 m

'Frühlingsmorgen'

Kordes GERMANY 1942
('E. G. Hill' × 'Cathrine Kordes') × *R. pimpinellifolia altaica*
Large, single flowers of cherry-pink and white with primrose centres and golden stamens. Sweetly perfumed. Starts flowering early and is occasionally recurrent. Upright. A well-foliated shrub with dark green leaves. Good maroon hips.
(SP) (P) (W) (H) (F) ● (MF) (AW)   6' × 4'   1.8 × 1.2 m

'Frühlingsschnee'

Kordes GERMANY 1954
'Golden Glow' × *R. pimpinellifolia altaica*
Large, single, pure white flowers opening early in the season. Upright in habit with plenty of thorns and dark green foliage.
(SP) (P) (W) (H) ● (MF) (AL)   6' × 4'   1.8 × 1.2 m

'Frühlingstag'

Kordes GERMANY 1949
'McGredy's Wonder' × 'Frühlingsgold'
Clusters of large, open, semi-double flowers of rich golden-yellow paling to soft yellow with age. Fragrant. Dark leathery foliage. Dark greenish-brown very thorny stems. Upright.
(SP) (P) (W) (H) ● (MF) (AL)   7' × 4'   2 × 1.2 m

'Frühlingszauber'

Kordes GERMANY 1942
('E. G. Hill' × 'Cathrine Kordes') × *R. pimpinellifolia altaica*

Large, almost single flowers of sil very-pink with abundant dark green foliage. An upright, rather thorny plant. Very healthy.
(SP) (P) (W) (H) ● (MF) (AL)   7' × 5'   2 × 1.5 m

'Glory of Edzell'

Single, clear pink with paler, almost white centres and pronounced stamens. Flowering very early each season. Foliage small but dense, growth upright, spiny.
(SP) (P) (W) (H) ● ☉ (AL)   5' × 4'   1.5 × 1.2 m

'Golden Wings'

Shepherd USA 1956
('Soeur Thérèse' × *R. pimpinellifolia altaica*) × 'Ormiston Roy'
Large, clear golden-yellow flowers, almost single with pronounced golden-brown stamens, produced abundantly both in clusters and singly, amid rich light green foliage. Flowers almost continuously from June to October, sweetly scented. An accommodating shrub in all respects.
(C) (P) (H) ☉ (SF) (AL)   5' × 4'   1.5 × 1.2 m

'Karl Förster'

Kordes GERMANY 1931
'Frau Karl Druschki' × *R. pimpinellifolia altaica*
A showy shrub. Large, semi-double flowers with prominent golden stamens when fully open. Bushy in growth with greyish light green foliage. A most useful, underrated rose with intermittent flowers produced later in summer.
(R) (P) (W) ● (SF) (AL)   5' × 4'   1.5 × 1.2 m

Top left: 'Frühlingsmorgen'
Left: 'Glory of Edzell'
Above: 'Frühlingsanfang'
Below: 'Karl Förster'

'Maigold'

Kordes GERMANY 1953
'Poulson's Pink' × 'Frühlingstag'
A superb climber. One of the first
to flower each season. Spectacular
when in full flush. In a good
summer will repeat with a good
crop of flowers in the autumn.

'Single Cherry'

R. × hibernica

'Stanwell Perpetual'

Fragrant semi-double flowers,
rich golden-yellow flushed
orange. Foliage rich green and
glossy. Strong stems covered in
reddish-brown thorns.
(SP) (T) (P) (N) ● (MF)
(AW) 12′ × 8′ 3.5 × 2.5 m

'Mary Queen of Scots'

A beautiful rose. Single flowers
with prominent stamens. Creamy-
white in the centre with lilac and
reddish brush marks which
deepen towards the edge of each
petal. These are followed by globular, blackish-maroon fruit on a
tidy, twiggy, well-foliated little
plant.
(SP) (P) (F) ● ☉ (SF)
(AL) 3′ × 3′ 90 × 90 cm

'Mrs Colville'

Thought to be *R. pimpinellifolia* ×
R. pendulina
A fascinating little shrub with
single, crimson-purple flowers,
having pronounced stamens and
a prominent white eye in the
centre. Less thorny than most of
its type, with reddish-brown
wood and small but plentiful
foliage.
(SP) (H) (P) (F) ● ☉
(AL) 4′ × 3′ 120 × 90 cm

'Ormiston Roy'

Doorenbos HOLLAND 1953
R. pimpinellifolia × *R. xanthina*
Single bright buttercup-yellow
flowers on a thorny, dense plant
with light green, fern-like leaves.
Large purple to black globular
hips in the autumn.
(SP) (H) (P) (F) ● ☉
(SF) (AL) 4′ × 3′ 120 × 90 cm

'Single Cherry'

Very bright, cherry-red, single
flowers with paler, blended
blotches of pink. Foliage grey-
green and plentiful on a short,
bushy plant. Small, rounded,
blackish hips later. One of the
nicest and most brightly coloured
of this group.
(SP) (H) (P) (F) ● ☉
(SF) (AL) 3′ × 3′ 90 × 90 cm

'Stanwell Perpetual'

Lee UK 1838
R. × damascena bifera ×
R. pimpinellifolia
A prickly, arching but graceful
shrub with numerous, greyish-
green leaves, sometimes becoming mottled-purple as though
diseased. Though unsightly, this
discoloration is not serious, nor,
as far as I know, contagious, and
it should not put you off this
superb, old variety. The long
flowering season – rare in this
group – amply compensates for a
few discoloured leaves. Flowers
fully-double, quartered, soft
blush-pink and scented. A favourite of mine.
(C) (H) (P) (W) ● ☉
(VF) (AW) 5′ × 5′ 1.5 × 1.5 m

'William III'

Semi-double flowers of rich
maroon paling to magenta, followed by dark chocolate-brown
hips. Dense foliage on a tidy
upright plant. Scented. An exquisite little rose.
(S) (P) (W) (F) ● ☉
(MF) (AL) 3′ × 3′ 90 × 90 cm

R. × hibernica

Templeton IRELAND 1765
R. pimpinellifolia × *R. canina*
A most interesting rose, discovered in Ireland at the end of the
18th century but now thought to
be extinct there in the wild. The
shrub is of medium size with
leaves midway between those of
R. pimpinellifolia and
R. canina. A special feature of this
shrub is its superb hips which are
coloured like those of *R. canina*
and shaped like those of *R. pimpinellifolia*, retaining its sepals in the
same fashion as the latter. The
flowers are single, medium-sized

and bright pink in colour. I have not found it remontant as is claimed for the Irish clone but it is possible – since the two parent species are obviously compatible – that other clones exist. Professor Nelson of Dublin Botanic Gardens has drawn my attention to the fact that a plant known to have come from Templeton's original is alive and well and growing in Belfast.

(S) (P) (F) (W) ☼ ☉
(MF) (AL) 4' × 4' 1.2 × 1.2 m

R. primula, 'Incense Rose'

CENTRAL ASIA, CHINA 1910
Beautiful species with strong, upright, dark-brown thorny stems supporting arching laterals. The glossy fern-like foliage has a strong aroma of incense. The flowers, which appear early in the season, are single and soft buttercup-yellow with pronounced stamens; they are strongly scented. A most useful and interesting shrub which sometimes sets small reddish fruit.

(SP) (W) (P) (A) ○ (VF)
(AL) 5' × 4' 1.5 × 1.2 m

R. × pteragonis

GERMANY 1938
R. hugonis × R. sericea
A medium-tall shrub with broad, dark red prickles similar to those of R. sericea but with primrose-yellow, five-petalled flowers after those of R. hugonis.

(SP) (W) (P) ● (AL)
6' × 4' 1.8 × 1.2 m

R. × reversa

S. EUROPE 1820
R. pendulina × R. pimpinellifolia
Flowers variable from pink to white, mostly pink. Medium-sized oval to round, pendulous, deep red hips. Growth slightly angular

with purple shoots, often quite bristly.

(SP) (W) (P) ● (AL)
4' × 3' 120 × 90 cm

R. × sabinii

N. EUROPE C. 1850
Very similar to R. × involuta, differing in having longer flower stamens, large hips and paler stems. Probably a cross between R. pimpinellifolia and R. mollis.

(S) (W) (P) ● (AL)
3' × 3' 90 × 90 cm

R. sericea pteracantha

'Hidcote Gold'

'Red Wing'

'Red Wing' foliage

R. sericea

FORMS AND HYBRIDS

CLASSIFICATION
BARB   Class 1
MR9   Class 55
WFRS   Class 10

R. sericea, R. omeiensis

HIMALAYAS, W. CHINA 1822
A vigorous shrub with fern-like foliage and stout branches armed with large, hooked thorns and numerous small spines. Thorns bright translucent red while young. Flowers white with pronounced, pale yellow stamens; unlike any other species of the genus, these are comprised of four petals only. Fruit bright red, almost oval but slightly pear-shaped. In some works R. omeiensis is listed as a separate species. Perhaps this is so, but they are so alike that one species is enough here.

(SP) (P) (F) (W) (A) (AL)
10' × 6' 3 × 1.8 m

R. sericea chrysocarpa

HIMALAYAS
The same in all aspects as R. sericea except that its fruit is bright yellow.

(SP) (P) (W) (F) (A) ●
(AL) 10' × 6' 3 × 1.8 m

R. sericea pteracantha, R. omeiensis pteracantha

CHINA Introduced 1890
Delicate, fern-like foliage con-

trasting with brown stems clad with huge, wedge-shaped thorns. When young these thorns are quite spectacular, being translucent and glowing like rubies against morning and evening sun. The small – at first sight rather insignificant – flowers are quite beautiful on close inspection, being white, single and made up of four petals only. These are followed by small, oval to round, bright orange-red hips.
(SP) (P) (F) (W) (A) ●
(AW)   10′ × 6′   3 × 1.8 m

R. sericea pteracantha atrosanguinea

As above, but with slightly deeper red, translucent thorns and darker red, almost black hips.
(SP) (P) (F) (W) (A) ●
(AW)   10′ × 6′   3 × 1.8 m

'Red Wing'

R. sericea pteracantha × *R. hugonis*
A gracefully-growing, arching plant with beautiful, red, wedge-shaped thorns. Flowers creamy-

yellow, single. A lovely shrub, not difficult to grow, but difficult to produce in the nursery.
(SP) (A) (W) ● (AL)
6′ × 4′   1.8 × 1.2 m

'Heather Muir'

Sunningdale Nurseries UK 1957
R. sericea seedling
Pure white, single flowers produced, for such a rose, over a long season. Foliage fern-like and stems heavily covered with wedge-like thorns. Upright growth. Produces rich orange fruit.
(SP) (W) (F) (A) ● (AL)
8′ × 6′   2.5 × 1.8 m

'Hidcote Gold'

Hilling and Co. UK 1948
R. sericea seedling
Bright yellow, single flowers in small clusters on a robust plant. Stems liberally covered with broad wedge-shaped thorns and ferny foliage.
(SP) (A) (W) ● (AL)
8′ × 6′   2.5 × 1.8 m

R. xanthina

FORMS AND HYBRIDS

CLASSIFICATION	
BARB	Class 1
MR9	Class 54
WFRS	Class 10

R. xanthina

CHINA 1906
An angular shrub with dark stems and thorns and dark green, fern-like foliage. Flowers small, loosely and raggedly semi-double, scented, rich yellow, produced early in the season.
(SP) (H) (MF) (AL)
10′ × 6′   3 × 1.8 m

R. xanthina lindleyii

NORTH CHINA, KOREA 1906
Medium-sized, double yellow flowers are produced from late spring to early summer. Foliage dark green and fern-like, the growth bushy.

(P) (H) (VF) ● ☉ (AL)
8′ × 6′   2.5 × 1.8 m

'Canary Bird', *R. xanthina spontanea*

CHINA c. 1908
Probably *R. hugonis* × *R. xanthina*
Tall, angular-growing shrub with dark wood and thorns, and dark green, fern-like foliage. Produces laterals of a graceful, pendulous habit on which the flowers are borne, making it a useful standard rose in good soils. Single flowers, rich canary yellow with prominent stamens, well scented. Sometimes rather temperamental, suffering partial die-back for no apparent reason; but if the dead wood is removed, it frequently recovers. Flowers sometimes appear intermittently in the autumn.
(SP) (H) (P) ● (MF)
(AW)   8′ × 6′   2.5 × 1.8 m

'Canary Bird'

ROSA Subgenus *Eurosa* (Rosa)

SECTION : *Gallicanae*

Growth between 3′ to 6′, 1 m to 2 m, upright or arching.
Stems variably armed.
Foliage large, usually made up of 5 leaflets.
Flowers solitary or in threes or fours on long stems.
Sepals reflex and drop from hips when ripe.

SPECIES

R. × *centifolia*
R. × *centifolia alba*
R. × *centifolia muscosa*
R. × *damascena*
R. × *damascena bifera*
R. × *damascena trigintipetala*
R. × *damascena versicolor*
R. *gallica*

R. *gallica officinalis*
R. *gallica versicolor*
R. *macrantha*
R. × *richardii*

GARDEN GROUPS

Gallicas (French roses)
Centifolias (Provence roses)
Damasks
Portlands

Gallicas

FORMS AND HYBRIDS

This group has had a considerable influence on the evolution of modern roses. These quietly unobtrusive garden hybrids, although seldom, if ever, remontant, deserve to be far more widely used.

Note: Included in this section are the few forms of *R. francofurtana* which are closely related to the Gallicas. In some works these are listed as a separate group.

CLASSIFICATION

BARB	Species: Class 19	Hybrids: Class 19
MR9	Species: Class 20	Hybrids: Class 20
WFRS	Species: Class 25	Hybrids: Class 25

ORIGIN AND DISTRIBUTION

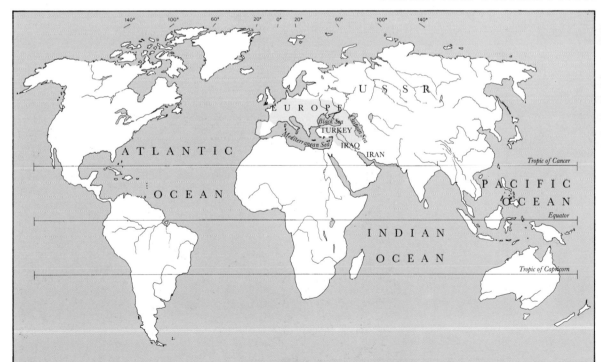

'James Mason'

R. gallica, R. rubra,
'French Rose'

EUROPE, S.W. ASIA Of great antiquity
A rather insignificant rose considering that its genes permeate – to a greater or lesser extent – many modern garden hybrids. Small shrub with upright habit, bearing medium to large, single

'Hippolyte' (enlarged to twice its actual average size)

flowers with pronounced powdery-yellow stamens, petals varying from deep to soft pink. Useful for group planting, perhaps in the wild garden.
(S) (W) (P) ● ☉ (SF) (AL) 4' × 3' 120 × 90 cm

R. gallica officinalis, 'The Apothecary's Rose, 'Red Rose of Lancaster', 'Rose of Provins', 'Double French Rose'

EUROPE, S.W. ASIA Of great antiquity
A showy shrub with erect yet bushy growth and slightly coarse, dark greyish-green leaves. Flowers light crimson, semi-double, quite large, highly scented and profuse in June. In the Middle Ages its scent-retaining properties were much valued by apothecaries. After a good summer, when fully ripe, in the autumn the small, oval hips are attractive.
(S) (P) (F) (H) ● ☉ ✂ (VF) (AW) 3' × 3' 90 × 90 cm

R. gallica versicolor, 'Rosa Mundi'

EUROPE, S.W. ASIA
Of great antiquity
A striking rose. A sport from *R. gallica officinalis* to which it is identical except in colour. Probably the oldest and best known of the striped roses, it is a varied

'Agatha'

mixture of light crimson and white. The most romantic of various legends surrounding this rose is that it was named after 'Fair Rosamund', mistress of Henry II.
(S) (F) (P) (H) ● ☉ (VF) ✂ (AW) 3' × 3' 90 × 90 cm

'Agatha', *R. × francofurtana agatha*

EUROPE, S.W. ASIA
Possibly *R. gallica* × *R. pendulina* Although somewhat taller, this charming rose is probably related to that lovely Gallica 'Empress Josephine'. Flowers slightly smaller and of a deeper pink shade than those of 'Josephine' and with a stronger scent. Densely arching in growth. Leaves soft to touch, yet quite crisp in texture. Few thorns of significance.
(S) (P) (H) ● ☉ (VF) (AL) 5' × 4' 1.5 × 1.2 m

'Agathe Incarnata'

EUROPE c. 1800
A highly scented rose with soft pink flowers. When fully open, the irregular petals create a tight, quartered effect, reminiscent of crumpled and torn crêpe paper. Foliage is grey-green and soft to touch. Growth dense, slightly arching and somewhat thorny. My particular clone seems fairly distinct but occasionally similar varieties crop up for identi-

'Anaïs Ségalas'

'Alain Blanchard'

fication, suggesting that others once existed as garden varieties. Graham Stuart Thomas suggests Damask influence in the 'Agathe' type Gallicas.
(S) (H) ☉ (VF) (P) (AL) 4' × 4' 1.2 × 1.2 m

'Alain Blanchard'

Vibert FRANCE 1839
Probably *R. × centifolia* × *R. gallica* Large flowers, slightly more than single in form, crimson smudged purple with very pronounced golden stamens. Foliage dark green; growth dense and bushy. A most pleasing rose with a good scent.
(S) (P) ● ☉ (H) (VF) (AL) 4' × 4' 1.2 × 1.2 m

'Anaïs Ségalas'

Vibert FRANCE 1837
A shortish growing, arching shrub, rather more Centifolia-like than Gallica. Perhaps the main feature is the superb form of the flowers, each one seemingly carefully groomed. Highly scented. Colour cerise to crimson, paling towards edges with age. Foliage small and dark green.
(S) (P) ☉ (VF) (AL) 3' × 3' 90 × 90 cm

'Antonia d'Ormois'

From the Roseraie de l'Hay collection FRANCE Pre-1848
Flowering slightly later than some other Gallicas. Fully double cupped flowers. The colour is of

'Camaieux'

'Charles de Mills'

soft pink paling to almost white with age, especially at the edges. Since 1986 I have come to know this rose well, and it gives me much pleasure each summer.
(S) (P) (MF) (AL)
5' × 3' 150 × 90 cm

'Assemblage des Beautés', 'Rouge Eblouissante'

Originated in Angers
FRANCE c. 1823
Double, bright crimson flowers changing to purple with age. They are scented and produced in abundance on a compact, bushy shrub. Foliage rich dark green; shoots bear few thorns. One of the nicest of the Gallicas.
(S) (P) ● ☉ (VF) (AL)
4' × 3' 120 × 90 cm

'Belle de Crécy'

Mid-19th century
Fairly reliable as a grower but temperamental in flower. At best can be one of the most beautiful in its group; at worst, horrid. Flowers are a pleasing mixture of pinks, greys and mauves, flat and quartered, often with a clearly defined, green eye in the centre. Highly scented. Growth upright, foliage grey-green. Stems almost thornless.
(S) (P) (H) ☉ (VF) M✂
(WW) (AW)
4' × 3' 120 × 90 cm

'Belle Isis'

Parmentier BELGIUM 1845
A small to medium-growing shrub with tidy, upright growth and grey-green foliage. The flowers, which are fully double and open flat, are a lovely delicate shade of pink and have a strong perfume.
(S) (P) ✂ (VF) (AW)
4' × 3' 120 × 90 cm

'Boule de Nanteuil'

Mid-19th century
A charming rose. Fully double flowers opening flattish and quartered. Colour deep pink, almost cerise with silver overtones. Like most Gallicas, it is scented. Growth robust and upright. Foliage dark green.
(S) (P) (H) ● ☉ (VF)
(AL) 4' × 3' 120 × 90 cm

'Camaieux'

Vibert FRANCE 1830
Striking, double, pale pink blooms striped purplish-crimson changing with age to a pleasing mixture of lavender and purple. These open rather loosely and are borne on arching stems amid grey-green foliage on a shortish, bushy plant.
(S) (P) (H) ☉ (VF) ✂
(AW) 3' × 3' 90 × 90 cm

'Cardinal de Richelieu'

Laffay FRANCE c. 1840
Beautifully formed rich purple flowers of a delicate velvety texture borne mostly in clusters. Sweetly scented. A compact bush with thin stems which are almost free of thorns. Foliage abundant, smooth and dark green, sometimes edged with maroon.
(S) (P) (H) ☉ (VF) (AW)
4' × 3' 120 × 90 cm

'Charles de Mills'

From the Roseraie de L'Hay collection. An old variety
A rose of uncertain origin but one of the best, especially in good soil. Vigorous, with dark green leaves. Large flowers open to a mixture of purple and deep red. Sometimes, the petals form perfect edges as if the rose were enclosed

'Cardinal de Richelieu' (enlarged to one and a half times its actual average size)

'Duchesse d'Angoulême'

R. gallica 'Complicata'

'Cosimo Ridolfi'

'D'Aguesseau'

'Duc de Guiche'

by an invisible, circular frame. When fully open, the flower is quartered and sometimes exposes a dark green eye in the centre.
(S) (P) (H) (VF) (AW)
4′ × 4′ 1.2 × 1.2 m

R. gallica 'Complicata'

Of unknown origin
An exceptional rose, good even in poor soils. Vigorous with arching branches bearing flat, single flowers of bright pink with paler centres and gold stamens, produced freely about mid-June. Foliage matt grey-green, growth quite vigorous. This rose can range in use from a specimen shrub to an effective pillar or climbing rose, or even a tall hedge. In some works it is attributed to *R. macrantha*.
(S) (P) (H) ● (VF) (AW)
10′ × 6′ 3 × 1.8 m

'Conditorum'

FRANCE An ancient variety
A very useful rose. Rich ruby-red double flowers abundantly produced on a tidy, upright, well-foliated bush. Scented. Foliage dark green.
(S) (H) ☉ (P) (AL)
4′ × 3′ 120 × 90 cm

'Cosimo Ridolfi'

Vibert FRANCE 1842
Shapely cupped flowers of smoky bluish lilac, opening fully double and flat. Scented. Foliage greyish-green. Growth compact. A little-known but delightful Gallica.
(S) (P) (H) ☉
3′ × 3′ 90 × 90 cm

'Cramoisi Picoté'

Vibert FRANCE 1834
An unusual rose. Compact, upright growth with thin, almost thornless shoots full of closely packed, small, dark green leaves. Flowers fully double, small and pompon-like when open. Initially crimson, later changing to deep pink with deeper flecks and markings. Sadly, little or no fragrance.
(S) ☉ (P) M⚬ (AL)
3′ × 2′ 90 × 60 cm

'D'Aguesseau'

Vibert FRANCE 1823
Bright crimson with deeper shadings. Flowers fully double, quartered when open; each with a dark green, button eye in the centre. Bush upright and vigorous with dark foliage.
(S) (SF) (AL)
4′ × 3′ 120 × 90 cm

'Duc de Fitzjames'

c. 1885
For some years I have grown a beautiful, deep pink Centifolia under this name. This must now remain a mystery variety. The correct variety, which I now have, is deep maroon-purple and vigorous.
(S) (P) (AL)
4′ × 3′ 120 × 90 cm

'Duc de Guiche'

Prévost 1835
An outstanding Gallica. Highly scented. Double, beautifully formed, rich violet-crimson flowers opening to a charming cupped shape. When fully open it reveals a pleasing central green eye. Foliage dark green. Rather sprawly in growth.
(S) (P) ● (VF) ✂ (AL)
4′ × 4′ 1.2 × 1.2 m

'Duchesse d'Angoulême', 'Duc d'Angoulême'

Vibert FRANCE 1835, perhaps earlier

Deep pink buds opening to fully double, small, delicate, saucer-shaped, blush-pink flowers. These appear suspended from the tops of smooth, light green shoots. Foliage crisp and bright green. Related to the Centifolias.
(S) (P) (H) ⊙ (VF) ✂
(WW) (AL)
4' × 3'   120 × 90 cm

'Duchesse de Buccleugh'

Robert FRANCE 1860
Almost thornless with rich grey-green foliage. This vigorous shrub flowers rather later than some of its group. Well-formed flowers opening flat; their colour is rich magenta-red with pink highlights.
(S) (P) (MF) (AL)
6' × 4'   1.8 × 1.2 m

'Duchesse de Montebello'

Laffay FRANCE 1829
A lovely member of the Gallica family. The small, fragrant, fully double flowers of soft feminine pink are produced on a tidy, upright plant with good, dark green foliage.
(S) (P) (H) ● ⊙ (VF)
✂ (AL)   4' × 3'   120 × 90 cm

'Empress Josephine', *R. × francofurtana*

Early 19th century
Thought to be *R. gallica* × *R. pendulina*
Heavily textured petals form large, loosely arranged, double, deep pink flowers with the added charm of heavy veining and lavender and paler pink highlights; only slightly scented. The bush has ample foliage, is rela-tively thornless and is rather sprawly, yet still remains dense.
(S) (P) (H) ● ⊙ (MF)
(AL)   5' × 4'   1.5 × 1.2 m

'Georges Vibert'

Robert FRANCE 1853
Colour variously described from carmine to purple but alters with the climate as do so many striped varieties. In this rose, though, the stripes are always present amid an abundance of petals. A tidy, com-pact plant suitable for small gar-dens. Foliage dark green but rather coarse.
(S) (P) (H) ⊙ (MF) (AL)
3' × 3'   90 × 90 cm

'Gloire de France'

Pre-1819
Very double, medium-sized flowers of pale pink with deeper centres, produced in great profu-sion, fading rapidly to soft pink, almost white in hot sunshine. Has dark, crisp foliage and is fairly low growing, almost spreading.
(S) (G) (P) ● ⊙ (VF)
(AL)   3' × 4'   90 × 120 cm

'Henri Foucquier'

Early 19th century
Fully double flowers of clear pink, reflexing when open and exposing a small, button eye. Scented. Rather sprawly, not over-tall, with dark green foliage.
(S) (H) (P) ⊙ (VF) (AL)
4' × 4'   1.2 × 1.2 m

'Hippolyte'

Early 19th century
One of the nicest of the Gallicas. Flowers exquisitely formed, magenta-purple with softer high-lights in the centre. Clusters of blooms on thin almost thornless

'Duchesse de Montebello'

stems, often arching downwards. Foliage plentiful, dark green and very smooth for a Gallica.
(S) (P) (H) ⊙ (VF) (AL)
4' × 4'   1.2 × 1.2 m

'Ipsilanté'

1821
Pale lilac pink, this lovely old rose deserves more attention. Fully double flowers, large, quartered and scented. Foliage, on prickly stems, dark green. Growth habit perhaps rather coarse but still quite dense.
(S) (H) (P) ⊙ (VF) (AL)
4' × 3'   120 × 90 cm

'James Mason'

Beales UK 1982
'Scharlachglut' × 'Tuscany Superb'
A beautiful new introduction to the Gallica group. Flowers slightly more than single, large, up to 4" (10 cm) across. Scented. Profuse flowering in mid-June. Flowers sometimes hidden amid abun-dant dark green foliage.
(S) (P) (H) ⊙ (VF) (AL)
5' × 4'   1.5 × 1.2 m

'Jenny Duval'

Mid-18th century
The true variety has flowers of rich crimson, but since *Classic Roses* was first published in 1985 I have come to the conclusion that all clones of this variety that I know, including my own, are in fact 'Président de Sèze', with the true 'Jenny Duval' now probably extinct commercially.

'La Belle Sultane', *R. gallica violacea*

Of considerable antiquity – pre-Redouté
Slightly more than single flowers, soft violet smudged-purple with very pronounced golden-yellow stamens, produced freely on an

'Henri Foucquier'

upright shrub with rather sparse, grey-green leaves.
(S) (P) (H) ● (SF) (AL)
5' × 4'   1.5 × 1.2 m

'La Plus Belle des Ponctuées'

A tall, vigorous Gallica with good and ample dark green foliage. The fully double, slightly crumpled flowers are clear rich pink with smudges of softer pink throughout, giving an overall mottled effect.
(S) (P) (H) (WW) (MF)
(AL)   6' × 4'   1.8 × 1.2 m

'Marcel Bourgouin'

Corboeuf-Marsault FRANCE 1899
Rich, deep red to purple flowers, semi-double, sometimes showing off yellow stamens. Petals have a velvety texture. Growth upright with smallish, dark green leaves. I was privileged to work for the late Edward LeGrice when he crossed this and 'Tuscany Superb', among others, with modern roses to breed his famous range of unusually coloured modern varieties.
(S) (H) (P) ● (VF) (AL)
4' × 3'   120 × 90 cm

'Maître d'Ecole'
see 'Rose du Maître d'Ecole'

'Nanette'

Double, bright crimson flowers opening flat, with a green eye, blotched or striped with purple. A short growing variety, ideal for the small garden or for growing in pots. Stems almost thornless, well foliated with dark green leaves.
(S) (P) (H) ● ☉ (VF)
(AL)   3' × 3'   90 × 90 cm

'Néron'

Laffay FRANCE 1841
One of the taller Gallicas if given its head. Rich red with a deeper centre, fully double and scented. Foliage mid-green and somewhat coarse in texture.
(S) (P) (H) ● (SF) (AL)
5' × 4'   1.5 × 1.2 m

'Nestor'

c. 1846
A fine old variety. Predominantly magenta but varying with weather, and perhaps soil, from deep pink to mauve. Double, opening flat. Almost free of

thorns, foliage crisp and mid-green.
(S) (P) ☉ (MF) ✄ (AL)
4' × 3'   120 × 90 cm

'Oeillet Flamand'

Vibert FRANCE 1845
I have grown this rose for a number of years, but am still unsure of its authenticity. Vigorous, upright in growth, large, abundant, dark green, rather coarse leaves. Flowers fully double, on erect stems, pinky-white with deeper pink, almost magenta stripes. Not my favourite, but interesting.
(S) (H) ☉ (P) (MF) (AL)
4' × 3'   120 × 90 cm

'Oeillet Parfait'

Foulard FRANCE 1841
Small-to-medium, pure white flowers erratically striped with bright crimson. Clustered flowers opening rather raggedly but fully double. Large, coarse leaves with plentiful thorns for a Gallica. Rather straggly.
(S) (P) (MF) (AL)
5' × 4'   1.5 × 1.2 m

'Ohl'

Vibert FRANCE 1830
A medium-sized plant but vigorous. Large, fully double flowers with deep crimson petals in the centre and violet petals around the edge. Highly scented, it should be grown more widely, for it is a unique colour combination. Foliage dark green on stout, strong stems with few thorns.
(S) (H) ☉ (P) (VF) (AL)
4' × 3'   120 × 90 cm

'Ombrée Parfaite'

Vibert FRANCE 1823
A lesser known but good rose. Flower head comprised of several

'La Belle Sultane'

'Président de Sèze'

'Nestor'

'Ohl'

'Rose du Maître d'Ecole'

blooms of different colours from purple to pink, sometimes blush-pink, each flower fully double and scented. A short-growing plant, tidy and accommodating, with good, mid-green foliage.
(S) (P) ☉ (VF) (AL)
3′ × 2′   90 × 60 cm

'Orpheline de Juillet'

Paul UK 1848
Probably related to the Damasks.

Large, fully double flowers of crimson-purple turning to fiery red in the centre. Upright growth, moderately vigorous with greyish-green leaves. Similar to 'Belle de Crécy'.
(S) (H) (P) ☉ (VF) (WW) (AL)   4′ × 3′   120 × 90 cm

'Pompon Panachée'

Quite old. Perhaps 18th century A short growing, wiry, upright plant with ample foliage. Double,

'Surpasse Tout'

shapely flowers of creamy-white to white with pronounced splashes and stripes of deep pink.
(S) (H) ⊙ (SF) (WW) (AL)
3' × 2'   90 × 60 cm

'Président de Sèze', 'Mme Hébert'

c. 1836
Unique mixture of magenta and lilac with paler edges. The centre of its large flower is packed with inward-folding petals to form a neat cushion. A superb and interesting rose of manageable proportions. Leaves grey-green. Shoots more thorny than most of its group. Synonymous with 'Jenny Duval' in UK.
(S) (P) ⊙ (VF) (WW) (AL)
4' × 3'   120 × 90 cm

'Rose du Maître d'Ecole'

Miellez FRANCE 1840
The large, fully double flowers, opening flat and quartered, are unusual, being predominantly pink with lilac highlights and magenta shadings. Heavy, well spaced flowers, in trusses on an upright bush with lush green foliage and few thorns.
(S) (H) (P) ⊙ (VF) (AL)
3' × 3'   90 × 90 cm

'Scharlachglut', 'Scarlet Fire'

Kordes GERMANY 1952
'Poinsettia' × 'Alika'
This rose is a staggering sight as a fully established shrub. The very large, single flowers are bright velvety-red with pronounced golden stamens. Foliage large, dark green tinted brownish-purple. Stems also brownish-purple and smooth, with a few vicious thorns. Fruit large, urn-shaped and bright orange when ripe. The persistent calyx, not typical of a Gallica, has prompted some to believe this rose to have *R. pimpinellifolia* in its make-up; a possibility also suggested by the shape of its thorns and early flowering habit. In addition to making an excellent, solid free-standing shrub, this rose is also good climbing into small trees, demonstrated admirably by a fine specimen, now well established and growing up into a white flowering cherry tree at Mannington Hall, Norfolk.
(S) (T) (P) (W) (F) (N)
● (SF) (AW)
10' × 6'   3 × 1.8 m

'Sissinghurst Castle', 'Rose des Maures'

Discovered at Sissinghurst, reintroduced in 1947. Old variety. Semi-double, deep maroon petals with paler edges and lighter reverses. Prominently displayed golden anthers add to the attractions of this rose. Scented. Foliage small but abundant. Stems thin and brittle with few thorns.
(S) (P) ● ⊙ (VF) (AL)
3' × 3'   90 × 90 cm

'Surpasse Tout'

Pre-1832
I have never had any great success with this rose but perhaps it is temperamental. At its best it is fully double, opening reflexed with tightly packed petals in the centre. Colour deep cerise-maroon, paling to softer shades with age. Highly scented. I find the plant rather leggy and rather short of foliage.
(S) (P) (SF) M🗡 (AL)
4' × 3'   120 × 90 cm

'Tricolore', 'Reine Marguerite'

Lahaye Père FRANCE 1827
Deep pink to crimson flowers with petal edges tinged lilac, shapely and fully double. Scented. Foliage dark green. Stems moderately thorny.
(S) (H) ⊙ (SF) ✂ (AL)
4' × 3'   120 × 90 cm

'Tricolore de Flandre'

Van Houtte BELGIUM 1846
Heavily striped with purple, the pale pink flowers are shapely, almost fully double and scented. Growth upright and accommodating. Ideal for the small garden or as a single rose in pot. Foliage plentiful, smooth and dark green.
(S) (H) (P) ⊙ (MF) ✂
(AL)   3' × 2'   90 × 60 cm

'Tuscany', 'Old Velvet Rose'

Beautiful rich dark red flower with pronounced stamens, seldom seen these days because it has been superseded by 'Tuscany Superb', a slightly more vigorous rose, deeper red, with equally prominent stamens and better foliage. 'Tuscany' may date back well before 1500.
(S) (P) (H) ⊙ (VF) (AL)
3' × 3'   90 × 90 cm

'Tuscany Superb'

Paul UK 1848
Probably a sport from 'Tuscany' A superb rose. Semi-double flowers large and rich velvety dark red, displaying a golden crown of stamens when fully open. Strongly perfumed. Large, dark green leaves. Strong stems with

'Tuscany Superb'

few thorns provide an upright effect, fitting comfortably into any small space.

(S) (P) (H) ☉ (VF) ✄ (AW) 4' × 3' 120 × 90 cm

'Velutinaeflora'

Date unknown, could be 19th century

Pointed buds with downy sepals open to fragrant, single, pinkish-purple flowers with pronounced stamens. A fascinating, short-growing shrub with dense, grey-green foliage. Stems thorny by Gallica standards.

(S) (P) ● ☉ (VF) (AL)
3' × 3' 90 × 90 cm

Centifolias (Provence Roses, Cabbage Roses)

FORMS AND HYBRIDS

Centuries old, these 'roses of the hundred leaves' make superb shrubs. Sometimes coarse and lax in growth, they are often very prickly. The more vigorous forms usually produce large flowers of exquisite shape and intoxicating perfume, with the shorter types producing very double flowers almost invariably in perfect proportion to the size of the plant. Although their flowering season varies from variety to variety they seldom produce any more flowers after mid-summer.

CLASSIFICATION

BARB	Class 21
MR9	Class 5
WFRS	Class 29

'Fantin Latour'

R. × *centifolia*,
'Cabbage Rose',
'Provence Rose'

EUROPE Pre-1600
The fully double flowers of *R.* × *centifolia* prohibit this rose from self-perpetuation from seed. Thus, although *R.* × *centifolia* is usually listed as a species, it is probably a quite complex hybrid with a genealogy comprising *R. canina*, *R. gallica*, *R. moschata* and others. A rose similar to the present form was cultivated before 1600. A rather lax, medium-sized shrub with thick, coarse, grey-green leaves and abundant thorns. Flowers deep pink, very double cupped or cabbage-shaped when open. Has a strong, heady perfume.

(S) (P) (W) (VF) (WW) M✄ (AW) 6' × 5' 1.8 × 1.5 m

'Blanchefleur'

R. × *centifolia alba*
see **'White Provence'**

R. × *centifolia muscosa*
see Mosses

'Blanchefleur'

Vibert FRANCE 1835
Flat, very double, sweetly scented flowers of white with occasional pink tints. Slightly tidier than some other Centifolias but the weight of blooms sometimes gives the plant a lax, open gait when in flower. Greyish-green foliage, soft to touch.

(S) (P) (H) ● (VF) (AL)
5' × 4' 1.5 × 1.2 m

'Bullata',
'Lettuce-leaved Rose'

Cultivated in 16th century
Very large leaves and fewer thorns distinguish this rose from others in the group. Leaves unique, being loosely crinkly both in appearance and touch. Flowers are almost identical to those of *R.* × *centifolia* as is its growth habit, except that the density of foliage gives the overall appearance of a tidier plant.

(S) (P) (W) (VF) (WW) M✄ (AL) 5' × 4' 1.5 × 1.2 m

'Duchesse de Rohan',
'Duc de Rohan'

c. 1860
A fine rose, although in typical Centifolia mould, being rather coarse in growth. I am not sure if it is a true Centifolia, but it fits. Many-petalled flowers fade slightly with age from rich, warm pink to lavender, exuding a characteristically heady, Centifolia perfume, and occasionally repeating, which is, of course, untypical. It could be an early Hybrid Perpetual.

(R) (W) (VF) (AL)
5' × 4' 1.5 × 1.2 m

'Petite Lisette' (enlarged to twice actual average size)

'Juno'

'Fantin Latour'

A suberb mystery rose with records conspicuously absent. The soft, delicate pink flowers and their form puts it into this group, although its foliage is smoother, darker green and more rounded than is typical. Its shoots too are less thorny. I find the all-pervading perfume rather more Alba-like than Centifolia.

(S) (P) (H) (W) (VF)
(AW)   5′ × 4′   1.5 × 1.2 m

'Juno'

1832
Not large but nevertheless an arching shrub. The globular, double flowers of pale blush-pink

are produced profusely and are highly scented.

(S) (H) (P) ☉ (VF) M⚬
(AL)   4′ × 4′   1.2 × 1.2 m

'La Noblesse'

1856
Exceptionally tidy for a member of this group and flowering rather later in summer. Highly scented, the well formed, fully double blooms open flat and are soft silvery-pink.

(S) (P) (H) (MF) (AL)
5′ × 4′   1.5 × 1.2 m

'Petite de Hollande', 'Pompon des Dames', 'Petite Junon de Hollande'

HOLLAND c. 1800
An attractive and compact small shrub producing many small, double flowers about 1½″ (4 cm) across. These are cupped until fully open, and clear pink with deeper centres. Scented.

(S) (P) ☉ (H) (VF) (AL)
4′ × 3′   120 × 90 cm

'Petite Lisette'

Vibert FRANCE 1817
Small pompon flowers, 1″ (2.5 cm) across, of deep rose pink, produced in considerable numbers in large, evenly-spaced heads. Small, deeply serrated, greyish-green pointed foliage. Makes a useful shrub for the front of borders.

(S) (H) ● ☉ (P) (VF)
(AL)   3′ × 3′   90 × 90 cm

'Petite Orléanaise'

c. 1900
Another Centifolia with small, pompon-like flowers but taller than the other small-flowered varieties. Ample foliage and a tidy disposition make this a useful

shrub for growing in large tubs or pots.

(S) (P) (H) ☉ (VF) ✂
(AL)   4′ × 3′   120 × 90 cm

'Pompon de Bourgogne', 'Burgundian Rose', 'Parvifolia', R. burgundica

Pre-1664
A superb little rose. Pompon flowers of rosy-claret to purple, some flecked with pink. Growth erect with foliage packed closely along clustered, thin, stiff stems. An ideal miniature rose for terrace, patio or pot.

(S) (H) ☉ (MF) (AL)
2′ × 2′   60 × 60 cm

'Prolifera de Redouté'

c. 1820
Clear deep rose pink with many petals, opening cabbage-like but with a high frequency of proliferation (another bud growing through the centre of the flower) which makes this a frustrating rose to enjoy. Highly scented. Growth lax, maturing to a medium-sized shrub with coarse, greyish-dark-green foliage.

(S) (P) (W) (VF) M⚬
(AL)   6′ × 5′   1.8 × 1.5 m

'Petite Orléanaise'

'Pompon de Bourgogne'

'Rose de Meaux'

'Reine des Centfeuilles'

BELGIUM 1824
Large, scented, double, clear pink flowers, reflexed when fully open, with spiky petals. Ample foliage, medium to tall and, in my experience, fairly disorderly in habit.
(S) (P) (MF) (AL)
5' × 3' 150 × 90 cm

'Robert le Diable'

FRANCE
A very useful and interesting small shrub rose, slightly procumbent and well endowed with foliage. Colour of flowers – produced later than most – difficult to describe but on the crimson side of red, with lilac and grey highlights and dark-purple shadings. Often exposes a small, green eye in the centre of each bloom.
(S) (P) ☉ (VF) M✄ (AL)
3' × 3' 90 × 90 cm

'Rose de Meaux'

Sweet UK Pre-1789
A short, erect, well-foliated bush with massed, small, double, pink flowers – not quite pompons, more like small Dianthus with slightly frilly petals. Scented. A superb shorter growing rose, temperamental in some soils, but most rewarding once established in good soil. Excellent in pots.
(S) (H) ☉ (MF) (AL)
2' × 2' 60 × 60 cm

'Rose de Meaux White'

As 'Rose de Meaux', but white.
(S) (H) ☉ (MF) (AL)
2' × 2' 60 × 60 cm

'Spong'

'Rose des Peintres', *R. × centifolia* 'Major', 'Centfeuille des Peintres'

A slightly more refined form of *R. × centifolia*. Large flowers opening fully double with a lovely clearly defined button eye in the centre. Clear deep pink in colour, with a delicate texture to the petals. Good dark green foliage on a sprawly plant.
(S) (P) (W) (VF) ✄ (AL)
6' × 5' 1.8 × 1.5 m

'Spong'

Spong FRANCE 1805
An unusual name for an unusual rose. Of medium stature, rather like 'Rose de Meaux' with larger flowers and taller growth. Scented. Flowers early and needs 'dead-heading' after flowering, especially in wet weather. Good plentiful greyish-green foliage.
(S) (P) (H) ● ☉ (VF) (WW) (AL)
4' × 3' 120 × 90 cm

'The Bishop'

'The Bishop'

Full, rosette-shaped flowers of an unusual mixture of magenta, cerise and purple. Fragrant. Flowering rather earlier than most of this group. Upright in habit. An excellent rose although some doubt exists as to its proper classification and, indeed, its true name.
(S) (P) (H) ☉ (MF) (AL)
4' × 3'   120 × 90 cm

'Tour de Malakoff', 'Black Jack'

Soupert and Notting
LUXEMBOURG 1856
A unique rose. Vivid magenta flowers flushed deep purple and fading to lilac-grey, each bloom large, double, but loosely formed. A lanky, lax plant which benefits from support.
(S) (P) (CL) (VF) ✂ (AL)
8' × 5'   2.5 × 1.5 m

'Village Maid', 'Belle des Jardins', 'La Rubanée', *R. × centifolia variegata*

Vibert FRANCE 1845
A vigorous, thorny rose with strong shoots. Rather more upright than most taller Centifolias. Soft, off-white blooms liberally streaked and striped with pink. Very floriferous when it blooms in late June. Scented. In my experience it occasionally repeats with an odd bloom in late summer.
(S) (P) (H) (VF) (AL)
5' × 4'   1.5 × 1.2 m

'White Provence', 'Unique Blanche', 'Vierge de Cléry', *R. × centifolia alba*

Discovery in UK 1775
Probably a sport from another Centifolia
In good weather, the flowers of this rose are quite the most beautiful of all white roses. Indeed, if we only had one good summer in ten, it would be worth waiting for just one of its perfect blooms. White silk is the nearest I can come to a simile. The shrub itself is not the most elegant, but who cares, when it yields such rewards?
(S) (P) (H) (VF) (WW)
(AL)   5' × 4'   1.5 × 1.2 m

'Village Maid'

Mosses

FORMS AND HYBRIDS

At some point in the evolution of the Centifolias, Nature decreed that some would have whiskers. Whiskers which take a variety of forms, from multiple stiff bristles to soft, downy glands resembling moss. There are no records of exactly when the first mossy mutation occurred, but they have probably been around far longer than the 285 years since the first one was recorded.

Controlled breeding was made possible by the discovery of a chance, single-flowered sport at the beginning of the 19th century. Thirst for novelty then led to the breeding of an abundance of Moss roses and soon between 30 and 40 varieties were commonly being listed in Victorian nurserymen's catalogues. Many, had they been naked, without the novelty of moss, would never have survived the competition and would quickly have faded into oblivion. They are not over-popular today and apart from a few which are underrated, I am not sure if they deserve to be. It would be sad, though, if they were to die out. The following are those still available, some of which merit wider recognition.

CLASSIFICATION	
BARB	Class 22
MR9	Class 47
WFRS	Class 27

R. × centifolia muscosa

17th century
Mossed form of *R. × centifolia*. Identical in all respects except for the moss, which is really closely packed reddish-brown bristles, brighter on young shoots and covering both stems and calyx. Rather prone to mildew.
(S) (P) (VF) M✿ (WW)
(AL)   6' × 5'   1.8 × 1.5 m

'Alfred de Dalmas', 'Mousseline'

Portemer FRANCE 1855
Any criticism made of Moss roses does not extend to this little charmer, which really belongs among the Portland Damasks. Blooms semi-double, creamy-pink and scented. It flowers continuously from mid-June to November. Foliage lush, growth tidy and manageable. Its moss is green, tinted pink, turning to russet on older shoots. Can fulfil a variety of roles from massed planting to an outdoor pot plant.
(C) (P) (H) ● ☉ (MF)
(AW)   3' × 2'   90 × 60 cm

'à longues pédoncules'

Robert FRANCE 1854
Soft lilac-pink double flowers on a vigorous sprawly shrub with ample, light greyish-green leaves. Flower stalks long with profuse green mossing around globular buds.
(S) (P) ● (W) (VF) (AL)
5' × 4'   1.5 × 1.2 m

'Alfred de Dalmas'

'Blanche Moreau'

'Capitaine Basroger'

'Baron de Wassenaer'

Verdier FRANCE 1854
Vigorous, with much dark foliage
and considerable moss. Flowers
rich bright red to crimson, fully

double, cupped, often borne in
clusters on strong stems, in the
way of 'William Lobb'.
(S) (P) (CL) (VF) (AL)
7′ × 4′   2 × 1.2 m

'Blanche Moreau'

Moreau-Robert FRANCE 1880
'Comtesse de Murinais'
× 'Quatre Saisons Blanc'
mousseux
The bristly, purple, almost black
moss on this rose is too often
marred by mildew for it to get
much attention, although it has
beautiful, fully double, pure
white, perfumed flowers.
(S) (P) ☉ (VF) M⚘ (WW)
(AL)   4′ × 3′   120 × 90 cm

'Capitaine Basroger'

Moreau-Robert FRANCE 1890
A distinct feature of this rose is
its ability to produce a sparse,
second flush of flowers in late
summer. Double, deep crimson,
scented flowers emerge from
tight, globular buds, sprinkled
rather than covered with moss.
Vigorous, better with support.
(R) (P) (VF) (AL)
6′ × 4′   1.8 × 1.2 m

'Capitaine John Ingram'

Laffay FRANCE 1856
Not over tall, one of the most
charming of the Moss roses,
deserving more attention. Well
endowed with reddish moss on
stems, receptacle and calyx.
Colour of the fully double flowers

'Chapeau de Napoléon'

varies with weather from dark
crimson to purple. Very strongly
scented.
(S) (P) (H) ☉ (VF) (AL)
4′ × 3′   120 × 90 cm

'Catherine de 'Würtemberg'

Robert FRANCE 1843
An upright-growing plant with
sparse reddish mossing and ample
small, red thorns. Flowers lilac-
pink and double, with faint scent.
(S) (P) (SF) (AL)
6′ × 4′   1.8 × 1.2 m

'Célina'

Hardy FRANCE 1855
Not exceptionally mossy. Flowers
are quite distinctive, of good size,
semi-double, and a mixture of
cerise, pink and lavender, display-

Above: 'Célina'

ing golden anthers when open. A
reasonably tidy shrub but somewhat prone to mildew later in the
season.
(S) (P) (H) (MF) M⚘
(AL)   4′ × 3′   120 × 90 cm

'Chapeau de Napoléon', 'Cristata', 'Crested Moss'

Vibert FRANCE 1826
Chance discovery
Fully double, highly scented,
cabbage-like, silvery deep pink
flowers enhanced by a fascinating
moss formation on the calyx. This
is shaped like a cocked-hat, hence
the name. Apart from that, it is a
useful shrub of medium size, well
dressed with foliage. Probably
better with support.
(S) (P) (H) (VF) ✂ (AW)
5′ × 4′   1.5 × 1.2 m

'Common Moss', 'Old Pink Moss', 'Communis'

FRANCE Pre-1700
Presumably so called because of its ubiquity, but I suspect it applies to a number of pink Mosses, which were, of course, very common in the 19th century. The rose I grow under this name could well be something else but I find it better than *R. × centifolia muscosa* in several respects. It is softer in colour, more regular in shape and tidier in growth habit. From cuttings sent to me over the years I believe that a number of different clones exist, all derivatives of *R. × centifolia muscosa*, but selected as better plants because of their more manageable dispositions. All are very well mossed and have an exceptionally strong perfume.
(S) (P) (VF) ✂ (AW)
4′ × 4′   1.2 × 1.2 m

'Comtesse de Murinais'

Robert FRANCE 1843
A tall rose, needing support but with much to commend it. Flowers soft pink paling to creamy-white when open, fully double, opening flat, even in wet weather. Moss clear rich green and rather bristly; if touched, it exudes a powerful, lingering, balsam-like odour. Scented moss is by no means unique but in this rose it is stronger than in most others.
(S) (VF) (AL)
6′ × 4′   1.8 × 1.2 m

'Crested Jewel'

R. S. Moore USA 1971
'Little Darling' × 'Chapeau de Napoléon'

A delightful, shorter growing Moss rose from that most talented hybridizer Ralph Moore. Conspicuous crested moss formations on the sepals of high-centred, bright pink, semi-double flowers. Tough, leathery mid to dark green foliage.
(S) (P) ☉ (SF) (AL)
3′ × 3′   90 × 90 cm

'Crested Moss'
see 'Chapeau de Napoléon'

'Crimson Globe'

W. Paul UK 1890
This sounds more like a vegetable than a rose and, frankly, I sometimes wonder if it is. Probably better in warmer climes.
(S) (VF) M✂ (AL)
4′ × 4′   1.2 × 1.2 m

'Cristata'
see 'Chapeau de Napoléon'

'Deuil de Paul Fontaine'

Fontaine FRANCE 1873
Deep red to blackish-purple best describes the colour of this rose. A relatively small, very thorny plant with somewhat coarse foliage. Will repeat in most seasons.
(R) (H) ☉ (MF) (AL)
3′ × 3′   90 × 90 cm

'Dresden Doll'

R. S. Moore USA 1975
I feel that this charming miniature Moss rose should be included although I am not sure it should be placed here. Raised recently, it is quite exquisite, with heavily mossed buds and stems

'Eugène Guinoisseau'

and lush green foliage. The small, pointed buds open to fully double, cupped scented flowers of soft pink. Ideal for pots on patios, or even in window-boxes.
(C) (P) (H) ☉ (MF) (AW)
9″ × 6″   25 × 15 cm

'Duchesse de Verneuil'

Portemer FRANCE 1856
A very refined Moss rose. Medium-tall and well foliated with light green leaves and dense darker green moss. Flattish flowers composed of many folded petals, these reflex to expose pale pink beneath and brighter pink above. Foliage, moss and flowers combine to pleasing effect.
(S) (P) (VF) (WW) (AL)
5′ × 3′   150 × 90 cm

'Eugénie Guinoisseau'

Guinoisseau FRANCE 1864
Scented flowers in a mixture of shades between deep pink, violet-grey and purple, substantial and more cupped in shape than most. Foliage is smooth with just a hint of gloss, moss is dark green. Bears a second crop of blooms in a good season, surprising in such a tall variety. Better grown with support.
(S) (P) (CL) (MF) (AL)
6′ × 4′   1.8 × 1.2 m

'Fairy Moss'

R. S. Moore USA 1969
('Pinocchio' × 'William Lobb') × 'New Penny'
Small mid-pink, semi-double flowers open from well mossed, pointed buds. Foliage tough light green. Growth vigorous and bushy.
(C) (P) ☉ (SF) (AL)
1′ × 1′   30 × 30 cm

'Félicité Bohain'

c. 1865
A little-grown variety, with plentiful but small foliage. Moss reddish, spreading to the edges of its young leaves. Smallish flowers have a button eye, surrounded by folded and crinkled, bright pink petals.
(S) (H) (P) ☉ (VF) (AL)
4' × 3' 120 × 90 cm

'Gabriel Noyelle'

Buatois FRANCE 1933
'Salet' × 'Souvenir de Mme Kreuger'
Shapely fully double flowers of bright salmon with highlights of orange and yellow. Fragrant. Foliage dark green, growth upright bushy. Recurrent.
(R) (H) ☉ (VF) (AL)
4' × 4' 1.2 × 1.2 m

'Général Kléber'

Robert FRANCE 1856
An excellent variety both for beauty of flower and garden value. Flowers very bright, almost shining pink, quite large with patternless petals, rather like small, crumpled, pink tissues. Foliage copious, large and lush bright green; thick stems covered in bright lime green moss extend-

'Gloire des Mousseaux'

'Général Kléber'

ing to the tips of the sepals. Very few thorns.
(S) (P) (H) ☉ (VF) (AL)
4' × 4' 1.2 × 1.2 m

'Gloire des Mousseux'

Laffay FRANCE 1852
This rose probably has the largest flowers of all the Mosses and, for once, big is beautiful. Huge, scented blooms of clear soft pink, fully double and reflexing, produced freely on a substantial plant with light green leaves and moss.
(S) (P) (H) ☉ (VF) (WW) (AL) 4' × 3' 120 × 90 cm

'Goethe'

P. Lambert GERMANY 1911
Several single Mosses existed in Victorian times but this later variety is the only true single available today. Rich magenta pink with yellow stamens. Reddish-brown moss and dark bluish green foliage. When young, the shoots are pinkish-red. Very vigorous.
(S) (P) (SF) M✿ (AL)
6' × 4' 1.8 × 1.2 m

'Golden Moss'

Pedro Dot SPAIN 1932
'Frau Karl Druschki' × ('Souvenir de Glaudius Pernet' × 'Blanche Moreau')
This relatively recent Moss rose has very little to commend it, apart from being the only yellow in its group. The flowers are pale yellow, cupped and fragrant, but

it detests wet weather and can be rather shy. Perhaps I have never seen it at its best?
(S) (H) (SF) (WW) (AL)
5' × 3' 150 × 90 cm

'Henri Martin', 'Red Moss'

Laffay FRANCE 1863
Clusters of medium-sized, bright crimson, scented flowers on sparsely mossed stems. Well worth growing for the sheer quantity of flowers produced. Foliage dark green, plentiful.
(S) (P) (H) (VF) (AL)
5' × 4' 1.5 × 1.2 m

'Hunslett Moss'

Beales UK 1984
Discovery by the late Humphrey Brooke
Undoubtedly one of the earliest English Moss roses. Known to have been grown by Humphrey Brooke's ancestors for several generations. Large, full and heavily mossed, deep pink with a strong perfume. Foliage dark on a sturdy upright plant.
(S) (P) (H) ☉ (VF) (AL)
4' × 3' 120 × 90 cm

'James Mitchell'

Verdier FRANCE 1861
Medium-sized, double flowers of rich, bright pink, produced plentifully in early July. Scented. A healthy plant, perhaps slightly short of foliage and moss, but makes an excellent, tidy shrub.
(S) (P) (H) ● (VF) (AL)
5' × 4' 1.5 × 1.2 m

'James Veitch'

Verdier FRANCE 1865
A most interesting, short-growing Moss rose. Royal purple with slate-grey highlights. Flowers

'Henri Martin' (enlarged to one and and half times its actual average size)

almost continuously throughout summer. But for mildew, which can be a problem, it is superb. Another Moss rose which could well be placed among the Portland Damasks.

(S) ☉ (VF) M⚭ (AL)
3' × 3'   90 × 90 cm

'Japonica'
see 'Mousseux de Japon'

'Jeanne de Montfort'

Robert FRANCE c. 1851
One of the tallest Moss roses, needing support if placed in a shrubbery. Moss dark maroon, leaves dark green and almost glossy. Flowers clear rose pink, borne in large clusters and scented. Worth growing as a small climber or pillar rose.

(S) (P) (CL) (VF) (AL)
8' × 5'   2.5 × 1.5 m

'Laneii', 'Lane's Moss'

Laffay FRANCE 1854
Very double, crimson flowers produced freely on a sturdy plant. Scented flowers initially cupped but opening flat and reflexed, exposing a large green eye in the centre. Moss slightly darker than the deep green foliage.

(S) (P) (H) ☉ (VF) (AL)
4' × 3'   120 × 90 cm

'Little Gem'

W. Paul UK 1880
Very popular in late Victorian times, this tidy, useful little rose is very free-flowering and colourful. Flowers in clusters, evenly spaced and pompon-like, bright crimson. Stems, which are amply clothed in moss, are provided with many small, closely packed, rich green leaves.

(R) (H) ☉ (VF) (AL)
3' × 2'   90 × 60 cm

'Louis Gimard'

Pernet Père FRANCE 1877
The fully double flowers open flat with rich, deep pink centres, paling towards borders to soft pink. Foliage very dark green with reddish veins and margins. Bristly moss, almost purple.

(S) (P) (H) (MF) (AL)
5' × 3'   150 × 90 cm

'Ma Ponctuée'

Guillot FRANCE 1857
A very unusual little Moss rose. Small double flowers produced intermittently throughout summer, pinkish-red with white flecks. Well mossed. It needs good soil to flourish. I suspect the variety has deteriorated over the years, perhaps by hosting some form of hard-to-detect growth-retarding virus.

(R) ☉ (C) (SF) M⚭ (AL)
3' × 3'   90 × 90 cm

'James Veitch'

'Little Gem'

'Mme de la Roche Lambert'

'Maréchal Davoust'

Robert FRANCE 1853
An effective rose where an unusual colour is desired. Each flower's many reflexing petals combine an extraordinary mixture of purples, greys, and pinks. The flower sometimes reveals a little green eye in the centre. Fairly tidy with very dark moss and grey-green foliage.

(S) (H) (P) ☉ (VF) (AL)
4' × 3'   120 × 90 cm

'Marie de Blois'

Robert FRANCE 1852
This free-flowering rose should be more popular. Shoots are well covered with reddish moss and bright green leaves. Flowers are made up of randomly-formed clusters of bright pink petals, heavily scented and produced freely each season.

(R) (P) (H) (MF) (AL)
5' × 4'   1.5 × 1.2 m

'Maréchal Davoust'

'Mme Louis Lévêque'

'Nuits de Young'

'Mme de la Roche-Lambert'

Robert FRANCE 1851
Globular flowers which open
flattish with many deep purple
petals, which hold their colour
even in hot sunshine. Scented.
Moss is also deep purple and
leaves dark green. An interesting
and useful medium shrub which
sometimes repeats its flowers well
into the autumn.
(R) (P) (H) ☉ (VF) M⚘
(AL) 4′ × 3′ 120 × 90 cm

'Mme Louis Lévêque'

Lévêque FRANCE 1898
I first saw this rose in Mr Maurice
Mason's famous garden at
Fincham, Norfolk. Probably then

at its best, it was as near perfect as
any rose I have ever seen. The
flowers are cup-shaped until fully
open, quite large and of soft
warm pink. More important then
the colour is the soft, silky texture
of the petals in their nest of moss.
The flowers are held on an erect,
mossy stem amid large, dark
green foliage.
(R) (P) (H) ☉ (VF) (AL)
4′ × 3′ 120 × 90 cm

'Monsieur Pélisson'
see **'Pélisson'**

'Mousseline'
see **'Alfred de Dalmas'**

'Mousseux du Japon', 'Moussu du Japon', 'Japonica'

Perhaps the most heavily mossed
of all roses, the moss creating an
illusion that the stems are far
thicker than they actually are.
Flowers semi-double, soft lilac-
pink with pronounced stamens.
Leaves – with mossed stalks –
darkish green.
(R) (H) ☉ (VF) (AL)
4′ × 3′ 120 × 90 cm

'Mrs William Paul'

W. Paul UK 1869
Short, strong stems bearing mossy
buds which open to double,
bright pink flowers with red
shadings. Quite vigorous for such

a short-growing shrub. This useful
rose should be better known
especially as it is recurrent.
(R) (H) ☉ (B) (VF) (AL)
3′ × 3′ 90 × 90 cm

'Nuits de Young', 'Old Black'

Laffay FRANCE 1845
Compact, erect shrub with small,
dark green leaves and small
almost double flowers, of very
dark, velvety maroon-purple
emphasized by golden stamens.
Although not heavily mossed, and
with somewhat small foliage, this
is certainly one of the best Mosses
for general effect, especially
where dark colour is needed.
(S) (P) (H) ☉ (VF) (AL)
4′ × 3′ 120 × 90 cm

'Old Pink Moss

see **'Common Moss'**

'Pélisson', 'Monsieur Pélisson'

Vibert FRANCE 1848
Double flowers, opening flat, red
changing to purple with age. A
vigorous, upright, shortish
grower. Foliage coarse dark green,
deeply veined. Stems have
stumpy thorns and darkish green
moss.
(S) (P) ☉ (VF) M & (AL)
4' × 3'   120 × 90 cm

'Princesse Adélaide'

Laffay FRANCE 1845
Foliage dark green, often variegated. Sparsely mossed. Flowers
large, shapely, double, soft pink
and well scented. Sometimes
classed as a Gallica.
(S) (P) (H) ☉ (MF) (AL)
4' × 3'   120 × 90 cm

'Reine Blanche'

Moreau FRANCE 1857
A lovely, short to medium Moss
rose which, for some reason, is
often ignored in favour of the
taller 'Blanche Moreau'. 'Reine
Blanche' has very good moss
which is light green, as is its
copious foliage. The fully double
flowers, although on a weak neck,
are shapely, pure white with
creamy centres, each with a tight,
button eye in the centre.
(S) (P) (H) ☉ (VF) (AL)
3' × 3'   90 × 90 cm

'René d'Anjou'

Robert FRANCE 1853
This rose is of the most feminine
shade of pink, with quite an
exquisite perfume. As a shrub, it
is not too vigorous, making it

ideal for the smaller garden,
especially as both foliage and
moss have bronze tints which are
most marked when young.
(S) (P) (H) ☉ (VF) (AL)
4' × 3'   120 × 90 cm

'Robert Léopold'

Buatois FRANCE 1941
A shapely, fully double Moss rose
of modern colouring, salmon with
deeper pink markings on an
orangey-yellow background.
Sounds a gaudy combination of
colour but is actually a pleasing
rose. Blooms held on sturdy,
stout, well mossed stems. Moss
brownish. Growth upright. Foliage dark green but rather coarse.
(R) (P) ☉ (MF) (AL)
4' × 3'   120 × 90 cm

'Salet'

Lacharme FRANCE 1854
A rose with considerable character, especially useful for the
smaller garden. Flowers clear rose
pink, deeper in the autumn,
double and somewhat muddled
when fully open. Not very mossy
but the leaves are bright green
especially when young.
(R) (P) (H) ☉ (VF) (AL)
4' × 3'   120 × 90 cm

'Shailer's White Moss'

Shailer UK c. 1788
Supposed to be the white form of
R. centifolia muscosa but unless I
have a different rose, I find it less
sprawly and with darker green
foliage. Well mossed, highly
scented; full, flat and quartered
flowers with the outer layer of
petals rather spiky, mostly white
but with occasional hints of pink.
Very free-flowering.
(S) (P) ● (VF) M & (AL)
5' × 4'   1.5 × 1.2 m

'Robert Léopold'

'Soupert et Notting'

Pernet Père FRANCE 1874
A useful, short-growing, dense
bush with well mossed stems and
buds. Flowers deep pinkish-red,
fully double and quartered when
fully open. Sadly, mildew needs
to be controlled to get the best
from the autumn blooms.
(R) (H) ☉ (VF) M & (AL)
3' × 2'   90 × 60 cm

'Souvenir de Pierre Vibert'

Moreau-Robert FRANCE 1867
The fully double flowers are a
mixture of red, deep pink and
violet, and are produced throughout summer. The shrub is somewhat lax for such a short plant
but effective if placed correctly.
Ample moss and foliage.
(R) (H) ☉ (VF) (AL)
4' × 3'   120 × 90 cm

'Striped Moss'

Not, I find, the most shapely of
roses, the small flowers are
various shades of pink with
random red markings. Its small
upright stature makes it an ideal
pot plant.
(S) (P) (H) ☉ (MF) (AL)
3' × 2'   90 × 60 cm

'Striped Moss'

'White Bath'

'William Lobb'

'White Bath', 'White Moss', 'Clifton Moss'

Salter UK c. 1817
Said to be sport of 'Common Moss'
Large fully double pure white flowers. Heavily scented. Foliage, stems and buds well mossed. Of medium vigour.
(S) (P) (H) ● ☉ (VF) M🍂 (AL) 4′ × 3′ 120 × 90 cm

'William Lobb', 'Duchesse d'Istrie', 'Old Velvet Moss'

Laffay FRANCE 1855
Very vigorous, often producing long stems each with large clus-

ters of flowers, so heavy as to bend almost to the ground. Best with support, perhaps of another rose, say a climber of similar colour such as 'Veilchenblau' or a vigorous creamy-white rambler. Well mossed, with ample, large leaves. Flowers large, semi-double and scented, a mixture of purple, grey, magenta and pink, slightly paler on the reverse.
(S) (P) (CL) (VF) (AL) 8′ × 5′ 2.5 × 1.5 m

'Zenobia'

W. Paul UK 1892
A tall-growing, rather lanky rose with well mossed buds and stems and thick, leathery foliage. Flowers fragrant, globular, reminiscent of an old Hybrid Perpetual in shape, even when fully open. Colour on the cerise side of pink.
(S) (P) (VF) (AL) 6′ × 4′ 1.8 × 1.2 m

'Zoe'

Vibert FRANCE 1830
A free-flowering Moss rose with medium sized bright pink, fully double flowers opening flat and made up of many narrow, fluted petals. Scented. Well endowed with brownish red moss. Foliage mid-green. An excellent example of this rose can be seen at Castle Howard, Yorkshire.
(S) (P) (H) ☉ (VF) (AL) 4′ × 3′ 120 × 90 cm

Damasks
FORMS AND HYBRIDS

There is little doubt that the Damasks have a close affinity to the Gallicas; the more I delve into the complex lineage of roses, the more confused I become about them. As a mere grower of roses I can only follow, or attempt to follow, the rules laid down by others.

CLASSIFICATION	
BARB	Class 20
MR9	Class 17
WFRS	Class 24

'Belle Amour'

'Blush Damask'

R. × *damascena bifera*
see **'Quatre Saisons'**

R. × *damascena trigintipetala*
see **'Kazanlik'**

R. × *damascena versicolor*
see **'York and Lancaster'**

'Autumn Damask'
see **'Quatre Saisons'**

'Belle Amour'

Discovered by Miss Nancy Lindsay 1950
Rich yellow stamens framed by two layers of crinkled, salmony-pink petals. Possibly related to the Albas but its foliage and growth, respectively greeny-grey and thorny, places it here among the Damasks.
(S) (P) (H) (W) (MF) (AL) 5′ × 3′ 150 × 90 cm

'Blush Damask'

A vigorous, dense but sprawly shrub, very floriferous when in bloom but with fleeting effect. The double medium-sized flowers are rich pink, paling to soft pink at the edges. Needs dead-heading, as the decayed flowers are very reluctant to fall. Probably of ancient origin.
(S) (P) (H) (W) (VF) M🍂 (WW) (AL) 4′ × 3′ 120 × 90 cm

'Botzaris' (enlarged to one and a half times its average size)

'Gloire de Guilan'

'Gloire de Guilan'

MIDDLE EAST
Introduced by Nancy Lindsay
1949
The flowers which are very double, and flat when open, are often beautifully quartered, clear pink in colour and richly fragrant. Flowering early summer, inclined to sprawl without support. Foliage light green, wood densely populated with small thorns. Probably of some antiquity.
(S) (P) (W) (VF) (AL)
6' × 4' 1.8 × 1.2 m

'Ispahan'

'Ispahan', 'Rose d'Isfahan'

MIDDLE EAST Pre-1832
Flowering for a long season compared with others of this group, the shapely double, light pink flowers hold both their shape and colour well. Very fragrant. It has attractive foliage and its stems are not over-thorny.
(S) (P) (H) ☉ (VF) (AL)
4' × 3' 120 × 90 cm

'La Ville de Bruxelles'

'Botzaris'

1856
Flattish, fully double flowers of creamy-white, often quartered when fully open. Another Damask with an affinity to the Albas, hence its quality perfume. Wood thorny, foliage rich light green. A superb rose which will never outgrow its welcome, even if left unpruned.
(S) (P) (W) (H) (VF) (AL)
4' × 3' 120 × 90 cm

'Celsiana'

Pre-1750
An attractive shrub in full bloom, its downy, light grey-green foliage and reasonably contained habit help make it quite unobtrusive whilst 'resting' in late summer. Flowers highly scented, borne in nodding clusters, semi-double, displaying yellow anthers to effect. Clear pink fading to pinkish-white in hot sun.
(S) (P) (H) (W) (VF)
(AW) 5' × 4' 1.5 × 1.2 m

'Coralie'

c. 1860
A rather thorny shrub of medium stature with small greyish-green leaves. Soft pink flowers open flat, rather more than semi-double, petals inclined to fold backwards when fully open. Still attractive when faded to blush-white in hot sun.
(S) (P) (H) (W) ☉ (VF)
(AL) 4' × 3' 120 × 90 cm

'Kazanlik'

'Kazanlik', 'Trigintipetala'

MIDDLE EAST Very ancient
A vigorous rose originating in the rose fields of Bulgaria as one of varieties used in the manufacture of 'attar of roses'. Ideal for making pot-pourri. The soft-textured petals are warm pink and very fragrant. Flower opens to a somewhat shaggy double bloom. Foliage dark green; although it makes a good shrub, it is better with support.
(S) (P) (W) ● (VF) (AL)
5′ × 4′   1.5 × 1.2 m

'La Ville de Bruxelles'

Vibert FRANCE 1849
Large, full, pure pink blooms with quartered and incurving centres. Highly scented. A strong, vigorous and upright shrub, which is good for specimen planting.
(S) (P) (W) (VF) M⚘
(AL)   5′ × 3′   150 × 90 cm

'Leda', 'Painted Damask'

Probably early 19th century
Double flowers, blush-pink to white, with interesting crimson markings on the margins of each petal. Scented. Tidy and compact for a damask, foliage downy grey-green.
(S) (P) (H) ☉ (VF) (AL)
3′ × 3′   90 × 90 cm

'Marie Louise'

c. 1813
Glowing pink, double flowers full and flat when fully open, well perfumed. Shrub compact, bushy with good foliage, fairly free of at least any vicious thorns.
(S) (P) (H) ☉ (VF) (AL)
4′ × 3′   120 × 90 cm

Above: 'Léda'; *right,* 'Marie Louise'

'Mme Hardy'

Hardy FRANCE 1832
An elegant and sumptuous rose which can hold its own against any in the shrubbery. Flowers pure white, fully double and quite large considering the number it produces. Centre petals are folded inwards, exposing a rich green eye. Strongly scented. Growth, although strong and vigorous, is accommodating. Foliage bright, almost lime-green especially when young.
(S) (P) (H) ● (VF) (AW)
5′ × 5′   1.5 × 1.5 m

'Mme Zöetmans'

Marest FRANCE 1830
Deserving more attention. Soft pink, double, sometimes quartered flowers, paling to blush-white, each with a prominent, green eye. A tidy compact shrub for a Damask, with darkish green foliage.
(S) (P) (H) ☉ (VF) (AL)
4′ × 3′   120 × 90 cm

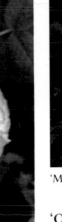

'Mme Zöetmans'

'Omar Khayyam'

1893
Undoubtedly of some antiquity. Propagated from a plant growing on Edward Fitzgerald's grave in Suffolk, planted there in 1893 from seed gathered from plants on Omar Khayyam's tomb in Nashipur. Medium-sized light pink flowers double and scented. Shrub shortish, foliage grey-green and downy.
(S) (H) ☉ (VF) (AL)
3′ × 3′   90 × 90 cm

'Mme Hardy'

'Omar Khayyam'

'Pink Léda'

Probably GERMANY Pre-1844
Bright clear pink. Identical in all
other respects to 'Leda' including
the red markings on the outer
edge of its petals. Perhaps 'Léda'
is a sport from this variety but
more likely the other way round.
(S) (P) (H) ⊙ (MF) (AL)
3' × 3'   90 × 90 cm

'Quatre Saisons',
R. × damascena bifera,
'Autumn Damask'

MIDDLE EAST Extremely ancient
Thought to be *R. gallica* ×
R. moschata
A very old rose, loosely double
with large, sometimes rather
crumpled, petals. Colour clear but
silky pink, highly scented. Shrub
rather sprawly, foliage greyish and
downy. Remontant, it tolerates
pruning better than most others
in this group. Good for making
pot-pourri.
(R) (P) (W) (H) (VF) M&
(AL)   4' × 3'   120 × 90 cm

'Quatre Saisons Blanc Mousseux'

Laffay FRANCE
'Quatre Saisons' sport
A name sometimes applied to

'St Nicholas'

other remontant Moss roses. This
variety is well endowed with
brownish-green moss on both
stems and buds. Otherwise,
except for its white colour, the
same as 'Quatre Saisons'. An
ancient rose.
(R) (P) ● (VF) M& (AL)
4' × 3'   120 × 90 cm

'Rose d'Hivers'

An odd little rose, placed here as
a sibling, for want of another
home. Rather un-Damask-like,
with small, grey foliage and
twiggy, yellowish-green shoots. Its
flowers are small, though quite
shapely; they pale towards the
margins from clear pink to white.
(R) (P) (H) (W) ● ⊙
(SF) (AL)   3' × 3'   90 × 90 cm

'St Nicholas'

James UK 1950
Possibly a chance seedling of an
unknown Damask × *R. gallica*
An odd rose but none the less
attractive for that. Short-growing,
the shrub has downy grey leaves
and vicious thorns. Flowers are
almost single, pink with rich
golden anthers. A charmer when
seen in early evening sunlight. If
not dead-headed, produces good,
attractive hips.
(R) (H) ⊙ (VF) M& (AL)
3' × 3'   90 × 90 cm

'Trigintipetala'
see 'Kazanlik'

'York and Lancaster',
R. × damascena versicolor

Pre-1551
Inconsistent blush-pink and white
flowers. Sometimes mottled,
sometimes with two colours on
different flowers on the same
head, semi-double and scented.
Inclined to be rather untidy. Foliage grey, thorns numerous. More
a collector's rose than of real garden merit.
(S) (P) (H) (W) ● (VF)
(AW)   5' × 4'   1.5 × 1.2 m

'York and Lancaster'

Portlands

Although in some works this group is classified as a sub-group of the Damasks, it is now generally accepted that they have enough unique common characteristics to be grouped together as a separate class. It is true that *R. damascena* and perhaps some of its hybrids played an important part in its early development but, as this class has evolved, its genealogy has become mixed and other influences dominate it, not least that of the Gallicas from where, I believe, several of its subjects have acquired their short, tidy growth habit.

Amongst the ranks of the Portlands are some of the most useful of the old garden roses for, with their accommodating nature and willingness to flower throughout the summer, they make ideal subjects for the smaller garden and for growing in containers.

CLASSIFICATION	
BARB	Class 23
MR9	Class 51
WFRS	Class 28

'Arthur de Sansal'

Cartier FRANCE 1855
A short-growing rose, well foliated and very free-flowering, sadly marred by a strong desire to mildew. Flowers very double, rosette-form, dark crimson-purple and scented.
(R)　(H)　⊙　(VF)　M&　(AL)
3' × 2'　90 × 60 cm

'Blanc de Vibert'

Vibert FRANCE 1847
White, double flowers with a touch of pale lemon in the base and a strong scent. Bush upright, well clothed with Gallica-like foliage. Very useful but quite rare these days.
(R)　(P)　(B)　⊙　(VF)　(AL)
3' × 3'　90 × 90 cm

'Comte de Chambord'

Moreau-Robert FRANCE 1863
'Baronne Prévost' × 'Portland Rose'
An outstanding member of this group with plentiful, large, grey-green foliage which sometimes hides the buds, at least until the flowers are fully open. Flowers are also large – for such a small plant – with many petals of rich warm pink, exuding a strong, heady perfume.
(C)　(P)　(H)　(B)　(VF)　✄
(AW)　3' × 2'　90 × 60 cm

'Comte de Chambord'

'Delambre'

Moreau-Robert FRANCE 1863
Fully double, deep reddish-pink flowers freely borne on a compact plant. Dark green, healthy foliage.
(P)　(H)　(B)　●　⊙　(VF)
(AL)　3' × 2'　90 × 60 cm

'Jacques Cartier'

Moreau-Robert FRANCE 1868
Very much like 'Comte de Chambord', especially in growth habit. Flowers, however, less cupped and much flatter in appearance, both when in bud and fully open; shortish petals give it an attractive, ragged look. The colour is deep pink fading towards the edges to soft pink. It is blessed with a good perfume. Strong, leathery dark green foliage. Note: 'Jacques Cartier' is grown and sold as 'Marquise Boeccella' in the USA and this may well be its correct name.
(C)　(P)　(H)　(B)　●　⊙
(VF)　✄　(AL)
3' × 2'　90 × 60 cm

'Marbrée'

Robert et Moreau FRANCE 1858
An interesting variety. Slightly taller than most of this group, with ample, dark-green foliage. Double flowers opening flat, deep pinkish purple, with paler mottling. Sadly, only slightly fragrant.
(R)　(H)　(P)　(B)　⊙　(SF)
(AL)　4' × 3'　120 × 90 cm

'Mme Knorr'

Verdier FRANCE 1855
Similar in stature to 'Jacques

'Arthur de Sansal'

Cartier' and 'Comte de Chambord', with slightly fewer leaves. Semi-double flowers of bright pink. Has a good strong fragrance.
(R) (H) (P) ☉ (VF) (AL)
3' × 3'   90 × 90 cm

'Pergolèse'

Moreau FRANCE 1860
A very good rose. Small to medium-sized, fully double, scented flowers, of rich purple-crimson sometimes paling to soft lilac-mauve, produced in small spaced clusters on a plant which is well endowed with darkish green foliage. If pruned regularly, will repeat in most seasons. Shows considerable Gallica influence, in my opinion.
(R) (P) (H) ☉ (VF) (AL)
3' × 3'   90 × 90 cm

'Duchess of Portland'

'Portland Rose', 'Duchess of Portland'

ITALY c. 1790
Parentage obscure, said to be 'Quatre Saisons' × 'Slater's Crimson China'
A very useful rose, of ancient origin, important as the progenitor of its race. Single to semi-double flowers freely borne on a short, well foliated plant, cerise-red with pronounced golden stamens. Scented. Useful for group planting but needs dead-heading for best effect.
(R) (P) (H) (B) ☉ (SF)
(AL)   3' × 2'   90 × 60 cm

'Rose du Roi', 'Lee's Crimson Perpetual'

Lelieur FRANCE 1815
'Portland Rose' × *R. gallica officinalis*?
An important rose. See page 00. Sometimes classified a Hybrid Perpetual, but I prefer to place it here. Flowers are double, red mottled purple, loosely formed when open and highly scented. Short growing but slightly straggly. Foliage small, rather pointed and dark green.
(R) (P) (H) ☉ (VF) (AL)
3' × 3'   90 × 90 cm

'Rose du Roi à Fleurs Pourpres', 'Roi des Pourpres', 'Mogador'

1819
Said to be a sport of 'Rose du Roi' An interesting rose, the red-violet-purple flowers are similar to those of 'Rose du Roi' and freely produced throughouot season. Plant short, bushy and slightly straggly.
(C) (P) (H) ☉ (VF) (AL)
3' × 3'   90 × 90 cm

'Rose de Rescht'

Discovered by Miss Nancy Lindsay
This is a fascinating little rose. Very Gallica-like in foliage, the only concession to Damask being a short flower stalk. Highly scented. The flowers, which are rich fuchsia-red in colour with strong purple tints, changing with age to magenta-pink, are tightly-formed rosette shaped, almost pompon and produced in small, upright clusters amid lots of foliage. Well worth a place in any garden. Very remontant especially when young: needs hard pruning to remain so when over five years old.
(R) (H) (P) (B) ● ☉
(VF) (AL)   3' × 2'   90 × 60 cm

'Rose du Roi'

'Jacques Cartier'

'Rose de Rescht'

R. macrantha

FORMS AND HYBRIDS

This species, if indeed it is a true wild rose, has many similarities to *R. gallica*, an exception being its very vigorous, speading habit, probably deriveed from *R. arvensis*. From it has come a number of very useful, delightfully pretty hybrids, all of which have inherited this wide-growing characteristic of their parent. They are all easy to grow but some, sadly, have a proneness to mildew. They are best used for partial ground cover or as specimen shrubs in their own right.

CLASSIFICATION

BARB	Species: Class 1	Hybrids: Class 1
MR9	Species: Class 55	Hybrids: Class 32
WFRS	Species: Class 38	Hybrids: Class 10

R. macrantha

c. 1880
Possibly of Gallica origin
A vigorous spreading and arching shrub bearing many attractive single flowers of clear pink, fading to white, with prominent stamens and a good fragrance. Plentiful dark, veined foliage. Globular red hips in autumn.
(S) (W) (F) (P) (G) (AL)
4′ × 6′   1.2 × 1.8 m

'Chianti'

Austin UK 1967
R. macrantha × 'Vanity'
Semi-double blooms of rich purple-maroon with pronounced golden anthers when fully open, these are produced in clusters on a well-foliated plant. Foliage matt, dark green. Scented.
(S) (P) (H) (W) (MF) ✄
(AL) 5′ × 4′   1.5 × 1.2 m

'Daisy Hill'

Kordes GERMANY 1906
Large, slightly more than single, rich pink flowers, well perfumed. Vigorous, rather wider than high in habit. Abundant dark foliage and globular red hips.
(S) (W) (F) (G) (MF) ≈
(AL) 5′ × 8′   1.5 × 2.5 m

'Harry Maasz'

Kordes GERMANY 1939
'Barcelona' × 'Daisy Hill'
A good but little known spreading rose with dark, greeny-grey foliage. Very vigorous. Single flowers large and cherry-red, paling to pink towards centre, each with a prominent arrangement of stamens. Scented.
(S) (P) (G) ● (W) (MF)
≈ (AL) 5′ × 8′   1.5 × 2.5 m

'Raubritter', 'Macrantha Raubritter'

Kordes GERMANY 1967
'Daisy Hill' × 'Solarium'
A trailing shrub of great charm. Excellent for banks and similar features. Trusses of clear, silvery-pink, semi-double blooms of cupped, Bourbon form. Flowers borne all along rather thorny branches amid dark, greyish-green, matt foliage. Inclined to suffer badly from mildew, but this can be excused as it usually occurs after flowering is finished in late summer.
(S) (P) (G) ● (MF) ≈
M ⚮ (AL) 3′ × 6′   90 × 180 cm

'Scintillation'

Austin UK 1967
R. macrantha × 'Vanity'
Clusters of blush-pink, semi-double flowers on a sprawly, useful-sized plant. Foliage grey-green and plentiful.
(S) (P) (G) (W) ● (SF)
≈ (AW) 4′ × 8′   1.2 × 2.5 m

'Harry Maasz'

'Raubritter'

R. × richardii, R. sancta, 'The Holy Rose'

ABYSSINIA 1897
Probably a Gallica hybrid of considerable antiquity
A low-growing, slightly sprawly plant with dark green, matt-finished leaves. Flowers single, beautifully formed, soft rose pink.
(S) (P) (G) (W) ● ☉ ≈
(MF) (AL)
3′ × 4′   90 × 120 cm

R. macrantha

ROSA Subgenus *Eurosa (Rosa)*

SECTION : *Caninae*

Growth upright and arching. Thorns usually hooked and numerous.
Foliage medium-sized, mostly greyish-green, 7 to 9 leaflets.
Flowers usually in small clusters.
Hips generally oval to round.
Sepals no consistent pattern.

CLASSIFICATION

BARB   Species: Class 1
MR9   Species: Class 55
WFRS   Species: Classes 38 and some 39
For classification of hybrids in this section
see under garden group headings.

SPECIES

R. agrestis
R. × alba
R. biebersteinii
R. britzensis
R. canina
R. collina
R. corymbifera
R. dumales
R. eglanteria
R. glauca
R. inodora
R. jundzillii
R. micrantha
R. mollis

R. orientalis
R. pulverulenta
R. serafinii
R. sherardii
R. sicula
R. stylosa
R. tomentosa
R. villosa

R. villosa duplex
R. waitziana

GARDEN GROUPS

Albas
Dog Roses
Sweet Briars

R. agrestis

S. EUROPE 1878
A tall shrub related to the better
known *R. eglanteria* to which it is
similar in many respects except
that the foliage is without scent
until the leaves are crushed.
(S) (W) (P) ● (AL)
10' × 8'   3 × 2.5 m

ORIGIN AND DISTRIBUTION

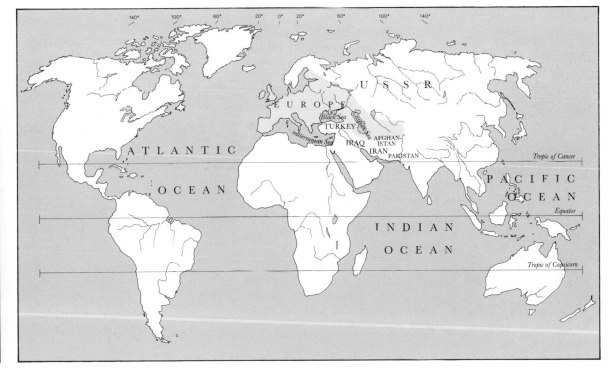

R. canina

'Maxima'

Albas

FORMS AND HYBRIDS

As a garden group the Albas are exceptionally healthy and comprise some of the most beautiful roses from the past. They are mostly of pastel shades and, without exception, are superbly scented. Notes on their history can be found on page 11. Of all the older roses they are perhaps the easiest to grow. They make agreeable specimen shrubs and the quiet charm of their flowers coupled with their greyish-green foliage makes them very compatible with other plants in shrubberies and herbaceous borders.

CLASSIFICATION

BARB	Class 28
MR9	Class 1
WFRS	Class 20

R. × alba,
'White Rose of York'

EUROPE Pre-16th century
A lovely shrub, closely related to the 'dog rose' and in many ways similar, both in shape of flower and growth habit. Single flowers pure white and sweetly scented. Foliage matt-grey and smooth. Stems light green with an average population of stout thorns. Seldom seen in gardens today.
(S) (P) (W) (H) (VF) ≈≈
(AL) 6' × 4' 1.8 × 1.2 m

'Félicité Parmentier'

'Amelia'

Vibert FRANCE 1823
One of the less vigorous Albas with possibly some Damask influence. Large, semi-double, pink flowers up to 3" (8 cm) with pronounced golden anthers. Superb scent. Grey-green foliage. Often confused with and grown as the Damask 'Celsiana'.
(S) (P) (W) (H) (VF) (AL)
4' × 3' 120 × 90 cm

'Blanche de Belgique', 'Blanche Superbe'

Vibert FRANCE 1817
Pure white flowers of good size and shape with a superb perfume. Foliage grey-green and healthy. Growth vigorous, bushy and upright.
(S) (P) (H) (W) ● (VF)
(AL) 6' × 4' 1.8 × 1.2 m

'Celestial', 'Celeste'

Very ancient
Beautiful, semi-double, soft pink flowers combining well with leaden grey foliage. A healthy robust yet charming rose with a superb, 'expensive' perfume.
(S) (W) (P) (H) ● (VF)
(AL) 6' × 4' 1.8 × 1.2 m

'Chloris', 'Rosée du Matin'

Very ancient
Not seen as often as some other Albas, it has the darkest green leaves of all, and is comparatively thornless. Flowers double with incurving petals curling into a tight central button. Colour soft satiny-pink. Scented.
(S) (W) (P) (H) ● (VF)
(AL) 5' × 4' 1.5 × 1.2 m

'Celestial'

'Félicité Parmentier'

Pre-1828
A tidy shrub bearing an abundance of flat, reflexing flowers similar in colour to pink coconut ice. Good healthy dark greyish-green foliage.
(S) (W) (P) (H) ● (VF)
✂ (AL) 4' × 3' 120 × 90 cm

'Jeanne d'Arc'

Vibert FRANCE 1818
Rather sprawly but nevertheless a very useful shrub. Darkish foliage shows off the creamy rather muddled flowers to advantage fading to white in hot sun.
(S) (P) (W) (H) ● (VF)
(AL)
6' × 5' 1.8 × 1.5 m

'Königin von Dänemark', 'Queen of Denmark'

1826
The individual flowers of this rose are slightly smaller than most other Albas and its colour a deeper pink. Shoots somewhat more than typically thorny and the foliage, although greyish-green, is more coarse. Superbly

'Königin von Dänemark'

scented, this rose is an excellent ambassador for the Albas as a whole.

(S) (P) (H) (W) ☉ ●
(VF) ✂ (AL)
5' × 4'   1.5 × 1.2 m

'Maiden's Blush Great', 'Cuisse de Nymphe', 'Incarnata', 'La Virginale', 'La Séduisante'

EUROPE 15th century or earlier
In France this rose is known by the very seductive name 'Cuisse de Nymphe', but, in England, Victorian prudery caused it to be known by the more refined but equally suggestive name 'Maiden's Blush'. This most lovely of roses combines all the best Alba attributes. Blush-pink, it has a refined perfume and is amply clothed with blue-grey leaves. 'Cuise de Nymphe Émue' is the name applied to more richly coloured clones of this variety.

(S) (P) (H) (W) (CL) ●
(VF) ✂ (AW)
6' × 5'   1.8 × 1.5 m

'Maiden's Blush Small'

Kew Gardens UK 1797
Parentage unknown, probably sport of 'Maiden's Blush Great' Similar in all respects to its sister but slightly smaller, both in stature and size of flower.

(S) (P) (H) (W) ☉ ●
(VF) ✂ (AL)
4' × 3'   120 × 90 cm

'Maxima', 'Jacobite Rose', 'Bonnie Prince Charlie's Rose', 'White Rose of York', 'Great Double White', 'Cheshire Rose'

EUROPE 15th century or earlier
Possibly *R. canina* × *R. gallica*
Pure white, sometimes creamy-white, very double flowers in an upright cluster of 6 to 8 blooms. Healthy, grey-green foliage. Sometimes with good narrowly oval shaped autumn fruit.

(S) (P) (W) (H) (VF) (AL)
6' × 4'   1.8 × 1.2 m

'Maiden's Blush'

'Mme Plantier'

'Pompon Blanc Parfait'

'Mme Legras de St Germain'

Early 19th century
A relatively thornless rose. Medium-sized, very double creamy-white flowers produced in large clusters, highly scented, standing up well to inclement weather. Light grey-green foliage, soft and downy to touch. Equally good as shrub or climber, when with support it will attain at least double its usual height.

(S) (P) (W) (CL) ● (N)
(VF) ✂ ≋ (AL)
7' × 6'   2 × 1.8 m

'Mme Plantier'

Plantier 1835
An interesting rose, best classified as an Alba. Probably an Alba/Moschata cross. Capable of climbing, when it will reach perhaps 20' (6 m) into small open trees, but good as lax shrub or pillar rose. Flattish flowers, made up of many convoluted petals, pale cream, changing to pure white, borne in very large clusters on long, sometimes arching stems. Foliage and stems light greyish-green. Few thorns.

(S) (T) (P) ● (N) (CL)
(VF) ✂ ≋ (AL)
12' × 8'   3.5 × 2.5 m

'Pompon Blanc Parfait'

c. 1876
An upright-growing variety not altogether typical of an Alba in growth habit, being rather stubby, apart from the occasional longer shoot. Smooth foliage and short leaf stalks. Scented, pure white flowers produced very freely in small clusters.

(S) (P) (W) (H) ☉ ●
(N) (VF) (AL)
4' × 3'   120 × 90 cm

'Semi-plena'

'Princesse de Lamballe'

An Alba seen mentioned from time to time but with which I am not familiar. Others, too, have become lost in the ravages of time. In fact, in one of my favourite old books, *The Flower Garden*, 1843, some 50 or so Albas are mentioned. Another old Alba which I have not seen is 'A Feuilles de Chauvre'. This is described as having small white semi-double flowers and growing to 3' (90 cm).
(Cultural information not available)

'Semi-plena',
R. × alba suavolens,
R. × alba nivea

EUROPE 16th century or earlier
Semi-double, sweetly scented, pure white flowers with pronounced anthers borne on an upright but graceful bush with matt, grey-green leaves. Good autumn fruit. An underrated form of *R. × alba*, deserving more attention, especially as an informal hedge or lax shrub in the wilder garden.
(S) (P) (W) (H) (CL) (N)
● (VF) (AW)
8' × 5'   2.5 × 1.5 m

R. biebersteinii,
R. horrida

EUROPE AND W. ASIA 1796
A curious, almost gooseberry-like bush with small, white flowers followed by globular red hips.
(S) (P) (F) (W) ☉
2' × 2'   60 × 60 cm

R. britzensis

MIDDLE EAST 1901
A tallish upright shrub with bluish-green, relatively thornless branches and greyish-green leaves. Flowers large, up to 3" (8 cm) across, blush-white and scented. Hips biggish, oval and dark red with sparse bristles.
(S) (F) (W) (P) ●
8' × 6'   2.5 × 1.8 m

'Abbotswood'

R. canina

FORMS AND HYBRIDS

The 'dog rose', *R. canina*, is one of our prettiest native hedgerow plants and I often think it surprising that more hybrids have not been developed from this species. Of those that have come forth, I mention just three here, although, scattered throughout the book, are a number of other roses with lesser amounts of *R. canina* in their make-up. These three are best allowed to have their heads in a woodland or wild garden setting.

CLASSIFICATION	
BARB	Class 1
MR9	Class 26
WFRS	Class 10

R. canina 'Dog Rose'

EUROPE Ancient species
The most common wild rose native to Britain and Europe, also occasionally found naturalized in other temperate areas such as North America. Although a coarse, somewhat awkward shrub, its individual flowers are quite beautiful. Usually pale or blush pink, they sometimes vary from district to district. I have recently found one of pure white. They also have a sweet scent. A distinctive feature is the abundance of orange-red hips produced in autumn. These are rich in vitamin C and used in rose hip syrup; they also make a good wine. Until superseded by 'Laxa', the common dog rose was the most widely used understock in Europe for the production of modern roses. *R. canina inermis* is a fairly thornless form now sometimes used as an understock.
(S) (F) (P) (N) ● (W)
(MF) ≈ (AW)
Up to 10' × 6'   3 × 1.8 m

'Abbotswood',
'Canina Abbotswood'

Hilling UK 1954
R. canina × unknown garden variety
A chance hybrid with scented, double, pink flowers, most useful where a well-armed, dense shrub is needed for a specific purpose.
(S) (P) (N) ● (W) (VF)
≈ (AL)   10' × 6'   3 × 1.8 m

'Andersonii'

Hillier UK 1935
Chance hybrid of *R. canina* × possibly *R. arvensis* or *R. gallica*
A deep pink, larger-flowered form of *R. canina* with fewer thorns and, in my experience, tidier habit.
(S) (F) (P) (N) ● (W)
(VF) ≈ (AL)
8' × 6'   2.5 × 1.8 m

'Pfander',
R. canina 'Pfander',
'Pfander's Canina'

Pfander GERMANY 1954
Not important as a garden plant although it produces an abundance of pale rosy-pink, single flowers and a good crop of bright red, sizeable oval hips. Its main use has been as an understock in the commercial production of roses.
(S) (P) (W) (H) ● (SF)
(F) (AL)   10' × 6'   3 × 1.8 m

'Andersonii'

R. eglanteria (Sweet Briars)

FORMS AND HYBRIDS

Very closely related to the dog rose, *R. eglanteria* is better known for the distinctive apple perfume of its foliage than for its flowers and, while some of its less vigorous hybrids make extremely useful and easy-going garden shrubs, the majority are best let loose to grow naturally. Failing that, they make very good impenetrable hedges, quite formal if pruned or clipped regularly, and a large plus in their favour is a regular crop of bright orangey-red hips each autumn.

CLASSIFICATION	
BARB	Class 29
MR9	Class 18
WFRS	Class 30

R. × collina,
R. corymbifera × R. gallica

CENTRAL EUROPE 1779
A medium growing shrub with sparse, reddish thorns and pale, greyish-green leaves. Flowers mid to pale pink followed by oval, bright red hips.
(S) (F) (W) (P) ● (SF)
≈≈ (AW) 6′ × 4′ 1.8 × 1.2 m

R. corymbifera

E. EUROPE AND ASIA 1838
Obviously related to *R. canina*, which it resembles both in size of plant and in foliage. Flowers are slightly larger in size, creamy white with hints of blush pink. Good orange-red hips, again similar to those of *R. canina*.
(S) (P) (W) (F) ● (SF)
(AL) 10′ × 6′ 3 × 1.8 m

R. × dumales

E. EUROPE, MIDDLE EAST 1872
A medium shrub related to, and similar to, *R. canina*, found

R. eglanteria hips
mostly in mountainous areas in southern Europe. Flowers large, 2½″ (7 cm), clear rose pink, scented. Large oval to round red fruit.
(S) (F) (W) (P) ● (SF)
(AL) 6′ × 5′ 1.8 × 1.5 m

'Amy Robsart'

R. eglanteria,
R. rubiginosa, 'Sweet Briar', 'Eglantine Rose'

EUROPE
Similar to *R. canina*, distinguished by its perfumed foliage and higher density of prickles. Flowers single, smallish and blush-pink. Fruits freely, the hips stay on the bush well into winter. Given its head it will reach 6′ or 7′ (1.8–2 m) in the open and twice this height if grown as a hedgerow plant, which it prefers. In the gar-

den, it is best clipped each year to encourage young growth, for it is the young tips which exude the strongest scent. *R. eglanteria* is a native of Europe and has probably been appreciated for its perfumed leaves since civilization began. Many varieties are listed in 19th-century catalogues, but most of these seem to have disappeared now.

(S) (P) (F) (H) (W) ●
☉ (VF) (AW)
12′ × 8′ 3.5 × 2.5 m

'Amy Robsart'

Penzance UK c. 1894
Dull for most of the year but spectacular in full bloom; a mass of scented, deep pink, almost single blooms in June on a vigorous bush. The hips, which do not always set, can compensate in late summer. Foliage only slightly scented.

(S) (P) (F) (H) W ●
(VF) ≈≈ (AL)
10′ × 8′ 3 × 2.5 m

'Anne of Geierstein'

Penzance UK c. 1894
This is a very vigorous member of its group with sweetly scented foliage and single, gold-centred crimson flowers, followed by oval scarlet hips in autumn.

(S) (P) (F) (H) (W) ●
(VF) ≈≈ (AL)
10′ × 8′ 3 × 2.5 m

'Catherine Seyton'

Penzance UK 1894
Lovely soft pink, single flowers with pronounced golden-yellow stamens. Rich green foliage on a vigorous shrub. Both flowers and foliage are scented. Orange-red hips in autumn.

(S) (P) (W) (F) (H) ●
(VF) (AL) 8′ × 5′ 2.5 × 1.5 m

'Edith Bellenden'

Penzance UK 1895
A good but little known Sweet Briar with well scented foliage. Its scented flowers are single, pale rosy-pink, produced very freely in season and followed by good, oval, red hips.

(S) (P) (W) (H) (F) ●
(VF) (AL) 8′ × 6′ 2.5 × 1.8 m

'Flora McIvor'

Penzance UK c. 1894
A medium tall vigorous shrub bearing single, deep pink flowers with white centres, followed by oval orange-red hips in late summer. Foliage scented, but leaves need to be rubbed between the fingers for this to be noticeable.

(S) (P) (F) (H) (W) ●
(VF) (AL) 8′ × 6′ 2.5 × 1.8 m

'Goldbusch'

Kordes GERMANY 1954
A most useful shrub which I would like to see grown more widely. Large, semi-double flowers produced freely in clusters amid an abundance of lush, light green, healthy, scented foliage. Flowers also well scented.

(S) (P) (H) (W) ● (CL)
(VF) BS⅋ (AL)
8′ × 5′ 2.5 × 1.5 m

'Flora McIvor', and *left:* 'Amy Robsart'

'Goldbusch'

reenmantle'

nzance UK 1894
igle rose-red with golden
mens. Fragrant foliage. A lesser
own Sweet Briar which should
more popular.
(P) (H) (W) ● (VF)
L) 8' × 5' 2.5 × 1.5 m

**lebe's Lip',
ubrotincta',
eine Blanche'**

. Paul UK Introduced 1912
ought to be R. × damascena ×
eglanteria
unknown but probably very
cient origin. Scented foliage.
owers almost single, white,
iged with red at the petal edges.
iorny with coarse foliage. Open
bit of growth.
) (P) (H) (W) ● ⊙
F) (AL) 4' × 4' 1.2 × 1.2 m

**lerbstfeuer',
.utumn Fire'**

ordes GERMANY 1961
lusters of large, semi-double,
irk red, fragrant flowers which
e occasionally repeated in the
itumn; these are produced on a
gorous bush with dark green,
ightly scented foliage. Very

ireenmantle'

large, elongated-pear shaped,
bright orange-red fruit. I have
never understood why this rose is
not better known. Foliage not
scented.
(R) (P) (W) (H) (F) ●
(A) (VF) (AL)
6' × 4' 1.8 × 1.2 m

**'Janet's Pride',
'Clementine'**

Paul UK Introduced 1892
Semi-double flowers, white with
bright pink markings at petal
edges. Scented. Not as vigorous as
some of this group. Coarse foliage
not unattractive. Interesting and
unique.
(S) (H) (P) (W) ● (VF)
(AL) 5' × 4' 1.5 × 1.2 m

'Herbstfeuer'

'Janet's Pride'

'Lady Penzance'

'Julia Mannering'

Penzance UK c. 1895
Bright, clear pink, heavily veined
single flowers. Good, dark foliage,
well scented as are the flowers.
(S) (H) (P) (W) ● (VF)
(AL) 6' × 4' 1.8 × 1.2 m

**'La Belle Distinguée',
'Scarlet Sweetbriar',
'La Petite Duchesse'**

Probably a very old variety. A
most interesting rose, not very tall
and of an upright, bushy habit
with numerous, small, slightly
aromatic leaves. At first sight, the
young bush is reminiscent of the
Centifolia 'Rose de Meaux'.
Flowers almost scarlet, fully
double and produced freely.
(S) (P) (H) ⊙ (MF) (AL)
5' × 4' 1.5 × 1.2 m

'Lady Penzance'

Penzance UK c. 1894
R. eglanteria × R. foetida bicolor
A dense, vigorous shrub, probably
the best known of the Sweet

Briars, with by far the strongest-
scented foliage. Flowers single,
coppery-salmon and pink with
pronounced yellow stamens, followed by bright red hips.
(S) (F) (P) (W) (H) ●
(VF) BS & (AW)
7' × 6' 2 × 1.8 m

'Lord Penzance'

Penzance UK c. 1890
R. eglanteria × 'Harrison's Yellow'
A vigorous, dense shrub with
sweetly scented foliage. Flowers
single, buff-yellow tinged pink,
followed by bright red hips.
(S) (F) (P) (W) (H) (VF)
BS & (AL) 7' × 6' 2 × 1.8 m

'La Belle Distinguée'

'Manning's Blush'

'Lucy Ashton'

Penzance UK 1894
Lovely, single, pure white flowers with the edges of each petal touched with pastel pink. Scented foliage. Makes a good vigorous shrub.
(S) (P) (H) (W) (F) (VF)
(AL) 6' × 5' 1.8 × 1.5 m

'Magnifica'

Hesse GERMANY 1916
'Lucy Ashton' seedling
A splendid shrub rose which should be more widely grown. Semi-double flowers purplish-red, of good size and quality. Foliage only slightly scented but dense and dark green. Makes a very good hedge.
(S) (P) (H) (W) ● (VF)
(AL) 6' × 5' 1.8 × 1.5 m

'Manning's Blush'

c. 1800
A very good shrub rose. Flowers large, white flushed pink, fully double, opening flat, and fragrant. Foliage scented, small and plentiful suggesting *R. pimpinellifolia* influence. The shrub is bushy and dense and, although it is not generally recurrent, I have seen the odd flower in early autumn.
(S) (P) (W) (H) ● ☉
(VF) (AL) 5' × 4' 1.5 × 1.2 m

'Mechtilde von Neuerburg'

Boden GERMANY 1920
Semi-double flowers of an attractive pinkish-red. Foliage slightly aromatic, dark and plentiful. Has a vague Gallica look, belied by its size.
(S) (P) (W) (F) (CL) ●
(VF) ≈≈ (AL)
10' × 8' 3 × 2.5 m

'Meg Merrilies'

Penzance UK c. 1894
An extremely vigorous and prickly shrub rose. Bright crimson semi-double flowers followed by an abundance of good red hips. One of the best of its group, with scented flowers and foliage.
(S) (P) (W) (H) (F) (VF)
≈≈ (AL) 8' × 7' 2.5 × 2 m

'Rose Bradwardine'

Penzance UK 1894
Clusters of single, clear rose-pink flowers on a vigorous, well-proportioned plant with good, dark green, aromatic leaves, good hips.
(S) (P) (H) (W) (F) ●
(VF) (AL) 6' × 5' 1.8 × 1.5 m

R. glauca

R. glauca (R. rubrifolia)

FORMS AND HYBRIDS

CLASSIFICATION	
BARB	Class 1
MR9	Class 54
WFRS	Class 10

R. glauca, R. rubrifolia

EUROPE 1830
A very useful, ornamental shrub with glaucous-purple stems and foliage. Clusters of small, rather inconspicuous, yet rather beautiful flowers of soft mauve-pink. Oval reddish-purple hips in autumn. Useful for flower-arranging, as one or two plants will give an almost unending supply of foliage for this purpose. For many years better known as *R. rubrifolia*. This is botanically erroneous, *R. glauca* now accepted as more accurate.
(S) (F) (N) (H) (W) (P)
(A) ● (SF) (AW)
6' × 5' 1.8 × 1.5 m

R. glauca hips

'Carmenetta'

Central Experimental
Farm CANADA 1923
R. glauca × R. rugosa
Slightly more vigorous and consequently less graceful than its seed parent. Foliage and stems glaucous-purple with numerous small thorns. Hips of similar size and colour, and flowers slightly larger than those of *R. glauca*.
(S) (F) (N) (H) (W) (P)
(A) (SF) ≈≈ (AL)
7' × 7' 2 × 2 m

'Sir Cedric Morris'

Sir Cedric Morris, introduced by Beales UK 1979
R. glauca × R. mulliganii
The identity of the male parent is an assumption by the late Sir Cedric. It was a foundling, growing among other *R. glauca* seedlings at his home, Benton End, Hadleigh, Suffolk, and introduced by me in 1979. A specimen of *R. mulliganii*, or what we know as such, was growing close by, flowering at the same time as *R. glauca*. I was staggered by my first sight of this rose. The glaucous-purple (not as purple as *R. glauca*) foliage is abundant and large. Stems are thick, also glaucous and very thorny. Flowers are evenly spaced in huge clusters and, when established, grow in massed

'Sir Cedric Morris'

profusion. These are single, pure white and display prominent golden anthers. The scent is strong, sweet and pervading. It bears a lavish crop of small, orange hips in autumn.
(S) (F) (T) (P) (W) (A) (N) (VF) ≋ (AL) 30′ × 20′   9 × 6 m

R. inodora, R. graveolens, R. obtusifolia

S. EUROPE 1905
A coarse, vigorous, thorny shrub with scented (Sweet Briar) foliage, ideal for naturalizing or growing into hedgerows, almost a less refined form of R. elanteria. Flowers single, soft pink to blush-white. Oval, bright red hips.
(S) (F) (W) (P) ● (SF) (AL) 8′ × 5′   2.5 × 1.5 m

R. jundzillii, R. marginata

E. EUROPE 1870
A handsome rose. Flowers single, quite large, bright pink, produced freely on a medium-sized, moderately prickly plant bearing ample darkish green, serrated leaves. Smooth bright red round to oval hips in autumn.
(S) (P) (F) ● (SF) (AL) 5′ × 4′   1.5 × 1.2 m

R. micrantha

E. EUROPE 1900
Similar to R. eglanteria but slightly less vigorous with smaller flowers and only slightly scented foliage.
(S) (F) (W) (P) ● (SF) (AL) 6′ × 4′   1.8 × 1.2 m

R. mollis

N. EUROPE 1818
A small, shrubby plant with greyish to red stems and grey, downy foliage. Flowers mid-pink, borne mostly in small clusters of three or four fragrant blooms in mid-summer. Bristly, occasionally smooth, globular hips.
(S) (F) (W) (P) ● (SF) (AL) 3′ × 3′   90 × 90 cm

R. orientalis

S. EUROPE/MIDDLE EAST 1905
A shrubby, short growing plant with slender, hairy branches. Leaves made up of five, seldom seven small, oval leaflets of bright green. Papery flowers of soft pink. Hips small, narrow, oblong and bright red.
(S) (W) (P) (F) (SF) (AL) 2′ × 2′   60 × 60 cm

R. pulverulenta, R glutinosa

MEDITERRANEAN REGIONS Introduced 1821
Short growing and prickly, with small, pinkish-white, single flowers followed by small globular hips. Foliage smells of pine.
(S) (P) (F) ● ⊙ (SF) (AL) 3′ × 3′   90 × 90 cm

R. serafinii

EASTERN MEDITERRANEAN 1914
Small, single, pink flowers on a short-growing, thorny, rather sprawly plant. Rounded, bright orange-red fruit. Foliage serrated and glossy.
(S) (P) (W) (F) ● (SF) (AL) 2′ × 2′   60 × 60 cm

R. sherardii, R. omissa

N. CENTRAL EUROPE 1933
Medium-sized shrub with angular sometimes zig-zag branches and bluish-green foliage. Deep pink flowers usually in small clusters followed by smallish, almost urn shaped hips.
(S) (W) (P) (F) ● (MF) (AL) 6′ × 4′   1.8 × 1.2 m

R. sicula

S. EUROPE AND N. AFRICA C. 1894
A short, free-suckering shrub similar to R. serafinii with reddish wood when young. Foliage is greyish-green and slightly scented as are the flowers which are soft pink in colour. Hips round to oval.
(S) (H) (P) (F) ● (SF) (AL) 3′ × 2′   90 × 60 cm

R. stylosa

EUROPE 1838
An arching shrub with small, narrow, oval, mid-green leaves. Its flowers are in small clusters, and individually are of medium size (1½″, 5 cm). They are blush-pink-ish-white followed by smooth, oval, red hips.
(S) (F) (W) (P) ● (SF) (AL) 10′ × 8′   3 × 2.5 m

R. tomentosa

EUROPE Ancient species
Tall shrub rose, similar in many respects to R. canina. Medium-sized, clear, soft pink flowers with a good display of soft, creamy-yellow stamens. Scented. Foliage matt grey-green, softer in both

R. villosa duplex

R. villosa

R. villosa hips

appearance and touch to that of the dog rose. Bright red, oval fruit. Grows wild in many parts of mainland Europe and the British Isles. I have come upon one or two in Norfolk hedgerows.
(S) (F) (P) (W) ● ≋
(VF) (AL) 10′ × 8′ 3 × 2.5 m

R. villosa,
R. pomifera,
'Apple Rose'

EUROPE/ASIA 1761
Medium-sized shrub with greyish, downy leaves, which are fragrant but this is barely perceptible in my plant. Flowers scented, clear pink and single. Fruit large, orange, apple-shaped and well covered with bristles.
(S) (P) (F) (E) (N) ●
(VF) ≋ (AL)
6′ × 5′ 1.8 × 1.5 m

R . villosa duplex,
R. pomifera duplex,
'Wolly Dodd's Rose'

Discovered in the garden of the Rev. Wolly-Dodd, Cheshire, c. 1900
Similar in most respects to *R. villosa* but slightly shorter in growth. Flowers semi-double and clear pink. Sets hips only rarely but repeats flowers intermittently when growing in good situations, suggesting hybrid origin.
(S) (P) (F) (W) (N) ●
(AL) 5′ × 4′ 1.5 × 1.2 m

R. × waitziana

EUROPE 1874
R. canina × *R. gallica*
A medium to tall shrub with stems and armature similar to those of *R. canina.* Medium sized, deep pink flowers. Fruit seldom sets fully in the cultivated form.
(S) (W) (P) ● (AL)
6′ × 4′ 1.8 × 1.2 m

ROSA Subgenus *Eurosa (Rosa)*

SECTION : *Carolinae*

Growth shortish, upright. Thorns short, usually in pairs, hooked.
Leaves composed of 7 to 9 leaflets – usually good in autumn.
Flowers mostly singly on short stalks.
Hips mostly roundish. Sepals drop when ripe.

CLASSIFICATION

BARB	Species: Class 1	Hybrids: Class 1
MR9	Species: Class 55	Hybrids: Class 54
WFRS	Species: Class 38	Hybrids: Classes 9 and 10

R. nitida

SPECIES

R. carolina
R. carolina alba
R. carolina plena
R. foliolosa
R. × kochiana
R. × mariae-graebnerae
R. nitida
R. palustris
R. virginiana

ORIGIN AND DISTRIBUTION

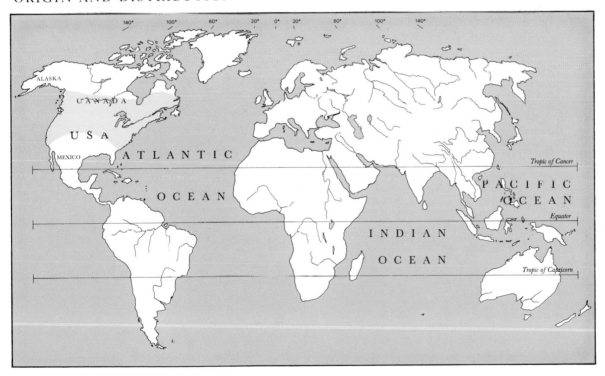

R. foliolosa

R. × kochiana

R. × kochiana autumn foliage

R. carolina

FORMS AND HYBRIDS

CLASSIFICATION – see section heading

R. carolina

N. AMERICA c. 1826
A useful, free-suckering rose –
when on its own roots – with
thin, relatively thornless shoots
and completely thornless lateral
branches. Ample, slightly glossy
foliage. Flowers clear, soft pink
borne solitarily, followed by
roundish, red hips.
(S) (F) (A) (P) ☉ (SF)
(AL)   3′ × 3′   90 × 90 cm

R. carolina alba, R. virginiana alba

Garden discovery USA 1867
But for its single, white flowers, it
is similar in most respects to *R.
carolina.* Slight differences in foliage suggest the influence of genes
from another species or variety.
This difference is most marked on
the underside of leaves, with
more numerous tiny hairs,
making them appear greyer than
those of the pink form.
(S) (F) (A) (P) (W) ● ○
3′ × 2′   90 × 60 cm

R. carolina plena
'The Double Pennsylvanian Rose'

USA c. 1790 (Lynes rediscovery
1955)
Charming, small, double flowers
of clear pink paling to almost
white at the edges. Foliage
smooth and dark green. Makes a

tidy, short-growing, free-suckering plant when on its own roots,
which is perhaps the best way it
can be reproduced and grown.
For more details of the rose and
its rediscovery, see Graham
Thomas's book *Shrub Roses for
Today.*
(S) (P) ☉ ● (AL)
2′ × 2′   60 × 60 cm

R. foliolosa

N. AMERICA 1880
Bright pink, solitary, slightly
ragged flowers amid strange,
narrow, elongated foliage. Free
suckering when on its own roots.
No thorns. Short-growing and tolerant of the wettest soils. Fruits
small, spherical and bright red.
(S) (P) (A) (F) (SF) (AL)
3′ × 3′   90 × 90 cm

R. × kochiana

N. AMERICA 1869
Probably *R. palustris* × *R.
pimpinellifolia*
I have become very fond of this
little shrub. The pleasing, bright
lime-green foliage remains
healthy all summer and changes
to a rich, russet-red in autumn.
Few but strong thorns on stiff,
thin, angular shoots. Flowers solitary and deep rose pink, reminiscent of those of the shrub *Cistus
crispus.*
(S) (P) (W) ☉ (A) (AL)
3′ × 2′   90 × 60 cm

R. × mariae-graebnerae

H. Dabel GERMANY 1900
R. Palustris × *R. virginiana*
A most useful, rare but striking
little shrub. Bright rose pink
flowers, produced at first in profusion and then intermittently
throughout the summer. Sparsely
thorned shoots with semi-glossy
foliage. Small, round hips and
good autumn colour.
(R) (F) (A) (W) (P) (G)
● (AL)   3′ × 2′   90 × 60 cm

R. nitida

N. AMERICA 1807
A free-suckering, short shrub with
thin, prickly stems and small,
dainty, fern-like foliage which
turns to rich crimson in the
autumn. Flowers small, single,
numerous and deep rose pink. A
useful shrub. Hips small, oval and
slightly bristly.
(S) (G) (F) (A) ● ☉
(AL)   3′ × 3′   90 × 90 cm

R. palustris, **'The Swamp Rose'**

N. AMERICA 1726
A vigorous rose with abundant,
mid- to dark-green foliage, reddish stems and an upright habit.
Single, deep pink flowers produced intermittently over a long
season, followed by oval hips in
the autumn. Will tolerate wet,
boggy conditions.
(S) (A) (P) (F) (W) ☉
(AL)   4′ × 3′   120 × 90 cm

R. virginiana

FORMS AND HYBRIDS

CLASSIFICATION – see section heading

R. virginiana

N. AMERICA C. 1807

At home in most soils, this very useful shrub does particularly well in light, sandy conditions. Well foliated with light green glossy leaves, very colourful in autumn. Upright and bushy in growth. Blooms single, rich clear pink with yellow stamens and a good scent. Flowers appear later than in some species, followed by orange, plump, round hips which remain on the plant well into winter.

(S) (H) (P) (W) (A) (F)
● (MF) (AL)
5′ × 3′   150 × 90 cm

'Rose d'Amour'

'Rose d'Amour', 'St Mark's Rose', *R. virginiana plena*

Pre-1870

Taller than *R. virginiana* but the plant has many characteristics in common with the species. Flowers beautiful, quite small, high-centred, and fully double with petals scrolled as they open, pastel pink deepening towards the centre of each bloom. An excellent example can be seen at The Royal Horticultural Society's Gardens at Wisley, Surrey, where it has grown quite tall as a wall plant.

(R) (P) (A) ● (MF)
(WW) (AL)   7′ × 5′   2 × 1.5 m

'Rose d'Orsay'

Flowers, foliage and colour of wood are almost identical to those of 'Rose d'Amour', but its habit of growth and freedom of flower is quite different, being shorter, more branchy and untidy, and flowering for a much longer season. A superb rose, one fault being a reluctance to shed its dead petals, thus dead-heading is important for the best results.

(C) (P) (A) ● (MF)
(WW) (AL)
4′ × 4′   1.2 × 1.2 m

Note

For a number of years I have grown seedlings of *R. virginiana* from imported seed. When young, the plants look identical but in their second year become more varied, some almost thornless, some densely thorny, others growing much taller, with variation in colour and size of hips. The only constant and typical feature is their leaves. At least one of these seedlings – mis-

R. virginiana autumn foliage

takenly sent to an anonymous buyer and presumably lost forever – had a few more than the expected number of petals. One day, perhaps, I will track down the source of this seed. I suspect it comes from somewhere near the eastern Mediterranean.

Mr Graham Thomas explained the difference between 'Rose d'Amour' and 'Rose d'Orsay', and the part he played in their respective identifications, in an article in The Royal National Rose Society's *Rose Annual*, 1977.

ROSA Subgenus *Eurosa* (Rosa)

SECTION : *Cassiorhodon* (*Cinnamomeae*)

Growth mostly shrubby and upright.
Variable from 3′ to 12′, 1 m to 4 m.
Thorns often large and in pairs.
Leaves with 5 to 9, sometimes 11, leaflets.
Flowers mostly in groups, colours usually red or pink
except in R. *wardii* and *rugosa*.
Hips are usually a special feature, large, variously shaped – sepals
held erect when ripe.

SPECIES

R. *acicularis nipponensis*
R. *amblyotis*
R. *arkansana*
R. *banksiopsis*
R. *beggeriana*
R. *bella*
R. *blanda*
R. *californica*
R. *californica plena*
R. *caudata*
R. *coriifolia*
R. × *coryana*
R. *corymbulosa*
R. *davidii*
R. *davurica*
R. *fargesii*
R. *farreri persetosa*
R. *fedtschenkoana*
R. *forrestiana*
R. *gymnocarpa*
R. *hemsleyana*
R. *holodonta*
R. × *kamtchatica*
R. × *kordesii*
R. *latibracteata*
R. × *l'heritierana*

R. *macrophylla*
R. *majalis*
R. *marretii*
R. *maximowicziana*

R. *melina*
R. *micrugosa*
R. × *micrugosa alba*
R. *mohavensis*
R. *moyesii*
R. *multibracteata*
R. *murielae*
R. *nanothamnus*
R. *nutkana*
R. *paulii*
R. × *paulii rosea*
R. *pendulina*
R. *pisocarpa*
R. *prattii*
R. *pyrifera*
R. *rugosa*
R. *rugosa alba*
R. *rugosa rubra*
R. *rugosa typica*
R. *sertata*
R. *setipoda*

R. *spaldingii*
R. *suffulta*
R. *sweginzowii macrocarpa*
R. *ultramontana*
R. *wardii*
R. *webbiana*
R. *willmottiae*
R. *woodsii*
R. *woodsii fendleri*
R. *yainacensis*

GARDEN GROUPS

Boursaults
Kordesii
Rugosas

ORIGIN AND DISTRIBUTION

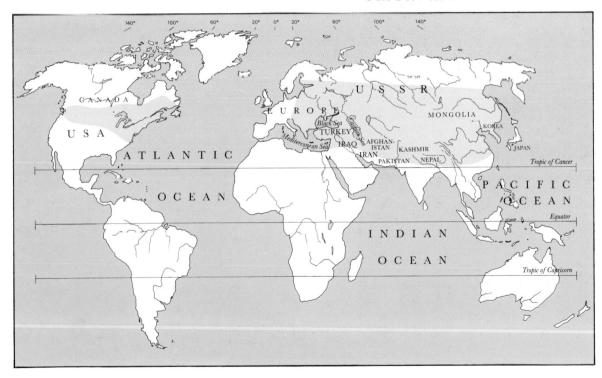

R. suffulta

CLASSIFICATION
BARB   Species: Class 1
MR9   Species: Class 54
WFRS   Species: Class 38
For classification of hybrids
in this section, see under
garden groups.

R. acicularis

N. E. ASIA, N. AMERICA AND
N. EUROPE 1805
Rich pink solitary flowers, 1½"
(4 cm) in diameter, occasionally
in twos or threes. Bright red,
plump, smooth, pear-shaped hips
of approximately 1" (2.5 cm) in
length. Foliage mid-green to grey
on a lax plant with thin shoots, an
abundant amount of variably
sized bristles and few real thorns.
(S) (P) (W) (H) (F) (MF)
(AL)   6' × 5'   1.8 × 1.5 m

R. acicularis nipponensis

JAPAN 1894
Solitary flowers of 1½" to 2"
(4–5 cm), deep pink, almost red,
followed by plump, pear-shaped
hips. Greenish-grey foliage.
Flower stalks and hips bristly,
with few real thorns.
(S) (P) (W) (H) (F) (MF)
(AL)   5' × 4'   1.5 × 1.2 m

R. amblyotis

N. E. ASIA 1917
An upright medium sized shrub
similar to R. majalis to which it is
obviously related. Medium sized,
red flowers followed by medium-
sized, globular to pear-shaped,
red hips.
(S) (F) (W) (P) ● (MF)
(AL)   6' × 4'   1.8 × 1.2 m

R. arkansana

USA 1917
A prickly, short growing dense
shrub with a fairly long flowering
season in mid-summer. Foliage
almost glossy and heavily veined
Flowers 1½" (5 cm), bright red
with yellow stamens, usually in
clusters. Small, round, reddish
hips.
(S) (P) (G) ● (MF) (AL)
2' × 2'   60 × 60 cm

R. banksiopsis

CHINA 1907
I lost my only plant of this in the
severe winter of 1981 and never
saw it flower. It is described in
Hillier's Manual of Trees and
Shrubs as being a medium-sized
shrub with small, rose-red flowers
followed by flask-shaped hips.
(S) (P) (F) (W) (SF) (AL)
5' × 4'   1.5 × 1.2 m

R. beggeriana

CENTRAL ASIA 1869
Not the most auspicious of
species but it has a long flowering
season from mid-summer onwards
when the early flowers, small and
white, are followed by small,
round, orange hips. Stems
covered with lightish coloured,
hooked thorns. Greyish-green
foliage.
(S) (P) (F) (W) ● (A)
(MF)   (AL)   8' × 7'   2.5 × 2 m

R. bella

CHINA 1910
An upright growing rather prickly
shrub with many of the characteristics of R. moyesii. Flowers single,
bright pink. Medium sized flask-
shaped orange fruit.
(S) (W) (P) (F) (S) (MF)
(AL)   8' × 6'   2.5 × 1.8 m

R. blanda,
'Smooth Rose', 'Meadow Rose', 'Hudson Bay Rose', 'Labrador Rose'

N. AMERICA 1773
Subtly similar to R. canina except
for fewer thorns and deeper pink
flowers. Also less vigorous. Hips
rather more pear-shaped than
oval. A few other strains exist but
none of great interest to the
gardener.
(S) (P) (W) (F) ● (MF)
(AL)   5' × 3'   150 × 90 cm

R. californica

N. W. AMERICA 1878
Uncommon in UK. Described in
McFarland's Modern Roses, as up

to 8' (2.5 m) with corymbs of
single pink flowers 1½" (4 cm)
across. A large specimen is growing at the John Innes Institute
near Norwich, but I have not seen
it flowering.
(S) (P) (SF) (AL)
8' × 4'   2.5 × 1.2 m

R. californica plena

Date attributed 1894
An excellent garden shrub with
lilac-pink flowers, shaped rather
like the individual bloom of a
semi-double hollyhock. The
shrub is healthy, upright in habit

R. acicularis nipponensis

R. acicularis nipponensis hips

and amply foliated with grey-green leaves. The wood is dark and has few thorns. Hips rounded orange-red.

(S) (P) (W) (F) ● (MF) (AL)   8′ × 5′   2.5 × 1.5 m

R. californica plena

R. californica plena hips

R. × coryana

R. caudata

CHINA 1907

Very similar to the better known *R. setipoda*, to which it could well be related. However, since it is usually listed as a separate species, I have followed that rule. It forms a dense shrub with thick, well armed branches. Flowers, produced in large clusters, are pale pink, followed by flagon-shaped, bristly hips.

(S) (P) (W) (F) ● (SF) (AL)   7′ × 5′   2 × 1.5 m

R. coriifolia froebelii, *R. dumetorum laxa*, 'Laxa'

EUROPE 1890

A dense shrubby rose, with greyish-green wood and foliage. Moderately thorny, flowers white, hips plump but oval. Of little use ornamentally but invaluable and widely used, especially in Europe, as an understock under the name 'Laxa'. Produces fewer suckers than most other understocks.

(S) (W)   5′ × 4′   1.5 × 1.2 m

R. × coryana

Cambridge Botanical Gardens
UK 1926

R. macrophylla × *R. roxburghii*
A medium-sized shrub with leanings towards *R. roxburghii* in appearances, and an ideal woodland subject. Large, single, deep pink flowers produced in early summer. Interesting but not significant.

(S) (P) (W) (SF) (AL) 6′ × 4′   1.8 × 1.2 m

R. corymbulosa

CHINA 1908

A medium, rather lax, almost thornless, thin-stemmed shrub;

R. californica

R. forrestiana

small leaves, with slightly hairy undersides, changing from green to deep purple in autumn. Flowers single, deep pinkish-red, with a white eye. Hips medium-sized, rounded and red.

(S) (P) (W) (F) (AL)
5′ × 4′   1.5 × 1.2 m

R. davidii

CHINA 1908

A useful, later (mid June) flowering species with soft pink flowers borne, sometimes in clusters, along the length of each stem, sometimes singly. Upright and vigorous, with heavily veined, light green foliage and orange-red flagon-shaped hips in autumn.

(S) (P) (F) (W) ● (MF) (AL)   10′ × 5′   3 × 1.5 m

R. davurica

N. CHINA AND ASIA 1910

A shortish, averagely thorned shrub with small leaves and medium-sized, pink flowers followed by small, oval hips.

(S) (F) (W) (P) ● (AL) 3′ × 3′   90 × 90 cm

R. farreri persetosa, 'Threepenny Bit Rose'

CHINA 1914

A charming, sprawly shrub with fine, fern-like leaves which turn purple and crimson in the autumn. Hips, produced in profusion, are bright orange-red. These features, together with its habit of growth, are perhaps more important than its small lilac-pink flowers. Shoots biscuit brown, densely covered in minute but fairly harmless thorns, giving an almost mossed effect. Rather enjoys partial shade.

(S) (F) (G) (W) (P) (A) ●   (AW)   5′ × 5′   1.5 × 1.5 m

R. fedtschenkoana

S. E. EUROPE/ASIA 1880

A most useful shrub with single white, papery flowers, produced at first in profusion then intermittently throughout summer. Foliage light grey-green and feathery. Sparsely bristled oval-to-pear-shaped hips. Slowly becoming better known and more widely grown – as indeed it should be.

(R) (P) (H) (W) (A) (MF) (AW)   5′ × 4′   1.5 × 1.2 m

R. forrestiana

W. CHINA 1918

Pinkish-crimson flowers with creamy-buff anthers freely produced in small clusters, followed by bottle-shaped red hips. Ample, purplish-green foliage. Growth

also purplish green, arching, dense and vigorous.
(S) (P) (F) (G) (W) (SF) (AW) 7′ × 7′ 2 × 2 m

R. gymnocarpa

N. AMERICA 1893
Graceful, vigorous shrub with moderately thorny, wiry shoots and numerous small roundish leaves. Flowers small, single, pale pink. Small, red, pear-shaped, smooth hips in autumn. My stock came direct from seed collected by a friend in Nova Scotia where it grows in the wild.
(S) (F) (P) (W) ● (MF) (AL) 8′ × 10′ 2.5 × 3 m

R. hemsleyana

CHINA 1904
Vigorous shrub similar to *R. setipoda*. Medium-sized, pink, single flowers borne in clusters, followed by bottle-shaped, bristly, orange-red hips.
(S) (F) (P) (W) ● ☉ (AL) 5′ × 4′ 1.5 × 1.2 m

R. × kamtchatica, R. ventenatiana

Kamchatka USSR c. 1770
R. rugosa × *R. amblyotis*?
Often seen listed as a form of *R. rugosa*, but despite an obvious affinity to that species, distinct. Flowers smallish, single, pink touching cerise. Slightly scented. Mid-green foliage; stems well armed but less so than *R. rugosa*. Hips small to medium, round and bright red.
(C) (W) (F) (P) (H) (A) ● (MF) (AL) 7′ × 6′ 2 × 1.8 m

R. × kordesii

FORM AND HYBRIDS

Most of these hybrids make excellent short climbers or specimen shrubs. If they have a fault it is a distinct dislike of orderliness, but this is easily overlooked when one considers that they will stand even the coldest climate and will flower on and on throughout every summer.

CLASSIFICATION

BARB Species and hybrids: Class 1
MR9 Species and hybrids: Class 45
WFRS Species and hybrids: Classes 2 and 14

R. × kordesii

Kordes GERMANY 1950
'Max Graf' seedling
This rose was never officially introduced by Herr Kordes but he used it extensively in the breeding of some very important hybrids. Offspring from this rose are particularly disease-resistant. Flowers double pinkish-red in small clusters. Foliage dark green, growth spreading foliage.
(R) ● (P) (AL) 5′ × 5′ 1.5 × 1.5 m

'Champlain'

Department of Agriculture CANADA 1982
R. kordesii × seedling × ('Red Dawn' × 'Suzanne')
Large, double, dark red flowers with a moderate fragrance. Foliage light green, small. Bushy growth. Amply armed with soft-yellow thorns. Very hardy.
(R) ● ☉ (H) (MF) (G) (AL) 4′ × 4′ 1.2 × 1.2 m

'Dortmund'

Kordes GERMANY 1955
Seedling × *R. kordesii*
Large, single, crimson flowers with a pale, almost white, central eye. Produced in large clusters on a vigorous, thorny plant with dark green foliage.
(R) (P) (N) ● (CL) (SF) (AW) 8′ × 6′ 2.5 × 1.8 m

'Hamburger Phoenix'

Kordes GERMANY 1954
R. kordesii × seedling
Clusters of large, semi-double, rich crimson flowers on a spreading, vigorous shrub or short climber with dark green foliage. Hips good in autumn.
(C) (P) (F) (N) (CL) ● (MF) (AL) 8′ × 5′ 2.5 × 1.5 m

'Henry Kelsey'

Department of Agriculture CANADA 1984
R. kordesii × seedling
Double, mid-red fragrant flowers in clusters on a wide-growing shrub with dark green, glossy foliage. Very hardy.
(R) ● ☉ (G) (MF) (AL) 4′ × 5′ 1.2 × 1.5 m

'John Cabot', and *above: R. × kordesii*

'John Cabot'

Department of
Agriculture CANADA 1978
R. kordesii × seedling
Clusters of large, fully double,
soft red, fragrant blooms amid
abundant light green foliage.
Growth vigorous and upright.
Extremely hardy. A useful rose.
(R) ● ☉ (H) (MF) (G)
(AL) 5′ × 4′ 1.5 × 1.2 m

'Karlsruhe'

'Parkdirektor Riggers'

'William Baffin'

'Karlsruhe'

Kordes GERMANY 1950
R. kordesii seedling
Large clusters of slightly fragrant,
deep rosy-pink, fully double
flowers cupped until fully open
and then flat. These repeat regularly each summer. Foliage plentiful, mid-green, glossy. Growth
vigorous, sprawling. An excellent,
little-known rose.
(R) (G) (CL) (T) (N) ●
(SF) (AL) 8′ × 6′ 2.5 × 1.8 m

'Leverkusen'

Kordes GERMANY 1954
R. kordesii × 'Golden Glow'
Semi-double, lemon-yellow
flowers which, when open, have
attractively ragged edges. Sweetly
scented, continues blooming all
summer. Attractive, glossy, light
green, deeply serrated foliage. As
so often with Kordes roses, rudely
healthy.
(C) (P) (N) (CL) ● (MF)
(AW) 10′ × 8′ 3 × 2.5 m

'Parkdirektor Riggers'

Kordes GERMANY 1957
R. kordesii × 'Our Princess'
A very good climbing rose. Large
clusters of deep red to crimson,
almost single, firm textured
flowers. Plant upright and
vigorous. Foliage health, dark
green and glossy.
(C) (P) (N) ● (CF) (SF)
(AL) 10′ × 6′ 3 × 1.8 m

'Raymond Chenault'

Kordes GERMANY 1960
R, kordesii × 'Montezuma'
Large, semi-double blooms of
bright red borne in clusters.
Fragrant. Foliage dark green and
glossy. Growth very vigorous,
spreading and bushy.
(R) ● (N) (G) (CL) (MF)
≈≈ (AL) 10′ × 8′ 3 × 2.5 m

'William Baffin'

Department of
Agriculture CANADA 1983
R. kordesii seedling
Clusters of large, semi-double to
double deep clear pink blooms on
a vigorous, wide-growing shrub
with abundant, glossy, mid-to-
dark green foliage. A marvellous
sight when, as a mature plant, it is
seen in full flush. Very hardy. Can
also be used as a climber.
(R) ● (N) (AL)
8′ × 6′ 2.5 × 1.8 m

R. latibracteata

CHINA 1936
Similar in most respects to
R. webbiana which is better
known but the lilac-pink flowers
are borne in small corymbs rather
than solitarily. Grey-blue foliage
as in *R. webbiana* but slightly
larger. Growth habit arching making a broad, solid plant. Hips
broadly bottle-shaped.
(S) (P) (H) (W) ● ☉
(AL) 7′ × 7′ 2 × 2 m

'Leverkusen'

Boursaults

FORMS AND HYBRIDS

The Boursaults are but few and until recently it was assumed that *R. × l'heritierana*, from which they descend, had occurred from a cross between *R. pendulina* and *R. chinensis*. Certainly their smooth stems, dark wood and leaf shape point in that direction. However, authoritative opinion varies, and chromosome counts seem to prove conclusively an error in this assumption. Thus I have placed them here.

CLASSIFICATION

BARB   Species and hybrids: Class 1
MR9   Species and hybrids: Class 4
WFRS   Species: Class 39   Hybrids: Class 22

'Amadis'

'Blush Boursault'

'Mme de Sancy de Parabère'

R. × l'heritierana

Probably EUROPE Pre-1820
Unarmed cane-like stems, variable from green to reddish-brown. Foliage dark green, rather blackberry-like, but smooth. Flowers double, opening flat, deep pinkish-red to blush-white. Smooth round hips, when and if they set.
(S) (W) (P) (A) (AL)
10' × 8'   3 × 2.5 m

'Amadis', 'Crimson Boursault'

Laffay FRANCE 1829
A climbing thornless rose with long, arching shoots changing from green when young to almost chocolate-purple when mature. Smooth dark green foliage. Flowers semi-double, deep reddish purple, rather ragged when open, produced both singly and in small clusters. Said to repeat but my plant has not done so to date.
(S) (P) (A) (SF) (AL)
10' × 6'   3 × 1.8 m

'Blush Boursault', 'Calypso', 'Rose de l'Isle'

1848
Probably FRANCE
Flowers fully double, opening flat, with slightly ragged petals of pale blush-pink. Long, arching, thornless branches less purple than 'Amadis' but reddening with age. Foliage, dark green and plentiful, gives good display of autumn colour.
(S) (P) (A) (SF) (AL)
15' × 10'   4.5 × 3 m

'Mme de Sancy de Parabère'

Bonnet FRANCE c. 1874
A beautiful rose of rich pink. Fully double, opening flat with the elongated outer layer of petals giving the effect almost of a ragged rose within a rose. Foliage handsome, darkish green. Thornless stems deepening from green to soft greeny-brown as they mature.
(S) (P) (A) ● (MF) (AL)
15' × 10'   4.5 × 3 m

'Morlettii', *R. inermis morlettii*, *R. pendulina plena*

Morlet FRANCE 1883
Slightly less vigorous than other Boursaults although foliage and stems similar. Foliage particularly colourful in autumn. Flowers deep pinkish-magenta, almost double, rather ragged when fully open.
(S) (P) (A) (SF) (AL)
8' × 6'   2.5 × 1.8 m

R. macrophylla

FORMS AND HYBRIDS

The few hybrids that have come forth from this Himalayan species are all robust and vigorous. With the odd exception, these are perhaps better grown for the size and quality of their hips rather than for any intrinsic beauty of their flowers.

CLASSIFICATION

BARB	Species and hybrids: Class 1	
MR9	Species: Class 55	Hybrids: Classes 46 and 54
WFRS	Species: Class 38	Hybrids: Classes 10 and 17

'Auguste Roussel'

R. macrophylla

HIMALAYAS 1818
Medium-tall shrub with bright, cerise-pink flowers amid large, purplish-green leaves. Wood purple and smooth. Large orange fruits hang conspicuously, rather like small, slim bristly pears.
(S) (P) (F) (W) (SF) (AL)
10′ × 4′   3 × 1.2 m

'Arthur Hillier'

Hillier UK 1938
R. macrophylla × *R. moyesii*
An erect rose of considerable vigour. Masses of small clusters of large, single, rosy-crimson flowers with prominent yellow stamens heavily laden with pollen. These start in mid-June and last well into July. Each flower is slightly concave. A special feature in autumn are the fiery-red hips which are in drooping clusters and flask-shaped. Foliage dark green with a dull gloss.
(S) (P) (W) (F) ● (SF)
(AL)   10′ × 6′   3 × 1.8 m

'Auguste Roussel'

Barbier FRANCE 1913
R. macrophylla × 'Papa Gontier'
A vigorous climber or large arching shrub with large, semi-double, bright pink flowers. Apart from its flowers, which are beautiful, this shrub lacks the character of others in its group, especially in fruit.
(S) (P) (F) ● (MF) (AL)
15′ × 8′   4.5 × 2.5 m

'Doncasterii'
R. doncasterii

E. Doncaster UK 1930
R. macrophylla seedling
A good rose, more arching than others of its type and less tall. Inherits dark, plum-coloured wood and purplish-green leaves

'Morlettii'

'Doncasterii'

'Doncasterii' hips

from *R. macrophylla*, together with large, pear-shaped hips. Flowers pink verging on red.

(S) (P) (F) (W) ● (AL)
6′ × 4′   1.8 × 1.2 m

'Master Hugh'

L. M. Mason UK 1966
R. macrophylla seedling
This rose provides us with some of the largest hips of all. They are orange-red in colour and flagon-shaped. The shrub is similar in other respects to its parent, except that its leaves are larger and it grows more vigorously.

(S) (P) (F) ● (W) (AL)
15′ × 8′   4.5 × 2.5 m

'Rubricaulis',
R. macrophylla rubricaulis

HIMALAYAS Of recent introduction by Hillier
Similar to the species but wood darker and often covered in a greyish bloom. Said to be less hardy but I have no experience to prove this.

(S) (F) (W) ● (AL)
8′ × 4′   2.5 × 1.2 m

'Master Hugh'

R. melina

R. majalis,
R. cinnamomea,
'Cinnamon Rose'

N. E. EUROPE 17th century or earlier
An upright-growing, yet branching rose with slightly downy greyish-green foliage and mauvish-purple stems. The flowers, which are variable from pale to mid-pink, occur quite early in summer or, in good seasons, late spring. Medium-sized round fruit.

(SP) (F) (W) (SF) (AL)
6′ × 4′   1.8 × 1.2 m

R. majalis plena,
R. cinnamomea plena,
'Rose du Saint Sacrement',
'Whitsuntide Rose'

N. AND W. ASIA Cultivated pre-1600
This is the double form of *R. majalis* and is the same in all respects except for its flowers, which are rather lovely for a short time in late spring to early summer. More commonly known as *R. cinnamomea plena*.

(SP) (F) (W) (AL)
6′ × 4′   1.8 × 1.2 m

R. × micrugosa

R. marretii

MIDDLE EAST 1908
An upright growing shrub with purple wood and medium sized, mid-green foliage. Flowers mid- to pale pink usually in small

clusters. Hips red, round and of medium size.

(S) (F) (W) (P) ● (SF)
(AL)   6′ × 4′   1.8 × 1.2 m

R. maximowicziana

N. E. ASIA 1905
Single white flowers in small spaced clusters, sometimes hidden among soft-textured, serrated foliage. Not tall. Mine, after three years, admittedly in a shady position, has reached 5′ (1.5 m), bushy with thin, sparsely spiny stems with many lateral branches on which flowers are produced. Perhaps a rogue hybrid, as none of its characteristics fit any other description I have found. Similar is *R. fedtschenkoana*.

(S) (P) (W) ● (AL)
6′ × 4′   1.8 × 1.2 m

R. × micrugosa alba

R. melina

N. AMERICA 1930
A short-growing, dense shrub
with large, soft rose pink flowers.
I have not met this rose as a
mature shrub. As a maiden, it has
greyish-green foliage.
(S) (P) (W) ● (AL)
3' × 3'   90 × 90 cm

R. × micrugosa

Foundling at Strasbourg Botanical
Institute c. 1905
R. roxburghii × *R. rugosa*
A dense, medium-sized shrub
with rugose foliage. Large, delicate, single, pale pink flowers
followed by stubbled, round,
orange-red hips.
(R) (H) (W) (F) (P) (A)
(MF) ● ☉ (AL)
5' × 4'   1.5 × 1.2 m

R × micrugosa alba

Dr Hurst UK 1910
Very beautiful white flowers with
pronounced stamens. Continuity
of bloom should encourage its
wider use. More upright in habit
than its parent *R. micrugosa*, but
otherwise similar in growth.
(R) (H) (W) (F) (P) (A)
● ☉ (MF (AL)
5' × 4'   1.5 × 1.2 m

R. mohavensis

S. USA c. 1930
A short-growing, dense shrub
with numerous slender stems and
an average population of thorns.
Small, mid-green leaves. Flowers
small, mid-to-soft pink. Rounded
red hips. Enjoys moisture.
(S) (F) (W) (P) ● ≈
(AL)   3' × 3'   90 × 90 cm

R. moyesii

FORMS AND HYBRIDS

It is not surprising that breeders, from time to time, have experi-
mented with this rose as a parent; for, as a species, it is one of the
best and most garden-worthy of all the wonderful wild to have
come to us from the wilds of China. I have selected here about a
dozen; representing, perhaps, the best of its several hybrids. Every
garden should have at least one, for not only do they produce a
good crop of flowers but, with one or two notable exceptions
where fruit is not important anyway, they all bear a heavy crop of
very attractive hips each autumn.

CLASSIFICATION

BARB	Species and hybrids: Class 1	
MR9	Species: Class 55	Hybrids: Class 33
WFRS	Species: Class 38	Hybrids: Class 10

R. moyesii

W. CHINA Discovery 1890, intro
duction 1894
Despite the very attractive deep
crimson flowers and distinctive
dark green foliage, it is undoubtedly the fruit that makes this rose
and its hybrids so popular.
Although the hips are not as large
as in some other species, the plant
can usually be relied upon to
yield a large crop each year. Produced pendulously, they are
orange-red and flagon shaped,
with a five-pointed crown of
sepals at the bottom. As a shrub it
is vigorous and solid but if
allowed to grow for too long
without pruning it gets gaunt and
coarse at the base. I have seen this
rose making a splendid, if
unusual, wall plant. Beware of
growing this rose from seed or
purchasing plants grown by this
means as many are sterile and
never produce hips.
(S) (P) (W) (F) ● ≈
(AL)   10' × 6'   3 × 1.8 m

'Eos'

R. moyesii, 'Pink Form'

CHINA
Similar in most respects to *R.
moyesii* except for the colour of
the flower which is, of course,
pink. Several variable forms seem
to have been distributed, presumably from seedlings, of *R. moyesii*
or its forms, raised deliberately or
by chance.
(S) (P) (W) (F) ● (AL)
10' × 6'   3 × 1.8 m

'Eddie's Crimson'

Eddie CANADA 1956
'Donald Prior' × *R. moyesii* hybrid
A double deep blood-red with
Moyesii-like foliage. In full flush
it makes an impressive shrub.
Upright in growth. Fruit not so
obviously Moyesii, spherical in
shape and deep red in colour.
(S) (P) (W) (F) (CL) ●
(SF) (AL)   10' × 6'   3 × 1.8 m

'Eddie's Jewel'

Eddie CANADA 1962
'Donald Prior' × *R. moyesii*
hybrid
Significant, in that I can vouch for
this rose repeating in good seasons. Each double flower bright
brick-red. Shoots dark browny-
red. Foliage in Moyesii mould.
Achieved from same cross as
'Eddie's Crimson'. In the first edition of *Classic Roses* I indicated
that I had not seen fruit set on
this variety. I now correct this: my
plant has now produced a good
crop of plump orange-red hips for
the last three years.
(R) (P) (W) (F) (CL) ●
(SF) (AL)   8' × 6'   2.5 × 1.8 m

'Eos'

Ruys USA 1950
R. moyesii × 'Magnifica'
An attractive shrub rose, very profuse in bloom with medium-sized,
almost single flowers of bright
pinkish-red with white centres,
produced all along rather stiff but
arching stems. Scented. Sometimes fails to set fruit.
(S) (F) (P) (W) (CL) ●
≈ (AL)   8' × 5'   2.5 × 1.5 m

'Fred Streeter'

Jackman UK 1951
R. moyesii seedling
A denser shrub than any other
Moyesii hybrid, with arching,
spindly growth, bearing bright
pink, single flowers along its
length, followed by pendulous,
large red hips.
(S) (P) (W) (F) (CL) ●
(SF) (AL) 8′ × 6′ 2.5 × 1.8 m

'Geranium'

Royal Horticultural Society UK
1938
R. moyesii seedling
The most widely grown and best
known of the Moyesii hybrids. Its
single flowers are a beautiful,
bright orange-red with a waxy
texture. Its creamy anthers often
powder the petals with pollen.
Less vigorous than its parent and
more angular in growth with
lighter green leaves, paler stems,
and larger, equally shapely but
less deep red fruits.
(S) (F) (P) (W) (CL) ●
(AL) 8′ × 5′ 2.5 × 1.5 m

'Geranium'

'Highdownensis'

Hillier UK 1928
R. moyesii seedling
Arching branches of single, light
crimson flowers on a bushy,
dense, tall shrub with ample
foliage. Fruit large, reddish-plum
coloured and flagon-shaped.
(S) (F) (P) (W) (CL) ●
≈≈ (AL) 8′ × 6′ 2.5 × 1.8 m

'Highdownensis' hips

'Hillierii'

'Hillieri',
R. × pruhoniciana hillieri

Hillier UK 1920
R. moyesii × *R. multibracteata*
Very dark red flowers, single with
prominent anthers. Fewer thorns
than others of this group with
smaller and perhaps fewer leaves.
Growth angular but stiff.
Vigorously graceful. Not all the
flowers set their fruit, which is
large, orange and flagon-shaped.
(S) (P) (W) (F) ● ≈≈
(AL) 8′ × 6′ 2.5 × 1.8 m

'Marguerite Hilling'

Hilling UK 1959
'Nevada' sport
This is a splendid, pink sport of
the well-known 'Nevada', which it
fully resembles except for its soft
rose-pink colour. In first flush this
rose is very showy and, like its
parent, very floriferous from late
May to mid-June, with intermittent flowers throughout the
remainder of summer, and well
into autumn.
(R) (P) (W) (H) (CL) ≈≈
(MF) (AL) 8′ × 7′ 2.5 × 2 m

'Nevada'

P. Dot SPAIN 1927
R. moyesii hybrid?
A superb shrub. Large, single,
slightly blowsy flowers produced
in profusion on a vigorous, dense
but tidy shrub in late May and
early June. Plentiful light green
foliage. Dark chocolate-brown
stems with sparse thorns. Usually
flowers on intermittently
throughout the summer, and
often gives a good display in the
autumn. Opinions vary as to its
proper parentage. It has some
affinity in looks with *R. moyesii*
and is usually placed here – a
course that I follow despite tending to agree with Mr Jack
Harkness, who suggests it might
be better placed among the *R.
pimpinellifolia* hybrids.
(R) (P) (W) (H) (CL) ≈≈
(MF) (AL) 8′ × 7′ 2.5 × 2 m

'Sealing Wax'

Royal Horticultural Society UK
1938

R. moyesii hybrid
A fine hybrid, very similar in habit and foliage to 'Geranium' except for its bright pink flowers. Fruit bright red in the expected flagon shape.
(S) (P) (W) (F) (CL) ●
(AL) 8' × 5' 2.5 × 1.5 m

'Wintoniensis'

Hillier UK 1928
R. moyesii × *R. setipoda*
Of interesting parentage, giving rise to a vigorous shrub which romps away, both in height and girth. Its light grey foliage is slightly scented. Its flowers are single, deep pink and its fruit are large and very hairy.
(S) (F) (P) (W) (CL) ●
(SF) (AL) 12' × 10' 3.5 × 3 m

R. fargesii

Veitch UK 1913
Very similar in stature to *R. moyesii* but slightly less vigorous. Flowers more pink than red and foliage smaller. Hips of the same shape but are usually larger and perhaps fewer.
(S) (F) (P) (W) (CL) ●
≈ (AL) 8' × 5' 2.5 × 1.5 m

R. holodonta

CHINA 1908
Glowing pink flowers in small clusters on an upright-growing, well-armed plant. Hips pendulous and flagon-shaped. This name is sometimes attributed to all pink forms of *R. moyesii*. It is now accepted that *R. holodonta* is distinct and more akin to *R. davidii* than to *R. moyesii*. See Bean, *Trees and Shrubs Hardy in the British Isles*, Vol. IV, 8th edition, 1981.
(S) (P) (W) (F) ≈ (AL)
10' × 6' 3 × 1.8 m

R. multibracteata

FORMS AND HYBRID

CLASSIFICATION

BARB	Species: Class 1	Hybrid: Class 1
MR9	Species: Class 55	Hybrid: Class 54
WFRS	Species: Class 38	Hybrid: Class 10

R. multibracteata

Top and *above*: 'Nevada'

'Cerise Bouquet'

R. multibracteata

CHINA 1908
An elegant shrub with fern-like leaves from thick stems with numerous, spiky thorns, usually in pairs. Single flowers are produced in bunched clusters, often at the ends of arching shoots; these are lilac-pink and produced on thin petioles which have alternating bracts along their length. Has a long flowering season although is never very floriferous. The small hips, which retain their sepals, are rounded, bright red and sparsely bristly.
(R) (F) (P) (W) ● (AL)
6′ × 5′   1.8 × 1.5 m

'Cerise Bouquet'

Kordes GERMANY 1958
R. multibracteata × 'Crimson Glory'
As so often with roses, one takes them for granted until a specimen is seen at its very best. At Helmingham Hall, Suffolk, Lord and Lady Tollemache have one shrub of this variety at least 12′ (3.5 m) high and 12′ (3.5 m) wide, standing alone in an open part of their garden and quite spectacular in full flush. Double bright cerise flowers are produced in profusion on long, arching branches amid dense greyish-green foliage.
(S) (P) (W) (CL) ● ≋
(SF) (AL)
12′ × 12′   3.5 × 3.5 m

R. murielae

W. CHINA 1904
A rare, medium growing, widish shrub with thin stems of reddish brown and mid-green to greyish foliage. White flowers in small corymbs. Hips small, flagon-shaped and a bright orange red.
(S) (F) (W) (P) ● (AL)
8′ × 6′   2.5 × 1.8 m

R. nanothamnus

CHINA, CENTRAL ASIA 1936
A close relative of the better-known R. webbiana and similar to this species in all respects except for its slightly smaller flowers and foliage.
(S) (P) (H) (W) ● ☉
(AL)   6′ × 6′   1.8 × 1.8 m

R. nutkana

FORMS AND HYBRIDS

The two hybrids of this American species described here are seldom seen outside botanical gardens and rose collections. This is a pity for both are easy-going and garden-worthy, and will do well in almost any garden.

CLASSIFICATION

BARB	Species: Class 1
MR9	Species: Class 37
WFRS	Species: Class 10

R. nutkana

N. AMERICA 1876
A strong-growing shrub liberally endowed with dark greyish-green foliage and strong, relatively thornless, nut-brown stems. The single flowers are clear lilac pink these are followed by smooth, rounded fruit left untouched by birds until well into winter. One of my favourite species.
(S) (P) (W) (F) ● ☉
(SF) (AL)   6′ × 4′   1.8 × 1.2 m

'Cantab'

Hurst UK 1939
R. nutkana × 'Red Letter Day'
A lovely rose which should be more widely used where a medium-sized shrub is required. The flowers which appear in July are large, single and deep pinkish-lilac with pronounced creamy-yellow stamens. These are followed by plumply-oval hips of clear deep red when ripe, which remain on the plant well into winter. The dark stems are moderately armed and the foliage greyish-green.
(S) (P) (W) (F) ● (AL)
8′ × 5′   2.5 × 1.5 m

'Schoener's Nutkana'

Schoener USA 1930
R. nutkana × 'Paul Neyron'
Vigorous shrub with large, single, clear rose-pink flowers. Quite fragrant. Growth arching but dense, with few thorns on darkish wood with grey-green foliage.
(S) (P) (H) (W) (F) ●
(AL)   5′ × 4′   1.5 × 1.2 m

R. × paulii, R. rugosa repens alba see 'Paulii'

R. × paulii rosea see 'Paulii Rosea'

R. pendulina, R. alpina, 'Alpine Rose'

EUROPE c. 1700
Arching, reddish-purple stems form a short, slightly spreading, almost thornless bush. Foliage dark green. Flowers single deep pink with pronounced yellow stamens, followed by handsome, elongated but plumpish hips.
(S) (A) (P) (F) (W) ●
(AL)   4′ × 4′   1.2 × 1.2 m

R. nutkana

R. × pisocarpa

N. AMERICA 1882
A medium-sized shrub with a
dense, slightly procumbent habit;
plentiful smallish leaves and
shoots covered in spines. Flowers
in little clusters, single and lilac-
pink. Fruit small, round, sometimes slightly elongated, bright
red.
(S) (A) (W) (F) ● ⊙
(AL) 3′ × 3′ 90 × 90 cm

R. prattii

W. CHINA 1908
An almost thornless, short to
medium shrub with purple stems.
Thorns that exist are yellow. Foliage greyish-green. Flowers pink,
in small corymbs followed by
small, oval, whiskery fruit.
(S) (W) (P) ● ⊙ (AL)
4′ × 3′ 120 × 90 cm

R. pendulina

R. pyrifera

W. USA c. 1931
A short to medium, quite dense
shrub. In many ways very similar
to the better known R. woodsii.
Flowers white, usually in
corymbs. Hips smallish, deep red
and almost pear-shaped.
(S) (F) (W) (P) ● ⊙
(AL) 3′ × 3′ 90 × 90 cm

Top: R. nutkana foliage, and above, R. pisocarpa hips

Rugosas

FORMS AND HYBRIDS

The many attributes of the Rugosa hybrids set them a race apart.
They are invariably healthy, will grow almost anywhere without
mollycoddling, and provide flowers throughout most of the
summer. They are becoming increasingly popular as subjects for
massed planting in parks, as barriers for motorways and as
trouble-free screens for factories. Yet in gardens, too, their
versatility can be harnessed to great and varied effect.

CLASSIFICATION

BARB	Species and hybrids: Class 30	
MR9	Species: Class 55	Hybrids: Class 39
WFRS	Species: Class 38	Hybrids: Class 2

R. rugosa alba

'Conrad Ferdinand Meyer'

R. rugosa

JAPAN/PARTS OF W. ASIA 1796
A vigorous, thorny shrub freely sending up long canes. Over the years various forms of this species have been used to produce standard roses. It is these which appear, almost from nowhere, in derelict gardens as the result of having reproduced themselves from the original root of a stan-

dard rose, having long ago cast off its enforced, more delicate charge. Its willingness, too, to chance-hybridize with other roses and produce seedlings with minor variations has led to uncertainty as to which form is the true species. All the semi-wild forms have lightish to mid-green, sometimes wrinkled but always rough-textured foliage. The scented flowers are single and in most clones have prominent, soft yellow stamens, their colours ranging from clear deep pink to deep cerise red. The hips are globular, usually rich red, and variable in size according to clone.
(C) (W) (F) (P) (H) (A)
● (VF) (AW)
7' × 6'   2 × 1.8 m

'Agnes'

R. rugosa alba

c. 1870
This is one of the best forms of *R. rugosa*, making a most useful garden plant. Flowers are large, pure white and scented. It is a vigorous, bushy plant with fine, deeply veined, coarse textured but slightly glossy leaves. Stems thick, buff-greyish and densely populated with small thorns of similar colouring. Fruit is large and tomato red in colour.
(C) (W) (F) (P) (H) (A)
● (VF) (AW)
7' × 6'   2 × 1.8 m

R. rugosa rubra, *R. rugosa atropurpurea*

JAPAN
Large deep crimson-purple flowers with creamy-yellow stamens. Habit of growth and foliage not unlike that of *R. rugosa typica*, though slightly more vigorous.
(C) (W) (F) (P) (H) (A)
● (VF) (AW)
6' × 5'   1.8 × 1.5 m

R. rugosa typica, *R. rugosa rugosa*

JAPAN c. 1796
Makes a dense, rounded shrub and probably nearest to the true, wild species. Single, scented flowers, deep reddish-carmine, followed by bright red, globular hips. This form makes a useful hedge and is frequently used in municipal planting schemes.
(C) (W) (F) (P) (H) (A)
● (VF) (AW)
5' × 5'   1.5 × 1.5 m

'Agnes'

Saunders Central Experimental Farms CANADA 1922
R. rugosa × *R. foetida persiana*

A bushy, dense rose with dark green, rather crinkled foliage on thorny stems, one of the few yellows of this group. Flowers fully-double and highly scented, amber yellow fading to white, repeated intermittently throughout season after a good first flush in June.
(R) (P) (H) ● ⊙ (VF)
(AL)   6' × 5'   1.8 × 1.5 m

'Belle Poitevine'

Bruant FRANCE 1894
Long pointed buds opening to large, almost double flowers of rich magenta pink. Foliage lush, heavily veined and dark green Slightly angular in growth but bushy. Occasionally sets large dark red fruit.
(R) (A) (P) (H) (F) ● ⊙
(VF) (AL)   6' × 5'   1.8 × 1.5 m

'Blanc Double de Coubert'

Cochet-Cochet FRANCE 1892
R. rugosa × 'Sombreuil'
One of the outstanding Rugosa hybrids. Pure white, almost fully double flowers, exuding a superb perfume. Foliage rich dark green, plant dense and bushy. Fruit, sometimes quite large, only sets intermittently. Good autumn colour.
(R) (F) (A) (P) (H) ● ⊙
(VF) (AL)   5' × 4'   1.5 × 1.2 m

'Calocarpa', *R. × calocarpa*, 'André'

Pre-1891
R. rugosa × *R. chinensis*
Single rosy pink flowers with pronounced stamens on a vigorous, sturdy plant with ample, deepish-green foliage. Sets abundant, sizeable, shapely hips.
(R) (P) (H) (A) (F) ●
(VF) (AL)   6' × 5'   1.8 × 1.5 m

'Belle Poitevine'

'Blanc Double de Coubert'

'Carmen'

'Carmen'

Lambert GERMANY 1907
R. rugosa × 'Princesse de Béarn'
Single blooms with prominent
stamens; deep, velvety crimson.
Dark foliage on a bushy plant. A
useful and under-used rose.
(R) (A) (P) (H) ● ☉
(VF) (AL) 4′ × 4′ 1.2 × 1.2 m

'Conrad Ferdinand Meyer'

F. Müller GERMANY 1899
R. rugosa hybrid × 'Gloire de
Dijon'
A very strong, robust rose with
stout stems and large thorns. Foliage rather coarse, dark green.
Flowers large and full,
unchanging silver-pink. Very
highly scented. Unfortunately
rather prone to rust, which can
invade very early in the season.
(R) (P) (W) (H) (VF) R⚭
(AW) 10′ × 8′ 3 × 2.5 m

'Corylus'

Hazel le Rougetel UK 1988
R. rugosa × *R. nitida*
More akin to *R. nitida* in appearance than *R. rugosa*. The beautiful, mid-silver-pink and sizeable
flowers are scented and have pronounced stamens. They are freely
produced among dense, feathery,
light green foliage. Bright orange-
red hips follow on. The foliage
turns a rich tawny-yellow in the
autumn. An upright and dense
rose, free-suckering making it
good for mass planting.
(C) (P) (SF) ● ☉ (AL)
3′ × 3′ 90 × 90 cm

'Corylus'

'Culverbrae'

'Fimbriata'

'Dr Eckener'

'Fru Dagmar Hartopp' hips

'Culverbrae'

Gobbee UK 1973
'Scabrosa' × 'Francine'
Very full, crimson-purple flowers
on a well-foliated, bushy plant.
Well scented. Size makes it a use-
ful variety. Slightly prone to mil-
dew late in the season.
(R) (W) (H) (VF) M❀
(AL) 5′ × 4′ 1.5 × 1.2 m

'Delicata'

Sizable, delicate textured, bright
rosy-to-mid-pink flowers in clusters, displaying creamy-yellow stamens to effect when fully open.
Sweety scented. Growth short by
Rugosa standards but making a
tidy, densish bush. Foliage quite
rugose, mid-green. Sets fruit intermittently.
(R) (H) ● ☉ (VF) (AL)
3′ × 3′ 90 × 90 cm

'Dr Eckener'

Berger GERMANY 1930
'Golden Emblem' × R. rugosa
hybrid
Huge, scented, semi-double
flowers of pale yellow and
coppery-bronze changing with
age to a slightly muddy pink; pronounced stamens when fully
open. Well scented. Foliage rather
coarse, growth vigorous and also
rather coarse. With spiteful
thorns.
(R) (W) (P) (H) ● (VF)
(AL) 10′ × 8′ 3 × 2.5 m

'Fimbriata', 'Phoebe's Frilled Pink', 'Dianthiflora'

Morlet FRANCE 1891
R. rugosa × 'Mme Alfred Carrière'
Not a typical Rugosa hybrid.
small double frilly petalled
flowers reminding one of
Dianthus, white with pale pink
blushes. Bushy, upright shrub
with numerous light green leaves.
(R) (P) (H) (W) (A) ●
☉ (VF) (AL)
4′ × 4′ 1.2 × 1.2 m

'F. J. Grootendorst'

de Goey HOLLAND 1918
R. rugosa rubra × 'Nobert
Levavasseur'
Clusters of small, crimson double
flowers with frilly petals. Copious
and somewhat coarse dark green
foliage on a vigorous bushy plant.
Continuously in flower through-
out the summer.
(C) (H) (P) (W) ● ☉
(VF) (AL)
4′ × 3′ 120 × 90 cm

'Fru Dagmar Hartopp', 'Fru Dagmar Hastrup', 'Frau Dagmar Hartopp'

Hastrup GERMANY 1914
Beautiful, clear, silver-pink
flowers with pronounced stamens
especially good in autumn.
Scented. Foliage dark green. Plant
bushy, growing wider than tall.
Excellent tomato-like hips.
Sold under all these names by
various nurseries around the
world but its correct name is Fru
Dagmar Hartopp.
(C) (P) (F) (W) (A) ●
(G) ☉ 3' × 4' 90 × 120 cm

'Fru Dagmar Hartopp'

'George Will'

Skinner USA 1939
(*R. rugosa* × *R. acicularis*) ×
unknown

This is a very good, interesting
rose. Deep pink, fully double
flowers in tight clusters with a
scent of cloves. Foliage follows its
Rugosa parent. Growth twiggy
but dense.
(C) (P) (H) ● ☉ (VF)
(AL) 4' × 3' 120 × 90 cm

'Hansa'

Schaum and Van Tol HOLLAND
1905
Very free-flowering. Double,
highly scented, reddish-purple
flowers. Vigorous, medium-sized
plant with dark green foliage.
Excellent red fruit. This is one of
the best all-round Rugosas.
(C) (H) (P) (F) (W) ●
☉ (VF) (AL)
4' × 3' 120 × 90 cm

'Hunter'

Mattock UK 1961
R. rugosa rubra × 'Independence'
Scented, fully double, bright
crimson flowers on a rugged,
medium-sized, bushy plant with
dark green foliage. A useful rose.
(C) (P) (W) ● ☉ (VF)
(AL) 4' × 3' 120 × 90 cm

'Grootendorst Supreme'

Sport from 'F. J. Grootendorst'
with deeper-red flowers.
(C) (H) (P) (W) ● ☉
(VF) (AL)
4' × 3' 120 × 90 cm

'Jens Munk'

Department of
Agriculture CANADA 1974
'Schneezwerg' × 'Fru. Dagmar
Hartopp'
This is a delightful rose in all
respects. Deliciously fragrant
flowers of soft lilac-pink, semi-
double when fully open with
pronounced primrose yellow
stamens, followed by smallish
round-to-oval hips. Foliage dark

'Hansa'. *Above right:* 'F. J. Grootendorst'

'Jens Munk'

green and plentiful. Dense, bushy
growth. Hardy.
(C) (P) (H) (F) (A) ☉
(VF) (AL)
4′ × 3′   120 × 90 cm

'Lady Curzon'

Turner UK 1901
R. macrantha × *R. rugosa rubra*
An arching shrub with very
thorny wood and dark green foliage. Lovely large, single, pale
rose-pink, fragrant flowers. A
vigorous, procumbent variety,
favouring its pollen parent in
most characteristics except habit

'Martin Frobisher'

which is why I place it here rather
than with *R. macrantha* hybrids.
(R) (P) (G) (W) ● ☉
(MF) (AL)   3′ × 6′   90 × 180 cm

'Marie Bugnet'

Bugnet USA 1963
('Thérèse Bugnet' × seedling)
× 'F. J. Grootendorst'
Pure white, very fragrant, double
flowers of a tousled form in small
clusters amid plentiful, light
green, crinkled foliage. Compact,
bushy growth. Hardy. A lovely
rose.
(C) ○   (H) (P) (VF) (AL)
4′ × 3′   120 × 90 cm

'Martin Frobisher'

Department of
Agriculture CANADA 1968
'Schneezwerg' seedling
Well scented shapely, double, soft
pink flowers. Foliage dark green,
growth upright and very prickly.
Not often seen but should be
more widely grown.
(R) (H) (P) (W) ● ☉
(SF) (AL)   4′ × 4′   1.2 × 1.2 m

'Mary Manners'

Leicester Rose Company UK 1970
Probably sport of 'Sarah Van
Fleet'
Pure white, semi-double flowers
in profusion on an upright,
thorny bush with ample, dark
green foliage. Highly scented. A
useful rose, if a little prone to
rust.
(C) (H) (P) (W) ● ☉
(VF) R⚭ (AL)
4′ × 3′   120 × 90 cm

'Max Graf'

Bowditch USA 1919
R. rugosa × *R. wichuraiana*
A trailing rose, ideal for banks,
etc. Single, deep silvery-pink
flowers paling slightly towards
the centre with pronounced stamens. Shoots heavily dressed with
large, dark, slightly glossy leaves.
Seldom sets any fruit.
(S) (F) (P) (G) ● (MF)
(AW)   2′ × 8′   60 × 250 cm

'Mary Manners'

'Mme Georges Bruant'

Bruant FRANCE 1887
R. rugosa × 'Sombreuil'
Loosely formed, semi-double,
creamy-white, scented flowers.
Ample, rather coarse, dark green
foliage on a vigorous, very thorny
bush. Makes an impenetrable
hedge.
(C) (W) (P) (H) ● (VF)
(AL)   5′ × 4′   1.5 × 1.2 m

'Moje Hammarberg'

Hammarberg SWEDEN 1931
Very fragrant, large, nodding,

'Hunter'

'Max Graf'

'Mme Georges Bruant'

'Nova Zembla'

Mees UK 1907
Pure white sport of 'Conrad F.
Meyer' with all the same charac-
teristics except colour of flower.
(R) (P) (W) (H) (VF) R☙
(AL) 4' × 5' 1.2 × 1.5 m

'Nyveldt's White'

Nyveldt HOLLAND 1955
(*R. rugosa rubra* × *R. majalis*)
× *R. nitida*
Large, pure white, single flowers
on a vigorous, dense, thorny bush.
Dark green stems and foliage.
Produces an excellent crop of
round, bright red hips unfailingly
each autumn.
(C) (F) (P) (W) (H) (A)
● (VF) (AL)
5' × 4' 1.5 × 1.2 m

'Parfum d l'Hay'
see 'Rose à Parfum de l'Hay'

deep purplish-red, fully double
blooms followed by large, red,
globular hips; together giving a
striking effect in late summer.
Growth vigorous with good,
tough, darkish-green foliage.
Extremely hardy.
(R) (P) (H) (A) (F) ●
(VF) (AL) 6' × 5' 1.8 × 1.5 m

'Mrs Anthony Waterer'

Waterer UK 1898
R. rugosa × 'Général Jacqueminot'
Semi-double, shapely, rich deep
crimson flowers, freely produced
on a vigorous, broad, thorny bush
with dark green foliage. Well
scented.
(C) (W) (P) (H) ● (VF)
M☙ (AL) 4' × 5' 1.2 × 1.5 m

'Mrs Anthony Waterer'

'Roseraie de l'Hay, and *top:* 'Rose à Parfum de l'Hay'

'Nyveldt's White'

'Pink Grootendorst'

Grootendorst HOLLAND 1923
'F. J. Grootendorst' sport
This rose is soft pink, otherwise
the same in all respects to its
parent. Tends to revert to red,
sometimes giving both colours on
the same head of blooms.
(C) (H) (P) (W) ● ☉
(VF) (AL)
4' × 3'   120 × 90 cm

'Robusta'

Kordes GERMANY 1979
R. rugosa × seedling
Large, single, rich scarlet-red
flowers on a strong, robust, dense,
thorny plant with good, dark if
somewhat coarse foliage. Scented.
Makes a very good, impenetrable
hedge.
(C) (P) (H) ● (VF) (AL)
5' × 4'   1.5 × 1.2 m

'Rose à Parfum de l'Hay', 'Parfum de l'Hay

Gravereaux FRANCE 1901
(R. damascena × 'Général
Jacqueminot') × R. rugosa
Large, globular buds opening flat
to rich, bright red flowers which
turn deeper in hot sun. It is fragrant and, at its best, very beautiful. The foliage is dark green on a

bushy plant with ample thorns. It
has a tendency to mildew later in
the season. Difficult to classify
but best here on account of
several R. rugosa characteristics.
(C) (W) ● ☉ (VF) M⚥
(AL)   4' × 3'   120 × 90 cm

'Roseraie de l'Hay'

Cochet-Cochet FRANCE 1901
Sport from unknown hybrid of
R. rugosa
One of the best loved of all the
Rugosa hybrids. Splendid, semi-
double flowers of crimson-purple,
large and opening loosely flat.
Strongly scented. Makes a dense,
vigorous, bushy shrub, and is
almost constantly in flower.
Foliage dark green. Sadly, only
occasionally sets fruit, but com-
pensates with very good autumn
foliage.
(C) (P) (W) (H) (A) ●
(VF) (AW)   6' × 5'   1.8 × 1.5 m

'Ruskin'

Van Fleet USA 1928
'Souvenir de Pierre Leperdrieux'
× 'Victor Hugo'
A bushy, well foliated, recurrent
rose which deserves more atten-
tion. Flowers large, fully double,
crimson and highly scented.
(R) (P) (H) ● ☉ (VF)
(AL)   4' × 3'   120 × 90 cm

'Ruskin'

'Sarah Van Fleet'

'Sarah Van Fleet'

Van Fleet USA 1926
R. rugosa × 'My Maryland'
Semi-double, silky-pink blooms
produced in profusion on a well-
foliated but viciously thorny
bush. Growth upright but bushy.
Foliage dark green. Seldom sets
fruit. Rather inclined to rust,
especially after its first flush of
flowers.
(C) (P) (W) (H) ● ☉
(VF) R⚥ (AW)
4' × 3'   120 × 90 cm

'Scabrosa'

Harkness UK introduced 1960
As often happens, this foundling
turned out well. Jack Harkness
tells the story of this rose in his

excellent book Roses. Sufficient to
say here that it came on the scene
through good observation. One of
my favourite Rugosas. Large,
single, rich silvery-cerise flowers
with prominent anthers, often
accompanied by large, tomato-
shaped hips which are produced
as abundantly as its flowers. Foliage dark, of thick texture, heavily
veined and almost glossy green.
Makes a dense, upright shrub.
Particularly good for hedging.
Very sweetly scented.
(C) (H) (P) (W) (A) ●
(VF) (AL)   6' × 4'   1.8 × 1.2 m

'Schneelicht'

Geschwind HUNGARY 1894
R. rugosa × R. phoenicia

'Scabrosa'

'Scabrosa' hips

Clusters of large, pure white, single flowers on a strong, impenetrable shrub with dark, viciously armed stems. Dark green foliage. Excellent as a dense hedge.
(R) (P) (W) (H) ● (VF)
(AL)   6′ × 4′   1.8 × 1.2 m

'Schneezwerg', 'Snow Dwarf'

P. Lambert GERMANY 1912
R. rugosa × a Polyantha rose
An interesting, slightly smaller member of the Rugosas. Pure white, semi-double, well-formed flowers with pronounced yellow stamens when fully open. Plenti-ful greyish-dark green foliage. Rich red medium-size hips set intermittently, often appearing together with the flowers later in the season.
(C) (F) (P) (W) (H) (A)
● ☉ (VF) (AL)
5′ × 4′   1.5 × 1.2 m

'Sir Thomas Lipton'

Van Fleet USA 1990
R. rugosa alba × 'Clotilde Soupert'
Not unlike 'Blanc Double de Coubert' in many ways, including colour, but with a few more petals in its flowers. Fragrant. Growth

'Nova Zembla'

vigorous and bushy with dark green, leathery foliage.
(C) (P) (H) (A) ● ☉
(VF) (AL) 5' × 4' 1.5 × 1.2 m

'Souvenir de Philémon Cochet'

Cochet-Cochet FRANCE 1899
'Blanc Double de Coubert' sport
Like its parent in all but colour.
Soft blush-pink with deeper tones
in the centre.
(C) (P) (H) (W) ● (VF)
(AL) 5' × 4' 1.5 × 1.2 m

'Thérèse Bugnet'

Bugnet CANADA 1950
(*R. acicularis* × *R.* × *kamtchatica*)
× (*R. amblyotis* × *R. rugosa plena*)
× 'Betty Bland'

'Schneezwerg'

'Schneezwerg' hips

'Thérèse Bugnet'

A very hardy rose. Large, double
flowers, clear red paling to pink.
Fragrant. Good foliage. *R. rugosa*
influence not immediately recognizable.
(C) (P) (H) ● (VF) (AL)
6' × 6' 1.8 × 1.8 m

'Vanguard'

Stevens USA 1932
(*R. wichuraiana* × *R. rugosa alba*)
× 'Eldorado'
A vigorous shrub, rather
untypically Rugosa, bearing semi-
double flowers of salmon bur-
nished bronze. Very fragrant.
Upright growth well foliated with
glossy, burnished leaves.
(R) (P) (W) (H) (F) ●
(VF) ≋ (AL)
8' × 6' 2.5 × 1.8 m

'White Grootendorst'

Eddy USA 1962
'Pink Grootendorst' sport
Identical to other 'Grootendorsts',
but with white flowers and lighter
green foliage.
(C) (P) (W) (H) ● ☉
(VF) (AL)
4' × 3' 120 × 90 cm

'Will Alderman'

Skinner USA 1954
(*R. rugosa* × *R. acicularis*) ×
unknown Hybrid Tea
Large, shapely, fully double, clear
pink flowers. Highly scented.
Growth upright but bushy.
Foliage mid-green. Hardy.
(R) (P) (H) ● ☉ (A)
(VF) (AL)
4' × 3' 120 × 90 cm

'Vanguard'

R. setipoda hips

R. sertata

W. CHINA 1904
A loose shrub with thinnish, arching, brownish branches with few
thorns and greyish-green leaves.
Deep pink flowers in small clusters followed by small, narrowly
oval, dark red hips.
(S) (F) (W) (P) ● (AL)
4' × 3' 120 × 90 cm

R. setipoda

CENTRAL CHINA 1895
A medium-sized, shrubby rose
with thick stems and well-spaced
strong thorns. Scented foliage,
noticeable only when leaves are
crushed. Exquisite flowers, produced in large clusters, clear, pale
pink, single and quite big, with
yellow stamens. Flower stalks

strangely purple. Finishes the season with large, pendulous plump, flagon-shaped, bristly deep red hips.

(S) (P) (W) (F) ● (SF)
(AL) 8′ × 5′ 2.5 × 1.5 m

R. spaldingii

R. suffulta

R. willmottiae foliage and hips

R. spaldingii

N. AMERICA 1915
Medium shrub with yellowish-green stems and soft greyish-green foliage. Flowers pink and slightly crinkled when fully open, flowering rather shyly and intermittently for a long season. I have the white form, which is rather charming. Small, round, red fruit in autumn.

(S) (P) (F) (W) (A) ● ⊙
(SF) (AL) 4′ × 3′ 120 × 90 cm

R. suffulta

Greene N. AMERICA 1880
Clusters of single, pink flowers followed by small orange hips. A short dense plant with soft grey foliage and thin, spiny stems.

(S) (W) (F) ● (SF) (AL)
4′ × 3′ 120 × 90 cm

R. sweginzowii macrocarpa

This garden form from GERMANY

Original from N. W. CHINA
The thick, smooth, light brown stems viciously armed with thorns belie the beauty of this rose. Flowers numerous, single and bright pink, followed by large, shiny, plump, flagon-shaped hips of rich bright red. Well foliated and rather angular in growth.

(S) (P) (F) (W) (A) ●
(SF) (AL)
10′ × 8′ 3 × 2.5 m

R. ultramontana

USA 1888
A short to medium shrub with few or no thorns of consequence. Small to medium sized clusters of pink flowers in mid-summer. Small, smooth, rounded, red hips.

(S) (W) (P) ● ⊙ (AL)
3′ × 3′ 90 × 90 cm

R. woodsii fendlerii

R. wardii

TIBET C. 1924
A medium-growing, lax shrub which now appears to be extinct in its native form. *R. wardii* 'Culta' was raised at Wisley from seed, from the original form, and introduced in this name. Flowers single and white, rather like those of *R. moyesii*, with distinct brownish stigmas and yellow stamens. Shoots brownish, thorns sparse but sharp. Foliage bright green.

(S) (F) (W) ● ⊙ (AL)
6′ × 5′ 1.8 × 1.5 m

R. webbiana

HIMALAYAS, E. ASIA 1879
A good and interesting shrub with long, arching, almost trailing, pliable shoots, densely clothed with small grey-blue foliage and fairly harmless thorns – at least until they become old and more stubborn. Small, numerous, soft pink, scented flowers, followed by small, orange-red, bottle-shaped hips in the autumn.

(P) (F) (W) ● ⊙ (MF)
(AL) 7′ × 7′ 2 × 2 m

R. willmottiae

W. CHINA 1904
A superb shrub with arching

stems of a darkish plum colour with a grey bloom. Grey-green, fern-like foliage, slightly scented when crushed. The plant, of arching angular habit, bears small, single, deep lilac-pink flowers with creamy-yellow anthers, followed by small, vaguely pear-shaped, orangey-red hips.

(S) (F) (W) (P) ● ⊙
(SF) (AL) 6′ × 6′ 1.8 × 1.8 m

R. woodsii
R. macounii

N. AMERICA 1820
Pink medium sized single flowers in small clusters, followed by sizeable, globose bright red hips. Foliage mid-green and healthy, colourful in the autumn. Growth bushy dense.

(S) (P) (A) (F) ● (H)
(W) (AL) 3′ × 3′ 90 × 90 cm

R. woodsii fendleri

N. AMERICA 1888
Makes a superb shrub of upright habit with numerous thin spiky thorns on greyish wood. The flowers plentifully produced on a well-foliated plant, are single, bright lilac-pink and followed by a crop of deep, waxy-red, globular hips which persist well into winter.

(H) (W) (P) (F) ● (SF)
(AL) 5′ × 5′ 1.5 × 1.5 m

R. yainacensis,
R. myriadenia

N. AMERICA C. 1912
Closely resembling *R. nutkana* to which it is obviously related. Smallish but numerous deep lilac-pink flowers followed by small, rounded, bright red hips. Growth strong with darkish-brown stems. Foliage grey-green.

(S) (P) (W) (F) ● (AL)
5′ × 4′ 1.5 × 1.2 m

ROSA Subgenus *Eurosa (Rosa)*

SECTION : *Synstylae*

Growth vigorous, climbing and flexible, 6' to 30 ' (2 m to 10 m)
Thorns variously sized, curved, some species sparse, others none.
Leaves mostly 5 to 7, sometimes 9, leaflets.
Flowers mostly in corymbs or clusters.
Hips mostly small, oval or round.
Sepals drop when hips are ripe.

CLASSIFICATION

BARB   Species: Class 1
MR9   Species: Class 55
WFRS   Species: Classes 38 and 39
For classification of hybrids in
this section, see under
garden group headings.

SPECIES

R. anemoneflora
R. arvensis
R. brunonii
R. × dupontii
R filipes
R. gentiliana
R. helenae
R. henryi
R. longicuspis
R. luciae
R. moschata
R. moschata nastarana
R. mulliganii
R. multiflora
R. multiflora carnea
R. multiflora cathayensis
R. multiflora grevillii
R. multiflora watsoniana
R. multiflora wilsonii
R. phoenicia
R. × polliniana
R. sempervirens
R. setigera
R. sinowilsonii
R soulieana
R. wichuraiana

Floribundas
Miniatures
Modern Shrubs
Modern Climbers
Patios
Polyanthas
Procumbents
Ramblers

GARDEN GROUPS

Ayrshires
Hybrid Musks

R. anemoneflora, R. triphylla

E. CHINA 1844
A climbing rose, the garden form
of which has small clusters of
double, white flowers (in the wild,
single). These are made up of
large outer petals and many
smaller ones in the centre. Quite
interesting and unique. Growth is
vigorous with few or no thorns.
Needs mollycoddling for best
results in colder climates.
(S) ☼ (T) (AL)
12' × 8'   3.5 × 2.5 m

ORIGIN AND DISTRIBUTION

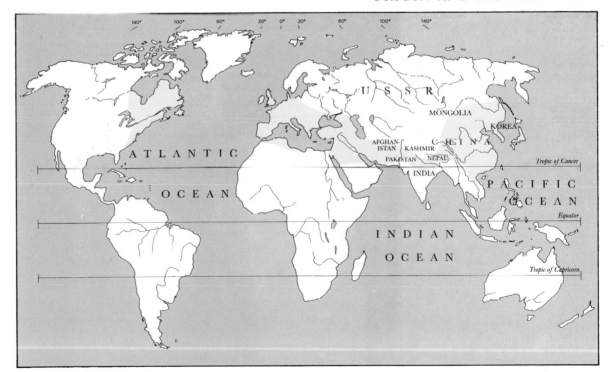

The Ayrshires (R. arvensis)

FORMS AND HYBRIDS

This interesting group of medium-sized ramblers and scramblers is useful for a variety of purposes, from tree climbing to ground covering. When compared to some other groups of ramblers, they may appear rather dull since their colour range is restricted to white and shades of pink but, to my mind, their flowers, without exception, have a simple refinement unsurpassed by those of any other equivalent group. At the same time, since they are derived from our native 'field rose', they are all very hardy and robust.

CLASSIFICATION	
BARB	Class 1
MR9	Class 2
WFRS	Class 16

R. arvensis, 'The Field Rose'

EUROPE
A beautiful, pure white single rose with medium-sized flowers and showy golden anthers. A ground-creeper or rambler with thin dark wood and foliage and well-spaced thorns. Frequently seen in hedgerows, especially in southern England.
(S) (P) (G) ● (F) (W)
(P) ≋ 20' × 10' 6 × 3 m

'Ayrshire Queen'

1835
Sadly, another which seems to have become extinct. Descriptions suggest it was creamy-white with a purple throat.

'Bennett's Seedling', 'Thoresbyana'

Bennett UK 1840
Another double white. Said to be fragrant and very free-flowering.
(S) (P) (G) (W) ● ≋
(MF) (AL) 20' × 10' 6 × 3 m

'Dundee Rambler'

Martin SCOTLAND c. 1850
A double white with flower rather smaller than R. arvensis and growth more dense.
(S) (P) (G) (W) ● ≋
(MF) (AL) 20' × 10' 6 × 3 m

'Düsterlohe'

Kordes GERMANY 1931
'Venusta Pendula' × 'Miss C. E. Van Rossen'.
Large, semi-double flowers of rich pink, paling towards centre. Foliage dark green and plentiful. Rather untidy but spreading to a dense wide shrub. Orange-red, plumpish, oval hips.
(S) (F) (P) (G) (MF) (AL)
5' × 8' 1.5 × 2.8 m

'Janet B. Wood'

Discovered by Mrs McQueen SCOTLAND 1984
Introduced by Beales UK 1989
R. arvensis hybrid
A delightful rediscovery to add to the important group of Ayrshire ramblers. The small, semi-double, pure white flowers are mostly produced in small clusters, but sometimes singly, having a slight scent. Foliage is ample and dark green, stems wiry, reddish and thorny. Since it is distinct from any other Ayrshire I know, I believe this to be an important rediscovery in that it complies in all respects with descriptions (admittedly somewhat scant) of the original Double Ayrshire of 1768. See page 23.
(S) (P) (T) (N) ● (SF)
(AL) 15' × 10' 4.5 × 3 m

'Ruga', R. × ruga

ITALY Pre-1830
R. arvensis × R. chinensis
Semi-double flowers in large, loose clusters. Pale pink and well scented. Darkish-green wood, well foliated with mid-green leaves. Very vigorous.
(S) (W) (P) (N) (T) ●
≋ (MF) (AL)
30' × 20' 9 × 6 m

'Splendens', 'The Myrrh-scented Rose'

A good semi-double rose. Shapely buds opening to cupped flowers, white with hints of pink at the edges of each petal. Has an unusual perfume, and is some-

'Splendens', and *top: R. arvensis* hips

'Venusta Pendula'

R. brunonii

R. brunonii

AND HYBRID

CLASSIFICATION

BARB   Class 1
MR9   Class 53 and 55
WFRS   Classes 39 and 14 or 16

---

times called the 'myrrh-scented' rose. Stems dark purplish-green, foliage dark green.
(S) (P) (G) (W) ● ≈≈
(VF) (AL) 20′ × 10′ 6 × 3 m

'Venusta Pendula'

Reintroduced Kordes 1928
Clusters of cascading, small, white flushed pink, fully double flowers on spindly, dark plum-red shoots with dark, dull-green foliage. Moderately thorny, little or no scent.
(S) (P) (G) (W) ● ≈≈
(MF) (AL) 18′ × 10′ 5.5 × 3 m

R. × dupontii

'La Mortola'

R. brunonii, R. moschata nepalensis

HIMALAYAS C. 1823
A densely foliated, vigorous climber. Leaves large, downy in texture and drooping, light grey-green. Shoots grey-green, with young wood a tarnished, pinkish brown. Extremely vigorous and armed with hooked thorns. Flower are single, tissuey in texture, creamy white, produced in clusters in July. Until recently this species was thought to belong under *R. moschata* but it is now accepted as distinct.
(S) (N) (P) (T) (W) ●
(VF) (AL)
25′ × 15′ 7.5 × 4.5 m

'La Mortola'

La Mortola Gardens ITALY c. 1936
Introduced to UK by Sunningdale Nurseries, 1959
Probably sport from *R. brunonii*
A more refined or less refined form, depending on your viewpoint, of *R. brunonii*. Foliage of the same texture but larger and more obviously grey. Flowers slightly larger and perhaps more numerous. Seems quite hardy here in Norfolk.
(S) (N) (P) (T) (W) ●
(VF) (AL) 20′ × 12′ 6 × 3.5 m

R. × dupontii

EUROPE Pre-1817
Possibly *R. gallica* × *R. moschata*
Beautifully shaped pure white flowers with pronounced golden-brown stamens. Sweetly scented. Flowering rather later than many species, linking it perhaps with *R. moschata*. Also it has an occasional flower later in the summer. Growth is strong with light green wood and ample greyish-green foliage. Fruit, when set, ripens very late in autumn.
(S) (P) (H) (W) (MF)
(AW) 7′ × 4′ 2 × 1.2 m

'Kiftsgate'

R. filipes

FORMS AND HYBRIDS

R. filipes is best known for its prowess as a climber and its few direct descendants have, without exception, inherited that trait. They are not candidates for the smaller garden, being capable of climbing the tallest tree and completely smothering an average-sized house. However, they have their place and no garden that can accommodate them should be without at least one, preferably all.

CLASSIFICATION
BARB Class 1
MR9   Class 53 and 55
WFRS Class 16 or 18

R. filipes

CHINA 1908

A vigorous species capable of growing 30′ (9 m) or more especially with the support of trees, and producing large panicles of single, creamy-white scented flowers each with golden stamens. Lush, light green foliage, numerous hips in autumn. Now more commonly seen in the better garden form, 'Kiftsgate'.

(S) (N) (P) (F) (G) (T)
(A) ● ≈ (MF) (AL)
30′ × 20′   9 × 6 m

'Brenda Colvin'

Colvin UK 1970
Probably 'Kiftsgate' seeding
Medium flowers of soft blush-pink to white, single, in clusters. Strongly perfumed. Very vigorous

R. filipes

and healthy. Foliage dark green and glossy.

(S) (P) (T) ● ≈ (VF)
(AL) 30′ × 20′ 9 × 6 m

'Kiftsgate'

Murrell UK 1954
Sport or form of R. filipes, found at Kiftsgate Court, Glos.
A strong, vigorous climber capable of climbing to considerable heights. The fragrant, creamy-white flowers with golden stamens are borne in huge, cascading trusses in mid-summer, followed by thousands of small, red hips in the autumn. The foliage is large, profuse and glossy, green tinted copper when young. It also changes to rich russet in autumn. It tolerates considerable shade and consequently it is an ideal subject for climbing into trees. Also an effective ground cover but only where its enthusiasm can be left unchecked.

(S) (N) (P) (F) (G) (T)
(A) ● ≈ (MF) (AL)
30′ × 20′   9 × 6 m

'Kiftsgate' autumn foliage

R. helenae hips

'Treasure Trove'

Treasure UK 1979
'Kiftsgate' × Hybrid Tea
A superb seedling from 'Kiftsgate' with all the vigour and performance of its parent. Large trusses of semi-double creamy-apricot flowers changing with age to blush pink. Quite outstanding, with a strong scent. Foliage changes from pinkish-red through to mid-green as it ages.

(S) (N) (P) (F) (G) (T)
(A) ● ≈ (VF) (AL)
30′ × 20′   9 × 6 m

R. gentiliana, erroneously R. polyantha grandiflora

CHINA 1907
Single to semi-double, creamy-white flowers produced in dense, cascading clusters from an exceptionally vigorous climbing plant, followed by small, orange hips in autumn. Very large, glossy foliage of light green with coppery overtones. Its stems which are similar in colour to its leaves are also shiny with a sparse mixture of broad, hooked thorns, and smaller, more numerous, bristles.

(S) (P) (F) (T) (A) ● ≈
20′ × 10′   6 × 3 m

R. helenae

AND HYBRID

CLASSIFICATION
BARB Class 1
MR9   Class 53 and 55
WFRS Class 16 or 18

R. helenae

CHINA 1907

A vigorous rose well worth its popularity as a climber into small trees. Foliage large, plentiful and grey-green. Stems thick, sometimes mottled brown. Single flowers, scented, creamy-white and borne in dense corymbs during mid-to-late June, followed by small, oval, red hips in early autumn, which alone can be quite spectacular.

(S) (F) (P) (W) (T) ● ≈
(AL) 20′ × 15′ 6 × 4.5 m

'Lykkefund'

Olsen DENMARK 1930
R. helenae × seedling
Huge trusses of single, scented, creamy-yellow flowers tinted pink. Foliage lush, light green tinted bronze. Shoots quite thornless and vigorous. Ideal for growing up into trees and sturdy enough to make a large specimen shrub.

(S) (P) (T) (W) ● (MF)
(AL) 18′ × 15′ 5.5 × 4.5 m

R. henryi

CHINA 1907
A vigorous shrub or small climber with ample almost glossy foliage and large, hooked thorns. Dense

corymbs of white flowers from early to mid-summer followed by masses of small, round, dark red hips.

(S) (P) (F) (T) ● (AL)
15′ × 10′   4.5 × 3 m

R. longicuspis

F. Kingdom Ward W. CHINA
c. 1915
Almost evergreen, this rose is very vigorous with profuse, long, leathery, serrated, dark green foliage, reddish-pink when young. Very floriferous, the huge, cascading panicles of bunched, medium-sized, single, white flowers each with pronounced yellow stamens. The growth is as tall but not as coarse as, for example, 'Kiftsgate'. The strong, wiry stems are excellent in assisting it to achieve great heights into trees. The flowers have little or no scent and are followed by small, oval, orange-red hips. Not totally hardy but well worth trying in the south. The species grown and sold as this variety in most modern-day catalogues is actually R. mulliganii.

(S) (G) (P) (T) (F) (N)
(VF) (AL)   30′ × 15′   9 × 4.5 m

R. luciae

E. ASIA c.1880
Very similar to the better known and more widely grown R. wichuraiana. A dense, spreading shrub with plentiful, almost glossy, dark green leaves. Clusters of medium-sized white flowers produced in late spring/early summer. Scented. It is now thought that this species was used to produce many of the hybrid Wichuraiana ramblers of late Victorian and Edwardian times.

(S) (W) (T) ● ≈≈ (MF)
(AL)   10′ × 8′   3 × 2.5 m

(R. moschata) Musks

FORMS AND HYBRIDS

R. moschata has a number of direct descendants, and currently growing in our gardens are many more a few generations removed, for genes from this species inhabit the chromosomes of many of our modern roses.

The following are those directly related; there were once others. William Paul listed nine, excluding 'noisettes', in the tenth edition of *The Rose Garden*. I will describe only those hybrids known to be available today and which are probably true to name.

CLASSIFICATION

BARB	Class 1
MR9	Class 34
WFRS	Classes 12 and 18

R. moschata, 'The Musk Rose'

S. EUROPE/MIDDLE EAST
An ancient variety probably introduced during the reign of Henry VIII
Medium to short-growing climber or shrub rose with grey-green, slightly drooping foliage. Stems also grey-green, sparsely populated with hooked thorns. Flowers, produced in large spaced clusters, are cream until fully open when they change to white. Starts flowering in July and continues until well into September. Hips, when produced, are small and oval.

(S) (P) (W) (T) (N) ●
(AL)   8′ × 6′   2.5 × 1.8 m

R. moschata floribunda

A very vigorous, spreading, dense, relatively thornless climber with large, long, lightish-green leaves and thick, green, slightly downy stems. The large, tightly packed clusters of single, white flowers are produced rather earlier in the

season than other Moschata hybrids. Each flower has an attractive ring of yellow stamens and emits a pleasant musk scent; they are followed by oval to round, orange hips. This is a pleasing and under-used variety.

(S) (P) (T) (F) (N) ●
(MF) (AL)   20′ × 15′   6 × 4.5 m

R. moschata grandiflora

Bernaix FRANCE 1866
An extremely vigorous climbing rose with typical Moschata-type foliage and extremely large clusters of single, white flowers, each with golden stamens. Very fragrant. Round orange hips in autumn.

(S) (P) (T) (F) (N) ●
(MF) (AL)   30′ × 20′   9 × 6 m

R. luciae

'Narrow Water'

R. moschata nastarana, 'Persian Musk Rose'

ASIA MINOR 1879
Possibly hybrid between R. moschata and R. chinensis
Similar in many respects to R. moschata but more vigorous in growth and with more numerous, smaller leaves. Flowers, although similar in form to those of the species, are semi-double and touched with pale lilac-pink; they can also be fractionally larger in some ideal situations. Flowers are provided well into autumn.

(S) (P) (W) (N) (T) ●
(VF) (AL)   10′ × 6′   3 × 1.8 m
15′ × 10′   4.5 × 3 m

'Autumnalis', R. moschata 'Autumnalis'

Probably R. moschata × R. chinensis
An interesting rose. The rose I describe is the variety I have grown under this name for many years but I have never been quite sure if it correct. It is a small climber similar to 'Princess of

R. moschata

Nassau' except more vigorous. Large clusters of semi-double, cupped flowers of creamy-white to pure white produced, it seems, with some reluctance from August through to early winter. Slightly scented. Foliage light green. Stems, almost thornless, also light green. Probably better in warmer climates than Norfolk.
(C) (T) (N) ● (SF) (AL)
10' × 6'   3 × 1.8 m

'Narrow Water'

Daisy Hill Nurseries IRELAND c. 1883
Not much is known about this rose, but it probably belongs in this section. A tallish shrub or small climber with dark foliage and large clusters of semi-double, lilac-pink flowers with a good scent. Particularly useful in that it flowers late into autumn. I have become very fond of it.
(R) (P) ● (VF) (AL)
8' × 6'   2.5 × 1.8 m

'Paul's Himalayan Musk'

W. Paul UK Probably late 19th century
Perhaps nearer to *R. multiflora* or even *R. sempervirens* than its name suggests. Its drooping leaves (a clue to *moschata*) are slightly glossy and darkish green, with hints of copper when young. Broad, hooked thorns on long, pliable wood. Very profuse when blooming in July. Flowers small, double, pinkish-lavender, produced in drooping clusters. Quite hardy, an outstandingly useful climbing rose.
(S) (P) (T) ● ≈ (SF)
(AL)   20' × 12'   6 × 3.5 m

'Paul's Perpetual White', 'Paul's Single White'

Paul UK 1882
The flowers, large and single, and the way they are displayed, solitarily or in small clusters, suggest a liaison with *R. laevigata*. The foliage and habit of growth, however, belie this. It is light green and well spaced on relatively thornless, almost lime-green shoots. Moderately vigorous. From the first flush which occurs in July, flowers continue to appear throughout the season until well into autumn. Not easy to grow.
(R) (P) ● (SF) (AL)
10' × 8'   3 × 2.5 m

'Princess of Nassau'

Probably early 19th century
A recent rediscovery, I believe by Graham Thomas, who sent me budwood in 1982. These flowered as maiden plants, coinciding with *R. moschata*, and going on well into autumn, fitting Paul's descriptions almost perfectly: 'Flowers, yellowish-straw, form-cupped, very sweet.' I add to this, light green foliage. I can now vouch for its hardiness since it survived the severe winter of 1984/85 with only moderate frost damage. Quite vigorous.
(R) (P) ● (MF) (AL)
10' × 8'   3 × 2.5 m

'The Garland'

Wills UK 1835
R. moschata × *R. multiflora*
Vigorous, spreading climber flowering in early July in great profusion. Masses of small, semi-double, daisy-like flowers, creamy-white, sometimes tinged pink. Very fragrant. Foliage mid-to-dark green and not as large as in most other Moschata hybrids. Stems are well armed with stout, hooked thorns. An excellent rose.
(S) (P) (N) (T) ● ≈
(VF) (AL)   15' × 10'   4.5 × 3 m

'The Garland'

'Princess of Nassau'

R. mulliganii

Forrest S. CHINA 1917
A medium vigorous species with broad, sharp, hooked thorns. Similar in many respects to *R. rubus*. Young shoots and foliage purplish-green; greyish-green when older. Flowers single in small spaced clusters, pure white and scented. Fruit small, red, round and conspicuous. Many of the plants grown and sold as *R. longicuspis* over recent years are actually this species and I confess myself in common with others to this error in identity.

(S) (G) (P) (T) (F) (N)
● ≈ (MF) (AL)
15′ × 10′   4.5 × 3 m

R. mulliganii

R. multiflora

FORMS AND HYBRIDS

R. multiflora has had great influence in the development of the modern rose and I could almost fill two books of this size with hybrids which have *R. multiflora* somewhere in their lineage. I will place a number of important groups under this heading since this is where in my opinion they are best placed in the family tree of roses.

I will first deal with the Multiflora species, and will then subdivide the hybrids of this lineage into their garden groups, each with a brief note of introduction as follows: Hybrid Musks, Multiflora Ramblers, Modern Shrubs, Polyanthas, Floribundas and Modern Climbers. Most of these groups, especially the Modern Shrubs, Floribundas and Modern Climbers, owe almost as much in lineage to section *Chinensis* as *Synstylae* but their cluster inflorescences place them here.

CLASSIFICATION	
BARB	Species: Class 1
MR9	Species: Class 35
WFRS	Species: Class 16

R. multiflora

E. ASIA Late 18th, early 19th century
Very floriferous, at least during its relatively short flowering season. Flowers small, single, creamy-white grow in large clusters on wood produced in the previous season. When in full flush, they almost obscure the leaves which are smooth and lightish-green. Stems also smooth and fairly free of thorns. Fruit is small, round to oval, smooth and red in colour. Until recently it was popular as an understock both from seed and – as it roots easily – from cuttings.

(S) (F) (P) (T) (N) ● ≈
(SF) (AL)   15′ × 10′   4.5 × 3 m

R. multiflora carnea

CHINA 1804
A fully double form of *R. multiflora* with stronger shoots and larger leaves. Flowers globular, white faintly tinted pink.

(S) (P) (W) (F) (T) (N)
● ≈ (MF (AL)
18′ × 10′   5.5 × 3 m

R. multiflora cathayensis

CHINA 1907
Pink form of *R. multiflora* with larger flowers and lighter-coloured foliage.

(S) (F) (P) (T) (N) ●
≈ (MF) (AL)
15′ × 10′   4.5 × 3 m

R. multiflora platyphylla, R. multiflora grevillei, 'Seven Sisters Rose'

CHINA 1816
A vigorous climbing rose with large, dark green, rather coarse foliage and stiff, dark green stems.

Hybrid musks

R. multiflora hips

Flowers are double, quite large, and borne in very big trusses; they vary from deep to soft pink with sometimes lilac and even deep red blooms all produced together in the same truss. Scented. Common in Victorian times, when it was called 'Seven Sisters', derived from the seven different colours to be seen in each truss of flowers, another rose bearing this nickname being 'Félicité et Perpétue', which is actually a *R. sempervirens* hybrid.
(S) (P) (T) (N) ● (VF) (AL)   12′ × 10′   3.5 × 3 m

R. multiflora watsoniana

JAPAN 1870
This unusual form of *R. multiflora* is probably an old garden hybrid. Slim, trailing stems with small, hooked thorns and small, narrow, light green leaves, often wavy at the edges. Large panicles of small, closely packed, single flowers of off-white to pale pink. Masses of small, globular, red hips in autumn and early winter. More of

a novelty than a useful garden plant. Not fully hardy.
(S) (F) ☼ (SF) (AL)
5′ × 4′   1.5 × 1.2 m

R. multiflora wilsonii

1915
Rounded trusses of medium-sized, single white flowers, produced very freely on a vigorous, moderately thorny plant bearing shiny foliage. Fruit orange, smooth, rounded but quite small.
(S) (W) (P) (T) (N) (F) ● (AL)   15′ × 10′   4.5 × 3 m

These are among the most useful of shrubs having, by and large, long flowering seasons and agreeable habits of growth. For details on their history see pages 21–2.

CLASSIFICATION	
BARB	Class 15
MR9	Class 34
WFRS	Class 2

'Autumn Delight'

Bentall UK 1933
Soft, buff-yellow from shapely, deeper coloured buds. The semi-double flowers are produced in large trusses on an almost thornless, upright but bushy shrub with dark green, leathery foliage.
(C) (P) (H) (SF) (AL)
4′ × 4′   1.2 × 1.2 m

'Ballerina'

Bentall UK 1937
An outstanding rose with many uses from bedding to growing in pots. Huge sprays of small, single, pink flowers, each with a white centre. These are delightfully and daintily displayed throughout the

'Autumn Delight'

R. multiflora carnea

R. multiflora platyphylla

'Belinda'

summer on a bushy, upright, dense shrub with plentiful, mid-green foliage.
(C) (P) (H) ● ☉ (SF)
(AW) 4' × 3' 120 × 90 cm

'Belinda'

Bentall UK 1936
Huge trusses of semi-double flowers of mid-pink. Very vigorous and strong with plenty of darkish green foliage. Fragrant. One of the less well known Hybrid Musks but well worth consideration where a long-flowering shrub or ornamental hedge is required.
(C) (P) (H) ● ☉ (MF)
(AL) 5' × 4' 1.5 × 1.2 m

'Bishop Darlington'

Thomas USA 1926
'Aviateur Blériot' × 'Moonlight'
Large flowers, semi-double, creamy-white to pink with a yellow base to each petal and a strong scent. Bush vigorous with mid- to dark-green foliage.
(R) (P) (H) (SF) (AL)
5' × 5' 1.5 × 1.5 m

'Buff Beauty'

'Clytemnestra'

'Bloomfield Dainty'

Thomas USA 1924
'Danaë' × 'Mme. Edouard Herriot'
Long, pointed, orange buds open to single blooms of soft clear yellow. Quite fragrant. Foliage glossy mid-green on a vigorous, upright-growing plant.
(R) (P) (N) ● (MF) (AL)
8' × 4' 2.5 × 1.2 m

'Buff Beauty'

Bentall UK 1939
'William Allen Richardson' × unknown
One of the best of its group. A vigorous shrub with spreading growth and dark green foliage. Flowers fully double, opening flat

'Danaë'

from tight, cupped buds and produced in large trusses. Colour varies with weather and, I suspect, the soil in which they are growing, from buff-yellow to almost apricot, at times paling to primrose. Strongly scented.
(C) (P) (H) ● ☉ (MF)
(AW) 5' × 5' 1.5 × 1.5 m

'Callisto'

Pemberton UK 1920
'William Allen Richardson' × 'William Allen Richardson'
Sizeable clusters of small, shapely, semi-double to double flowers of rich yellow, paling to soft yellow with age. Quite vigorous in that its flowers are carried on long, sometimes arching stems, giving the effect of a rather open plant. Medium-sized foliage of lightish green. Few thorns.
(C) (P) (H) ● ☉ (AL)
5' × 4' 1.5 × 1.2 m

'Clytemnestra'

Pemberton UK 1915
'Trier' × 'Liberty'
Large clusters of soft lemony-beige flowers gently suffused salmon with pronounced anthers of golden yellow. Fragrant. Individually an untidy flower but very effective *en masse*. Foliage dark

green and leathery on a wide, vigorous shrub. This rose should be far better known.
(C) (P) (H) ● ☉ (MF) (AL) 4' × 4' 1.2 × 1.2 m

'Cornelia'

Pemberton UK 1925
Conspicuous bronzy foliage produced on long, dark brownish shoots. The small, fully double flowers, which are produced in large clusters, blend superbly with the foliage, being apricot-pink flushed deep pink with paler highlights. Particularly good in the autumn.
(C) (P) (H) ● ☉ (MF) (AW) 5' × 5' 1.5 × 1.5 m

'Danaë'

Pemberton UK 1913
'Trier' × 'Gloire de Chédane-Guinoisseau'
Clusters of semi-double, bright yellow flowers changing to buff and then to cream with age. A healthy, vigorous plant with dark foliage. A most useful lesser-known Hybrid Musk, well worth growing, where a shrub of this colour is sought.
(C) (P) (H) ● (MF) (AL) 5' × 4' 1.5 × 1.2 m

'Daphne'

Pemberton UK 1912
One of the first Pemberton Musks and one of the least known. Clusters of soft pink to blush, semi-double flowers with a good

perfume. Growth moderately vigorous. Foliage mid-green, semi-glossy.
(C) (P) (H) ☉ ● (MF) (AL) 4' × 4' 1.2 × 1.2 m

'Daybreak'

Pemberton UK 1918
'Trier' × 'Liberty'
Rather less than double flowers, lemon-yellow paling to primrose, produced on strong stems in medium-sized, well-spaced clusters. Foliage coppery, especially when young. Seldom gets very tall and never outgrows its welcome in any garden.
(C) (P) (H) ☉ (MF) (AL) 4' × 3' 120 × 90 cm

'Eva'

Kordes GERMANY 1938
'Robin Hood' × 'J. C. Thornton'
Trusses of good-size, almost single, bright carmine to red flowers which pale towards the centre to white. This lesser-known variety is well scented. Dark green foliage on a fairly tall-growing plant.
(C) (P) (H) (AL) 6' × 4' 1.8 × 1.2 m

'Felicia'

Pemberton UK 1928
'Trier' × 'Ophelia'
This rose is among the best of its group. The fully double flowers open from a rather muddled bud to shapely blooms of quite a charming mixture of rich pink with salmon shadings; they pale slightly with age but I find this an added attraction. Foliage crisp, slightly crinkled at the edges and dark green. The bush retains its shape well with judicious pruning, making it ideal for specimen planting.
(C) (P) (H) ☉ (MF) (AW) 4' × 4' 1.2 × 1.2 m

'Francesca'

Pemberton UK 1928
'Danaë' × 'Sunburst'
Large sprays of semi-double, apricot-yellow flowers on strong, dark stems with glossy dark green foliage. Useful, since its strong yellow colour is rare amongst shrub roses generally.
(C) (P) (H) ● ☉ (SF) (AL) 4' × 4' 1.2 × 1.2 m

'Kathleen'

Pemberton UK 1922
'Daphne' × 'Perle des Jeannes'
Very vigorous rose. Dark green foliage rather sparse for my taste. Stems greyish-green. Flowers almost single, medium-sized, best described as clear pink with deeper shadings.
(R) (P) (MF) (AL) 8' × 4' 2.5 × 1.2 m

'Lavender Lassie'

Kordes GERMANY 1960
Large trusses of beautiful, double, lavender-pink flowers, opening flat, produced throughout the summer on a healthy bush with dark green foliage. An ideal rose which can fulfil a variety of roles in the modern garden.
(C) (P) (H) ● (MF) (AL) 5' × 4' 1.5 × 1.2 m

'Cornelia', and *top:* 'Francesca'

'Felicia'

'Kathleen'

'Moonlight'

'Moonlight'

Pemberton UK 1913
'Trier' × 'Sulphurea'
Long, well-foliated stems with clusters of creamy-white almost single flowers with pronounced stamens. Scented. Vigorous and healthy.
(C) (P) (H) ● (MF) (AL)
5' × 4'   1.5 × 1.2 m

'Mozart'

Lambert GERMANY 1937
'Robin Hood' × 'Rote Pharisäer'

Small, single, carmine flowers with white centres are produced freely in massive clusters. Foliage mid-green on a dense and bushy plant.
(C) (P) (B) (H) ☉ (AL)
4' × 3'   120 × 90 cm

'Nur Mahal'

Pemberton UK 1923
'Château de Clos Vougeot' × Hybrid Musk seedling
Large clusters of bright crimson, semi-double flowers well perfumed. An interesting rose with much to commend it, not least its healthy dark foliage.
(C) (P) (H) ● (MF) (AL)
5' × 4'   1.5 × 1.2 m

'Nur Mahal'

'Pax'

Pemberton UK 1918
'Trier' × 'Sunburst'
Very large semi-double flowers, creamy-white to pure white, with obvious golden stamens. Blooms produced in large, well-spaced clusters which are held on long, arching stems. Foliage crisp and very dark green. A superb rose.
(C) (P) (H) ● (MF) (AW)
6' × 5'   1.8 × 1.5 m

'Penelope'

Pemberton UK 1924
'Ophelia' × 'Trier'
A favourite amongst the Hybrid Musks. This very pretty rose has large, semi-double flowers which,
when open, show off to advantage the slightly frilled petal edges; creamy-pink with deeper shadings, especially on frilled edges. Scented. Foliage dark green with plum-red shadings, likewise the stems. A little prone to mildew.
(C) (P) (H) ● ☉ M ⚘
(SF) (AW)   5' × 4'   1.5 × 1.2 m

'Pax'

'Lavender Lassie'

'Penelope'

'Prosperity'

'Pink Prosperity'

Bentall UK 1931
Large trusses of small, clear pink,
fully double blooms with deeper
shadings on an upright bush with
dark green foliage. Scented.
(C) (P) (H) ☉ (SF) (AL)
4′ × 4′   1.2 × 1.2 m

'Thisbe'

'Prosperity'

Pemberton UK 1919
'Marie-Jeanne' × 'Perle des
Jardins'
Large, double, creamy-white
flowers produced in large even
clusters on strong arching shoots
with dark green foliage. The arching effect, caused largely by bend-
ing from the weight of flowers,
rather than any tendency to sprawl,
adds to its attraction. Well worth
growing.
(C) (P) (H) ● (MF) (AW)
5′ × 4′   1.5 × 1.2 m

'Robin Hood'

'Sadler's Wells'

'Wilhelm'

'Robin Hood'

Pemberton UK 1927
Seedling × 'Miss Edith Cavell'
Large clusters of medium-sized
flowers, rather more than single,
bright scarlet ageing to crimson.
Good, dark green foliage with a
bushy, tidy growth habit.
(C) (H) ☉ (SF) (AL)
4' × 3'   120 × 90 cm

'Sadler's Wells'

Beales UK 1983
'Penelope' × 'Rose Gaujard'
The newest member of this
group. Makes a fine continuous-
flowering shrub. Semi-double
slightly scented flowers produced
in large, well-spaced clusters on a
vigorous but tidy bush. The background colour is silvery-pink,
with each petal laced with cherry
red, especially at the edges. The
autumn flowers are particularly
good, when the enriched colouring seems almost impervious to
inclement weather. When cut, the
sprays last very well in water.
Foliage is dark green and glossy.
(C) (P) (H) ● (NF) (AL)
4' × 3'   120 × 90 cm

'Thisbe'

Pemberton UK 1918
'Daphne' sport
Sulphur-straw coloured, the
flowers are semi-double rosettes
borne in large clusters on a bushy
upright shrub with glossy, mid-
green foliage.
(C) (P) (H) ☉ (MF) (AL)
4' × 4'   1.2 × 1.2 m

'Vanity'

Pemberton UK 1920
'Château de Clos Vougeot' ×
seedling
Large sprays of fragrant, rose-
pink, almost single flowers of
considerable size, produced freely
on a vigorous, bushy but somewhat angular shrub. Rather short
on foliage for my taste, but
brightness and density of flowers
probably makes up for this minor
fault.
(C) (P) (MF) (AL)
6' × 5'   1.8 × 1.5 m

'Wilhelm', 'Skyrocket'

Kordes GERMANY 1944
'Robin Hood' × 'J. C. Thornton'
Clusters of crimson, almost single
flowers on stout, strong stems. A
very useful rose since good red
varieties are scarce among the
Hybrid Musks. Foliage is dark
green and healthy. Gives a good
display of hips if not dead-
headed.
(C) (H) (F) (P) ● (AL)
5' × 4'   1.5 × 1.2 m

'Will Scarlet'

'Vanity'

'Will Scarlet'

Hilling UK 1947
'Wilhelm' sport
Almost identical to 'Wilhelm',
except being brighter red.
(C) (F) (H) (P) ● (AL)
5' × 4'   1.5 × 1.2 m

Multiflora Ramblers

The Multiflora Ramblers were developed towards the end of the Victorian era and were very popular, alongside the Wichuraianas, for the first quarter of this century. As a group, they span a wide colour range and all are very floriferous for about four weeks in early summer. Generally speaking they are robust, healthy and easy to grow and an advantage in the eyes of many gardeners is that, relatively speaking, they have few thorns. Although their popularity has declined since the advent of modern remontant climbers, they are far from out of place in the modern garden.

'Blush Rambler'

CLASSIFICATION

BARB	Class 15
MR9	Class 35
WFRS	Class 16

'Apple Blossom'

Burbank USA 1932
'Dawson' × *R. multiflora*
Huge trusses of apple blossom-like, pink flowers with crinkled petals. Foliage rich green with copper overtones. Wood is similar in colour to its foliage with few or no thorns.
(S) (P) ● (SF) (AW)
10′ × 6′   3 × 1.8 m

'Aglaia', 'Yellow Rambler'

Schmitt FRANCE 1896
R. multiflora × 'Rêve d'Or'
Small, semi-double flowers of pale primrose yellow. Growth upright, stems almost thornless. Foliage bright light green with bronzy tints, especially when young. Important as one of the roses used initially by Pemberton in breeding his race of Hybrid Musks.
(S) (P) ● (N) (SF) (AL)
8′ × 6′   2.5 × 1.8 m

'Apple Blossom'

'De la Grifferaie'

'Astra Desmond'

This rose, I feel, must be included in any serious book of roses for it is one of the loveliest of the vigorous climbers. So far, all I can discover about its origin is that it was named after an opera singer. Its flowers are small and semi-double, off-white to cream and they are produced very freely in huge trusses from mid-June to mid-July. Fragrant. The foliage is light green and crisp. Growth is very vigorous.
(S) (T) ● (N) (MF) (AL)
20′ × 10′   6 × 3 m

'Bleu Magenta'

c. 1900
One of the daintiest of flowers. Rich deep purple with yellow stamens peeping from beneath folded, centre petals. Sweetly scented. Foliage dark and free of thorns. Although not recurrent, flowers later in summer than most.
(S) (P) (N) ● (MF) (AL)
12′ × 10′   3.5 × 3 m

'Blush Rambler'

B. R. Cant UK 1903
'Crimson Rambler' × 'The Garland'
A vigorous, almost thornless rose, popular as a cottage rambler in Edwardian days. Fragrant flowers blush-pink in colour, borne in cascading clusters. Foliage plentiful and light green.
(S) (P) (SF) (AL)
12′ × 10′   3.5 × 3 m

'Bobbie James'

Sunningdale Nurseries UK 1961
Capable of considerable climbing feats especially into trees and hedges. I rate this rose as one of the best for this purpose. The individual white flowers are of cupped shape and quite large, rather more than single, highly scented, and displayed in large, drooping clusters. The foliage is rich coppery green and polished. Stems are strong and well equipped with sharp, hooked thorns.
(S) (A) (P) (T) (N) ●
(VF) (AW)   30′ × 20′   9 × 6 m

'Crimson Rambler', 'Turner's Crimson', 'Engineer's Rose'

JAPAN 1893
More important as a stud rose in the development of ramblers than as a garden plant. Semi-double crimson flowers produced in clusters. Foliage light green. Rather disease-prone, which is the main reason for its virtual disappearance from modern gardens.
(S) (SF) (AL)
12' × 10'   3.5 × 3 m

'De la Grifferaie'

Vibert FRANCE 1845
A vigorous, dark, rather coarse-foliage plant, extensively used in the past as an understock, hence frequently found in old gardens. Trusses of spaced, fully double flowers of magenta fading to dirty white. Well scented, not of great garden value.
(S) (P) (N) ● (VF) (AL)
8' × 4'   2.5 × 1.2 m

'Francis E. Lester'

Lester Rose Gardens USA 1946
'Kathleen' × unnamed seedling
Very large trusses of well-spaced, medium-sized, single flowers, white with splashes of pink on the edges of each petal. A special feature is its strong perfume. The shrub is vigorous but not overpowering, with lush, coppery-tinted, glossy foliage. Small red hips in autumn.
(S) (T) (F) (P) (N) ●
(MF) (AL)   15' × 10'   4.5 × 3 m

'Ghislaine de Féligonde'

Turbat FRANCE 1916
'Goldfinch × unknown
A small climber or, if space permits, can be grown as a large shrub. Fully double, orange-

'Bobbie James'

yellow flowers in very large clusters. Healthy, large, glossy foliage. Almost thornless. I can't think of a good reason why this rose has not gained the popularity it deserves.
(R) (P) (N) ● (MF) (AL)
8' × 8'   2.5 × 2.5 m

'Goldfinch'

W Paul UK 1907
'Hélène' × unknown
Less vigorous than some but very useful where a small rambler or climber is required. Small cupped flowers a mixture of golden-yellow and primrose with pronounced golden-brown anthers, still charming even when fading to cream in hot sun. Almost thornless greenish brown stems and glossy foliage.
(S) (P) (N) ● (MF) (AL)
8' × 5'   2.5 × 1.5 m

'Hiawatha'

Walsh USA 1904
'Crimson Rambler' × 'Paul's Carmine Pillar'
Single, deepish pink to crimson

flowers with paler, almost white centres. These are borne in clus-

'Ghislaine de Féligonde'

ters on a vigorous, free-growing plant with lightish green leaves. Another rose awkward to classify, but probably best here, because of obvious Multiflora influence.
(S) (P) ● (T) (AL)
15' × 12'   4.5 × 3.5 m

'Francis E. Lester'

'Goldfinch'

'Lauré Davoust', 'Marjorie W. Lester'

Laffay FRANCE 1934
Flowers which are small, cupped and double change with age from bright pink through to soft pink and then white. Foliage mid-green. Growth fairly upright and healthy. A useful, lesser known small rambler or tall shrub.
(S) (P) ● (MF) (AL)
10′ × 8′   3 × 2.5 m

'Leuchtstern'

J. C. Schmidt GERMANY 1899
'Daniel Lacombe' × 'Crimson Rambler'
Clusters of medium-sized, single deep pink flowers with centres paling to white. Good, mid-green foliage. Not often seen but a good, shorter rambler.
(S) (P) (N) ● (AL)
10′ × 8′   3 × 2.5 m

'Mme d'Arblay'

Wills UK 1835
R. multiflora × R. moschata
Drooping clusters of small, flattish-topped yet slightly cupped flowers comprised of randomly arranged, shortish petals, fragrant, blush-pink paling to white. A very vigorous climber with darkish green foliage. Now quite rare.
(S) (P) (T) (N) ● (VF)
(AL)   20′ × 20′   6 × 6 m

'Madeleine Selzer', 'Yellow Tausendschön'

Walter FRANCE 1926
'Tausendschön' × 'Mrs Aaron Ward'
Attractive, almost thornless rose with bronzy-green foliage, bearing trusses of fully double, scented, lemon to white flowers. Quite a spectacle when in full flush. An excellent medium-growing rambler.
(S) (P) (SF) (AL)
10′ × 6′   3 × 1.8 m

'Mrs F. W. Flight'

Cutbush UK 1905
'Crimson Rambler' × unknown
For some reason, this rose has escaped me. So I can only discuss it from a photograph and cribbed descriptions. Small, semi-double, rose-pink flowers in large clusters. On a short to medium-growing plant with large, soft mid-green foliage.
(S) (SF) (AL)
8′ × 6′   2.5 × 1.8 m

'Paul's Scarlet'

W. Paul UK 1916
'Paul's Carmine Pillar' × 'Rêve d'Or'
Double, bright scarlet flowers in small spaced clusters. One of the brightest and most popular ramblers of its day. Foliage dark green, as are its relatively thorn-less stems. I am not sure it should be in this group, but where else to place it?
(S) (P) (N) ● (AL)
10′ × 8′   3 × 2.5 m

'Paul's Scarlet'

'Phyllis Bide'

Bide UK 1923
'Perle d'Or' × 'Gloire de Dijon'
Small, slightly ragged, large pyramidal clusters of flowers of mixed colouring including yellow,

'Madeleine Selzer'

'Paul's Scarlet'

cream and pink, sometimes deepening with age and becoming mottled. Foliage plentiful but each leaf quite small. Growth vigorous and relatively thorn-free. A superb and important rose flowering continuously throughout the season, perhaps nearer to the section *Chinensis* than *Synstylae*.

(R) (P) (N) ● (SF) (AL)
10′ × 6′   3 × 1.8 m

'Phyllis Bide'

'Russelliana'

'Rambling Rector'

'Rambling Rector'

Very old variety

Large clusters of fragrant, semi-double flowers, creamy to begin with, then opening white to display rich yellow stamens. These are produced in abundance on a vigorous, healthy, scrambling shrub. Plentiful foliage, small, grey-green and downy. Superb as a tree or hedgerow climber. Pro-

'Tea Rambler'

'Rambling Rector' hips

duces a good display of small hips in the autumn. Many an old corrugated iron shed would become less of an eyesore if supporting 'Rambling Rector'.

(S) (P) (W) (F) (T) (N)
● (VF) (AL)
20′ × 15′   6 × 4.5 m

'Rose Marie Viaud'

Igoult FRANCE 1924
'Veilchenblau' seedling
Very double flowers of rich purple produced in small trusses on a vigorous rambler with light green foliage and relatively thornless, light green shoots.

(S) (P) ● (AL)
15′ × 6′   4.5 × 1.8 m

'Russelliana', 'Old Spanish Rose', 'Russell's Cottage Rose', 'Scarlet Grevillei'

Probably SPAIN 1840
Probably a cross between *R. multiflora* and *R. setigera*
A rose of some antiquity with very double, small flowers borne in clusters. Its colour is a mixture of crimson and mild purple, giving an overall red appearance. Well worthy of garden space. Foliage dark green and stems rather thorny, belying its Multiflora ancestry. Good specimens can be seen at both Cranborne House, Dorset, and Mottisfont Abbey, Hants.

(S) (P) (N) (T) ● (VF)
(AL)   10′ × 10′   3 × 3 m

'Seagull'

Pritchard UK 1907
R. multiflora × 'Général Jacqueminot'
Bright yellow stamens surrounded by a double layer of white petals. Highly scented flowers borne in large clusters on a vigorous, well-foliated plant which has grey-green leaves. An established plant in full flush of flower is a sight to remember.

(S) (P) (N) (T) ● (MF)
(AL)   25′ × 15′   7.5 × 4.5 m

'Veilchenblau'

'Seagull'

'Tausendschön', 'Thousand Beauties'

J. C. Schmidt GERMANY 1906
'Daniel Lacombe' × 'Weisser Herumstreicher'
An interesting rose. The flowers which are large, double and borne in loose clusters, are pink with white towards their centre. Growth is strong with thornless shoots, amply clothed with mid-green foliage.
(S) (P) (SF) (AL)
10' × 8'   3 × 2.5 m

'Tea Rambler'

W. Paul UK 1904
'Crimson Rambler' × a Tea rose
Fragrant, double, soft pink flowers with brighter highlights on a vigorous plant with mid-green foliage.
(S) (P) (T) ● (SF) (AL)
15' × 8'   4.5 × 2.5 m

'Thalia', 'White Rambler'

Schmitt FRANCE Introduced by P. Lambert GERMANY 1895
Quite a good rose, not often seen today. Flowers white, smallish, double and highly scented, produced profusely in large clusters. Growth vigorous and only moderately thorny. Foliage mid-green and mildly glossy.
(S) (P) (T) (N) ● (SF) (AL)   12' × 8'   3.5 × 2.5 m

'Trier'

P. Lambert GERMANY 1904
'Aglaia' × unknown
An upright-growing climber or, if preferred, tall shrub with small, creamy-yellow, single or near-single flowers in clusters. Foliage small, almost daintily so. Used much by breeders earlier this century, especially in development of Hybrid Musks.
(R) (P) ● (SF) (AL)
8' × 6'   2.5 × 1.8 m

'Turner's Crimson' see 'Crimson Rambler'

'Veilchenblau'

J. C. Schmidt GERMANY 1909
'Crimson Rambler' × unknown seedling
A vigorous rambler sometimes called 'The Blue Rose'. Bear large trusses of small, semi-double flowers of lavender-purple occasionally flecked with white, especially in their centres. They mature to bluish-lilac and fade to lilac-grey. Scented. An ideal companion for cream and white ramblers, when the respective flowers can merge to good effect.
(S) (P) (T) (N) ● (MF)
(AL)   15' × 12'   4.5 × 3.5 m

'Violette'

Modern Climbing Roses

In recent years a most useful trend has occurred in modern roses: the development of a number of continuously flowering climbers. To be more accurate, they are really large shrubs which, if placed by a wall or given support, will behave rather like climbers. They do not send up long climbing shoots as do, for example, climbing Hybrid Teas (which are placed elsewhere despite the BARB classification that puts many of them into that group). They usually flower on wood produced in the same season. As for classification, they are a mixed bunch and now very hybrid indeed. But much of their vigour and floriferousness must be derived from *R. multiflora*, which enables me to place them here.

Most have been raised as seedlings and are not climbing sports. More and more are coming in each year and it is difficult to keep up to date, but those chosen for inclusion are all well-tried varieties.

'Violette'

Turbat FRANCE 1921
Very double, cupped, rosette flowers of rich violet-purple with hints of yellow in their base. Flowers in clusters, scented. Foliage rich dark green. Growth is vigorous and shoots have few thorns.
(S) (P) (T) ● (MF) (AL)
15′ × 10′   4.5 × 3 m

'White Flight'

I have yet to find this rose described anywhere, and suspect it to be wrongly named. It is perhaps a sport from 'Mrs W. Flight' but I have never seen this to check. Less vigorous than most of its type. Huge corymbs of small, single, pure white flowers amid an abundance of smallish, light green foliage. Growth thin, wiry and yet dense. Supplied to me by the late Mr Humphrey Brooke of Claydon, Suffolk.
(S) (P) (N) ● (MF) (AL)
12′ × 8′   3.5 × 2.5 m

'Wind Chimes'

Lester USA Pre-1946
Clusters of small, double, rosy-pink blooms on a very vigorous shrub or small climber with good clear mid-green foliage.
(C) (P) (W) ● (VF) (AL)
12′ × 8′   3.5 × 2.5 m

CLASSIFICATION

BARB	Classes 10, 11 and 12. Some 7
MR9	Class 46
WFRS	Classes 13 and 17

'Alchemist'

'Agatha Christie', 'Ramira' (Kormeita)

Kordes GERMANY 1990
Large, classical, clear pink blooms freely produced throughout the summer, set off by striking, dark green glossy foliage.
(C) (P) (SF) ✖ (AL)
8′ × 4′   2.5 × 1.2 m

'Alchemist'

Kordes GERMANY 1956
'Golden Glow' × *R. eglanteria* hybrid
An unusual but beautiful medium-growing, climbing rose with rich green foliage and thorny

'Aloha'

strongly fragrant. Healthy, dark bronze foliage. Has an upright habit and is seldom not in flower throughout the summer. In all respects a first-class rose.

(C) (P) ✂ (VF) (AW)
10' × 6'   3 × 1.8 m

'Altissimo'

Delbard-Chabert FRANCE 1967
'Ténor' × unknown
Large, bright red, single flowers borne in small-spaced clusters, sometimes singly amid dark green foliage. A superb rose for pillar work or trellis. Does not do well as a wall plant, at least for me.

(C) (P) (SF) (AL)
10' × 6'   3 × 1.8 m

'America'

Warriner USA 1976
'Fragrant Cloud' × 'Tradition'
Fully double flowers of rich salmon with lighter reverses. Very fragrant. Foliage mid-green. Growth vigorous.

(R) (P) (VF) (AW)
15' × 10'   4.5 × 3 m

'Antique',
'Antike '89' (Kordalen)

Kordes GERMANY 1989
Large, fully double, Centifolia-like flowers of rose pink, paler in the centres. Foliage lush. Growth vigorous.

(C) (P) (SF) (AL)
8' × 4'   2.5 × 1.2 m

'Ash Wednesday',
'Aschermittwoch'

Kordes GERMANY 1955
Said to be *R. eglanteria* hybrid. Although of Eglanteria descent, this rose is probably better placed here among modern climbers since I can detect no perfume from its foliage. Trusses of ashen-white to soft lilac, double blooms on a vigorous, thorny, well-foliated plant.

(S) (P) (N) ● (SF) (AL)
10' × 6'   3 × 1.8 m

wood. The very double flowers, mostly opening quartered, are a rich mixture of yellow and yolky-orange with a strong scent. These are produced quite early in the season; some of the first flowers are much paler than the later ones. Black spot can be trouble-some.

(S) (P) ● (VF) (AL) BS✂
12' × 8'   3.5 × 2.5 m

'Aloha'

Boerner USA 1949
'Mercedes Gallart' × 'New Dawn'
A sumptuous and most attractive rose comprising 60 or more rose-pink petals, each with a deeper reverse and shadings of magenta,

'Altissimo'

'Ash Wednesday'

'Autumn Sunlight'

Gregory UK 1965
'Danse de Feu' × 'Goldilocks'
Large clusters of fully double,
orange-vermilion flowers. Foliage
rich mid-green. Growth upright
and tall.
(C) (P) (SF) (AL)
12' × 8' 3.5 × 2.5 m

'Bantry Bay'

'Casino'

'Bantry Bay'

McGredy UK 1967
'New Dawn' × 'Korona'
Large, scented, semi-double
flowers opening rather blowsily,
deep pink with quieter reflections. Foliage lush and dark green.
One of the best and most free-
flowering of its type.
(P) (C) (MF) (AW)
12' × 8' 3.5 × 2.5 m

'Breath of Life'

Harkness UK 1981
'Red Dandy' × 'Alexander'
Rich but not dazzlingly so. Apricot flowers are shapely, Hybrid
Tea-like, and scented. Foliage
dark green. A good and apparently reliable rose for those who
like the orange shades, which are
never the easiest of roses to grow.
(C) ✄ (MF) (AL)
10' × 6' 3 × 1.8 m

'Butterscotch' (Jactan)

Warriner USA 1986
('Buccaneer' × 'Zorina') × 'Royal
Sunset'
Double, shapely, tan-to-orangey-
yellow flowers opening cupped,
produced in clusters on a vigorous, dense plant with mid-green,
semi-glossy foliage.
(C) (P) ☼ (SF) (AL)
10' × 6' 3 × 1.8 m

'Casino'

McGredy UK 1963
'Coral Dawn' × 'Buccaneer'
Clusters of large, full, globular,
clear yellow scented blooms on
strong, dark stems with contrasting light green, glossy foliage. Can
be relied upon as a good pillar
rose.
(R) (VF) (AL)
10' × 8' 3 × 2.5 m

'City of York', with whole plant *above*

'City of York',
'Direktor Benschop'

Tantau GERMANY 1960
'Prof Gnau' × 'Dorothy Perkins'
A good vigorous climber with
ample glossy foliage. Flowers
creamy-white with lemon centres,
semi-double and cupped. Individually beautiful and produced very
freely to give a superb overall
effect. Scented.
(S) (P) (W) (N) (T) ●
(MF) (AL) 15' × 10' 4.5 × 3 m

'Clair Matin'

Meilland FRANCE 1960
('Fashion' × 'Independence')
× unnamed Multiflora seedling

'Clair Matin'

Free-branching, with large trusses of clear pink blooms, each with cream highlights. Almost but not quite single. A free flowering habit makes this rose outstanding. Foliage dark green and stems chocolate-purple. Also makes a good free-standing shrub or tall hedge.
(C) (P) (N) ● (SF) (AL)
8' × 4'   2.5 × 1.2 m

'Colcestria'

B. R. Cant UK 1916
A beautiful, large, full flower of silvery-pink with reflexing petals opening flat. Very fragrant. Foliage light green. Growth – a little reluctant but well worth the effort.
(R) ☉ (Gh) ☼ (VF) ✄
(AL)   8' × 5'   2.5 × 1.5 m

'Columbian Climber'

Strictly speaking I should ignore this rose because I can find out very little about it, but it is too good a rose to pretend it doesn't exist. Undoubtedly, it has another name. The blooms are large, full, highly scented and rosy-pink in colour. They are produced amid good mid-green foliage on a medium-vigorous plant. My thanks to Vivian Russell for introducing me to this seductive variety.

'Constance Spry'

'Compassion'

(R) ☉ (Gh) ☼ (VF) ✄
(AL)   8' × 5'   2.5 × 1.5 m

'Compassion'

Harkness UK 1974
'White Cockade' × 'Prima Ballerina'
Dark green, glossy foliage on dark wood bearing shapely blooms of apricot and copper with yellow highlights. Scented.
(R) ✄ (VF) BS✿ (AW)
10' × 6'   3 × 1.8 m

'Constance Spry'

Austin UK 1960
'Belle Isis' × 'Dainty Maid'
A beautiful rose in the old-fashioned style. Large, clear, bright pink, very full with a myrrh-like perfume. Copious grey-green foliage on a vigorous, quite thorny plant. Ideal for most situations. Particularly good on a tripod.
(S) (P) (H) ● (VF) M✿
(AL)   20' × 10'   6 × 3 m

'Coral Dawn'

Boerner USA 1952
'New Dawn' × unnamed yellow Hybrid Tea
Large, full, rather plump, coral-pink blooms amid ample dark green, healthy foliage. Scented. A first-class free-flowering rose.
(R) (N) ● (SF) (AL)
12' × 8'   3.5 × 2.5 m

'Danse de Feu', 'Spectacular'

Mallerin FRANCE 1953
'Paul's Scarlet' × unnamed Multiflora seedling
So bright, this rose almost screams, which makes it difficult to place with other climbers. Nevertheless, an excellent, free-flowering rose with shapely buds opening flat and fully double. Colour bright brick-red. Copious foliage but I find this variety rather prone to black spot.
(C) ● BS✿ (AW)
12' × 8'   3.5 × 2.5 m

'Coral Dawn'

'Danse de Feu'

'Dublin Bay'

'Danse des Sylphes'

Mallerin FRANCE 1959
'Danse de Feu' × ('Peace' ×
'Independence')
Rich bright red, a seedling from
'Danse de Feu'. Almost as bright
but far more refined.
(C) ● (SF) (AL)
12' × 8'   3.5 × 2.5 m

'Etude'

'Golden Showers'

'Don Juan', 'Malandrone'

Jackson and Perkins USA 1958
'New Dawn' seedling × 'New
Yorker'
Fully double, cupped flowers of
velvety-dark-red, very fragrant
and borne in clusters. Foliage
glossy, dark green and leathery.
Growth upright but branching.
(R) (P) (VF) ✂ (AW)
10' × 6'   3 × 1.8 m

'Dreaming Spires'

Mattock UK 1977
'Buccaneer' × 'Arthur Bell'
Shapely, high-centred, deep yellow flowers with discreet touches
of orange, fading to primrose with
age. Fine, dark foliage on a vigorous plant.
(C) (P) (SF) (AL)
12' × 8'   3.5 × 2.5 m

'Dublin Bay'

McGredy UK 1976
'Bantry Bay' × 'Altissimo'
A very good pillar rose with large,
glossy leaves. Clusters of
medium-sized, rich blood-red
flowers. Almost constantly in
flower throughout the summer.
Can also be grown successfully as
a large shrub.
(C) (P) (SF) (AL)
7' × 5'   2 × 1.5 m

'Eden Rose '88' (Meiviolin)

Meilland FRANCE 1987
Its fully double flowers are in the
old-fashioned style, their colour is
creamy-white shaded with lavender-pink at the base of the petals.
Foliage dark green and glossy.
Growth upright and bushy.
(C) (SF) (AL)
8' × 6'   2.5 × 1.8 m

'Etude'

Gregory UK 1965
'Danse de Feu' × 'New Dawn'
Clusters of semi-double, deep
rose-pink blooms with a good
fragrance. Glossy, light green
foliage on a vigorous, upright-
growing plant.
(C) (P) (N) ● ✂ ☼
(MF) (AL) 10' × 8'   3 × 2.5 m

'Fugue' (Meitam)

Meilland FRANCE 1958
'Alain' × 'Guinée'
A very good but little known
variety with fully double flowers
of rich, deep red. Dark glossy foliage and vigorous growth. A useful
pillar rose.
(C) (P) (SF) (AL)
10' × 6'   3 × 1.8 m

'Galway Bay'

McGredy UK 1966
'Heidelberg' × 'Queen Elizabeth'
Large, double, shapely flowers, of
salmon-pink. Scented. Foliage
profuse and glossy dark green.
The plant is vigorous and has a
tidy growth habit.
(C) (P) ● (SF) (AL)
12' × 8'   3.5 × 2.5 m

'Golden Showers'

Lammerts USA 1956
'Charlotte Armstrong' × 'Captain
Thomas'
Large, loosely formed, rather
raggedly formed flowers, of deep
golden-yellow fading quickly to
cream. Flowers continuously from
June to October. Foliage rich dark
green and glossy. Also capable of
making a good free-standing
shrub.
(C) (P) ● (SF) (AW)
10' × 6'   3 × 1.8 m

'Golden Showers'

'Grand Hotel' (Mactel)

McGredy UK 1972
'Brilliant' × 'Heidelberg'
Semi-double, sizeable flowers of
rich scarlet borne in clusters. Foliage dark green and semi-glossy.
Growth upright and bushy.
(C) (P) (SF) (AL)
8′ × 4′ 2.5 × 1.2 m

'Handel'

McGredy UK 1956
'Columbine' × Heidelberg'
A good variety with dark stems
and glossy dark green, almost

'Malaga'

'Handel'

purple leaves. Large, semi-double
flowers, cupped until fully open,
silver-white with pink to red
markings especially on the petal
edges. These markings intensify
with age. An excellent rose, but
somewhat 'pretty' for my taste.
(C) (P) (SF) (AW)
12′ × 8′ 3.5 × 2.5 m

'Highfield'

Harkness UK 1982
A paler sport of 'Compassion',
preferred by some because it is
less severe in colour.
(C) ✄ (VF) (AL)
8′ × 6′ 2.5 × 1.8 m

'Ilse Krohn Superior'

Kordes GERMANY 1957
'Golden Glow' × *R. kordesii*
Fully double, pure white flowers
from shapely, pointed buds.
Slightly scented. Foliage rich
green and glossy. Growth vigorous.
(S) (T) (N) (P) ● (SF)
(AW) 12′ × 10′ 3.5 × 3 m

'Köln am Rhein'

Kordes GERMANY 1956
Fragrant, double, deep salmon-
pink flowers produced in clusters
on a healthy robust plant. Foliage
rich dark green and glossy. Not
often seen, but well worth garden
space.
(R) (P) (N) ● (AL)
15′ × 10′ 4.5 × 3 m

'Laura Ford' (Chewarvel)

Warner UK 1989
Although 'climbing miniature' is
in some ways a contradiction in
terms, this one is delightful with
small flowers and small leaves, as
one would expect in a miniature.
Strong yellow with amber shades
– especially in the autumn. Constantly in flower, it makes a good
pillar rose.
(C) ☉ (AL)
8′ × 3′ 250 × 90 cm

'Lavinia', 'Lawinia' (Tanklewi)

Tantau GERMANY 1980
Large, fragrant, cupped, double
flowers of mid-pink borne amid
large, mid-green, semi-glossy foliage on a vigorous, wide-growing
plant.
(R) (T) (VF) ✄ (AW)
12′ × 8′ 3.5 × 2.5 m

'Leaping Salmon' (Peamight)

Pearce UK 1986
('Vesper' × 'Aloha') × ('Paddy
McGredy' × 'Maigold') × 'Prima
Ballerina'
Large salmon-pink, fragrant,
almost double flowers produced
freely on a bushy, upright plant
amid plentiful, mid-green, glossy
foliage.
(R) (P) (SF) ✄ (AL)
10′ × 6′ 3 × 1.8 m

'Laura Ford'

'Malaga'

McGredy UK 1971
('Hamburger Phoenix' × 'Danse
de Feu') × 'Copenhagen'
Large, deep rose-pink flowers in
good clusters on a medium but
vigorous plant with dark green
foliage. A special feature is the
distinctive sweet briar fragrance.
(R) (P) ✄ (VF) (AL)
8′ × 4′ 2.4 × 1.2 m

'Morning Jewel'

Cocker UK 1968
'New Dawn' × 'Red Dandy'
Large, semi-double flowers,
fragrant, rich pink. Very free
flowering with glossy, clear green
foliage.
(R) (P) (MF) (AL)
10′ × 8′ 3 × 2.5 m

'Rosy Mantle'

'Night Light' (Poullight)

Poulsen DENMARK 1982
'Westerland' × 'Pastorale'
Sizeable sprays of large, double,
deep yellow flowers. Foliage dark
green and glossy. Growth upright.
(C) (SF) (AL)
10' × 8'   3 × 2.5 m

'Norwich Gold'

Kordes GERMANY 1962
Fragrant flowers of yellow shaded
orange, very full, opening flat.
Foliage rather dull green.
(R) (P) (MF) (AL)
10' × 8'   3 × 2.5 m

'Norwich Pink'

Kordes GERMANY 1962
Semi-double, bright cerise flowers
with a strong fragrance. Foliage
dark and glossy.
(R) (P) (VF) (AL)
10' × 8'   3 × 2.5 m

'Norwich Salmon'

Kordes GERMANY 1962
Fully double, soft salmon-pink
flowers produced in large clusters
on a vigorous, bushy plant. Foliage dark green and glossy.
(R) (SF) (AL)
10' × 8'   3 × 2.4 m

'Parade'

Boerner USA 1953
'New Dawn' seedling × 'World's
Fair'
Cerise-red to crimson flowers,
fully double and scented. Foliage
glossy, profuse and healthy.
Excellent both as a pillar rose
or free-standing shrub.
(C) (P) ● ✂ (SF) (AL)
10' × 8'   3 × 2.5 m

'Pinata'

Susuki JAPAN 1978
Fully double, high-centred
flowers of clear yellow overlaid
vermilion. Slightly fragrant. Foliage large, light to mid-green.
Growth vigorous, dense.
(C) (P) ● (SF) (AL)
10' × 6'   3 × 1.8 m

'Pinkie' Climber

Dering, Armstrong Nurseries USA
1952
Sport from bush form. Swim USA
1947
'China Doll' × seedling
This is an outstandingly free-
flowering climber. When in full
flush its mass of semi-double,
bright pink flowers are a sight to
behold. The foliage, soft to touch,
is a glossy light green. Growth

America and the Antipodes. I
recall seeing a particularly good
plant at The Antique Rose Emporium, Brenham, Texas.
(R) (P) ☉ ☼ (MF) (AL)
10' × 8'   3 × 2.5 m

'Pink Perpétue'

Gregory UK 1965
'Danse de Feu' × 'New Dawn'
One of the outstanding modern
climbers. Its colour is perhaps
rather hard for some tastes, but it
can be relied upon to produce
masses of double, deep pink,
rather cupped, semi-double
flowers throughout the summer.
Its very dark green foliage has
glossy purple overtones making
an excellent foil for the flowers.
(C) (P) (N) ● (MF) (AL)
12' × 8'   3.5 × 2.5 m

'Rhonda'

Lissmore USA 1968
'New Dawn' × 'Spartan'
Large, fully double flowers in
clusters, deep carmine-rose.
Fragrant. Foliage mid-green,
semi-glossy. Growth vigorous and
upright.
(R) (P) (SF) (AW)
10' × 6'   3 × 1.8 m

'Ritter von Barmstede'

'Swan Lake'

'Ritter von Barmstede'

Kordes GERMANY 1959
Deep pink, double flowers in
large clusters. Somewhat untidy
in growth but has excellent, glossy
dark green foliage.
(R) (P) ● (AL)
10' × 10'   3 × 3 m

'Rosy Mantle'

Cocker UK 1968
'New Dawn' × 'Prima Ballerina'
Silver-pink, fully double flowers

'Parade'

'Pinkie'

'Pink Perrpétue'

with a strong perfume. Rather sprawly if not tethered, but very showy when in full flush. Good, glossy dark green foliage.
(C) (N) ● ✂ (VF) (AL)
8′ × 8′   2.5 × 2.5 m

'Royal Gold'

Morey USA 1957
'Goldilocks' × 'Lydia'
Not the most free-flowering of climbers, but its flowers are usually of good quality, golden-yellow, almost non-fading, of classic Hybrid Tea shape, opening loosely-formed and quite large. Foliage glossy, mid- to dark-green. Needs a warm sheltered position to ensure against a slight tenderness.
(C) ☼ ✂ (VF) (AL)
8′ × 8′   2.5 × 2.5 m

'Schoolgirl'

'Royal Gold'

'Warm Welcome'

'White Cockade'

'Schoolgirl'

McGredy UK 1964
'Coral Dawn' × 'Belle Blonde'
Rich, coppery-orange flowers Hybrid Tea-shaped in bud, opening loosely flat and semi-double. Highly scented. A little short on foliage and, in my opinion, rather overrated.
(C) ✂ (VF) (AW)
10′ × 8′   3 × 2.5 m

'Soldier Boy'

LeGrice UK 1953
Unnamed seedling × 'Guinée'
A rose of considerable beauty. Flowers are single, rich scarlet with pronounced golden anthers. Foliage profuse and matt dark green. Repeats intermittently throughout summer.
(R) (P) (N) ● (VF) (AL)
10′ × 8′   3 × 2.5 m

'Sparkling Scarlet', 'Iskra' (Meihaiti)

Meilland FRANCE 1970
'Danse des Sylphes' × 'Zambra'
Clusters of semi-double, very bright scarlet flowers, with large, mid-green, semi-glossy foliage on an upright, branching plant.
(C) (P) (VF) (AL)
10′ × 8′   3 × 2.5 m

'Spectacular'
see 'Danse de Feu'

'Summer Wine' (Korizont)

Kordes GERMANY 1985
Its large, semi-double, deep pink flowers have red stamens and come in clusters. Foliage mid-green and semi-glossy. Growth upright and bushy.
(C) (P) (MF) (AL)
10′ × 6′   3 × 1.8 m

'Swan Lake'

McGredy UK 1968
'Memorium' × 'Heidelberg'
A beautiful rose, shapely in bud, opening large and fully double, white with a pale pink flush in the centre, and produced freely all summer. Rounded, dark green foliage, liberally produced on an upright, tidy plant.
(C) (P) ✄ (SF) (AW)
8' × 6'   2.5 × 1.8 m

'Sympathie'

Kordes GERMANY 1964
Fragrant, dark red, fully double and shapely blooms produced freely and continuously throughout summer. Foliage dark green and glossy.
(C) (P) (MF) (AL)
10' × 8'   3 × 2.5 m

'Tempo'

Warriner USA 1975
'Climbing Ena Harkness' × unknown
Fully double, shapely, fragrant, deep red flowers in profusion. Growth vigorous. Foliage dark green, glossy.
(R) (P) (VF) (AW)
15' × 10'   4.5 × 3 m

'Warm Welcome' (Chewizz)

Warner UK 1990
Another good miniature-flowered climber from the raiser who brought out 'Laura Ford'. This one is very bright indeed and described by Warner as 'lively orange-vermilion'. Good leathery foliage.
(C) ☉ (AL)
8' × 3'   250 × 90 cm

'White Cockade'

Cocker UK 1969
'New Dawn' × 'Circus'
A thorny, upright climber with small but ample, dark, glossy foliage, combining well with fully double, pure white flowers which open into rather triangular shapes, hence its name. One of the best white climbers, but not the most vigorous; good grown as a pillar rose.
(C) ✄ (SF) (AL)
8' × 6'   2.5 × 1.8 m

'Angelina'

'Applejack'

Modern Shrub Roses

An increasing demand for shrub roses has prompted breeders to produce and introduce many and varied tall varieties, all with long flowering seasons. These, as with modern climbers, are of very mixed progeny; and many, in addition to making excellent shrubs, may also be adapted to make admirable small climbers or pillar roses. Some also make very good hedges, both informal and formal.

CLASSIFICATION	
BARB	Class 7
MR9	Class 54
WFRS	Classes 1 and 2

'Alexander'

Harkness UK 1972
'Super Star' × ('Ann Elizabeth' × 'Allgold')
Shapely pointed buds opening to large, slightly ragged flowers of a very bright luminous vermilion, displaying creamy yellow stamens to good effect. Foliage rich green and healthy. Growth upright, with strong thorny stems.
(C) (P) (H) ● ✄ (SF)
(AW)   6' × 4'   1.8 × 1.2 m

'Angelina'

Cocker UK 1976
('Super Star' × 'Carina') × ('Cläre Grammerstorf' × 'Frühlingsmorgen')
An extremely free-flowering, shortish shrub rose, not yet widely distributed, but as it becomes better known it is sure to become a firm favourite. The fragrant flowers are large, slightly fuller than single, and bright rose-pink. These are produced in large clusters on upright stems with dark green foliage.
(C) (H) (P) ☉ (MF)
(AL)   4' × 3'   120 × 90 cm

'Anna Zinkeisen'

Harkness UK 1983
A shrubby rose with good mid-green foliage. Fully double flowers ivory-white with golden-yellow tones in the base, borne in clusters. Has a distinctive perfume.
(C) (G) (P) ● ☉ (VF)
(AL)   4' × 3'   120 × 90 cm

'Applejack'

Buck USA 1973
'Goldbusch' × ('Josef Rothmund' × R. laxa retzius)
Small, pointed buds open to loose, semi-double flowers of deepish rose-pink discreetly dappled red, very fragrant, very free-flowering. Foliage profuse, mid-green, leathery. Growth vigorous and widely bushy. A delightful all-rounder. Hardy. I have never seen this rose in the UK but I have happy memories of several good specimens in America.
(P) (H) ☉ (VF) ✄ (AL)
8' × 7'   2.5 × 2.1 m

'Alexander'

'Armada'

'Autumn Sunset'

'Armada'
(Haruseful)

Harkness UK 1988
'New Dawn' × 'Silver Jubilee'
The rich clear pink blooms hold
their colour well. They are semi-
double and come in large clusters,
leaving handsome hips in the
autumn. Foliage bright green and
glossy. Upright, bushy growth.
(C) (H) (CL) ☉ (AL)
5′ × 3′   150 × 90 cm

'Autumn Bouquet'

Jacobus USA 1948
'New Dawn' × 'Crimson Glory'
Long, pointed buds open to large
and fully double, carmine to
silvery-deep-pink flowers. Foliage
leathery and dark green. Growth
upright and bushy.
(C) (P) (VF) (H) ☉ ●
✄ (AL)   4′ × 3′   120 × 90 cm

'Autumn Sunset'

Lowe USA 1987
Sport from 'Westerland'
The medium-sized flowers, fully
double, cupped and loosely
formed, are apricot with touches
of orange and deep yellow.
Glossy, mid-green foliage.
Growth tall and bushy.
(C) (P) (MF) (H) ● ✄
(AL)   6′ × 4′   1.8 × 1.2 m

'Ballerina' *see* Hybrid Musks

'Berlin'

Kordes GERMANY 1949
'Eva' × 'Peace'
Large single flowers, bright, rich
red, paling towards the centre to
white. Pronounced yellow stamens. Upright but not tall. Foliage dark and crisp. The young
wood especially is dark, with lots
of thorns.
(C) (P) (H) (AL)
5′ × 3′   150 × 90 cm

'Biddulph Grange'
(Frydarkeye)

Fryer UK 1988
An unusually coloured rose,
velvety-bright-red, deeper in the
centre of each petal and deepening with age. The base and reverse
of each petal is white. Borne in
large clusters on a shrubby small
plant with good healthy foliage.
(C) ☉ (H) (G) (AL)
4′ × 3′   120 × 90 cm

'Bonica '82'
(Meidomonac)

Meilland FRANCE 1982
The double flowers are made up
of rather frilled petals of delicate
pink with deeper centres; these
are produced along strong arching
stems throughout the summer.
Foliage coppery-light green and
glossy. Not to be confused with
another rose of this name raised
by Meilland in 1953.
(C) (P) (G) (H) ☉ (AW)
3′ × 6′   90 × 180 cm

'Bonn'

Kordes GERMANY 1950
'Hamburg' × 'Independence'
Freely produced semi-double
flowers of bright orange-red
fading rather with age, though
not offending the eye in so doing.

'Autumn Sunset'

'Cardinal Hume'

A vigorous upright bush, with rich dark green foliage.
(C) (P) (H) (SF) (AL)
6' × 4'   1.8 × 1.2 m

'Butterfly Wings'

Gobbee UK 1976
'Dainty Maid' × 'Peace'
A beautiful rose. Large, refined, single flowers of blush-white with touches of red around their edges. Ample, dark green foliage. Not over-tall.
(C) ☉ ☼ (AL)
4' × 3'   120 × 90 cm

'Canterbury'

Austin UK 1969
('Monique' × 'Constance Spry') × seedling
Large, silky, fragrant, almost single flowers of pure rose-pink with well displayed golden stamens in their centres. Foliage mid-green, plentiful. Growth, bushy.
(R) ☉ (H) (MF) (AL)
3' × 3'   1 × 1 m

'Cardinal Hume' (Harregale)

Harkness UK 1984
[('Lilac Charm' × 'Sterling Silver') × ('Orangeade' × 'Lilac Charm')]

× [('Orange Sensation' × 'Allgold') × *R. californica*] × 'Frank Naylor'
A most unusual rose. The rich tyrian purple flowers are double, made up of a multitude of many narrow petals, and borne in clusters which remain close to the plant, almost amongst the plentiful dark green foliage. Slightly wider than tall, but not wide enough to qualify as procumbent.
(R) (G) (P) ● BS𝄇 (VF)
(AL)   3' × 4'   90 × 120 cm

'City of London'
(Harukfore)

Harkness UK 1987
'New Dawn' × 'Radox Bouquet'
Large, shaggy, blush-pink blooms with a heady perfume are produced in clusters. Large, bright green leaves on an upright and bushy plant.
(C) (P) (H) (VF) (CL)
(AL)   5' × 3'   150 × 90 cm

'Cocktail'

Meilland FRANCE 1959
('Independence' × 'Orange Triumph') × 'Phyllis Bide'
A bright rose with clusters of burnished red, single flowers each with yellow centres; the red intensifies with age. Upright,

'Bonn'

thorny growth with numerous, deep green, deeply serrated leaves.
(C) (P) (H) ● ☉ (SF)
(AL)   6' × 4'   1.8 × 1.2 m

'Bonica '82'

'Copenhagen'

Poulsen DENMARK 1964
Seedling × 'Ena Harkness'
Double, scarlet flowers in clusters on an upright plant with good, bronzy foliage. Can also make a good, short-growing climber.
(C) (P) (CL) (AL)
8' × 4'   2.5 × 1.2 m

'Country Dancer'

Buck USA 1973
'Prairie Princess' × 'Johannes Boettner'
Large, fully double flowers of rosy-red. Fragrant. Borne on a bushy, upright-growing plant with abundant, glossy dark green foliage.
(R) ☉ (H) ● (VF) (AL)
3' × 3'   90 × 90 cm

'Cymbeline'
(Austeen)

Austin UK 1983
Seedling × 'Lilian Austin'
Greyish-pink, loosely double,
myrrh-scented flowers are borne
in clusters on a spreading but
bushy plant with abundant mid-
green, semi-glossy foliage.
(R) (G) (P) (VF) (AL)
5′ × 5′   1.5 × 1.5 m

'Dapple Dawn'

Austin UK 1983
Sport from 'Red Coat'
Large, single, slightly scented,
delicate pink flowers in clusters
on a vigorous, upright-growing
plant. Thorny with dark green
foliage.
(R) (H) (CL) (P) ● (SF)
(AL)   5′ × 4′   1.5 × 1.2 m

'Copenhagen'

'Dorothy Wheatcroft'

'Dentelle de Malines', 'Lens Pink'

Lens BELGIUM 1983
A tallish spreader. Trusses of
blush-pink to white, cupped
flowers on an arching shrub with
plentiful, mid-green foliage. A
lovely rose with much to commend it.
(R) ☉ ● (SF) (W) (G)
(H) ≈ (AL)
4′ × 5′   1.2 × 1.5 m

'Dr Jackson'

Austin UK 1987
Sprays of single, brilliant scarlet-

crimson flowers on a strong-
growing, widely bushy plant with
darkish green foliage.
(S) (H) (B) (P) ● (SF)
(AL)   3′ 6″ × 3′   110 × 90 cm

'Dorothy Wheatcroft'

Tantau GERMANY 1960
Large, semi-double, bright red
flowers, made up of petals that
are slightly crimped on their outer
edges. These are borne in large
clusters on a vigorous, well-
foliated, thorny shrub.
(C) (P) (H) (AL)
5′ × 4′   1.5 × 1.2 m

'Cocktail'

'Elmshorn'

'Erfurt'

'Elmshorn'

Kordes GERMANY 1951
'Hamburg' × 'Verdun'
Large clusters of smallish, vivid
pink, double flowers on a vigorous bush, carrying abundant,
slightly crinkled, dark-greyish-
green foliage. A very good, free-
flowering shrub rose, deservedly
popular.
(C) (P) (H) ● ⊙ (AL)
5' × 4'   1.5 × 1.2 m

'Erfurt'

Kordes GERMANY 1939
'Eva' × 'Réveil Dijonnais'
Single flowers of rich, cerise pink,
paling towards the centre to
almost white; prominent brown
anthers. The rather beautiful

'Fred Loads'

flowers are enhanced by healthy,
plentiful coppery-green foliage.
Stems are coppery-brown with
numerous hooked thorns. An outstanding shrub rose.
(C) (P) (H) ● (SF) (AL)
5' × 4'   1.5 × 1.2 m

'Fountain'

Tantau GERMANY 1972
Sizeable, blood-red flowers in
clusters on a medium-growing
shrub with thick, dark green
foliage. A good, healthy variety.
(C) (P) (H) ⊙ ✂ (SF)
(AW)   7' × 4'   2 × 1.2 m

'Frank Naylor'

Harkness UK 1978
[('Orange Sensation' × 'Allgold') ×
('Little Lady' × 'Lilac Charm')] ×
[('Blue Moon' × 'Magenta') ×
('Cläre Grammerstorf' ×
'Frühlingsmorgen')]

'Fountain'

'Fred Loads'

Clusters of single red flowers with
yellow centres. Good, healthy
dense growth. Foliage long and
reddish-green. A very good,
shorter-growing shrub rose where
a bright colour is needed.
(P) (H) ⊙ (SF) (AL)
4' × 3'   120 × 90 cm

'Fred Loads'

Holmes UK 1968
'Dorothy Wheatcroft' × 'Orange
Sensation'
Large, almost single blooms in
impressive sized trusses, rich,
bright salmon-pink. A vigorous
and upright rose with large,
leathery leaves.
(C) (P) (H) (AW)
5' × 4'   1.5 × 1.2 m

'Fritz Nobis'

Kordes GERMANY 1940
'Joanna Hill' × 'Magnifica'
A beautiful rose, flowering only
once each season, but nonetheless
useful. A dense shrub, extremely
healthy, with small but numerous
grey-green leaves. Flowers are soft
blush-pink to quiet salmon, fully
double and produced in great
abundance; followed in autumn
by an impressive crop of small
but colourful orange hips.
(S) (P) (H) (F) ● (AW)
5' × 4'   1.5 × 1.2 m

'Grandmaster'

Kordes GERMANY 1954
'Sangerhausen' × Sunmist'
Pointed buds opening to large,
semi-double flowers of apricot-

'Fritz Nobis'

pink with lemon shadings.
Scented. Foliage light green on a
bushy plant.
(C) (P) (SF) (AL)
5' × 4' 1.5 × 1.2 m

'Heidelberg'

Kordes GERMANY 1958
'World's Fair' × 'Floradora'
Very bright rose, crimson-scarlet
splashed deep orange, fully
double, produced in large trusses.
Foliage dark green and tough-
looking.
(C) (P) (AL)
6' × 5' 1.8 × 1.5 m

'Hon. Lady Lindsay'

N. J. Hanson USA 1938
'New Dawn' × 'Rev. F. Page Rob-
erts'
Double flowers of clear pink with
deeper pink reverses. Foliage dark
green on a widely bushy plant.
Enjoys a good hot summer or
warmer climates.
(C) (H) (P) ☼ (Gh) ☉
(SF) (AL) 3' × 3' 90 × 90 cm

'Jacqueline du Pré'
(Harwanna)

Harkness UK 1989
'Radox Bouquet' × 'Maigold'
A delightful large, ivory white,
almost single rose with prominent
golden-red stamens and a good
scent (musk). These are freely
produced on a strong-growing
shrub which bears abundant
darkish green foliage.
(R) (P) (H) ☉ (VF) (AL)
6' × 5' 1.8 × 1.5 m

'Jayne Austin'
(Ausbreak)

Austin UK 1990
Parentage Noisette-related
Flowers beautifully shaped rosette
form with a button eye, produced

'Jacqueline du Pré'

in clusters. Soft apricot-yellow in
colour. Very fragrant. Foliage
plentiful light green. Widely
bushy. Vigorous.
(R) (II) (G) ✂ ☉ (VF)
(AL) 4' × 3' 120 × 90 cm

'John Franklin'

Department of
Agriculture CANADA 1980
'Lilli Marlene' × unnamed
seedling
Sizeable, double (25 petals),
fragrant red flowers borne in
small clusters. Rounded leaves of
mid-to-dark green on an upright,
bushy plant amply endowed with
yellowish-cream thorns.
(R) (N) ● ☉ (H) (MF)
(AL) 5' × 4' 1.5 × 1.2 m

'Joseph's Coat'

'Joseph's Coat'

Armstrong & Swim USA 1964
'Buccaneer' × 'Circus'
Often listed as a climber, but I
feel it is better as a free-standing
shrub or, at most, a pillar rose.
Loosely formed flowers from
shapely buds, borne in large
trusses on a thorny, upright plant
with light green, glossy foliage.
(C) (P) (H) (CL) (MF)
(AW) 7' × 4' 2 × 1.2 m

'Kassel'

Kordes GERMANY 1957
'Obergärtner Wiebicke' ×
'Independence'
Trusses of closely spaced, double
flowers on strong stems; orange-
scarlet deepening with age to
bright red. Foliage leathery,

'Kassel'

slightly glossy. Upright bushy growth. Stems brownish-red.
(C) (P) (H) ☉ (AL)
5′ × 4′   1.5 × 1.2 m

'Kathleen Ferrier'

Buisman HOLLAND 1952
'Gartenstolz' × 'Shot Silk'
Small clusters of semi-double, rich salmon-pink flowers. Vigorous and upright growth with dark green, glossy foliage. A first-class rose.
(C) (H) (SF) (AL)
5′ × 4′   1.5 × 1.2 m

'Lafter'

Brownell USA 1948
['V for Victory' × ('Général Jacqueminot' × 'Dr Van Fleet')] × 'Pink Princess'
A most useful shrub. Clusters of semi-double, rather loosely formed flowers of salmon pink and apricot, with hints of yellow. Foliage dark green, slightly glossy but leathery. Upright but bushy growth.
(C) (P) (H) (SF) (AL)
5′ × 4′   1.5 × 1.2 m

'Kathleen Ferrier'

'Lafter'

'La Sevillana'

'La Sevillana' (Meigekanu)

Meilland FRANCE 1982
Very healthy, abundant rich red, semi-double flowers which hold their colour well, even in hot sun. Rich dark green foliage. Dense bushy but spreading growth.
(C) (H) (P) (G) (AW)
4′ × 5′   1.2 × 1.5 m

'Lady Sonia'

Mattock UK 1961
'Grandmaster' × 'Doreen'
A free-flowering, semi-double rose of deep golden-yellow. Shapely in bud and well formed when open. Foliage dark and leathery. Growth upright and free-branching.
(C) (P) ✄ (AL)
5′ × 4′   1.5 × 1.2 m

'Lichtkönigin Lucia' (Korlilub)

Kordes GERMANY 1966
'Zitronenfalter' × Cläre Grammerstorf'
Clusters of closely arranged, canary-yellow, semi-double flowers with a good fragrance. Foliage mid-to-light green, glossy. Medium-tall, bushy growth. A useful yellow shrub rose.
(C) ☉ (H) (P) (MF) ✄ (AL)   4′ × 3′   120 × 90 cm

'L'Oréal Trophy' (Harlexis)

Harkness UK 1982
Sport from 'Alexander'
Softer in colour than its parent, otherwise identical.
(C) (P) (H) (SF) ☉ ✄ (AL)   6′ × 4′   1.8 × 1.2 m

'Marjorie Fair'

'Magenta'

Kordes GERMANY 1954
Yellow Floribunda seedling × 'Lavender Pinocchio'
A moderately vigorous shrub bearing double flowers of unusual shades, fawn and purple with pink and lilac highlights, opening flat in the old-fashioned style and produced in large clusters. Foliage dark green and growth openly bushy. This rose can be frustratingly temperamental.
(C) (H) ☉ (VF) (AL)
4′ × 4′   1.2 × 1.2 m

'Malcolm Sargent' (Harwharry)

Harkness UK 1988
'Herbstfeuer' × 'Trumpeter'
Hybrid Tea-shaped flowers of shining crimson-scarlet, with rich green sparkling foliage on a bushy, upright plant.
(C) (H) ☉ ✄ (AL)
4′ × 3′   120 × 90 cm

'Märchenland', 'Exception'

Tantau GERMANY 1951
'Swantje' × 'Hamburg'
Very large trusses of well-spaced, almost single flowers, bright pink with deeper shadings. Very free-flowering. Foliage dark green,

'Lichtkönigin Lucia'

'Märchenland'

slightly glossy and plentiful.
Upright bushy growth. This is a
most underrated shrub rose.
(C) (P) ☉ (AL)
5' × 4'   1.5 × 1.2 m

'Marjorie Fair'

Harkness UK 1978
'Ballerina' × 'Baby Faurax'
A good shorter shrub rose bred
from 'Ballerina, and which could

perhaps be included among the
Hybrid Musks. The flowers,
which are produced in large
trusses, are small, single and red
with a pinkish-white eye. Foliage
plentiful and mid-green. Growth
bushy and tidy.
(C) (H) (P) ☉ ● (AW)
4' × 3'   120 × 90 cm

**'Mary Hayley Bell',
'Abunancia'** (Korparau)

Kordes GERMANY 1989
Clusters of pretty, soft pink, semi-
double blooms amid good mid-
green foliage. Growth bushy.
(C) ☉ (H) (P) (SF) (AL)
5' × 4'   1.5 × 1.2 m

'Nymphenburg'

'Mary Hayley Bell'

'Malcolm Sargent'

'Mountbatten'

Harkness UK 1952
('Anne Cocker' × 'Arthur Bell') ×
'Southampton'
Huge clusters of clear yellow,
fully double flowers on an
upright but thorny plant with
good, clean, light green foliage.
Makes an excellent hedging rose.
(C) (H) (P) ☼ ☉ ✂
(MF) (AW)
5' × 3'   150 × 90 cm

'Nymphenburg'

Kordes GERMANY 1954
'Sangerhausen' × 'Sunmist'
A vigorous upright shrub or pillar
rose. Semi-double flowers,
salmon-pink with lemon and
deeper pink highlights. Very free-
flowering. Foliage dark green and
glossy.
(C) (P) (H) (MF) (AW)
6' × 4'   1.8 × 1.2 m

'Parkjuwel',
'Parkjewel'

Kordes GERMANY 1956
'Independence' × a red Moss rose
A vigorous shrubby plant with
wrinkled, rather leathery foliage
and good well mossed buds.
Flowers large, very double, globu-
lar, light soft pink. Loses nothing
by not repeating.
(S) (P) (H) ● ☉ (SF)
(AL) 6' × 4'   1.8 × 1.2 m

'Peach Blossom'
(Ausblossom)

Austin UK 1990
Large yet delicate, semi-double,
rose-pink flowers in clusters, produced very freely throughout the
summer, with a slight fragrance.
These are followed by a good
crop of hips in the autumn. Foliage mid-green, plentiful. Growth
shrubby and wide.
(R) ☉ (H) ● (SF) (AL)
4' × 3'   120 × 90 cm

'Pike's Peak'

Gunter USA 1940
R. acicularis × 'Hollywood'
Light red with a yellow centre
paling with age, semi-double,
borne in clusters. Light green,
wrinkled foliage. Bushy, vigorous
growth.
(S) (H) (P) (AL)
5' × 3'   150 × 90 cm

'Pink La Sevillana',
'Rosy La Sevillana'
(Meigeroka)

Meilland FRANCE 1983
Sport from 'La Sevillana'
A pink sport from 'La Sevillana'
with all its parent's characteristics
except colour.
(C) (P) (H) (SF) (AL)
4' × 4'   1.2 × 1.2 m

'Radway Sunrise'

'Sally Holmes'

'Pleine de Grâce' (Lengra)

Lens BELGIUM 1983
'Ballerina' × R. filipes
An outstanding shrub or climber.
Large trusses of single, creamy-
white flowers, fragrant, borne on
arching branches well covered
with light green foliage.
(S) (T) (N) ● (W) ≈
(VF) (AL) 10' × 13' 3 × 4 m

'Poulsen's Park Rose'

Poulsen DENMARK
'Great Western' × 'Karen Poulsen'
An outstanding shrub, vigorous,
dense and broad in habit with
trusses of large, shapely, silvery
pink flowers and good clean dark
green foliage.
(R) (P) ● (VF) (AL)
6' × 6'   1.8 × 1.8 m

'Prairie Princess'

Buck USA 1972
'Carrousel' × ('Morning Stars' ×
'Suzanne')
Large, semi-double, soft coral-
pink flowers in profusion amid
abundant large, dark green leaves.
Growth upright and bushy.
(C) (H) ☉ (SF) (AL)
5' × 4'   1.5 × 1.2 m

'Prestige'

Kordes GERMANY 1957
'Rudolph Timm' × 'Fanal'
Large, semi-double, light crimson
flowers are carried in clusters with
plentiful, dark green, matt foliage
on a bushy plant.
(C) (P) (H) (SF) (AL)
4' × 3'   120 × 90 cm

'Rachel Bowes Lyon'

Harkness UK 1981
'Kim' × ('Orange Sensation' ×
'Allgold') × R. californica
Semi-double, peachy-pink flowers

of medium size in large clusters
on a medium-tall but bushy, well-
foliated plant.
(C) (P) (H) (AL)
5' × 4'   1.5 × 1.2 m

'Radway Sunrise'

Waterhouse Nurseries UK 1962
'Masquerade' seedling
A striking, moderately vigorous
shrub bearing clusters of single
flowers; these are a mixture of
flame, cerise-pink and yellow. The
colours are suffused to give the
general effect of glowing warmth,
eye-catching but not gaudy. Foliage dark green and glossy.
(C) (P) (H) ☉ (SF) (AL)
4' × 3'   120 × 90 cm

'Red Coat'

Austin UK 1973
Seedling × 'Golden Showers'
Large, single, slightly scented, rich
crimson flowers produced in
clusters and in great profusion
throughout summer. Foliage dark
green. Growth upright and
thorny.
(R) (H) (W) (CL) (P) (SF)
(AL) 5' × 4'   1.5 × 1.2 m

'Roundelay'

Swim USA 1953
'Charlotte Armstrong' ×
'Floradora'
An upright, free-flowering shrub
with large trusses of cardinal-red
flowers, fully double, opening flat.
Has a good perfume. Healthy
dark green foliage. Deserves more
attention.
(C) (P) (H) ☉ (VF) (AL)
4' × 3'   120 × 90 cm

'Sally Holmes'

Holmes UK 1976
'Ivory Fashion' × 'Ballerina'

'Roundelay'

A short-growing, almost Floribunda-type rose with an upright habit and good foliage. Trusses of single flowers of soft, pale pink to white.
(C) (H) ☉ ● (AL)
4' × 3' 120 × 90 cm

'Shropshire Lass'

Austin UK 1968
'Mme Butterfly' × 'Mme Legras de St Germain'
Large, flat, almost single flowers of delicate flesh-pink fading to white with age, prominent stamens. Fragrant. Foliage plentiful mid-green. Growth robust bushy.
(S) (H) (W) (P) (CL) (SF)
(AL) 6' × 4' 1.8 × 1.2 m

'Sparrieshoop'

Kordes GERMANY 1953
('Baby Château' × 'Else Poulsen')
× 'Magnifica'
An interesting shrub with pointed buds opening to large, pale pink flowers, borne in trusses but sometimes singly. Upright bushy growth and healthy foliage.
(R) (P) ● (SF) (AL)
5' × 4' 1.5 × 1.2 m

'Summer Wind'

Buck USA 1975
('Fandango' × 'Florence Mary Morse') × 'Applejack'
Large, fragrant (clove), not quite single flowers of orangey-red.

Leathery, dark green foliage. Growth upright and bushy.
(R) (H) ● (MF) (AL)
4' × 3' 120 × 90 cm

'Till Uhlenspiegel'

Kordes GERMANY 1950
'Holstein' × 'Magnifica'

An arching tall shrub with large almost burnished, glossy green leaves. Large single flowers of glowing dark red with white centres. Scented.
(S) (P) ● (MF) (AL)
10' × 8' 3 × 2.5 m

'Uetersen'

'Uetersen'
'Zenith'

Tantau GERMANY 1939
'K of K' × 'Stämmler'
Large, semi-double flowers of glowing pinkish-red in clusters. Slightly fragrant. Foliage dark green, glossy. Growth bushy and vigorous. A useful, underrated and little seen shrub rose.
(R) (CL) (H) (T) ● (SF) (AL) 8' × 6' 2.5 × 1.8 m

'Uncle Walter'

McGredy UK 1963
'Detroiter' × 'Heidelberg'
Hybrid Tea-shaped flowers borne in clusters and opening to an attractively muddled shape; bright red, good for cutting. Foliage is dark green and plentiful. Often listed as a Hybrid Tea, but is much too vigorous and is better placed amongst shrub roses.
(C) (P) (H) ✂ (AW) 5' × 4' 1.5 × 1.2 m

'White Spray'

LeGrice UK 1974
Seedling × 'Iceberg'
A superb white variety deserving of more attention. An accommodating sized shrub with good, mid-green foliage. Flowers white to cream, fully double, shapely and produced in large clusters on a bushy plant.
(C) (P) (H) ☉ ● (AL) 4' × 4' 1.2 × 1.2 m

'Wild Flower'

Austin UK 1986
Fragrant, medium to small, single flowers of lemon-yellow set off by attractive stamens and dark green foliage. Growth compact, dense and branching.
(C) (B) (H) ☉ (MF) (AL) 2' × 2' 60 × 60 cm

'Uncle Walter'

'William and Mary'

Beales UK 1988
Seedling × 'Constance Spry'
Large, fully double, blowsy blooms in the old-fashioned style. Deep silvery-pink with crimson and carmine highlights, produced singly and in clusters. Foliage greyish-green and matt. Growth bushy and upright.
(S) (P) (H) (VF) (CL) ✂ (AL) 6' × 4' 1.8 × 1.2 m

'Windrush' (Ausrush)

Austin UK 1984
Seedling × ('Canterbury' × 'Golden Wings')
Clusters of semi-double, soft medium-yellow flowers with pronounced stamens. Very fragrant. Foliage sizeable, light green. Growth bushy, branching but fairly dense.
(C) (H) (VF) (AL) 4' × 4' 1.2 × 1.2 m

'Yesterday'

Harkness UK 1974
('Phyllis Bide' × 'Shepherd's Delight') × 'Ballerina'
An aptly named variety. Masses of small, almost single, rich pinky-purple, slightly scented

flowers in large trusses on a sturdy, rather spreading bush.
(C) (P) (G) (H) ☉ ● (SF) (AW) 4' × 4' 1.2 × 1.2 m

Top: 'William and Mary', *and above:* 'Yesterday'

Polyanthas

From the beginning of this century until the early 1940s, Dwarf Polyanthas reigned supreme as bedding roses and many new varieties were introduced. Ironically, they only lost their supremacy when they were put to stud with the Hybrid Teas and became parents to the larger-flowered Hybrid Polyanthas. As their popularity has declined their numbers have inevitably dwindled and several good varieties are now lost for ever. Those that remain are fairly widely available and I have briefly described most of them here. Several are sports from others, mainly 'Orléans Rose'. Their colours are, in fact, rather unstable, and variations can occur within a flower cluster from time to time.

These little roses are very easy to grow and have numerous uses, from massed display to hedging and edging. In groups they look most effective among herbaceous plants and are quite at home providing prolonged colour at the front of shrubberies. They also make useful, decorative plants in tubs, urns and other containers, and they are not at all out of place in modern settings; in fact, when planted closely, they readily take on the role of a 'Patio' rose (a term for the 'Compact Floribundas' described in the next section). They also last quite well in water when they are cut and taken indoors.

CLASSIFICATION	
BARB	Class 13
MR9	Class 52
WFRS	Classes 5 and 6

'Baby Faurax'

Lille FRANCE 1924
Large clusters of double, violet-coloured, fragrant, small blooms on a short, bushy plant with small, mid-green foliage.
(C) ● (G) (H) ☉ (B)
(AW)   1′ × 1′   30 × 30 cm

'Cameo'

de Ruiter HOLLAND 1932
'Orléans Rose' sport
Dense clusters of small, semi-double, cupped flowers of soft salmon-pink, deepening with age; these are produced on stocky, bushy plants which have strong shoots, these bearing a few large, cruel thorns and many smaller, kinder ones. Foliage plentiful and light greyish-green.
(C) (P) (G) (H) ● ☉
(AL)   2′ × 2′   60 × 60 cm

'Cameo'

'Gloria Mundi'

'Golden Salmon Superior'

'Clotilde Soupert'

Soupert and Notting
LUXEMBOURG 1890
'Mignonette' × 'Mme Damaizin'
Large clusters of very double, small, soft, creamy-white blooms with soft pink centres. Fragrant. Foliage rich light green. Growth bushy.
(C) ● (G) (H) ☉ (B)
(AL)   1′ 6″ × 1′ 6″   45 × 45 cm

'Dick Koster'

Koster HOLLAND 1931
Sport of 'Anneke Koster'
Large, tidy clusters of globular, deep orange-pink flowers on a compact, short shrubby little plant with good mid-green foliage.
(C) ● (G) (H) ☉ (B)
(AL)   1′ × 1′   30 × 30 cm

'Gloria Mundi'

de Ruiter HOLLAND 1929
'Superb' sport
Similar to 'Cameo' in flower shape and form, except with slightly fewer petals. Rich, scarlet-red with occasional flecks of white on the inner petals. Upright growth. Foliage dark green.
(C) (P) (G) (H) ● ☉
(AL)   2′ × 2′   60 × 60 cm

'Golden Salmon Superior'

de Ruiter HOLLAND 1926
'Superb' sport
Of similar flower formation and growth habit to the previous two but with a strong, orange-salmon colouring. One of the best for a massed, bright effect.
(C) (P) (G) (H) ● ☉
(AL)   2′ × 2′   60 × 60 cm

'Jean Mermoz'

Chenault FRANCE 1937
R. wichuraiana × a Hybrid Tea
Fully double, reddish-pink, small blooms in dense corymbs. Slightly fragrant. Foliage rather small, glossy and dark green. Vigorous and bushy.
(C) ● (G) ☉ (B) (SF)
(AL)   2′ × 1′ 6″   60 × 45 cm

'Katharina Zeimet', 'White Baby Rambler'

P. Lambert GERMANY 1901
'Etoile de Mai' × 'Marie Parvie'
Rather different from others in that the flowers, although in large clusters, are more widely spaced. Growth too is more angular, the foliage darker and perhaps less dense.
(C) (P) (G) (H) (AL)
2′ × 2′   60 × 60 cm

'The Fairy'

'Margo Koster'

Koster HOLLAND 1931
Sport of 'Dick Koster'
Large, tidy clusters of globular,
salmon flowers on a compact,
short, shrubby little plant with
good mid-green foliage.
(C) ● (G) (H) ☉ (B)
(AL) 1′ × 1′ 30 × 30 cm

'Mignonette'

Guillot Fils FRANCE 1880
R. chinensis × *R. multiflora*
Small globular, double, blush-
pink to white flowers, borne in
large clusters. Plant dwarf and
compact. Probably the earliest
bred Polyantha still available.
(C) (G) (P) (AL)
1′ × 1′ 30 × 30 cm

'Miss Edith Cavell'

de Ruiter HOLLAND 1917
'Orléans Rose' sport
Rich red to scarlet sometimes
overlaid crimson. Flowers in
clusters, globular in bud, opening
semi-double and flattish. Foliage
dark green, stems slightly lighter.
Like others of its race, has little or
no scent.
(C) (P) (G) (H) (AL)
2′ × 2′ 60 × 60 cm

1985 was the 70th anniversary of
the execution of Nurse Edith
Cavell. For a time we lived near
her birthplace, the village of
Swardeston near Norwich. As part
of the planned commemorative
events, the vicar of Swardeston,
Rev. Philip McFadyen, asked me
if I could obtain some plants of
the 'Cavell' rose for him to plant
in the village. After an initial
search and enquiries in the rose
trade, I was force to conclude that
the rose had become extinct.

Philip set about proving me

wrong by writing to the *Eastern
Daily Press*, while I sped all over
Norfolk looking at potential res-
urrections, none of them this elusive rose. Finally I called on a
charming and spritely octogena-
rian, Mrs Doris Levine, at
Brundall, a village adjacent to the
Norfolk Broads. She and her late
husband George had been given
half a dozen plants of 'Miss Edith
Cavell' soon after they were mar-
ried in 1934. Fifty years on, only
one rather gnarled bush remained
alive; from this I was able to
propagate some ten plants and
the life of another, almost extinct
rose was rekindled, together with
a little bit of Norfolk heritage.

'Pinkie'

Swim USA 1947
'China Doll' × unknown
Large trusses of cupped, semi-
double flowers of bright rosy-pink
very freely produced. Very fragrant. The foliage is bright green
and glossy, soft to touch. Growth
vigorous and bushy.
(C) ☉ (G) (H) (B) (VF)
(AL) 2′ × 1′ 6″ 60 × 45 cm

'The Fairy'

Bentall UK 1932
'Paul Crampel' × 'Lady Gay' (not
a 'Lady Godiva' sport, as often
stated)
After a spell in obscurity, this rose
is currently enjoying a new lease
of life, and deservedly so. The
small, globular, pink flowers are
produced in profusion all over a
dense, spreading bush with attractive foliage. It is procumbent
enough to be used for partial
ground cover as well as for group
planting and patio work.
(C) (P) (G) (H) ● ☉
(AW) 2′ × 4′ 60 × 120 cm

Floribundas

The classification 'Floribunda' covers all bush cluster-flowered
roses other than Miniature Polyanthas and the groups known in
the BARB classification as 'Patio' roses.

Many hundreds and probably thousands have been raised and
introduced worldwide during the last fifty or so years and it would
be impossible to include them all. I have selected those which I
believe to be a fair representation of the best available today,
together with a few classics from the past, and if the latter are not
readily available, they are included as being important and
oustanding examples of their type.

Floribundas have many uses, the most common of which is for
bedding. Many make excellent hedging plants and most can be
used for group planting in herbaceous borders or among other
shrubs. Not a few, especially the shorter ones, make very good pot
plants for urns, tubs and the like. Others, especially the taller ones,
make ideal cut flowers.

CLASSIFICATION	
BARB	Class 6
MR9	Class 19
WFRS	Class 5

'Abundance'

Gandy UK 1974
Seedling × 'Firecracker'
Clusters of full double, mid-pink
blooms on a sturdy and low-
growing bush with dark, matt-
green foliage.
(C) (P) (H) (SF) (B) ☉
(AL) 1′ 6″ × 1′ 6″ 45 × 45 cm

'Alison Wheatcroft'

Wheatcroft UK 1959
Sport from 'Circus'
Large clusters of shapely, cupped,
fully double flowers, deep yellow
and apricot flushed crimson. Foliage plentiful and glossy. Growth
upright.
(C) (P) (H) (SF) (B) (AL)
2′ 6″ × 2′ 75 × 60 cm

'Alison Wheatcroft'

'Allgold'

'Allgold'

LeGrice UK 1956
'Goldilocks' × 'Ellinor LeGrice'
An outstanding old variety, with
loosely arranged clusters of clear
golden-yellow, semi-double
flowers. Its foliage is small, mid-
green and glossy. Growth upright.
(C) (P) (SF) (B) ☉ ✂
(AW) 2' × 2' 60 × 60 cm

'Amanda' (Beesian)

Bees UK 1979
'Arthur Bell' × 'Zambra'
Globular buds open to clear
yellow flowers which are fully
double and produced in good,
large clusters. Small, plentiful,
light green foliage. Upright
growth.
(C) (SF) (B) (AL)
2' × 2' 60 × 60 cm

'Ambassador' (Meinuzeten)

Meilland FRANCE1979
Seedling × 'Whisky Mac'
Large, cupped flowers of orangey-
red with reverses a blend of
golden-orange. Foliage dark green
and glossy. Growth bushy.
(C) ☉ (B) (H) (AW)
2' × 2' 60 × 60 cm

'Amberlight'

LeGrice UK 1962
(Seedling × 'Lavender Pinocchio')
× 'Marcel Bourgouin'
Fully double, rather muddled
flowers of bright amber yellow are
produced, well spaced in large
clusters. Darkish green and semi-
matt foliage. Growth bushy.
(C) (MF) (H) (B) (WW)
(AL) 2' 6" × 2' 75 × 60 cm

'Anisley Dickson'

'Amber Queen' (Harroony)

Harkness UK 1984
'Southampton' × 'Typhoon'
Large, well-packed clusters of
fully double blooms of amber-
yellow. The foliage is large,
maroonish, almost glossy. Growth
bushy.
(C) (MF) (B) (Gh) ☉ ✂
(AW) 2' × 2' 60 × 60 cm

'American Pride'

Warriner USA 1974
Rounded buds open to high-
centred, fragrant, deep red
blooms. Foliage dark green, semi-
glossy. Growth tall, upright and
bushy.
(C) ☉ (B) (H) (E) (Gh)
✂ (VF) (AW)
4' × 3' 120 × 90 cm

'Angel Face'

Swim USA 1968
('Circus' × 'Lavender Pinocchio')
× 'Sterling Silver'
Fully double, shapely buds of
deep lavender mauve with deeper

colouring on the edge of each
petal. These are fragrant and produced freely in trusses on a
bushy, upright plant with leathery
dark green foliage.
(C) (B) (H) ☉ (VF) ✂
(AL) 3' × 2' 90 × 60 cm

'Anisley Dickson', 'Dicky', 'München Kindl' (Dickimono)

Dickson UK 1983
'Coventry Cathedral' ×
'Memento'
Deep salmon-pink, lighter on the
reverse, large, fully double flowers
in clusters. Foliage mid-green and
glossy. Growth bushy.
(C) (P) (SF) (B) ☉ (AL)
2' 6" × 2' 75 × 60 cm

'Anita'

Christensen USA 1982
'Rumba' × 'Marmalade'
A blend of assorted pinks, its
clusters of large, fully double
blooms are borne on an upright

'Amber Queen'

plant with good, glossy foliage and large, spiteful thorns.
(C) (SF) (B) (H) (AL)
2′ 6″ × 2′   75 × 60 cm

'Ann Aberconway'

Mattock UK 1976
'Arthur Bell' × seedling
Largish, double-formed flowers of apricot-orange are borne in medium-sized clusters. Foliage dark and leathery. Growth upright.
(C) (SF) (B) (H) (AL)
2′ 6″ × 2′   75 × 60 cm

'Anna Livia' (Kormetter)

Kordes GERMANY 1989
Sizeable clusters of clear pink, double flowers well endowed with perfume. Foliage leathery, semi-glossy, mid-green. Growth upright.
(C) ☉ (B) (H) (MF) ✄
(AL)   2′ 6″ × 2′   75 × 60 cm

'Anna Wheatcroft'

Tantau GERMANY 1958
'Cinnabar' seedling × unknown
Very large, single blooms are produced in huge clusters of bright salmon, almost vermilion, with pronounced yellow stamens. Foliage dark, semi-glossy. Growth vigorous.
(C) (SF) (B) (H) (AL)
3′ × 2′   90 × 60 cm

'Anne Cocker'

Cocker UK 1970
'Highlight' × 'Colour Wonder'
The very double, small, bright vermilion flowers are closely packed in large clusters, with light to mid-green, crisp and glossy foliage, and very prickly stems. Growth upright. Lasts a good time in water when cut.
(C) (P) (B) (H) M✄ ✄
(AW)   3′ 6″ × 2′   105 × 60 cm

'Anne Harkness'
(Harkaramel)

Harkness UK 1979
'Bobby Dazzler' × [('Manx Queen' × 'Prima Ballerina') × ('Chanelle' × 'Piccadilly')]
Medium-sized, full blooms in very large clusters, apricot-yellow with a deeper base. Semi-glossy foliage. Growth upright and tall.
(C) (P) (SF) (B) (H) (Gh)
☉ ✄ (AW)
3′ 6″ × 2′   105 × 60 cm

'Antigua'

Warriner USA 1974
'South Seas' × 'Golden Masterpiece'
Fragrant flowers, globular at first with high centres opening fully double. A blend of apricot and

'Anna Livia'

'Anne Harkness'

'Arthur Bell'

'Astrid Späth Striped'

soft pink, shaded deeper on the reverse. Foliage glossy, mid-green. Growth bushy. Prefers warm summers.
(C) ☉ (B) (Gh) ✄ (MF)
(AL)   3′ × 2′   90 × 60 cm

'Apricot Nectar'

Boerber USA 1965
Seedling × 'Spartan'
The buff-yellow and apricot flowers are large and cupped, several in each cluster, and with good scent. Foliage dark and glossy. Growth bushy.
(C) (VF) (B) (H) (AW)
2′ × 2′   60 × 60 cm

'Arcadian',
'New Year'
(Macnewye)

McGredy NEW ZEALAND 1982
'Mary Sumner' × seedling
Medium-sized, fully double flowers are borne in clusters, a blend of orange and gold. Foliage dark green and glossy. Growth upright.
(C) (P) (SF) (B) (H) ☉
✄ (AL)   2′ 6″ × 2′   75 × 60 cm

'Ards Beauty' (Dicjoy)

Dickson UK 1986
('Eurorose' × 'Whisky Mac') × 'Bright Smile'
Large, Hybrid Tea-like flowers are produced in good-sized clusters, soft yellow and well scented. Foliage mid-green and glossy. Growth bushy.
(C) (MF) (B) (H) (AL)
2′ × 2′   60 × 60 cm

'Arthur Bell'

McGredy UK 1965
'Clare Grammerstorf' × 'Piccadilly'
Shapely buds open to well-formed, semi-double flowers of rich deep yellow, fading to lemon with age, in large clusters, though occasionally singly. The foliage is mid- to light green and glossy. Growth densely upright.
(C) (MF) (B) (H) ☉ ✄
(AW)   2′ 6″ × 2′   75 × 60 cm

'Astrid Späth Striped'
'Frau Astrid Späth Striped'

Spath GERMANY 1933
Sport of 'Frau Astrid Späth', in turn a sport of 'Lafayette'
Abundant semi-double blooms of carmine-pink striped and blotched white, produced in large clusters on an upright plant with dark green foliage.
(C) ☉ (B) (H) (AL)
2′ × 2′   60 × 60 cm

'August Seebauer',
'The Queen Mother'

Kordes GERMANY 1944
'Break o' Day' × 'Else Poulsen'
Large, double, clear pink and high-centred blooms are carried in sizeable clusters. Foliage small but plentiful, mid-green and

'August Seebauer'

'Beautiful Britain'

'Betty Prior'

'Bonfire Night'

semi-glossy. Growth bushy and vigorous.
(C) (P) (SF) (B) (H) ⊙
(AL)   2′ 6″ × 2′   75 × 60 cm

'Avignon'

Cant UK 1974
'Zambra' × 'Allgold'
Clear yellow, medium-sized and double flowers are borne in clusters. Foliage light green and glossy. Growth upright and vigorous.
(C) (P) (SF) (B) (H) (AL)
3′ 6″ × 2′   105 × 60 cm

'Avocet' (Harpluto)

Harkness UK 1984
'Dame of Sark' × seedling
Produces very large clusters of semi-double blooms, orange faintly edged pink to copper. Foliage plentiful, dark green and glossy. Growth bushy.
(C) (P) (SF) (B) (H) ⊙
✄ (AL)   2′ 6″ × 2′   75 × 60 cm

'Baby Bio'

Smith UK 1977
'Golden Treasure' × seedling
Very large clusters of double, deep yellow blooms are produced on a well-foliated, dark green, glossy, short and bushy plant. A most useful rose.
(C) (SF) (B) (H) ⊙ (AW)
1′ 6″ × 1′ 6″   45 × 45 cm

'Beautiful Britain' (Dicfire)

Dickson UK 1983
'Red Planet' × 'Eurorose'
Shapely blooms of rich orange-tomato-red, well spaced in large clusters. Foliage mid-green and semi-glossy. Growth bushy and upright. A good, bright variety.
(C) (P) (SF) (B) (H) ⊙
✄ (AW) 2′ 6″ × 2′   75 × 60 cm

'Beauty Queen' (Canmiss)

Cant UK 1984
'English Miss' × seedling
Its mid-pink blooms are well arranged in large clusters and are very double. Foliage dark green and glossy. Growth upright.
(C) (MF) (B) (H) ⊙ (AL)
2′ 6″ × 2′   75 × 60 cm

'Betty Prior'

Prior UK 1935
'Kirsten Poulsen' × seedling
Clusters of largish, single, slightly cupped flowers of rich carmine-pink. Slightly fragrant. Foliage profuse, dark green, matt. Growth vigorous and bushy. One of the best Floribundas from the '30s.
(C) ⊙ (B) (H) (P) (SF)
(AL)   3′ × 2′   90 × 60 cm

'Bonfire Night'

McGredy UK 1971
'Tiki' × 'Variety Club'
Bears large clusters of semi-double, sizeable flowers of orange-scarlet and yellow.

Foliage dark green, matt and well serrated. Growth bushy.
(C) (SF) (B) (H) (AL)
2′ 6″ × 2′   75 × 60 cm

'Bright Smile' (Dicdanse)

Dickson UK 1980
'Eurorose' × seedling
Flattish, convex blooms, semi-double and clear yellow, are borne in good-sized clusters. Foliage dense and mid-green with dark thorns. Bushy upright growth.
(C) (SF) (B) (H) (AW)
2′ × 2′   60 × 60 cm

'Brown Velvet', 'Colorbreak' (Macultra)

McGredy NEW ZEALAND 1982
'Mary Sumner' × 'Kapai'
Deep orangey blooms tinted brownish, and very double, are produced in large clusters – an unusual combination. Foliage dark green and glossy. Growth upright.
(C) (SF) (B) (H) ⊙ ✄
(AL)   3′ × 2′   90 × 60 cm

'Buck's Fizz'

'Centenaire de Lourdes'

'Buck's Fizz' (Poulgay)

Poulsen DENMARK 1990
Seedling × 'Mary Sumner'
Classy, Hybrid Tea-shaped
blooms of soft orange in clusters.
Scented. These are borne on a
tallish, upright plant with dark
green glossy foliage.
(C) ☉ (B) (H) (VF) ✄
(AW)   3' × 2'   90 × 60 cm

'Burma Star'

Cocker UK 1974
'Arthur Bell' × 'Manx Queen'
Largish, double, apricot yellow
flowers are carried in large
clusters on a tall, well-foliated
plant, the leaves large and glossy.
Growth upright.
(C) (P) (MF) (B) (H) (AL)
3' × 2'   90 × 60 cm

'By Appointment' (Harvolute)

Harkness UK 1990
'Anne Harkness' × 'Letchworth
Garden City'
Apricot-shaded-buff, fully double,
shapely, produced in large
clusters on a tallish, upright-
growing plant with good dark
green foliage.
(C) ☉ (B) (H) (SF) ✄
(AW)   3' × 2'   90 × 60 cm

'Cairngorm'

Cocker UK 1973
'Anne Cocker' × 'Arthur Bell'
Gold heavily overlaid with tangerine, fully double flowers borne
in large clusters. Foliage dark
green and glossy. Growth upright.
(C) (P) (SF) (B) (H) (AL)
2' 6" × 2'   75 × 60 cm

'Centenaire de Lourdes', 'Mrs Jones', 'Delge'

Delbard-Chabert FRANCE 1958
('Frau Karl Druschki' × seedling)
× seedling
Huge clusters of well-spaced
flowers, each shapely both in bud
and when fully open, of bright
shrimp-pink. Foliage large, dark

'Chanelle'

green and shiny. Growth bushy
and upright. A little tender for
cold districts, but a superb variety.
(C) (P) (SF) (B) (H) (AL)
3' × 2'   90 × 60 cm

'Champagne Cocktail' (Horflash)

Horner UK 1985
'Old Master' × 'Southampton'
Medium-sized, double flowers of
soft yellow splashed with pink,
several blooms in a cluster. Foliage mid green. Growth bushy.
(C) (SF) (B) (H) (AL)
2' 6" × 2'   75 × 60 cm

'Chanelle'

McGredy UK 1959
'Ma Perkins × ('Fashion' × 'Mrs
William Sprott')
Large clusters of semi-double,
creamy apricot flowers are carried
on a vigorous plant with good,
dark green, glossy foliage. Growth
bushy.
(C) (MF) (B) (H) (AW)
2' 6" × 2'   75 × 60 cm

'By Appointment'

'Charles Aznavour' (Meibeausai)

Meilland FRANCE 1987
A profusion of shapely, creamy-white flowers tinged pink, produced amid an abundance of mid-green foliage on a compact, bushy plant.
(C) ☉ (B) (Gh) (H) (AL)
2' × 2'   60 × 60 cm

'Charleston' (Meiridge)

Meilland FRANCE 1963
'Masquerade' × ('Radar' × Caprice')
Clusters of semi-double blooms of soft yellow heavily flushed crimson, deepening with age. Foliage leathery. Growth bushy.
(C) (SF) (B) (H) BS ✄
(AL)   2' 6" × 2'   75 × 60 cm

'Cherish' (Jacsal)

Warriner USA 1980
'Bridal Pink' × 'Matador'
Clusters of fully double, high-centred flowers of coral pink. Slightly fragrant. Foliage plentiful, dark green. Growth compact, bushy.
(C) ☉ (B) (H) (P) (SF)
(AL)   2' 6" × 2'   75 × 60 cm

'Chinatown' (Ville de Chine)

Poulsen DENMARK 1963
'Columbine' × 'Cläre Grammerstorf'
The very large, fully double flowers of clear yellow are often flushed pink. These are displayed in medium-sized clusters amid lush, light green foliage. Growth upright and vigorous. This variety could well be used as a free-standing shrub rose.
(C) (P) (VF) (B) (H) (AW)
4' × 3'   120 × 90 cm

'Chorus' (Meijulito)

Meilland FRANCE 1975
'Tamango' × ('Sarabande' × 'Zambra')
Sizeable, double, bright red flowers are borne in large clusters. Foliage mid-green and glossy. Growth vigorous and upright.
(C) (P) (SF) (B) (H) (AL)
2' 6" × 2'   75 × 60 cm

'Chuckles'

Shepherd USA 1958
('Jean Lafitte' × 'New Dawn') × 'Orange Triumph'
Large, semi-double flowers of

deep orange-pink with a central white eye are produced in large clusters on a bushy plant.
(C) (SF) (B) (H) (AL)
2' × 2'   60 × 60 cm

'Circus'

Swim USA 1956
'Fandango' × 'Pinocchio'
The large clusters of shapely, cupped, fully double flowers are yellow flushed orange, and the foliage is plentiful and glossy. Growth upright.
(C) (P) (H) (SF) (B) (AL)
2' 6" × 2'   75 × 60 cm

'City of Belfast'

'Chinatown'

'Clydebank Centenary'

'City of Belfast' (Macci)

McGredy UK 1968
'Evelyn Fison' × ('Circus' × 'Korona')
The bright scarlet-red, very eye-catching blooms are borne in large clusters. Foliage plentiful and glossy. Growth bushy.
(C) (P) (B) (H) (AW)
2' × 2'   60 × 60 cm

'City of Birmingham' (Korholst)

Kordes GERMANY 1989
Large trusses of crimson-scarlet flowers, fully double. Foliage rich dark green and glossy. Growth compact, bushy.
(C) ☉ (B) (H) ✄ (AW)
2' × 2'   60 × 60 cm

'City of Leeds'

McGredy UK 1965
'Evelyn Fison' × ('Spartan' × 'Red Favourite')
Large, semi-double, salmon-pink flowers are produced in good-sized clusters. Foliage dark and leathery. Growth upright and bushy.
(C) (P) (B) (H) (SF) (AL)
2' 6" × 2'   75 × 60 cm

'City of Portsmouth'

Cant UK 1975
'Arthur Bell' × seedling
Coppery-orange and yellow with pink highlights, the flowers are large and borne in sizeable clusters. Foliage bronzy-green. Growth vigorous and upright.
(C) (P) (B) (SF) (H) (AL)
3' × 2'   90 × 60 cm

'Clydebank Centenary' (Cocdazzle)

Cocker UK 1987
Seedling × 'Darling Flame'

'City of Birmingham'

'Dearest'

'Dainty Maid'

LeGrice UK 1940
'D. T. Poulsen' × unknown
The beautiful, large, single flowers of silvery-pink have a deeper reverse and pronounced yellow stamens, and are carried in large clusters. Foliage dark green and leathery. Growth upright.
(C) (P) (B) (H) (AL)
3' × 2'   90 × 60 cm

'Dame of Sark'

Harkness UK 1976
('Pink Parfait' × 'Masquerade') × 'Tablers' Choice'
A striking variety, a mixture of orange and yellow with red marbling on fully double flowers in large clusters. Foliage dark green. Growth bushy and upright.
(C) (P) (B) (H) ● (AW)
2' 6" × 2'   75 × 60 cm

'Dame Wendy' (Canson)

Cants UK 1990
'English Miss' × 'Memento'
Unfading, fully double flowers of pure mid-pink in clusters. Foliage greyish-green and glossy. Growth medium but slightly spreading. Named after the actress Dame Wendy Hiller.
(C) ⊙ (BP) (H) (SF) ✂ (AL)   2' × 2' 6"   60 × 75 cm

'Dearest'

Dickson UK 1960
Seedling × 'Spartan'
Large, semi-double, salmon-pink blooms are borne in sizeable clusters, and have a fine scent. Foliage dark greyish-green and matt. Growth bushy.
(C) (B) (H) (VF) (WW) (AW)   2' × 2'   60 × 60 cm

'Deb's Delight' (Legsweet)

LeGrice UK 1983
'Tip Top' × seedling
A delightful blend of silvery-salmon and pink, fully double blooms in large clusters. Foliage mid-green and semi-glossy. Growth bushy and upright.
(C) (B) (H) (MF) ⊙ (AL)
2' × 2'   60 × 60 cm

'Dicky' *see* 'Anisley Dickson'

'Disco Dancer' (Dicinfra)

Dickson UK 1984
Coventry Cathedral' × 'Memento'
The very bright scarlet blooms have orange reflections, and are

Well-formed Hybrid Tea-like flowers of sparkling orange-vermilion with a yellow reverse. A rose of good foliage and upright growth.
(C) (B) (H) (SF) ⊙ (AL)
2' 6" × 2'   75 × 60 cm

'Daily Sketch' (Macai)

McGredy UK 1961
'Ma Perkins' × 'Grand Gala'
Hybrid Tea-shaped, fully double blooms of silver edge pink are produced in clusters. Foliage dark green and semi-glossy. Growth vigorous and upright.
(C) (P) (B) (SF) (H) (AL)
2' 6" × 2'   75 × 60 cm

'Dame Wendy'

'Dusky Maiden'

'Elizabeth of Glamis'

semi-double and produced in large clusters. Mid-green glossy foliage. Bushy and vigorous.
(C) (P) (B) (H) (SF) ☉
(AW) 3′ × 2′ 90 × 60 cm

'Dreamland', 'Traumland'

Tantau GERMANY 1958
'Cinnabar Improved' × 'Fashion'
Peachy-pink, fully double and shapely blooms, in large clusters.

'Escapade'

Foliage dark green and leathery. Growth short and bushy.
(C) (P) (B) (H) (SF) ☉
(AW) 1′ 6″ × 1′ 6″ 45 × 45 cm

'Dusky Maiden'

LeGrice UK 1947
(Daily Mail Scented Rose' × 'Etoile de Hollande') × 'Else Poulsen'
Large, single, deep velvety-red blooms are borne in clusters on an upright, sturdy plant with dark green foliage. A superb old variety.
(C) (P) (B) (H) (VF) ☉
✄ (AL) 2′ × 2′ 60 × 60 cm

'Edith Holden', 'Edwardian Lady' (Chewlegacy)

Horner UK 1988
Bred by an amateur. This is a very good rose with a difference. Warm brown suffused gold, very free-flowering with a strong bushy growth. Named to commemorate the author of *Diary of an Edwardian Lady*.
(C) ☉ (B) (H) (SF) ✄
(AL) 2′ × 2′ 60 × 60 cm

'Elizabeth of Glamis', 'Irish Beauty' (Macel)

McGredy UK 1964
'Spartan' × 'Highlight'
The superbly formed, well-scented double flowers of rich salmon-pink are produced in large clusters. Foliage dark green, matt. Growth upright. Needs protection in cold districts.
(C) (B) (H) (VF) ☉ BS⚘
M⚘ ✄ (AW)
2′ 6″ × 2′ 75 × 60 cm

'English Miss'

Cant UK 1977
'Dearest' × 'Sweet Repose'
Soft, blush-rose-pink, shapely, individual flowers in large, tight clusters. Foliage dark green overlaid purple. Growth bushy and upright.
(C) (P) (B) (H) (SF) ☉
(AW) 2′ × 2′ 60 × 60 cm

'Escapade' (Harpade)

Harkness UK 1967
'Pink Parfait' × 'Baby Faurax'
Scented, semi-double blooms of rosy-violet with hints of lavender are borne in large clusters. Foliage light green and semi-glossy, on an upright and branching bush.
(C) (P) (B) (H) (MF) ☉
✄ (AW) 3′ × 2′ 90 × 60 cm

'Europeana'

de Ruiter NETHERLANDS 1963
'Ruth Leuwerik' × 'Rosemary Rose'
Beautifully formed, fully double, deep red flowers opening flat and quartered are produced in large, heavy clusters. Foliage very dark green heavily overlaid with maroon. Stems dark, with few thorns. Bushy and angular growth.
(C) (B) (H) (SF) ☉ M⚘
(AL) 2′ × 2′ 60 × 60 cm

'Evelyn Fison', 'Irish Wonder' (Macey)

McGredy UK 1962
'Moulin Rouge' × 'Korona'
Large clusters of evenly spaced flowers, fully double and bright red. Foliage dark to mid-green. Growth bushy.
(C) (P) (B) (H) (SF) ☉
(AW) 2′ 6″ × 2′ 75 × 60 cm

'Evening Star'

Warriner USA 1974
'White Masterpiece' × 'Saratoga'
Large clusters of double flowers
of pure white with lemon
shadings, high-centred and
shapely. Foliage dark green and
leathery. Upright, bushy growth.
(C) (P) (B) (H) (SF) (AW)
2' 6" × 2'   75 × 60 cm

'Everest Double Fragrance'

Beales UK 1979
'Dearest' × 'Elizabeth of Glamis'
The large, fully double and
shapely blooms are borne in
trusses, a soft powder-pink sometimes almost coral, and highly
scented. Dark green, leathery and
heavily veined foliage, and stout
stems with prickles, on a plant of
upright and vigorous growth.
(C) (P) (B) (H) (VF) R♣
✂ (AL)   4' × 2'   120 × 60 cm

'Eyepaint',
'Tapis Persan'
(Maceye)

McGredy NEW ZEALAND 1975
Seedling × 'Picasso'
Medium-sized, single blooms of
scarlet with a white eye, in large
clusters. Foliage dark green, the
leaves numerous but small.
Growth bushy and tall.
(C) (P) (B) (H) ☉ (AL)
3' × 2'   90 × 60 cm

'Fashion'

Boerner USA 1949
'Pinocchio' × 'Crimson Glory'
Rich salmon to coral, shapely,
high-centred flowers are carried
in large clusters. Dark green,
glossy foliage and brownish
wood, the growth bushy.
(C) (B) (H) ☉ R♣ (AL)
2' × 2'   60 × 60 cm

'Europeana'

'Fergie' (Ganfer)

Gandy UK 1987
Eye-catching, Hybrid Tea-like
flowers of orange-buff and ginger
with a shell-pink edge to the
petals. Grey-green foliage on a
plant of compact growth.
(C) (B) ☉ (AL)
1' 6" × 1' 6"   45 × 45 cm

'Firecracker'

Boerner USA 1956
'Pinocchio' seedling × 'Numa Fay'
seedling
Large, semi-double flowers in
sizeable clusters, scarlet on
yellow. Foliage light green and
leathery. Compact and upright
growth.
(C) (B) (H) (SF) ☉ (AL)
2' × 2'   60 × 60 cm

'Florence Nightingale'
(Ganflor)

Gandy UK 1989
Trusses of buff-flecked-pink buds
open up to silvery-white. Very
fragrant. Foliage shiny olive
green. Growth bushy and branching.
(C) ☉ (B) (H) (VF) ✂
(AW)   2' × 2'   60 × 60 cm

'Everest Double Fragrance'

'French Lace'

'Fragrant Delight'

Tysterman UK 1978
'Chanelle' × 'Whisky Mac'
Soft orange-salmon blooms, large
and semi-double, are produced in
huge trusses on a well-balanced
plant with glossy reddish foliage.
Growth upright.
(C) (B) (H) ☉ (AW)
2' 6" × 2'   75 × 60 cm

'French Lace'

Warriner USA 1981
'Dr A. J. Verhage' × 'Bridal Pink'
Pointed buds in clusters open to
fully double blooms of ivory and
soft apricot paling to white.
Foliage small, plentiful and dark
green. Growth bushy.
(C) ☉ (B) (H) (P) (Gh)
(E) ✂ (AL)
2' 6" × 2'   75 × 60 cm

'Frensham'

Norman UK 1946
Floribunda seedling × 'Crimson
Glory'
Shapely, pure crimson flowers are
borne in clusters on a vigorous,

'Evelyn Fison'

'Frensham'

'Geraldine'

'Glad Tidings'

angular plant with bright green foliage and vicious thorns.
(C) (P) (B) (H) M⚘ (AL)
4 × 2' 6"   120 × 75 cm

'Frenzy', 'Prince Igor' (Meihigor)

Meilland FRANCE 1970
('Sarabande' × 'Dany Robin') × 'Zambra'
Shapely little flowers of orange-red with a yellow reverse, and abundant, darkish and matt-green foliage. Bushy growth.
(C) (P) (B) (H) (SF) ☉
(AL)   2' × 2'   60 × 60 cm

'Garnette'

Tantau GERMANY 1951
('Rosenelfe' × 'Eva') × 'Heros'
Never at its best out of doors but excellent under glass, this is still used extensively as a florist's rose. The flowers are cupped, double, garnet-red and are borne in clusters. Foliage dark green. Growth upright.
(C) (Gh) ☉ ✄ (AL)
2' × 2'   60 × 60 cm

'Geraldine' (Peahaze)

Pearce UK 1984
Seedling × seedling
A pleasing combination of

oranges in clusters very full of semi-double flowers. Foliage light green and semi-glossy. Growth upright.
(C) (B) (H) (SF) (AW)
2' 6" × 2'   75 × 60 cm

'Living Fire'

'Gilda' (Peahigh)

Pearce UK 1986
Very fragrant, soft-shell-pink flowers in clusters complemented by a profusion of leathery pale green, matt foliage. Growth vigor-

ous and shrubby. In fact, if lightly pruned, would make an excellent, small specimen shrub.
(C) (B) (H) ✄ (VF) (AL)
3' 6" × 2' 6"   110 × 75 cm

'Glad Tidings' (Tantide)

Tantau GERMANY 1988
This rose produces masses of large clusters of semi-double, deep crimson flowers. Foliage is dark glossy green. Growth upright and bushy. British 'Rose of the Year' 1989.
(C) ☉ (B) (H) ✄ (AW)
2' 6" × 2'   75 × 60 cm

'Glenfiddich'

Cocker UK 1976
'Arthur Bell' × ('Sabine' × 'Circus')
Large, well-shaped, full flowers of rich amber-yellow, in large clusters. Foliage dark green and glossy on a plant of upright growth. Not hardy in cold districts.
(C) (B) (H) (SF) ☉ (AW)
3' × 2'   90 × 60 cm

'Gold Badge' see 'Gold Bunny'

'Gold Bunny', 'Gold Badge', 'Rimosa '79' (Meigronuri)

Paulino FRANCE 1978
'Poppy Flash' × ('Charlston' × 'Allgold')
Full, fairly large blooms of clear yellow are borne in large clusters on a bushy plant with mid-green foliage.
(C) (B) (H) (SF) ☉ BS⚘
(AL)   2' × 2'   60 × 60 cm

'Golden Quill' (Tanellelog)

Tantau GERMANY 1990
Slightly fragrant, large clusters

of fully double, golden-yellow flowers amid glossy light green foliage on a medium-sized bushy plant.
(C) ☉ (B) (SF) ✂ (AW)
2′ 6″ × 2′   75 × 60 cm

'Golden Slippers'

Von Abrams USA 1961
'Goldilocks' × seedling
Loosely formed, semi-double flowers of orange and yellow are produced in large clusters on an upright and bushy plant with glossy, leathery foliage.
(C) (B) (H) (SF) ☉ (AL)
2′ × 2′   60 × 60 cm

'Golden Years' (Harween)

Harkness UK 1990
Golden-yellow, double flowers very freely produced and complemented superbly by glossy mid-green foliage. Slightly fragrant. Growth compact and bushy.
(C) ☉ (B) (H) (SF) ✂ (Gh) (AW)
2′ 6″ × 2′   75 × 60 cm

'Grace Abounding'

Harkness UK 1968
'Pink Parfait' × 'Penelope'
Clusters of semi-double, fragrant, ivory blooms on a bushy plant with glossy dark green foliage.
(C) ☉ (B) (H) (MF) (AL)
2′ 6″ × 2′   75 × 60 cm

'Great Ormond Street'

Beales UK 1991
Seedling × (Arthur Bell' × 'Allgold')
Clusters of shapely, semi-double flowers of golden-yellow – not harsh but soft – changing with age to pineapple yellow and then to creamy yellow. A special feature is a prominent display of golden-brown anthers. Slight

'Gold Bunny'

fragrance. Foliage is large, mid-to-dark green and semi-glossy. Growth bushy compact. Well armed with creamy-yellow thorns.
(C) ☉ (B) (SF) ✂ (AL)
1′ 6″ × 1′ 6″   45 × 45 cm

'Greensleeves' (Harlenten)

Harkness UK 1980
('Rudolph Timm' × 'Arthur Bell') × [('Pascali' × 'Elizabeth of Glamis') × ('Sabine' × 'Violette Dot)]
An unusual rose, its semi-double, chartreuse-green flowers with a pink overlay are borne in large clusters. Dark green, matt foliage on a plant of upright growth.
(C) (B) (H) (Gh) ☉ ✂ (AL)   2′ 6″ × 2′   75 × 60 cm

'Grüss an Aachen'

Geduldig GERMANY 1909
'Frau Karl Druschki' × 'Franz Deegen'
A charmer from the past, its fully double, creamy-white flowers have soft pink and peachy highlights and are very freely pro-

duced in smallish clusters. Foliage matt dark green. Growth bushy, upright.
(C) (B) (H) (Gh) (SF) ☉ (AL)   1′ 6″ × 1′ 6″   45 × 45 cm

'Hannah Gordon' (Korweiso)

Kordes GERMANY 1983
Seedling × 'Bordure'
Large clusters of blooms, full and shapely, white to cream touched deep pink. Foliage of good size, mid-green and semi-glossy. Growth bushy and upright.
(C) (P) (B) (H) (SF) ☉ (AW)   3′ × 2′   90 × 60 cm

'Great Ormond Street'

'Harold Macmillan'
(Harvestsun)

Harkness UK 1989
'Avocet' × 'Remember Me'
Medium-sized clusters of semi-double blooms of bright orange-red with a barely detectable perfume. Foliage shiny dark green on a vigorous, bushy plant.
(C) ☉ (B) (H) ✂ (SF)
(AL)   3' × 2' 6"   90 × 75 cm

'Harvest Fayre' (Dicnorth)

Dickson UK 1990
Large clusters of semi-double, apricot-orange flowers on a healthy, strong, bushy plant with glossy mid-green foliage. Starts flowering rather later than most Floribundas but more than makes up for this by improving steadily later in the year when its colour is enhanced by autumn light. British 'Rose of the Year' 1990.
(C) ☉ (B) (H) ✂ (SF)
(AL)   3' × 2' 6"   90 × 75 cm

'Heaven Scent'

Poulsen DENMARK 1968
'Pernille Poulsen' × 'Isabel de Ortiz'
Soft salmon, fully double, large blooms are produced in large clusters. Good, mid-green foliage. Bushy growth.
(C) (B) (H) (VF) ☉ ✂
(AL)   2' × 2'   60 × 60 cm

'Highland Laddie' (Cocflag)

Cocker UK 1989
'National Trust' × 'Dainty Dinah'
Clusters of rich scarlet, semi-double flowers, petals slightly crinkled. Moderate fragrance. Foliage mid-green. Growth upright.
(C) ☉ (B) (H) (SF) (AL)
3' × 2'   90 × 60 cm

'Honeymoon', 'Honigmond'

Kordes GERMANY 1960
'Cläre Grammerstorf' × 'Spek's Yellow'
Sizeable clusters of clear yellow blooms each fairly large with ruffled petals. Foliage exceptionally good, rich mid-green, semi-glossy and veined. Growth upright and dense.
(C) (P) (B) (H) ☉ (AL)
3' × 2'   90 × 60 cm

'Horstmann's Rosenresli'

Kordes GERMANY 1955
'Rudolph Timm' × 'Lavender Pinocchio'
Pure white, fully double flowers in large clusters. Foliage mid-green, semi-glossy on a plant of bushy and upright growth. An excellent variety.
(C) (P) (B) (H) (SF) ☉
(AL)   2' 6" × 2'   75 × 60 cm

'Iceberg', 'Schneewittchen', 'Fée des Neiges' (Korbin)

Kordes GERMANY 1958
'Robin Hood' × 'Virgo'
One of the best Floribundas ever raised, its shapely little buds open to loosely formed flowers of pure white which are carried in large trusses. Foliage light green and glossy, the stems also light green. Growth upright and bushy.
(C) (P) (B) (H) (Gh) (MF)
☉ ✂ (AW)
3' × 2'   90 × 60 cm

'Iced Ginger'

Dickson UK 1971
'Anne Watkins' × unknown
Pale pink to ivory flowers with a

'Harold Macmillan'

'Harvest Fayre'

coppery reverse, large and full, in sizeable clusters. Foliage overlaid red and heavily veined on an upright plant.
(C) (B) (H) (SF) ☉ ✂
(AL)   3' × 2'   90 × 60 cm

'Impatient' (Jacdew)

Warriner USA 1984
'America' × seedling
Trusses of orangey-red, semi-double flowers with a slight fragrance produced on a compact, bushy plant with glossy, light green foliage.
(C) ☉ (B) (H) (P) (SF)
(AL)   2' × 2'   60 × 60 cm

'Inner Wheel' (Fryjasso)

Fryer UK 1984
'Pink Parfait' × 'Picasso'
Carmine-pink flowers edged rosy-pink, full, shapely and in large trusses with reddish, matt foliage. Growth bushy.
(C) (B) (H) (SF) ☉ (AL)
2′ 6″ × 2′   75 × 60 cm

**'Intrigue',
'Lavaglut',
'Lavaglow'**
(Korlech)

Kordes GERMANY 1978
'Grüss an Bayern' × seedling
Shapely, rounded flowers with slightly crumpled petals, very dark red, in large clusters. This rose stands sun very well. Foliage dark green and glossy. Growth bushy. More than one variety has this name.
(C) (B) (H) (SF) ☉ (AW)
2′ 6″ × 2′   75 × 60 cm

'Intrigue' (Jacum)

Warriner USA 1984
'White Masterpiece' × 'Heirloom'
Large double flowers of reddish-purple, foliage dark green, semi-glossy. Growth bushy.
(C) (B) (H) (VF) (AL)
2′ 6″ × 2′   75 × 60 cm

**'Invincible',
'Fennica'**
(Runatru)

de Ruiter NETHERLANDS 1983
'Rubella' × 'National Trust'
Large clusters of semi-double, clear red blooms on a tidy and bushy plant with mid-green, glossy foliage.
(C) (B) (H) (SF) ☉ (AL)
2′ 6″ × 2′   75 × 60 cm

**'Irene of Denmark',
'Irene von Dänemark'**

Poulsen DENMARK 1948
'Orléans Rose' × ('Mme Plantier' × 'Edina')
Very double, shapely flowers of pure white with a creamy base which are cupped until fully open, then flat and well formed. Foliage mid-green and glossy. Growth upright and bushy.
(C) (P) (B) (H) (MF) ☉
✂ (AL)   2′ 6″ × 2′   75 × 60 cm

'Iceberg'

'Horstmann's Rosenresli'

'Irene of Denmark'

'Irène Watts'

'Ivory Fashion'

'Irène Watts'

Guillot FRANCE 1896
Although it was raised in 1896, I could not resist including this charming little rose, for it is well placed even ninety years on and has superbly shaped, scented blooms of ivory with pinkish-orange shadings, especially deep in the centre. Foliage dark green, matt. Growth bushy and short.
(C) (B) (H) (MF) (Gh) ☉ (AL) 1′ 6″ × 1′ 6″ 45 × 45 cm

'Irish Mist', 'Irish Summer'

McGredy UK 1966
'Orangeade' × 'Mischief'
Large clusters of semi-double blooms of orange-salmon. Foliage dark green and semi-glossy. Growth bushy.
(C) (B) (H) (SF) ☉ (AL)
2′ 6″ × 2′ 75 × 60 cm

'Ivory Fashion'

Boerner USA 1958
'Sonata' × 'Fashion'
Globular buds open up to shapely, cupped, semi-double, ivory-white, fragrant flowers in large clusters. Foliage leathery

dark green. Growth bushy and compact. A delightful older variety that should never disappear from our gardens no matter how many upstarts arrive on the scene.
(C) ☉ (B) (H) (MF) (Gh) ✄ (AL)
  1′ 6″ × 1′ 6″ 45 × 45 cm

'Jenny Wren'

Ratcliff UK 1957
'Cécile Brünner' × 'Fashion'
Small, exquisite flowers of creamy-apricot, their reverses are soft salmon, and they are borne in

large sprays in the fashion of 'Cécile Brünner'. Foliage dark and semi-glossy. Growth bushy.
(C) (B) (Gh) ☉ ✄ (AL)
2′ × 2′ 60 × 60 cm

'Jiminy Cricket'

Boerner USA 1954
'Goldilocks' × 'Geranium Red'
Shapely buds open to loosely formed blooms of pinkish-coral-orange in medium-sized clusters on a twiggy but dense plant with good, dark, glossy foliage.
(C) (B) (H) ☉ (AL)
2′ 6″ × 2′ 75 × 60 cm

'Jiminy Cricket'

'Jocelyn'

LeGrice UK 1970
Fully double flowers of mahogany age to bluish-brown on a compact and bushy plant with dark green foliage.
(C) (B) ☉ ✄ (AL)
2′ × 2′ 60 × 60 cm

'Joyfulness', 'Frohsinn'

Tantau GERMANY 1963
'Horstmann's Jubiläumsrose' × 'Circus'
Large clusters of semi-double flowers of orange-red to salmon with some cream are carried on a bushy, upright plant with mid-green glossy foliage.
(C) (B) (H) (SF) (AL)
2′ 6″ × 2′ 75 × 60 cm

'Julie Cussons' (Fryprincess)

Fryer UK 1988
Plentiful, shapely flowers in clusters of brilliant orange-salmon with a delightful fragrance. Good mid-to-dark green foliage on a vigorous, bushy plant.
(C) ☉ (B) (H) (VF) (AL)
3′ × 2′ 90 × 60 cm

'Kim'

Harkness UK 1973
('Orange Sensation' × 'Allgold') × 'Elizabeth of Glamis'
A delightful little free-flowering rose, its very large clusters of

'Jocelyn'

small, fully double flowers of clear yellow are suffused red. Foliage small, mid-green and matt-finished. Growth bushy.
(C) (B) (H) ☉ (AL)
1' 6" × 1' 6"   45 × 45 cm

'Korona' (Kornita)

Kordes GERMANY 1955
'Obergärtner Wiebicke' × 'Independence'
An outstanding rose from the 1950s whose rich orange-scarlet flowers, double and shaggy when open, come in large clusters on tall stems with deep green, matt foliage. Growth upright and vigorous.
(C) (P) (B) (H) ☉ (AW)
3' × 2'   90 × 60 cm

'Korp', 'Prominent'

Kordes GERMANY 1970
'Colour Wonder' × 'Zorina'
The blooms are borne in small clusters, individually quite large for a Floribunda, cupped and full and vivid orange-red. The foliage is light green on a bushy and upright plant.
(C) (P) (B) (H) ☉ ✁
(AW) 3' × 2'   90 × 60 cm

'Korresia', 'Fresia', 'Friesia', 'Sunsprite'

Kordes GERMANY 1977
'Friedrich Wörlein' × 'Spanish Sun'
Rounded buds arranged in large flat clusters open to fully double bright yellow flowers on a sturdy, bushy plant. Foliage lightish green.
(C) (P) (B) (H) (VF) ☉
(AL) 2' × 2'   60 × 60 cm

'Lady Cecily Gibson' (Evebright)

Everett UK 1990
'Southampton' seedling
Flowers coral-red in bud opening to coppery apricot with a slight fragrance. Medium, vigorous bushy growth with dense, glossy foliage. Bred by a most promising amateur.
(C) ☉ (B) (H) (SF) (AL)
2' × 2'   60 × 60 cm

'Lady Romsey'

Beales UK 1985
('Fragrant Cloud' × 'Pascali') × seedling
Shapely and high-centred when half-open, the flowers open large, full and flattish, white with cream and pink highlights and scented. The foliage is large, glossy and light green touched pink when young on a bushy, upright and shortish plant.
(C) (P) (B) (II) (SF) (Gh)
☉ ✁ (AL)
1' 6" × 1' 6"   45 × 45 cm

'Lagoon'

Harkness UK 1973
'Lilac Charm' × 'Sterling Silver'
I cannot resist including this beautiful variety. Clusters of lovely, single, scented, lilac blooms with deeper reverses and prominent golden stamens. Foliage dark green and glossy. Growth moderately vigorous, bushy. Perhaps slightly shy in flowering but this is easily forgiven.
(C) ☉ (B) (Gh) (MF)
1' 6" × 1' 6"   45 × 45 cm

'Korona'

'Lady Romsey'

'Langdale Chase' (Fryrhapsody)

Fryer UK 1990
Superbly formed flowers of a lovely combination of cream and peachy-apricot in large clusters, produced on long stout stems from a vigorous yet bushy plant with dense green foliage.
(C) ☉ (B) (H) ✁ (Gh)
(AL) 2' 6" × 2'   75 × 60 cm

'La Paloma '85' (Tanamola)

Tantau GERMANY 1985
Elegant buds open to shapely, pure white flowers produced freely in large trusses on a plant with clear green foliage. Growth upright.
(C) (B) (H) (SF) (AL)
2' 6" × 2'   75 × 60 cm

'Laurence Olivier', 'Wapiti' (Meinagre)

Meilland FRANCE 1988
Shapely, pointed buds open to bright red, high-centred flowers very freely produced on an upright but bushy, vigorous plant bearing good mid-to-dark green foliage.
(C) ☉ (B) (II) (Gh) ✁
(SF) (AW) 3' × 2'   90 × 60 cm

'Lavaglut' see 'Intrigue'

'Lavender Pinocchio'

Boerner USA 1948
'Pinocchio' × 'Grey Pearl'
This variety has figured in the parentage of many off-beat-coloured roses since its introduction. Large trusses of fully double flowers are a rather tousled mixture of soft brown, pink and lavender. Foliage mid-green and leathery. Growth bushy.
(C) (P) (B) (H) (SF) ☉
✁ (AL) 2' × 2'   60 × 60 cm

'Len Turner' (Dicjeep)

Dickson UK 1984
'Mullard Jubilee' × 'Eyepaint'
The ivory-white to cream flowers, heavily flushed deep pink edged carmine, are full, large and shapely and are carried in large clusters. The foliage is mid-green and glossy, on a shortish bushy plant. A worthy rose to honour Mr Len Turner, MBE, Secretary of the Royal National Rose Society for eighteen years.
(C) (P) (B) (H) (SF) ☉
(AW) 2' × 2'   60 × 60 cm

'Léonie Lamesch'

P. Lambert GERMANY 1899
'Aglaia' × 'Kleiner Alfred'
One of the first Polyanthas.

Placed here because it was ahead of its time when introduced. A short variety with rather stubby growth but ample, leathery, dark green foliage. Flowers are small, full double, borne in clusters and an odd mixture of yellow, orange and red.
(P) ☉ (C) (AL)
2′ × 2′   60 × 60 cm

'Lilac Charm'

LeGrice UK 1952
Bred from a *R. californica* seedling
A beautiful rose, with large clusters of single, or almost single, soft pastel-mauve flowers which have pronounced gold and red stamens. Foliage dark matt-green. Growth sturdy and bushy.
(C) (P) (B) (H) (MF) ☉
(AL)   2′ × 2′   60 × 60 cm

'Lilli Marlene' (Korlima)

Kordes GERMANY 1958
('Our Princess' × 'Rudolph Timm') × 'Ama'
An outstanding rose with superbly formed flowers of deep velvety-red; these are large and well spaced in flattish clusters. Foliage dark green and leathery, the stems very thorny. Growth bushy and upright.
(C) (P) (B) (H) BS⚘
(AW)   2′ 6″ × 2′   75 × 60 cm

'Little White Pet'
see **'White Pet'**

'Liverpool Echo'

McGredy NEW ZEALAND 1971
('Little Darling' × 'Goldilocks') × 'München'

'Ma Perkins'

'Manx Queen'

The soft salmon-pink blooms, fairly full and large, are produced in sizeable clusters on a vigorous and upright plant with light green foliage.
(C) (P) (B) (H) (SF) ☉
✂ (AL)   3′ × 2′   90 × 60 cm

'Living Fire'

Gregory UK 1972
'Super Star' × unknown
Generous clusters of full flowers of rich orange-scarlet and yellow with smallish, plentiful, dark green and leathery foliage, the stems thorny. Growth very upright.
(C) (P) (B) (H) (AL)
2′ 6″ × 2′   75 × 60 cm

'Lloyds of London' (Canlloyd)

Cants UK 1991
A pleasing bicolour. Trusses of orange and yellow flowers on a strong-growing plant with leathery mid-green foliage. Initially offered exclusively to members of Lloyds of London.

'Lilli Marlene'

(C) ☉ (B) (H) (Gh) ✄
(SF) (AL) 3' × 2' 90 × 60 cm

'Manx Queen', 'Isle of Man'

Dickson UK 1963
'Shepherd's Delight' × 'Circus'
The large, semi-double flowers
are an eye-catching mixture of
red, orange, yellow and bronze.
The foliage is dark green and
leathery on a bushy plant.
(C) (P) (B) (H) (SF) (AL)
2' 6" × 2' 75 × 60 cm

'Ma Perkins'

Boerner USA 1952
'Red Radiance' × 'Fashion'
Not widely available, but this
variety demands inclusion
because it is both beautiful and a
representative of the Floribundas
of the 1950s. A lively mixture of
salmon, shell-pink and cream
flowers, large and full, are pro

'Margaret Merril'

duced in generous clusters. Foliage glossy and rich green. Growth
bushy and upright.
(C) (B) (H) (Gh) (MF) ☉
✄ (AL) 2' × 2' 60 × 60 cm

'Margaret Merril' (Harkuly)

Harkness UK 1977
('Rudolph Timm'
× 'Dedication') × 'Pascali'
A superb variety, the flowers are
white with blushes of soft pink
and have pronounced golden stamens when fully open. They are
highly scented and are carried in
small clusters. Foliage dark green,
matt. Growth sturdy and upright.
(C) (P) (B) (H) (Gh) (VF)
☉ ✄ (AW)
2' 6" × 2' 75 × 60 cm

'Marie-Jeanne'

Turbat FRANCE 1913
Clusters of fully double, rosette-
shaped flowers of soft pink to
almost white with deeper
coloured centres. Slightly scented.
Foliage glossy light green tinted
bronze, especially when young.
Vigorous. Can be left unpruned
to produce an excellent, shortish
shrub.
(C) (H) (P) ☉ ● (AL)
3' × 3' 90 × 90 cm

'Marie Parvie'

Alégatière FRANCE 1888
Clusters of small, white to blush-
pink flowers on an upright but
bushy plant. Slightly short on
foliage but free-flowering enough
to compensate for this short-
coming.
(C) ☉ (AL)
3' × 2' 90 × 60 cm

'Marina', 'Rinakov'

Kordes GERMANY 1974
'Colour Wonder' × seedling
Pointed buds open to high-
centred, double flowers of bright
vermilion-orange with yellow
tints deep in the base. Slightly fra-
grant. Foliage dark green glossy.
Growth upright, bushy.
(C) (B) ☉ (H) ✄ (Gh)
(SF) (AW) 2' × 2' 60 × 60 cm

'Marlena'

Kordes GERMANY 1964
'Gertrud Westphal' × Lilli
Marlene
A discreet mixture of red and
crimson flowers, semi-double,
large and flattish when fully open.
Foliage dark green. Growth bushy
and compact.
(C) (P) (B) (H) ☉ (AW)
1' 6" × 1' 6" 45 × 45 cm

'Masquerade'

Boerner USA 1949
'Goldilocks' × 'Holiday'
The forerunner of many brightly
coloured Floribundas. Semi-
double flowers of bright yellow
changing through pink and
orange to deep red with age are
produced in very large clusters.
Foliage small, dark and leathery.
Growth upright. The hips set
easily and therefore must be
dead-headed in order to encourage the autumn flowers.
(C) (P) (B) (H) ☉ (AW)
2' 6" × 2' 75 × 60 cm

'Matangi' (Macman)

McGredy NEW ZEALAND 1974
Seedling × 'Picasso'
The large clusters of bright vermilion-red, double flowers with a
white eye and silver reverse are
spectacular. Foliage small, mid-
green and matt on a bushy and
upright plant.
(C) (P) (B) (H) (AW)
3' × 2' 90 × 60 cm

'Matthias Meilland' (Meifolio)

Meilland FRANCE 1985
Clusters of bright red flowers
amid an abundance of healthy
dense, mid-green foliage on a
vigorous, upright yet bushy plant.
(C) ☉ (B) (H) (AW)
3' × 2' 90 × 60 cm

Top: 'Marlena', and *above*, 'Matangi'

'Melody Maker'

'Megiddo'

Gandy UK 1970
'Coup de Foudre' × 'S'Agaró'
Large sprays of semi-double,
bright scarlet flowers on a strong-
growing and upright plant with
large, olive-green matt-finished
foliage.
(C) (P) (B) (H) BS✄ (AL)
3' × 2'   90 × 60 cm

'Melody Maker' (Dicqueen)

Dickson UK 1991
Very large, well proportioned
clusters of shapely, light vermilion flowers with a silver lining.
Foliage dense dark green on a
medium-height, bushy plant. British 'Rose of the Year' 1991.
(C) ⊙ (B) (H) (SF) ✄
(Gh) (AW)   2' × 2'   60 × 60 cm

'Memento' (Dicbar)

Dickson UK 1978
'Bangor' × 'Korbel'
Salmon, red and bright pink
blooms of fair size in very large
clusters, with deep green and
leathery foliage on a bushy plant.

(C) (P) (B) (H) (SF) (AW)
2' 6" × 2'   75 × 60 cm

'Meteor'

Kordes GERMANY 1959
'Feurio' × 'Gertrud Westphal'
Closely packed clusters of many,
small, double, orange-scarlet
flowers on a compact and
upright-growing plant with
lightish green foliage.
(C) (P) (B) (H) ⊙ (AL)
1' 6" × 1' 6"   45 × 45 cm

'Mevrouw Nathalie Nypels'
see 'Nathalie Nypels'

'Nancy Steen'

Sherwood NEW ZEALAND 1976
'Pink Parfait' × ('Ophelia' ×
'Parkdirektor Riggers')
The large, fully double, fragrant
flowers are borne in clusters and
are blush-pink with hints of
salmon, the centre cream. Foliage
lush and glossy, dark bronzy-
green. Growth bushy and upright.
(C) (P) (B) (H) (MF) ⊙
✄ (AL)   2' 6" × 2'   75 × 60 cm

'Nancy Steen'

'Nathalie Nypels', 'Mevrouw Nathalie Nypels'

Leenders HOLLAND 1919
'Orléans Rose' × ('Comtesse du
Cayla' × R. foetida bicolor)
One of the best and most reliable
of the cluster-flowered roses from
the past. Large clusters of double,
silky-textured, deep pink to
salmon flowers are borne on
strong stems from a bushy and
branching plant with good, dark
green foliage.
(C) (P) (B) (H) ⊙ (AL)
2' 6" × 2'   75 × 60 cm

'New Horizon' (Dicplay)

Dickson UK 1991
Almost perfectly formed blooms
of salmon with subtle shades of

pink and yellow make this a most
attractive rose. Mid-green glossy
foliage adds to the pleasing effect.
Growth upright but bushy.
(C) ⊙ (B) (H) (Gh) (AW)
2' × 2'   60 × 60 cm

'Nathalie Nypels'

'News' (Legnews)

LeGrice UK 1968
'Lilac Charm' × 'Tuscany Superb'
An unusual colour, beetroot-purple, the flowers are semi-double and arranged in large cluster. Foliage olive-green and semi-glossy. Growth bushy and upright.
(C) (P) (B) (H) (SF) ☉
✕ (AW) 2' 6" × 2' 75 × 60 cm

'New Year' see 'Arcadian'

'Nina Weibull'

Poulsen DENMARK 1962
'Fanal' × 'Masquerade'
Trusses of semi-double, dark blood-red flowers on a thorny, upright and bushy plant with dark green, semi-glossy foliage.
(C) (P) (B) (H) ☉ (AL)
2' 6" × 2' 75 × 60 cm

'Norwich Castle'

Beales UK 1979
('Whisky Mac' × 'Arthur Bell') ×
seedling
Closely packed clusters of Hybrid

Tea-shaped flowers, flat when fully open, of deep coppery-orange paling to soft apricot. Very free-flowering, with light green, shiny foliage and of upright growth.
(C) (P) (B) (H) (Gh) ☉
✕ (AL)   2' 6" × 2' 75 × 60 cm

'Norwich Union'

Beales UK 1975
'Arthur Bell' × (seedling ×
'Allgold')
Large, fully double, cupped flowers of deep clear yellow paling to lemon with age, but

'Norwich Union'

losing nothing in doing so, are produced in small, upstanding clusters. Foliage bright green and glossy. Growth stocky and upright.
(C) (B) (H) (Gh) (VF) ●
☉ ✕ (AL)
1' 6" × 1' 6" 45 × 45 cm

'Olala',
'Ohlala'

Tantau GERMANY 1956
'Fanal' × 'Crimson Glory'

Blood-red flowers with light red centres, semi-double and large, are carried in very large trusses. Foliage dark green and leathery. Growth bushy and upright.
(C) (P) (B) (H) ☉ (AL)
3' × 2' 90 × 60 cm

'Old Master' (Macesp)

McGredy UK 1974
('Maxi' × 'Evelyn Fison') ×
('Orange Sweetheart' ×
'Frühlingsmorgen')
The flowers are semi-double, their silvery-white petals liberally painted inside with carmine which pales towards the edges to leave brush strokes. Foliage mid-green and semi-glossy. Growth bushy and upright.
(C) (P) (B) (H) ☉ ✕
(AW) 3' × 2' 90 × 60 cm

'New Horizon'

Top: 'Old Master'. *Above:* 'Norwich Castle'

'Orangeade'

McGredy UK 1959
'Orange Sweetheart' × 'Independence'
Very large trusses of single, bright vermilion-orange flowers on a vigorous plant with large, leathery and glossy foliage.
(C) (P) (B) (H) (SF) (AL)
3' × 2'   90 × 60 cm

'Orange Sensation'

de Ruiter UK 1961
The bright orange, semi-double flowers are well spaced in large trusses. The foliage is mid-green and matt-finished on a rather sprawling but bushy plant.
(C) (P) (B) (H) (SF) (AL)
2' 6" × 2'   75 × 60 cm

'Orange Silk'

McGredy UK 1968
'Orangeade' × ('Ma Perkins' × 'Independence')
Lots of blooms per cluster, semi-double, orange-vermilion, medium-sized and cupped. Foli-

'Orange Triumph'

age dark green and glossy. Growth bushy.
(C) (P) (B) (H) (SF) (AL)
2' 6" × 2'   75 × 60 cm

'Orange Triumph'

Kordes GERMANY 1937
'Eva' × 'Solarium'
Individually small, cupped flowers of many petals are borne in large clusters. The name is misleading, as the colour is nearer to clear red. Plentiful, large, dark green and glossy foliage on a robust, upright plant.
(C) (P) (B) (H) (AL)
3' × 2'   90 × 60 cm

'Paddy McGredy' (Macpa)

McGredy UK 1962
'Spartan' × 'Tzigane'
Tubby, Hybrid Tea-shaped, high-centred individual blooms of carmine to rose-pink are produced in large clusters. Foliage dark green and leathery. Growth bushy and strong.
(C) (P) (B) (H) (M) ☉
BS⌘ (AW)
2' 6" × 2'   75 × 60 cm

'Paint Box'

Dickson UK 1963
Seedling × 'St Pauli'
Large, semi-double blooms of red

'Orange Sensation'

and yellow, shedding the yellow with age to become deep red, are carried in large clusters, with dark green, matt foliage. Growth upright and vigorous.
(C) (B) (H) (AL)
3' × 2'   90 × 60 cm

'Penelope Plummer'

Beales UK 1970
'Anna Wheatcroft' × 'Dearest'
Large, semi-double blooms of flamingo-pink to salmon are produced in small, upright clusters. Foliage dark and matt-finished on a short, bushy plant.
(C) (B) (H) (SF) BS⌘
(AL)   1' 6" × 1' 6"   45 × 45 cm

'Pensioners' Voice' (Fryrelax)

Fryer UK 1989
Tints of pink and vermilion on a bright orange-apricot background make this an unusually coloured rose. The fragrant blooms are well spaced in clusters on a strong, sturdy, bushy plant; the whole set-off by an abundance of tough luxuriant foliage.
(C) ☉ (B) (H) (Gh) ✄
(SF) (AL)   2' 6" × 2'   75 × 60 cm

'Pernille Poulsen'

Poulsen DENMARK 1965
'Ma Perkins' × 'Columbine'
Semi-double, salmon blooms are borne in large clusters, and are very freely produced. Foliage pointed, light green and profuse. Growth bushy and shortish.
(C) (P) (B) (H) ✄ (AW)
2' × 2'   60 × 60 cm

'Picasso' (Macpic)

McGredy UK 1971
'Marlena' × ['Evelyn Fison' × ('Frühlingsmorgen' × 'Orange Sweetheart')]
Semi-double flowers are pro-

'Penelope Plummer'

'Picasso'

'Pinocchio'

'Pernille Poulsen'

'Plentiful'

duced in clusters, their petals deep rose-pink, the edges and reverse silvery. The foliage is small and dark green on a bushy plant. This was the first of several 'hand-painted' roses, as their raiser calls them.
(C) (P) (H) ⊙ BS❦ (AL)
2' 6" × 2'   75 × 60 cm

'Piccolo' (Tanolokip)

Tantau GERMANY 1983
Small, double, orange-red flowers come in clusters, with dark green, glossy foliage on an upright plant.
(C) (B) (H) (AW)
2' 6" × 2'   75 × 60 cm

'Pillarbox' (Chewaze)

Gandy UK 1987
A tall, upright-growing rose bearing clusters of vivid vermilion, fully double flowers set off by an abundance of healthy mid-green foliage.
(C) ⊙ (H) (B) (Gh) ✄
(SF) (AL)   3' × 2'   90 × 60 cm

'Pink Parfait'

Swim USA 1960
'First Love' × 'Pinocchio'
Attractive buds open to large, semi-double blooms made up of several shades of pink which are produced in large numbers in clusters of variable size. The foliage is semi-glossy and leathery, the growth upright and bushy. Without any doubt, this is an outstanding rose.
(C) (P) (B) (H) (SF) (Gh)
⊙ ✄ (AL)
3' × 2'   90 × 60 cm

'Pinocchio', 'Rosenmärchen'

Kordes GERMANY 1940
'Eva' × 'Golden Rapture'
Small, cupped blooms open rather raggedly but profusely in medium-sized clusters, their colour pink suffused salmon with a hint of yellow in the base, on a bushy plant of leathery foliage. An important rose as a parent in the development of the Floribundas.
(C) (P) (B) (H) (SF) ⊙
(AL)   2' × 2'   60 × 60 cm

'Plentiful'

LeGrice UK 1961
Large, deep pink and scented flowers packed with petals of different lengths to create a very old-fashioned, quartered effect when

fully open. Foliage dark green, leathery and veined. Growth angular with many thorns.
(C) (P) (B) (MF) ⊙ ✄
(AL)   2' 6" × 2' 6"   75 × 75 cm

'Poppy Flash', 'Rusticana' (Meiléna)

Meilland FRANCE 1971
('Dany Robin' × 'Fire King') × ('Alain' × 'Mutabilis')
Large clusters of bright vermilion blooms, fully double, on a vigorous, bushy plant with good, deep green and glossy foliage.
(C) (P) (B) (H) (AL)
3' × 2'   90 × 60 cm

'Princess Michael of Kent' (Harlightly)

Harkness UK 1981
'Manx Queen' × 'Alexander'
Bright yellow, large and full blooms are carried in small clusters. Foliage mid-green and glossy. Growth bushy.
(C) (P) (B) (H) (VF) ⊙
✄ (AL)   2' × 2'   60 × 60 cm

'Princess Michiko'

Dickson UK 1966
'Circus' × 'Spartan'
The large clusters of orange-red blooms with a yellow base are semi-double and of medium size. Dark, glossy foliage on a bushy plant.
(C) (B) (H) (SF) ⊙ BS❦
(AL)   2' × 2'   60 × 60 cm

'Priscilla Burton' (Macrat)

McGredy NEW ZEALAND 1978
['Maxi' ×['Evelyn Fison' × ('Orange Sweetheart' × 'Frühlingsmorgen')]] × [[('Little Darling' × 'Goldilocks') × ['Evelyn

Fison' × 'Coryana' × 'Tantau's Triumph')]] × ('John Church' × 'Elizabeth of Glamis')]
A mixture of red and carmine with a paler, painted reverse, the blooms are semi-double, large and are borne in clusters. Foliage dark green and glossy. Growth upright and vigorous.
(C) (P) (B) (H) (SF) (AW)
2' 6" × 2'   75 × 60 cm

'Prominent' see 'Korp'

'Queen Elizabeth', 'The Queen Elizabeth Rose'

Lammerts USA 1954
'Charlotte Armstrong' × 'Floradora'
This outstanding rose has deserved all the attention it has ever received. Long, high-centred buds open to large blooms of clear pink, produced in clusters. The foliage is large, dark green, leathery and glossy on a very vigorous, upright plant.
(C) (P) (H) (Gh) (SF) ⊙
✄ (AW)
5' × 2' 6"   150 × 75 cm

'Radox Bouquet', 'Rosika' (Harmusky)

Harkness UK 1980
('Alec's Red' × 'Piccadilly') × ['Southampton' × 'Cläre Grammerstorf' × 'Frühlingsmorgen')]
The rose-pink flowers, many-petalled with an old-fashioned form, are borne in large clusters on a vigorous, upright plant with good, mid-green, glossy foliage.
(C) (P) (B) (H) (VF) ⊙
✄ (AL)   3' 6" × 2'   105 × 60 cm

'Razzle Dazzle'

Warriner USA 1977
Aptly named. Large clusters of
very bright red flowers with white
reverses. Slightly fragrant. Foliage
dark green, leathery. Growth
bushy.
(C) ⊙ (B) (H) (P) (SF)
(AL) 2' × 2' 60 × 60 cm

'Queen Elizabeth'

'Radox Bouquet'

'Ripples'

'Ripples'

LeGrice UK 1971
('Tantau's Surprise' × 'Marjorie
LeGrice') × (Seedling × 'Africa
Star')
The semi-double flowers are lilac-
lavender with wavy petals when
fully open. Foliage dark green and
leathery. Growth bushy.
(C) (P) (B) (H) (SF) ⊙
✂ (AL) 2' × 2' 60 × 60 cm

'Rob Roy' (Corob)

Cocker UK 1970
'Evelyn Fison' × 'Wendy Cussons'
Rich deep red, superbly formed,
high-centred flowers of substance
are borne in clusters. Good, glossy
and dark foliage. Growth bushy
and upright.
(C) (P) (B) (H) (Gh) (SF)
⊙ ✂ (AL)
3' × 2' 90 × 60 cm

'Rosabell' (Cocceleste)

Cocker UK 1986
Seedling × 'Darling Flame'
Full flowers of bright rose-pink,
their petals incurved when open
to give an old-fashioned look, are
very freely produced. Growth
short and bushy.
(C) (B) (H) ⊙ (AL)
1' 3" × 12" 38 × 30 cm

'Rob Roy'

'Rosemary Rose'

de Ruiter HOLLAND 1954
'Grüss an Teplitz' × a Floribunda
seedling
The fully double, flattish carmine-
red flowers are crammed, it
seems, with petals in *R. centifolia*
style, and likewise are occasionally quartered. They are carried in
large, heavy clusters. Foliage
darkish green to maroon, the
stems plum-red. Growth, though
bushy, is often bent by the sheer
weight of flowers.
(C) (B) (H) ⊙ ✂ M✿
(AL) 2' 6" × 2' 75 × 60 cm

'Rosenelfe'

Kordes GERMANY 1939
'Else Poulsen' × 'Sir Basil
McFarland'
Medium-sized buds opening to
high-centred, double flowers of
silvery-pink, well scented and
produced in great abundance.
Foliage light green, leathery and
glossy. Growth vigorous and
bushy. I am grateful to Mrs Cam-
pion of Norwich for giving me
this rose.
(C) (P) (H) ● ⊙ (AL)
5' × 3' 150 × 90 cm

'Royal Occasion' (Montana)

Tantau GERMANY 1974
'Walzertraum' × 'Europeana'
Large clusters of semi-double,
orange-scarlet flowers produced
on a tallish and upright plant.
Foliage mid-green and glossy.
3' 6" × 2' 105 × 60 cm

'Rumba'

Poulsen DENMARK 1958
'Masquerade' × ('Poulsen's
Bedder' × 'Floradora')
The medium-sized, fully double
blooms of bright yellow are
heavily flushed with bright red

'Rosemary Rose'

and deepen with age. They are
produced in large clusters. Foliage
dark green and glossy. Growth
bushy and upright.
(C) (P) (B) (H) ⊙ (AL)
2' × 2' 60 × 60 cm

'Save the Children'
(Hartred)

Harkness UK 1986
'Amy Brown' × 'Red Sprite'
Cupped, bright red, semi-double
flowers in clusters. Fragrant.
Abundant, narrow, semi-glossy
foliage on a bushy, compact plant.
(C) ⊙ (B) (H) (MF) (AL)
2' × 2' 60 × 60 cm

'Scarlet Queen Elizabeth'

Dickson UK 1963
('Korona' × seedling) × 'Queen
Elizabeth'
Globular buds open to loosely
formed, cupped, double blooms
of bright scarlet and in generous
clusters. The foliage, a particular
feature, is dark green and
leathery. Growth upright and tall,
and relatively thornless.
(C) (P) (B) (H) (AW)
3' 6" × 2' 105 × 60 cm

'Scented Air'

'Scherzo'

'Sexy Rexy'

'Scented Air'

Dickson UK 1965
'Spartan' seedling × 'Queen Elizabeth'
Well-formed, very double flowers
of rich salmon are borne in large
clusters, with good, dark green
foliage on an upright and vigorous plant.
(C) (P) (B) (H) ⊙ ✄
(AW)   3′ × 2′   90 × 60 cm

'Scherzo' (Meipuma)

Paolino FRANCE 1975
'Tamango' × ['Sarabande' ×
('Goldilocks' × 'Fashion')]
Full, shapely blooms of bright
scarlet-vermilion with paler off-
white, splashed crimson on the
reverse, are produced in large
clusters. Foliage dark green and
glossy. Growth bushy and
upright.
(C) (P) (B) (N) ⊙ (AW)
3′ × 2′   90 × 60 cm

'Sea Pearl', 'Flower Girl'

Dickson UK 1964
'Perfecta' × 'Montezuma'
A delightful combination of soft
pinky-peach with a soft yellow
reverse, the blooms are fully
double, shapely, flat when fully
open and are carried in large
clusters. Dark, leathery foliage on
an upright and vigorous plant.
(C) (P) (B) (H) (Gh) ⊙
✄ (AL)   3′ × 2′   90 × 60 cm

'Sexy Rexy' (Macrexy)

McGredy NEW ZEALAND 1984
'Seaspray' × 'Dreaming'
Very double flowers opening flat,
in large clusters, of pink and soft
salmon. Foliage light green and
glossy. Growth bushy.
(C) (B) (H) (SF) ⊙ (AW)
2′ × 2′   60 × 60 cm

'Sheila's Perfume' (Harsherry)

Sheridan UK 1985
'Peer Gynt' × ['Daily Sketch' ×
('Paddy McGredy' × 'Prima
Ballerina')]
Medium-sized, fairly full blooms
are borne in small clusters, clear
yellow edged red. Foliage dark
green and semi-glossy on a bushy
and upright plant.
(C) (B) (H) (Gh) (VF) ⊙
✄ (AL)   2′ 6″ × 2′   75 × 60 cm

'Shona' (Dicdrum)

Dickson UK 1982
'Bangor' × 'Korbel'
Large clusters of loosely double
blooms of soft coral pink. Foliage
mid-green and semi-glossy, the
growth bushy.
(C) (P) (B) (H) (SF) (AL)
2′ × 2′   60 × 60 cm

'Showbiz', 'Ingrid Weibull', 'Bernhard Daneke Rose' (Tanweieke)

Tantau GERMANY 1981
Large clusters of light red flowers,
double, produced on a healthy,
bushy plant amid dark green,
glossy foliage.
(C) ⊙ (B) (H) (P) (AL)
2′ 6″ × 2′   75 × 60 cm

'Southampton', 'Susan Ann'

Harkness UK 1972
('Ann Elizabeth' × 'Allgold') ×
'Yellow Cushion'
Large, fully double blooms of rich
apricot flushed orange and scarlet, some yellow in certain
weather conditions, produced in
clusters. Foliage dark green and
glossy. Growth upright.
(C) (P) (B) (H) (MF) ⊙
(AW)   3′ × 2′   90 × 60 cm

'Stargazer'

Harkness UK 1977
'Marlena' × 'Kim'
Flowers almost single, large,
orange-red and borne in large
clusters. Mid-green, matt-
finished foliage on a bushy plant.
(C) (B) (SF) ⊙ (AL)
1′ 6″ × 1′ 6″   45 × 45 cm

'St Boniface' (Kormatt)

Kordes GERMANY 1980
'Diablotin' × 'Träumerei'
Very double, medium-sized
blooms of orange-red are carried
in large clusters. Foliage dark
green and semi-glossy. Of bushy
growth.
(C) (B) (H) (SF) ⊙ (AL)
2′ × 2′   60 × 60 cm

'St Bruno' (Lanpipe)

Sealand UK 1985
'Arthur Bell' × 'Zambra'
Large, fully double, deep golden-
yellow flowers borne in sizeable
clusters on a bushy plant with
mid-green, semi-glossy foliage.
(C) (B) (H) (VF) ⊙ (AL)
2′ × 2′   60 × 60 cm

'Strawberry Ice'

Bees UK 1975
[('Goldilocks' × 'Virgo') ×
('Orange Triumph' × 'Yvonne
Rabier')] × 'Fashion'
The flowers are large, semi-
double and creamy-white, heavily
flushed pink and deepening at the
edges. Good, dark green foliage
on a compact, bushy plant.
(C) (B) ⊙ (AL)
2′ × 2′   60 × 60 cm

'Southampton'

'Sue Lawley', 'Spanish Shawl' (Macspash)

McGredy NEW ZEALAND 1980 [('Little Darling' × 'Goldilocks') × ['Evelyn Fison' × ('Coryana' × 'Tantau's Triumph')]] × [('John's Church' × 'Elizabeth of Glamis') × ['Evelyn Fison' × ('Orange Sweetheart' × 'Frühlingsmorgen')]] The semi-double, carmine-red flowers, their edges brushed white and pink, are borne in clusters. The foliage is mid- to dark green, the growth bushy.
(C) (B) (H) (SF) ☉ ✄
(AL) 2′ × 2′ 60 × 60 cm

'Sue Ryder' (Harlino)

Harkness UK 1983 'Southampton' × [('Highlight' × 'Colour Wonder') × ('Parkdirektor Riggers' × 'Piccadilly')]

'Strawberry Ice'

'Tango'

'Sue Lawley'

The variable salmon-orange to soft vermilion blooms, yellowish on the reverse, are fully double and are carried in large clusters. Foliage mid-green and semi-glossy on a bushy plant.
(C) (P) (B) (H) ✄ (AL)
3′ × 2′ 90 × 60 cm

'Summer Fashion', 'Arc de Triomphe' (Jacale)

Warriner USA 1985 'Precilla' × 'Bridal Pink' Fragrant double flowers borne in small clusters, or singly, are soft yellow-flushed-pink, both shades deepening with age. Foliage large, mid-green, semi-glossy. Growth bushy.
(C) (B) ☉ (H) ✄ (MF)
(AW) 2′ 6″ × 2′ 75 × 60 cm

'Sunfire' (Jacko)

Warriner USA 1974 'Super Star' × 'Zorina' Clusters of bright orangey-red flowers, high-centred, slightly fragrant. Foliage ample, large and leathery. Growth upright but dense.
(C) ☉ (B) (H) (P) (SF)
(AL) 3′ × 2′ 90 × 60 cm

'Taora'

'Sunsilk'

Fryer UK 1974 'Pink Parfait × a 'Redgold' seedling Fully double, shapely blooms of soft yellow are produced in medium-sized clusters. Foliage dark green and leathery. Growth upright.
(C) (P) (B) (H) (SF) ✄
(AW) 3′ × 2′ 90 × 60 cm

'Sunsprite' see 'Korresia'

'Tanamola' see 'La Paloma '85'

'Tango' (Macfirwal)

McGredy NEW ZEALAND 1989 'Sexy Rexy' seedling A blend of orange and pale yellow flowers are produced in great abundance on a tall, bushy plant with plentiful mid-green foliage.
(C) ☉ (B) (H) (Gh) ✄
(SF) (AW)
2′ 6″ × 2′ 75 × 60 cm

'Taora' (Tanta)

Tantau GERMANY 1968 'Fragrant Cloud' × 'Schweizer Grüss' Shapely buds open to double flowers of orange-red. Ample

'The Times Rose'

glossy foliage on a bushy plant.
(C) (B) (SF) ☉ (AL)
3′ × 2′ 90 × 60 cm

'The Times Rose' (Korpeahn)

Kordes GERMANY 1984 'Tornado' × 'Redgold' Large clusters of fully double, blood-red flowers on a compact and bushy plant with dark green, leathery foliage.
(C) (B) (H) (SF) ☉ ✄
(AL) 2′ × 2′ 60 × 60 cm

'Tip Top'

Tantau GERMANY 1963 The loose, semi-double flowers opening from shapely buds are soft rose-salmon and are produced freely in large clusters. Foliage dark green and matt on a compact bushy plant. Not to be confused with 'Tip-Top' (1909).
(C) (B) (H) ☉ BS✄
(AW) 1′ 6″ × 1′ 6″ 45 × 45 cm

'Topsi'

Tantau GERMANY 1972 'Fragrant Cloud' × 'Signalfeuer' Semi-double blooms of orange-scarlet to red are borne in large clusters. Foliage mid-green. Growth bushy and compact.
(C) (B) (H) ☉ (AW)
1′ 6″ × 1′ 6″ 45 × 45 cm

'Trumpeter' (Mactrum)

McGredy NEW ZEALAND 1977
'Satchmo' × seedling
Rounded buds open to fully
double blooms of bright oranged-
red, in sizeable clusters. Foliage
mid-green and glossy on a bushy,
compact plant.
(C) (B) (H) ☉ (AL)
1' 6" × 1' 6"   45 × 45 cm

'Valentine Heart' (Dicogle)

Dickson UK 1989
An aptly named, sweetly scented
rose of lilac-pink with hints of
deep scarlet at its base. Petals are
serrated at the edges and very
resistant to rain. The plant is of
medium height and produces
purple new growth, with this

'White Pet'

'Willhire Country'

same colour overlaying the dark
green foliage; the whole making
up a delightfully different rose.
(C) ☉ (H) (B) ✂ (VF)
(AL)   3' × 2'   90 × 60 cm

'Violet Carson' (Macio)

McGredy UK 1964
'Mme Léon Cuny' × 'Spartan'
Shapely, full blooms of light
peachy-pink with primrose
reverses to the petals produced in
large clusters. Foliage dark green
and glossy. Growth bushy.
(C) (B) (H) (SF) ✂ (AW)
2' × 2'   60 × 60 cm

'Vital Spark' (Cocacert)

Cocker UK 1982
['Anne Cocker' × ('Sabine' ×
'Circus')] × 'Yellow Pages'
Large, full, shapely blooms of rich
fiery-red and yellow are produced
in large clusters. Foliage dark
green and glossy. Bushy growth.
(C) (P) (B) (H) (SF) ○
✂ (AL)   2' × 2'   60 × 60 cm

'Viva'

Warriner USA 1974
Seedling × seedling
Clusters of rounded buds open to
high-centred, fully double blooms
of rich dark red. Slightly fragrant.
Foliage glossy, dark green.
Growth upright, dense.
(C) (B) ☉ (H) ✂ (SF)
(AL)   4' × 2' 6"   120 × 75 cm

'Warrior'

LeGrice UK 1977
'City of Belfast' × 'Ronde
Endiablée'
Shapely, full blooms of bright
glowing red are carried in large
clusters. Foliage light green and
semi-glossy. Growth bushy.
(C) (B) (H) (SF) ☉ (AL)
2' × 2'   60 × 60 cm

'Yvonne Rabier'

'White Pet', 'Little White Pet'

P. Henderson USA 1879
'Félicité et Perpétue' sport
Large clusters of small, white,
fully double, rosette flowers on a
bushy plant which is abundantly
clothed in dark green foliage. A
useful and superb little rose for
any garden. Should strictly be
under forms of R. sempervirens,
but as the only dwarf in that section is better placed here.
(C) (P) (G) ● ☉ (AW)
2' × 2'   60 × 60 cm

'White Queen Elizabeth'

Banner UK 1965
Sport from 'Queen Elizabeth'
See 'Queen Elizabeth', from
which this rose differs only in that
it is pure white.

'Willhire Country'

Beales UK 1979
('Elizabeth of Glamis' × 'Arthur
Bell') × 'Allgold'
A tall, upright rose bearing trusses

of rich orange, salmon and yellow
fully double blooms with a strong
perfume. Foliage is leathery dark
green and stems well endowed
with thorns. An excellent hedging
variety.
(C) ☉ (B) (H) ✂ (VF)
(AL)   3' 6" × 2'   100 × 60 cm

'Wishing', 'Georgie Girl' (Dickerfuffle)

Dickson UK 1984
'Silver Jubilee' × 'Bright Smile'
Deep salmon and shapely blooms
are borne in large clusters. Matt-
green, semi-glossy foliage on a
bushy plant.
(C) (B) (H) (SF) ☉ (AL)
2' 6" × 2'   75 × 60 cm

'Valentine Heart'

'Woburn Abbey'

Sibley & Cobley UK 1962
'Masquerade' × 'Fashion'
Tight, oval buds open to double,
loosely formed blooms of clear
orange-yellow, sometimes faintly
touched with red. Foliage dark
green and leathery, semi-glossy,
the stems grained brownish.
Growth upright.
(C) (P) (B) (H) (SF) ☉
✂ R⚘ (AW)
2' 6" × 2'   75 × 60 cm

'Yellow Queen Elizabeth'

Vlaeminck UK 1964
Sport from 'Queen Elizabeth'
See 'Queen Elizabeth', from
which this rose differs only in that
it is bright yellow.

'Yvonne Rabier'

Turbat FRANCE 1910
R. wichuraiana × a Polyantha rose
Often listed amongst Polyanthas
but its flowers are larger and the
plant taller. Its true place would
be among Wichuraiana hybrids,
but in garden terms it is too short
for this. Semi-double, pure white
blooms in clusters on a healthy,
well-foliated plant. Leaves light
rich green; the stems, also light
green, are almost free of thorns.
(C) (P) (G) ● ☉ (AL)
3' × 2'   90 × 60 cm

'Zambra' (Meialfi)

Meilland FRANCE 1961
('Goldilocks' × 'Fashion')
× ('Goldilocks' × 'Fashion')
Rounded buds open to small,
semi-double blooms of clear
orange with a yellow reverse.
They are borne in large clusters.
Foliage leathery, glossy and light
green. Growth bushy.
(C) (P) (B) (H) (SF) ☉
BS⚘ (AW)
2' 6" × 2'   75 × 60 cm

Climbing Floribundas

Floribunda roses occasionally produce climbing sports. For some
reason, these are not nearly as numerous as climbing Hybrid Teas,
but since Floribunda numbers are fewer, I suspect they occur in
roughly the same ratio. I describe seven, not necessarily as my
favourites, but as a representative selection of those which should
be available commercially and which will perform well in any situation. They provide a profusion of flowers on vigorous plants, and
therefore have wider applications than some of the more modern,
long-flowering climbers, which sometimes lack climbing ability.

CLASSIFICATION

BARB	Class 11
MR9	Class 9
WFRS	Class 18

'Allgold' Climbing

Bush form LeGrice UK 1958
'Goldilocks' × 'Ellinor LeGrice'
This form Gandy UK 1961
An excellent climber and, since
good yellow climbers are scarce,
well worth consideration where
such colour is needed. Clear
yellow, almost unfading flowers
open to semi-double blooms produced in upright clusters on
strong stems. Slightly scented.
Leaves small but numerous, rich
dark green.
(S) (P) (MF) (AW)
15' × 10'   4.5 × 3 m

'Arthur Bell' Climbing

Bush form McGredy UK 1965
'Cläre Grammerstorf' ×
'Piccadilly'
This form Pearce UK 1979
Clusters of deep yellow, double
flowers paling to soft yellow with
age on a tall, upright plant with
exceptionally glossy, deep green
foliage.
(S) (P) (VF) ✂ (AL)
12' × 8'   3.5 × 2.5 m

'Fashion' Climbing

Bush form Boerner USA 1949
'Pinocchio' × 'Crimson Glory'
This form Boerner USA 1951
Another identical climbing form
introduced by Mattock UK in
1955
This rose has fallen from favour
as a bush because of its proneness
to rust, but this does not seem to
be a problem for the climbing
form, probably because of its
extra vigour. Clusters of double,
bright coral-salmon flowers in
profusion on a fairly thornless
plant with coppery-green shoots
and foliage.
(S) (P) ☼ (MF) (AL)
15' × 10'   4.5 × 3 m

'Iceberg' Climbing, 'Schneewittchen'

Bush form Kordes GERMANY 1958
'Robin Hood' × 'Virgo'
This form Cant UK 1968
A shortage of good white climbers
justifies the inclusion of this rose,
which retains all the good
qualities of the bush with the
added dimensions of a climber.
Freely produced, large trusses of
almost double, pure white
flowers. Climbing shoots almost
thornless with crisp, shiny, pale
green leaves.
(S) (P) (N) ● (SF) (AL)
18' × 10'   5.5 × 3 m

'Korona' Climbing

Bush form Kordes GERMANY 1955
'Obergärtner Wiebicke' ×
'Independence'
This form Kordes GERMANY 1957
Clusters of semi-double, bright
orange-scarlet flowers on a vigorous, fairly thorny plant with dark
green foliage. Rather bright for
my taste but included for its
remarkable resistance to rain and
inclement weather.
(S) (P) (N) ● (AL)
15' × 10'   4.5 × 3 m

'Masquerade' Climbing

Bush form Boerner USA 1949
'Goldilocks' × 'Holiday'
This form Gregory UK 1958
Clusters of semi-double flowers
opening soft yellow, changing to
soft pink and then to almost
crimson as they age. Vigorous,
moderately thorny stems. Dark
green foliage.
(S) (P) (SF) (AL)
18' × 10'   5.5 × 3 m

'Queen Elizabeth' Climbing

Bush form Lammerts USA 1954
'Charlotte Armstrong' ×
'Floradora'
This form Wheatcroft UK 1960
A very vigorous climber, almost
too vigorous since its flowers are
often borne too high up in the
branches to be enjoyed. Flowers
rich, clear silvery-pink, produced
in large clusters. Foliage large,
healthy and dark green.
(S) (P) (AW)
20' × 10'   6 × 3 m

'Iceberg' Climbing as a pillar rose at the Ruston Rose Gardens, Renmark, South Australia

Procumbent Shrub Roses (Ground-Cover Roses)

Roses have been planted for ground cover since the nineteenth century. In those days however the main sources of material were the relaxed ramblers such as the Ayrshires and the Evergreens (the Sempervirens). Later, mostly during the first two decades of this century, the introduction of the flexible Wichuraiana hybrids provided a greater range of colour. The weakness of most ramblers is, of course, their relatively short flowering season, which means that although they are ideal for covering banks and mounds, they are seldom used for this purpose today; the more's the pity.

Since the Second World War, and with landscape gardeners demanding cost-effective plants, ground-cover roses have been in great demand and breeders have not been slow to react, developing a steadily increasing number of both once-flowering and remontant varieties.

Personally, I have never been happy with the term 'ground cover' for roses of any kind. Although I accept that some are suitable for the purpose, only a very few that I know of are sufficiently dense to suppress weeds in the same way as more traditional ground-cover plants such as *Hypericum calcinum* and *Vinca major*. In fact, spreading roses can make weed-infested ground more rather than less difficult to cultivate, and so may create a problem rather than solve one. I prefer the term 'procumbent' which adequately describes their habit with no misleading connotations.

Procumbent roses can be used in a variety of ways. They are most commonly planted for massed displays to give colour to municipal and industrial landscapes. In the garden they can serve useful purposes on banks or in beds where too much height is undesirable. They also look good planted in groups to provide colour lower down in shrubberies and many are excellent grown in tubs, pots or urns, or cascading down from short walls or troughs. One or two smaller varieties make fine rockery subjects.

One clear advantage of this type of rose is that many flourish on their own roots, thus eliminating any difficulties in removing suckers.

Most modern catalogues and, indeed, most good garden suppliers now offer a considerable range of these roses; it has not been an easy task to choose those for inclusion. Those selected, however, are a fair cross-section of old and new, and most can be obtained without difficulty both in the UK and abroad.

There are quite a number of roses other than those described in this section which fall into the procumbent category, but for reasons of heredity I have placed them under their rightful family group headings.

CLASSIFICATION

BARB	Class 17
MR9	No specific class; best covered by Class 54
WFRS	Classes 3 and 11

'Alba Meidiland' (Meiflopan)

Meilland FRANCE 1987
With tight, heavy clusters of pure white and fully double flowers, which are good for cutting. Foliage mid-green. Growth dense and spreading.
(C) (G) (H) (SF) ● ☉ ✂ (AL) 3' × 4' 90 × 120 cm

'Bonica' (Meidomonac)
see Modern Shrub Roses

'Candy Rose' (Meiranovi)

Meilland FRANCE 1980
(*R. sempervirens* × 'Mlle Marthe Carron') × [('Lilli Marlene' ×

'Evelyn Fison') × ('Orange Sweetheart' × 'Frühlingsmorgen')]
Semi-double flowers of deep pink with a reddish reverse. Foliage small, light green and glossy. Growth bushy and spreading.
(C) (G) (P) ☉ (AL) 4' × 6' 1.2 × 1.8 m

'Cardinal Hume' (Harregale)
see Modern Shrub Roses

'Carefree Beauty' (Bucbi)

Buck USA 1977
Seedling × 'Prairie Princess'
Semi-double, fragrant, creamy-buffy-pink flowers produced in large quantities throughout the

'Candy Rose'

summer. Foliage plentiful, deep green, semi-glossy. Growth bushy and wide. A good rose in all respects.
(C) ☉ (P) (H) (G) (SF) (AW) 5′ × 4′ 1.5 × 1.2 m

'Caterpillar' *see* 'Pink Drift'

'Daisy Hill' *see* page 172

'Dunwich Rose'
see Forms and Hybrids of *R. pimpinellifolia*

'Essex' (Poulnoz)

Poulsen DENMARK 1987
Small, deep pink, single blooms in profusion. After the habit of 'Nozomi'. Very free-flowering.
(C) ☉ (G) ● (AW)
2′ × 5′ 60 × 180 cm

'Eyeopener' (Interop)

Ilsink HOLLAND 1987
(Seedling × 'Eyepaint') × (Seedling × 'Dortmund')
Its bright flowers have white centres. Foliage dense and mid-green on a vigorous, spreading bush.
(C) (P) (G) ● (AL)
1′ × 3′ 30 × 90 cm

'Eyeopener'

'Essex'

'Fairy Damsel'

'Fairy Changeling' (Harnumerous)

Harkness UK 1981
'The Fairy' × 'Yesterday'
Plump little buds open to small, cupped, fully double flowers of soft clear pink in large trusses. Foliage small, dark green and semi-glossy. Growth bushy and spreading.
(C) (P) (G) (SF) ☉ (AL)
1′ 6″ × 2′ 45 × 60 cm

'Fairy Damsel' (Harneatly)

Harkness UK 1981
'The Fairy' × 'Yesterday'
Dark red, small, double flowers, cupped at first then flattish in small trusses. Foliage dark green and glossy. Growth bushy and spreading.
(C) (P) (G) (SF) ☉ (AL)
2′ × 5′ 60 × 150 cm

'Fairyland' (Harlayalong)

Harkness UK 1980
'The Fairy' × 'Yesterday'
Soft pink, cupped, small, fully double flowers are borne in large trusses. Foliage mid-green and glossy. Growth bushy and spreading.
(C) (P) (G) (SF) ☉ (AL)
2′ × 5′ 60 × 150 cm

'Ferdy' (Keitoli)

Suzuki JAPAN 1984
Climbing seedling × 'Petite Folie' seedling
Has deep salmon-pink flowers, small and fully double. Foliage small, plentiful and light green. Growth bushy, spreading and dense.
(C) (P) (G) ☉ (AW)
2′ × 3′ 60 × 90 cm

'Fairyland'

'Fiona' (Meibeluscen)

Meilland FRANCE 1982
'Sea Foam' × 'Picasso'
Large clusters of dark red flowers,
slightly paler in the centre. Small-
ish, dark green and glossy foliage.
Growth bushy and spreading.
(C) (P) (G) (MF) (H) ☉
(AW) 3' × 4' 90 × 120 cm

'Flamingo Meidiland' (Meisolroz)

Meilland FRANCE 1990
Attractive, clear pink flowers produced in profusion throughout
summer followed by bright red-
orange hips. Good foliage on a
dense, wide-growing but bushy
plant. Could also make a useful
specimen shrub or dense hedge. A
good landscape rose.
(C) (H) ☉ (F) (G) ●
(AW) 3' × 4' 90 × 120 cm

'Flower Carpet' (Noatram)

Noack GERMANY 1990
Huge trusses of sizeable, double,
deep pink flowers produced in
abundance throughout the summer. Foliage glossy light green.
Growth dense and wide. Has won
several awards for excellence.
(C) ☉ (G) (AW)
1' 6" × 4' 45 × 120 cm

'Francine Austin' (Ausram)

Austin UK 1988
Sprays of small, pompon-like,

'Fiona'

fully double flowers of pure
glistening white. Foliage light
green and plentiful. Growth
vigorous, bushy and wide.
(R) ☉ (G) (P) ● (AL)
3' × 4' 90 × 120 cm

'Grouse', 'Immensee' (Korimro)

Kordes GERMANY 1982
'The Fairy' × R. wichuraiana seedling
Clusters of small, single, white
flowers with pink blushes and

prominent stamens. Foliage mid-green and glossy on a prostrate, spreading plant.

(R) (P) (G) (MF) ● (AW)
2' × 10'   60 × 300 cm

'Hampshire' (Korhamp)

Poulsen DENMARK 1989
A ground-hugging shrub. Small, single flowers of bright scarlet. Good foliage.

(R) ☉ (G) ● (AL)
2' × 4'   60 × 120 cm

'Harry Maasz' *see* Forms and Hybrids of *R. macrantha*

'Heidekönigin' *see* 'Pheasant'

'Grouse'

'Kent'

'Laura Ashley'

'Hertfordshire' (Kortenay)

Kordes GERMANY 1991
Single, carmine blooms borne in great profusion on a low, spreading plant liberally endowed with good, healthy foliage.

(R) (V) (G) (AL)
1' 6" × 3'   45 × 100 cm

'Immensee' *see* 'Grouse'

'Kent', 'White Cover' (Poulcov)

Poulsen DENMARK 1987
Trusses of semi-double, white flowers produced in great quantities. Impervious to weather, it is said. Compact and wide.

(R) ☉ ● (G) (AL)
1' 6" × 3'   45 × 100 cm

'Lady Curzon' *see* Forms and Hybrids of *R. rugosa*

'Laura Ashley' (Chewharla)

Warner UK 1990
Pretty lilac-pink flowers in clusters. Sweetly scented. Very free-flowering. Foliage mid-green. Growth dense and wide.

(C) ☉ (G) (MF) (AL)
2' × 3'   60 × 90 cm

'Norfolk'

'Max Graf' *see* Forms and Hybrids of *R. rugosa*

'Norfolk' (Poulfolk)

Poulsen DENMARK 1989
One of the very few procumbents with any yellow in their make-up. This one has clusters of small, double, bright yellow flowers amid good foliage.

(R) ☉ ● (G) (AL)
1' 6" × 2'   45 × 60 cm

'Northamptonshire' (Mattdor)

Mattock UK 1990
Shapely, small flowers (similar to 'Cécile Brünner') of soft pink borne amid fresh green foliage on a dense, ground-hugging plant.

(R) ☉ ● (G) (AL)
1' 6" × 3'   45 × 100 cm

'Hertfordshire'

'Nozomi'

Onodera JAPAN 1968
'Fairy Princess' × 'Sweet Fairy'
Small, single, star-like flowers of
pearly-pink in small trusses. The
foliage is very small, plentiful,
dark green and glossy, with arching plum-coloured young stems,
the older wood dark green.
Growth very dense and spreading.
(S) (G) (P) (H) ● ☉
(AW)   3′ × 6′   90 × 180 cm

'Northamptonshire'

'Nozomi'

'Partridge',
'Weisse Immensee'
(Korweirim)

Kordes GERMANY 1984
'The Fairy' × *R. wichuraiana* seedling
Small, single, white flowers come
from pink buds in clusters. Foliage small, dark green and glossy,
though bronzy when young.
Growth prostrate and spreading.
(R) (P) (G) (MF) ● (AL)
2′ × 10′   60 × 300 cm

'Paulii',
R. × paulii

Paul UK *c.* 1903
R. arvensis × *R. rugosa*
The large, single, white flowers
have 5 spaced petals and promi-

'Partridge'

'Paulii'

nent yellow stamens. Foliage slender, rugose, light to mid-green,
the young wood pinkish, and with
many thorns. Growth prostrate.
(S) (G) (SF) ● M☙ (AL)
3′ × 10′   90 × 300 cm

'Paulii Rosea',
R. × paulii rosea

c. 1912
A possible sport from 'Paulii' but
there are many differences
The large, single, soft rose-pink
flowers, their petals less spread
than 'Paulii', have pronounced
yellow stamens. Foliage mid-
green and rugose, the stems
thorny. Young wood is lime-
green. Its growth is prostrate but
denser than 'Paulii'.
(S) (G) (SF) M☙ (AL)
3′ × 10′   90 × 300 cm

'Pearl Drift' (Leggab)

LeGrice UK 1980
'Mermaid' × 'New Dawn'
Sizeable, semi-double, white
flowers flushed pink borne in
large trusses. Foliage dark green
and semi-glossy. Growth dense,
bushy and spreading.
(C) (P) (G) (MF) ● ☉
(AW)   3′ × 4′   90 × 120 cm

'Paulii Rosea'

'Pearl Meidiland' (Meineble)

Meilland FRANCE 1989
The raiser describes this rose as
pale ochre, flowers produced in
clusters on a dense, spreading
plant with glossy foliage.
(R) ⊙ (G) ● (AW)
2′ × 4′   60 × 120 cm

'Pheasant', 'Heidekönigin' (Kordapt)

Kordes GERMANY 1986
'Zwerkonig '78' × R. wichuraiana
seedling
Modest clusters of small, deep

'Queen Mother'

rose-pink, double flowers, with
mid-green glossy foliage on a
plant of prostrate, spreading
growth.
(R) (P) (G) (MF) ● (AL)
2′ × 10′   60 × 300 cm

'Pink Bells' (Poulbells)

Poulsen DENMARK 1983
'Mini Poul' × 'Temple Bells'
Small, fully double, bright pink

'Pearl Drift'

flowers borne in profusion. Foliage mid-green, semi-glossy, small
but plentiful. Growth dense and
spreading.
(S) (P) (G) (SF) ● ⊙
(AW)   2′ × 4′   60 × 120 cm

'Pink Chimo' (Interchimp)

Ilsink HOLLAND 1990
Attractively formed deep pink
flowers on a dense, wide-growing
plant with good leathery foliage.
(C) ⊙ ● (G) (AL)
2′ × 3′   60 × 90 cm

'Pink Drift', 'Kiki Rose', 'Caterpillar' (Poulcat)

Poulsen DENMARK 1984
'Temple Bells' × seedling
Large trusses of small, semi-
double, light pink blooms are
freely produced. Foliage plentiful,
small, dark green and glossy.
Growth bushy and spreading.
(C) (P) (G) (MF) ● ⊙
(AL)   2′ × 3′   60 × 90 cm

'Pink Meidiland', 'Schloss Heidegg' (Meipoque)

Meilland FRANCE 1983
'Anne de Bretagne' × 'Nirvana'
The single flowers of deep pink
have a white eye. foliage smallish,
mid-green and semi-glossy. A
bushy, spreading habit of growth.
(C) (G) (H) (SF) ● ⊙
(AW)   2′ × 2′   60 × 90 cm

'Pink Wave' (Mattgro)

Mattock UK 1983
'Moon Maiden' × 'Eyepaint'
Soft pink, semi-double flowers are
borne in clusters. Foliage mid-
green and semi-glossy. Growth
bushy and spreading.
(C) (P) (G) (MF) ● ⊙
(AL)   2′ × 3′   60 × 90 cm

'Queen Mother' (Korquemu)

Kordes GERMANY 1991
Pure soft pink semi-double
flowers produced in great profusion and set off by plentiful glossy
foliage. Growth rounded, bushy
and slightly spreading.
(C) ⊙ (B) (SF) (G) (AW)
1′ × 1′ 6″   30 × 45 cm

'Raubritter', 'Macrantha Raubritter'

see Forms and Hybrids of
R. macrantha

'Red Bells' (Poulred)

Poulsen DENMARK 1983
'Mini-Poul' × 'Temple Bells'
Small, fully double, red flowers
are produced in great abundance.
Foliage mid-green, semi-glossy,
small and plentiful. Growth dense
and spreading.
(S) (P) (G) (SF) ● ⊙
(AL)   2′ × 4′   60 × 120 cm

'Pink Bells'

'Red Blanket' (Intercel)

Ilsink HOLLAND 1979
'Yesterday' × unnamed seedling
The flowers, semi-double and
medium-sized, are borne in small
clusters and are deep pink to
almost red. Foliage dark green
and glossy. Growth dense and
spreading.
(C) (P) (G) (SF) ● ☉
BS& (AW)
3' × 4'   90 × 120 cm

'Red Max Graf',
'Rote Max Graf'
(Kormax)

Kordes GERMANY 1980
R. kordesii × seedling
Bright red, medium-sized, single
flowers are borne in large clusters.
The abundant foliage is matt,
dark green and leathery on a
coarsely spreading plant.
(C) (P) (G) (SF) ● (AW)
3' × 6'   90 × 180 cm

'Red Trail' (Intcrim)

Ilsink HOLLAND 1991
Large quantities of bright red
flowers on a vigorous, wide-growing, ground-covering plant with
ample foliage.
(R) (G) ● (AL)
3' × 5'   90 × 150 cm

'Red Blanket'

'Red Max Graf'

'Red Trail'

'Repens Meidiland'
(Meilontig)

Meilland FRANCE 1987
Small, single, white flowers in
profusion. Foliage small, mid-
green and glossy. Growth very
prostrate and vigorous.
(S) (P) (G) ● (AL)
6" × 10'   15 × 300 cm

'Rosy Carpet' (Intercarp)

Ilsink HOLLAND 1983
'Yesterday' × seedling
Light pink, single blooms are very
freely produced in large clusters.
Foliage dark green and glossy.
Growth prickly, dense and
spreading.
(R) (P) (G) (MF) ● ☉
(AL)   2' × 4'   60 × 120 cm

'Rosy Cushion' (Interall)

Ilsink HOLLAND 1979
'Yesterday' × seedling
Soft pink, almost single blooms
are borne in large clusters. Foliage
dark green and glossy. Growth
dense, bushy and spreading.
(R) (P) (G) (SF) ● ☉
(AW)   3' × 4'   90 × 120 cm

'Rutland' (Poulshine)

Poulsen DENMARK 1988
Masses of small, single, pink
blooms on a compact cushion-
like plant. Foliage ample, deep
green and glossy.
(R) ☉ ● (G) (AL)
1' × 1'   30 × 30 cm

'Scarlet Meidiland'
(Meikrotal)

Meilland FRANCE 1987
Heavy clusters of bright cherry-
red flowers, with dark green,
glossy foliage on a dense and
spreading bush. Particularly good
in the autumn.
(C) (G) (H) (SF) ● ☉
✂ (AL)   3' × 4'   90 × 120 cm

'Scintillation' *see* Forms and
Hybrids of *R. macrantha*

'Rosy Cushion'

'Sea Foam'

E. W. Schwartz USA 1964
('White Dawn' × 'Pinocchio')
× ('White Dawn' × 'Pinocchio')
× ('White Dawn' × 'Pinocchio')
Double whitish-cream flowers in
sizeable clusters. Slightly fragrant.
Foliage glossy. Growth very vigorous and spreading.
(R)   (SF)   (G)   (CL)
4' × 6'   1.2 × 1.8 m

'Simon Robinson'

'Suffolk'

'Simon Robinson'
(Trobwich)

Robinson UK 1982
R. wichuraiana × 'New Penny'
Medium to small, single, mid-pink flowers are borne in clusters.
Foliage dark green and glossy.
Growth bushy and spreading.
(C)   (P)   (G)   (SF)   ●   ☉
(AL)   2' 6" × 4'   75 × 120 cm

'Sussex'

'Smarty' (Intersmart)

Ilsink HOLLAND 1979
'Yesterday' × seedling
Large clusters of almost single,
smallish blooms of light pink.
Foliage bright green and matt-finished. Growth quite thorny,
bushy and spreading.
(R)   (P)   (G)   (SF)   ●   ☉
(AL)   3' × 4'   90 × 120 cm

'Snow Carpet' (Maccaryse)

McGredy NEW ZEALAND 1980
'New Penny' × 'Temple Bells'
Small, very double, pure white
flowers are produced in small
clusters. Foliage small, light green
and semi-glossy. Growth prostrate and spreading.
(R)   (MF)   (G)   ●   (AW)
1' × 3'   30 × 90 cm

'Suffolk',
'Bassimo'
(Kormixal)

Kordes GERMANY 1988
Scarlet, single blooms on a wide,

creeping plant with ample light
green foliage.
(R)   ☉   ●   (B)   (AW)
2' × 4'   60 × 120 cm

'Suma' (Harsuma)

Onodera JAPAN 1989
Parentage includes 'Nozomi'
Fully double flowers of ruby-red
open to display golden stamens
creating a most colourful effect.
Foliage plentiful, small and glossy
dark green. Growth dense, wide
and trailing. A first-class variety.
(R)   ☉   ●   (G)   (AW)
1' × 3'   30 × 90 cm

'Surrey',
'Summerwind' (Korlanum)

Kordes GERMANY 1987
Clusters of soft pink, double
blooms produced in profusion on
a wide-growing plant.
(R)   ●   ☉   (G)   (AL)
2' × 4'   60 × 120 cm

'Sussex' (Poulave)

Poulsen DENMARK 1991
Double flowers of apricot to pink
and buff, produced in large
clusters. Foliage plentiful, mid-green. Growth dense and
spreading.
(R)   ☉   (G)   (AL)
2' × 3'   60 × 90 cm

'Sea Foam'

'Surrey'

'Swany' (Meiburenac)

Meilland FRANCE 1978
R. sempervirens × 'Mlle Marthe Carron'
Yields large clusters of very double, cupped flowers of pure white. Foliage dark green and glossy with bronze overtones. Growth vigorous, bushy and spreading.
(C) (P) (G) ● ⊙ (AW)
3' × 5'   90 × 150 cm

'Tall Story' (Dickooky)

Dickson UK 1984
'Sunsprite' × 'Yesterday'
Medium-sized, soft yellow, semi-double flowers in clusters along arching branches. Foliage light green and semi-glossy on an arching and spreading plant.
(C) (P) (G) (VF) ● ⊙
(AL)   2' × 4'   60 × 120 cm

'Temple Bells'

Morey USA 1971
R. wichuraiana × 'Blushing Jewel'
Small, single, white flowers open in profusion at first, then spasmodically. Foliage small and light green. Its hugging, prostrate growth makes this rose well suited to rockeries.
(R) (G) ● ⊙ (AW)
2' × 4'   60 × 120 cm

'The Fairy'
see Polyantha Roses

'Warwickshire' (Korkandel)

Kordes GERMANY 1991
Freely produced, single blooms of deep rosy-red each with a prominent white eye. Foliage dark green, glossy. Growth dense and spreading.
(C) ⊙ (G) (SF) (AL)
1' 6" × 3'   45 × 100 cm

'Swany'

'Weisse Immensee'
see 'Partridge'

'White Bells' (Poulwhite)

Poulsen DENMARK 1983
'Mini-Poul' × 'Temple Bells'
The white, fully double flowers have hints of soft yellow. Foliage

'White Bells'

'White Max Graf'

'Warwickshire'

small, mid-green and semi-glossy. Growth dense, bushy and spreading.
(S) (P) (G) (SF) ● ⊙
(AW)   2' × 4'   60 × 120 cm

'White Max Graf', 'Weisse Max Graf' (Korgram)

Kordes GERMANY 1983
Seedling × *R. wichuraiana* seedling
Pure white, single flowers, slightly cupped, in clusters. Foliage light green and semi-glossy. Growth vigorous and spreading.
(C) (G) (H) (SF) ● ⊙
(AW)   3' × 6'   90 × 180 cm

'White Meidiland' (Meicoublan)

Meilland FRANCE 1986
Bears pure white flowers in clusters on a bushy, spreading plant with plentiful, smallish, mid-green and semi-glossy foliage.
(C) (G) (H) (SF) ● ⊙
(AW)   2' × 4'   60 × 120 cm

Miniatures and Patios
(Compact Floribundas)

Miniature roses enjoyed a brief spell of popularity during the early years of the nineteenth century, but the colour range of the first varieties was limited and they soon fell from favour and disappeared from cultivation until rediscovery in 1918 (*see* 'Rouletii'). Since then they have established themselves as a very important group and many hundreds of varieties have been raised and introduced; far too many to cover comprehensively so I have selected 120 or so, including some of the more recent 'Patio' varieties. The Patios are slightly more bushy and taller than the Miniatures but shorter and of smaller proportions than the dwarf Floribundas.

Both Miniatures and Patios grow well on their own roots and, with the advent of micropropagation, more and more are being produced in this way. Own-root Miniatures are usually smaller than those produced by other methods of propagation such as grafting or budding, so it is wise to enquire how they have been grown before purchase. In the garden their uses are several, from close-density bedding and edging to group-planting among other subjects. They also make useful pot plants and will do well in window boxes. They never enjoy growing indoors as house plants.

CLASSIFICATION

BARB	Classes 8 and 9
MR9	Class 48
WFRS	Class 8

**'Air France',
'Rosy Meillandina',
American Independence'**
(Meifinaro)
[Miniature]

Meilland FRANCE 1982
'Minijet' × ('Darling Flame' × 'Perla de Montserrat')
Fully double blooms of medium size and clear rose-pink are carried in clusters. Foliage dark green. Growth bushy and upright.
(C) ⊙ (AW) 1' 30 cm

'Amorette' *see* **'Snowdrop'**

'Amruda' *see* **Red Ace**

**'Angela Rippon',
'Ocaru', 'Ocarina'**
[Miniature]

de Ruiter HOLLAND 1978
'Rosy Jewel' × 'Zorina'
Largish blooms, fully double and coral-pink to salmon are borne in clusters on a bushy, compact plant with mid-green foliage.
(C) (MF) ⊙ (AW)
1' 30 cm

'Angelita' *see* **'Snowball'**

'Air France'

'Apricot Sunblaze'

'Anna Ford'

'Clarissa'

'Anna Ford' (Harpiccolo)
[Patio]

Harkness UK 1980
'Southampton' × 'Darling Flame'
Its orange-red flowers, with yellow deep down in their base, are semi-double and come in clusters. Foliage glossy and dark green. Growth dense and bushy, slightly spreading.
(C) ⊙ ● (AL) 1' 6" 45 cm

**'Apricot Sunblaze',
'Mark One'**
(Savamark) [Patio]

Savile USA 1984
'Sheri Anne' × 'Glenfiddich'
Bright orange-red blooms are borne profusely in small compact clusters. Foliage glossy, on a plant of bushy, tidy and dense habit.
(C) (B) (MF) ⊙ (AW)
15" 38 cm

'Arctic Sunrise' (Bar. Arcsun)
[Patio]

Barrett UK 1989
Large clusters of buds start pink, gradually changing to white as they open (displaying a creamy centre) to semi-double flowers. These are borne in clusters on a bushy, spreading plant with mid-green glossy foliage.
(C) ⊙ (G) (Gh) (AL)
1' 6" × 2' 45 × 60 cm

'Baby Darling' [Miniature]

Moore USA 1964
'Little Darling' × 'Magic Wand'
Apricot-orange flowers, quite large and double, borne in medium-sized clusters, with mid-green foliage. Growth upright and bushy. Quite nice when cut for miniature flower arrangements.
(C) (B) (SF) ⊙ ✂ (AW)
1' 30 cm

**'Baby Gold Star',
'Estrellita de Oro'**
[Miniature]

Dot SPAIN 1940
'Eduardo Toda' × 'Rouletii'
Sizeable, semi-double flowers of
deep yellow bordering on apricot
are borne in generous clusters,
with plentiful small, mid-green
foliage. Growth open and bushy.
(C) (P) ☉ BS✂ (AW)
1' 30 cm

**'Baby Masquerade',
'Baby Carnaval',
'Tanbakede' (Tanba)**
[Miniature]

Tantau GERMANY 1956
'Peon' × 'Masquerade'
The almost double blooms, in
sizeable clusters, are yellow with
red, the red deepening with age.
Foliage dark green, almost glossy,
and leathery. Growth upright and
bushy.
(C) (P) (B) (SF) ✂ (AW)
1' 6" 45 cm

'Baby Sunrise' (Macparlez)
[Miniature]

McGredy NEW ZEALAND 1984
'Benson & Hedges Special' ×
'Moana'
Smallish, shapely blooms of apricot with coppery overtones, and
semi-double, are borne in sizeable
clusters. Foliage semi-glossy and
mid-green on a bushy plant.
(C) (SF) ☉ (AL) 1' 30 cm

**'Benson & Hedges Special',
'Dorola'** (Macshana)
[Miniature]

McGredy NEW ZEALAND 1982
'Darling Flame' × 'Mabella'
Deep clear yellow, fully double
and shapely flowers are produced

in sizeable clusters. Foliage mid-
green and semi-glossy. Growth
bushy and upright.
(C) (SF) ☉ (AW) 1' 30 cm

'Bianco' (Cocblanco) [Patio]

Cocker UK 1983
'Darling Flame' × 'Jack Frost'
The fully double, pure white
flowers come in clusters. The foliage is of fair size, mid-green and
semi-glossy. Growth bushy and
wide.
(C) (G) (SF) ☉ (AL)
1' 6" 45 cm

'Bit o' Sunshine' [Miniature]

Moore USA 1956
'Copper Glow' × 'Zee'
Semi-double flowers, shapely in
bud and bright yellow, are carried
in clusters. Foliage mid-green and
semi-glossy. Growth upright and
bushy.
(C) (MF) ☉ (AW)
1' 30 cm

**'Blue Peter',
'Azulabria',
'Bluenette'**
(Ruiblun)
[Miniature]

de Ruiter HOLLAND 1983
'Little Flirt' × seedling
Full, lilac-purple blooms are in
clusters. Foliage smallish, light
green and semi-glossy on a bushy,
upright plant.
(C) (SF) ☉ (AW)
1' 30 cm

'Boys' Brigade' (Cockdinkum)
[Patio]

Cocker UK 1984
('Darling Flame' × 'Saint Alban')
× ('Little Flirt' × 'Marlena')
The small, bright red flowers have
a creamy-white eye and are in

large clusters. Foliage mid-green
and semi-glossy. Growth dense
and bushy.
(C) (P) (B) ☉ (AL)
1' 6" 45 cm

'Brass Ring'
see **'Peek a Boo'**

'Buttons' (Lembut) [Miniature]

Dr M. Lemrow USA 1980
Cross between two unnamed
seedlings
A very compact little miniature
with globular, pure white, fully
double flowers borne singly but
profusely amid tiny, mid-green
leaves. Few or no thorns.
(C) ☉ (Gh) (AL)
1' 30 cm

'Cider Cup' (Dicladida) [Patio]

Dickson UK 1988
Shapely, Hybrid Tea-like flowers
of deep apricot produced in
clusters. Foliage mid-green and
glossy. Growth bushy and wide.
(C) (B) (H) ☉ ✂ (AL)
1' 6" 45 cm

'Cinderella' [Miniature]

De Vink HOLLAND 1953
'Cécile Brünner' × 'Peon'
Very double, slightly fluffy
blooms of white tinged pink. Foliage light green. Growth dense,
upright and almost thornless.
(C) (P) (SF) ☉ ✂ (AW)
1' 30cm

'Clarissa' (Harprocrustes)
[Patio]

Harkness UK 1983
'Southampton' × 'Darling Flame'
The shapely blooms of rich
orangey-yellow are very freely

'Cinderella'

'Boys' Brigade'

'Guernsey Love'

produced in large clusters. Foliage dark green and glossy. Growth dense and upright.
(C) (P) (B) (H) ☉ ✄
(AW) 2′ 60 cm

'Colibri' (Meimal) [Miniature]

Meilland FRANCE 1958
'Goldilocks' × 'Perla de Montserrat'
Buff-yellow flushed orange, double flowers in medium-sized clusters. Foliage dark green and glossy on a plant of upright, bushy habit.
(C) ☉ BS✄ (AW) 1′ 30 cm

'Colibri '79' (Meidanover) [Miniature]

Meilland FRANCE 1979
Its yellow flowers, heavily flushed pink and orange, and fully double, are produced in clusters. Foliage semi-glossy and mid-green. Growth upright and bushy.
(C) (MF) ☉ (AW)
1′ 30cm

'Conservation' (Cocdimple) [Patio]

Cocker UK 1986
[('Sabine' × 'Circus') × 'Maxi'] ×'Darling Flame'
The semi-double, shapely, apricot-pink blooms are in clusters. Foliage mid-green and glossy. Growth dense, bushy and wide.
(C) (B) (SF) (GC) ☉ (AL)
1′ 6″ 45 cm

'Coralin', 'Carolin', 'Carolyn', 'Karolyn', 'Perla Corail' [Miniature]

Dot SPAIN 1955
'Méphisto' × 'Perla de Alcañada'
Large, full, coral-pink blooms, variable to soft red in some conditions. They are produced in clusters. Foliage mid-green and semi-glossy. Growth upright and bushy.
(C) (MF) ☉ (AW)
15″ 38 cm

'Coral Reef' (Cocdarlee) [Patio]

Cocker UK 1985
('Darling Flame' × 'St Albans') × 'Silver Jubilee'
Semi-double, shapely flowers of

'Conservation'

'Cricri'

orange-salmon, slightly fragrant, produced on a bushy plant with dense, mid-green, glossy foliage.
(C) ☉ (B) (SF) (Gh) (AL)
1′ 30cm

'Cricri', 'Gavolda' (Meicri) [Miniature]

Meilland FRANCE 1958
('Alain' × 'Independence') × 'Perla de Alcañada'
Clusters of small, fully double, rosette flowers of soft salmon shaded coral on an upright plant with leathery, mid-green foliage.
(C) (P) (B) ☉ (AW)
1′ 30cm

'Dainty Dinah' (Cocamond) [Patio]

Cocker UK 1981
'Anne Cocker' × 'Wee Man'
Soft salmon-pink, semi-double and shapely blooms in clusters. Foliage mid-green and semi-glossy. Growth bushy and wide.
(C) (B) (SF) ☉ (AL)
1′ 6″ 45 cm

'Darling Flame', 'Minuette', 'Minuetto' (Meilucca) [Miniature]

Meilland FRANCE 1971
('Rimosa' × 'Rosina') × 'Zambra'

'Eleanor'

The double, shapely flowers of orange-red have pronounced yellow stamens when fully open and are borne in large clusters. The foliage is dark green and glossy on an upright, bushy plant. This rose is between a Miniature and a Compact Floribunda in size and it has proved an outstanding parent to other Miniatures.
(C) (P) (B) (SF) ☉ ✄
(AW) 1′ 6″ 45cm

'Dorola'
see 'Benson & Hedges Special'

'Dwarfking', 'Zwergkönig' [Miniature]

Kordes GERMANY 1957
'World Fair' × 'Peon'
Clusters of semi-double, reddish-carmine blooms, which are initially cupped and are occasionally borne singly. Foliage dark green and glossy. Growth upright and slender.
(C) (SF) ☉ (AW)
1′ 30 cm

'Easter Morning', 'Easter Morn' [Miniature]

Moore USA 1960
'Golden Glow' × 'Zee'
Its very shapely buds are exquisitely scrolled until fully open, the flowers very full and ivory-white in medium-sized clusters. Foliage glossy. Growth upright and bushy.
(C) ☉ (AW) 1′ 30 cm

'Eleanor' [Miniature]

Moore USA 1960
(R. wichuraiana × 'Floradora') × (Seedling × 'Zee')
The double, coral-pink flowers deepen with age and are produced in large clusters on an

upright, bushy plant with glossy, mid-green foliage.
(C) (SF) ☉ (AW)
1' 30cm

'Fashion Flame' [Miniature]

Moore USA 1977
'Little Darling' × 'Fire Princess'
Peachy-red to orange blooms, fully double, shapely and in clusters. Good, mid-green, leathery foliage. Growth bushy.
(C) (S) ☉ (AW) 1' 30 cm

'Finstar' *see* **'Mini Metro'**

'Fire Princess' [Miniature]

Moore USA 1969
'Baccara' × 'Eleanor'
Full, medium-sized, orange-scarlet flowers. Mid-green and glossy foliage. Upright and bushy growth.
(C) (SF) ☉ ✄ (AW)
1' 30 cm

'Freegold'
see **'Penelope Keith'**

'Gentle Touch' (Diclulu) [Patio]

Dickson UK 1986
Pale pink, the large clusters of shapely double flowers are borne on a compact, widish bush with good mid-green foliage.
(C) (H) (SF) (GC) ☉ (AL)
1' 30 cm

'Gingernut' (Coccrazy) [Patio]

Cocker UK 1988
('Sabine' × 'Circus') × 'Darling Flame'
Well spaced clusters of double flowers of bronzy-orange with reddish reverses opening flat from shapely buds. Foliage mid-green glossy. Growth upright bushy.
(C) ☉ (B) (SF) (Gh) ✄
(AL) 1' 6" 45 cm

'Gold Coin' [Miniature]

Moore USA 1967
'Golden Glow' × 'Magic Wand'
Rich buttercup-yellow, semi-double to double flowers come in

'Gentle Touch'

clusters. Foliage mid-green. Growth bushy and upright.
(C) (MF) ☉ (AL)
1' 30 cm

'Golden Angel' [Miniature]

Moore USA 1975
'Golden Glow' × ('Little Darling' × seedling)
Very double, shapely flowers of deep yellow emerge from tiny round buds. Foliage matt-finished and mid-green on a bushy plant.
(C) (VF) ☉ (AL) 1' 30 cm

'Green Diamond' [Miniature]

Moore USA 1975
Polyantha × 'Sheri Anne'
Greenish soft pink, fully double, small flowers are borne in clusters. Foliage mid-green and leathery. Growth bushy and upright.
(C) (SF) ☉ (AL) 1' 30 cm

'Guernsey Love' (Troblove) [Patio]

Robinson GUERNSEY 1990
Deep red buds open to fully double, velvety red flowers in clusters. Very fragrant. Dark green glossy foliage. Growth bushy spreading.
(C) ☉ (B) (H) (Gh) (VF)
(AL) 1' 30 cm

'Guiding Spirit' (Harwolave) [Patio]

Harkness UK 1989
Seedling × 'Little Prince'
Beautifully formed rosette-shaped flowers in clusters, soft rosy-red in colour. Foliage small, dark green. Growth upright and bushy. Named to commemorate the centenary of the birth of Olave Baden-Powell who started the Girl Guide movement.
(C) ☉ (H) (Gh) (B) (SF)
(AL) 1' 30 cm

'Gypsy Jewel' [Miniature]

Moore USA 1975
'Little Darling' × 'Little Buckaroo'
Its shapely, large blooms are fully double and deep rose-pink. Foliage dark green and glossy. Growth bushy and upright.
(C) ☉ ✄ (AL) 1' 30 cm

'Happy Hour' (Savanhour) [Miniature]

Saville USA 1983
('Tamango' × 'Yellow Jewel') × 'Zinger'
Semi-double, bright red flowers with a yellow centre are borne in large clusters. Foliage dark green and glossy. Growth bushy and spreading.
(C) (MF) ☉ (AL) 1' 30 cm

'Happy Thought' [Miniature]

Moore USA 1978
(*R. wichuraiana* × 'Floradora') × 'Sheri Anne'
The flowers are a blend of pink, coral and yellow. They are fully double and bunch in clusters. Foliage mid-green and glossy on a bushy plant.
(C) (SF) ☉ (AW) 1' 30 cm

'Hello' (Cochello) [Patio]

Cocker UK 1990
'Darling Flame' × seedling
Clusters of crimson flowers each with a white eye. Slightly fragrant. Small, mid-green leaves. Growth upright, bushy.
(C) ☉ (B) (Gh) (H) (SF)
(AL) 1' 6" 45 cm

'Hombre' [Miniature]

Jolly USA 1982
'Humdinger' × 'Rise 'n' Shine'
The apricot-pink flowers have a

paler reverse. They are fully double and high-centred, opening flat in clusters on a plant with mid-green, semi-glossy foliage and of bushy habit.
(C) (SF) ☉ (AW)
1′ 30 cm

'Honeybunch' (Cocglen) [Patio]

Cocker UK 1989
Seedling × 'Bright Smile'
Fully double, shapely flowers of honey-yellow brushed with soft salmon and light red, borne in well formed clusters. Good scent. Foliage is mid-green and growth vigorously bushy.
(C) ☉ (Gh) (B) (H) ✀
(VF) (AL) 1′ 6″ 45 cm

'Hotline' (Aromiker) [Patio]

Armstrong USA 1981
'Honest Abe' × 'Trumpeter'
Rounded buds slightly mossed open to bright red, fragrant, double flowers of Hybrid Tea shape, usually borne singly on a compact, bushy plant amply endowed with good healthy mid-green foliage.
(C) ☉ (B) (H) (Gh) (SF)
(AW) 1′ 30 cm

'Hotline'

'Judy Fischer'

'Hula Girl' [Miniature]

Williams USA 1975
'Miss Hillcrest' × 'Mabel Dot'
The fully double flowers from long, pointed buds are bright orange-salmon. Foliage mid-green, glossy and leathery. Growth bushy.
(C) (SF) ☉ (AW) 1′ 30 cm

'Jenny Robinson' (Trobette) [Miniature]

Robinson GUERNSEY 1983
'Rumba' × 'Darling Flame'
Double flowers of orange-brushed-pink. Fragrant. Foliage small, dark green and glossy. Growth bushy.
(C) ☉ (Gh) (VF) (AW)
1′ 30 cm

'Joan Ball' (Troball) [Miniature]

Robinson GUERNSEY 1989
Shapely buds of bright clear pink, very fragrant. Good dark green foliage. Growth bushy.
(C) ☉ (Gh) (VF) (SF)
(AW) 1′ 30 cm

'Judy Fischer' [Miniature]

Moore USA 1968
'Little Darling' × 'Magic Wand'
Fully double, deep pink, shapely flowers in clusters. Foliage bronzy dark green. Growth bushy.
(C) (SF) ☉ ✀ (AW)
1′ 30 cm

'June Time' [Miniature]

Moore USA 1963
(R. wichuraiana × 'Floradora') × [('Etoile Luisante' seedling × 'Red Ripples') × 'Zee')]
Very double, light pink flowers with a deeper reverse, in large clusters. Foliage mid-green and glossy. Growth bushy.
(C) (SF) ☉ (AW) 1′ 30 cm

'Lavender Jewel' [Miniature]

Moore USA 1978
'Little Chief' × 'Angel Face'
Fully double, shapely, high-centred flowers of lavender-mauve. Foliage dark green and semi-glossy. Growth bushy.
(C) (SF) ☉ (AW) 1′ 30 cm

'Lavender Lace' [Miniature]

Moore USA 1968
'Ellen Poulsen' × 'Debbie'
Small, fully double, high-centred flowers in clusters with plentiful, small, mid-green, glossy foliage. Growth bushy, though very short.
(C) ☉ (AL) 9″ 23 cm

'Lavender Sweetheart' (Willash) [Miniature]

Williams USA 1984
'Double Feature' × seedling
Almost double, deep lavender, shapely, high-centred blooms are carried singly on strong stems. Foliage dark green and semi-glossy. Growth upright.
(C) (E) ☉ ✀ (AL)
1′ 30 cm

'Little Buckaroo'

'Jenny Robinson'

'Joan Ball'

'Lavender Jewel'

'Little Flirt'

'Lemon Delight' [Miniature]

Moore USA 1978
'Fairy Moss' × 'Gold Moss'
Semi-double, clear lemon flowers come from well mossed, pointed buds. Foliage mid-green, the stems mossy. Growth upright and bushy.
(C) (SF) ⊙ (AL) 1' 30 cm

'Little Artist', 'Top Gear' (Macmanly) [Miniature]

McGredy NEW ZEALAND 1982
'Eyepaint' × 'Ko's Yellow'
Semi-double flowers, red with an off-white centre and reverse. Foliage plentiful, small, mid-green and semi-glossy on a compact, bushy plant. Almost but not quite a 'Patio'.
(C) (B) ⊙ (AL) 15" 38 cm

'Little Breeze' [Miniature]

McCann EIRE 1981
'Anytime' × 'Elizabeth of Glamis'
Slim buds open to semi-double, orange-red flowers paling to pink. Foliage mid-green and semi-glossy. Growth upright and bushy.
(C) ⊙ (AL) 1' 30 cm

'Little Buckaroo' [Miniature]

Moore USA 1956
(*R. wichuraiana* × 'Floradora') × ('Oakington Ruby' × 'Floradora')
Double, loosely formed, bright red flowers with white centres are borne in clusters. Foliage bronzy and glossy. Growth upright and tallish.
(C) (B) ⊙ ✂ (AW) 15" 38 cm

'Little Flirt' [Miniature]

Moore USA 1961
(*R. wichuraiana* × 'Floradora') × ('Golden Glow' × 'Zee')
Fully double, shapely flowers of rich orange-yellow, with clear yellow on the reverse, their pointed petals giving a star-like appearance. Foliage light green on a bushy plant.
(C) (B) ⊙ BS ✿ (AW) 15" 38 cm

'Little Jewel' (Cocabel) [Patio]

Cocker UK 1980
'Wee Man' × 'Belinda'
Freely produced, fully double, deep pink rosette-shaped flowers are carried in sizeable clusters. Foliage dark green and glossy. Growth bushy and compact.
(C) (H) (B) ⊙ (AL) 1' 6" 45 cm

'Little Prince' (Coccord) [Patio]

Cocker UK 1983
'Darling Flame' × ('National Trust' × 'Wee Man')
The bright orange-red flowers have hints of yellow deep down in their centre and are semi-double in large clusters. Foliage small, plentiful, mid-green and semi-glossy. Growth upright, compact and bushy.
(C) (H) (B) ⊙ (AL) 1' 6" 45 cm

'Little Prince'

'Mini Metro'

'Lollipop' [Miniature]

Moore USA 1959
(*R. wichuraiana* × 'Floradora')
× 'Little Buckaroo'
Bright red, double flowers borne
in clusters, with glossy foliage on
a plant of vigorous, bushy habit.
(C) (SF) ⊙ (AW)
15″ 38 cm

'Orange Sunblaze'

'Mabel Dot' [Miniature]

Dot SPAIN 1966
'Orient' × 'Perla de Alcañada'
Small, fully double, rosy-coral
blooms borne in clusters. Foliage
semi-glossy. Growth upright.
(C) ⊙ ✂ (AW) 1′ 30 cm

'Magic Carousel'
(Morrousel) [Miniature]

Moore USA 1972
'Little Darling' × 'Westmont'
Its fully double, shapely blooms
are white tipped pink and are
produced in small clusters. Foliage glossy, leathery and mid-
green. Growth upright.
(C) (SF) ⊙ ✂ (AW)
1′ 30 cm

'Pandora'

'Mark One'
see 'Apricot Sunblaze'

'Meillandina' (Meirov)
[Patio]

Paolino FRANCE 1975
'Rumba' × ('Dany Robin' × 'Fire
King')
Currant-red, fully double flowers,
cupped. Foliage matt and deep
green. Growth bushy and wide.
(C) (H) (B) (GC) ⊙ (AW)
15″ 38 cm

'Mini Metro',
'Finstar' (Rufin)
[Patio]

de Ruiter HOLLAND 1979
'Minuette' × seedling
Shapely, small, orange-salmon
blooms produced in clusters. Foliage mid-green and semi-glossy on
a bushy, upright plant.
(C) (H) (B) ⊙ (AW)
15″ 38 cm

'Mona Ruth' [Miniature]

Moore USA 1959
[('Soeur Thérèse' × 'Wilhelm') ×
(Seedling × 'Red Ripples')] × 'Zee'
Mid-pink, fully double flowers in
clusters. Foliage mid-green and
leathery. Growth bushy.
(C) (SF) ⊙ (AL) 1′ 30 cm

'Mood Music' [Miniature]

Moore USA 1977
'Fairy Moss' × 'Gold Moss'
Very full, orange-pink flowers in
small clusters, the calyx heavily
mossed. Foliage plentiful, mid-
green and matt, the stems also
mossed. Growth bushy and
upright.
(C) (B) (H) ⊙ (AW)
1′ 30 cm

'Mr Bluebird' [Miniature]

Moore USA 1960
'Old Blush' × 'Old Blush'
Small, rounded buds in clusters
produce semi-double, lavender-
blue flowers in profusion. Foliage
dark and matt-finished. Growth
upright and bushy.
(C) ⊙ (AW) 1′ 30 cm

'My Valentine' [Miniature]

Moore USA 1975
'Little Chief' × 'Little Chief'
Very double, high-centred, deep
red flowers borne in small
clusters. Foliage glossy, dark to
mid-green tinted bronze. Growth
bushy and upright.
(C) ⊙ ✂ (AW) 1′ 30 cm

'New Penny' [Miniature]

Moore USA 1962
(*R. wichuraiana* × 'Floradora') ×
seedling
Stumpy buds open to double
flowers of orange-red paling to
coral pink. Foliage leathery but
glossy. Growth bushy and short.
(C) (MF) ⊙ (AW)
10″ 26 cm

'Orange Honey' [Miniature]

Moore USA 1979
'Rumba' × 'Over the Rainbow'
High-centred flowers, fully
double, orange-yellow and
cupped with mid-green, matt-
finished foliage. Growth bushy
and wide.
(C) (VF) ⊙ (AL) 1′ 30 cm

'Orange Sunblaze',
'Orange Meillandina'
(Meijikatar) [Patio]

Meilland FRANCE 1982
'Parador' × ('Baby Bettina' ×
'Duchess of Windsor')

'Penelope Keith'

Bright orange-red, double, cupped flowers are borne in profusion in small clusters. Foliage plentiful, light-green and matt. Growth bushy and dense.
(C) (P) (B) (SF) (GC) ☉ (AW) 15″ 38 cm

'Perestroika'

'Painted Doll' (Lavpaint) [Miniature]

Laver CANADA 1985
'Party Girl' × 'Dwarf King '78'
Double flowers of orange with yellow reverses. Slightly fragrant. Foliage light green matt. Growth bushy, dense.
(C) ☉ (Gh) (SF) (AL) 1′ 30 cm

'Paint-Pot' (Trobglow) [Miniature]

Robinson GUERNSEY 1984
Unnamed seedling × 'Darling Flame'
Medium-sized, shapely, double, orange-red flowers. Very fragrant. Foliage small, mid-green. Growth upright, bushy.
(C) ☉ (Gh) (VF) (AL) 1′ 30 cm

'Pandora' (Harwinner) [Miniature]

Harkness UK 1990
'Clarissa × 'Darling Flame'
A delightful little rose. Full, rosette-shaped flowers of yellowish-white amid small dark green foliage. Growth bushy.
(C) ☉ (B) (H) (Gh) (SF) (AL) 1′ 30 cm

'Para Ti' *see* **'Pour Toi'**

'Party Girl' [Miniature]

Saville USA 1979
'Rise 'n' shine' × 'Sheri Anne'
Pointed buds open to shapely, high-centred, double flowers of soft apricot-yellow. Spicy fragrance. Foliage mid-green. Growth compact, bushy.
(C) ☉ ✂ (Gh) (VF) (AW) 1′ 30 cm

'Peach Sunblaze' (Meixerul) [Patio]

Meilland FRANCE 1990
Large quantities of peachy-pink flowers on a compact bushy plant with good mid-green, healthy foliage.
(C) ☉ (H) (Gh) (AW) 1′ 30 cm

'Peachy White' [Miniature]

Moore USA 1976
'Little Darling' × 'Red Germain'
Semi-double flowers in clusters, white tinted peachy-pink. Foliage leathery and mid-green. Growth bushy and upright.
(C) (MF) ☉ ✂ (AW) 1′ 30 cm

**'Peek-a-Boo',
'Brass Ring'** (Dicgrow) [Patio]

Dickson UK 1980
'Memento' × 'Nozomi'
Double, flattish flowers of rich copper-orange, paling to pink with age, are borne in large clusters. Glossy, mid-green foliage. Upright, widish growth.
(C) (B) (G) (AW) 1′ 6″ 45 cm

**'Penelope Keith',
'Freegold'** (Macfreego) [Patio]

McGredy NEW ZEALAND 1983
'Seaspray' × 'Benson & Hedges Special'
Double, shapely flowers, high-centred, of golden-yellow with a deeper reverse. Foliage light green and semi-glossy. Growth upright and bushy.
(C) (B) (E) (MF) ☉ ✂ (AW) 1′ 6″ 45 cm

**'Peon',
'Tom Thumb'** [Miniature]

de Vink NETHERLANDS 1936
'Rouletii' × 'Gloria Mundi'
Its small, semi-double flowers are deep red with a white centre. Foliage light green and leathery on a bushy, compact plant. A rose with a place in the pedigree of many Miniatures.
(C) ☉ (AL) 9″ 23 cm

'Perestroika', 'Sonnenkind' (Korhitom) [Patio]

Kordes GERMANY 1990
Classically formed bright yellow blooms on a sturdy, bushy plant amid abundant mid-green foliage.
(C) ☉ (H) (Gh) (AW) 1′ 30 cm

'Perla de Alcañada', 'Baby Crimson', 'Pearl of Canada', 'Titania', 'Wheatcroft's Baby Crimson' [Miniature]

Dot SPAIN 1944
'Perle des Rouges' × 'Rouletii'
Semi-double, carmine flowers are produced either in small clusters or singly. Foliage dark green and glossy. Growth bushy, compact habit. This is an important early Miniature, parent to several good varieties and in the pedigree of many more.
(C) ☉ (AL) 9" 23 cm

'Perla de Montserrat' [Miniature]

Dot SPAIN 1945
'Cécile Brünner' × 'Rouletii'
Very shapely blooms borne in upright sprays reminiscent of its parent, 'Cécile Brünner'. They are of soft pink deepening towards the centre. Foliage darkish green and matt. Growth upright and bushy.
(C) ☉ ✂ (AW) 9" 23 cm

'Petit Four' (Interfour) [Patio]

Ilsink HOLLAND 1982
'Marlena' seedling × seedling
Clusters of semi-double, mid-pink blooms. Foliage mid-green, glossy. Growth widish and bushy. The shoots very thorny.
(C) (B) (H) (MF) ☉ (AL)
15" 38 cm

'Phoebe' (Harvander) [Miniature]

Harkness UK 1990
'Clarissa' × (Seedling × 'Mozart')
Very double, fragrant, rosette-like flowers of blush-pink open from

'Phoebe'

slim buds which are borne on a twiggy open plant with small, mid-green leaves.
(C) ☉ (MF) (Gh) (AL)
1' 30 cm

'Phoenix' (Harvee) [Miniature]

Harkness UK 1990
'Clarissa' × ('Wee Man' × Seedling)
Small, pretty, full rosette flowers of rich carmine with orange highlights. Foliage tiny but profuse. Growth compact and dense.
(C) ☉ (MF) (Gh) (AL)
1' 30 cm

'Pink Posy' (Cocanelia) [Patio]

Cocker UK 1982
'Trier' × 'New Penny'
Large sprays of soft pink, almost lilac, fully double flowers on a bushy, wide-growing plant with dark green, matt-finished foliage.
(C) (B) (H) (MF) ☉ (AL)
1' 6" 45 cm

'Robin Redbreast'

'Red Ace'

'Pink Sunblaze', 'Pink Meillandina' (Meijidiro) [Patio]

Meilland FRANCE 1983
Sport from 'Orange Sunblaze'
Identical to its parent except in colour, which is bright mid-pink.
(C) (P) (B) (SF) ☉ (AL)
15" 38 cm

'Pixie Rose', 'Pink Pixie' [Miniature]

Dot SPAIN 1961
'Perla de Montserrat' × 'Coralin'
High-centred, cupped, deep pink flowers are carried in clusters of variable size. Dark green, semi-glossy foliage. Growth branching and bushy.
(C) ☉ (AW) 9" 23 cm

'Plum Pudding' (Wilplpd) [Miniature]

J. B. Williams USA 1984
'Angel Face' × unnamed seedling
Double flowers of lavender

washed purple and red. Fragrant. Foliage small, dark green, semi-glossy. Growth upright, bushy.
(C) ☉ (Gh) (MF) (AL) 1′ 30 cm

'Pot Black' (Peanut)
[Miniature]

Pearce UK 1985
Small, shapely, fully double dark velvety-red flowers are borne in clusters. Foliage mid-green and matt. Growth bushy.
(C) ☉ ✂ (AL) 1′ 30 cm

'Pour Toi',
'For You',
'Para Ti',
'Wendy' [Miniature]

Dot SPAIN 1946
'Eduardo Toda' × 'Pompon de Paris'
Semi-double flowers, white with yellow deep in the centre, produced in small clusters. Foliage mid-green and glossy. Growth short and bushy.
(C) ☉ (AW) 9″ 23 cm

'Regensberg'

'Prince Meillandina',
'Prince Starblaze' (Meirutral)
[Miniature]

Meilland FRANCE 1988
The flowers which are borne in large clusters are velvety-red with a remarkable propensity for retaining their colour. Good foliage of mid-green on a spreading bushy plant. Good, both outdoors and under glass.
(C) ☉ (Gh) ✂ (G) (AW) 1′ 30 cm

'Red Ace',
'Amruda',
'Amanda' [Miniature]

de Ruiter HOLLAND 1977
'Scarletta' × seedling
Shapely, double, deep red flowers are carried in small clusters. Foliage mid-green and semi-glossy. Growth compact and bushy.
(C) (SF) ☉ (AW) 1′ 30 cm

'Red Rascal' (Jacbed) [Patio]

Warriner USA 1986
Seedling × seedling
Sprays of fully double, cupped, satiny textured red flowers on a compact bush with mid- to dark-green foliage.
(C) (B) (H) ☉ (AL) 1′ 6″ 45 cm

'Regensberg',
'Young Mistress',
'Buffalo Bill' (Macyoumis)
[Patio]

McGredy NEW ZEALAND 1979
'Geoff Boycott' × 'Old Master'
Its double flowers of soft pink with their petals edged white have prominent yellow stamens.

'Rise 'n' Shine'

Foliage plentiful and mid-green. Growth compact, spreading and bushy.
(C) (B) (H) (VF) (G) ☉ (AL) 1′ 6″ 45 cm

'Rise 'n' Shine',
'Golden Meillandina',
'Golden Sunblaze' [Patio]

Moore USA 1978
'Little Darling' × 'Yellow Magic'
Clear yellow, shapely, double flowers come in clusters with plentiful, mid-green foliage. Growth upright and bushy.
(C) (B) (H) (E) ☉ ✂ (AW) 1′ 6″ 45 cm

'Robin Redbreast' (Interrob)
[Patio]

Ilsink HOLLAND 1984
Seedling × 'Eyepaint'
Small, single blooms of dark red with creamy-yellow centres and silvery reverses are produced in profusion. Mid-green, glossy foliage, the stems thorny. Growth bushy and spreading.
(C) (B) (H) (G) ☉ (AL) 1′ 6″ 45 cm

'Rosina',
'Josephine Wheatcroft',
'Yellow Sweetheart'
[Miniature]

Dot SPAIN 1951
'Edouardo Toda' × 'Rouletii'
Semi-double, clear yellow flowers

are produced in small clusters. Foliage mid-green and glossy. Growth upright and bushy.
(C) (SF) ⊙ (AW)
9″ 23 cm

'Rouletii', *R. rouletii* [Miniature]

Correvon SWITZERLAND 1922
Variety of *R. chinensis minima*
The first of the modern Miniatures, discovered growing in pots on a window ledge in Switzerland by Major Roulet in 1918. Double flowers of deep rose-pink produced singly or in small clusters. Foliage dark green and matt. Growth bushy and compact.
(R) ⊙ (AL) 9″ 23 cm

'Royal Salute', 'Rose Baby' (Macros) [Miniature]

McGredy NEW ZEALAND 1976
'New Penny' × 'Marlena'
Double, shapely flowers of rosy-red carried in small clusters. Foliage dark green and semi-glossy.

Growth upright and bushy.
(C) (SF) ⊙ (AL)
1′ 30 cm

'Scarlet Gem', 'Scarlet Pimpernel' (Meido) [Miniature]

Meilland FRANCE 1961
('Moulin Rouge' × 'Fashion') × ('Perla de Montserrat' × 'Perla de Alcañada')
Very double, cupped flowers of rich scarlet are borne in clusters. Dark green, glossy foliage on a plant of bushy and upright habit.
(C) (SF) ⊙ (AW)
9″ 23 cm

'Sheri Anne' (Morsheri) [Miniature]

Moore USA 1973
'Little Darling' × 'New Penny'
Semi-double, orange-red flowers with a yellow base are borne in large clusters. Foliage mid-green and glossy. Growth bushy and upright.
(C) ⊙ ✄ (AW) 1′ 30 cm

'Scarlet Gem'

'Silver Tips' [Miniature]

Moore USA 1961
(*R. wichuraiana* × 'Floradora') × 'Lilac Time'
Very double pink flowers with silvery tips to each petal and an even more silvery reverse, paling with age to soft lavender. Foliage mid-green and leathery. Growth dense and bushy.
(C) ⊙ ✄ (AW) 1′ 30 cm

'Snookie' (Tinsnook) [Miniature]

Bennett USA 1984
'Torchy' × 'Orange Honey'
The double flowers of deep orange turn red with age. Foliage mid-green and semi-glossy. Growth bushy and small.
(C) ⊙ (AL) 9″ 23 cm

'Snowball', 'Angelita' (Macangel) [Miniature]

McGredy NEW ZEALAND 1982
'Moana' × 'Snow Carpet'
Fully double, white, globular blooms are produced in clusters. Foliage light green and dense. Growth bushy.
(C) ⊙ (AW) 1′ 30 cm

'Snowdrop', 'Amoretta', 'Amorette' (Amoru) [Miniature]

de Ruiter HOLLAND 1979
'Rosy Jewel' × 'Zorina'
Its double, white, shapely flowers with ivory centres are usually borne singly. Foliage mid-green and glossy. Growth upright.
(C) (SF) (Gh) ⊙ ✄ (AW)
1′ 30 cm

'Sheri Anne'

'Stacey Sue' [Miniature]

Moore USA 1976
'Ellen Poulsen' × 'Fairy Princess'
Very double globular blooms of soft pink are born in small clusters. Foliage mid-green and glossy. Growth bushy and upright.
(C) (Gh) ⊙ (AW)
1′ 30 cm

'Starina' (Meigabi) [Miniature]

Meilland FRANCE 1965
('Dany Robin' × 'Fire King') × 'Perla de Montserrat'
Orange-scarlet, fully double flowers with mid-green, glossy foliage on a very bushy plant.
(C) ⊙ (AW) 1′ 30 cm

'Stars 'n' Stripes' [Miniature]

Moore USA 1976
'Little Chief' × ('Little Darling' × 'Ferdinand Pichard')
Double flowers, eye-catchingly striped red and white, shapely and high-centred, are produced in clusters. Foliage mid-green and of bushy, upright habit.
(C) ⊙ ✄ (AW) 1′ 30 cm

'Striped Meillandina' (Mormum) [Patio]

Meilland FRANCE 1988
No two flowers of this variety are alike in markings but each has a striped red and white effect. Buds mossed, making it unique. Foliage

mid-green. Growth bushy compact.
(C) ☉ (Gh) (B) (AL)
1' 30 cm

**'Sunblaze',
'Sunny',
'Sunny Meillandina'**
(Meiponal) [Patio]

Meilland FRANCE 1985
('Sarabande' × 'Moulin Rouge')
× ('Zambra' × 'Meikim')
Orangey-yellow, fully double
blooms in clusters. Foliage plentiful, dark green and matt-finished.
Growth bushy and dense.
(C) (B) (H) ☉ (AW)
15" 38 cm

'Sweet Dream' (Fryerminicot)
[Patio]

Fryer UK 1987
Masses of double, peachy-apricot
blooms in clusters. Foliage plentiful and mid-green. Growth wide
and bushy.
(C) (B) (H) ☉ (AL)
1' 6" 45 cm

'Sweet Dream'

'Sweet Fairy' [Miniature]

de Vink HOLLAND 1946
'Tom Thumb' × seedling
Fully double flowers, soft blush-pink and cupped. Foliage dark
green and semi-glossy. Growth
bushy and very dwarf.
(C) (Gh) (SF) ☉ (AW)
6" 15 cm

'Sweet Magic' (Dicmagic)
[Patio]

Dickson UK 1987
The semi-double, shapely orange
blooms are freely produced in
clusters. Foliage mid-green and
glossy. Growth bushy, wide and
dense.
(C) (SF) (B) (H) ☉ (AW)
1' 6" 45 cm

'Tear Drop' (Dicomo)
[Patio]

Dickson UK 1988
White, semi-double flowers display prominent yellow anthers
when fully open. Fragrant. Foliage
mid-green and healthy. Growth
bushy and robust.
(C) ☉ (Gh) (B) (AW)
15" 38 cm

'Top Gear' see **'Little Artist'**

'Toy Clown' [Miniature]

Moore USA 1966
'Little Darling' × 'Magic Wand'
Semi-double flowers open slightly
cupped and in clusters, white-edged and shaded pinkish-red.
Foliage mid-green and leathery.
Growth bushy, dense and upright.
(C) (Gh) ☉ ✄ (AW)
1' 30 cm

'Wee Jock' (Cocabest)
[Patio]

Cocker UK 1980
'National Trust' × 'Wee Man'
Fully double, bright red flowers
borne in sizeable clusters. Foliage
plentiful, mid-green and glossy.
Growth compact and bushy.
(C) (B) (H) ☉ (AL)
15" 38 cm

**'Wee Man',
'Tapis de Soie'** [Miniature]

McGredy NEW ZEALAND 1974
'Little Flirt' × 'Marlena'
Semi-double flowers of rich scarlet in clusters. Foliage dark green
and glossy. Growth bushy.
(C) ☉ BS✄ (AL)
1' 30 cm

'White Meillandina'
see **'Yorkshire Sunblaze'**

'Wee Jock'

'Yellow Doll' [Miniature]

Moore USA 1962
'Golden Glow' × 'Zee'
Its shapely, fully double flowers of creamy-yellow are not unlike miniature Hybrid Teas. Foliage mid-green and glossy. Growth vigorous and bushy.
(C) (Gh) (SF) ☉ ✄ (AW)
1′   30 cm

**'Yellow Sunblaze',
'Yellow Meillandina'**
(Meitrisical) [Patio]

Meilland FRANCE 1980
['Poppy Flash' × ('Charleston' × 'Allgold')] × 'Gold Coin'
Double, yellow flowers edged with pink. Foliage dark green and semi-glossy. Growth bushy.
(C) (B) (H) ☉ (AL)
15″   38 cm

**'Yorkshire Sunblaze',
'White Meillandina'**
(Meiblam) [Patio]

Meilland FRANCE 1983
'Katherina Zeimet' × 'White Gem'
Small, densely packed clusters of semi-double white flowers. Foliage plentiful, light green and semi-glossy on a compact, bushy plant.
(C) (MF) (B) (H) ☉
(AL)   1′   30 cm

R. phoenicia

MIDDLE EAST 1885
A very vigorous, slender growing climber with few thorns. Ample greyish-green leaves. White flowers in large corymbs. Hips small, round and dark red. Not easy to grow but interesting enough to warrant the effort. Has

'Yorkshire Sunblaze'

a particular liking for dry, sandy soils. An important if seldom seen species that is now recognized as part of the complex genealogy of *R. × centifolia*.
(S) (MF) (AL)
20′ × 10′   6 × 3 m

R. × polliniana

CENTRAL EUROPE c. 1880
Single, blush-pink flowers on a sprawly plant with dark green stems and foliage. The stems are moderately thorny, not a contender for space in today's gardens, but could be useful in woodland.
(S) (W) (P) ● (AL)
15′ × 10′   4.5 × 3 m

R. rubus, 'Blackberry Rose'

MIDDLE EAST 1907
A vigorous climber with numerous thorns, greenish-purple stems and glossy, dark green foliage. Young shoots are a clear purplish-red. Fragrant white flowers in large clusters, similar to those of the wild blackberry from which it gets its name. Small, round, red hips in profusion in autumn.
(S) (P) (F) (T) ☼ (AL)
20′ × 15′   6 × 4.5 m

R. sempervirens
FORMS AND HYBRIDS

These were known as evergreen roses in Victorian days and, indeed, it is true that they retain their lush foliage in most winters. I suspect that, like *R. arvensis*, this species has had more influence on our modern climbers than has ever been acknowledged. Most of the hybrids described here have been with us for many years; few, in fact, have been introduced since early Victorian times. They make useful dense ramblers and scramblers and ideal subjects for arches, pergolas and trellises as well as for walls. They are healthy, and easy to grow and to live with.

CLASSIFICATION	
BARB	Class 1
MR9	Class 40
WFRS	Class 37

R. sempervirens

S. EUROPE 17th century
White, fragrant, single flowers produced in small clusters on a semi-vigorous plant. Foliage mid- to dark green, as near evergreen as a rose can be. Small, orange-red fruit in late autumn.
(C) (P) (W) (F) (T) ● ≈
(SF) (AL)   20′ × 8′   6 × 2.5 m

'Adélaide d'Orléans'

Jacques FRANCE 1826
R. sempervirens hybrid
Clusters of small, shapely, semi-double, powder-pink to white flowers cascading in profusion from a well foliated, evergreen climber. Vigorous in a rather refined way.
(S) (P) (T) (H) ● (MF)
(AL)   15′ × 10′   4.5 × 3 m

'Félicité et Perpétue'

Jacques FRANCE 1827
Vigorous climber bearing clusters of small, creamy-white, fully double, cupped, rosette-shaped flowers often with a hint of pink. Well scented. Makes an admirable climber, with dark green, glossy leaves offsetting the flowers to good effect. Relatively thornless. Often thought of, mistakenly, as the 'Seven Sisters Rose'. The dwarf form of this rose, 'White Pet', is described among the Floribunda roses.
(P) (T) (N) ● ≈ (S)
(MF) (AL)   15′ × 10′   4.5 × 3 m

'Félicité et Perpétue'

'Flora'

Jacques FRANCE 1829
Good, medium-sized climber
with dark green foliage and
growth. The flowers, produced in
clusters, are cupped, open flat and
are full of small, folded petals.
Colour lilac and soft whitish-pink.
Has a refined perfume.
(S) (P) (T) (N) ● (VF)
(AL) 12′ × 8′ 3.5 × 2.5 m

'Princesse Louise'

Jacques FRANCE 1829
Double, cupped flowers of
creamy-white with lilac-pink
shadings. A beautiful rose produced in cascading clusters on a
healthy, almost evergreen plant.
(S) (P) (T) (N) ● (MF)
(AL) 15′ × 8′ 4.5 × 2.5 m

'Princesse Marie'

Jacques FRANCE 1929
Large cascading clusters of
cupped flowers filled with numerous shortish petals which open
flattish but fully double and
charmingly ragged. Colour bright
pinkish lilac on an off-white
ground. Foliage dark green on
long pliable stems with few
thorns.
(S) (P) (T) (N) ● (MF)
(AL) 15′ × 10′ 4.5 × 3 m

'Spectabilis'

c. 1850
A useful, shorter-growing, climbing rose with small, cupped,
double flowers, creamy-lilac to
white, produced in clusters, sometimes giving a surprise repeat performance later in the summer.
Dark, almost evergreen foliage.
(R) (P) (N) ● (MF) (AL)
10′ × 6′ 3 × 1.8 m

R. setigera

AND HYBRIDS

From this species has come a most useful group of ramblers which
for some reason, probably availability, since they seem to be quite
hardy, are far more popular on the other side of the Atlantic than
they are here. 'Baltimore Belle', probably the best known, seems
to crop up everywhere one goes in America, and a great deal of
pleasure it gives. My favourite, though, is the lesser known,
fragrant, pure white, double variety 'Long John Silver'.

Following the character of their parent, the hybrids are all well
endowed with healthy foliage and they almost all flower rather
later in the season and, in some cases, for longer than most of their
better-known counterparts.

CLASSIFICATION	
BARB	Class 1
MR9	Class 41
WFRS	Class 18

R. setigera, 'The Prairie Rose'

N AMERICA 1810
A trailing but shrubby species
with lightish green foliage and
long, arching branches. The
flowers, which are produced in
clusters, are single, deep pink
paling to soft pinkish-white, followed by small, globular, red hips.
(S) (W) (F) (P) (G) (A)
● ≋ (SF) (AL)
5′ × 6′ 1.5 × 1.8 m

'Baltimore Belle'

Feast USA 1843
R. setigera × R. gallica hybrid
A healthy, climbing rose bearing
smallish clusters of very double
pale pink flowers in profusion.
Foliage mid-green. Flowering
somewhat later than most
climbers and remaining in flower
for rather longer.
(S) (P) (T) (N) ● (MF)
(AL) 15′ × 8′ 4.5 × 2.5 m

'Doubloons'

Howard USA 1934
R. setigera hybrid × R. foetida
bicolor hybrid
Double, cupped flowers of deep
rich yellow borne in clusters on
strong, stout stems. Fragrant.
Foliage plentiful and glossy mid-
green. Sometimes repeats its
flowers in the autumn.
(R) (P) (T) (N) ● (VF)
(AL) 15′ × 8′ 4.5 × 2.5 m

'Erinnerung an Brod', 'Souvenir de Brod'

Geschwind HUNGARY 1886
R. setigera hybrid
My plant has recently passed

'Baltimore Belle'

away, so I have not, so far, met
this variety as a mature plant. I
include it because it crops up
from time to time as a parent to
other roses. Flowers double, deep
pink to magenta-purple.
(S) (P) (T) (N) ● (SF)
(AL) 12′ × 8′ 3.5 × 2.5 m

'Jean Lafitte'

Horvath USA 1934
R. setigera seedling
× 'Willowmere'
Rich green leathery foliage and
strong stems among which are
produced many rich pink,
cupped, double flowers each with
a good perfume.
(R) (P) (T) (N) ● (VF)
(AL) 12′ × 8′ 3.5 × 2.5 m

'Long John Silver'

Horvath USA 1934
R. setigera seedling × 'Sunburst'
This rose deserves more attention,
being seldom seen, at least in Britain. Flowers large, double, and
cupped rather like a small, silky-
white water-lily, produced freely
on strong stems amid large,
leathery leaves. Very vigorous and
scented.
(S) (P) (T) (N) ● ≋
(VF) (AL) 15′ × 10′ 4.5 × 3 m

'Queen of the Prairies', 'Beauty of the Prairies', 'Prairie Belle'

Feast USA 1843
R. setigera × R. gallica
Clusters of large, fully double,
plumpish blooms of bright pink,
most but not all having a few distinctive white flecks or stripes.
Very fragrant. It is vigorous and
very hardy with ample mid- to
dark green foliage. I find it interesting that such a cross should
produce such offspring.
(S) (W) (P) (T) (N) ●
(VF) (AL) 15′ × 8′ 4.5 × 2.5 m

R. sinowilsonii
AND HYBRID

R. sinowilsonii

CHINA 1904

A large, climbing rose with superb, glossy, heavily veined foliage. Flowers white, large, single and produced in flat trusses followed by small, red fruit. Said not to be hardy but seems to survive our Norfolk winters, even that of 1983 when temperatures dropped to 15°F (−9°C).
(S) (A) (F) ● ≈≈ (AL)
12′ × 8′ 3.5 × 2.5 m

'Wedding Day' (Climbing)

Stern UK 1950

R. sinowilsonii × unknown
An outstanding rose with bright green, glossy foliage and clear green, relatively thornless wood. Flowers large, compared with other such roses. These are single with prominent yellow stamens and are produced in large trusses. Growth is rampant, capable of considerable climbing feats when festooning trees, seeming not to mind the shade.
(S) (P) (N) '(T) ● ≈≈
(VF) (AL) 30′ × 15′ 9 × 4.5 m

R. soulieana
AND HYBRIDS

R. soulieana

CHINA 1896

A vigorous, dense shrub with thin, arching branches bearing grey-green, rather fluffy foliage and numerous small spines. Single white flowers, produced in trusses, followed by bunches of oval, orange-red hips.
(S) (P) (F) (W) ● ≈≈
(AL) 10′ × 6′ 3 × 1.8 m

'Kew Rambler'

'Chevy Chase'

'Chevy Chase'

N.J. Hansen USA 1939

R. soulieana × 'Eblouissant'
A spectacular rose which, in full flush, has large clusters of small, very double, fragrant blooms of rich deep crimson produced in great profusion in early summer. Abundant, light green, crinkled foliage on a dense, vigorous plant. Until now this rose has not been seen in the UK but it is widely grown in America.
(S) (P) (W) (N) ● (MF)
(AL) 15′ × 10′ 4.5 × 3 m

'Kew Rambler'

Royal Botanic Gardens Kew UK 1912

R. soulieana × 'Hiawatha'
An interesting, vigorous rambler showing the influence of its seed parent *R. soulieana* in the small, plentiful greyish-green foliage, and of its pollen parent 'Hiawatha' in the shape and colour of its flowers, which are individually single, small, pink with a central white eye, and produced in packed clusters. Stems thorny and stiffish but still pliable. Good orange hips in the autumn.
(S) (W) (F) (T) (N) ●
≈≈ (MF) (AL)
18′ × 12′ 5.5 × 3.5 m

'Ohio'

Shepherd USA 1949
R. soulieana × 'Grüss an Teplitz'
seedling
Interesting, recurrent rose, bushy
but vigorous with semi-double,
bright red flowers. Very hardy.
(R) (H) (P) ⊙ (SF) (AL)
4' × 3'   120 × 90 cm

'Wickwar'

Steadman UK 1960
Seedling of *R. soulieana*
An unusual and pleasing rose
which should perhaps have
received more attention in the 25
or so years since its introduction.
A short to medium, dense-
growing climber with small, greyish-green foliage. Medium-sized,
single, creamy-white flowers. Very
fragrant.
(S) (P) (N) ● ≈ (VF)
(AL)   12' × 5'   3.5 × 1.5 m

R. wichuraiana

AND HYBRIDS

R wichuraiana has contributed much to modern roses, being
directly or indirectly responsible for many ramblers and climbers,
especially those with glossy foliage.* A number of breeders used
them with much success around the turn of the century, and many
a rusty iron arch remains standing, supported by such a rose
planted fifty or more years ago. Apart from a proneness to mildew
in a few varieties, these are among our healthiest roses. They are
easy to grow and amongst their ranks can be found a colour to suit
every taste. For the best results prune them immediately after
flowering.

CLASSIFICATION

BARB	Class 16
MR9	Class 53
WFRS	Class 16

R. wichuraiana hips

* Graham Thomas now believes that *R. luciae* was the parent of some of these hybrids and he puts forward some good and interesting reasons for this being so.

It could be that both *R. wichuraiana* and *R. luciae* were involved, with breeders in America and Europe using separately these two very similar species.

'Albertine'

R. wichuraiana

CHINA 1860
An almost evergreen species,
making a dense, procumbent
shrub or short climber. Foliage
dark green and glossy. Shoots dark
and pliable. Flowers single, white
profusely if briefly produced in
mid-July. The small oval dark red
hips are much enjoyed by birds.
Ideal as a ground cover plant.
(S) (P) (G) (W) ● ≈
(SF) (AW)
6' × 20'   1.8 × 6 m

'Albéric Barbier'

Barbier FRANCE 1900
R. wichuraiana × 'Shirley
Hibbard'
Superb glossy foliage produced
on long, pliable stems. Flowers
shapely, slightly scrolled in bud,
opening to semi-double, creamy-
white flushed lemon-yellow.
Healthy. One of the best
ramblers.
(S) (P) (T) (N) ● (SF)
(AW)   15' × 10'   4.5 × 3 m

'Albertine'

Barbier FRANCE 1921
R. wichuraiana × 'Mrs Arthur
Robert Waddell'
A famous old rambler with glossy
leaves, heavily burnished with
coppery-red, especially when
young. Shoots vigorous, equipped
with large, spiteful, hooked
thorns. Very floriferous in full

'Albéric Barbier'

flush. Flowers open from shapely buds to rather muddled, full blooms of lobster pink each with a golden base, and paling to blush-pink with age. Highly scented. Rather prone to mildew, but usually only after flowering.
(S) (P) (T) (VF) M✿
(AW) 15′ × 10′ 4.5 × 3 m

'Alexander Girault'

Barbier FRANCE 1909
R. wichuraiana × 'Papa Gontier'
Vigorous with dark green, glossy foliage on pliable shoots. Very prostrate if not trained as a rambler. Flowers are double, opening flat with muddled centres. These are borne in clusters, and are a mixture of deep rose-pink and copper with hints

'American Pillar'

of yellow. Has a strong, fruity scent.
(S) (G) (P) ● (VF) (AL)
12′ × 12′ 3.5 × 3.5 m

'Alida Lovett'

Van Fleet USA 1905
'Souvenir de Président Carnot' × *R. wichuraiana*
Fragrant, large, double flowers of soft shell-pink with a yellow base; opening flat, and borne in clusters on a vigorous, relatively thornless plant with dark green, glossy foliage.
(S) (P) (T) (MF) (AL)
12′ × 10′ 3.5 × 3 m

'American Pillar'

Van Fleet USA 1909
(*R. wichuraiana* × *R. setigera*) × 'Red Letter Day'
A vigorous, almost coarse rose with strong, thorny, green stems and large, glossy leaves. Single flowers, at first reddish-pink, paling to deep pink with off-white centres, usually in large trusses.

'Alida Lovett'

(S) (P) (T) ● (SF) (AW)
15′ × 10′ 4.5 × 3 m

'Améthyste'

Nonin FRANCE 1911
'Non Plus Ultra' sport
Trusses of tightly packed, double, violet to crimson flowers, produced on long, firm but arching shoots. Foliage glossy.
(S) (P) (T) (N) ● (SF)
(AL) 12′ × 10′ 3.5 × 3 m

'Auguste Gervais'

Barbier FRANCE 1918
R. wichuraiana × 'Le Progrès'
Very vigorous, with smallish but plentiful shiny dark green leaves. Flowers large by the standards of its type, semi-double, coppery-yellow suffused salmon, paling quickly with age to creamy-white. Very fragrant.
(S) (N) (P) (T) (VF) (AL)
12′ × 8′ 3.5 × 2.5 m

'Aviateur Blériot'

Fauque FRANCE 1910
R. wichuraiana × 'William Allen Richardson'
Vigorous but more upright than most of its kind and rather less thorny. Large trusses of scented, double, orange-yellow flowers, fading to creamy-yellow with age. Foliage dark green, burnished bronze, healthy.
(S) (P) (MF) (AL)
12′ × 6′ 3.5 × 1.8 m

'Awakening', 'Probuzini'

Blatna Nurseries
CZECHOSLOVAKIA 1935
Reintroduced Beales UK 1990
Sport of 'New Dawn'
A form of 'New Dawn' with all its parent's attributes except that each bloom is made up of twice the number of petals, creating a sumptuous, old-fashioned, muddled effect. An outstanding rose in all respects.
(C) (P) (N) ● ☉ (VF)
✂ (AL) 10′ × 8′ 3 × 2.5 m

'Blaze'

Kallay USA 1932
'Paul's Scarlet' × 'Grüss an Teplitz'
Similar to 'Paul's Scarlet' both in colour and form but with the considerable advantage of repeat flowering. Cupped, double flowers of bright scarlet in clusters. Scented. Foliage leathery dark green. Growth upright and vigorous.
(R) (P) (N) (T) ● (MF)
✂ (AL) 10′ × 8′ 3 × 2.5 m

'Breeze Hill'

Van Fleet USA 1926
R. wichuraiana × 'Beauté de Lyon'
Very double, cupped flowers, clear pink flushed tawny-orange, produced in clusters on a vigorous plant with glossy, dark green foliage. Not too well known but worth growing especially as a tree climber. An excellent specimen festoons an apple tree at Sheldon Manor, near Chippenham, Wiltshire, home of Major and Mrs Gibbs.
(S) (P) (N) (T) ● ≈
(MF) (AL) 18′ × 12′ 5.5 × 3.5 m

'Cadenza'

Armstrong USA 1967
'New Dawn' × climbing 'Embers'
Double, dark red flowers of some size and substance produced freely in clusters. Fragrant. Abundant, glossy, dark green foliage on a medium sized plant which can be used as either a small climber or a large shrub.
(P) ☉ (R) (MF) (AL)
10′ × 6′ 3 × 1.8 m

'Chaplin's Pink', 'Chaplin's Pink Climber'

Chaplin Bros UK 1928
'Paul's Scarlet' × 'American Pillar'
This rose of mixed pedigree might have been better placed among the Multiflora climbers but its main characteristics are derived from R. wichuraiana. Glossy, mid-green foliage and pliable growth. Flowers semi-double, bright, startling pink, accentuated by yellow stamens. Very free-flowering; not for those who like a quiet life.
(S) (P) (N) (T) ● (MF)
(AL) 15′ × 10′ 4.5 × 3 m

'Chaplin's Pink Companion'

Chaplin & Sons UK 1961
'Chaplin's Pink' × 'Opera'
Semi-double flowers of bright silvery-pink. Less 'noisy' than 'Chaplin's Pink' but still brightly coloured. Foliage glossy dark green. Vigorous growth.
(S) (P) (N) (T) ● (MF)
(AL) 15′ × 10′ 4.5 × 3 m

'Crimson Showers'

Norman UK 1951
'Excelsa' seedling
Crimson, pompon-like blooms, slightly scented, in large, pendulous clusters on a wiry, vigorous plant. Foliage mid-green and glossy.
(S) (P) (T) (G) ● (SF)
(AL) 15′ × 8′ 4.5 × 2.5 m

'Debutante'

Walsh USA 1902
R. wichuraiana × 'Baroness Rothschild'
Clusters of small, fragrant, fully-double blooms of soft rose-pink, borne amid dark green, glossy foliage to good effect. Vigorous, healthy and of slightly spreading habit.
(S) (P) (G) (T) ● (SF)
(AL) 12′ × 10′ 3.5 × 3 m

'Dorothy Perkins'

Jackson & Perkins USA 1902
R. wichuraiana × 'Gabriel Luizet'
A very famous rose known, by name at least, to most gardeners. Colourful cascades of clear pink flowers with the occasional almost white bloom among the cluster. Foliage, when free of mildew early in the season is bright, glossy dark green. Growth is pliable and semi-vigorous. Well scented.
(S) (P) (G) (VF) (AL)
10′ × 8′ 3 × 2.5 m

'Dr Huey', 'Shafter'

Thomas USA 1920
'Ethel' × 'Grüss an Teplitz'

'Aviateur Blériot'

'Awakening'

'Chaplin's Pink'

'Debutante'

'Dr Huey'

Showy, sizeable, semi-double
blooms of crimson-maroon with
prominent yellow anthers.
Slightly fragrant. Borne in clusters
on a vigorous upright plant with
rich green, semi-glossy foliage.
Used extensively as an understock
under the name 'Shafter', especially in the USA and Australia.
Consequently it crops up frequently as a garden plant in its
own right, and so it should.
(S) (P) ☉ (SF) ● (N)
(AW) 12′ × 8′ 3.5 × 2.5 m

'Dr W. Van Fleet'

Van Fleet USA 1910
R. wichuraiana × 'Safrano'
A vigorous, well-foliated plant
with rather thorny stems and dark
green glossy leaves. Flowers are
shapely in bud and open to semi-
double, soft blush-pink. Perfumed.
(S) (P) (T) (N) ● (MF)
(AL) 15′ × 10′ 4.5 × 3 m

'Easlea's Golden Rambler'

Easlea UK 1932
Placed here because of its rich
glossy foliage. Could well have
been included among the climbing Hybrid Teas. An aristocrat of
yellow climbers, with shapely,

rich golden-yellow flowers on
long, strong stems. Growth vigorous and extremely healthy, with
plenty of reddish thorns.
(S) (P) (T) ● (MF) (AL)
20′ × 15′ 6 × 4.5 m

'Elegance'

Brownell USA 1937
'Glenn Dale' × ('Mary Wallace'
× 'Miss Lolita Armour')
Large, shapely, fully double, clear
yellow flowers, losing none of
their charm as they pale with age
to lemon. Good, healthy, dark
green foliage. Sometimes gives a
subdued repeat performance in
autumn.
(R) (P) (SF) (AL)
10′ × 8′ 3 × 2.5 m

'Emily Gray'

A. H. Williams UK 1918
'Jersey Beauty' × 'Comtesse du
Cayla'
An outstanding rose with shapely
buds opening to almost double
yellow flowers, which pale with
age to lemon. Fragrant. Very
floriferous on a vigorous plant
with rich green, highly polished
foliage.
(S) (P) (T) (N) ● (MF)
(AW) 15′ × 10′ 4.5 × 3 m

'Ethel'

Turner UK 1912
'Dorothy Perkins' seedling
Large, cascading clusters of
mauve-pink, double flowers on a
vigorous, scrambling-type plant

'Emily Gray'

with glossy foliage and ample
thorns. A most useful rose, much
healthier than its parent.
(S) (P) (T) (N) ● (VF)
(AL) 20′ × 15′ 6 × 4.5 m

'Evangeline'

Walsh USA 1906
R. wichuraiana × 'Crimson
Rambler'
Healthy, leathery foliage provid-
ing an ideal foil for the clusters of
single, soft pinkish-white flowers.
These are produced advanta-
geously rather later in the season
than those of most others of its
type.
(S) (P) (T) (N) ● (SF)
(AL) 15′ × 12′ 4.5 × 3.5 m

'Excelsa',
'Red Dorothy Perkins'

Walsh USA 1909
Large trusses of small, crimson
flowers, densely produced on
strong, pliable shoots. Foliage
exceptionally dark green. Rather
inclined to mildew after flowering, especially around the soft,
immature thorns. A most useful
rambler or prostrate rose, flowering well into August.
(S) (T) (P) (G) (N) ● ≈
(SF) (AL) 15′ × 12′ 4.5 × 3.5 m

'Evangeline'

'Ethel'

'François Juranville and *top right*, 'Gardenia'

'François Juranville'

Barbier FRANCE 1906
R. *wichuraiana* × 'Mme Laurette Messimy'
A tangle of petals create an unusual individual bloom. Spectacular in full flush, this rose, clear pink with deeper shadings, is a rather refined 'Albertine', with which it is sometimes confused. Foliage dark green, burnished bronze. Growth pliable and dense, with few thorns of consequence.
(S) (T) (P) (G) (N) ●
(SF) (AL) 15' × 10' 4.5 × 3 m

'Fräulein Octavia Hesse'

Hesse GERMANY 1909
R. *wichuraiana* × 'Kaiserin Auguste Viktoria'
Creamy-white, semi-double flowers with a fruity scent, produced in small clusters on vigorous, wiry growth with dark green foliage.
(S) (P) (G) (MF) (AL)
12' × 10' 3.5 × 3 m

'Gardenia'

Manda USA 1899
R. *wichuraiana* × 'Perle des Jardins'
Shapely, fully double flowers of creamy-white. These open from pointed buds to give a lovely muddled effect with deeper creamy-yellow centre petals. They are produced in small clusters on short, lateral stems along strong but pliable branches of the previous year's growth. Pleasing fragrance reminiscent of apples.

Foliage dark green and glossy, growth very vigorous. Quite rare these days.

(S) (P) (T) ● ≈ (MF) (AL) 20′ × 15′ 6 × 4.5 m

'May Queen'

'Minnehaha'

'New Dawn'

'Gerbe Rose'

Fauque FRANCE 1904
R. wichuraiana × 'Baroness Rothschild'
A vigorous, healthy climber with abundant, green foliage. The large, double flowers, opening flat, are soft rosy-pink with a faint but sweet fragrance.

(S) (T) (N) ● (MF) (AL) 10′ × 8′ 3 × 2.5 m

'Golden Glow'

Brownell USA 1937
'Glenn Dale' × (Mary Wallace' × a Hybrid Tea)
Shapely, cupped, almost double flowers of golden-yellow, retaining their colour fairly well as they age. Foliage crisp, dark green and plentiful. Growth strong with an average number of thorns.

(S) (P) (N) ● (AL) 10′ × 8′ 3 × 2.5 m

'Jersey Beauty'

Manda USA 1899
R. wichuraiana × 'Perle des Jardins'
Clusters of good-sized, single, whitish to creamy yellow, sweetly scented flowers with deep golden stamens. Flowers show up well against lush, dark green, glossy foliage. Interesting single with the same parents as 'Gardenia' which is fully double.

(S) (P) (T) (N) ● ≈ (SF) (AL) 15′ × 10′ 4.5 × 3 m

'Léontine Gervais'

Barbier FRANCE 1903
R. wichuraiana × 'Souvenir de Claudius Denoyel'
Clusters of medium-sized, fully-double, flat flowers opening rather muddled, deep salmon with yellow, red and orange high-

lights. A semi-vigorous, pliable plant with ample, dark green, glossy foliage.

(S) (P) (T) (N) ● ≈ (SF) (AL) 15′ × 10′ 4.5 × 3 m

'Mme Alice Garnier'

Fauque FRANCE 1906
R. wichuraiana × 'Mme Charles Small'
Slender branches carrying small but numerous, glossy, dark green leaves. Medium-sized clusters of scented, double flowers, bright orange-pink with yellow centres. Vigorous and, when required, procumbent.

(S) (P) (N) (G) ● (SF) (AL) 10′ × 8′ 3 × 2.5 m

'Mary Wallace'

Van Fleet USA 1924
R. wichuraiana × a pink Hybrid Tea
Warm pink almost double flowers, with a good perfume, produced freely on a vigorous, relatively upright plant amid dark, shiny but not glossy foliage. Leaves spaced rather wider apart than others of this family.

(S) (P) (N) ● (MF) (AL) 10′ × 8′ 3 × 2.5 m

'May Queen'

Manda USA 1898
R. wichuraiana × 'Champion of the World'
Free-flowering. The semi-double, lilac-pink flowers are well scented. They appear in clusters on a vigorous, densely growing climber with darkish thorns and dark green foliage.

(S) (G) (N) (T) ● (VF) (AL) 15′ × 8′ 4.5 × 2.5 m

'Minnehaha'

Walsh USA 1905
R. wichuraiana × 'Paul Neyron'

Large clusters of cascading, pink flowers which pale almost to white with age. The plant is well endowed with small, dark green, glossy leaves.

(S) (P) (N) (T) (G) ● ≈ (MF) (AL) 15′ × 8′ 4.5 × 2.5 m

'New Dawn'

Somerset Rose Company USA 1930
'Dr Van Fleet' sport
An outstanding rose, one of the most useful sports ever discovered. Well scented flowers identical to those of 'Dr Van Fleet' with slightly tubby buds opening to semi-double flowers of soft blush-pink. Foliage dark green and glossy. Its greatest advantage over all others of this group is its remontancy. Flowers freely from June to October. In fact, the ideal, smaller rambling rose.

(C) (P) (N) ● (VF) (AW) 10′ × 8′ 3 × 2.5 m

'Paul Transon'

Barbier FRANCE 1900
R. wichuraiana × 'l'Idéal'
Medium-sized, fully-double flowers opening flat, rich salmon with coppery overtones and a creamy-yellow base to each petal. Foliage shiny, coppery tinted, light green, combining beautifully with the flowers to give a pleasing overall effect. Sometimes repeats in autumn, especially if placed in a warm position.

(R) ☼ (P) ● (MF) (AL) 10′ × 8′ 3 × 2.5 m

'Purity'

Hoopes Bros & Thomas USA 1917
Unnamed seedling × 'Mme Caroline Testout'

'Sanders White'

'Sanders White'

Large, pure white, shapely flowers opening semi-double and perfumed. Foliage light green and glossy on a vigorous, somewhat thorny plant.
(S) (P) ● (MF) (AL)
12' × 8' 3.5 × 2.5 m

'René André'

Barbier FRANCE 1901
R. wichuraiana × 'l'Idéal'
The semi-double flowers, which open flat, are a mixture of coppery-pink and yellow, changing with age to carmine and soft pink. Growth is very vigorous with ample, dark green, slightly glossy leaves. The flowers occasionally repeat.
(R) (G) (N) ● (AL)
15' × 8' 4.5 × 2.5 m

'Sanders White', 'Sanders White Rambler'

Sanders & Sons UK 1912
One of the best white ramblers. Abundant, almost rosette-shaped, pure white flowers in cascading clusters, sometimes singly. Foliage is dark green and growth pliable with ample, stubby thorns.
(S) (P) (T) (G) (N) ● ≈
(SF) (AL) 12' × 8' 3.5 × 2.5 m

'Snowdrift'

Walsh USA 1913
Small, pure white, fully double flowers in large clusters produced in great profusion on a medium-sized yet vigorous plant with large, light green foliage. A useful rose which is not widely enough known.
(S) (P) (N) (T) ● (AL)
12' × 8' 3.5 × 2.5 m

'Thelma'

Easlea UK 1927
R. wichuraiana × 'Paul's Scarlet'
A pleasing mixture of coral-pink and deeper pink with a hint of lemon faintly visible in the centre Semi-double and quite large when open. Foliage rather coarse deep green and glossy. Growth robust with few but large thorns.
(S) (P) (T) ● (SF) (AL)
12' × 8' 3.5 × 2.5 m

'Wickmoss'

Barbier FRANCE 1911
R. wichuraiana × 'Salet'
Sizeable clusters of shapely, well mossed buds open to small, soft, creamy white flushed pink, semi-double flowers with a good fragrance. An unusual rambler with ample dark green, leathery foliage.
(S) (P) (T) (MF) M⚹
(AL) 10' × 8' 3 × 2.5 m

'Sénateur Amic'

ROSA Subgenus *Rosa* (*Eurosa*)

SECTION : *Chinensis*

Growth very variable, usually upright from 3′–10′, 1 m–7 m.
Thorns sparse or relatively so, usually hooked.
Leaves 5 to 7 leaflets.
Flowers in small clusters.
Hips mostly roundish.
Sepals dropping when hips ripe.

SPECIES

R. chinensis (R. indica, R. sinica)
R. × borboniana
R. × odorata
R. gigantea

GARDEN GROUPS

Chinas
Teas
Noisettes
Bourbons
Hybrid Perpetuals
Hybrid Teas
Climbing Hybrid Teas
English Roses

ORIGIN AND DISTRIBUTION

CLASSIFICATION

BARB	Species:	Class 1
MR9	Species:	Class 55
WFRS	Species:	Class 39

For classifications of hybrids see under garden group headings.

R. gigantea

HYBRIDS

This species is very important both historically and genetically, in that it gave rise to the old Tea-Scented roses cultivated in China long before they found their way to the West. Sadly, it is not hardy enough to perform well in the UK except perhaps in the southwest. A few interesting hybrids have been raised direct from this species over the years and these are described here. Some, like their parent, are a little tender but all are well worth growing.

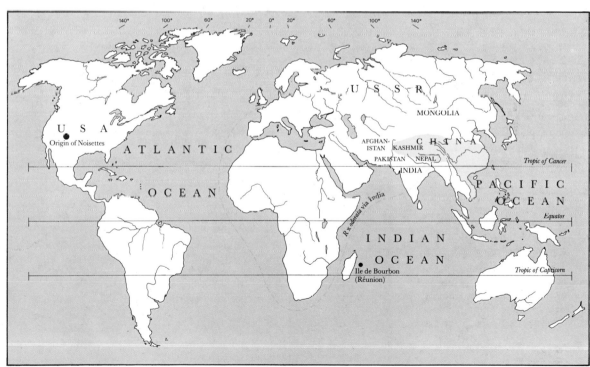

'Bloomfield Abundance'

R. gigantea

HIMALAYAS 1889
In specific form this rose has little garden value in cold districts of the world, but it is excellent and quite beautiful in warm temperate zones. Flowers large, white and single, produced somewhat reluctantly on a vigorous, thorny, climbing shrub with crisp, dark foliage. I believe a less vigorous clone exists, since I have seen an obviously aged plant no more than 5' (1.5 m) tall and 6' (1.8 m) wide at the Huntington Botanic Gardens, California.
(S) (P) (T) ● (VF) (AL)
40' × 10'   12 × 3 m

R. gigantea

'Belle Portugaise', 'Belle of Portugal'

Cayeux PORTUGAL c. 1900
R. gigantea × 'Reine Marie Henriette'?
Flowers semi-double, made up of loosely arranged petals of pale pink with deeper shadings. Makes a good climbing rose, flowering profusely and growing vigorously. Needs a warm sheltered position to give of its best. Foliage dark green and slightly crumpled.
(S) (T) ● (MF) (AL)
15' × 10'   4.5 × 3 m

'La Follette'

Busby FRANCE c. 1900
R. gigantea × unknown
A very attractive rose, sadly not hardy enough for British gardens. Makes a good climber for growing under glass or in warmer climates, with large, fragrant, deep pink flowers and dark, abundant foliage.
(R) (Gh) (VF) (AL)
20' × 15'   6 × 4.5 m

'Lorraine Lee'

Clarke AUSTRALIA 1924
'Jessie Clarke' × 'Capitaine Millet'
Falls into this group as a second-generation hybrid, 'Jessie Clarke' being a *R. gigantea* seedling which is now seemingly extinct in Europe. Double, fragrant rich pinkish apricot, with lush green, very glossy foliage. Not hardy enough for northern Europe. Excellent in Australia.
(S) (Gh) (VF) (AL)
10' × 6'   3 × 1.8 m

'Belle Portugaise'

'Sénateur Amic'

P. Nabonnand FRANCE 1924
R. gigantea × 'General MacArthur'
Much hardier than given credit for. I know an old, established plant growing as a dense, pillar rose in south Norfolk, which must have survived many a biting north-easterly. Quite beautiful, the flowers are semi-double, large, loosely formed when open, rich pink with hints of yellow at the base and prominent stamens. Superb scent. Growth not as thorny as one would expect. Foliage dark with a dull gloss.
(R) (VF) (AL)
10' × 8'   3 × 2.5 m

Chinas (R. chinensis)

FORMS AND HYBRIDS

These roses were, initially, the group that brought the valuable remontancy factor into modern varieties.

As garden plants they have a wide range of uses, from group planting and bedding in some cases, to specimen and shrubbery planting in others. In Northern European climates however the majority are best used as conservatory subjects, when they come into their own, especially when grown in tubs, pots or urns. I have learned to appreciate their quiet charm and relaxed behaviour far more since I have seen them growing in warmer parts of the world than East Anglia. Having said all this, all those who love and enjoy their roses, no matter where in the world, will derive a great deal of pleasure from the little extra care they will need to take in growing these.

Note: Amongst the roses described in this group are a few varieties which, in appearance at least, have an obvious affinity to other types, in particular, the Gallicas. In the United States and, to a lesser extent, other parts of the world, the 'less obvious' Chinas have become known by a separate collective name, 'Hybrid Chinas'. There is probably a good case to be made for this term although I, personally, find it confusing since, broadly speaking, almost any modern rose is a 'Hybrid China'. However, where such a classification is thought appropriate, I have indicated it.

CLASSIFICATION

BARB	Class 2
MR9	Class 6
WFRS	Class 23

R. chinensis, **'China Rose'**, **'Bengal Rose'**, *R. indica*, *R. sinica*, *R. nankiniensis*

It is not known whether the originally discovered species still exists, but this is the name given to the species thought to have been the parent of wide and varied Chinese hybrids which reached us, by way of India, in the early 18th century. The last recorded sighting in China itself is reported to have been made around 1885, but this remains speculative. This rose is described as single, red to white, of variable height from 4' to 20' (1.2 to 6 m). Hardly the description of a species, although such erratic heights and colour variations are characteristic of several China hybrids; so possibly it does have chameleon-like qualities.

'Anne-Marie de Montravel'
[Hybrid China]

Rambaud FRANCE 1880
A Polyantha × 'Mme de Tartas'
A short-growing, rather sprawly China but nevertheless dense in growth. Pure white flowers, fully double, globular and produced in great profusion.
(C) (Gh) (B) ⊙ (AL)
2' × 3'   60 × 90 cm

'Archduke Charles', 'Archiduc Charles'

Laffay FRANCE c. 1825
Freely produced, shapely, rounded buds open to almost double flowers of claret with paler reverses, sometimes marbled. Growth branching, perhaps awkward. Temperamental, does better in warmer climates but quite hardy.
(C) ⊙ ✿ (Gh) (H) (AL)
4' × 3'   120 × 90 cm

'Arethusa'

W. Paul UK 1903
The double flowers, which are a mixture of sulphur yellow, lemon and apricot, are made up of a host of rather ragged petals and are produced in clusters. Foliage shiny but somewhat sparse.
(C) (P) ⊙ (SF) (AL)
3' × 3'   90 × 90 cm

'Beauty of Rosemawr'

Van Fleet USA 1904
A twiggy but dense, upright-growing variety producing loosely formed, sweetly scented flowers of soft carmine with softer veining. Rather short of foliage for my taste.
(C) (Gh) (P) ⊙ ✿ (AL)
4' × 2'   120 × 60 cm

'Bloomfield Abundance', 'Spray Cécile Brünner'

Thomas USA 1920
Said to be 'Sylvia' × 'Dorothy Page-Roberts'
One of the tallest bush Chinas. The small compact blooms of shell-pink are exquisite and are produced freely throughout summer in huge, well-spaced clusters, each on a lengthy stalk – ideal for buttonholes. Wood smooth, brownish-purple, sometimes spindly, with few thorns. Foliage dark green and also

'Archduke Charles'

'Arethusa'

'Brennus'

'Cécile Brünner'

smooth. The individual blooms are very similar to and sometimes confused with 'Cécile Brünner', which is a much shorter grower. The most marked difference, however, is seen in the sepals – on 'Bloomfield Abundance' long and extending well beyond the petals, and visible, even when the flower is fully open; on 'Cécile Brünner' shorter, sometimes but not always folding back towards the receptacle. Nurserymen have for many years added to a confusion between these two roses. 'Bloomfield Abundance' is unquestionably easier to produce, yet 'Cécile Brünner' sells better, leading one to wonder sadly, how many mistakes have been deliberate?

Note: Over recent years there has been, and still is, some controversy about 'Bloomfield Abundance'. In America it is now sometimes listed as 'Spray Cécile Brünner'. This name has not been adopted elsewhere in the world so far. Climate, without doubt, influences the China roses more than most and the present rose may not be the one originally given this name by its raiser. In my opinion, however, it is not a sport from 'Cécile Brünner', a conclusion reached after observing the behaviour and habits of both varieties in my nursery over several years. It is easy to become dogmatic in matters such as this and I must keep an open mind, but unless the true 'Bloomfield Abundance' is found alive and well I can see no reason to change the name of the one we have now, at least here in the UK, especially so since, as an apprentice nurseryman, I recall growing 'Bloomfield Abundance' in the early 1950s under the late, respected Edward LeGrice, the very same rose which he had been growing under that name since the 30s, well before 'Spray Cécile Brünner' was introduced in America in 1940.

(C) (H) (P) ☉ (SF) (AW)
6' × 4'   1.8 × 1.2 m

'Brennus' [Hybrid China]

1830
Probably a China × Gallica cross
Bears little resemblance at first sight to a typical China, being more upright and less branchy, with larger, more plentiful and less shiny foliage. Flowers cupped, full, rich reddish-carmine.

(R) (P) (SF) (AL)
5' × 4'   1.5 × 1.2 m

'Camellia Rose'

Prévost FRANCE pre-1830
Clusters of rounded buds on rather weak necks open to fully double, ragged, camellia-shaped blooms of lilac-pink, sometimes flecked deeper, with an occasional whitish streak in some petals. This description perhaps sounds

'Cécile Brünner' Climbing

off-putting but, in fact, the overall effect is quite delightful. Foliage semi-glossy, mid-green and plentiful. Growth vigorous with many thinnish, upright shoots, making a dense plant.

(C) ☉ (H) (Gh) ● (AL)
5' × 3'   150 × 90 cm

'Cécile Brünner', 'The Sweetheart Rose', 'Mignon', 'Maltese Rose'

Pernet-Ducher FRANCE 1881
A Polyantha rose × 'Mme de Tartas'
Without doubt, one of the most charming of roses, sometimes temperamental, but capable of giving a lifetime of pleasure. Colour and shape of flowers already discussed under 'Bloomfield Abundance'. Although the plant is short, spindly and rather lacking in foliage, this is fairly typical of the Chinas and should not put you off this superb little rose. Flowers faintly but distinctively scented.

(C) (Gh) ☉ (MF) (AW)
4' × 2'   120 × 60 cm

'Cécile Brünner' Climbing

Hosp USA 1904
'Cécile Brünner' sport
Contradicts its parent by growing into a very vigorous climber indeed. Well endowed with dark green foliage and tolerant of most soils. Flowers, identical to those of the bush form, freely produced but sometimes hidden by dense foliage. Ideal for growing into trees or over unsightly buildings.

(S) (P) (B) (N) (T) (Gh)
● (MF) (AL)
25' × 20'   7.5 × 6 m

'Comtesse du Cayla'

'Cécile Brünner' White

Fauque FRANCE 1909
'Cécile Brünner' sport
White with a hint of yellow and
peach. Quite rare nowadays. In all
other respects the same as its
parent.
(C) (Gh) (B) ☉ (MF)
(AL) 4′ × 2′ 120 × 60 cm

'Comtesse du Cayla'

Guillot FRANCE 1902
A most useful, brightly coloured
variety. Almost single flowers of
orange and pink with red highlights. Angular growth and
vigorous, its lack of foliage amply
compensated by its free-flowering
habit. One of the most highly
scented China roses.
(C) (Gh) (P) ☉ (VF) (AL)
3′ × 3′ 90 × 90 cm

'Cramoisi Supérieur'

Coquereau FRANCE 1832
An outstanding China rose forming a compact, tidy bush. The
flowers, which are produced in
large clusters, are semi-double
and cupped, especially when in
bud. Their colour is clear,
unfading red with paler centres
and with the odd petal sometimes
faintly streaked with white. Has
little or no perfume.
(C) (P) (B) ☉ (AL)
3′ × 2′ 90 × 60 cm

'Gloire des Rosomanes'

'Cramoisi Supérieur' Climbing

Couturier FRANCE 1885
'Cramoisi Supérieur' sport
This sport from the bush from
makes an extremely good, healthy
climber and is well worth a prominent position since few red
climbers retain their colour so
well, even in hot sun.
(S) (P) ☉ (AL)
12′ × 8′ 3.5 × 2.5 m

'Duke of York'

1894
The double flowers are variably
mixed rosy-pink and white and
produced freely on a bushy,
branching shrub, with dark shiny
foliage.
(C) (Gh) ☉ (SF) (AL)
3′ × 2′ 90 × 60 cm

'Fabvier'

Laffay FRANCE 1832
A very showy rose, tidy in habit
and ideal for massed bedding
where an older variety is needed.
Bright crimson flowers, semi-
double, and produced in large
clusters. Foliage is very dark,
glossy and tinted purple.
(C) (P) (B) ☉ (AW)
3′ × 2′ 90 × 60 cm

'Cramoisi Supérieur'

'Fabvier'

'Fellemberg', 'La Belle Marseillaise'

Fellemberg GERMANY 1857
Cupped, fully double, cerise to

'Fellemberg'

crimson flowers, borne in trusses on a vigorous plant. Attractive, cascading habit if grown free of support. Makes a useful pillar rose. Foliage mid-green and generously produced. Stems more thorny than most other Chinas. Some authorities list it as a Noisette.

(C) (P) (AW)
7′ × 4′   2 × 1.2 m

'Gloire des Rosomanes', 'Ragged Robin', 'Red Robin'

Vibert FRANCE 1825
A vigorous hybrid China, semi-double flowers of bright crimson-cerise, very floriferous. Once used extensively as an understock, especially in the USA. Was important in the early breeding of the Bourbons.

(C) (P) (N) ☉ ● (SF)
(AL)   4′ × 4′   1.2 × 1.2 m

'Grüss an Teplitz' [Hybrid China]

Geschwind HUNGARY 1897
('Sir Joseph Paxton' × 'Fellemberg') × ('Papa Gontier' × 'Gloire de Rosomanes')
Rather difficult to classify but has enough China characteristics to

'La Vésuve'

'Louis XIV'

be placed here. Shapely, crimson flowers deepening with age, borne in loose clusters but sometimes individually. Good light green foliage but rather inclined to mildew if not in good soil. Sometimes used successfully as a small climber. Makes a good hedge. Sometimes listed as a Bourbon.

(C) (H) (SF) (AL) M❀
6′ × 4′   1.8 × 1.2 m

'Hermosa', 'Armosa', 'Mélanie Lemaire', 'Mme Neumann'

Marcheseau FRANCE 1840
Definitely a good rose for the front of a border or for the smaller garden, where it is best grown in groups of three. Full, globular buds opening to cup-shaped flowers of delicate bright mid-pink. Leaves greyish-green, rather small but numerous.

(C) ● ☉ (SF) (AL)
3′ × 2′   90 × 60 cm

'Le Vésuve'

Laffay FRANCE 1825
Very free-flowering, this rose has shapely, pointed buds which open to loosely formed, sometimes quartered flowers of silvery-pink with carmine highlights. Needs mollycoddling to give of its best. Good under glass.

(C) ☼ (Gh) ☉ (SF) (AL)
3′ × 3′   90 × 90 cm

'L'Ouche' [Hybrid China]

Buatois FRANCE 1901
Large, full, pointed buds open to fully double, cupped blooms of flesh pink lightly flecked with buff-yellow. Scented. Not entirely typical of a China, being rather upright in growth with fairly dark, thick foliage.

(C) (MF) (AL)
4′ × 3′   120 × 90 cm

'Louis Philippe'

Guérin FRANCE 1834
(Another rose of this name was introduced by Hardy (France) in 1824)
Deep crimson to purple with some petals white at the margins, as though the dye has been removed. Flowers loosely double, retaining their cupped shape throughout. An interesting rose, which prefers good soil. Foliage moderately sparse, growth angular and twiggy.

(C) ☼ (Gh) ☉ (SF) (AL)
2′ × 2′   60 × 60 cm

'Louis XIV'

Guillot Fils FRANCE 1859
Well scented, rich deep crimson, semi-double to double flowers displaying golden stamens when fully open, and produced on a rather angular plant amid glossy but somewhat sparse foliage. Relatively thornless.

(C) ☼ (Gh) ☉ (AL)
2′ × 2′   60 × 60 cm

'Mme Laurette Messimy'

Guillot FRANCE 1887
'Rival de Paestum' × 'Mme Falcot'
One of the best hybrid Chinas. A healthy rose with multitudes of semi-double flowers of bright pink bordering on salmon, each

petal suffused yellow at its base. The shrub, fairly tall for a China, is bushy but upright in growth with ample glossy leaves of grey-ish-green. Good for bedding.

(C) (Gh) (B) ☉ ● (SF)
(AL)   2′ × 2′   60 × 60 cm

'Minima', R. chinensis minima, 'Miss Lawrance's Rose', 'Fairy Rose'

CHINA 1815
Not so important as a garden rose as for its role in the lineage of modern miniature roses. Single flowers, soft creamy-pink with rather pointed, well-spaced petals, tips slightly deeper coloured. Dwarf spreading habit with ample small leaves and few thorns.

(C) ☼ (Gh) ☉ (AL)
1′ × 2′   30 × 60 cm

'Mutabilis', 'Tipo Ideale', R. turkistanica

CHINA 1932
Although thought by some to be a species, this rose is probably an old Chinese garden hybrid with characteristically mysterious origins. An interesting and useful garden shrub which, I am convinced, has a well developed sense of humour. Capable of reaching a height of 6′ (1.8 m) but more likely to stay relatively dwarf, continuously producing single flowers of honey-yellow, orange and red. Sometimes when fully open, the petal formation is rather like a butterfly. Extremely healthy and very much older than the given date.

(C) (P) (H) (CL) ☉ (N)
● (SF) (AL)
3′ × 2′   90 × 60 cm

**'Old Blush',
'Parson's Pink',
'Monthly Rose',
'Pallida',
'Common Monthly'**

Parson CHINA 1789
Introduced to Europe 1789
An important rose. This is one of
the most garden-worthy of the
old Chinas, silvery-pink with a
deeper flush. Highly scented. The
bush is practically thornless,
upright in stature and, if grown as
a small climber, will attain 6'–8'
(1.8–2.5 m) in height. Has probably been cultivated in China for
many centuries. I have seen a
climbing form listed in some
catalogues but have never seen
it myself.
(C) (P) (N) (CL) ● ○ (VF)
(AL) 6' × 4' 1.8 × 1.2 m

'Papa Hémeray'

Hémeray-Aubert FRANCE 1912
A very good China rose. Clusters
of small bright pink to rosy-red
flowers, single, with a pronounced
white central eye. Growth bushy
but upright, foliage dark green.
Stems have few thorns.
(C) (P) ○ ☼ (AL)
2' × 2' 60 × 60 cm

'Papillon'

Probably FRANCE 1900
A vigorous, angular shrub. This
rose is well named. The roughly
triangular petals which form the
semi-double flowers often stand
up charmingly like butterfly
wings. Colour predominantly
shrimp-pink with copper and
yellow reflections from a deeper
base. Foliage deep green and
coppery.
(C) ☼ (Gh) ○ (SF) (AL)
4' × 3' 120 × 90 cm

**'Perle d'Or',
'Yellow Cécile Brünner'**

Dubreuil FRANCE 1884
R. multiflora seedling × 'Mme
Falcot'
Clusters of spaced, small, exquisitely shaped, creamy-buff yellow
flowers with hints of pink.
Slightly perfumed. Ample rich
dark green foliage with twiggy,
almost thornless stems. Quite
vigorous and dense in growth.
Can be temperamental. In good
situations will attain a height of
over 6' (1.8 m) but normally only
4' (1.2 m). Remarkably similar to
'Cécile Brünner' in many respects,
save in colour, casting doubt on
its recorded parentage.

'Papillon'

'Mutabilis'

(C) (Gh) (SF) (AW)
4' × 2' 120 × 60 cm

'Pompon de Paris' Climber'

Bush form 1839
A fascinating climber, dainty in
growth but vigorous with small,
greyish-green foliage and twiggy
growth. Flowers small and button-like, produced profusely in
small clusters. An excellent plant
can be seen at the Royal Horticultural Society's Gardens, Wisley,
Surrey. Also good when grown as
prostrate shrub rose.
(S) (G) (Gh) ○ (AL)
12' × 6' 3.5 × 1.8 m

**'Pompon de Paris' Dwarf
form**

1839
A fashionable mid-19th century
pot plant variety in Paris. I
acquired this from Mr Frank
Buckley of Lancaster. Said to be
synonymous with 'Rouletii' but I
find it fairly distinctive.
(C) ☼ (Gh) ○ (AL)
1' × 1' 30 × 30 cm

**'Pumila',
'Bengale Pompon'**

Colville UK c. 1806
Small, double, almost star-like

'Perle d'Or'

flowers usually borne singly on a
short, slightly spreading, miniature plant with long (for size of
plant) thin mid-green leaves.
(R) ☼ (Gh) ○ (R) (AL)
1' × 1' 30 × 30 cm

'Queen Mab'

W. Paul UK 1896
Fully double flowers; an interesting mixture of soft apricot and
pink with deeper shadings, paler
on the reverse with hints of
purple. Foliage dark green.
Growth bushy.
(C) ○ ☼ (AL)
4' × 3' 120 × 90 cm

'Rouletii' *see* Miniature and
Patio rose section.

'Saint Prist de Breuze'

Desprez FRANCE 1838
Globular flowers fully double and
muddled when open. Rich dark
red with centre petals paler and
sometimes discreetly streaked
white. Bush twiggy in growth,
upright with ample foliage, similar to 'Louis Philippe'.
(C) ○ (Gh) ☼ (AL)
4' × 3' 120 × 90 cm

**'Sanguinea',
'Miss Lowe's Rose'**

Probably CHINA Discovered in
1887
Seedling of 'Slater's Crimson'.
Single titian-red, colour deepening with age. Angular growth.
Interesting more for its historic
and genetic associations than for
its garden value.
(C) ☼ ○ (AL)
3' × 2' 90 × 60 cm

'Viridiflora'

'Slater's Crimson China', 'Semperflorens', 'Old Crimson China'

Discovered in CHINA
Introduced to UK by Slater 1792
A medium to short, branching
bush with darkish green foliage
and sparse, broad, flattish thorns.
Semi-double flowers of crimson
to red with the centre petals
sometimes slightly streaked with
white. Good as a small wall plant.
(C) ☼ ☉ (AL)
3′ × 3′   90 × 90 cm

'Sophie's Perpetual'

UK An old variety reintroduced
1960
Discovery by the late
Mr Humphrey Brooke
A superb shrub or small climber.
Globular flowers, pale blush-pink
heavily overlaid with deep pink
and cerise red. Ample healthy,
dark green foliage. Almost
thornless stems.
(C) (P) (VF) (AL)
8′ × 4′   2.5 × 1.2 m

'Tipo Ideale' *see* 'Mutabilis'

'Triomphe de Laffay'

Laffay FRANCE c. 1930
Double flowers of considerable
size for a China, off-white heavily
flushed pink. Growth medium
short. Foliage small, dark green.
(C) ☉ (Gh) ☼ (AL)
3′ × 3′   90 × 90 cm

'Viridiflora', 'The Green Rose', *R. viridiflora*

c. 1833
A strange and novel rose, very
easy to grow and quite without
any disease problems. Flowers
formed by a multitude of green
and brown bracts with no petals
in the accepted sense. These are
produced quite freely, making
this rose useful for the flower
arranger's collection, especially as
they change to purplish-brown
with age.
(C) (P) ☉ ● (AL)
3′ × 3′   90 × 90 cm

'Sophie's Perpetual'

Bourbons

The origin of the Bourbons is discussed in an earlier chapter but, briefly, they arose from a cross between *R. chinensis* or one of its hybrids and *R × damascena bifera* 'The Autumn Damask' on the Isle de Bourbon in 1817. They reigned supreme during the mid-nineteenth century. Making excellent shrubs and being relatively easy to grow in most climates, a Bourbon can usually be found to fulfil any role asked of it in the modern garden. Amongst their ranks are some of the most beautiful and well loved of the old 'Classics'.

CLASSIFICATION

BARB	Class 24
MR9	Class 3
WFRS	Class 21

R. × *borboniana*, 'Bourbon Rose'

FRANCE 1817
Thought to be 'Old Blush' × 'Quatre Saisons'
This, the first Bourbon, is either now extinct or synonymous with 'Rose Edward' no one can be sure. The flowers are said to be deep red, repeating in the autumn; the plant, vigorous.
(R)   4' × 3'   120 × 90 cm

'Adam Messerich'

P. Lambert GERMANY 1920
'Frau Oberhofgärtner Singer' × ('Louise Odier' seedling × 'Louis Philippe')
Semi-double, bright rosy-red flowers produced in clusters abundantly throughout the season. The shrub is upright and well foliated. Flowers fade to a soft but still pleasing pink in very hot weather and have a good scent.
(C)   (P)   ✂   (MF)   (AL)
5' × 4'   1.5 × 1.2 m

'Adam Messerich'

'Blairii No. 1'
see Climbing Bourbons

'Blairii No. 2'
see Climbing Bourbons

'Boule de Neige'

Lacharme FRANCE 1867
'Blanche Lafitte' × 'Sappho'
A fine shrub, upright in growth with dark green almost glossy foliage and few thorns. Flowers fully double, globular, sometimes tinged reddish-purple on the petal edges while in bud, but opening to pure white with a strong fragrance.
(R)   (H)   ☉   (VF)   (AL)
4' × 3'   120 × 90 cm

'Bourbon Queen', 'Queen of Bourbons', 'Reine des Iles Bourbon', 'Souvenir de la Princesse de Lamballe'

Mauget FRANCE 1834
A sturdy shrub with thick branches and copious foliage. Semi-double, rose-pink flowers large and cupped when fully open. Highly scented but, sadly, seldom repeats in the autumn. I recall finding a very old plant of this growing wild on the south-east side of the mound of Pembroke Castle where it was competing admirably with brambles and had been doing so for many years, proving a very strong constitution.
(S)   (P)   (H)   ●   (VF)   (AL)
6' × 4'   1.8 × 1.2 m

'Boule de Neige'

'Charles Lawson'

Lawson UK 1853
Not often seen today, probably because of its relatively short flowering season and rather ungainly habit. With support, however, this rose, soft pink with

'Bourbon Queen'

'Commandant Beaurepaire'

'Coupe d'Hébé'

deeper shadings, is a useful shrub.
(S) ● (CL) (MF) (AL)
6′ × 4′   1.8 × 1.2 m

'Commandant Beaurepaire'

Moreau-Robert FRANCE 1874
A strong, dense bush with plentiful, fresh green leaves. Large, double, crimson flowers streaked pink and purple and marbled white. An interesting rose worthy of a place in any shrubbery.
(R) (P) (H) ● (MF) (AL)
5′ × 5′   1.5 × 1.5 m

'Coquette des Blanches'

Lacharme FRANCE 1867
'Blanche Lafitte' × 'Sappho'
Fully double, fragrant flowers, at first cupped but opening flat, white brushed delicately with soft pink. Foliage mid-green, plentiful. Growth vigorous.
(R) (P) (H) ☉ (MF) ✂
(AL)   5′ × 4′   1.5 × 1.2 m

'Gipsy Boy'

'Coupe d'Hébé'

Laffay FRANCE 1840
Bourbon hybrid × China hybrid
Tall shrub bearing attractive, light green foliage, can be marred later in the season by mildew if precautions are not taken in time. Very free-flowering, especially in first flush. The globular, pale pink, fully double flowers have a good scent.
(R) (P) (CL) M✂ (AL)
7′ × 5′   2 × 1.5 m

'Eugène E. Marlitt', 'Mme. Eugène Marlitt'

Geschwind HUNGARY 1900
Fully double flowers of bright carmine splashed scarlet. Good mid-green foliage. Growth vigorous with few thorns of consequence. A bright sensation in its heyday, now very rare.
(R) (P) (H) ☉ (MF) (AL)
4′ × 3′   120 × 90 cm

'Fulgens', 'Malton'

Guérin FRANCE 1830
This rose is thought to have been one parent in the early development of the Hybrid Perpetuals. Bright cerise-crimson, semi-double flowers. Although the plant is somewhat sprawly, it nevertheless makes a useful shrub.
(R) (MF) (AL)
5′ × 4′   1.5 × 1.2 m

'Gipsy Boy', 'Zigeunerknabe'

P.Lambert GERMANY 1909
'Russelliana' seedling
Where space permits this rose is probably best grown as a shrub but it can also be happy as a small climber. Coarse, rather Centifolia-like foliage should not put you off this lovely rose. Double flowers of deep crimson to almost purple-black with primrose yellow anthers.
(S) (P) ● (CL) (VF) (AW)
6′ × 4′   1.8 × 1.2 m

'Giuletta'

Laurentius FRANCE 1859
Delightful, fully double, quartered, initially cupped then flattish flowers of soft blush-pink

with a lovely fragrance. Greyish-green foliage on a bushy, upright growing plant.
(R) (P) ⊙ M⚷ (VF) (AL)
3′ × 3′ 90 × 90 cm

'Great Western'

Laffay FRANCE 1838
Once flowering, this rose has large, full, quartered flowers of maroon-purple. Its foliage is dark green and its shoots well endowed with thorns.
(S) (P) ● (VF) (AL)
5′ × 4′ 1.5 × 1.2 m

'Gros Choux d'Hollande'

Obviously an old variety with full, cupped, very double, soft pink blooms. Very fragrant and very vigorous.
(R) (P) (CL) (VF) (AL)
7′ × 5′ 2 × 1.5 m

'Honorine de Brabant'

One of the most acceptable striped roses. Delicate shades of lilac with purple markings on a large, cupped flower, which is sometimes hidden by large, lush foliage. Vigorous, with few thorns. I have also seen this rose grown successfully as a climber.
(C) (P) ● (CL) (VF) (AL)
6′ × 5′ 1.8 × 1.5 m

'Kronprinzessin Viktoria'

'Kathleen Harrop'
see Climbing Bourbons

'Kronprinzessin Viktoria'

1888
'Souvenir de la Malmaison' sport
Has the beautiful petal formation of its parent, together with its superb perfume and grace. Creamy-white with lemon shadings. Very free-flowering and ideal for small gardens, but dislikes wet weather.
(C) ⊙ (WW) ☼ M⚷
(MF) (AL)
4′ × 3′ 120 × 90 cm

'La Reine Victoria'

Schwartz FRANCE 1872
A slender, erect bush bearing soft green leaves and beautiful, rich lilac-pink, cupped blooms with silky textured petals. The overall picture is sometimes spoilt by a proneness to black spot and a dis-like of all but the best soils.
(C) ⊙ ✂ BS⚷ (VF) (AL)
4′ × 3′ 120 × 90 cm

'Lewison Gower', 'Malmaison Rouge'

Béluze FRANCE 1846
'Souvenir de la Malmaison' sport
A bright pink to red variety with all the virtues and faults of its parent, though with its harder colouring it loses some of Malmaison's sophistication. One of Mr Arthur Wyatt's rediscoveries.
Note: Mr Wyatt did much to rekindle interest in the old roses in the 1950s and 1960s and led a successful search for many old varieties that were then in danger of extinction.
(C) ⊙ (WW) ☼ M⚷
(VF) (AL)
4′ × 3′ 120 × 90 cm

'La Reine Victoria'

'Louise Odier'

Margottin FRANCE 1851
Very double, almost camellia-like, bright rose-pink flowers on a vigorous bush. Flowers are produced in dense clusters which sometimes weigh down the slender branches to give an arching effect. Superbly perfumed.
(C) (H) ● ✂ (MF) (AL)
5′ × 4′ 1.5 × 1.2 m

'Mme Dubost'

Pernet Père FRANCE 1890
Shapely, fully double flowers of
soft pink with deeper shading in
the centres. Fragrant. Foliage crisp
mid-green. Growth bushy.
(R) ⊙ (MF) (AL)
4' × 3'   120 × 90 cm

'Mme Ernst Calvat'

Schwartz FRANCE 1888
'Mme Isaac Pereire' sport
Large, shaggy, pale rose-pink
blooms with a strong perfume.
Slightly less vigorous than its
famous parent, otherwise the
same in all but colour.
(C) (P) ● (VF) (AL)
5' × 4'   1.5 × 1.2 m

'Mme Isaac Pereire'

Garçon FRANCE 1881
Huge, shaggy, purplish deep-pink
blooms exuding a heady perfume
and carried on a large, strong
bush. Has its critics, but few other
Bourbons can rival its bold
character. Early blooms can sometimes suffer from malformation
but this should not put you off.
Equally good as a small climber.
(C) (P) (CL) ● (VF) (AL)
7' × 5'   2 × 1.5 m

'Mme Lauriol de Barny'

Trouillard FRANCE 1868

'Louise Odier'

The flat, quartered, fully-double
blooms of deep silver-pink are
blessed with an unusual but
pleasant, fruity perfume. The
plant is vigorous and healthy. A
very worthwhile variety, especially good if 'pegged down' in the
old style of training.
(R) (P) ● (VF) (AL)
5' × 4'   1.5 × 1.2 m

'Mme Pierre Oger'

Verdier FRANCE 1878
'La Reine Victoria' sport
Very pale silvery-pink, translucent, cupped flowers with the
form of small water-lilies, sweetly
scented. The flowers are borne on
a bush of medium vigour, sadly
marred by the same disease problems as its parent, 'La Reine
Victoria', but what are a few

'Mme Isaac Pereire'

'black spots' between friends?
(C) ⊙ ✄ BS⚘ (VF) (AL)
4' × 4'   1.2 × 1.2 m

'Malton' *see* 'Fulgens'

'Martha'
see Climbing Bourbons

'Michel Bonnet', 'Catherine Guillot'

Guillot FRANCE 1861
'Louise Odier' × unknown
Large, fully double, quartered,
deep cerise-crimson flowers. Well
scented. Foliage purplish when
young, maturing to deep mid-
green. Growth vigorous and arching. Also makes a useful small
climber.
(R) ⊙ (VF) (CL) (AL)
7' × 5'   2 × 1.5 m

'Mrs Paul'

W. Paul UK 1891
Large, soft pale pink to white,
fully double though somewhat
blowsy flowers borne amid
plentiful if rather coarse foliage.
Vigorous.
(R) (VF) (AL)
5' × 3'   150 × 90 cm

'Parkzierde'

P. Lambert GERMANY 1909
Very floriferous for a short period
in early summer. Scarlet-crimson
flowers on long stems, useful for
cutting. Foliage dark green.
(S) ● (P) (S) (VF) (AL)
5' × 4'   1.5 × 1.2 m

'Paul Verdier'

Verdier FRANCE 1866
A very good rose which deserves
more attention, useful as shrub or
climber. Fully double, slightly
frilly flowers of deep rose pink,
opening flat from globular bud,
produced along the length of
arching, rather thorny canes amid
dark green foliage.
(R) (P) (VF) (AL)
5' × 4'   1.5 × 1.2 m

'Prince Charles'

Pre-1918
A medium-tall if somewhat lax

'Mme Lauriol de Barny'

'Parkzierde'

'Prince Charles'

'Queen of Bedders'

Noble UK 1871
Seedling from 'Sir Joseph Paxton'
A compact-growing Bourbon. Out
of date now for bedding but very
useful as a shorter growing variety
for the front of shrubberies,
herbaceous borders or for growing in pots. Shapely, double
flowers of deep carmine softening
to deep pink with age.
(R) ☉ (B) (VF) (AL)
3′ × 2′   90 × 60 cm

'Queen of Bourbons' *see* 'Bourbon Queen'

'Reverend H. d'Ombrain'

Not well known, this rose has
flattish, double flowers of clear
rose pink with a quiet, refined
perfume. Matt green foliage
rather prone to mildew but the
bush is of quite tidy habit.
(R) (VF) M & (AL)
5′ × 4′   1.5 × 1.2 m

'Rivers George IV', 'George IV'

Rivers UK 1820
R. × *damascena* × a China Rose
Loose, double cupped flowers of
deep red to maroon-crimson.
Foliage and growth rather China-
like. Not the most distinguished
Bourbon but one of the very first
introductions.
(S) ☉ (VF) (AL)
4′ × 4′   1.2 × 1.2 m

'Robusta'

Soupert and Notting
LUXEMBOURG 1877
Well scented flowers opening
from tight, rounded buds to
shapely rosettes, flat and quartered. Rich crimson dusted purple

borne in small, tightly packed
clusters on long, thin, arching
branches. Foliage plentiful.
Growth upright openly bushy.
Not to be confused with the
modern Rugosa of this name.
(R) ☉ (VF) (AL)
6′ × 5′   1.8 × 1.5 m

'Rose Edouard', 'Rose Edward'

Bréon, ILE DE RÉUNION c. 1818
'Old Blush' × 'Quatre Saisons'?
Two roses of this name existed in
the early days of the Bourbons.
Which one I have I do not know.
Richly perfumed, it forms a lax

'Queen of Bedders'

'Robusta'

bush bearing heavily veined
crimson to maroon flowers of
considerable size when fully open,
tending to fade slightly but
enhanced by golden yellow
anthers. The bush has large, thick

leaves with a heavy texture. Its
origin is a mystery and the exact
date unknown to me.
(S) (H) (P) ● (VF) (AL)
5′ × 4′   1.5 × 1.2 m

bush with fragrant reddish scarlet double flowers. Trevor Griffiths of New Zealand sent me the budwood, having received if from his friend, the late Nancy Steen, who, in turn, had obtained it from India.

(R) (P) ● M❀ (VF) (AL)
4′ × 4′   1.2 × 1.2 m

'Sir Joseph Paxton'

Laffay FRANCE 1852
Shapely, fully double flowers of deep carmine to red tinted violet. Fragrant. Foliage greyish-green on a moderately vigorous shrub.

(R) ☉ (MF) M❀ (AL)
4′ × 3′   120 × 90 cm

'Souvenir de la Malmaison', 'Queen of Beauty and Fragrance'

Beluze FRANCE 1843
'Mme Desprez' × a Tea Rose
This rose, at its best, is the most beautiful of all Bourbons, but at its worst can be horrid. It hates wet weather and in such conditions seldom opens properly without help. Flowers blush-white with face-powder-pink shadings, each bloom beautifully proportioned and opening to a flat, quartered shape. The finest example I ever knew was at Lime Kiln, Claydon, Suffolk, the home of the late Mr Humphrey Brooke, who did so much to promote 'old roses'. It was a plant of huge proportions, an unforgettable sight in full flush. This plant, however, was not typical and no others I know have reached this size. Sadly, Lime Kiln is no longer open to the public.

(C) ☉ (WW) M❀ (VF)
(AL) 6′ × 6′   1.8 × 1.8 m

'Souvenir de la Malmaison' Climbing Form
see Climbing Bourbons

'Souvenir de Mme Auguste Charles'

Moreau-Robert FRANCE 1866
Fully double, slightly fimbriated, large blooms opening flat and quartered, flesh pink to soft rosy-pink, fragrant. Foliage mid-greyish-green, almost rugose. Growth wide but bushy.

(R) ☉ (MF) (AL)
4′ × 4′   1.2 × 1.2 m

'Souvenir de St Anne's'

Hilling UK 1950
Sport of 'Souvenir de la Malmaison'
A semi-double form of 'Souvenir de la Malmaison'. Its fewer petals enable it to open better in wet weather. Like its parent, very free-flowering and although not quite as refined, it is none the less attractive. Deliciously scented.

(C) ☉ (H) (VF) (AL)
5′ × 4′   1.5 × 1.2 m

'Souvenir de St Anne's'   'Vivid'

'Variegata di Bologna'

Bonfiglioli ITALY 1909
Double, cupped flowers with pronounced, irregular stripes of purple on a creamy-white background, reminding me of the semolina and blackcurrant jam of school dinner days. A tall, rather

lax bush with somewhat sparse and rather coarse foliage.

(R) (P) M❀ (VF) (AL)
6′ × 5′   1.8 × 1.5 m

'Vivid'

Paul UK 1853
A very brightly coloured rose of vivid magenta-pink to red. Vigorous, upright and rather prickly. Occasionally repeating.

(R) (P) (VF) (AL)
5′ × 4′   1.5 × 1.2 m

'Zéphirine Drouhin'
see Climbing Bourbons

'Zigeunerknabe'
see 'Gipsy Boy'

'Souvenir de la Malmaison'

'Kathleen Harrop'

Climbing Bourbons

FORMS AND HYBRIDS

CLASSIFICATION

BARB	Class 24
MR9	Class 3
WFRS	Class 21

'Blairii No. 1'

Blair UK 1845
Similar in most respects to the better known and more widely grown 'Blairii No. 2' but more clearly and consistently soft pink. Has a few more petals and is quite beautiful at its best, but rather shy.
(R) M☀ (VF) (AL)
12′ × 6′   3.5 × 1.8 m

'Blairii No. 2'

Blair UK 1845
This rose can be excused a slight proneness to mildew late in the season for it is very beautiful. Large, flattish blooms pale pink with deeper shadings towards centre. Growth and foliage is somewhat coarse but this is not a problem. The overall effect of an established climber in full flush is staggering. Particularly good when grown on a tripod or similar supporting structure.
(R) (VF) M☀ (AL)
12′ × 6′   3.5 × 1.8 m

'Kathleen Harrop'

Dickson UK 1919
'Zéphirine Drouhin' sport
Oblivious to weather, this rose flowers on from mid-June well into winter. Flowers semi-double, shell-pink and fragrant. Can be grown in children's play areas or by the front door since, like its parent 'Zéphirine Drouhin', it is completely thornless.
(C) (N) (P) ● (VF) (AL)
10′ × 6′   3 × 1.8 m

'Martha'

Zeiner FRANCE 1912
'Zéphirine Drouhin' sport
Thornless and very long-flowering. The colour is a slightly paler pink than 'Zéphirine', with a creamy touch to the centre of each flower.
(C) (N) (P) ● (VF) (AL)
9′ × 6′   2.8 × 1.8 m

'Souvenir de la Malmaison' Climbing form

Bush form Beluze 1843
This form Bennett UK 1893
Unlike the bush form, this rose repeats only in good years, but flowers generously in late June, so is well worth growing where space permits. Best on a south wall where it is less likely to encounter too much rain, which, like its parent, it hates.
(R) (WW) M☀ (VF) (AL)
12′ × 8′   3.5 × 2.5 m

'Blairii No. 2'

'Blairii No. 1'

'Zéphirine Drouhin'

'Zéphirine Drouhin'

Bizot FRANCE 1868
Lovely though the flowers are, this legendary rose would hardly have gained such popularity had it not been for its long flowering season and its thornless shoots. Flowers semi-double, cerise-pink and distinctly fragrant. Young shoots and leaves are bronzy-red in the first stages of growth, changing to dull greyish-green when mature. In spite of my earlier comments, a fine rose.
(C) (N) (P) ● (VF) (AL)
10′ × 6′   3 × 1.8 m

'Alister Stella Gray'

Noisettes

The development and popularity of the Noisettes ran roughly parallel to that of the Bourbons and Teas. Most significantly, they added a new range of colours, especially yellow, to the rather dull climbing and rambler roses of those early days. Many are still with us, and deservedly so, adding much charm to the modern garden.

It is worth remembering that the Noisettes have a certain reputation for tenderness. My experience of growing them in chilly Norfolk leads me to believe that they can stand more frost than they are ever given credit for. In the winters of 1981 and 1987 – our coldest recently – one or two were badly frosted, but most came through with no more than a little damage, from which they quickly recovered. Apart from this and a slight propensity to mildew these most beautiful of roses are quite easy to grow.

CLASSIFICATION

BARB	Class 3
MR9	Class 50
WFRS	Class 36

'Aimée Vibert', 'Bouquet de la Mariée, 'Nivea'

Vibert FRANCE 1828
'Champney's Pink Cluster' × R. sempervirens hybrid
Small clusters of scented, double, pure white flowers on a vigorous, almost thornless plant with lush healthy, light green leaves. As with several Noisettes, this rose comes into flower a week or two later than, say, the Bourbon climbers, and repeats its flowers in a good season.
(R) (P) ● (VF) (AL)
12′ × 10′   3.5 × 3 m

'Alister Stella Gray', 'Golden Rambler'

A. H. Gray UK 1894
Clusters of double, shapely flowers in cascading clusters. Yellow with 'eggy' centres paling to cream and, eventually, white at the edges. Highly perfumed – of tea, it is said. Shrub vigorous, producing long, slightly spindly branches ideal for arches and trellises. Fairly free of thorns with ample, darkish green foliage. Repeats intermittently.
(R) ☼ (T) ● (MF) (AL)
15′ × 10′   4.5 × 3 m

'Aimée Vibert'

'Blush Noisette'

'Crépuscule'

'Blanc Pur'

Mauget FRANCE 1827
A vigorous yet shorter growing
Noisette, at least with me.
Flowers full and large, opened
quartered, produced sometimes
singly, sometimes in small clusters.
Pure white and scented. Foliage
large and mid- to dark green.
More thorny than most of its
group. Probably closer to a Tea
than a Noisette.
(R) ☉ ☼ (CL) (MF) (AL)
8' × 6'   2.5 × 1.8 m

'Blush Noisette'

Noisette USA 1825
Seedling from 'Champneys Pink
Cluster'
An attractive rose of gentle
growth producing large clusters of
semi-double flowers of blush-
lilac-pink with pronounced
stamens. Can, given time, make a
useful short climber or pillar rose
but also makes a good, free-standing shrub. Few thorns and dark
green foliage. One of the first
Noisettes introduced.
(C) (P) (N) ● (MF) (AL)
7' × 4'   2 × 1.2 m

'Bouquet d'Or'

Ducher FRANCE 1872
'Gloire de Dijon' × unknown
seedling
A vigorous rose with fully double,
quartered or muddled, coppery
salmon and yellow flowers,
slightly scented. Growth vigorous,
foliage dark green and semi-
glossy.
(R) ☼ (Gh) (AL)
10' × 6'   3 × 1.8 m

'Céline Forestier'

Trouillard FRANCE 1842
Large flowers opening attractively
to flat blooms with muddled
centre petals, primrose yellow
with deeper shadings, sometimes
tinged pink, scented. Makes an
excellent free-flowering small
climber. Seldom without a flower
throughout the summer. Growth
vigorous, not in any way coarse,
with profuse, light green, healthy
foliage.
(C) (P) (Gh) ☉ (MF) (AL)
8' × 4'   2.5 × 1.2 m

'Champneys' Pink Cluster'

Champneys USA 1802
R. chinensis × R. moschata
If not the first, then one of the
first Noisettes. Long clusters of
semi-double to double flowers of
blush-pink, flushed deep pink,
highly scented. Growth vigorous,
extremely healthy with mid-to-
dark green foliage.
(S) (P) (T) (MF) (AL)
15' × 8'   4.5 × 2.5 m

'Claire Jacquier'

Bernaix FRANCE 1888
Possibly R. multiflora × a Tea
Rose
A very useful rose with considerable prowess as a climber. Flowers
shapely, double, not large, rich
egg yolk yellow, paling to cream
with age and produced in large
clusters, pleasingly perfumed.
Foliage rich, lightish green.
Repeats in most seasons.
(R) (N) (T) ● (MF) (AL)
15' × 8'   4.5 × 2.5 m

'Cloth of Gold', 'Chromatella'

Coquereau FRANCE 1843
'Lamarque' seedling
Fully double flowers, of soft
sulphur-yellow with deeper
centres, fragrant, born on
long stems. Copious light green
foliage. Quite vigorous, needs
molly-coddling in cold districts.
Excellent under glass.
(R) ☼ (Gh) ☉ (VF) (AL)
12' × 8'   3.5 × 2.5 m

'Crépuscule'

Dubreuil FRANCE 1904
Double if rather muddled flowers
of rich apricot. An excellent
variety but somewhat tender.
Foliage light green with darker
shoots with few thorns.
(R) ☼ (Gh) (MF) (AL)
12' × 5'   3.5 × 1.5 m

'Deschamps'

Deschamps FRANCE 1877
Cupped flowers, of bright cerise
to cherry red, opening full almost
blowsy. Very free-flowering. Foli-

'Bouquet d'Or'

age large and darkish mid-green. Vigorous with few thorns.
(R) (P) (Gh) ● (MF) (AL)
15' × 10' 4.5 × 3 m

'Desprez à Fleurs Jaunes', 'Jaune Desprez'

Desprez FRANCE 1835
'Blush Noisette' × 'Park's Yellow China'
A beautiful, double, quartered rose in the style of the Tea Rose 'Gloire de Dijon'. Flowers are a mixture of yellow, orange and buff, with a fruity scent, borne in clusters, often at the end of long shoots. Growth is vigorous and the foliage light green. A particular feature of this variety is a dark mottling on the stems, which is particularly prominent in winter and should not cause any concern.
(R) (P) (Gh) (T) ● (MF)
(AL) 20' × 10' 6 × 3 m

'Duchesse d'Auerstädt'

A. Bernaix FRANCE 1888
'Rêve d'Or' sport
A little known variety which deserves more attention. The scented flowers are fully double, opening quartered but rather muddled, with an intense colouring of buff, apricot and gold.

'Duchesse d'Auerstädt'

Growth is vigorous and foliage dark.
(R) (Gh) ☼ (VF) (AL)
10' × 8' 3 × 2.5 m

'L'Abundance'

Moreau-Robert FRANCE 1887
A small climber of distinction, although little known. Flowers are flesh-pink and double in well-spaced clusters. Growth moderately vigorous and foliage mid-green. Repeats only in the best seasons.
(S) (P) (MF) (AL)
10' × 6' 3 × 1.8 m

'Lady Emily Peel'

Lacharme FRANCE 1862
'Blanche Lafitte' × 'Sappho'
White, double flowers with blush to carmine highlights. Fragrant. Tall and vigorous with ample mid-green foliage. Needs that little extra care to give of its best. Better in warmer climates than in this part of the world.
(R) ☼ (T) (Gh) (MF)
(AL) 15' × 10' 4.5 × 3 m

'Lamarque'

Maréchal FRANCE 1830
'Blush Noisette' × 'Park's Yellow China'
This very beautiful rose will thrive if given a warm, sheltered position but needs cold greenhouse protection in colder areas. Fragrant, pure white blooms borne on long stems amid copious, mid to light green foliage under glass, darker outdoors. Stems have few thorns.
(R) (Gh) ☼ ✂ (VF) (AL)
15' × 8' 4.5 × 2.5 m

'Desprez à Fleurs Jaunes'

'Leys Perpetual', 'Lais'

Damaizin FRANCE 1867
This may well be the climbing form of an original bush Tea rose for it behaves in every way as one would expect of a climbing sport. It is a rose that gives me much pleasure. Fully double, shapely flowers open flat and quartered in a muddled sort of way. Lemon-yellow and deliciously fragrant. Good foliage of darkish-green.
(R) ☼ ⊙ (Gh) (VF) (AL)
12' × 8' 3.5 × 2.5 m

'Louise d'Arzens'

Lacharme FRANCE 1860
Pinkish buds open to fully double flowers of creamy-white. Foliage mid-green and glossy. Growth moderately vigorous. Rare and

unusual but well worth growing especially in warmer climates although it seems to be quite hardy.
(R) ⊙ ☼ (Gh) (SF) (AL)
10' × 6' 3 × 1.8 m

'Mme Alfred Carrière'

J. Schwartz FRANCE 1879
A superior rose. The lovely, rather loosely formed flowers are large and white with occasional hints of soft pink, highly scented. Growth is vigorous with sparse thorns. Leaves large, plentiful and light green. This rose flowers almost continuously throughout the season and is quite tolerant of a north wall situation.
(C) (Gh) (P) ● (T) ✂
(MF) (AL) 15' × 10' 4.5 × 3 m

'Mme Driout'

Thiriat FRANCE 1902
Sport of 'Reine Marie Henriette'
Shapely buds opening flat and
quartered. Deep reddish-pink
with flecks of white. Foliage quite
large, dark green. Growth moderately vigorous. Needs extra attention to behave at its best.
(R) ☼ ☉ (MF) ✂ (AL)
10' × 8' 3 × 2.5 m

'Manettii'

R. noisettiana manetti

Botanic Gardens, Milan ITALY
1837
Not an important garden rose.
Once used extensively as a
rootstock, especially in the USA.
A dense shrub with pale pink
semi-double flowers. Wood
reddish when young, streaked or
mottled when older. Well
endowed with dark thorns.
(S) (P) (H) (W) ● ☉
(SF) (AL) 6' × 4' 1.8 × 1.2 m

'Maréchal Niel'

Pradel FRANCE 1864
Seedling from 'Cloth of Gold'
Huge, golden-yellow, double
flowers emerging from shapely,
pointed buds. Very fragrant.
Needs a warm, sheltered position
or greenhouse to survive in colder
climates. Growth vigorous with
large, dark, coppery-green foliage.
(R) ☼ (Gh) ✂ ☉ (VF)
(AL) 15' × 8' 4.5 × 2.5 m

'Reine Olga de Wurtemberg'

G. Nabonnand FRANCE 1881
Rich red, fully double blooms
of medium size, initially high-
centred, opening flat. Fragrant. A
vigorous climber with good mid-
to dark green foliage.
(R) (P) ☼ (T) (MF) (AL)
15' × 8' 4.5 × 2.5 m

'Rêve d'Or'

Ducher FRANCE 1869
'Mme Schultz' seedling
This is a very good rose. Shapely,
fully double blooms in the mould
of 'Gloire de Dijon'. Buff to
yellow with sometimes a hint of
pink. Fragrant. Growth is strong
and the foliage dark green. Rather
tender.
(R) ☼ (Gh) ☉ ✂ (VF)
(AL) 12' × 8' 3.5 × 2.5 m

'William Allen Richardson'

Ducher FRANCE 1878
'Rêve d'Or' sport
Medium-sized, fully double buff
to apricot flowers, very free-
flowering. This climber needs a
warm, sheltered spot to really
flourish. Stems are dark with dark
green, copper-tinted foliage.
(R) (Gh) ☉ ☼ ✂ (VF)
(AL) 15' × 8' 4.5 × 2.5 m

'Rêve d'Or'

The Teas

Teas were very popular garden roses in Europe during the latter
half of the 19th century. Sadly many have now become extinct, but
some of the best have survived and a few still have sufficient
stamina – with our help – to go on for a long time yet. Gardeners in
colder zones, concerned with overall effect, should avoid growing
these roses. However, they make excellent subjects under glass
and for growing in tubs and urns. They are best just lightly pruned,
reacting against hard pruning with a reduced yield of flowers. The
climbing forms are, unless absolutely necessary, best left
unpruned. In warmer climates they are undoubtedly excellent
garden subjects, and readers should bear in mind that the dimensions indicated in these descriptions are those for the UK, and they
could well attain double these sizes where winters are not as cold.

CLASSIFICATION	
BARB	Class 4
MR9	Class 56
WFRS	Class 31

'Adam', 'The President'

Adam UK 1833
A large, fully double rose of buff,
amber and apricot, with tints of
pink deep in the centre. The fully
open flowers are often quartered.
Said to be the first of the Tea
roses. Probably a vigorous bush
but better as a climber on a short
wall, where it can enjoy protection from the severest weather of
winter. Well foliated with large
dark green leaves.
(R) ☼ (Gh) ☉ (VF) (AL)
7' × 5' 2 × 1.5 m

'Anna Oliver'

Ducher FRANCE 1872
A mixture of flesh pink and deep
rose. Fragrant. Shapely, high-
centred blooms on a vigorous,
branching bush with good mid-
green foliage.

Note: A soft primrose-yellow
mystery Tea rose is sometimes
grown and sold erroneously as
this variety. I think it could be an
old variety called 'Léda'.
(C) ☼ (Gh) ☉ ✂ (MF)
(AL) 3' × 3' 90 × 90 cm

'Archiduc Joseph'

G. Nabonnand FRANCE 1872
Seedling from 'Mme Lombard'
One of the outstanding Tea roses.
Flowers opening flat, are made up
of many petals, the whole a pleasing mixture of pink, purple,
orange and russet with tints of
gold and yellow in the centre. The
foliage is dark, glossy and abundant. The stems have few thorns.
Apparently quite hardy. Can be
used both as a shrub and small
climber.
Note: In the USA the rose
described here and grown under
the name 'Archiduc Joseph' in the
UK is known and sold as 'Mons.
Tillier'.
(C) (P) (Gh) ☉ ☼ (MF)
(AL) 5' × 3' 150 × 90 cm

'Archiduc Joseph' (Mons. Tillier, USA)

'Adam'

'Baronne Henriette de Snoy'

'Baronne Henriette de Snoy'

A Bernaix FRANCE 1897
'Gloire de Dijon' × Mme
Lombard'
The scented flowers are flesh pink
with a deeper reverse, and open
double from fairly high-centred
buds. The bush is angular and the
leaves large and mid-green.
(C) ☼ (Gh) ☉ (VF) (AL)
4′ × 3′ 120 × 90 cm

'Belle Lyonnaise'

Levet FRANCE 1870
A climbing Tea rose which is not
often seen but worthy of any
warm, sheltered garden or cold
greenhouse. Not over-vigorous
but quite generous with its
flowers which are large, scented,
full, flat, quartered and soft
yellow fading to creamy-white
with age.
(R) ☼ (Gh) ☉ (VF) (AL)
10′ × 6′ 3 × 1.8 m

'Bon Silène'

Hardy FRANCE 1839
Fragrant, fully double, deep rosy-
red flowers produced in profusion
on a compact, vigorous plant.
Foliage mid-green and stems
moderately thorny.
(C) ☼ (Gh) ☉ (VF) (AL)
4′ × 3′ 120 × 90 cm

'Bon Silène'

'Catherine Mermet'

Guillot Fils FRANCE 1869
Shapely, high-centred buds opening to semi-double, lilac-pink
flowers, held on longish stems.
Well-foliated and bushy with
healthy, mid-green, coppery
tinged leaves. An excellent greenhouse variety but equally at home
in an open, sunny, warm position.
(C) ☼ (Gh) ☉ ✄ (MF)
(AL) 4′ × 3′ 120 × 90 cm

'Clementina Carbonieri'

Bonfiglioli ITALY 1913
An outstanding Tea rose. Fully
double flowers opening flat and
quartered, their colour is a grand
mixture of orange, pink and
salmon, all on a bright mustard-

yellow background. They are
freely produced and scented. Foliage dark green on an angular but
dense plant with an average number of thorns.
(C) ☼ (GH) ☉ (MF) (AL)
3′ × 2′ 90 × 60 cm

'Dean Hole'

A. Dickson UK 1904
Large by Tea rose standards. The
flowers are an interesting combination of silvery-pink, flushed
apricot and gold. Growth is vigorous and thorny with darkish
green foliage.
(S) ☼ (Gh) ☉ (VF) (AL)
3′ × 2′ 90 × 60 cm

'Devoniensis', 'Magnolia Rose'

Foster UK 1838
Very large flowers, creamy-white
with an occasional blush of pink.
A refined rose which needs plant-

'Catherine Mermet'

'Clementina Carbonieri'

ing in a warm, sheltered position
or under glass to be appreciated
fully. Ample, light to mid-green
foliage and few thorns. Foliage
darker outdoors.
(R) ☼ (Gh) ☉ (AL)
12′ × 7′ 3.5 × 2 m

'Dr Grill'

Bonnaire FRANCE 1886
'Ophirie' × 'Souvenir de Victor
Hugo'
A branching, angular plant which
would be better with more foliage. Flowers exquisite, pink
overlaid with copper. High-
centred in bud but opening flat
and full, sometimes quartered.
Fragrant.
(C) ☼ (Gh) ☉ (VF) (AL)
3′ × 2′ 90 × 60 cm

'Devoniensis'

'Francis Dubreuil'

'Duchesse de Brabant', 'Comtesse de Labarthe', 'Comtesse Ouwaroff'

Bernède FRANCE 1857
Very double flowers, clear pink to rose, shapely, cupped and free-flowering. The bush has a spreading habit and is well-foliated for Tea. Beautiful. This variety is known as 'Shell' in Bermuda.
(C) ☼ (Gh) ☉ (VF) (AL)
3' × 3'   90 × 90 cm

'Étoile de Lyon'

Guillot FRANCE 1881
Rich golden-yellow flowers held on flimsy flower stalks on a twiggy, angular bush with sparse foliage. Its main attributes are a strong colour and a strong scent.
(R) (Gh) ☼ ☉ (AL)
2' × 2'   60 × 60 cm

'Fortune's Double Yellow', 'Beauty of Glazenwood', 'San Rafael Rose'

Fortune Discovered in CHINA 1845
An old Chinese garden rose brought back to Europe by Robert Fortune. Slightly tender. The plant is best grown with support. Loosely formed, double flowers of buff-yellow with faint tints of orange. Scented. Foliage dark green and glossy, few thorns.
(R) ☼ (Gh) (CL) (VF)
(AL)   8' × 4'   2.5 × 1.2 m

'Francis Dubreuil'

Dubreuil FRANCE 1894
Long pointed buds opening to large high-centred flowers, blowsy when fully open, dark crimson red paling slightly with age. Foliage somewhat sparse, glossy, dark green. Stems moderately thorny.
(R) ☼ (Gh) ☉ (MF) (AL)
3' × 2'   90 × 60 cm

'Freiherr von Marschall'

P. Lambert GERMANY 1903
'Princess Alice de Monaco' × 'Rose d'Evian'
Pointed buds opening to flattish flowers of rich carmine and red. Foliage particularly good, being plentiful, dark green and heavily tinted with red.
(C) ☼ (Gh) ☉ (VF)
(AL)   3' × 2'   90 × 60 cm

'Général Galliéni'

G. Nabonnand FRANCE 1899
'Souvenir de Thérèse Levet' × 'Reine Emma des Pays-Bas'
One of the most popular roses of its day. Main colour buff, but heavily overlaid with red and pink with hints of yellow in the base. Vigorous and relatively free of thorns, with good, mid-green foliage.
(R) ☼ (Gh) ☉ (VF) (AL)
4' × 3'   120 × 90 cm

'Dr Grill'

'Etoile de Lyon'

'Général Schablikine'

'Duchesse de Brabant'

'Gloire de Dijon'

'Général Schablikine'

G. Nabonnand FRANCE 1878
A useful rose. Very double
flowers opening flat, combining
copper-red and cherry to good
effect. A compact and well
foliated plant.
(C) ☼ (Gh) ☉ (MF) (AL)
3′ × 2′   90 × 60 cm

'Homère'

'Gloire de Dijon'

Jacotot FRANCE 1853
Unknown Tea rose × 'Souvenir de
la Malmaison'
This is a deservedly well-loved
old variety, made famous by the
writings of the Rev. Dean
Reynolds-Hole, first president of
the National Rose Society. It was
his favourite rose. Large, perfumed flowers, full, opening flat
and quartered, of buff-apricot to
orange, often giving a second
flush in the autumn. Foliage dark
green but slightly prone to black
spot, especially after the first
flush. Flowers dislike wet
weather. With all her faults, well
worth living with.
(R) ☼ (Gh) (VF) (AL)
12′ × 8′   3.5 × 2.5 m

'Grüss an Coburg'

Felberg-Leclerc GERMANY 1927
'Alice Kaempff' × 'Souvenir de
Claudius Pernet'
Shapely, globular flowers of
yellow flushed orange-apricot
with a tawny-pink reverse. Very
fragrant. Foliage bronzy-deep-
green. Growth angular. Vigorous.
Perhaps a Hybrid Tea?
(C) ☼ ☉ (Gh) (VF) (AL)
4′ × 3′   120 × 90 cm

'Homère'

Robert and Moreau FRANCE 1858
If some of the other Teas are not
fully hardy, 'Homère' definitely is.
Shapely, cupped flowers are a
pleasing mixture of soft blush-
pink and pure white, sometimes
with the margins of petals
blushed-red. A relatively thornless
bush with a twiggy growth habit
and dark foliage.
(C) (Gh) ☉ (AL)
4′ × 2′   120 × 60 cm

'Hume's Blush Tea-scented China',
'Odorata',
R. × odorata

Fa Tee Nurseries, Canton CHINA
1810
Thought to be *R. chinensis × R.
gigantea*
Found cultivated in China, this,
the first Tea rose from that country, is probably the result of a
spontaneous cross but could have
been deliberate hybridization by
an early Chinese gardener.
Flowers vary from off-white –
sometimes with hint of lemon –
to blush-pink, sometimes almost
brownish-pink, semi-double to
almost single. Growth vigorous
but erratic. Foliage slightly glossy,
mid-green. My stock arrived by a

circuitous route from
Sangerhausen, East Germany, and
I believe it to be correct.
(R) ☼ (Gh) (VF) (AL)
variable from 4′ × 4′ to 15′ × 10′
1.2 × 1.2 m to 4.5 × 3 m

'Isabella Sprunt'

Sprunt USA 1855
Sport from 'Safrano'
Semi-double to double flowers of
rich sulphur yellow. Shapely buds
open to attractively ragged, full
blooms. Foliage plentiful, mid-
green. Bush open and branching.
(C) ☉ (Gh) ☼ (SF) ✂
(AL) 4′ × 3′   120 × 90 cm

'Jean Ducher'

Ducher FRANCE 1873
Peachy-pink overlaid salmon-
orange, full and rounded blooms
on a fairly vigorous, relatively
hardy plant with good foliage.
(C) ☉ (Gh) ☼ (MF) (AL)
4′ × 3′   120 × 90 cm

'Lady Hillingdon'

Lowe and Shawyer UK 1910
'Papa Gontier' × 'Mme Hoste'
An outstandingly good rose,
deservedly popular since its introduction. The long, pointed buds
are rich yoky-yellow, opening to
large, blowsy, semi-double
flowers with a lovely perfume.
Leaves glossy, dark purplish-
green, combining superbly with
relatively thornless, plum-
coloured shoots.
(C) (Gh) ☉ ✂ (VF) (AL)
3′ × 2′   90 × 60 cm

'Lady Hillingdon' Climbing

Hicks UK 1917
Undoubtedly outstanding as a
climber. Its plum-coloured wood
and dark foliage are great assets.
Needs careful placing but its

reputation for tenderness is some-what exaggerated; although some-times forcibly pruned by frost, it will survive most winters.

(R) ☼ (P) ✂ (VF) (AL)
15′ × 8′   4.5 × 2.5 m

'Lady Plymouth'

A. Dickson UK 1914
A lovely, old variety. Flowers ivory-white to flushed cream and blush-pink, well formed and evenly spaced. Slightly scented. Bush dense and thorny, although it would be better with more of its darkish green foliage.

(C) ☼ (Gh) ☉ (MF) (AL)
3′ × 3′   90 × 90 cm

'Lady Roberts'

F. Cant UK 1902
Sport of 'Anna Olivier'
A brightly coloured Tea rose, apricot with deeper base heavily burnished with reddish-orange. Fully double, shapely. Good scent. Foliage dark green. Growth bushy.

(C) ☉ (Gh) ☼ (VF) (AL)
4′ × 3′   120 × 90 cm

'Mme Antoine Mari'

Mari FRANCE 1901
Fragrant with shapely flowers, especially in the late bud stage. Pink in bud opening to soft flesh pink with lavender-lilac high-lights. Foliage light to mid-green on an angular but tidy plant.

(R) ☼ (Gh) ☉ (MF) (AL)
3′ × 3′   90 × 90 cm

'Mme Berkeley'

Bernaix FRANCE 1899
A mixture of salmon, pink, cerise and gold. Flowers initially high-centred, opening somewhat muddled, but attractively so. Extremely free-flowering on a vigorous plant.

(C) ☼ (Gh) ☉ (MF) (AL)
3′ × 2′   90 × 60 cm

'Mme Bravy', 'Adèle Pradel', 'Mme de Sertot'

Guillot Père FRANCE 1846
One of the early Teas. Large, double, creamy-white flowers with pink shadings. Very free-flowering and with a strong, sup-posedly 'tea' fragrance. Plant dense and bushy.

(C) ☼ (Gh) (B) ☉ ✂
(MF) (AL)   3′ × 2′   90 × 60 cm

'Mme de Tartas'

Bernède FRANCE 1859
An important rose, used extensively at stud in Victorian times. Flowers large, full and cupped, blush-pink, scented. Bush vigorous, rather sprawly in habit

'Maman Cochet'

'Maman Cochet' (white)

but none the less charming. Foli-age dark green and leathery. Quite hardy, probably one of few Teas better outdoors than in.

(C) ☼ (P) ☉ (MF) (AL)
3′ × 3′   90 × 90 cm

'Mme de Watteville'

Guillot Fils FRANCE 1883
A dense medium-growing plant with small but plentiful dark green foliage and several thorns. Flowers shapely, fully double, soft yellow with pinkish tinges to the petal edges, scented.

(C) ☼ ☉ (SF) (AL)
3′ × 3′   90 × 90 cm

'Mme Jules Gravereaux'

Soupert and Notting
LUXEMBOURG 1901
I am very fond of this accommo-dating climbing rose and can only assume that its suspect hardiness has prevented more widespread distribution. Shapely, fully double, sometimes quartered blooms of yellowish-buff, shaded peach with hints of pink as undertones. It is scented. Foliage lush, dark green and the wood also dark. The best plant I know is at Mottisfont Abbey, Hants.

(R) ☼ (Gh) ✂ (VF) (AL)
8′ × 6′   2.5 × 1.8 m

'Mme Lombard'

Lacharme FRANCE 1878
'Mme de Tartas' seedling
Flowers full, very double, salmon with deeper centres, scented. Bush vigorous with dark green foliage. Similar, save in colour, to Mme de Tartas.

(C) ☼ ☉ (MF) (AL)
3′ × 3′   90 × 90 cm

'Mme Wagram', 'Comtesse de Turin'

Bernaix FRANCE 1895

'Mme Berkeley'

'Mme de Tartas'

'Mme Jules Gravereaux'

Large, rosy-red petals with yellow bases make up fully double, globular flowers, borne freely on a healthy bush with dark green foliage.

(C) (Gh) ☉ (SF) (AL)
3′ × 3′   90 × 90 cm

'Maman Cochet'

Cochet FRANCE 1893
'Marie Van Houtte' × 'Mme Lombard'
A very free-flowering rose, initially globular, opening blowsy, pale pink flushed deeper pink with a lemon centre. The bush is vigorous with few thorns, carrying dark green foliage of a leathery texture.
Note: A white form of this rose exists and in some districts the two have become confused. I confess my own guilt at being caught up in this in the past.
(C) ☼ (Gh) ☉ ✄ (MF) (AL) 3' × 2' 90 × 60 cm

'Marie Lambert' *see* 'Snowflake'

'Marie van Houtte'

Ducher FRANCE 1871
'Mme de Tartas' × 'Mme Falcot'
Bright pink tinged with orange and suffused cream. Fragrant and very free-flowering. Rich green foliage on a vigorous but sprawly plant.
(C) ☼ (Gh) ☉ (VF) (AL) 3' × 2' 90 × 60 cm

'Mons. Tillier'

Bernaix FRANCE 1891
A good but little known rose better endowed than most Teas with foliage. Large loosely double flowers, blood red with violet smudges, freely produced on a vigorous bush. Growth quite tall and lax. The rose sold under this name in the USA is the one sold in the UK as 'Archiduc Joseph'.
(C) (Gh) ☉ (SF) (AL) 4' × 3' 120 × 90 cm

'Mme Wagram'

'Mrs B. R. Cant'

B. R. Cant UK 1901
Soft rose pink, deeper base with buffish undertones. Petals deeper on the reverse. Well scented. Cupped until fully open. Foliage mid- to dark green, leathery. Growth vigorous, branching and bushy.
(C) ☉ (Gh) ☼ (MF) ✄ (AL) 4' × 3' 120 × 90 cm

'Mrs Campbell Hall'

Hall, introduced by Dickson UK 1914
Creamy-white-edged salmon flowers with deeper salmon centres, quite large and high-centred in bud, opening full and somewhat blowsy. Dark, leathery foliage on a vigorous bush.
(C) ☼ (Gh) ☉ (SF) (AL) 4' × 3' 120 × 90 cm

'Mrs Dudley Cross'

W. Paul UK 1907
Fully double blooms of soft yellow deepening with age, especially in full sun, to become,

at first, flushed with pink and then crimson. Slight fragrance. Foliage darkish-green on almost thornless stems. Growth vigorous, open and bushy. Seems quite hardy.
(C) ☉ ☼ (Gh) (SF) (AL) 4' × 3' 120 × 90 cm

'Niphetos'

Bush form Bougère FRANCE 1843
Climbing form Keynes, Williams and Co. UK 1889
Used extensively as florist's rose during late Victorian and Edwardian times. Lovely, creamy buds open to pure white, with

pointed petals creating a muddled, star-like shape. Foliage light green under glass, darker outdoors. Makes a vigorous climber but needs placing under glass for the best blooms.
(R) ☼ (Gh) ☉ (VF) (AL)
Bush form 4' × 3' 120 × 90 cm
Climbing form 10' × 6' 3 × 1.8 m

'Noella Nabonnand' Climber

Nabonnand FRANCE 1901
'Reine Marie Henriette' × 'Bardou Job'
Not often seen, perhaps because it seldom repeats and because of its reputation for tenderness. Nevertheless, a fine variety. Globular yet pointed buds open to a blowsy, large, rose of velvety

'Niphetos'

'Mons. Tillier'

'Papa Gontier'

'Perle des Jardins'

crimson. Foliage mid-green and quite healthy.
(S) (Gh) (P) (VF) (AL)
10' × 6' 3 × 1.8 m

'Papa Gontier'

G. Nabonnand FRANCE 1883
Used extensively as a forcing rose in its early career. Flowers rich-pink, almost red, sometimes slightly mottled and with a deeper reverse, semi-double and slightly scented. Growth habit rather twiggy; I would prefer to see more of its dark green glossy foliage.
(C) ☼ (Gh) ☉ ✂ (SF)
(AL) 3' × 2' 90 × 60 cm

'Parks Yellow Tea-scented China', *R. × odorata ochroleuca*

CHINA 1824
Said to be the original Tea Rose. I believe I have this rose, but sadly have no recollection or record of whence or from whom it came. Perhaps a reader will remember and remind me to acknowledge. It is an angular-growing climber with fairly large, double, cupped flowers of soft, sulphur-yellow, unusually perfumed, although I fail to detect any resemblance to tea. The foliage, although large, is none the less typical of a China or Tea. It has but few thorns.
(R) ☼ (Gh) ☉ (MF) (AL)
6' × 4' 1.8 × 1.2 m

'Perle des Jardins'

F. Levet FRANCE 1874
'Mme Falcot' seedling
A fragrant, many-petalled rose often opening quartered. Sulphur-yellow to buff on a sturdy compact plant. Apparently quite hardy out of doors but probably better under glass in cold or wet districts, since it fails to open properly in such conditions.
(C) (Gh) ☉ ☼ (VF) (AL)
3' × 2' 90 × 60 cm

'Rival de Paestum'

Paul UK 1848
Fully double flowers, ivory white tinged pink, more so in the bud stage. Scented. Bush well foliated with dark green leaves. Twiggy in habit.
(C) (Gh) ☉ (MF) (AL)
3' × 2' 90 × 60 cm

'Rosette Delizy'

P. Nabonnand FRANCE 1922
'Général Galliéni' × 'Comtesse Bardi'
Pleasing combination of rose-pink, buff and apricot with deeper colouring on the outside of each petal. Bush branchy but nevertheless refined in habit with good foliage.
(C) ☼ (Gh) ☉ ✂ (SF)
(AL) 3' × 2' 90 × 60 cm

'Safrano'

Beauregard FRANCE 1839
This rose, one of the oldest of the Teas, is still worthy of consideration, especially if planted in groups or in pots. Will not enjoy an exposed position. Very floriferous, each flower fully double, opening flat from a high-centred bud, buff and pinkish-

'Sombreuil' Climbing

apricot with a sulphur yellow base. Foliage mid-green and plentiful.
(C) ☼ (Gh) ☉ (MF) (AL)
3' × 2' 90 × 60 cm

'Snowflake', 'Marie Lambert', 'White Hermosa'

E. Lambert FRANCE 1866
Sport of 'Mme Bravy'
Pure white, unblemished in good weather. Large and fully double. Exceptionally free-flowering with a good fragrance. Growth dense and bushy. Foliage mid-green and plentiful.
(C) ☼ (Gh) ☉ (SF) ✂
(AL) 3' × 2' 90 × 60 cm

'Solfaterre', 'Solfatare'

Boyau FRANCE 1843
Seedling from 'Lamarque'
A beautiful, large, double, pale sulphur yellow rose, which needs extra loving care and a warm, sheltered site or greenhouse to flourish, when it can be most rewarding.
(R) ☼ ☉ (MF) (AL)
10' × 8' 3 × 2.5 m

'Sombreuil' Climbing

Robert FRANCE 1850
A fully double, flattish flower, pure white with hints of cream in the base, sweetly scented. A beautiful rose which, with loving care, is most rewarding. With its

'Souvenir d'un Ami'

'The Bride'

ample, lush green foliage it makes a dense shrub or small climber.
(R) (Gh) ✂ (VF) (AL)
8' × 5'   2.5 × 1.5 m

'Souvenir d'Elise Vardon'

Marest FRANCE 1855
A shapely, fragrant rose of cream overlaid coppery-yellow. Foliage leathery and glossy. Rather tender.
(C) ☼ (Gh) ☉ (SF) (AL)
3' × 2'   90 × 60 cm

'Souvenir de Mme Léonie Viennot' Climbing

Bernaix FRANCE 1897
Fragrant, shapely flowers. A mixture of primrose yellow with variable coppery-orange overtones, sometimes veined pink. A very good climbing rose. My stock

came from Keith Money, whose mother sent it to him from New Zealand, wrapped in polythene, in a pencil case.
(R) ☼ (Gh) ● (VF) (AL)
12' × 8'   3.5 × 2.5 m

'Souvenir d'un Ami'

Bélot-Defougère FRANCE 1846
Fully double flowers of rose-pink tinted deeper pink to salmon. Highly scented. Foliage rich green on a vigorous plant.
(R) (P) (Gh) (VF) (AL)
8' × 4'   2.5 × 1.2 m

'The Bride'

May USA 1885
'Catherine Mermet' sport
Pure white with a mere hint of pink on each petal edge. William

Paul said of it 'in all respects a first class rose'. Quite vigorous. Good foliage.
(C) (Gh) ☉ ✂ (VF) (AL)
4' × 3'   120 × 90 cm

'Tipsy Imperial Concubine'

Introduced Beales UK 1982
Large double flowers of soft pink, subtly overlaid with tones of yellow and red. Very free flowering. Came from China and is believed to be an old Chinese garden variety. It was discovered by Hazel le Rougetel.
(C) ☼ (Gh) ☉ (SF) (AL)
2' × 2'   60 × 60 cm

'Triomphe de Luxembourg'

Hardy FRANCE 1839
Fully double flowers; salmon-pink to pinkish-buff. Foliage dark green. I dated this rose from an old catalogue of 1839, when it was priced at 7s. 6d. (37.5 pence) each – a week's wages for a gardener in those days.
(C) (Gh) ☉ (MF) (AL)
3' × 2'   90 × 60 cm

'William R. Smith', 'Charles Dingee', 'Blush Maman Cochet', 'President William Smith', 'Jeanette Heller'

Bagg USA 1909
Flowers creamy-white flushed pink with buff and gold at the base, blowsy when fully open but produced on a tidy plant.
(C) (Gh) ☉ ✂ (MF) (AL)
3' × 2'   90 × 60 cm

Bermuda Roses

As mentioned in an earlier chapter (pages 17–18), the Bermuda Rose Society, since its formation in 1945, has rescued and gathered together these roses, many of them very old. Most were probably taken there by settlers or imported by the keen gardeners of the island during the nineteenth century. They are an important little group and appear to be unique to Bermuda. Some are, undoubtedly, roses now extinct in the rest of the world, which, in the course of time, have lost their true identity. Others may simply be climatically induced variations of varieties we already know, but sufficiently different to defy identification. A clue to their age is that most are akin to the Teas and Chinas. In truth they would struggle to survive in the colder climates but, in their new-found identities, they fully deserve to be reintroduced to the rest of the world. Anyway they are safe in Bermuda for not only are they now grown extensively in private gardens there but the full collection, along with the other named roses which have been rescued, has been planted in a newly created public rose garden in the grounds of what was once the Premier's residence, the historic Camden House.

Although I have now come to know some of these fascinating roses it would be presumptuous of me to attempt to describe them and so I am delighted that Lorna Mercer, a past President of the Bermuda Rose Society, has agreed to do so for me. The photographs in this section are by Bill Mercer.

MYSTERY ROSES IN BERMUDA
By Lorna Mercer

The mystery roses in Bermuda are those whose original name or provenance is unknown, but which have grown here for many years. Most of these roses have been given the name of the area where they were found, or sometimes the name of the owner of the garden. The mystery roses, which are all old garden roses, have now been included in the Bench Competitions of the Bermuda Rose Society and at the annual Agricultural Exhibition. A trophy was given in 1987 by Peter Beales to the Bermuda Rose Society and this is awarded annually for Mystery Roses.

'Brightside Cream'

Probably a Noisette. Large vigorous climber with clusters of double cream flowers. Flowers about 3″ (8 cm) across. Strong scent. Foliage mid-green. Blooms all year round. Called Brightside after the home of a past president of the Bermuda Rose Society.
(C) (Gh) (VF) ☼ (AL)
12′ × 8′   3.5 × 2.5 m

'Carnation'

Deep pink double flowers with a mauve tinge. Petals have frilly edges. Very like a carnation! This rose is inclined to hang its head. Bush has dark green foliage.
(C) (Gh) ☉ ☼ (AL)
3′ × 3′   90 × 90 cm

'Maitland White'

Large double white rose with a pink blush near the centre. Tall stick-like bush with mid-green foliage. Good fragrance. Found a few years ago in the garden of a Mr Maitland.
(C) (Gh) ☉ ☼ (VF) (AL)
6′ × 4′   1.8 × 1.2 m

'Miss Atwood'

This large bush has double apricot-coloured flowers. Rather untidy when fully open but with a lovely fragrance. Mid-green foliage and large hips. This rose was found in the garden of a very old house belonging to Miss Atwood, which has since been demolished.
(C) (Gh) ☉ (VF) (AL)
6′ × 4′   1.8 × 1.2 m

'Pacific'

Some say this is a Hybrid Perpetual. According to Bermuda legend this rose was brought to the Island about 100 years ago by a Captain Nelmes, who while sailing in the Pacific Ocean gave water to a French ship and was given this rose as a thank you. Deep pink or red, very double flower. Has mid-green foliage. A thin spindly bush which never grows very tall.

'Maitland White'

Captain Nelmes was the great-grandfather of the founding President of the Bermuda Rose Society.

(C) (Gh) ☉ ☼ (AL)
3' × 3'   90 × 90 cm

'Smith's Parish'

Large bush with very light green foliage. The flowers are semi-double – sometimes all white, sometimes with one or more red stripes. Sometimes the bush will have an all red flower. Very pale yellow stamens. Originally found in Smith's Parish, hence the name.

(C) (Gh) ☉ (AL)
6' × 5'   1.8 × 1.5 m

'Spice'

Pale pink rose, semi-double with loose petals in the centre. Small mid-green foliage on a small bush – it grows to no more than 4' (1.2 m). This rose has been named 'Spice' because of its strong spice scent. It has been in Bermuda a very long time and it is suspected that it might be 'Hume's Blush Tea-scented China'.

(C) (Gh) ☉ (VF) ☼ ✄
(AL)   4' × 3'   120 × 90 cm

'Trinity'

Pure white, semi-double rose, buds touched with pink. Dark

'Trinity'

'Vincent Godsiff'

green shiny foliage. Bush grows to about 5 ft (1.5 m). This mystery rose was found in the graveyard of Holy Trinity Church.

(C) (Gh) ☉ ☼ (AL)
5' × 4'   1.5 × 1.2 m

'Vincent Godsiff'

A deep pink single rose. Dark green foliage. A small spindly bush. Possibly a seedling.

(C) (Gh) ☉ ☼ (AL)
3' × 3'   90 × 90 cm

There are also a great many Teas which do very well in the Bermuda climate and have grown large and strong over the years. Some of these are as follows – 'Duchesse de Brabant', 'Mme Lombard', 'Dr Grill', 'Maman Cochet' and 'White Maman Cochet', 'Niles Cochet', 'Papa Gontier', 'Rosette Delizy', 'Mme Berkeley', 'General Schablikine', 'W. R. Smith', 'Baronne Henriette de Snoy' and 'Homère'.

Hybrid Perpetuals

The Hybrid Perpetuals emerged in the 1830s and were born from a varied and complex union, in which the Chinas, Portlands, Bourbons, Noisettes and, later, the Teas all played their part.

Few were completely perpetual, but most were remontant to some degree. After a few years of uncertain popularity in competition with the Bourbons, they became one of the major groups of roses.

Throughout Queen Victoria's reign they led the field as exhibition roses, and as flower shows became fashionable, breeders felt impelled to seek ever larger, more shapely blooms. Despite this quest for size of flower, many very useful garden shrubs emerged and, as such, many have come down to us today, as true aristocrats from an important era in rose development.

CLASSIFICATION

BARB	Class 25
MR9	Class 38
WFRS	Class 4

'Alfred Colomb'

Lacharme FRANCE 1865
'Général Jacqueminot' × unknown
A large, full rose, rounded in late bud and high-centred, brickish-red with flecks of deep pink and carmine. Slightly vulgar but nevertheless appealing. Growth tidy and foliage abundant.

(R) (P) ☉ ✄ (SF) (AL)
4' × 3'   120 × 90 cm

'American Beauty', 'Mme Ferdinand Jamin'

Lédéchaux FRANCE 1875
First introduced as a forcing variety, its longish, strong stems making it ideal for bouquets. Also a useful garden plant. Crimson, high-centred flowers rather modern in appearance. The bush was perhaps rather ahead of its

time in being very Hybrid Tea-like in stature.

(R) (Gh) ☉ ✄ (MF) (AL)
3' × 3'   90 × 90 cm

'Anna de Diesbach', 'Gloire de Paris'

Lacharme FRANCE 1858
'La Reine' × seedling
A tall rose with many fragrant flowers of rich, deep rose-pink with deeper shadings, initially quite large and cupped, later opening rather flat. Bush tall, a little ungainly, but well foliated.

(R) ☉ (MF) (AL)
4' × 3'   120 × 90 cm

'Archiduchesse Elizabeth d'Autriche'

Moreau-Robert FRANCE 1881
Soft rose-pink flowers, fully double, opening flat. I find the

'Ardoisée de Lyon'

plant rather inclined to sprawl, but effective if pruned hard each season. Obviously enjoys full sun.
(R) ☼ (SF) (AL)
5′ × 4′   1.5 × 1.2 m

'Ardoisée de Lyon'

Damaizin FRANCE 1858
Superb, fully double, quartered flower of rich cerise with violet and purple shadings, held on a strong neck and exuding a rich perfume. Ample greyish-green foliage on a compact, tidy plant with numerous thorns. Little known but a splendid rose.
(R) (P) ☉ (VF) (AL)
4′ × 3′   120 × 90 cm

'Ards Rover'

Dickson UK 1898
Excellent old pillar rose. Shapely, crimson flowers opening blowsily, with a strong scent. Definitely has a place in the modern garden, especially since good, deep red climbers are so few. Of medium stature, it can fulfil the role of either wall climber or pillar rose to considerable effect, especially as it is sometimes, in good seasons, recurrent. Foliage quite lush and dark green. Needs attention for mildew early each season for it to give of its very best.
(R) ✁ (VF) M✿ (AL)
10′ × 6′   3 × 1.8 m

'Arrillaga'

Schoener USA 1929
(R. centifolia × 'Mrs John Laing') × 'Frau Karl Druschki'
Freely produced flowers of very bright pink with hints of gold in the base, large and full and held on strong stems. Good mid-green foliage.
(R) (P) (H) ☉ (VF) ✁
(AL)   5′ × 4′   1.5 × 1.2 m

'Baron de Bonstetten'

Liabaud FRANCE 1871
'Général Jacqueminot' × 'Géant des Batailles'
Very double, very dark red and very fragrant. Upright and vigorous in growth and rather thorny with mid to dark green foliage.
(R) ☉ (VF) (AL)
4′ × 3′   120 × 90 cm

'Baron Girod de l'Ain'

Reverchon FRANCE 1897
'Eugène Fürst' sport
A popular novelty since its introduction, this unusual rose is well worth garden space. Its very double flowers are bright crimson, and they open cup-shaped, with the petal edges rather ragged-looking, an illusion enhanced by the fringe of white edging the margins. As a shrub it is rather straggly but quite dense with firm, stout thorns and leathery dark green leaves.
(R) (P) (MF) M✿ (AL)
4′ × 3′   120 × 90 cm

'Baroness Rothschild', 'Baronne Adolphe de Rothschild'

Pernet Père FRANCE 1868
'Souvenir de la Reine d'Angleterre' sport
A superior member of its group.

Large, full flowers remain slightly cupped when fully open, held erect on strong, stout stems. Petals are of a soft to clear rose-pink colour and have a soft silky texture. Highly scented. Bush well covered with large grey-green foliage.
(R) (P) (H) (B) ☉ ✁
(VF) (AL)   4′ × 3′   120 × 90 cm

'Baronne Prévost'

Desprez FRANCE 1842
Deep rose pink scented flowers opening flat and double from globular buds. A reliable rose of considerable longevity, with many bushes still growing in cottage gardens, having survived from its heyday. Somewhat coarse in growth and rather thorny, it still makes a most useful shrub.
(R) (P) (VF) (AL)
5′ × 4′   1.5 × 1.2 m

'Black Prince'

W. Paul UK 1866
Vigorous variety with good foliage, if rather prone to mildew. Flowers large and cupped, opening from shapely buds of rich dark crimson to almost black. Scented.
(R) (VF) M✿ (AL)
5′ × 3′   150 × 90 cm

'Baron Girod de l'Ain'

'Baroness Rothschild'

'Charles Lefèbvre'

'Candeur Lyonnaise'

Croibier FRANCE 1914
'Frau Karl Druschki' seedling
Large, fully double flowers open
from shapely, pointed buds. Soft
yellow to pure white. Vigorous
with sizeable mid green leaves.
(R) (P) (H) ☉ (AL)
5' × 4'   1.5 × 1.2 m

'Captain Hayward' Climbing

Bush form Bennett UK 1893
'Triomphe de l'Expedition' seed-
ling
This form W. Paul 1906
A tall rose, needing support as a

shrub. Ideal as pillar rose when its
healthy disposition can be fully
appreciated. Pinkish crimson
flowers large and cupped until
fully open, when they then
become rather blowsy. Does not
always repeat. Hips large and
quite attractive so dead-heading
best avoided.
(R) (P) (VF) (AL)
8' × 4'   2.5 × 1.2 m

'Champion of the World', 'Mrs de Graw'

Woodhouse UK 1894
'Hermosa' × 'Magna Charta'
A presumptuous name, probably
describing the size of its deep
rosy-pink flowers. A bush of
medium stature, rather sprawly,
leaves dark green.
(R) (P) ☉ (MF) (AL)
4' × 3'   120 × 90 cm

'Charles Gater'

W. Paul UK 1893
An upright-growing plant which
can be slotted into the smallest
space. Flowers clear bright red
and globular throughout their

life. Scented. Good strong foliage.
Stems rather thorny. Inclined to
mildew after the first flush.
(R) ☉ M✿ (VF) (AL)
4' × 2'   120 × 60 cm

'Charles Lefèbvre'

Lacharme FRANCE 1861
'Général Jacqueminot' × 'Victor
Verdier'
Very large, many-petalled flowers
of rich crimson shaded maroon,
high-centred, opening cupped,
held on a strong, firm neck. Foliage dark green and sufficient.
(R) ☉ ✂ (VF) (AL)
4' × 3'   120 × 90 cm

'Clio'

W. Paul UK 1894
Clusters of fully double, initially
cupped, fragrant, soft silvery-pink
flowers on strong, almost arching
stems. Rich leathery foliage on a
vigorous, if somewhat sprawly
plant, with ample thorns.
(R) (VF) (AL)
4' × 4'   1.2 × 1.2 m

'Comtesse Cécile de Chabrillant'

Marest FRANCE 1858
The clear mid-pink flowers are
shapely, full and globular, and
strongly perfumed. They are supported on strong flower stalks.
Growth is upright, and the rose is
very free-flowering which
qualifies this excellent variety for
general use.
(R) ☉ (VF) (AL)
4' × 4'   1.2 × 1.2 m

'Countess of Oxford', 'Comtesse d'Oxford'

Guillot Père FRANCE 1869
William Paul spoke highly of this
rose. Double globular flowers
opening cupped, of rich carmine-
red and scented. A vigorous, tidy
plant with ample healthy foliage.
(R) (P) ☉ (VF) (AL)
4' × 3'   120 × 90 cm

'Crown Prince'

W. Paul UK 1880
A free-flowering fully double
rose of purple and red. Tidy and

'Baronne Prévost'

'Captain Hayward' Climbing (a first year plant)

'Comtesse Cécile de Chabrillant'

compact in growth with dark green foliage.
(R) ⊙ (MF) (AL)
3' × 3'   90 × 90 cm

'Dembrowski'

Vibert FRANCE 1849
Very shapely, fully double, reddish-purple flowers on a strong but medium-growing plant with mid-green foliage.
(C) (MF) (AL)
4' × 3'   120 × 90 cm

'Dr Andry'

E. Verdier FRANCE 1864
Very bright red with deeper shadings towards the centre of each fully double flower. Only a slight scent. Vigorous growth with dark green foliage.
(R) ⊙ (SF) (AL)
4' × 3'   120 × 90 cm

'Duke of Edinburgh'

Paul UK 1868
'Général Jacqueminot' × unknown
Not easy to grow except in the very best soils where it can be rewarding. Shortish in stature and slightly spreading in habit, it produces semi-double flowers of bright scarlet to crimson, sweetly scented.
(R) ⊙ (VF) (AL)
2' × 2'   60 × 60 cm

'Duke of Wellington'

Granger FRANCE 1874
A surprising name for a French rose? Large, shapely, high-centred flowers of deep crimson, these tend to dislike hot sun which turns their outer petals somewhat blackish. Upright in growth, the blooms are produced on thick, stout, thorny stems with dark foliage.
(R) ⊙ (VF) (AL)
4' × 3'   120 × 90 cm

'Dupuy Jamain'

Jamain FRANCE 1868
I place this rose high on my list of favourite Hybrid Perpetuals. Large, full, cerise-red flowers held on strong necks, with a good, strong perfume. The shrub is healthy with an abundance of lush, grey-green leaves. Relatively free of thorns, upright growth.
(R) (P) ⊙ ✄ (MF) (AL)
4' × 3'   120 × 90 cm

'Dr Andry'

'Duke of Wellington'

'Eclair'

'Eclair'

Lacharme FRANCE 1833
'Général Jacqueminot' × unknown
Well scented, very dark red, almost black flowers, opening flat in rosette shape. Not the easiest of roses to grow but well worth some extra loving care. Upright in growth. Can perhaps be faulted by its rather sparse foliage. Almost fits the Portlands in type. Sent to me by Margaret Wray of Langport, near Taunton. A valuable rediscovery.
(R) ⊙ ✄ (VF) (AL)
4' × 3'   120 × 90 cm

'Elisa Boelle'

Guillot Père FRANCE 1869
A vigorous rose having shapely, cupped, whitish-pink, scented flowers, with incurving centre petals. Ample foliage on a tidy, well-groomed plant.
(R) ⊙ (MF) (AL)
4' × 3'   120 × 90 cm

'Empereur du Maroc', 'Emperor of Morocco'

Guinoisseau FRANCE 1858
'Géant des Batailles' seedling
Very double flowers, opening flat; deep crimson tinged maroon. A superb rose when weather permits. Flowers borne in large clusters which are sometimes too heavy for the thorny branches to support, but hard pruning helps correct this fault over the years. Needs precautions against both black spot and mildew.
(R) (VF) BS ✷ M ✷ (AL)
4' × 3'   120 × 90 cm

'Enfant de France'

Lartay FRANCE 1860
For a number of years I have grown the rose here described

'Enfant de France'

'Eugène Fürst'

under this name uncertain as to whether it is correct, but it fits the descriptions I have read in old books and catalogues. Whatever its name, such a good rose should not be omitted. The fully double flowers, which are sometimes quartered, are silky pink and beautifully perfumed. Growth is upright and foliage plentiful. Rather in the Portland mould.
(R) (Gh) (P) ⊙ (VF) (AL)
3′ × 2′   90 × 60 cm

'Eugène Fürst'

Soupert and
Notting LUXEMBOURG 1875
'Baron de Bonstetten' × unknown
Ragged edged, crimson-purple, cupped flowers of considerable

size, highly scented. The bush is upright in growth and the flowers are borne on strong necks amid good, dark green foliage.
(R) ⊙ M❀ (VF) (AL)
4′ × 3′   120 × 90 cm

'Everest'

Easlea UK 1927
'Candeur Lyonnaise' × 'Mme Caristie Martel'
One of the last Hybrid Perpetuals introduced, and one of the most beautiful. Substantially sized, high-centred flowers of creamy-white. Foliage light green. Growth low, making a wide, bushy plant.
(R) (P) (H) ⊙ ✄ (VF)
(AL)   3′ × 3′   90 × 90 cm

'Ferdinand de Lesseps'

Verdier FRANCE 1869
An interesting rose bearing shapely flowers of lavender, shaded purple and magenta, opening flat, with many petals in the Centifolia form. Bush shrubby and vigorous.
(R) (VF) (AL)
4′ × 3′   120 × 90 cm

'Ferdinand Pichard'

Tanne FRANCE 1921
Flowers of rich, carmine red, heavily laced and striped with white, opening large and cup-shaped with a distinct scent; these combine well with rich green foliage and are produced on a vigorous, healthy shrub. One of the best of the striped roses available today.
(R) (P) (H) (VF) (AL)
5′ × 4′   1.5 × 1.2 m

'Ferdinand Pichard'

'Fisher Holmes', 'Fisher and Holmes'

Verdier FRANCE 1865
'Maurice Bernardin' seedling
Well-formed, double flowers from shapely, pointed buds. Shades of scarlet and crimson. Scented. Bush of medium height and moderately vigorous with good foliage. Rather prone to disease, the result perhaps of over-propagation, for it was very popular in Victorian times.
(C) ⊙ (VF) M❀ R❀ (AL)
3′ × 3′   90 × 90 cm

'Frau Karl Druschki', 'Snow Queen', 'Reine des Neiges', 'White American Beauty'

P. Lambert GERMANY 1901
'Merveille de Lyon' × 'Mme Caroline Testout'
For many years the most popular white rose, and deservedly so, its only significant faults being a lack of scent and a dislike of wet weather. Pure white blooms large

and globular, with high centres in bud. Shrub vigorous and strong with plenty of leathery, lightish green leaves.
(R) (P) (AL)
5′ × 3′   150 × 90 cm

'Frau Karl Druschki' Climbing

Lawrenson UK 1906
As bush form, except that it makes a vigorous and useful climber.
(S) (P) (AL)
15′ × 8′   4.5 × 2.5 m

'Général Jacqueminot', 'General Jack', 'Jack Rose'

Roussel FRANCE 1853
'Gloire des Rosomanes' seedling
Clear red, shapely, pointed buds opening to well-formed, perfumed flowers, produced on fairly long stems. A vigorous shrub with rich green foliage. Rather prone to rust from mid-summer onwards.
(R) (VF) R❀ (AL)
5′ × 4′   1.5 × 1.2 m

'Général Jacqueminot'

'Georg Arends', 'Fortuné Besson'

W. Hinner GERMANY 1910
'Frau Karl Druschki' × 'La France'
A first-class rose. Large, initially
high-centred but blowsy blooms
of clear rose-pink paling to soft
pink. Free-flowering, fragrant and,
as a shrub, vigorous with plenty
of large, grey-green leaves.
(C) (H) (P) ✕ (MF) (AL)
5′ × 4′   1.5 × 1.2 m

'Gloire de Bruxelles', 'Gloire de l'Exposition'

Soupert and
Notting LUXEMBOURG 1889
'Souvenir de William Wood' ×
'Lord Macaulay'
Sixty or more velvety petals make
up a flower which opens flat in
large rosette form, dark red to
crimson-purple and scented. The
shrub is loose and untidy despite
small stature but well worth the
effort of support.
(R) (VF) M✕ (AL)
4′ × 4′   1.2 × 1.2 m

'Gloire de Chédane-Guinoisseau'

Chédane-Pajotin FRANCE 1907
'Gloire de Ducher' × unknown
Shapely cupped flowers produced

in considerable numbers, bright
rich pinkish red, scented. Foliage
dark green and abundant on a
vigorous quite healthy plant.
(R) (P) ☉ (VF) (AL)
4′ × 3′   120 × 90 cm

'Gloire de Ducher'

Ducher FRANCE 1865
More credit is due to this rose
than it has ever received. Huge,
fully double blooms of deep purplish-red, somewhat blowsy in
structure, produced freely along
long, arching branches amid dark
grey-green leaves. Well scented.
(R) (P) (VF) M✕ (AL)
6′ × 4′   1.8 × 1.2 m

'Gloire de l'Exposition' *see* 'Gloire de Bruxelles'

'Gloire de Bruxelles'

'Gloire de Ducher'

'Georg Arends'

'Gloire de Paris' *see* 'Anna de Diesbach'

'Gloire d'un Enfant d'Hiram'

Vilin FRANCE 1899
Large, bright pink, scented,
cupped flowers on a strong,
sturdy, upright growing plant
with few thorns and good,
greyish-green leathery foliage.
(R) (P) ☉ (MF) (AL)
4′ × 3′   120 × 90 cm

'Gloire Lyonnais'

Guillot Fils FRANCE 1885
'Baron Rothschild' × 'Mme
Falcot'
A favourite of mine, this creamy-
white rose has semi-double
flowers that open flat with a good
perfume. The shrub is upright in
growth with strong stems supporting the flowers without arching. Few thorns, foliage is dark
green and healthy. Should be
more widely grown.
(C) (P) (H) (B) ☉ (VF)
(AL)   4′ × 2′   120 × 60 cm

'Hans Mackart'

E. Verdier Fils FRANCE 1885
Double flowers of bright but deep
pink opening flat from cupped

'Gloire Lyonnaise'

buds, inclined to sprawl. Ample lightish-green foliage with but few thorns.
(R) (P) (VF) (AL)
5' × 3'   150 × 90 cm

'Heinrich Münch'

W. Hinner GERMANY 1911
'Frau Karl Druschki' × ('Mme Caroline Testout' × 'Mrs W. J. Grant')
Fully double, large, soft blush pink blooms with a good fragrance, produced on a strong, branching shrub with good, mid to dark green foliage. A good rose for the 'pegging down' system of training.
(R) (P) (VF) ✗ (AL)
6' × 4'   1.8 × 1.2 m

'Heinrich Schultheis'

Bennett UK 1882
'Mabel Morrison' × 'E. Y. Teas'
A Victorian exhibition rose which probably won many prizes for size alone. Flowers high-centred until fully open, then cupped, flat topped and slightly ragged, rich pink with hints of a deeper shade in the base, scented. Vigorous, well-foliated and upright. Worth growing.
(C) ☉ ✗ (VF) (AL)
4' × 3'   120 × 90 cm

'Heinrich Schultheis'

'Henry Nevard'

Cants UK 1924
Fragrant, bright crimson, cupped flowers of considerable size. Bushy growth with dark green, leathery leaves.
(R) (MF) (AL)
4' × 3'   120 × 90 cm

'Her Majesty'

Bennett UK 1885
'Mabel Morrison' × 'Canary'
Huge, fully double blooms of clear pink. Another Victorian exhibition rose well worth growing today. Foliage large and grey, but inclined to mildew. Shrub vigorous but less tall than most of its type.
(R) ☉ (VF) M✗ (AL)
3' × 2'   90 × 60 cm

'Horace Vernet'

Guillot Fils FRANCE 1866
'Général Jacqueminot' × unknown
A high-centred rose of rich crimson, retaining its shape well into maturity, fragrant. The shrub is upright and tidy in habit with abundant dark foliage.
(R) ☉ (MF) (AL)
4' × 3'   120 × 90 cm

'Hugh Dickson'

Dickson UK 1905
'Lord Bacon' × 'Grüss an Teplitz
A tall lanky rose from the latter end of the Hybrid Perpetual cycle. Rich dark red, powerfully perfumed flowers borne on long, arching stems, making it an ideal rose for 'pegging-down' or for pillars. Can be grown as a shrub but needs support. Foliage rich, dark green with hints of maroon.
(R) (P) ✗ (VF) (AL)
8' × 5'   2.5 × 1.5 m

'John Hopper'

'Kaiserin Auguste Viktoria'

'James Bourgault'

Renault FRANCE 1987
Shapely, soft pink to white blooms, fully double and fragrant. A little known Hybrid Perpetual with much to commend it. Foliage ample, dark green. Growth vigorous and upright.
(R) (P) (H) ☉ (MF) ✗ (AL)   4' × 3'   120 × 90 cm

'Jean Rosenkrantz'

Portemer FRANCE 1864
Big flowers of neatly formed, deep pinkish-red petals with perfume. The shrub is well foliated, vigorous and upright.
(R) ☉ (MF) (AL)
4' × 3'   120 × 90 cm

'John Hopper'

Ward UK 1862
'Jules Margottin' × 'Mme Vidot'
The large fragrant flowers are a pleasing combination of bright pink and lilac, with deeper centres produced on an upright vigorous plant which remains tidy and seems to enjoy most soils. A first-class rose.
(R) (H) (P) ☉ (VF) (AL)
4' × 3'   120 × 90 cm

'Jules Margottin'

Margottin FRANCE 1853
'La Reine' seedling
This rose has lots of thick, dark green foliage on strong, thorny stems. From these emerge equally strong, pointed buds opening into large, flattish flowers of deep carmine each with a strong scent.
(R) (VF) (AL)
4' × 3'   120 × 90 cm

'Juliet'

W. Paul UK 1910
'Captain Hayward' × 'Soleil d'Or'
A multi-coloured rose. Flowers open from shapely, golden-yellow to a rich pink to a deep rosy-red on the inside of each petal with clear tawny-gold on the outside. Fragrant. Plentiful wrinkled dark green foliage. Quite vigorous and bushy.
(R) (Gh) (VF) ☉ ✗ (AL)
4' × 3'   120 × 90 cm

'Kaiserin Auguste Viktoria'

P. Lambert GERMANY 1891
'Coquette de Lyon' × 'Lady Mary Fitzwilliam'
Shapely, very double flowers open flattish from high-centred buds. Pure white with lemon centres and a delicious perfume. Mid-green foliage on a vigorous if

somewhat twiggy, bushy plant.
(R) (P) ☉ (Gh) (VF) ✄
(AL) 3′ × 3′ 90 × 90 cm

'La Reine', 'Reine des Français'

Laffay FRANCE 1842
Large, globular almost portly
blooms, high-centred as buds but
opening to cupped blooms with

'Mabel Morrison'

'Marguerite Guillard'

flattish tops, the numerous petals
giving an almost serrated effect.
Colour silvery rose-pink with an
undertone of lilac. The shrub is
upright, well foliated but not too
tall. One of the first Hybrid Perpetuals, its influence can still be
seen in roses to this day.
(C) ☉ (VF) (AL)
3′ × 2′ 90 × 60 cm

'Le Havre'

Eudes FRANCE 1871
Scented, very double, almost vermilion-red flowers on a healthy,
strong plant with dark green,
leathery foliage.
(R) ☉ (VF) (AL)
4′ × 3′ 120 × 90 cm

'Mabel Morrison'

Broughton UK 1878
'Baroness Rothschild' sport
A white sport of the excellent
'Baroness Rothschild', inheriting
most of her attributes except
height, as this rose – for me at
least – is somewhat shorter.
Flowers pure white with flecks of
pink in hot weather.
(R) (P) (H) (B) ☉ (VF)
(AL) 4′ × 3′ 120 × 90 cm

'Mme Ferdinand Jamin' *see* 'American Beauty'

'Mme Gabriel Luizet'

Liabaud FRANCE 1877
Large, often quartered, fully
double flowers of deep glowing
pink with paler petal edges when
fully open. Very vigorous with
good foliage and stout strong
stems. Seldom remontant
although the occasional autumn
bloom can be rewarding.
(S) (P) (VF) (AL)
6′ × 4′ 1.8 × 1.2 m

'Mme Scipion Cochet'

S. Cochet FRANCE 1873
Attractively wrinkled, cup-shaped
flowers, deep purplish-pink paling to softer shades at the edges,
good, dark green foliage and
vigorous, bushy growth.
(R) (VF) (AL)
4′ × 3′ 120 × 90 cm

'Mme Victor Verdier'

E. Verdier FRANCE 1863
'Sénateur Vaisse' × unknown
Huge buds open to shaggy, but
attractive, double, light crimson
to carmine flowers with slightly
weak necks. Plenty of good, dark-
green foliage. Shrub vigorous and
healthy.
(R) (P) (H) (VF) (AL)
5′ × 4′ 1.5 × 1.2 m

'Magna Charta'

W. Paul UK 1876
Bright pink flowers with deeper
carmine shadings, fully double
and cupped when fully open.
Scented. Dark green, leathery
foliage. Bushy, tidy growth.
(P) (R) ☉ (VF) (AL)
3′ × 3′ 90 × 90 cm

'Marchioness of Londonderry'

Dickson UK 1893
Fragrant white blooms tinted soft
pink, large and full. Good mid-
green foliage. Very vigorous.
(R) (P) (VF) ✄ (AL)
6′ × 4′ 1.8 × 1.2 m

'Marguerite Guillard'

Chambard FRANCE 1915
'Frau Karl Druschki' sport
Has fewer petals than its parent,
enabling it to open in wet
weather. Otherwise similar in
both colour and habit.
(R) (AL) 5′ × 3′ 150 × 90 cm

'Merveille de Lyon'

Pernet Pere FRANCE 1882
Sport of 'Baroness Rothschild'
Large, full flowers, cupped when
fully open and held on strong,
stout stems. Pure white flushed
soft pink, especially at the petal
edges. Scented. Very free-flowering. Foliage large, greyish-dark

'Merveille de Lyon'

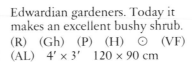

Edwardian gardeners. Today it makes an excellent bushy shrub.
(R) (Gh) (P) (H) ☉ (VF) (AL) 4′ × 3′ 120 × 90 cm

'Paul Neyron'

Levet FRANCE 1869
'Victor Verdier' × 'Anna de Diesbach'
This sturdy, healthy variety should be grown more extensively. Very large unfading, rich, warm pink flowers with a pleasing, muddled appearance when fully open. Scented. Growth strong and upright, with large, matt, dark green leaves.
(R) (Gh) (P) (H) (B) ☉ (VF) (AL) 3′ × 2′ 90 × 60 cm

'Paul Neyron'

'Paul Ricault'

Portemer FRANCE 1845
A rose with large, almost Centifolia-like, fully double flowers opening flat and

'Mrs John Laing'

green. Growth sturdy and upright. A little prone to mildew but well worth living with.
(R) (P) (H) ☉ (Gh) (VF) ✄ (AW)
4′ × 3′ 120 × 90 cm

'Mrs John Laing'

Bennett UK 1887
'François Michelon' seedling

Undoubtedly one of the superior Hybrid Perpetuals and one of the best from Henry Bennett's stable in late Victorian times. Upright in growth with large, grey-green leaves. A healthy plant producing an abundance of scented, shapely, silver-pink flowers, which would have been used extensively for exhibition by Victorian and

'Mme Victor Verdier'

'Paul Ricault'

quartered, borne along long, arching stems on a vigorous, thorny, well-foliated shrub.
(R) (P) (VF) (AL)
5′ × 4′ 1.5 × 1.2 m

'Paul's Early Blush', 'Mrs Harkness'

W. Paul UK 1893
'Heinrich Schultheis' sport
Blush-pink flowers, which as the name suggests, appear a few days earlier than most, large, very double and scented, produced on a strong, thorny bush, with thickish branches. Foliage dark green.
(R) (P) ☉ (VF) M❦ (AL)
4′ × 3′ 120 × 90 cm

'Pierre Notting'

Portemer FRANCE 1863
'Alfred Colomb' seedling
An upright grower with deep crimson, globular flowers. Highly scented. One of many such types from the middle of the 19th century, presumably owing their survival to a strong constitution, which this rose certainly has.
(R) (P) (VF) (AL)
4′ × 3′ 120 × 90 cm

'Prince Camille de Rohan', 'La Rosière'

E. Verdier FRANCE 1861
'Général Jacqueminot' × Géant des Batailles'
Can be faulted by its very weak neck, otherwise a fascinating rose. Deep blackish-red blooms of colossal size, opening flat and deepening with age. The shrub is rather sprawly and until mature has difficulty in carrying the weight of the blooms on its thinnish stems. Foliage dark green.
(R) ☉ (VF) BS❦ M❦
(AL) 4′ × 3′ 120 × 90 cm

'Reine des Violettes', 'Queen of the Violets'

Millet-Malet FRANCE 1860
'Pius IX' seedling
If I had to choose just one Hybrid Perpetual, it would have to be this one. An upright-growing and almost thornless shrub with stout, erect branches. Foliage grey-green and soft to touch. Flowers, sometimes charmingly hidden among the foliage, with which they blend so well, are soft, velvety violet, opening flat and quartered. To cap all this, it has a lovely perfume. Flowers shatter very quickly after reaching perfection, but this small fault helps me appreciate it even more.
(C) (P) (H) ☉ (VF) (AL)
5′ × 3′ 150 × 90 cm

'Roger Lambelin'

Schwartz FRANCE 1890
'Fisher Holmes' sport
A strange rose, whose addiction to mildew and other diseases renders it no more than a novelty. Flowers double and crimson-maroon with white streaks and stripes, especially on the edges of the petals.
(R) ☉ M❦ R❦ (VF) (AL)
4′ × 3′ 120 × 90 cm

'Ruhm von Steinfurth', 'Red Druschki'

Weigand GERMANY 1920
'Frau Karl Druschki' × 'Ulrich Brunner Fils'
An old exhibition variety. Plump, double, high-centred flowers of ruby red fading to cerise, cupped when open. Scented. Bush upright and sturdy with leathery, dark green foliage. A Hybrid Tea in all but pedigree.
(R) (P) ☉ (VF) (AL)
3′ × 2′ 90 × 60 cm

'Reine des Violettes'

'Ruhm von Steinfurth'

'Sidonie'

Vibert FRANCE 1847
Almost a Portland. Scented, slightly fimbriated, fully double flowers of medium size and of clear glowing pink, usually in well-spaced clusters. Has a short tidy habit but is vigorous with good if somewhat coarse foliage and an unfortunate addiction to black spot.
(C) (P) ☉ BS❦ (VF)
(AL) 3′ × 2′ 90 × 60 cm

'Snow Queen' *see* **'Frau Karl Druschki'**

'Sidonie'

'Roger Lambelin'

'Souvenir d'Alphonse Lavallée'

Verdier FRANCE 1884
For years there has been some confusion between this rose and another Hybrid Perpetual, 'Souvenir du Docteur Jamain'. 'Lavallée' is a lovely full, scented rose, combining several shades of crimson and purple. Inclined to wander if grown as a shrub unless tethered to a stake or a tripod. Best grown as a small climber. More thorny than 'Jamain'.
(R) (P) (VF) (AL)
8' × 6'   2.5 × 1.8 m

'Souvenir de Jeanne Balandreau'

Robichon FRANCE 1899
The large, double, cupped flowers, of deep cerise with pink stripes and vermilion highlights, are shapely and held erect on strong necks amid good dark grey-green foliage on an upright, tidy shrub.
(R) (P) (H) ☉ (VF) (AL)
4' × 3'   120 × 90 cm

'Souvenir du Docteur Jamain'

Lacharme FRANCE 1865
'Charles Lefèbvre' seedling
A superb rose if kept away from scorching sun, which it hates. Flowers are rich ruby-red and, although semi-double, open to a cupped shape, sometimes showing off their anthers to good effect. Foliage is dark green and the stems relatively thornless. Scented. At its best it is of rare beauty and even at its worst can still be enjoyed.
(R) (N) (P) ● (VF) (AL)
10' × 7'   3 × 2 m

'Souvenir du Docteur Jamain'

'Spencer'

W. Paul UK 1892
'Merveille de Lyon' sport
Fully double flowers opening flat from globular buds, soft satin-pink, with paler, almost white reverse. Growth vigorous but tidy, with good dark foliage.
(R) ☉ (VF) (AL)
4' × 3'   120 × 90 cm

'Star of Waltham'

W. Paul UK 1875
Flowers rich carmine-red opening shapely, slightly cupped to flat with tidily arranged petals. Fragrant and held on a strong neck. Foliage large, darkish-green. Stems fairly free of prickles. Growth upright and bushy.
(R) (H) ☉ (Gh) (VF) M☙
(AL)   3' × 3'   90 × 90 cm

'Surpassing Beauty', 'Woolverstone Church Rose'

Rediscovery by the late Mr Humphrey Brooke
Reintroduced Beales UK 1980
An old variety of climbing rose discovered growing at Woolverstone Church, Suffolk. Flowers deep red to crimson, blowsy when open and very strongly fragrant, appearing par-ticularly early each season. Well worth its reintroduction. Growth relaxed and vigorous.
(R) (P) (VF) M☙ (AL)
8' × 6'   2.5 × 1.8 m

'Ulrich Brunner Fils', 'Ulrich Brunner'

A. Levet FRANCE 1882
Confused parentage – probably 'Paul Neyron' sport
Large, plump, initially high-centred blooms opening rather loosely but attractively; rosy-carmine fading to pink with age. Sweetly scented. The bush is upright and well endowed with dark green foliage. Stems have few thorns.
(R) (H) (P) ☉ (VF) (AL)
4' × 3'   120 × 90 cm

'Vick's Caprice'

Vick USA 1891
'Archiduchesse Elizabeth d'Autriche' sport
Large, double, cupped flowers with high centres. An unusual colour combination of pale pink and lilac with white, flecked and striped deeper pink. Foliage large, attractively light green, taking an upright stance on relatively thornless shoots.
(C) (H) ☉ (P) (MF) (AL)
4' × 3'   120 × 90 cm

'Victor Hugo'

J. Schwartz FRANCE 1884
('Charles Lefebvre' × unknown) × unknown
Fragrant, large flowers of deep rosy-red shaded purple, fully double and cupped. Foliage leathery, dark green. Growth vigorous and bushy.
(R) ☉ (Gh) (VF) (AL)
4' × 3'   120 × 90 cm

'Victor Verdier'

Lacharme FRANCE 1859
'Jules Margottin' × 'Safrano'
Large, fully double, clear bright rose-pink flowers held on a firm neck, with a good perfume. Stems strong and thorny with good dark green foliage. Upright in growth. An important stud rose.
(R) (P) ☉ (VF) (AL)
4' × 3'   120 × 90 cm

'Vick's Caprice'

English Roses

Over the past twenty-five or so years, a range of very interesting roses have been developed which, because of their obvious differences from the general run of modern roses, have emerged as a new group in their own right. These differences are most obvious in the shape and structure of the flowers which are seldom high-centred but either cupped or flat or both, and invariably made up of many more smaller petals than, say, the average Hybrid Tea.

Further differences also show up in many varieties in both foliage and thorn patterns and, sometimes, in the general demeanour of the plant. They are almost all fragrant to some degree.

With one or two exceptions all these varieties have been developed by the English rose producer and hybridizer David Austin; prompted, no doubt, by his own taste in roses and by the realization that a certain section of the public prefer the charm of the 'old' to what they consider the brashness of the 'new'. David, to his eternal credit, set about capturing the best of both worlds and, slowly at first, but of late rapidly, this is exactly what he has done, creating remontant varieties in the style of the old Gallicas, Centifolias, Damasks and Bourbons, but with the growth habit of the modern Shrub Roses, Floribundas and Hybrid Teas.

Such has been the success of what David has called his 'English Roses' that, wherever I have been in the world, I have come upon them growing in some very prominent places and, furthermore, whatever he prefers to call them himself, they are generally known as 'Austin' roses, a testimony indeed to him and his work.

Having said all this, David, I feel, would be the first to admit that some of the roses in this group need a little extra loving care to give of their best and a small minority are martyrs to mildew and black spot; but then so are many modern roses, so this criticism should be seen in that context only and should not put anyone off growing any of these charming, excellent varieties.

I am not sure if I have placed these rightfully in the correct order of things in this book but, since their remontancy no doubt owes its allegiance to the Chinas, the section *Chinensis* would seem to be correct.

CLASSIFICATION

BARB   Class 26
MR9   Class 54
WFRS   Classes 1 and 2

'Yolande d'Aragon'

'Xavier Olibo'

Lacharme FRANCE 1865
'Général Jacqueminot' sport
This rose has all the attributes and faults of 'Général Jacqueminot', but its colour is a much darker red.
(R) (VF) R ⚜ (AL)
5′ × 4′   1.5 × 1.2 m

'Yolande d'Aragon'

Vibert FRANCE 1843
Flat, fully double flowers of considerable size, bright purplish to rich pink, scented. A good, healthy shrub with strong upright growth and light green foliage.
(R) (P) ☉ (VF) (AL)
4′ × 3′   120 × 90 cm

'Abraham Darby'

'Abraham Darby' (Auscot)

Austin UK 1985
Full, large, cupped blooms in shades of apricot and yellow with a fruity fragrance. Strong, arching growth habit, quite thorny with dark green, leathery foliage.
(R) ☉ (P) (VF) ⚜ (AW)
5′ × 4′   1.5 × 1.2 m

'Admired Miranda' (Ausmira)

Austin UK 1983
'The Friar' × 'The Friar'
Large, fully double, light pink blooms opening flat and reflexing. Foliage mid-green and semi-glossy. Growth upright.
(C) (VF) ☉ (AL)
3′ × 2′   90 × 60 cm

'Ambridge Rose' (Auswonder)

Austin UK 1990
Medium sized flowers at first cupped, later loosely rosette-shaped. Deep apricot-pink paling towards the edges. Foliage mid-green. Growth bushy.
(C) ☉ (B) (H) (SF) (AL)
2′ 6″ × 2′   75 × 60 cm

'Belle Story' (Auselle)

Austin UK 1984
('Chaucer' × 'Parade') × ('The Princess' × 'Iceberg')
Freely produced pale pink flowers of an unusual formation, described by its raiser as 'wide but incurving with a pronounced boss of stamens at the centre'. These are produced on an open shrub with few thorns and mid-green, glossy foliage.
(R) ⊙ (H) (VF) ✄ (AL)
4' × 4' 1.2 × 1.2 m

'Bibi Maizoon' (Ausdimindo)

Austin UK 1989
Very full flowers, deeply cupped and fragrant, of pure clear rich pink, outer petals paler. Growth slightly arching but bushy. Foliage mid-green and plentiful.
(R) ⊙ (H) (VF) ✄ (AW)
3' 6" × 3' 6" 1.1 × 1.1 m

'Bredon' (Ausbred)

Austin UK 1984
'Wife of Bath' × 'Lilian Austin'
Medium to small sized, fragrant, fully double, neatly formed flowers of buffy-yellow. Foliage light green, matt. Growth upright, bushy.
(C) ⊙ (P) (H) (VF) (AL)
3' × 2' 90 × 60 cm

'Claire Rose'

'Brother Cadfael' (Ausglobe)

Austin UK 1990
Richly fragrant, huge, fully double, globular peony-like flowers of soft pink. Foliage large, mid-green. Growth stout, bushy.
(R) ⊙ (H) (VF) ✄ (AL)
3' 6" × 3' 110 × 90 cm

'Charles Austin'

Austin UK 1973
'Chaucer' × 'Aloha'
Large, cupped, full blooms of apricot-yellow paling slightly with age. Very fragrant. Foliage mid-green, plentiful. Growth arching.
(R) (H) (P) (CL) (VF) ✄
(AL) 5' × 5' 1.5 × 1.5 m

'Charles Rennie Mackintosh' (Ausren)

Austin UK 1988
Fully double flowers, cupped with muddled petals when fully open. Lilac-pink with a very strong perfume. Foliage plentiful, mid-green on a rugged, thorny, bushy shrub.
(C) ⊙ (B) (H) (CL) (VF)
✄ (AL) 3' 6" × 3' 110 × 90 cm

'Charmain' (Ausmain)

Austin UK 1982
Seedling × 'Lilian Austin'
Clusters of fully double, rich deep pink flowers opening flat with reflexing outer petals. Fragrant. Foliage semi-glossy, mid-green. Growth spreading and bushy.
(C) ⊙ (B) (H) (P) (VF)
(AL) 3' 6" × 3' 6" 1.1 × 1.1 m

'Chaucer'

Austin UK 1970
Seedling × 'Constance Spry'
Mid-pink blooms open cupped and quartered with a strong scent, produced in small clusters. Foliage mid-green. Growth vigorous

'Brother Cadfael'

but bushy with a multitude of pink, viciously hooked thorns.
(R) ⊙ (B) (H) (VF) M✥
(AL) 3' 6" × 3' 110 × 90 cm

'Claire Rose' (Auslight)

Austin UK 1986
Fragrant, initially cupped flowers, open to many-petalled, flat, large, rosette-shapes, clear blush-pink in colour fading to almost white when fully open. Foliage large, light green. Growth upright, vigorous.
(R) (H) (P) (WW) (MF)
M✥ (AL) 4' × 3' 120 × 90 cm

'Cottage Rose'

Austin UK 1991
Medium-sized, fully double cupped blooms of warm pink produced throughout the summer. Fragrant. Foliage plentiful. Growth free branching, bushy.
(C) ⊙ (H) (MF) (AL)
3' 6" × 3' 110 × 90 cm

'Country Living'

Austin UK 1991
Delicate pink flowers fading to almost white, cupped and made up of a multitude of short petals to form a perfect rosette. Foliage plentiful, small. Growth twiggy and bushy.
(C) ⊙ (SF) (AL)
4' × 3' 120 × 90 cm

'Cressida'

Austin UK 1983
Beautiful, large, apricot-pink flowers open full, flat with somewhat muddled petals adding to its attractiveness and exuding a distinct myrrh-like fragrance. Foliage coarse, darkish-green. Growth vigorous, upright and thorny.
(R) (H) (CL) (P) (MF) M✥
(AL) 5' × 4' 1.5 × 1.2 m

'Dark Lady'

Austin UK 1991
Large peony-like, fully double, loosely arranged flowers of deep rosy-red, strongly fragrant. Foliage dark green. Wider than tall.
(R) ⊙ (G) (H) (SF) (AL)
3' × 3' 6" 90 × 110 cm

'Dove' (Ausdove)

Austin UK 1984
'Wife of Bath' × 'Iceberg' seedling
Fully double, Hybrid Tea-like flowers at first, opening to loose, rosette form. Colour soft blush-pink to white and produced in small clusters. Slightly fragrant. Growth wide, bushy. Foliage mid-to-dark green, semi-glossy.
(C) (B) (P) ✄ (SF) (AL)
3' 6" × 4' 1.1 × 1.2 m

'Ellen' (Auscup)

Austin UK 1984
Flowers fully double, cupped, rich apricot in colour, deepening towards the centre. Very fragrant. Foliage large, mid-green. Growth dense, wide and bushy.
(C) (H) (B) ✂ (VF) M ⚘
(AL)   4' × 4'   1.2 × 1.2 m

'Emanuel'

Austin UK 1985
Freely produced large, rosette-shaped blooms of delicate blush pink with hints of gold deep in the centre of each bloom. Very fragrant. Foliage mid-green. Growth bushy, upright.
(C) ⊙ (H) (B) ✂ (VF)
(AL)   4' × 3'   120 × 90 cm

'English Elegance'

Austin UK 1986
Large, fully double blooms, blush pink at the edges with tints of bright pink, salmon and orange in the centres. Foliage mid-green, growth arching, bushy and vigorous.
(C) ⊙ (H) (P) ✂ (SF)
M ⚘ (AL)
4' × 3' 6"   1.2 × 1.1 m

'English Garden' (Ausbuff)

Austin UK 1987
The flat, rosette-like flowers, sizeable and with many petals, are pale yellow deepening towards the centre. Foliage mid-green. Growth compact and upright.
(C) (H) (VF) ⊙ (AL)
4' × 3'   120 × 90 cm

'Evelyn'

Austin UK 1991
Shallow, cup-shaped, fully double flowers of bright orange-apricot. Richly fragrant. Foliage plentiful mid-green. Growth vigorous, bushy.
(R) ⊙ (H) ✂ (SF) (AL)
4' × 3'   120 × 90 cm

'Fair Bianca' (Ausca)

Austin UK 1982
Very double flowers opening flat and quartered, soft yellow and white in colour with reflexed edges. Fragrant. Foliage semi-glossy, mid to light green. Growth short, upright and bushy.
(C) ⊙ (B) (H) ✂ (MF)
M ⚘ (AL)   3' × 2'   90 × 60 cm

'Financial Times Centenary' (Ausfin)

Austin UK 1988
Highly fragrant, deep clear pink, globular flowers opening flat but blowsy. Foliage rich dark green. Growth strong and upright.
(C) ⊙ (B) (H) ✂ (VF)
(AL)   3' 6" × 3'   110 × 90 cm

'Fisherman's Friend' (Auschild)

Austin UK 1987
Rich crimson flowers, very large and full in the old style. Mid-green foliage on a robust plant.
(C) (H) (VF) ⊙ (AL)
4' × 3'   120 × 90 cm

'English Garden'

'Fair Bianca'

Top: 'Warwick Castle', and *above*, 'Country Living'

'Gertrude Jekyll' (Ausbord)

Austin UK 1987
Its deep pink, fully double
flowers are in the old style, and
are very fragrant. Greyish-green
foliage comes on an upright,
bushy plant.
(C) (H) (VF) (AL)
4′ × 3′ 120 × 90 cm

'Graham Thomas' (Ausmas)

Austin UK 1983
Seedling × ('Charles Austin' ×
'Iceberg' seedling)
A very good variety, the large,
fully double, many-petalled
flowers are in the old-fashioned
style but with the modern colour
of rich yellow with a deeper

'Graham Thomas'

'Gertrude Jekyll'. *Top left:* 'Fisherman's Friend', and *right*, 'Heritage'

centre. Fragrant. Foliage dark
green and glossy on a bushy
plant.
(C) (P) (H) (VF) ☉ (AW)
4′ × 3′ 120 × 90 cm

'Heritage' (Ausblush)

Austin UK 1984
Seedling × 'Iceberg' seedling
Cupped, fully double flowers of
light pink with deeper centres.
Foliage smallish and dark green
with a slight gloss. Growth bushy.
(C) (H) (P) (VF) ☉ (AL)
4′ × 4′ 1.2 × 1.2 m

'Hero' (Aushero)

Austin UK 1983
'The Prioress' × seedling
The eye-catching mid-pink
blooms are cupped and moderately full. Foliage mid-green and
semi-glossy. Growth upright and
bushy.
(C)   (H)   (VF)   ☉   (AL)
4′ × 4′   1.2 × 1.2 m

'Hilda Murrell' (Ausmurr)

Austin UK 1984
Seedling × ('Parade' × 'Chaucer')
Shapely, fully double flowers
opening flat and quartered, of a
rich clear pink colouring and with
a pure fragrance. Foliage mid-
green, matt. Growth upright,
bushy, a little shy in autumn.
(R)   ☉   (H)   (P)   (VF)   ✄
(AW)   4′ × 4′   1.2 × 1.2 m

'Kathryn Morley' (Ausvariety)

Austin UK 1990
Clear soft pink, cup-shaped
flowers with a delicious perfume
produced very freely on a broad,
bushy, low-growing plant amid
plentiful, light green foliage.
(C)   ☉   (B)   (H)   ✄   (VF)
(AL)   3′ × 3′   90 × 90 cm

'L. D. Braithwaite' (Auscrim)

Austin UK 1988
The Squire' × 'Mary Rose'
Richly fragrant, fully double,
heavy flattish blooms of rich
glowing crimson with a hint of
cerise. Very freely produced on a
vigorous, wide-growing, bushy
plant amid good greyish-green
foliage.
(R)   ☉   (G)   ✄   (VF)   (AL)
3′ × 4′   90 × 120 cm

'L. D. Braithwaite'

'Leander' (Auslea)

Austin UK 1982
'Charles Austin' × seedling
Fragrant shapely flowers are made
up of a multitude of deep apricot
petals, to give a finished bloom in
the style of the Gallica 'Charles de
Mills'. Foliage glossy, dark green.
Growth, tall bushy and wide.
(R)   ☉   (G)   (B)   (Gh)   (VF)
M ⚘   (AL)   6′ × 5′   1.8 × 1.5 m

'Lilian Austin'

Austin UK 1973
'Aloha' × 'The Yeoman'
The semi-double flowers of
salmon-pink tinged apricot, deep
ening towards the centre, open
flat and are produced in clusters.
Foliage mid-green and glossy.
Growth bushy and arching.
(C)   (SF)   (AL)
4′ × 4′   1.2 × 1.2 m

'Lucetta'

Austin UK 1983
Clusters of very large, semi-
double, scented flowers of soft
blush-pink paling with age to
white. Foliage mid-green. Growth
wide and spreading.
(R)   ☉   (H)   (G)   ●   (VF)
(AL)   4′ × 4′   1.2 × 1.2 m

'Mary Rose' (Ausmary)

Austin UK 1983
Seedling × 'The Friar'
Very double flowers in the old-
fashioned form, warm-mid-pink
with a deeper centre and cupped.
Foliage glossy and mid-green.
Upright and bushy growth.
(C)   (B)   (VF)   ☉   (AW)
4′ × 3′   120 × 90 cm

'Othello' (Auslo)

Austin UK 1983
Rich dusky-crimson flowers,
large, fully double and cupped
changing to purple with age.
Good perfume. Foliage dark
green. Growth dense, bushy and
upright bearing numerous vicious
thorns.
(C)   ☉   (B)   (H)   ✄   (VF)
M ⚘   (AL)
3′ 6″ × 2′ 6″   110 × 75 cm

'Perdita'

Austin UK 1983
Very fragrant, apricot-blush
coloured, fully double, flat, quartered flowers borne amid dark

green foliage on a dense, bushy
plant.
(C)   ☉   (B)   (H)   ✄   (SF)
(AL)   3′ 6″ × 2′ 6″   110 × 75 cm

'Potter & Moore'

Austin UK 1988
'Wife of Bath' seedling
Large, rose pink flowers of many

'Othello'

'Mary Rose'

'Perdita'

'Sharifa Asma'

petals in the cupped style of the old Bourbons. Scented and very freely produced on a short, bushy plant with plenty of mid-green foliage.
(C) ☉ (B) (H) ✄ (VF) (AL) 3' × 3' 90 × 90 cm

'Pretty Jessica'

Austin UK 1983
Shapely, cupped blooms, fully double, of rich warm pink with a lovely perfume, produced in abundance on a bushy, tidy plant with ample mid-green foliage.
(C) ☉ (B) (H) ✄ (VF) (AL) 2' 6" × 3' 75 × 90 cm

'Prospero' (Auspero)

Austin UK 1983
'The Knight' × unnamed seedling
Very dark red, fully double, very well formed flowers in the style of the old double Gallicas, ageing to purple. Very fragrant. Foliage matt, dark green. Growth spreading. Needs extra special care to thrive.
(C) ☉ (B) (Gh) ✄ (VF) M ✿ BS ✿ (AL) 2' × 3' 60 × 90 cm

'Queen Nefertiti' (Ausap)

Austin UK 1988
Rosette blooms of good size, soft yellow brushed apricot. Fragrant. Foliage plentiful, mid-green. Growth bushy, branching freely.
(C) ☉ (B) (H) ✄ (VF) (AL) 3' × 2' 6" 90 × 75 cm

'St Cecilia' (Ausmit)

Austin UK 1986
Well spaced, lovely creamy-buff-shaded-pinkish-orange flowers, cupped until fully open, then flattish with muddled centres. Very fragrant. Foliage soft green tinted bronze. Growth open, bushy.
(C) ☉ (B) (H) ✄ (VF) (AL) 3' 6" × 3' 6" 1.1 × 1.1 m

'Sir Clough'

Austin UK 1986
Clusters of semi-double flowers of bright pink with golden stamens displayed to advantage when fully open. Foliage leathery dark green. Growth upright, branching. Named after the architect Sir Clough William-Ellis.
(R) (H) (W) (P) (CL) (MF) (AL) 5' × 4' 1.5 × 1.2 m

'Sir Walter Raleigh' (Ausspry)

Austin UK 1985
Its peony-like flowers, cupped with open centres displaying golden stamens, are clear warm pink. Foliage large and mid-green. Growth bushy.
(C) (H) (VF) ☉ (AL) 4' × 4' 1.2 × 1.2 m

'Sharifa Asma' (Ausreef)

Austin UK 1987
Fragrant, cupped flowers open reflexed to form a very double rosette of delicate blush-pink, fading with age to almost pure white on the outer petals. Foliage mid-green. Growth arching and bushy.
(C) ☉ (B) (H) ✄ (VF) (AL) 3' × 2' 6" 90 × 75 cm

'Swan' (Auswhite)

Austin UK 1987
Huge, pure white, fully double, flat, rosette-shaped flowers with hints of buff as they open. Fragrant. Foliage soft mid-green. Growth vigorous, upright and shrubby.
(R) (H) (W) ✄ (VF) (AL)· 4' × 3' 6" 1.2 × 1.1 m

'Sweet Juliet' (Ausleap)

Austin UK 1989
Noisette-related
Shallow, cupped, fragrant, apricot-yellow flowers produced in profusion on a bushy plant with plentiful, mid-green foliage.
(C) (B) (H) ✄ (VF) (AL) 3' 6" × 3' 110 × 90 cm

'The Countryman'

'Evelyn'

'Symphony' (Auslett)

Austin UK 1986
Related to 'Comte de Chambord'
Soft yellow rosette-shaped
flowers freely produced on a
bushy, upright plant with an
abundance of light green foliage.
A delightful rose.
(C)   ☉   (B) (H)   ✂   (VF)
(AL)   3' 6" × 3'   110 × 90 cm

'The Countryman' (Ausman)

Austin UK 1987
Related to 'Comte de Chambord'
Flat, many-petalled, rosette-
shaped, old-fashioned style, fra-
grant flowers of bright rose pink.
Foliage is abundant dark greyish-
green. Growth dense and arching.
(R)   ☉   (B) (H)   ✂   (VF)
(AW)   3' × 3' 6"   90 × 110 cm

'The Miller'

Austin UK 1970
'Baroness Rothschild' × 'Chaucer'
Rounded buds open to fully
double, rosette-shaped blooms of
mid-pink produced in small,
evenly spaced clusters. Foliage
mid-green, matt. Growth vigorous, upright, bushy and well
armed with reddish thorns.
(R)   (H) (P)   ✂   (VF)   (AL)
6' × 5'   1.8 × 1.5 m

'The Nun'

Austin UK 1987
Sprays of deeply cupped (tulip-
shaped) semi-double flowers of
pure white, the deep-down stamens are displayed to advantage.
Foliage mid-green. Growth
twiggy and upright.
(C)   ☉   (H) (B)   ✂   (SF)
(AL)   4' × 3'   120 × 90 cm

'The Pilgrim'

Austin UK 1991
Delicate, pure yellow, fully
double flowers opening flat and
evenly shaped. A special feature is
its pleasing softness of texture.
Very fragrant. Foliage healthy
mid-green. Growth strong and
bushy.
(C)   (H)   ✂   (SF)   (AL)
3' 6" × 3' 6"   1.1 × 1.1 m

'The Prince' (Ausvelvet)

Austin UK 1990
Initially cupped, the flowers open
to full rosette form, starting off as
rich crimson and changing to
royal purple as they develop. Very
fragrant. Foliage is dark dusky
green. Growth is low and bushy.
(C)   ☉   (B) (H)   ✂   (VF)
(AL)   2' × 2'   60 × 60 cm

'The Prioress'

Austin UK 1969
'La Reine Victoria' × seedling
Semi-double, chalice-shaped
flowers of blush-white displaying
stamens to advantage when fully
open. Fragrant. Foliage mid-
green. Growth vigorously upright.
(R)   ☉   (H)   ✂   (MF)   BS ✿
(AL)   4' × 3'   120 × 90 cm

'The Reeve'

Austin UK 1979
'Lilian Austin' × 'Chaucer'
Its deep pink, very double flowers
are in the old fashioned style and
are produced in clusters. Reddish-
green foliage. Growth bushy,
spreading.
(R)   (H) (VF)   ☉   ✂   (AL)
4' × 4'   1.2 × 1.2 m

'The Prince'

'The Squire'

Austin UK 1977
'The Knight' × 'Château de Clos
Vougeot'
Very full, deeply cupped flowers
of dark crimson. Fragrant. Foliage
coarse dark green. Growth
sparsely bushy, thorny.
(R)   ☉   (G) (MF)   M ✿
(AL)   3' × 3' 6"   90 × 110 cm

'The Yeoman'

Austin UK 1969
'Ivory Fashion' × ('Constance
Spry' × 'Monique')
The very full flattish flowers are
salmon-pink and apricot. Mid-
green foliage on a compact bush.
(C)   (H) (VF) (B)   ☉   ✂
(AL)   3' × 2'   90 × 60 cm

'Troilus'

Austin UK 1983
Deeply cupped, fully double
flowers of honey-buff. Fragrant.
Foliage mid-green. Growth sturdy
and upright.
(R)   (II)   ✂   (VF)   M ✿   (AL)
4' × 4'   1.2 × 1.2 m

'Warwick Castle' (Auslian)

Austin UK 1986
Shapely blooms of glowing pink
packed with a multitude of small
petals to form flat rosettes, produced in small, well spaced
clusters. Fragrant. Foliage greyish-
dark-green. Growth spreading
and bushy.
(C)   ☉   (B)   ✂   (MF)   BS ✿
(AL)   2' × 2' 6"   60 × 75 cm

'Wenlock' (Auswen)

Austin UK 1984
'The Knight' × 'Glastonbury'
Large, cupped, medium-full, fragrant blooms of mid-crimson,
freely produced amid plentiful,

'Wife of Bath'

dark green, semi-glossy foliage on a bushy, vigorous plant.
(C) (H) ✄ (VF) (AL)
4' × 3' 120 × 90 cm

'Wife of Bath'

Austin UK 1969
'Mme Caroline Testout' × ('Ma Perkins' × 'Constance Spry')
Flowers deep rose-pink with a paler reverse, semi-double and cupped. Foliage small and mid-green. Growth compact and bushy.
(C) (H) (VF) (B) ☉ ✄
(AW) 3' × 2' 90 × 60 cm

'William Shakespeare'

(Ausroyal)

Austin UK 1987
Fully double flowers in the old-fashioned style of rich crimson turning to purple with age. Foliage dark green. Growth bushy.
(C) (H) (VF) (B) ☉ ✄
(AL) 4' × 3' 120 × 90 cm

'Winchester Cathedral'

(Auscat)

Austin UK 1988
Sport from 'Mary Rose'
All the characteristics of its parent 'Mary Rose' except colour, which is white brushed buff in the centres.
(C) ☉ (B) (H) (VF) (AW)
4' × 3' 120 × 90 cm

'Wise Portia' (Ausport)

Austin UK 1982
'The Knight' × seedling
Very fragrant, mauve to purple, fully double flowers in profusion on a bushy plant with dark green, semi-glossy foliage.
(C) ☉ (B) (H) ✄ (VF)
M✄ (AL)
2' 6" × 2' 6" 75 × 75 cm

'William Shakespeare'

'Winchester Cathedral'

'Yellow Button'

Austin UK 1975
'Wife of Bath' × 'Chinatown'
Soft yellow, full, button-like rosettes with deeper centres, produced freely on a wide-growing, compact bush well endowed with dark green foliage.
(C) ☉ (B) (H) (G) ✄
(SF) (AL) 3' × 3' 90 × 90 cm

'Yellow Charles Austin'

Austin UK 1981
Sport from 'Charles Austin'
All the characteristics of its parent 'Charles Austin' except colour, which is lemon-yellow.
(R) (H) (P) (CL) (VF) ✄
(AL) 5' × 5' 1.5 × 1.5 m

Hybrid Teas

The classification 'Hybrid Tea' covers all 'Hybrids of the Teas' but whilst a high-centred shape of flower is their main recognition feature, many modern varieties now have a far more complex genealogy than the earlier ones.

Thousands have been raised and introduced since the first was named 'La France' in 1867 and many, probably deservedly, have quickly fallen by the wayside. In this Dictionary I have described the best of the up-to-date varieties and quite a few of my special favourites but, above all, I have tried to present a fair representation of the history of this much loved and auspicious group of roses.

Their uses are numerous. Many of the modern varieties are almost as floriferous as Floribundas and lend themselves readily to bedding and massed display. Many will grow happily among other plants; in a herbaceous border, for example, they can be very effective. Only a few are good as hedging plants, but most, if not all, will make themselves at home growing in urns or tubs. Almost without exception they are good for providing flowers for cutting and taking indoors. Some, in the right hands, will win prizes at shows, and quite a few more will be quite happy grown under glass.

CLASSIFICATION

BARB	Class 5
MR9	Class 44
WFRS	Class 4

'Abbeyfield Rose' (Cocbrose)

Cocker UK 1985
'National Trust' × 'Silver Jubilee'
Free-flowering, with deep rosy pink blooms not over-full of petals but adequate to make this a shapely rose. Growth bushy with mid-green foliage.
(C) (SF) (B) (AL)
3' × 2' 90 × 60 cm

'Ace of Hearts', 'Asso di Cuori', 'Toque Rouge' (Korred)

Kordes GERMANY 1981
Shapely crimson to scarlet blooms with firm, crisp petals. Slightly scented. Sturdy, upright growth with dark green, glossy foliage.
(C) (MF) (B) (AL)
3' × 2' 90 × 60 cm

'Admiral Rodney'

Trew UK 1973
Huge but shapely clear rose-pink flowers on a bushy, well-foliated plant. This variety is well loved by those keen on exhibiting but, sadly, lacks the vigour and floriferousness to make a good garden plant.
(C) (MF) (E) (W) BS✿ (AL)   2' × 2'   60 × 60 cm

'Adolf Horstmann'

Kordes GERMANY 1971
'Colour Wonder' × 'Dr A. J. Verhage'
Deep yellow flowers flushed orange-pink which are large and shapely, especially so at the almost open stage. Upright and tidy growth with mid-green glossy foliage.
(C) (SF) (E) (AL)
3' × 2'   90 × 60 cm

'Alec's Red' (Cored)

Cocker UK 1970
'Fragrant Cloud' × 'Dame de Coeur'
Crimson to cherry-red flowers are produced in abundance, the buds large and plump, almost black until they start to open. Strong necked, with dark green foliage and thorny stems. A good all-rounder.
(C) (B) (VF) (P) (AW)
2' 6" × 2'   75 × 60 cm

'Alexander' see Modern Shrub Roses

'Alpine Sunset'

Cant UK 1974
'Dr A. J. Verhage' × 'Grandpa Dickson'
Soft peachy-yellow, large, full and shapely flowers are held on strong

'Alec's Red'

'Benson and Hedges Gold'

necks. Shortish, bushy but upright growth. Mid-green foliage.
(C) (B) (E) (VF) (AW)
2' 6" × 2'   75 × 60 cm

'Amatsu-Otome'

Teranishi JAPAN 1960
'Chrysler Imperial' × 'Doreen'
Very large blooms of bright yellow flushed orange and coppery-red, held upright on leggy stems. Foliage veined, mid-green, slightly glossy.
(C) (E) BS✿ (AL)
4' × 3'   120 × 90 cm

'Angèle Pernet'

Pernet-Ducher FRANCE 1924
'Bénédicte Sequin' × a Hybrid Tea
A beautiful rose of exquisite form

and one of the most lovely to have come from the auspicious stable of Pernet-Ducher. Not an easy rose to grow and not the most free with its flowers, which are coppery-orange with no trace of garishness. Rich, dark, glossy foliage.
(C) (MF) ☉ (AL)
2' × 2'   60 × 60 cm

'Anna Pavlova'

Beales UK 1981
A beautiful, full, many-petalled variety with a strong scent, each flower of blush-pink with deeper shadings held on a very strong neck. When fully open, some petals are fimbriated. Foliage large, rounded and rich dark green. In poorer soils this rose is best left unpruned.
(C) (VF) (E) (Gh) (WW)
✿ ☉ ✂ (AL)
4' × 3'   120 × 90 cm

'Anne Diamond' (Landia)

Sealand UK 1988
Apricot suffused with pink blooms produced in great profusion. Highly scented. Foliage dark green and glossy on a vigorous, tall-growing, bushy plant.
(C) (B) (H) ✂ (VF) (AL)
3' 6" × 2' 6"   105 × 75 cm

'Augustine Halem'

'Anne Watkins'

Watkins UK 1962
'Ena Harkness' × 'Grandmère Jenny'
Creamy-pink blooms with peachy shadings and of exquisite, high-centred shape on a strong neck. Foliage dark green. Growth moderately vigorous with dark stems.
(C) (MF) (Gh) ☉ ✂ (AL)
2' × 2'   60 × 60 cm

'Apricot Silk'

Gregory UK 1965
Unknown × 'Souvenir de Jacques Verschuren'
A large and free rose with shapely orange-apricot to red flowers. Vigorous to a medium height but needs a good soil really to flourish.
(C) (MF) (B) ☉ BS✿
M✿ (AL)   2' × 2'   60 × 60 cm

'Arianna' (Meidali)

Meilland FRANCE 1968
'Charlotte Armstrong' × ('Peace' × 'Michèle Meilland')
Deep carmine blooms laced and suffused with coral; large, full and with crisp petals and high-centred until fully open. Dark green foliage. Vigorous and upright in habit.
(C) (E) (B) (MF) (P) (AL)
3' × 3'   90 × 90 cm

'Asso di Cuori' see 'Ace of Hearts'

'Augustine Guinnoisseau', 'White La France'

Guinoisseau FRANCE 1889
Sport of 'La France'
A white form of the first ever Hybrid Tea which occurred soon after its introduction and has remained stable ever since.

Flowers of the same high-centred form as 'La France' with just a hint of pink overlaying the pure white colouring, otherwise the same in all respects.
(R) ⊙ (Gh) (B) (MF) (AL)
4' × 3'   120 × 90 cm

'Augustine Halem'

Guillot FRANCE 1891
One of the earliest Hybrid Teas introduced, looks to be related to 'La France'. Deep coppery-cerise heavily tinged purple, veined. Shapely. Scented. Foliage dark green. Growth upright, bushy.
(R) ○ (Gh) (B) (MF) (AL)
2' × 2'   60 × 60 cm

'Baccara' (Meger)

Meilland FRANCE 1954
'Happiness' × 'Independence'
A vigorous, well-foliated, upright grower with strong, dark green stems and big thorns. The flowers are rich bright red when grown under glass where it flourishes; deeper red out of doors. Although now quite old, 'Baccara' is still unsurpassed as a long-stemmed florist's rose. No appreciable scent.
(C) (Gh) ⊙ ✿ ✄ (AL)
3' × 2'   90 × 60 cm

'Beauté'

'Barbara Richards'

'Barbara Richards'

Dickson UK 1930
An old Hybrid Tea not freely available but I could not resist including it. Shapely, fully double flowers of yellow flushed with pink, though too big for a rather weak neck. Very free-flowering. Bushy growth with good, dark foliage.
(C) (VF) ⊙ (AL)
2' × 2'   60 × 60 cm

'Barkarole' (Tanelorak)

Tantau GERMANY 1989
Shapely blooms of very deep red produced on long stems and very fragrant. Foliage dark green and glossy. Growth upright, bushy.
Note: Not to be confused with 'Barkarolle', another red rose introduced by Laperrière in 1959.
(C) (E) (B) (H) (Gh) ✄ (VF) (AL)   3' × 2'   90 × 60 cm

'Basildon Bond' (Harjosine)

Harkness UK 1980
('Sabine' × 'Circus') × ('Yellow Cushion' × 'Glory of Ceylon')

Freely produced large blooms, reasonably well filled with apricot petals. Short and bushy in its habit of growth, and with good foliage.
(C) (B) (MF) ⊙ (AL)
2' × 2'   60 × 60 cm

'Beauté'

Mallerin FRANCE 1953
'Mme Joseph Perraud' × seedling
I hope this rose never goes out of fashion. Long, shapely buds open to delightfully semi-double flowers of rich apricot to orange. Not over-blessed with foliage and not the easiest rose to grow but well worth the effort. Upright in growth.
(C) (SF) (B) ⊙ ✄ (AL)
2' 6" × 2'   75 × 60 cm

'Belle Blonde'

Meilland FRANCE 1955
'Peace' × 'Lorraine'
Freely produced, full and slightly globular blooms of clear yellow. Good leathery foliage in the fashion of its parent, 'Peace', but far

less healthy. Growth bushy.
(C) (SF) (B) ⊙ BS ✿ (AL)
2' × 2'   60 × 60 cm

'Benson & Hedges Gold' (Macgem)

McGredy NEW ZEALAND 1979
'Yellow Pages' × ('Arthur Bell' × 'Cynthia Brooke')
Deep golden-yellow blooms, large and full; quite shapely and free-flowering. Good, clean foliage. Growth bushy and vigorous.
(C) (MF) (B) ⊙ (AW)
2' 6" × 2'   75 × 60 cm

'Bettina' (Mepal)

Meilland FRANCE 1953
'Peace' × ('Mme Joseph Perraud' × 'Demain')
A well-loved variety. Shapely buds of almost copper open to flattish, full blooms of soft orange-peach with deeper-coloured veins. Dark green foliage. Sadly, 'Bettina' is not fully hardy but is well worth growing in warmer climates.
(C) (Gh) (SF) ⊙ BS ✿ ✿ (AL)   2' × 2'   60 × 60 cm

'Betty Uprichard'

Dickson UK 1922
A fine old variety whose well-shaped, soft salmony-pink blooms have a deeper, cloudy-pink reverse. It is very free-flowering. Growth habit upright and vigorous, with good, leathery foliage.
(C) (VF) M ✿ ✄ (AL)
3' × 2'   90 × 60 cm

'Big Chief', 'Portland Trailblazer'

Dickson UK 1975
'Ernest H. Morse' × 'Red Planet'
Very large, deep crimson blooms

'Blessings'

ideal for the exhibitor but not very suitable for the garden. Tall, leggy growth.
(R) (SF) (E) (Gh) (AW)
3′ 6″ × 2′   105 × 60 cm

'Black Beauty'

Delbard FRANCE 1973
('Gloire de Rome' × 'Impeccable') × 'Papa Meilland'
Large, deep garnet-red blooms, quite fine. Its growth is bushy. Like many dark reds, this rose is not easy to grow.
(C) (SF) ☉ (AL)
2′ 6″ × 2′   75 × 60 cm

'Blessings'

Gregory UK 1967
'Queen Elizabeth' × seedling
A very free-flowering, shapely rose of soft salmon, producing ample foliage on dark stems. Its growth is fairly dense but upright. A good rose for massing in beds.
(C) (MF) (B) (P) ✄ (AW)
2′ 6″ × 2′   75 × 60 cm

'Blue Moon', 'Blue Monday', 'Mainzer Fastnacht', 'Sissi' (Tannacht)

Tantau GERMANY 1964
'Sterling Silver' seedling × seedling

'Blue Moon'

Shapely buds open to large, full blooms of silvery-lilac, variable almost to lavender. Upright in growth with good foliage. 'Blue Moon' is certainly one of the best of the 'blues'.
(C) (VF) (B) (E) ☉ ✄
(AW)   2′ 6″ × 2′   75 × 60 cm

'Blue Parfum' (Tanfifum)

Tantau GERMANY 1978
Mauve semi-double blooms with a soft grey-and-pink overlay. Growth upright. Needs loving care to give of its best.
(C) (VF) (B) ☉ (WW)
(AL)   2′ 6″ × 2′   75 × 60 cm

'Bobby Charlton'

Fryer UK 1974
'Royal Highness' × 'Prima Ballerina'
Its deep rose-pink blooms have a paler reverse and can be very large in good soils. Growth upright and vigorous, though inclined to legginess.
(C) (VF) (E) ☉ (AL)
3′ × 2′   90 × 60 cm

'Bonnie Scotland'

Anderson UK 1976
'Wendy Cussons' × 'Percy Thrower'

'Briarcliff'

Large, full, clear rose-pink and shapely flowers on an upright, medium-sized plant.
(C) (SF) (B) (AL)
2′ 6″ × 2′   75 × 60 cm

'Bonsoir'

Dickson UK 1968
Seedling × seedling
Peachy blooms with a pink overlay – large, shapely and full. Growth upright, but not very free-flowering. Good for exhibition.
(R) (SF) (E) (Gh) ☉ (WW)
(AL)   2′ 6″ × 2′   75 × 60 cm

'Brandy' (Arocad)

Swim and Christensen USA 1981
'First Prize' × 'Dr A. J. Verhage'
Long, pointed buds open to high-centred, deep apricot, fragrant blooms, each produced on long stems. Foliage mid-green. Growth upright and bushy.
(C) ☉ (H) (E) (Gh) ✄
(VF) (AW)
2′ 6″ × 2′   75 × 60 cm

'Briarcliff'

Pierson USA 1926
Sport of 'Columbia'
A shapely, slim, high-centred rose which, despite its age, can still hold its own against many a modern forcing rose when grown under glass. The colour is soft blush-pink with rose-pink shadings deep in the centre. Foliage mid-green, matt. Growth upright, tidy.
(R) (Gh) ☼ ✄ (SF) (AL)
2′ 6″ × 2′   75 × 60 cm

'Broadway' (Burway)

Perry USA 1986
('First Prize' × 'Golden Glow') × 'Sutters Gold'

'Broadway'

Beautifully formed flowers of golden-yellow-brushed-pink. Fragrant. Foliage large, dark green and semi-glossy. Growth upright.
(C) (B) (H) ● (VF) (AW)
2' 6" × 2'   75 × 60 cm

'Buccaneer'

Swim USA 1952
'Golden Rapture' × ('Max Krause' × 'Captain Thomas')
A tall, upright rose classified as a Grandiflora in its home country. Although it is not often seen these days, I have included this rose partly from sentiment – I remember it well as a youth – and partly because it ranks as one of the best yellows. Long, pointed buds open to slightly shaggy, clear yellow blooms. Very free-flowering and healthy.
(C) (P) (H) (MF) ✂ (AL)
4' × 2'   120 × 60 cm

'Cambridge Rose' (Meifersi)

Meilland FRANCE 1989
Fully double, high-centred, bright red, slightly perfumed flowers on a strong-growing, bushy plant well endowed with an abundance of dark, semi-matt green foliage.
(C) ☉ (B) (H) (Gh) ✂
(SF) (AL)
3' 6" × 2' 6"   110 × 75 cm

'Canadian White Star', 'Dr Wolfgang Poschi'

Manda CANADA 1980
'Blanche Mallerin' × 'Pascali'
Flowers fully double, white, high-centred opening attractively into the shape of a many-pointed star. These are scented and usually borne singly on strong stems bearing dark green, glossy foliage. Growth upright.
(C) ☉ (B) (H) (Gh) ✂
(MF) (AL)   3' × 2'   90 × 60 cm

'Can Can' (Legglow)

LeGrice UK 1982
'Just Joey' × ('Superior' × 'Mischief')
Large, deep orange-red blooms are freely produced on a robust, bushy plant. Good foliage.
(C) (MF) (B) (AL)
2' × 2'   60 × 60 cm

'Cary Grant' (Meimainger)

Meilland FRANCE 1987
Shapely, large, high-centred, fragrant (spicy) flowers of eye-catching orange held upright on strong stems. Dark green, glossy foliage on a vigorous plant. Excellent for exhibition.
(C) (E) (B) (H) ✂ (Gh)
(VF) (AL)   3' × 2'   90 × 60 cm

'Champion'

Fryer UK 1976
'Grandpa Dickson' × 'Whisky Mac'
Soft creamy-yellow blooms, flushed pink, which are shapely, large and very full. Its growth is short but bushy.
(R) (MF) (E) ☉ BS✤
(AW)   2' × 2'   60 × 60 cm

'Champs-Elysées'

Meilland FRANCE 1957
'Monique' × 'Happiness'
Abundant, medium-sized, fully double and rich crimson flowers produced on an angular, bushy plant with good foliage. In view of the shortage of fine red bedding varieties, only its lack of scent can have condemned this excellent rose to the sidelines.
(C) (P) (B) ☉ (AL)
2' × 2'   60 × 60 cm

'Cheshire Life'

Fryer UK 1972
'Prima Ballerina' × 'Princess Michiko'
Freely produced, moderately full, shapely blooms of rich vermilion. Upright with good foliage.
(C) (SF) (B) (AW)
2' 6" × 2'   75 × 60 cm

'Chicago Peace'

Johnston USA 1962
Sport from 'Peace'
Identical to 'Peace' except for colour, which is shaded variably from rich yellow to primrose, heavily overlaid with copper and orange.
(C) (P) (SF) (B) (H) (E)
✂ (AW)   4' × 3'   120 × 90 cm

'Christian Dior' (Meilie)

Meilland FRANCE 1959
('Independence' × 'Happiness') × ('Peace' × 'Happiness')

'Chicago Peace'

'Christian Dior'

Large, full, shapely, bright red blooms are held on a strong neck on a plant of upright growth. With a little extra attention, 'Christian Dior' can be superb. No scent.
(C) (E) M✄ (WW) ✄
(AL) 3' × 2' 90 × 60 cm

'Chrysler Imperial'

Lammerts GERMANY 1952
'Charlotte Armstrong' × 'Mirandy'
Pointed buds open to large, full, somewhat muddled, deep velvety-red flowers. Its foliage is dark green, its growth bushy and vigorous. This rose has a fair scent.
(C) (SF) (B) (E) (AL)
2' 6" × 2' 75 × 60 cm

'Cilla' (Lanjoy)

Sealand UK 1980
High-centred, shapely flowers of bright red with a straw-yellow reverse to each petal. Fragrant. Growth neat and compact with reddish-green foliage.
(C) ⊙ (B) (MF) (AL)
2' × 2' 60 × 60 cm

'Cleo' (Beebop)

Bees UK 1981
'Perfecta' × 'Prima Ballerina'
Soft rosy-pink blooms, large and full. Bushy but upright in habit and free-flowering.
(C) (SF) (B) (E) (AL)
2' 6" × 2' 75 × 60 cm

'Colorama', 'Dr R. Maag' (Meirigalu)

Meilland FRANCE 1968
'Suspense' × 'Confidence'
Bright red blooms with a yellow reverse, large and full. Growth upright but bushy. No scent.
(C) (B) ⊙ (AL)
2' 6" × 2' 75 × 60 cm

'Colour Wonder', 'Queen of Roses', 'Königin der Rosen', 'Reine des Roses' (Korbico)

Kordes GERMANY 1964
'Perfecta' × 'Super Star'
Very large, full blooms of orange and soft pink with a creamy reverse; very free-flowering .
Bushy, upright growth.
(C) (SF) (B) (E) ⊙ (AW)
2' 6" × 2' 75 × 60 cm

'Comtesse Vandal'

Leenders HOLLAND 1932
('Ophelia' × 'Mrs Aaron Ward') × 'Souvenir de Claudius Pernet'
A very beautiful rose, especially to those who like their roses classically high-centred. Pointed, orange-toned buds open to pinky-apricot with deepening tones in the centre. A superb old variety, vigorous, bushy and well-foliated.
(C) (MF) (Gh) (B) (E) ⊙
✄ (AL) 2' 6" × 2' 75 × 60 cm

'Congratulations', 'Sylvia' (Korlift)

Kordes GERMANY 1978
'Carina' × seedling
A tall, healthy rose of upright growth. Clear rose-pink, shapely and fully double blooms, with good foliage.
(C) (P) (SF) (E) (AW)
4' × 2' 120 × 60 cm

'Comtesse Vandal'

'Corso'

Cocker UK 1976
'Anne Cocker' × 'Dr A. J. Verhage'
Tall and upright, with large and full bright orange blooms on strong necks. This rose needs a little extra care to give of its best. Good, glossy foliage.
(C) (B) (E) (Gh) BS✄
M✄ (AL) 4' × 2' 120 × 60 cm

'Country Lady' (Hartsam)

Harkness UK 1988
'Alexander' × 'Bright Smile'
Flowers orange-salmon to pinkish-salmon. Shapely. Pointed in bud opening to large, full blooms with a slight perfume. Growth robust and bushy. Foliage abundant, dark green tinged reddish especially when young.
(C) ⊙ (B) (H) (Gh) ✄
(SF) (AL)
3' × 2' 6" 90 × 75 cm

'Chrysler Imperial'

'Curley Pink'

'Congratulations'

'Crimson Glory'

Kordes GERMANY 1935
'Catherine Kordes' seedling ×
'W. E. Chaplin'
A fine old rose from the past, its
large, globular, deep velvety-red
blooms are superbly scented.
They are, however, carried on a
rather weak neck. Its foliage is
dark green and a little sparse, with
thorny stems on a bushy, angular
plant.

(C) (Gh) (B) (WW) (AL)
2′ × 2′ 60 × 60 cm

'Duke of Windsor'

'Dame Edith Helen'

'Curley Pink'

Brownell USA 1948
'Pink Princess' × 'Crimson Glory'
Very freely produced rosy-red,
pointed buds open to fully
double, curly petalled flowers of
mid-to-rose-pink. Fragrant.
Growth is vigorous and bushy
bearing abundant, glossy, dark
green foliage. I recall being most
impressed with this old rose when
I saw it for the first time at The
Cranford Rose Garden, Brooklyn
Botanic Garden, New York.

Should not be allowed to disappear from catalogues.
(C) ⊙ (B) (H) (MF) (AL)
3′ × 2′ 90 × 60 cm

'Cynthia Brooke'

McGredy UK 1943
'Le Progrès' × ('Mme Mélanie
Soupert' × 'Le Progrès')
Very large, fully double, globular
flowers of deep burnished gold,
brushed with salmon. An old variety which deserves more attention today. This rose has ample
leathery foliage, is sparsely
thorned, and is of stout and
angular growth.
(C) (VF) (B) (P) ⊙ (AL)
2′ 6″ × 2′ 75 × 60 cm

'Dainty Bess'

Archer UK 1925
'Ophelia' × 'K of K'
A superb, single, Hybrid Tea
whose large, silvery-rose-pink
flowers are produced in well-
spaced clusters. The effect is considerably enhanced by rich,
golden-brown stamens. Sweetly

'Cynthia Brooke'

'Dainty Bess'

scented, with large, healthy foliage.
(C) (P) (H) (MF) ☉ (AL)
3' × 2' 90 × 60 cm

'Dame Edith Helen'

Dickson UK 1926
Very large, many-petalled, cupped flowers, sometimes opening quartered in the old-fashioned style, of rich, deep, silvery-pink. The blooms are held on a strong neck. Glossy, mid-green foliage and of upright but bushy growth.
(R) (VF) ☉ (WW) (AL)
3' × 2' 90 × 60 cm

'Dave Hessayon'
(Driscobruce)

Driscoll UK 1990
'Silver Jubilee' × 'Pink Favourite'

'Diamond Jubilee'

An eye-catching, shapely rose of deep rose pink highlighted with pearl. Foliage glossy and healthy. Growth bushy, upright.
(C) ☉ (B) (H) ✄ (MF)
(AL) 2' 6" × 2' 75 × 60 cm

'Deep Secret', 'Mildred Scheel'

Tantau GERMANY 1977
The reasonably full, large, shapely, deep crimson flowers are held on a strong neck. Good glossy foliage on an upright plant.
(C) (P) (VF) (B) ✄ (AW)
2' 6" × 2' 75 × 60 cm

'Denham'

Sealand UK 1988
The full, shapely blooms of soft creamy-yellow with a strong fragrance are produced in large quantities on a vigorous, upright yet bushy plant which is well endowed with dark green, semi-glossy foliage.
(C) ☉ (B) (H) (E) (Gh)
✄ (VF) (AL)
3' × 2' 90 × 60 cm

'Diamond Jubilee'

Boerner UK 1947
'Maréchal Neil' × 'Feu Pernet-Ducher'
One of the classic Hybrid Teas. Shapely, buff-apricot blooms are produced freely on a strong, healthy plant with leathery, dark green foliage.
(C) (P) (E) (B) ☉ (Gh)
✄ (AL) 3' × 2' 90 × 60 cm

'Diorama'

de Ruiter HOLLAND 1965
'Peace' × 'Beauté'
Shapely and large blooms of yellow flushed red are carried on a bushy plant of medium height with good foliage.
(C) (B) (P) ☉ ✄ (AW)
3' × 2' 90 × 60 cm

'Dolly Parton'

Winchel USA 1983
'Fragrant Cloud' × 'Oklahoma'
Bright orange-red flowers, fully double and very fragrant. Foliage mid-green, semi-glossy. Growth upright.
(C) (B) (H) (E) (SF) ✄
(AW) 3' × 2' 90 × 60 cm

'Doreen'

Robinson UK 1951
'Lydia' × 'McGredy's Sunset'
The very deep yellow flowers of medium size, heavily veined and suffused with orange, open muddled and are freely produced on a short, bushy, dense plant. The foliage is coppery-green and the stems are very thorny.
(C) (MF) (P) (B) (AL)
1' 6" × 2' 45 × 60 cm

'Doris Tysterman'

Tysterman UK 1975
'Peer Gynt' × seedling
An upright grower with good bronzy-green foliage. Medium-sized, globular blooms of bright tangerine to orange, bronzing with age. Very free-flowering.
(C) (P) (H) (Gh) (SF) ☉
✄ (AW) 3' × 2' 90 × 60 cm

'Double Delight' (Andeli)

Swim & Ellis USA 1977
'Granada' × 'Garden Party'
Blooms large and reasonably full, creamy-white with pinkish-red brush strokes on the edge of the petals. A superb rose at its best but not easy to grow.
(C) (Gh) (VF) ☉ ☼ (WW)
(AW) 3' × 2' 90 × 60 cm

'Doris Tysterman'

'Double Delight'

'Dr A. J. Verhage', 'Golden Wave'

Verbeek HOLLAND 1963
'Tawny Gold' × ('Baccara' × seedling)
Shapely flowers of yellow with deeper shadings, the petal edges paling attractively in sunlight to buffy-cream. A useful forcing variety with good foliage, perhaps better under glass than outside.
(C) (Gh) (B) (P) ☉ ✄
(AL) 2′ 6″ × 2′ 75 × 60 cm

'Dr John Snow'

Gandy UK 1979
'Helen Traubel' × seedling
Large, full, creamy-white and scented flowers on a tall plant of upright growth with good foliage.
(C) (B) (P) (VF) ✄ (AL)
4′ × 2′ 120 × 60 cm

'Dr McAlpine' (Peafirst)

Pearce UK 1983
Large, fine blooms, shapely and deep rose-pink. Short, bushy, rather sprawling growth.
(C) (VF) (B) (AL)
1′ 6″ × 2′ 45 × 60 cm

'Duet'

Swim USA 1960
'Fandango' × 'Roundelay'
Large, shapely, high-centred blooms of light pink with deeper reverses. Slightly fragrant. Growth upright and vigorous. Foliage mid-green, leathery.
(C) ☉ (B) (H) (Gh) ✄
(SF) (AL) 3′ × 2′ 90 × 60 cm

'Duet'

'Eden Rose'

'Duke of Windsor', 'Herzog von Windsor'

Tantau GERMANY 1969
'Prima Ballerina' × seedling
Shapely, pointed buds open quite formally to full, flattish, highly scented flowers held on a strong neck. A rose of stout, upright, thorny growth which needs extra attention to thrive.
(C) (VF) (B) ☉ M✿ (AW)
2′ 6″ × 2′ 75 × 60 cm

'Dutch Gold'

Tysterman UK 1978
'Peer Gynt' × 'Whisky Mac'
Large, globular, clear yellow blooms with hints of orange. An upright and healthy rose.
(C) (SF) (B) (E) (Gh) ✄
(AW) 3′ × 2′ 90 × 60 cm

'Eden Rose'

Meilland FRANCE 1950
'Peace' × 'Signora'
Large and shapely, deep pink blooms with a paler silvery-pink reverses are held on a strong neck. Growth vigorous and robust, the stems stout and thorny with dark green foliage.
(C) (P) (Gh) (MF) (E)
(AW) 3′ 6″ × 2′ 105 × 60 cm

'Elizabeth Harkness'

Harkness UK 1969
'Red Dandy' × 'Piccadilly'
The large blooms are very full and shapely, creamy-white to ivory flushed pink, a superb colour combination. Medium, bushy growth with good foliage.
(C) (P) (SF) (B) (E) (AW)
2′ 6″ × 2′ 75 × 60 cm

'Ellen Willmott'

Archer UK 1936
'Dainty Bess' × 'Lady Hillingdon'
A charming, single variety. Pronounced golden anthers framed

'Elizabeth Harkness'

by wavy petals of cream and pink. Growth vigorous and bushy with dark green foliage.
(C) ☉ (B) (SF) (AL)
4′ × 3′ 120 × 90 cm

'Ena Baxter' (Cocbonne)

Cocker UK 1989
Seedling × 'Silver Jubilee'
A very free-flowering rose of salmony-red with 25 or so petals, just qualifies as fully double. Produced both singly and in small trusses. Growth vigorous, bushy with large, shiny, mid-green leaves.
(C) ☉ (B) (SF) (AL)
2′ × 2′ 60 × 60 cm

'Ernest H. Morse'

'Ellen Willmott'

'Ena Harkness'

Norman UK 1946
'Crimson Glory' × 'Southport'
Bright velvety-crimson blooms, very shapely and free-flowering though held on a weak neck. The foliage is a little sparse with thorny stems.
(C) (P) (Gh) (MF) (B) (WW) (AL)
2′ × 2′ 60 × 60 cm

'Ernest H. Morse'

Kordes GERMANY 1964
Shapely, dark buds open to loosely formed, bright crimson flowers held on a strong neck. The foliage is dark green, the stems almost purple. Growth upright.
(C) (P) (Gh) (MF) (H) (B) ✂ (AW) 3′ × 2′ 90 × 60 cm

'Eroica', 'Erotika'

Tantau GERMANY 1968
Surprisingly, for the 1960s, the name was changed to 'Eroica' when it left Germany. Full, dark red blooms on an upright plant with good, dark, glossy foliage.
(C) (VF) (B) (AL)
3′ × 2′ 90 × 60 cm

'Etoile de Hollande'

Verschuren NETHERLANDS 1919
'General MacArthur' × 'Hadley'
'Etoile de Hollande' is seldom seen today except as a climber, but merits inclusion as an important rose from the past. Very fragrant, cloudy red blooms with dark green foliage, soft to the touch, on a plant of bushy, angular growth. A good forcer in its day.
(C) (VF) (Gh) M♂ ✂ (AL) 2′ × 2′ 60 × 60 cm

'Félicité' (Lanken)

Sealand UK 1985
'Fragrant Cloud' × 'Mildred Reynolds'
Fully double, shapely, salmon-orange blooms with large, mid-green, leathery foliage. Growth bushy.
(C) ☉ (B) (Gh) ✂ (AL)
2′ × 2′ 60 × 60 cm

'First Love', 'Premier Amour'

Swim USA 1951
'Charlotte Armstrong' × 'Show Girl'
Long, pointed buds open to loose, semi-double flowers of soft blush-pink with deeper shadings. The blooms are held on a strong neck on a narrow, upright plant. Very

'Etoile de Hollande'
free-flowering, with good foliage.
(C) (P) (Gh) (MF) ☺ ✂ (AL) 3′ × 1′ 6″ 90 × 45 cm

'First Prize'

Boerner USA 1970
'Enchantment' seedling × 'Golden Masterpiece' seedling

'First Love'

Pointed buds open to large, high-centred blooms of rose pink with buffish-ivory centres and a strong fragrance. Foliage dark green and leathery. Growth upright. As its name suggests, a good rose for the exhibitor.
(C) ☉ (B) (E) (Gh) ✂
(VF) (AW) 3' × 2' 90 × 60 cm

'Forgotten Dreams'

Bracegirdle UK 1981
'Fragrant Cloud' × 'Tenerife'
Bright cardinal-red blooms open semi-double. Foliage mid-green and semi-glossy on a plant of bushy, upright growth.
(C) (B) (VF) (AL)
3' × 2' 90 × 60 cm

'Fragrant Cloud', 'Duftwolke', 'Nuage Parfumé' (Tanellis)

Tantau GERMANY 1968
Seedling × 'Prima Ballerina'
Its coral-red blooms are freely produced. They are highly scented and variable in colour: sometimes muddy, sometimes quite bright. Growth slightly open. Foliage dark.
(C) (B) (VF) ☉ (AW)
2' 6" × 2' 75 × 60 cm

'Fragrant Dream' (Dicodour)

Dickson UK 1989
Very fragrant, large, shapely flowers freely produced and, in colour, a blend of apricot and salmon with lighter veins. Foliage large, mid-green and glossy. Growth sturdy and bushy.
(C) ☉ (B) (H) (Gh) ✂
(VF) (AL)
2' 6" × 2' 75 × 60 cm

'Fragrant Cloud'

'Fragrant Gold', 'Duftgold' (Tandugoft)

Tantau GERMANY 1982
Blooms deep yellow and semi-double when fully open. Upright growth. Good, glossy foliage.
(C) (B) (VF) ☉ (AW)
2' 6" × 2' 75 × 60 cm

'Fulton Mackay' (Cocdana)

Cocker UK 1988
'Silver Jubilee' × 'Jana'
Well-formed flowers of apricot and gold with a delicious perfume. Foliage abundant, mid-green and glossy. Growth bushy and upright. A worthy rose to commemorate a distinguished Scottish actor.
(C) ☉ (B) (H) (Gh) ✂
(VF) (AL)
2' 6" × 2' 75 × 60 cm

'Gail Borden'

Kordes GERMANY 1956
'Mrs A. Verschuren' × 'Viktoria Adelheid'
A large, many-petalled, shapely rose, cupped when almost fully open. The rosy-pink blooms have a soft creamy-yellow reverse. Free-flowering, and very bushy with good foliage.
(C) (P) (SF) (B) ☉ (AW)
2' 6" × 2' 75 × 60 cm

'Garden Party'

Swim USA 1959
'Charlotte Armstrong' × 'Peace'
Tubby buds open to large-ish, fully double, cupped, high-centred flowers of soft yellow to creamy-white; like its famous parent – each petal edged and tinged pink. Foliage glossy, dark green. Growth bushy and branching.
(C) ☉ (B) (H) (E) (Gh)
✂ (SF) (AL)
2' × 2' 60 × 60 cm

'Gay Gordons'

Cocker UK 1969
'Belle Blonde' × 'Karl Herbst'
An aptly named rose whose orange and yellow blooms are suffused red, full, shapely and free-flowering. Growth bushy, with slightly glossy foliage and thorny stems.
(C) (SF) (B) ☉ BS✿
(AW) 2' × 2' 60 × 60 cm

'Gina Lollobrigida' (Meilivar)

Meilland FRANCE 1989
Large, very fragrant, abundantly produced, very full blooms of rich golden-yellow produced on a strong, upright plant with dense, mid-green foliage.
(C) (B) (H) (E) (VF) (AL)
3' × 2' 90 × 60 cm

'Gold Crown', 'Corona de Oro', 'Couronne d'Or', 'Goldkrone'

Kordes GERMANY 1960
'Peace' × 'Spek's Yellow'
A tall and upright, rather stiff and lanky plant. The deep yellow blooms, occasionally with outer petals splashed red, are large and full, sometimes quartered when fully open, and produced on long stems. The foliage is glossy and the stems are dark.
(C) (P) (MF) ✂ (AL)
3' 6" × 2' 105 × 60 cm

'Golden Days' (Rugolda)

de Ruiter HOLLAND 1980
'Peer Gynt' × seedling
Large, fully double, deep yellow flowers on a bushy plant with good, mid-green, slightly glossy foliage.
(C) (SF) (B) (AL)
2' 6" × 2' 75 × 60 cm

'Golden Jubilee' (Cocagold)

Cocker UK 1981
'Peer Gynt' × 'Gay Gordons'
Large, shapely, clear yellow
blooms, brushed pink, a plant of
upright growth with good, clean
foliage. (Another 'Golden Jubilee'
was introduced by Jacobus of the
USA in 1948.)
(C) (SF) (B) ⊙ (AL)
2' 6" × 2'   75 × 60 cm

**'Golden Melody',
'Irene Churruca'**

La Florida USA 1934
'Mme Butterfly' × ('Lady
Hillingdon' × 'Souvenir de
Claudius Pernet')
A beautiful rose, one of the best
from the 1930s, with large,
shapely, high-centred, moderately

full blooms of soft yellowish-buff
flushed pink with deeper centres.
It has dark green foliage, with
darker, almost maroon, stems and
large, sparse thorns. A plant of
angular growth.
(C) (VF) (B) (E) ⊙ ✄
(AL) 2' 6" × 2'   75 × 60 cm

'Golden Sceptre' *see* **'Spek's Yellow'**

'Golden Times'

Cocker UK 1970
'Fragrant Cloud' × 'Golden
Splendour'
Clear lemon-yellow blooms,
loosely formed when fully open.
Upright and free-flowering with
good foliage.
(C) (SF) (B) (AL)
2' 6" × 2'   75 × 60 cm

'Grace de Monaco'

'Golden Wave' *see* **'Dr A. J. Verhage'**

**'Goldstar',
'Point du Jour'** (Candide)

Cant UK 1983
'Yellow Pages' × 'Dr A. J. Verhage'
Medium to large, deep yellow
blooms are freely produced on an
upright, medium-sized plant.
Good foliage.
(C) (SF) (B) (AL)
2' 6" × 2'   75 × 60 cm

'Grace Darling'

Bennett UK 1884
A very useful, older Hybrid Tea;
indeed, one of the first to be
introduced. Globular flowers of
creamy-white with petal edges

touched pink, scented and produced freely on rather angular but
sturdy plants with dark, neat,
grey-green foliage.
(B) (R) ☼ ⊙ (SF) (AL)
3' × 2'   90 × 60 cm

'Gay Gordons'

'Golden Melody'

'Grace de Monaco' (Meimit)

Meilland FRANCE 1956
'Peace' × 'Michèle Meilland'
The very large, globular blooms
have satiny petals of silvery-pink.
Its growth is dark and rather
angular, the foliage dark green
and leathery.
(C) (VF) (B) ☉ (WW)
(AL) 2′ 6″ × 2′ 75 × 60 cm

'Grand Masterpiece'

Warriner USA 1978
Seedling × 'Tonight'
Shapely, mid-red flowers of considerable substance held on long
stems, making it an ideal rose for
cutting. Lasts well in water.
Slightly fragrant. Foliage mid-
green. Growth upright and vigorous.
(C) ☉ (H) (Gh) ✂ (E)
(SF) (AW)
4′ × 3′ 120 × 90 cm

'Grandmère Jenny'

Meilland FRANCE 1950
'Peace' × ('Julien Potin' ×
'Sensation')
The blooms are mostly soft
yellow heavily brushed with pink,
variable, sometimes deeper,
flushed burnt orange. A shapely
rose, a slimmer version of 'Peace'
and beautiful when behaving
itself. Upright growth with semi-
glossy and leathery foliage.
(C) (SF) (B) ☉ BS✿ ✂
(AL) 2′ 6″ × 2′ 75 × 60 cm

'Grandpa Dickson', 'Irish Gold'

Dickson UK 1966
('Perfecta' × 'Governador Braga
da Cruz') × 'Piccadilly'
Very large, graceful, shapely
lemon-yellow blooms, sometimes
faintly brushed pink. Fully open,
they are often splashed pink.
Strong and upright growth with
ample, mid-green foliage, and
very thorny.
(C) (SF) (B) (E) (AW)
2′ 6″ × 2′ 75 × 60 cm

'Gustav Grünerwald'

P. Lambert GERMANY 1903
'Safrano' × 'Mme Caroline
Testout'
Shapely, carmine-pink blooms
suffused soft pink at the edges
and yellow in the centres. Good
perfume. Foliage mid-green.
Growth bushy. A very good old
Edwardian variety deservedly
popular in its day and not out of
place in any modern garden.
(R) ☉ (B) (Gh) ✂ (MF)
(AL) 2′ × 2′ 60 × 60 cm

'Harry Wheatcroft' (Caribia)

Wheatcroft UK 1972
Sport from 'Piccadilly'
The orange-red blooms are
striped and splashed with yellow,
flamboyant, deeper when fully
open. Growth upright and strong,
with plentiful and almost glossy
foliage.
(C) (SF) (B) ☉ R✿ (AL)
2′ 6″ × 2′ 75 × 60 cm

'Headliner' (Jactu)

Warriner USA 1985
'Love' × 'Color Magic'
Shapely, high-centred blooms of
creamy-white heavily edged with
cerise, the cerise deepening with
age, ruffled when fully opened.
Slight fragrance. Glossy, mid-
green foliage. Growth upright and
vigorous.
(C) ☉ (B) (H) (E) (SF)
(Gh) ✂ (AW)
4′ × 3′ 120 × 90 cm

'Grandpa Dickson'

'Gustav Grünerwald'

'Harry Wheatcroft'

'Heirloom'

'Hector Deane'

McGredy UK 1938
'McGredy's Scarlet' × 'Lesley
Dudley'
A fine old variety with freely produced, high-centred, full flowers
of orange and pink flushed and
shaded deeper. Good, glossy foliage and of bushy growth.
(C) (VF) (P) (B) ☉ (AL)
2′ × 2′ 60 × 60 cm

'Heirloom'

Warriner USA 1972
Seedling × seedling
Long, pointed buds open to semi-
double, very fragrant flowers of
deep clear lilac ageing to magenta,
richly scented. Foliage leathery,
mid to dark green. Growth
vigorous, bushy.
(C) ☉ (B) (H) (Gh) ✂
(VF) (AW)
4′ × 3′ 120 × 90 cm

'Helen Traubel'

Swim USA 1951
'Charlotte Armstrong' × 'Glowing
Sunset'
A beautiful rose with long,
pointed buds opening to pinkish-
apricot. Rather a weak neck but
many good points to make
amends for this. Tall and upright,
with large and darkish green foliage.
(C) (H) (MF) (B) (WW)
(AL) 3′ 6″ × 2′ 105 × 60 cm

'Helmut Schmidt' *see* 'Simba'

'Honor', 'Michèle Torr' (Jacolite)

Warriner USA 1980
Very large, loose blooms of pure white freely produced and fragrant on a bushy plant with leathery, dark green foliage.
(C) ☉ (B) (H) (Gh) ✂
(MF) (AW) 3' × 2' 90 × 60 cm

'Indian Summer' (Peaperfume)

Pearce UK 1991
Creamy-orange, full flowers with a superb perfume. Foliage abundant, glossy and mid-green. Growth compact and bushy.
(C) ☉ (B) (VF) (AL)
2' × 2' 60 × 60 cm

'Ingrid Bergman' (Poulman)

Poulsen DENMARK 1983
Seedling × seedling
Fully double, dark red blooms on a free-flowering plant of upright growth with good, mid to dark green, semi-glossy foliage.
(C) (SF) (B) ☉ (AL)
2' × 2' 60 × 60 cm

'Intermezzo'

Dot SPAIN 1963
'Grey Pearl' × 'Lila Vidri'
The fully double, sometimes quartered, flowers of greyish-lavender with a pinkish sheen are produced in clusters, the buds rounded. A bushy plant, thorny and well endowed with glossy foliage.
(C) (P) (MF) (B) ☉ (AL)
1' 6" × 1' 6" 45 × 45 cm

'Irene Churruca' *see* 'Golden Melody'

'Irish Elegance'

Dickson UK 1905
A lovely single from the beginning of this century with large, orange-scarlet blooms shaded bronze, and of vigorous, upright growth and good foliage. Seldom seen now, but I could not resist including it as a representative of the early, single Hybrid Teas.
(R) (MF) ☉ M✂ (AL)
2' 6" × 2' 75 × 60 cm

'Irish Gold' *see* 'Grandpa Dickson'

'Isobel Harkness'

Norman UK 1957
'Phyllis Gold' × 'McGredy's Yellow'
Very large blooms appear semi-double when fully open and are bright yellow paling slightly with age. Leathery, dark green foliage on a bushy plant.
(C) (MF) (B) BS✂ ✂ (AL)
2' × 2' 60 × 60 cm

'Jardins de Bagatelle' (Meimafris)

Meilland FRANCE 1986
Very fragrant, full, shapely flowers, high-centred, of creamy-yellow lightly brushed orange. Very freely produced on a strong, bushy-growing plant with good, healthy, mid-green foliage.
(C) ☉ (B) (VF) (AL)
2' × 2' 60 × 60 cm

'Jean Sisley'

Bennett UK 1879
'Adam' × 'Emilie Hansburg'
A delightful, old variety dating

back to the beginning of the Hybrid Teas. I cannot resist including it although it is, perhaps, now surpassed by others of similar colouring. Soft lilac-pink, shapely and fragrant. Good foliage if a little prone to mildew. Growth bushy. Good under glass.
(R) ☉ (B) (Gh) (MF) M✂
(AL) 2' × 2' 60 × 60 cm

'Jema'

Astor Perry USA 1982
'Helen Traubel' × 'Lolita'
Very full and shapely apricot blooms on a plant of upright growth with light green foliage and lightly coloured thorns.
(C) (MF) (B) ✂ (AL)
4' × 2' 120 × 60 cm

'Jennifer Hart'

Swim USA 1982
'Pink Parfait' × 'Yuletide'
High-centred, very double, dark red blooms are held on a strong neck with mid-green, semi-glossy foliage.
(C) (MF) (B) (Gh) ✂ (AL)
3' × 2' 90 × 60 cm

'Joanna Hill'

Hill USA 1928
'Mme Butterfly' × 'Miss Amelia Gude'
Long, pointed buds open to high-centred, full flowers of creamy-yellow flushed orange in the base. Like its famous parent, 'Mme Butterfly', expensively perfumed and classy. Foliage dark and

'Ingrid Bergman'

'Joanna Hill'

leathery. Growth bushy. At times, temperamental.
(C)　⊙　(B)　(Gh)　✂　(VF)
(AL)　2' × 2'　60 × 60 cm

'John F. Kennedy'

Boerner USA 1965
Unnamed seedling × 'White Queen'
Greenish tinted, shapely buds open pure white with creamy centres, fully double and fragrant. Foliage leathery, mid-green. Growth upright and vigorous.
(C)　(B)　(H)　(E)　(Gh)　✂
(VF)　(AW)　3' × 2'　90 × 60 cm

'Johnnie Walker' (Frygran)

Fryer UK 1982
'Sunblest' × ('Arthur Bell' × 'Belle Blonde')

Quite large apricot (whisky-coloured) blooms, moderately full and semi-double when fully open. Growth upright and bushy with mid-green matt foliage.
(C)　(MF)　(B)　⊙　✂　(AW)
3' 6" × 2'　105 × 60 cm

'John Waterer'

McGredy UK 1970
'King of Hearts' × 'Hanne'
Large, full, high-centred, crimson blooms are freely produced on an upright plant with good, dark green foliage.
(C)　(P)　(B)　⊙　✂　(AL)
3' × 2'　90 × 60 cm

'Josephine Bruce'

Bees UK 1949
'Crimson Glory' × 'Madge Whipp'
At its best a superb and beautiful rose with shapely velvet-crimson blooms. Sturdy, slightly angular growth and matt greyish-green foliage. Can be temperamental.
(C)　(VF)　(B)　⊙　M✂　(AW)
2' × 2'　60 × 60 cm

'Joyce Northfield'

Northfield UK 1977
'Fred Gibson' × 'Vienna Charm'
Pointed buds open to large high-centred flowers of deep orange. Dark foliage on a vigorous and upright plant.
(C)　(P)　(SF)　(B)　✂　(AL)
3' × 2'　90 × 60 cm

'Just Joey'

'King's Ransom'

'Julia's Rose'

Tysterman UK 1976
'Blue Moon' × 'Dr A. J. Verhage'
The small but full, deep coppery-tan blooms are blended with pink – this is an unusual rose. Its dark foliage has reddish undertones and is borne on an upright but not over-tall bush.
(C)　(SF)　(B)　✂　(AL)
2' × 2'　60 × 60 cm

'Just Joey'

Cant UK 1972
'Fragrant Cloud' × 'Dr A. J. Verhage'
A superb rose, its large, ragged-edged flowers are coppery-orange with soft pink paling at the edges when the flowers open. The foliage is dark green, leathery and semi-glossy on a rather angular plant.
(C)　(MF)　(B)　⊙　(AW)
2' × 2'　60 × 60 cm

'Kan-pai'

Suzuki JAPAN 1980
['Yu-ai' × ('Happiness' × 'American Beauty')] × 'Pharaoh'
High-centred, deep red blooms on a strong neck. An upright grower with dark green foliage.
(C)　(P)　(MF)　(B)　(AL)
2' 6" × 2'　75 × 60 cm

'Keepsake', 'Esmeralda' (Kormalda)

Kordes GERMANY 1981
Seedling × 'Red Planet'
A pleasing mixture of pinks from carmine to blush in very full, large blooms, the outer petals reflexed when partially open. Dark green foliage with stout stems bearing many large thorns. Its growth is upright but dense.
(C)　(P)　(MF)　(B)　(AL)
2' 6" × 2'　75 × 60 cm

'King's Ransom'

Morey USA 1961
'Golden Masterpiece' × 'Lydia'
Shapely, full, high-centred,
golden-yellow flowers are held on
strong necks amid an abundance
of glossy bright green foliage.
Upright and amply thorned.
(C) (Gh) (MF) (B) ☉
(AW) 2' 6" × 2' 75 × 60 cm

'Kordes' Perfecta' *see*
'Perfecta'

'Korsaun' *see* **'Royal William'**

'Kronenbourg',
'Flaming Peace' (Macbo)

McGredy UK 1965
Sport from 'Peace'
The large, full blooms are a mix-
ture of plum-red and buff with a
soft yellow reverse. Identical to
'Peace' in all other respects.
(C) (P) (H) (SF) (B) (E)
☉ (AL) 4' × 3' 120 × 90 cm

'Lady Belper'

'Lady Sylvia'

'Lady'

Weeks USA 1984
'Song of Paris' × 'Royal Highness'
Medium-sized flowers of mid-
pink are freely produced on a
compact plant with semi-glossy
mid-green foliage.
(C) (B) (SF) ☉ (AL)
2' × 2' 60 × 60 cm

'Lady Alice Stanley'

McGredy UK 1909
The full and very double flowers,
made up of more than 70 densely
packed petals, are flesh-pink with
a deeper reverse. The foliage is
rich green, the growth angular
and branching. This is a fine old
variety.
(B) (VF) ☉ (Gh) (WW)
(AL) 2' × 2' 60 × 60 cm

'Lady Barnby'

Dickson UK 1930
Very large, double, high-centred
bright pink blooms with leathery,
rich green foliage. A short and
bushy plant.
(R) (B) (VF) (Gh) ☉ (AL)
1' 6" × 2' 45 × 60 cm

'Lady Beauty'

Kono JAPAN 1984
'Lady' × 'Princess Takamatsu'
Rounded buds open large and are
pale pink flushed creamy-yellow,
the reverse deeper. The foliage is
plentiful, mid-green and glossy on
an upright and vigorous bush.
(P) (SF) (Gh) ☉ ✂ (AL)
3' × 2' 90 × 60 cm

'Lady Belper'

Verschuren HOLLAND 1948
'Mrs G. A. van Rossem' ×
seedling

A shapely, slightly tubby, high-
centred rose whose coppery-
yellow blooms are heavily
overlaid with burnt orange. Dark
green, glossy foliage on a vigorous
bush of medium growth.
(C) (P) (B) (VF) ☉ (AL)
2' × 2' 60 × 60 cm

'Lady Diana'

Hill USA 1983
'Sonia' × 'Caress'
A forcing variety with soft pink,
high-centred blooms on long
stems with mid-green foliage.
(C) (SF) (Gh) ☉ ✂ ☼
(AL) 4' × 2' 120 × 60 cm

'Lady Elgin' *see* **'Thaïs'**

'Lady Forteviot'

B.R. Cant UK 1928
A famous, old variety very popular during the 1930s. High-
centred, golden-yellow to deepish
apricot. Very fragrant flowers produced quite freely on a bushy
plant with plentiful, glossy,
bronze-green foliage.
(R) ☉ (Gh) ☼ ✂ (SF)
(AL) 2' × 2' 60 × 60 cm

'Lady Mary Fitzwilliam'

Bennett UK 1882
'Devoniensis' × 'Victor Verdier'
Large, freely produced, soft pink
flowers, flushed deeper pink.
Shapely, high centred and
scented. Not over vigorous but
quite bushy. Ample, good, dark
green foliage. This is a famous old
rose; parent to many of the early
British Hybrid Teas. A rediscovery
at Caston, Norfolk, by Keith
Money in 1975.
(C) (MF) (B) ☉ (AL)
2' × 2' 60 × 60 cm

'Lady Rose' (Korlady)

Kordes GERMANY 1979
Seedling × 'Träumerei'
Long, pointed buds open to large,
high-centred flowers of orange-
salmon. Bushy with good, mid-
green foliage.
(C) (VF) (B) ☉ (AL)
2' 6" × 2' 75 × 60 cm

'Lady Sylvia'

Stevens UK 1926
Sport from 'Mme Butterfly'
A beautiful, shapely variety of
upright growth with pale pink
flowers and dark green, semi-
glossy foliage. Still popular in
spite of its age.
(C) (P) (VF) (B) (Gh) ☉
✂ (AL) 2' × 2' 60 × 60 cm

'La France'

Guillot Fils FRANCE 1865
Probably 'Mme Falcot' seedling
Said to be the first Hybrid Tea
ever introduced. High-centred
flowers of silvery-pink borne in
small clusters and scented, opening to show rather muddled
centres. Bush upright and foliage
mid-green. A beautiful if somewhat inconspicuous rose to carry
the mantle of being the first of its
race.
(R) (Gh) (B) ☉ (VF) (AW)
4' × 3' 120 × 90 cm

'Lakeland'

Fryer UK 1976
'Fragrant Cloud' × 'Queen
Elizabeth'
Large, fully double flowers of
light pink with ample good foliage on an upright plant. A good
rose for exhibiting.
(C) (SF) (E) ☉ (AL)
3' × 2' 90 × 60 cm

'Kronenbourg'

'Las Vegas' (Korgane)

Kordes GERMANY 1981
'Ludwigshafen am Rhein' ×
'Feuerzauber'
Large, high-centred, deep orange
flowers with a paler reverse, and
semi-glossy, mid-green foliage.
Bushy and upright growth.
(C) (P) (B) (MF) (AL)
2' 6" × 2' 75 × 60 cm

'Lincoln Cathedral' (Glanlin)

Langdale UK 1985
'Silver Jubilee' × 'Royal Dane'
The flowers are pink deepening to
orange in the centre with a yellow
reverse, shapely, quite large, and
freely produced. Glossy, mid-
green foliage on a bushy and very
thorny plant.
(C) (P) (SF) (B) ⊙ (AL)
2' 6" × 2' 75 × 60 cm

'Liselle' *see* 'Royal Romance'

'Liverpool Remembers' (Frystar)

Fryer UK 1990

'Lincoln Cathedral'

Long, pointed buds open to substantial well-formed flowers of
unfading, glowing vermilion, fragrant; these are produced very
freely on an upright, bushy plant
which is well clothed with dark
green, disease-resistant foliage.
    Named for the Hillsborough
Family Support Group following
the Hillsborough Stadium soccer
disaster of 1989.
(C) ⊙ (B) (E) (H) ✄
(VF) (AL)
2' 6" × 2' 6" 75 × 75 cm

'Lolita', 'Litakor' (Korlita)

Kordes GERMANY 1973
'Colour Wonder' × seedling
Soft orange blooms on a tall,
upright plant with good foliage.
(C) (B) (MF) ⊙ (AL)
3' 6" × 2' 105 × 60 cm

'Los Angeles'

Howard USA 1916
'Mme Segond Weber' × 'Lyon
Rose'
A shapely rose, its pointed buds
opening to fully double flowers of
coral pink with a deep gold base.
Its growth is somewhat spreading
with leathery, dark green foliage.
Well ahead of its time when
introduced and has since proved
valuable at stud.
(C) (P) (VF) (B) ⊙ (AL)
2' × 2' 60 × 60 cm

'Louisville Lady'

Weddle USA 1986
'Osiria' × seedling
An exhibition-sized rose, pink
with a silvery reverse, and with
dark green, glossy foliage. Dense
and upright growth.
(C) (E) (VF) (AL)
3' × 2' 90 × 60 cm

'Love'

'Love' (Jactwin)

Warriner USA 1980
Unknown × 'Red Gold'
High-centred, shapely flowers of
glowing scarlet with silvery-white
reverses, produced on a tallish,
upright plant with good, mid-
green foliage. If disbudded makes
an excellent exhibition rose.
(C) ⊙ (B) (H) (E) (Gh)
(AW) 3' × 2' 90 × 60 cm

'Lovely Lady', 'Dickson's Jubilee' (Dicjubell)

Dickson UK 1986
'Silver Jubilee' × ('Eurorose' ×
'Anabell')
Mid-pink, fully double, shapely
flowers on a bushy plant with
glossy, mid-green foliage.
(C) (B) (VF) (AL)
2' × 2' 60 × 60 cm

'Lovers' Meeting'

Gandy UK 1980
Seedling × 'Egyptian Treasure'
High-centred, shapely blooms of
bright vermilion-orange on an
upright, tallish plant with bronzy
green foliage.
(C) (P) (VF) (B) ✄ (AW)
3' × 2' 90 × 60 cm

'Loving Memory', 'Burgund '81', 'Red Cedar' (Korgund '81)

Kordes GERMANY 1981
Seedling × 'Red Planet' seedling
Large, fully double, high-centred,
bright crimson blooms are borne
on strong stems. Bushy and
upright growth with glossy foliage.
(C) (MF) (B) (E) (Gh) ✄
(AW) 3' 6" × 2' 105 × 60 cm

'Luis Brinas'

Dot SPAIN 1934
'Mme Butterfly' × 'Federico
Casas'
Cupped, pinkish-orange blooms
are carried on strong stems. The
foliage always appears to be
slightly limp. A vigorous old
variety well worth growing today.
(R) (VF) (Gh) (B) ✄ (AL)
3' × 2' 90 × 60 cm

'Lyon Rose'

Pernet-Ducher FRANCE 1907
'Mme Mélanie Soupert' × a 'Soleil
d'Or' seedling
Coral-pink, yellow and red
blooms, a colour combination
that sounds more startling than
it is. Bushy growth and good
foliage. An important old stud
variety.
(R) (VF) (Gh) ⊙ (AL)
2' × 2' 60 × 60 cm

'Mme Butterfly'

Hill USA 1918
Sport from 'Ophelia'
The soft blush-pink flowers,
deeper in the centre with hints of
yellow at the base, are beautiful
when fully open and showing off
golden anthers. The foliage is
darkish green and semi-glossy.
Growth upright. An exquisite all-

rounder from the past.
(C) (P) (VF) (B) (Gh) ⊙
✂ (AL)   2' × 2'   60 × 60 cm

'Mme Eliza de Vilmorin'

Leveque FRANCE 1864
One of the first Hybrid Teas.
Large, heavily scented, deep carmine, shapely blooms somewhat
shyly produced but held upright
on a bushy plant which is well
foliated with dark green, matt
foliage.
(R) ⊙ (B) (Gh) (VF) M&
(AL)   3' × 3'   90 × 90 cm

'Mme Louis Laperrière'

Laperrère FRANCE 1951
'Crimson Glory' × seedling
Rich deep crimson flowers are
produced in profusion on an
upright yet bushy plant with dark
green, matt foliage. A very good
variety, especially for bedding.
(C) (P) (VF) (B) ⊙ (AL)
2' × 2'   60 × 60 cm

'Maestro' (Mackinju)

McGredy NEW ZEALAND 1980
'Picasso' seedling × seedling
Sizeable blooms of soft crimson
brushed whitish-cream, the colour
variable but always eye-catching.
Dark green foliage on a prickly
bush.
(C) (SF) (B) ⊙ (AL)
2' 6" × 2'   75 × 60 cm

'Mala Rubinstein'

Dickson UK 1971
'Sea Pearl' × 'Fragrant Cloud'
Rich coral-pink, very full and
shapely blooms, extremely free-
flowering, with matt, dark green
foliage on an upright and bushy
plant.
(C) (VF) (B) BS& (AW)
2' 6" × 2'   75 × 60 cm

'Marchioness of Salisbury'

'McGredy's Yellow'

'Manuela'

Tantau GERMANY 1968
Large, shapely blooms of rich
rosy-pink, glossy foliage and a
bushy habit of growth.
(C) (VF) (B) (E) (WW)
(AW)   2' × 2'   60 × 60 cm

'Marchioness of Salisbury'

Pernet FRANCE 1890
Scented, very large, globular yet
high-centred flowers of rich deep
red, held erect by short, very stout
stems. Foliage abundant with
dark green leaves very closely
packed on stems. Growth bushy
and upright. One of the first deep
red Hybrid Teas introduced.
(R) ⊙ (B) (Gh) ✂ (VF)
(AL)   2' × 2'   60 × 60 cm

'Michèle Meilland'

'Marijke Koopman'

Fryer UK 1979
Reasonably large blooms of soft
satin-pink with a deeper centre
and a yellow base, mid-green foliage and upright growth.
(C) (P) (B) (SF) (AL)
3' × 2'   90 × 60 cm

'Marion Harkness'
(Harkantabil)

Harkness UK 1979
[('Manx Queen' × 'Prima Ballerina') × ('Chanelle' × 'Piccadilly')]
× 'Piccadilly'
The shapely, deep yellow blooms
are brushed orange, deepening
with age. Upright, bushy growth,
and well foliated.
(C) (P) (SF) (B) ⊙ (AL)
2' 6" × 2'   75 × 60 cm

'Marianne Tudor' (Frymartor)

Fryer UK 1988
Shapely, large, very bright red
flowers borne erectly on strong
stems bearing good dark green
foliage. Growth vigorous and tall.
(C) (B) (H) (E) (Gh) ✂
(AL)   4' × 2' 6"   120 × 75 cm

'Mischief'

'Mary Donaldson', 'Lady Donaldson' (Canana)

Cant UK 1984
'English Miss' × seedling
Large, full, salmon-pink flowers
are produced on a strong, healthy,
upright plant with plentiful, dark
green, glossy foliage. (This rose is
sometimes classified as a
Floribunda.)
(C) (P) (VF) (B) (E) ☉
(AL) 2' 6" × 2' 75 × 60 cm

'McGredy's Yellow'

McGredy UK 1934
'Mrs Charles Lamplough' × ('The
Queen Alexandra Rose' × 'J. B.
Clark')
Superbly shaped, unfading prim-
rose-yellow blooms on a sturdy
plant with dark, bronzy, semi-
glossy foliage. Bushy and vigor-
ous. Unsurpassed today in its
colour range.
(C) (P) (SF) (B) ☉ ✂
(AL) 2' × 2' 60 × 60 cm

'Medallion'

Warriner USA 1973
'South Seas' × 'King's Ransom'
Fully double, large, fragrant
flowers of glowing light apricot.
Very fragrant. Large, leathery,
light green foliage. Growth bushy,
vigorous. Good in warm climates.
(C) (B) (H) (Gh) ✂ (VF)
(AW) 3' 6" × 2' 6" 105 × 75 cm

'Message', 'White Knight'

Meilland FRANCE 1955
('Virgo' × 'Peace') × 'Virgo'
A good old white variety, high-
centred and full; not large but
free-flowering. Foliage small and

'Mme Butterfly'

darkish on an upright, thorny
plant.
(C) (SF) (Gh) ☉ ✂ M⚘
(AL) 3' × 2' 90 × 60 cm

'Michèle Meilland'

Meilland FRANCE 1945
'Joanna Hill' × 'Peace'
A classic from the past, its exqui-
sitely formed creamy-buff blooms
are shaded pink and salmon.
Free-flowering on a bushy,
upright plant with dark foliage
and stems.
(C) (MF) (B) (Gh) ☉ ✂
✿ (AL) 2' × 2' 60 × 60 cm

'Mikado', 'Ko-Sai' (Kohsai)

Suzuki JAPAN 1987
Very bright red flowers with
golden-yellow deep down in the
centres. Shapely and produced on
longish stems with good foliage
of mid-green, on a bushy, upright
plant.
(C) (B) (H) (Gh) ✂ (AW)
3' × 2' 90 × 60 cm

'Milestone'

Warriner USA 1985
'Sunfire' × 'Spellbinder'
Large, bright cerisey-red with
reverses overlaid silvery-red,

lighter centres. The whole deepening with age to finish glowing
red. Fully double. Slightly fragrant. Foliage mid-green and
semi-glossy. Growth upright,
bushy.
(C) (B) (H) (Gh) ✂ (SF)
(AW) 3' 6" × 2' 6" 105 × 75 cm

'Mischief' (Macmi)

McGredy UK 1961
'Peace' × 'Spartan'
A very free-flowering, rich
salmon-pink rose, the colour
deeper in the autumn. Bushy,
free-branching yet of upright
growth. Sadly, its ample, matt,
dark green foliage is often marred
by black spot.
(C) (P) (B) ☉ BS⚘ ✂
(AL) 3' × 2' 90 × 60 cm

'Miss All-American Beauty', 'Maria Callas' (Meidaud)

Meilland FRANCE 1965
'Chrysler's Imperial' × 'Karl
Herbst'
Rounded buds open to large, very
fragrant, fully double flowers of
rich deep pink. Foliage leathery,
mid-green. Growth bushy,
upright.
(C) ☉ (B) (H) (E) (Gh)
✂ (VF) (AW)
3' × 2' 90 × 60 cm

'Miss Harp', 'Oregold', 'Silhouette', 'Anneliese Rothenberger'

Tantau GERMANY 1975
'Piccadilly' × 'Colour Wonder'
Shapely, high-centred, deep
yellow blooms on a robust, bushy
plant with dark green, glossy foliage.
(C) (B) (SF) ☉ (AL)
3' × 2' 90 × 60 cm

'Mme Louis Laperrière'

'Mrs Oakley Fisher'

'Mister Lincoln'

Swim USA 1964
'Chrysler Imperial' × 'Charles Mallerin'
Dark red flowers of good size and shape, and cupped when almost open, are held on a strong neck. Dark, leathery, matt foliage on an upright and vigorous plant.
(C) (P) (VF) (B) (Gh) ✂
(AW) 3' × 2' 90 × 60 cm

'Mojave'

Swim USA 1954
'Charlotte Armstrong' × 'Signora'
Heavily veined, apricot-orange flowers tinted russet-red are held prominently on long, strong necks. The foliage is glossy and plentiful, the growth upright and vigorous.
(C) (P) (MF) (B) (Gh) ☉
☼ ✂ (AL)
3' × 2' 90 × 60 cm

'Monique'

Paolino FRANCE 1949
'Lady Sylvia' × seedling
Shapely buds open to lovely, large, but well-proportioned flowers, cup-shaped with flattish tops, their colour an exquisite mixture of pinks. Matt, mid-green foliage and of upright and tidy growth.
(C) (VF) (B) ☉ ✂ (AL)
2' 6" × 2' 75 × 60 cm

'Montezuma'

Swim USA 1955
'Fandango' × 'Floradora'
Plump, urn-shaped buds open to large, well-proportioned and high-centred blooms of salmony red. A vigorous rose with leathery, dark, semi-glossy foliage.

'Mountbatten'

(C) (P) (SF) (B) (Gh) ☉
✂ (AL) 2' 6" × 2' 75 × 60 cm

'Moriah' (Ganhol)

Holtzman ISRAEL 1983
'Fragrant Cloud' × seedling
Large, shapely blooms of soft orange with a deeper reverse. Foliage good, matt and dark green. Growth bushy.
(C) (VF) (B) ☉ ☼ ✂
(AL) 2' 6" × 2' 75 × 60 cm

'Mrs Oakley Fisher'

Cant UK 1921
Large clusters of evenly spaced, deep buff-yellow, single flowers with pronounced amber stamens, and dark green, bronzy and semi-glossy foliage. The stems are plum-coloured and thorny. An

eye-catcher from the past.
(C) (P) (MF) (B) ☉ (AL)
2' × 2' 60 × 60 cm

'Mrs Pierre S. du Pont'

Mallerin FRANCE 1929
[('Ophelia' × 'Rayon d'Or') × 'Ophelia'] × ('Constance' × 'Souvenir de Claudius Pernet')
Shapely, pointed yet rounded buds open to fully double, golden-yellow flowers brushed faintly orangey-red, paling with age to primrose flushed pink. Very fragrant. Foliage mid-green, matt. Growth bushy.
(C) ☉ (B) (Gh) ✂ (VF)
(AL) 2' × 2' 60 × 60 cm

'Mrs Sam McGredy'

McGredy UK 1929
('Donald Macdonald' × 'Golden Emblem') × (seedling × 'The Queen Alexandra Rose')
Large, slightly shaggy blooms of burnt-salmon-orange with their reverses flushed red and their centres yellow, and bronzy and glossy foliage, the stems dark. Awkward, angular growth.
(R) (P) (NF) (B) ☉ (AL)
3' × 2' 90 × 60 cm

'Mrs Wakefield Christie-Miller'

McGredy UK 1909
Flowers high-centred, of soft pink-shaded-salmon with brighter reverses. Foliage leathery, light green. Growth short, bushy.
(R) ☉ (B) (MF) M✃ (AL)
2' × 2' 60 × 60 cm

'Mullard Jubilee', 'Electron'

McGredy UK 1970
'Paddy McGredy' × 'Prima Ballerina'
Large, deep rose-pink, high-

'Monique'

'Mullard Jubilee'

centred flowers are freely produced on strong stems. The foliage is dark and plentiful on a plant of bushy growth.
(C) (P) (MF) (B) ✄ (AL)
2' × 2'   60 × 60 cm

'My Choice'

'My Choice'

LeGrice UK 1958
'Wellworth' × 'Ena Harkness'
Large, urn-shaped, high-centred blooms of dusky salmon-pink with a soft yellowish-buff reverse.

'National Trust'

The foliage is matt greyish-green. Growth upright.
(C) (P) (VF) (B) (E) (AL)
2' 6" × 2'   75 × 60 cm

'National Trust', 'Bad Naukeim'

McGredy UK 1970
'Evelyn Fison' × 'King of Hearts'
A very free-flowering rose, with superbly shaped, high-centred flowers of bright red, larger if disbudded. Dark foliage on an upright and bushy plant.
(C) (P) (SF) (B) ⊙ (AW)
2' × 2'   60 × 60 cm

'Olympiad' (Macauck)

McGredy NEW ZEALAND 1984
'Red Planet' × 'Pharaoh'
Bright red, almost luminous, large and full blooms. Its growth is upright and bushy, with mid-green, matt foliage.
(C) (SF) (E) (B) ✄ (AL)
3' × 2'   90 × 60 cm

'Opéra'

Gaujard FRANCE 1950
'La Belle Irisée' × seedling
Long buds open to fairly plump, cupped blooms of rich scarlet-red with a yellow base. The foliage is leathery and mid to light green.
(C) (P) (MF) (B) (AL)
3' × 2'   90 × 60 cm

'Ophelia'

Paul UK 1912
Probably a seedling from 'Antoine Rivoire'
A classic, the superbly shaped soft pink blooms have a soft yellow base. Beautiful in bud and when fully open, display golden stamens to advantage. Dark green foliage on a plant of upright growth. The progenitor of several

'Olympiad'

sports of equal stature, in particular 'Mme Butterfly' and 'Lady Sylvia'.
(C) (P) (VF) (B) (Gh) ⊙
✄ (AL)   2' × 2'   60 × 60 cm

'Oregold' see 'Miss Harp'

'Orient Express'

Wheatcroft UK 1978
'Sunblest' × seedling
Large and full, shapely blooms of coral-pink, with plentiful dark green-bronzy foliage. Growth vigorous and bushy.
(C) (P) (H) (VF) (B) ⊙
(AL)   3' 6" × 2'   105 × 60 cm

'Pacemaker' (Harnoble)

Harkness UK 1981
'Red Planet' × 'Wendy Cussons'
Clear, bright reddish-pink, high-centred blooms. Very free-flowering. Large, dark green foliage on a plant of upright and bushy growth.
(C) (P) (H) (VF) (B) ⊙
(AL)   3' × 2'   90 × 60 cm

'Painted Moon' (Dicpaint)

Dickson UK 1989
Large, shapely blooms of primrose-ivory heavily flushed

with pinkish-scarlet, discreet changes occurring in their colour combination as the flowers age. Foliage large, mid-green on a bushy, upright-growing plant.
(C) ⊙ (B) (H) (Gh) ✂
(E) (AL) 3' × 2' 90 × 60 cm

'Papa Meilland' (Meisar)

Meilland FRANCE 1963
'Chrysler Imperial' × 'Charles Mallerin'
Superb, deep velvety-crimson blooms with obvious veining. Mid to dark green, semi-glossy foliage on an upright plant with large thorns. Not an easy rose to grow but well worth the effort.
(R) (VF) (M) BS✦ (AW)
3' × 2' 90 × 60 cm

'Paradise', 'Burning Sky' (Wezeip)

Weeks USA 1978
'Swarthmore' × seedling
Shapely, fragrant flowers, fully double, silvery-lavender-brushed-

'Painted Moon'

pink at first, deepening with age to soft purple-brushed-red. Foliage dark green, glossy. Growth upright and bushy.
(C) ⊙ (B) (H) (E) ✂
(MF) (AL) 4' × 3' 120 × 90 cm

'Pascali' (Lenip)

Lens BELGIUM 1963
'Queen Elizabeth' × 'White Butterfly'
Well-formed flowers of almost pure white with a creamy base, held erect. Foliage dark green and semi-matt. Upright growth.
(C) (P) (Gh) (B) ⊙ ✂
(AW) 3' × 2' 90 × 60 cm

'Paul Shirville', 'Heart Throb' (Harqueterwife)

Harkness UK 1983
'Compassion' × 'Mischief'
The blooms are blended soft salmon and peach, shapely and elegant in form. Slightly spreading in habit with large, dark green, almost glossy leaves.
(C) (P) (VF) (B) ⊙ (AW)
3' × 2' 6" 90 × 75 cm

'Peace', 'Gloria Dei', 'Mme A. Meilland', 'Gioia'

F. Meilland FRANCE 1945
('George Dickson' × 'Souvenir de Claudius Pernet') × ('Joanna Hill' × 'Chas. P. Kilham') × 'Margaret McGredy'
Perhaps the best known and one of the best loved roses of all time. Large, high-centred, opening cupped, sometimes delightfully ragged. Tending to vary in colour from soil to soil and even from day to day in the same garden.

'Paul Shirville'

'Peaudouce'

Most often creamy-yellow (sometimes almost golden-yellow in cooler weather), with a pinkish edging to each petal intensifying almost to red as the flower ages. Can be rather shy at times. Subtly perfumed. Beautiful deep green, glossy foliage plus a strong constitution makes this a superb rose for any garden. Unpruned in good soil much taller than the height stated.
(C) (P) (H) (E) ✂ (SF)
(AW) 4' × 3' 120 × 90 cm

'Peaudouce', 'Elina' (Dicjana)

Dickson UK 1985
'Nana Mouskouri' × 'Lolita'
Very full, large, shapely blooms of ivory and soft yellow. Bushy and upright growth with ample foliage.
(C) (P) (SF) (B) (E) (AL)
2' 6" × 2' 75 × 60 cm

'Peer Gynt' (Korol)

Kordes GERMANY 1968
'Colour Wonder' × 'Golden Giant'
Large, shapely flowers of rich clear yellow brushed red at the edges of the petals, and very full. Good, mid-green and semi-glossy foliage on a vigorous, bushy plant.
(C) (P) (H) (SF) (B) ⊙
✂ (AW) 2' 6" × 2' 75 × 60 cm

'Penthouse', 'Westcoast' (Macngaura)

McGredy NEW ZEALAND 1988
Fragrant, large blooms of mid-

pink made up of a multitude of scalloped-edged petals held on strong necks. Foliage is matt mid-green. Growth strong and bushy.
(C) ⊙ (B) (H) (E) (Gh)
✄ (MF) (AL)
3′ × 2′   90 × 60 cm

'Perfect Moment'
(Korwilma)

Kordes GERMANY 1991
Shapely, high-centred buds open to large, full flowers of a blend of bright scarlet, orange and yellow. These are held on strong necks amply clothed with rich mid-green, glossy foliage. Growth upright.
(C) ⊙ (B) (H) (E) (Gh)
✄ (AL)   4′ × 2′ 6″   120 × 75 cm

'Perfecta', 'Kordes' Perfecta'
(Koralu)

Kordes GERMANY 1957
'Spek's Yellow' × 'Karl Herbst'
Very large, shapely blooms of soft cream heavily flushed deep pink and crimson with hints of yellow in the base. Free-flowering on an upright, thorny plant with dark, glossy and well-serrated foliage.
(C) (P) (H) (MF) (B) ⊙
(AW)   2′ 6″ × 2′   75 × 60 cm

'Perfume Delight'

Weeks USA 1973
'Peace' × [('Happiness' × 'Chrysler's Imperial') × 'El Capitan']

Pointed buds open to full, cupped blooms of deep clear pink, beautifully perfumed. Foliage large, leathery and dark green. Growth bushy and upright.
(C) ⊙ (B) (H) (Gh) ✄
(E) (VF) (AW)
4′ × 3′   120 × 90 cm

'Pharisaer'

Hinner GERMANY 1903
'Mrs W. J. Grant' seedling
High-centred flowers of white-painted-soft pink and salmon held, unfortunately, on rather thin, weak necks. Fragrant and beautiful. Foliage bronzy-green. Growth moderately bushy.
(P) ⊙ (B) (Gh) (SF) (AL)
2′ × 2′   60 × 60 cm

'Piccadilly'

McGredy UK 1960
'McGredy's Yellow' × 'Karl Herbst'
Shapely buds open to loosely formed blooms of scarlet and yellow, high-centred at the mid-way stage. Foliage dark and glossy. Stems very thorny. A dense, upright and very floriferous plant.
(C) (P) (H) (SF) (B) ⊙
R⚘ BS⚘ (AW)
2′ 6″ × 2′   75 × 60 cm

'Picture'

McGredy UK 1932
A fine old rose. At the half-open stage, the clear pink flowers are beautifully scrolled; fully open,

'Perfume Delight'

'Penthouse'

they are tidy and symmetrical. Foliage grey-green, matt. Growth short and bushy.
(C) (P) (SF) (B) (Gh) ⊙ ✂ (AL)
1′ 6″ × 1′ 6″   45 × 45 cm

'Pink Favourite'

Von Abrams USA 1956
'Juno' × ('Georg Arends' × 'New Dawn')
A very free, large, cupped rose. Its pink flowers are produced on a bushy plant with glossy, mid to bright green foliage.
(C) (SF) (B) (E) (AL)
2′ 6″ × 2′   75 × 60 cm

'Pink Peace' (Meibil)

Meilland FRANCE 1959
('Peace' × 'Monique') × ('Peace' × 'Mrs John Laing')
Very large, globular blooms of bright, silvery deep pink with prominent veining. A vigorous, upright plant with mid-green, matt-finished foliage.
(C) (P) (H) (VF) (E) R✿ φ (AW)
3′ 6″ × 2′ 6″   105 × 75 cm

'Pink Pearl' (Kormasyl)

Kordes GERMANY 1989
Sport from 'Congratulations'
A tall, upright-growing, healthy rose with full, shapely blooms of pearly-pink. Foliage good mid-green.
(C) ⊙ (B) (H) (P) (Gh) ✂ (AL)   4′ × 2′   120 × 60 cm

'Pinta'

Beales UK 1973
'Ena Harkness' × 'Pascali'
Very free-flowering, with clusters of shapely, creamy-white flowers on a robust, slightly angular plant with dark green stems and mid-

green, matt-finished foliage. A special feature is the distinct fragrance of eglantine.
(C) (P) (H) (VF) (E) R✿ (W) ⊙ (AW)
3′ 6″ × 2′ 6″   105 × 75 cm

'Polar Star', 'Polarstern' (Tanlarpost)

Tantau GERMANY 1982
A free-flowering rose, its creamy-white, shapely blooms are held on a strong neck. Light green foliage and prickly stems.
(C) (P) (B) (AW)
3′ × 2′   90 × 60 cm

'Polly'

Beckwith UK 1927
'Ophelia' seedling × 'Mme Caroline Testout'
Pale yellow, pointed buds open high-centred, creamy with pink and soft orangey shadings in the centre, paling to almost white with age. Foliage mid-green, semi-glossy. Growth upright, bushy. A famous old forcing variety.
(C) ⊙ (B) (H) (Gh) ✂ (MF) (AL)   2′ × 2′   60 × 60 cm

'Portland Trailblazer' see 'Big Chief'

'Pot o' Gold' (Dicdivine)

Dickson UK 1980
'Eurorose' × 'Whisky Mac'
Clear, bright yellow blooms touched gold, large and full. Foliage mid-green and heavily veined purple. Growth bushy but tidy, quite thorny.
(C) (P) (H) (B) (VF) ⊙ ✂ (AW)   2′ 6″ × 2′   75 × 60 cm

'Picture

'Precious Platinum', 'Red Star', 'Opa Pötschke'

Dickson UK 1974
'Red Planet' × 'Franklin Englemann'
Bright red blooms with an almost luminous sheen, shapely and of good deportment. Glossy, leathery, mid-green foliage. Upright and bushy growth.
(C) (P) (H) (B) (VF) (Gh) д ✂ (AW)
3′ × 2′   90 × 60 cm

'President Herbert Hoover'

Coddington USA 1930
'Sensation' × 'Souvenir de Claudius Pernet'
Long, pointed flowers, orange-pink with a buffy-gold reverse, open flattish and are held on strong, long necks. The foliage is leathery and semi-matt. Growth vigorous and upright, almost lanky. An excellent old variety.
(R) (H) (P) (VF) ✂ (AL)
4′ × 3′   120 × 90 cm

'Pink Favourite'
'Prima Ballerina'

'Prima Ballerina', 'Première Ballerine'

Tantau GERMANY 1957
Seedling × 'Peace'

The deep rose-pink, shapely and quite large flowers open blowsily. Foliage dark matt, with dark and thorny stems. Growth upright and sturdy.
(C) (VF) (B) M♨ (AW)
2′ 6″ × 2′ 75 × 60 cm

'Prima Donna'

Dickson UK 1944
'Heinrich Werland' seedling
Fully double, deep rich salmon-pink blooms brushed buff-yellow. High-centred even when fully open. A good old rose that continues to stand the test of time. Still very popular, especially in America. Not to be confused with a forcing variety by this name raised in Japan in 1983.
(C) ☉ (B) (E) (Gh) ✄
(SF) (AL)
3′ × 2′ 6″ 90 × 75 cm

'Princess Margaret of England'

Meilland FRANCE 1968
'Queen Elizabeth' × ('Peace' × 'Michèle Meilland')
Bright rose-pink, full, shapely and large blooms. Upright growth with leathery, matt foliage.
(C) (SF) (B) ☉ (AL)
2′ 6″ × 2′ 75 × 60 cm

'Pristine' (Jacpico)

Warriner USA 1978
'White Masterpiece' × 'First Prize'
White flowers with a pink blush, quite large and shapely. Dark green foliage on an upright, dense but tidy plant.
(C) (P) (H) (VF) (B) (Gh)
✄ (AW)
3′ 6″ × 2′ 105 × 60 cm

'Promise', 'Poesie'

Warriner USA 1976
'South Seas' × 'Peace'
High-centred, fully double flowers of fragrant, clear pink. Good glossy, mid-green foliage. Growth upright.
(C) ☉ (B) (E) (Gh) ✄
(MF) (AL)
4′ × 3′ 120 × 90 cm

'Proud Land'

Moray USA 1969
'Chrysler's Imperial' × seedling
Globular buds open to fragrant, very full flowers of rich deep red very freely produced on a bushy plant with dark green, leathery foliage.
(C) ☉ (B) (H) (E) (Gh)
✄ (VF) (AW)
3′ × 2′ 90 × 60 cm

'Queen Charlotte' (Harubondee)

Harkness UK 1989
Large, shapely flowers, slightly less than fully double when open, salmony-red in colour with a pleasing perfume. Foliage lustrous mid-green. Growth bushy, upright. Raised to commemorate the 250th Anniversary of Queen Charlotte's Hospital, London.
(C) ☉ (B) (P) (H) (Gh)
✄ (VF) (AL)
4′ × 3′ 120 × 90 cm

'Rebecca Claire'

Law UK 1984
'Blessing' × 'Redgold'
Double blooms of coppery-orange with coral edges to the petals. Very fragrant. Foliage mid-green, semi-glossy. Growth bushy.
(C) ☉ (B) (Gh) ✄ (P)
(VF) (AL) 3′ × 2′ 90 × 60 cm

'Queen Charlotte'

'Red Devil', 'Coeur d'Amour' (Dicam)

Dickson UK 1970
'Silver Lining' × 'Prima Ballerina'
Very large, high-centred blooms of rosy-scarlet, the reverse lighter, not over-freely produced. Foliage semi-glossy, mid-green. Growth upright and robust with strong, thorny stems.
(C) (P) (SF) (E) (WW) ✄
(AW) 3′ 6″ × 2′ 105 × 60 cm

'Red Masterpiece'

Warriner USA 1974
('Siren' × 'Chrysler Imperial') × ('Carousel' × 'Chrysler Imperial')
Very large, high-centred, fully double, very fragrant flowers of rich deep red deepening to burgundy with age. Foliage dark green, leathery. Growth bushy, upright.
(C) ☉ (B) (H) (Gh) ✄
(E) (VF) (AW)
4′ × 3′ 120 × 90 cm

'Red Devil'

'Red Planet'

Dickson UK 1970
'Red Devil' × seedling
Large, fully double, bright crimson blooms. Foliage mid-green and glossy. Growth bushy but tidy. A good exhibition variety.
(C) (P) (VF) (B) (AL)
3' × 2'   90 × 60 cm

'Remember Me' (Cocdestin)

Cocker UK 1984
'Ann Letts' × ('Dainty Maid' × 'Pink Favourite')
A rich mixture of copper and orange shades, not over-full but shapely blooms, and freeflowering. Ample, smallish, dark green foliage. Bushy and upright growth.
(C) (P) (SF) (B) (AW)
2' 6" × 2'   75 × 60 cm

'Rev. F. Page-Roberts'

Cant UK 1921
'Queen Mary' × seedling
An old, flamboyant variety, still worthy of a place in the garden. Fully double yellow blooms brushed and shaded red. Foliage good, glossy. Growth bushy and slightly angular.
(R) (VF) ☉ (AL)
2' × 2'   60 × 60 cm

'Roddy MacMillan' (Cocared)

Cocker UK 1982
('Fragrant Cloud' × 'Postillion') × 'Wisbech Gold'
Large, shapely, fully double blooms of rich apricot. Foliage mid-green and almost glossy. Growth bushy.
(C) (P) (MF) (B) ☉ (AL)
2' × 2'   60 × 60 cm

'Rose Gaujard' (Gaumo)

Gaujard FRANCE 1957
'Peace' × 'Opéra' seedling
Not a colour that always appeals, but one of the best all-round roses ever produced. Very large cherry-red and silver blooms with a paler reverse, sometimes opening split or quartered. Strong, dark wood liberally clothed with dark green and glossy foliage. Upright and rudely healthy.
(C) (P) (H) (SF) (B) (E) (WW) ✄ (AW)
4' × 3'   120 × 90 cm

'Rosy Cheeks'

Anderson UK 1975
'Beauty of Festival' × 'Grandpa Dickson'
A big rose, slightly tubby in shape. Carmine to red blooms with a soft yellow reverse. Foliage dark green and matt. Growth bushy.
(C) (MF) (B) ☉ (AL)
2' 6" × 2'   75 × 60 cm

'Roxburghe Rose' (Cocember)

Cocker UK 1990
'Anne Cocker' × 'Elizabeth of Glamis'
Bright, fully double, glowing vermilion flowers with a slight fragrance, freely produced on an upright plant with ample glossy, mid-green foliage.
(C) ☉ (B) (H) ✄ (SF) (AL)   3' × 2'   90 × 60 cm

'Royal Albert Hall'

Cocker UK 1972
'Fragrant Cloud' × 'Postillion'
An interesting, unusually coloured rose, deep wine-red with a soft primrose reverse. The fully double blooms open cupped and

'Royal Highness'

imbricated. Foliage small but plentiful, dark green. Growth upright and bushy.
(C) (VF) (B) BS✄ R✄ (AL)   2' × 2'   60 × 60 cm

'Royal Dane' *see* 'Troika'

'Royal Highness', 'Königliche Hoheit'

Swim UK 1962
'Virgo' × 'Peace'
A beautiful rose when at its best in fine weather, with long, pointed buds opening to large, full, high-centred flowers of soft pearly-pink. Foliage lush dark green, the stems sturdy and upright.
(C) (MF) (B) (E) (WW) ✄ (AW)   4' × 2'   120 × 60 cm

'Royal Romance', 'Liselle' (Rulis)

de Ruiter NETHERLANDS 1980
'Whisky Mac' × 'Esther Ofarim'
Medium-sized, shapely flowers, a mixture of soft salmony-orange and peach. Foliage large, dark green and semi-glossy. Growth bushy and upright.
(C) (B) ☉ (AL)
2' 6" × 2'   75 × 60 cm

'Rose Gaujard'

'Sandringham Centenary'

'Royal Smile'

Beales UK 1980
'Fragrant Cloud' × 'Pascali'
Creamy-white flowers with delicate soft pink shadings deepening
towards the centre, high-centred
and shapely. A special feature is
their strong perfume. The foliage
is matt dark green and its growth
bushy. Good in a warm climate.
(C) (B) (Gh) (VF) ⊙ R✿
✿ ✂ (AL)
2′ 6″ × 2′   75 × 60 cm

'Royal Velvet' (Meilotup)

Meilland FRANCE 1986
('Exciting' × 'Suspense') × 'Duke
of Windsor'
Dark red, fully double, shapely
blooms with a slight fragrance
freely produced on a bushy plant
with mid-green foliage.
(C) ⊙ (B) (H) (Gh) ✂
(SF) (AL)
3′ 6″ × 2′ 6″   105 × 75 cm

'Royal Volunteer'
(Cocdandy)

Cocker UK 1988
'Yellow Pages' × 'Alexander'
Shapely, fragrant blooms a blend
of golden-apricot and orange with
yellow reverses. Foliage light
green. Growth bushy, upright.
Named in honour of the
Women's Royal Voluntary Serv-
ice.
(C) ⊙ (B) (H) ✂ (SF)
(AL)   3′ × 2′   90 × 60 cm

'Royal William',
'Duftzauber '84'
(Korzaun)

Kordes GERMANY 1984
'Feuerzauber' × seedling
High-centred, deep red and
shapely blooms are freely produced on an upright plant with
dark green, semi-glossy foliage.
(C) (B) (MF) ⊙ ✂ (AW)
2′ 6″ × 2′   75 × 60 cm

'Ruby Wedding'

Gregory UK 1979
'Mayflower' × unknown
Shapely, ruby-red flowers of
medium size, with loosely
arranged petals when fully open.
Foliage mid-green. Growth bushy
and tidy.
(C) (Gh) (SF) (B) ⊙ ✂
(AL)   2′ × 2′   60 × 60 cm

'Sandringham Centenary'

Tysterman UK 1981
'Queen Elizabeth' × 'Baccara'
Large, rich burnt-orange flowers
paling slightly with age to
salmon-pink, their colour particularly rich when almost fully open.
Strong, vigorous and upright
growth with plentiful, mid-green
and semi-glossy foliage.
(C) (P) (H) (Gh) (SF) ✂
(AL)   4′ × 2′ 6″   120 × 75 cm

'Savoy Hotel' (Harvintage)

Harkness UK 1989
'Silver Jubilee' × 'Amber Queen'
Rounded buds open to high-
centred flowers of substance.
Bright light pink in colour, slight
scent. Foliage dark green and
plentiful. Growth bushy, upright.
(C) ⊙ (B) (H) (P) (Gh)
(E) ✂ (SF) (AL)
3′ × 2′ 6″   90 × 75 cm

'Seashell'

Kordes GERMANY 1976
Seedling × 'Color Wonder'
Rounded yet pointed buds open
to fully double, salmon-apricot-
orange blooms which are scented
and borne in great profusion on
an upright, bushy plant with dark
green, crinkled, shiny foliage.
(C) ⊙ (B) (H) (E) ✂
(MF) (AL)   4′ × 3′   120 × 90 cm

'Sheer Bliss' (Jactro)

Warriner ·USA 1987
'White Masterpiece' × 'Grand
Masterpiece'
Large, white blooms with pink
centres and a spicy fragrance
borne singly on long stems with
abundant mid-green, matt foliage.
Growth medium-tall, upright.
(C) ⊙ (B) (Gh) (MF)
(AL)   3′ × 2′   90 × 60 cm

'Sheer Elegance'

Twomey USA 1989
Shapely, initially high-centred
flowers opening cupped and flat-
topped. Clear pink deepening to
salmon in the base. Produced on
long stems well endowed with
dark green, glossy foliage. Growth
upright, bushy.
(C) ⊙ (B) (H) (E) ✂
(Gh) (SF) (AL)
3′ 6″ × 2′ 6″   105 × 75 cm

'Royal William'

'Shot Silk'

Dickson UK 1924
'Hugh Dickson' seedling ×
'Sunstar'
Without doubt one of the best of
the Dickson roses from before
World War II. Globular, full,
high-centred flowers of near
salmon with a yellow base and a
silky sheen. Luxuriant foliage,
plentiful and glossy. Growth
bushy, upright and shortish.
(C) (H) (Gh) (B) (MF) ☉
✂ (AL)
1' 6" × 1' 6" 45 × 45 cm

'Silver Jubilee'

'Savoy Hotel'

'Silver Jubilee'

Cocker UK 1978
[('Highlight' × 'Colour Wonder')
× ('Parkdirektor Riggers' ×
'Piccadilly')] × 'Mischief'
A shapely, very free-flowering
rose of silvery-pink and apricot
with a deeper reverse. The flowers
are produced in clusters;
disbudded, they become huge.
Foliage glossy. Growth very
bushy but upright, the stems
amply endowed with thorns. One
of the best roses ever raised.
(C) (P) (MF) (H) (Gh) (B)
(E) ☉ ✂ (AW)
3' 6" × 2' 105 × 60 cm

'Shot Silk'

'Silver Lining'

Dickson UK 1958
'Karl Herbst' × 'Eden Rose'
Soft blush flowers with deeper
pink highlights, and exquisitely
shaped: bulbous but with high
centres and held on strong necks.
Foliage a little sparse, dull, matt
green. Stems stout and thorny.
(C) (P) (B) (SF) ☉ ✂
(AL) 2' × 2' 60 × 60 cm

'Silver Lining'

'Silver Wedding'

Gregory UK 1976
A superb, underrated rose, with shapely blooms of creamy-white. Foliage matt, mid-green. Growth medium bushy.
(C) (SF) (B) (Gh) ☉ ✄
(AL)   2′ 6″ × 2′   75 × 60 cm

'Simba',
'Goldsmith',
'Helmut Schmidt'
(Korbelma)

Kordes GERMANY 1981
'Korgold' × seedling
Clear, bright yellow flowers, very large and fairly full of petals, held upright on a vigorous and bushy plant with good matt-green foliage.
(C) (SF) (B) ☉ ✄ (AL)
2′ 6″ × 2′   75 × 60 cm

'Sir Frederick Ashton'

Beales UK 1985
Sport from 'Anna Pavlova'
Very highly scented, large, full

blooms of pure white with creamy centres. Foliage large, rounded and dark matt green. Stems strong from upright growth.
(C) (VF) (E) (Gh) (WW)
☼   (AL)   4′ × 3′   120 × 90 cm

'Sir Harry Pilkington',
'Melina' (Tanema)

Tantau GERMANY 1974
'Inge Horstmann' × 'Sophia Loren'
Large, shapely, bright red and very full blooms. Foliage dark. Growth bushy and upright.
(C) (SF) (B) (E) (AL)
2′ 6″ × 2′   75 × 60 cm

'Smoky'

Combe USA 1968
Double flowers opening flat, smoky-deep-plum-red ageing to burgundy, variably, sometimes paler. Scented. Foliage mid to dark green. Growth upright, bushy.
(C) ☉ (B) (Gh) (MF)
(AL)   3′ × 2′   90 × 60 cm

'Soleil d'Or'

Pernet-Ducher FRANCE 1900
'Antoine Ducher' × *R. foetida persiana*
An important rose, being with 'Rayon d'Or' one of the 'Pernettiana' roses, significant as the source of most of the yellow and

bright colours in today's roses. This classification has since been dropped and such roses are now included in Hybrid Teas. 'Soleil d'Or' is very large and double, opening to a cupped, flattish flower with a muddled centre, fragrant, deep orange-yellow to tawny-gold shaded red. Foliage rich green on a thorny plant.
(R) (Gh) (P) ☉ (WW)
(VF) (AL)   3′ × 3′   90 × 90 cm

'Sonia',
'Sweet Promise',
'Sonia Meilland'
(Meihelvet)

Meilland FRANCE 1974
'Zambra' × ('Baccara' × 'Message')
Soft silky-salmon blooms, superbly shaped, rounded but high-centred. A free-flowering rose, excellent under glass. Foliage mid-green and semi-matt. Growth dense but upright.
(C) (SF) (B) (Gh) ☉
(WW) ✄ (AW)
2′ 6″ × 2′   75 × 60 cm

'Souvenir du Président Carnot'

Pernet-Ducher FRANCE 1894
Seedling × 'Lady Mary Fitzwilliam'
Long, pointed buds in clusters open to full, high-centred, fragrant, shell-pink flowers with deeper centres. Foliage ample mid-green, matt. Growth upright,

'Stella'

'Sonia'

'Sunblest'

quite vigorous. A useful old variety for the connoisseur.
(R) ☉ (B) (Gh) (MF) (AL)
3' × 2'   90 × 60 cm

'Spek's Yellow', 'Golden Sceptre'

Spek HOLLAND 1950
'Golden Rapture' × seedling
Long, pointed buds open to loose, deep golden-yellow flowers on long stems. This rose needs disbudding to produce sizeable blooms. Foliage rich light green. Growth rather sprawly. Good under glass.
(C) (MF) (B) (Gh) ✄
(AL)   3' × 2'   90 × 60 cm

'Spirit of Youth', 'Senator Burda', 'Victor Hugo' (Meivestal)

Meilland FRANCE 1985
Highly perfumed, bright red flowers, fully double and shapely. Growth upright and bushy. Foliage mid-green, leathery.
(C)   ☉   (B) (P) (H) (Gh)
✄   (E) (VF) (AW)
3' × 2'   90 × 60 cm

'Stella'

Tantau GERMANY 1958
'Horstmann's Jubiläumsrose' × 'Peace'
A plump yet high-centred rose of soft pink flushed deeper pink held on a strong neck, but not very free-flowering. Foliage dark green and leathery. Growth strong and bushy.
(C) (SF) (B) ☉ BS ✄ ✄
(AL)   2' 6" × 2'   75 × 60 cm

'Summer Dream' (Jacshe)

Warriner USA 1985
'Sunshine' × unnamed seedling
High-centred, shapely, double flowers borne singly on strong stems, apricot-pink. Fragrant. Foliage matt mid-green. Growth tall, upright.
(C)   ☉   (B) (H) (E) (Gh)
✄ (MF) (AW)
4' × 2' 6"   120 × 75 cm

'Summer Sunshine', 'Soleil d'Eté'

Swim USA 1962
'Buccaneer' × 'Lemon Chiffon'
A tall, almost carefree rose bearing an abundance of loosely formed blooms from long, pointed buds. Foliage mid-green and leathery. Growth upright.
(C) (P) (H) (Gh) (SF) ✄
(AL)   3' × 2'   90 × 60 cm

'Sunblest', 'Landora'

Tantau GERMANY 1970
Seedling × 'King's Ransom'
A very free-flowering bedding rose. The flowers from slim buds are rich yellow, fairly large and full, and are held on strong necks. Foliage mid-green, glossy. Growth bushy and upright.
(C) (SF) (B) (Gh) ☉ ✄
(AW)   3' × 2'   90 × 60 cm

'Sunbright'

Warriner USA 1984
Unnamed seedling × 'New Day'
Long, pointed buds open to double flowers of clear mid-yellow opening flattish. Slight fragrance. Foliage glossy, dark green. Growth upright.
(C) (R) (H) (P) (SF) (AL)
4' × 3'   120 × 90 cm

'Sun Flare' (Jacjem)

Warriner USA 1983
'Sunsprite' × seedling
Pointed buds open to clear yellow, fully double flowers in clusters. Foliage small, mid-green, glossy. Growth compact, bushy.
(C) ☉ (B) (SF) (AL)
1' 6" × 1' 6"   45 × 45 cm

'Sunny South'

Clark AUSTRALIA 1918
'Gustav Grünerwald' × 'Betty Berkeley'
Large, globular, highly scented flowers of mid-pink flushed carmine with a yellow base, and semi-double when fully open. Foliage plentiful and rich green. Growth bushy and vigorous. A beautiful rose superbly representative of Australia.
(R) (VF) (B) (Gh) ☉ ✄
(AL)   3' 6" × 3' 6"   105 × 105 cm

'Sunset Song' (Cocasun)

Cocker UK 1981
('Sabine' × 'Circus') × 'Sunblest'
With amber yellow blooms overlaid copper, this is a shapely, full rose of personality. Good, light green, glossy foliage. Upright, bushy growth.
(C) (SF) (B) ☉ ✄ (AW)
3' × 2'   90 × 60 cm

'Super Star', 'Tropicana' (Tanorstar)

Tantau GERMANY 1960
(Seedling × 'Peace') × (Seedling × 'Alpine Glow')

Large, full, high-centred blooms of bright coral-vermilion. Foliage matt-grey, with thorny stems. Growth angular.
(C) (H) (MF) (B) ☉ M ❀
✂ (AW)
3′ 6″ × 3′   105 × 90 cm

'Super Sun'

Bentley UK 1967
Sport from 'Piccadilly'
Deep yellow flowers brushed and veined orange with a paler reverse, shapely and opening loosely formed. Foliage dark green and glossy, the stems very thorny. Growth dense and upright.
(C) (P) (H) (SF) (B) ☉
BS ❀ (AL)
2′ 6″ × 2′   75 × 60 cm

'Susan Hampshire' (Meinatac)

Paolino FRANCE 1972
('Monique' × 'Symphonie') × 'Miss All American Beauty'
A free-flowering rose with amply proportioned, full, high-centred, bright rose-pink flowers. Foliage mid-green and matt. Growth upright and dense.
(C) (P) (H) (SF) (B) ☉
✂ (AW)
2′ 6″ × 2′   75 × 60 cm

'Sutter's Gold'

Swim USA 1950
'Charlotte Armstrong' × 'Signora'
Very free-flowering, the slim buds held on long, strong necks open to loosely formed, attractive flowers of deep yellow brushed and shaded with orange and pink. Foliage mid-green and semi-glossy. Growth upright but bushy.
(C) (P) (MF) (B) (Gh) ☉
✂ (AW)   3′ × 2′   90 × 60 cm

'Super Star'

'Sweetheart' (Cocapeer)

Cocker UK 1980
'Peer Gynt' × ('Fragrant Cloud' × 'Gay Gordons')
Large and full blooms of deep glowing pink. Foliage mid-green. Growth upright and tall.
(C) (P) (SF) (B) ✂ (AL)
3′ 6″ × 2′   105 × 60 cm

'Sweet Promise' see 'Sonia'

'Sutter's Gold'

'Sweet Surrender'

Weeks USA 1987
Seedling × 'Tiffany'
Large, cupped flowers of mid-silvery-pink with a very heady perfume. Foliage dark green and leathery. Growth bushy and upright.
(C) ☉ (B) (H) (Gh) ✂
(SF) (AW)
3′ 6″ × 2′ 6″   105 × 75 cm

'Sylvia' see 'Congratulations'

'Susan Hampshire'

'Talisman'

Montgomery USA 1929
'Ophelia' × 'Souvenir de Claudius Pernet'
Fully double blooms open attractively flat-topped, not large but held on strong stems which makes them ideal for cutting. Golden-yellow in colour though tinged orange-copper. Foliage light green and glossy. Growth upright. A good and much-loved older variety.
(C) (MF) (P) (Gh) (B) ☉
✂ (AL)   3′ × 2′   90 × 60 cm

'Tallyho'

Swim USA 1948
'Charlotte Armstrong' × seedling
Large, globular buds open to large, cupped flowers of very deep pink, almost maroon. Foliage leathery. Very dark wood on a bushy plant.
(C) (P) (VF) (B) ☉ (AL)
3′ × 2′   90 × 60 cm

'Tenerife'

Bracegirdle UK 1972
'Fragrant Cloud' × 'Piccadilly'
Large, very full flowers of orange-red with a peach-yellow reverse. Foliage glossy. Growth upright.
(C) (P) (VF) (B) ☉ (AL)
2′ 6″ × 2′   75 × 60 cm

'Tequila Sunrise' (Dicobey)

Dickson UK 1989
('Eurorose' × 'Typhoon') × 'Bright Smile'
Pointed buds opening to full-petalled flowers of scarlet and gold. Foliage large, glossy, mid-green. Growth bushy, upright.
(C) ☉ (B) (H) (AL)
2′ 6″ × 2′   75 × 60 cm

'Super Sun'

'Tequila Sunrise'

'Texas Centennial'

'Texas Centennial'

Watkins USA 1935
Sport from 'President Herbert Hoover'
Long, pointed buds, held on long strong necks, open to flattish blooms of bright vermilion-red with a gold base. Foliage leathery and semi-matt. Growth vigorous, upright. A rose that can be used as a free-standing shrub.
(R) (H) (P) (VF) ✂ (AL)
4' × 3' 120 × 90 cm

'Thaïs',
'Lady Elgin'

Meilland FRANCE 1954
'Mme Kriloff' × ('Peace' × 'Genève')
I could not resist including this old variety, despite its rarity. Rounded buds open to full, cupped flowers of apricot-buffish-

yellow washed and veined orange. Foliage dark green and leathery. Growth upright.
(C) (P) (VF) (E) ☉ ✂ (AL) 3' × 2' 90 × 60 cm

'The Coxswain' (Cocadilly)

Cocker UK 1985
('Super Star' × 'Ballet') × 'Silver Jubilee'
Blended shades of pink and cream. The large and full flowers are freely produced. Foliage mid-green and semi-glossy. Bushy, upright growth.
(C) (P) (B) (H) (E) ☉ ✂ (AL) 2' 6" × 2' 75 × 60 cm

'The Doctor'

Howard USA 1936
'Mrs J. D. Eisele' × 'Los Angeles'
A famous variety which, despite a martyrdom to black spot, should not be allowed to vanish into oblivion. It has large flowers of rich silver-pink with a satin sheen, shapely and high-centred at the mid-open stage. Foliage matt grey-green. Growth vigorous and upright.
(C) (VF) (B) (E) ☉ BS✂ (WW) ✂ (AL)
2' 6" × 2' 75 × 60 cm

'The Lady' (Fryjingo)

Fryer UK 1985
'Pink Parfait' × 'Redgold'
Very large, exhibition-sized blooms of honey yellow brushed salmon. Semi-glossy, mid-green foliage. Upright growth.
(C) (P) (MF) (E) ☉ ✂ (AL) 2' 6" × 2' 75 × 60 cm

'Tiffany'

Linquist USA 1954
'Charlotte Armstrong' × 'Girona'
Blends of yellow and pink make

up the colouring of this shapely, high-centred, very fragrant rose. Foliage dark green and plentiful. Growth bushy, upright. One of the best roses to have come down to us from the 50s.
(C) ☉ (B) (H) (E) (Gh) ✂ (P) (VF) (AW)
3' × 2' 90 × 60 cm

'Torvill & Dean' (Lantor)

Sealand UK 1984
'Grandpa Dickson' × 'Alexander'
Glowing, mid-pink blooms with a cream underlay and base, large and shapely. Foliage mid-green and semi-glossy. Growth habit upright.
(C) (SF) (B) (E) ☉ (AL)
2' 6" × 2' 75 × 60 cm

'Touch of Class',
'Maréchal de Clerc' (Kricarlo)

Kriloff FRANCE 1984
'Micaële' × ('Queen Elizabeth' × 'Romantica')
Large, shapely, fragrant blooms of mid-pink highlighted cream and shaded coral held on long stems. Foliage dark green and semi-glossy. Growth upright.
(C) (B) (H) (E) (P) (Gh) ✂ (MF) (AL)
3' × 2' 90 × 60 cm

'Velvet Hour'

'Tranquillity',
'Handout' (Barout)

Barrett UK 1982
'Whisky Mac' × 'Pink Favourite'
Large, peachy-pink blooms flushed apricot and yellow. Foliage dark green and glossy. Growth upright and bushy.
(C) (SF) (B) ☉ (AL)
2' 6" × 2' 75 × 60 cm

'Troika',
'Royal Dane'

Poulsen DENMARK 1971
['Super Star' × ('Baccára' × 'Princesse Astrid')] × 'Hanne'
The large, full, colourful blooms are a blend of orange and pink. Foliage large, dark and glossy. Growth bushy and upright.
(C) (MF) (B) (H) ☉ ✂ (AW) 2' 6" × 2' 75 × 60 cm

'Tropicana' see 'Super Star'

'Typhoon' (Taifun)

Kordes GERMANY 1972
'Dr A. J. Verhage' × 'Colour Wonder'
Medium-sized blooms, a blend of salmon and yellow. Foliage mid-green and semi-matt. Growth upright.
(C) (MS) (B) (H) ☉ ✂ (AL) 2' 6" × 2' 75 × 60 cm

'Uncle Bill'

Beales UK 1984
Sport from 'Alec's Red' (discovered by Rev. W. Temple-Bourne)
Soft, silky, mid-pink blooms are produced in abundance from large and plump buds. Half open, the flowers are high-centred. Foliage mid-green, matt, the stems thorny. Growth bushy and upright.
(C) (VF) (B) (P) (AL)
2' 6" × 2' 75 × 60 cm

'Velvet Hour'

LeGrice UK 1978
Freely produced, medium-sized, full, blood-red flowers on strong necks, with a very good scent. Foliage dark and semi-glossy. Growth upright.
(C) (P) (H) (SF) (B) ⊙ φ ✂ (AL) 2' 6" × 2' 75 × 60 cm

**'Vienna Charm',
'Charming Vienna',
'Wiener Charme',
'Charme de Vienne'**
(Korschaprat)

Kordes GERMANY 1963
'Chantré' × 'Golden Sun'
Large, pointed buds open to large, full blooms of coppery-orange, well scented. Foliage dark and semi-glossy. Growth tallish, upright. Not totally hardy.
(C) (H) (MF) (B) ⊙ ☼ ✂ (AL) 3' 6" × 2' 105 × 60 cm

'Violinista Costa'

Camprubi SPAIN 1936
'Sensation' × 'Shot Silk'
Shapely flowers, freely produced, of deep orange-pink with deeper undertones and a yellow base, at times almost red. Foliage mid-green, glossy, the stems well armed with thorns. Growth angular.
(C) (P) (H) (B) (SF) ⊙ (AL) 2' 6" × 2' 75 × 60 cm

**'Virgo',
'Virgo Liberationem'**

Mallerin FRANCE 1947
'Blanche Mallerin' × 'Neige Parfum'
Shapely, pointed buds open to loose blooms of good size on strong stems, pure white. Foliage mid-greyish-green and semi-matt. Growth slender and upright.
(C) (MF) (B) (Gh) ⊙ ✂ (AL) 2' 6" × 2' 75 × 60 cm

'Viva'

Warriner USA 1974
Seedling × seedling
Rounded buds open to high-centred flowers of rich dark red. Fragrant. Glossy dark green foliage. Vigorous, upright growth.
(C) ⊙ (B) (H) (P) ✂ (SF) (AL)
3' 6" × 2' 6" 110 × 75 cm

'Wendy Cussons'

Gregory UK 1963
Seedling from 'Independence'
Superbly shaped, high-centred blooms of deep cerise-red are freely produced on a strong, angular, rather awkward plant with dark matt-green foliage.
(C) (P) (VF) (E) (WW) (AW)
2' × 2' 60 × 60 cm

'Uncle Bill'

'Violinista Costa'

'Virgo'

'Wendy Cussons'

'Whisky Mac'

'Whisky Mac' (Tanky)

Tantau GERMANY 1967
Shapely blooms of rich gold and amber with dark green, glossy foliage. Growth angular but upright. Not totally hardy.
(C) (P) (VF) (B) (Gh) ⊙ ✂ BS✋ R✋ (AW)
2′ 6″ × 2′ 75 × 60 cm

'White Knight' *see* **'Message'**

'White Masterpiece'

Boerner USA 1969
Very large, slightly scented, shapely flowers of pure white open from pointed buds. Foliage mid-green. Growth upright.
(C) (B) (H) (P) (Gh) (E) ✂ (SF) (AW)
4′ × 2′ 6″ 120 × 75 cm

'White Wings'

Krebs USA 1947
'Dainty Bess' × seedling
Long, pointed buds open to large, single, pure white flowers with pronounced chocolate-brown stamens. A beautiful rose when the right situation is found. Foliage mid-green and matt. Growth bushy.
(C) (MF) ⊙ ☼ (AL)
3′ 6″ × 3′ 6″ 110 × 75 cm

'Wiener Charme' *see* **'Vienna Charme'**

'Wisbech Gold'

McGredy UK 1964
'Piccadilly' × 'Golden Star'
The large, shapely blooms which are held upright on strong necks are golden-yellow edged pink. Foliage dark green and glossy. Growth upright.
(C) (P) (MF) (B) (Gh) ⊙ ✂ (AL) 2′ 6″ × 2′ 75 × 60 cm

'With Love' (Andwit)

Anderson UK 1983
'Grandpa Dickson' × 'Daily Sketch'
Freely produced, medium-sized blooms of clear yellow edged pink. Foliage mid-green and glossy. Growth upright.
(C) (MF) (B) ⊙ ✂ (AL) 2′ 6″ × 2′ 75 × 60 cm

'White Wings'

'Yorkshire Bank', 'True Love' (Rutrulo)

de Ruiter HOLLAND 1979
'Pascali' × 'Peer Gynt'
Large white blooms with hints of pink, freely produced amid bright green semi-glossy foliage. Growth bushy.
(C) (P) (B) (MF) ⊙ (AL)
2′ × 2′ 60 × 60 cm

'Allen Chandler'

Climbing Hybrid Teas

From time to time during their lifetimes, some varieties of Hybrid Teas (as with Floribundas, see page 000) have spontaneously produced a climbing shoot from an otherwise non-climbing plant. The reason is genetic and the survival of the new form depends upon the nurseryman reproducing the shoot by budding and grafting. Many Hybrid Teas make very worthy climbers, the best of which are described here. They make good wall subjects, but because of their vigour and lanky growth need training to give of their best.

CLASSIFICATION

BARB   Class 10
MR9   Class 12
WFRS   Class 17

'Allen Chandler'

Chandler USA 1923
'Hugh Dickson' × seedling
A sturdy, healthy rose of brilliant red. Large, semi-double flowers displaying golden stamens to advantage. A good, repeat flowering variety with dark green foliage.
(R) (P) (SF) (AL)
12' × 8'   3.5 × 2.5 m

'Bettina' Climbing

Bush form Meilland FRANCE 1953
'Peace' × ('Mme Joseph Perraud' × 'Demain')
This form Meilland FRANCE 1958
Shapely, cupped flowers opening flat; orange suffused with salmon. Foliage very dark green on relatively thornless stems. Needs a sheltered, warm situation to thrive.
(S) ☼ ✂ (VF) (AL)
15' × 8'   4.5 × 2.5 m

'Blessings' Climbing

Bush form Gregory UK 1967
'Queen Elizabeth' × seedling
This form Gregory UK 1968
A shapely rose of soft salmon, highly scented. Growth vigorous with ample mid-green foliage.
(S) (P) (MF) ✂ (AL)
15' × 8'   4.5 × 2.5 m

'Captain Christy' Climbing

Bush form Lacharme FRANCE 1873
'Victor Verdier' × 'Safrano'
This form Ducher FRANCE 1881
Semi-double soft pink with deeper pink centres, cupped until fully open. Flowers generously produced and fragrant, occasionally repeated in the autumn. Growth upright and vigorous with mid-green foliage.
(R) (P) (VF) (AL)
15' × 8'   4.5 × 2.5 m

'Château de Clos Vougeot' Climbing

Bush form Pernet-Ducher FRANCE 1908
This form Morse UK 1920
Flowers of a superb, deep velvety red, highly scented. An awkward rose, however, with angular growth and sprawly habit. Shoots relatively thornless. Foliage dark green but rather sparse.
(S) (VF) (AL)
15' × 8'   4.5 × 2.5 m

'Christine' Climbing

Bush form McGredy UK 1918
This form Willink IRELAND 1936
Shapely flowers of rich golden yellow, semi-double and unusually well-scented for a yellow. Growth upright and foliage medium-sized, mid to light green.
(S) (P) (VF) (AL)
12' × 8'   3.5 × 2.5 m

'Comtesse Vandal' Climbing

Bush form Leenders HOLLAND 1932
('Ophelia' × Mrs Aaron Ward') × 'Souvenir de Claudius Pernet'
This form Jackson & Perkins USA 1936
A very beautiful, rather elegant rose with long pointed buds opening to loosely formed flowers of silvery-buff pink with orange shadings and deeper reverse. Slightly scented. Growth vigorous and upright. Foliage large and dark green.
(S) (P) ✂ (SF) (AL)
12' × 8'   3.5 × 2.5 m

'Château de Clos Vougeot' Climbing

'Captain Christy' Climbing

'Crimson Conquest'

Chaplin Bros UK 1931
'Red Letter Day' sport
Medium-sized, semi-double, rich
crimson flowers on a healthy
plant with dark green, glossy foliage. An excellent, underrated
climbing rose, perpetuating a
famous old bush Hybrid Tea now
extinct.
(S) (N) (P) ● (SF) (AL)
15' × 8' 4.5 × 2.5 m

'Crimson Glory' Climbing

Bush form Kordes GERMANY
1935
'Cathrine Kordes' seedling × 'W.
E. Chaplin'
This form Jackson & Perkins USA
1946
The climbing form of this famous
Hybrid Tea makes an excellent
specimen. The colour speaks for
itself. Blooms velvety and very
full of petals. Its notoriously weak
neck is an advantage since, as it
climbs higher, the flowers can
hang down to effect. Has a strong,
heady perfume. Wood reddish-
brown and foliage dark green.
(S) (P) ✄ (VF) (AL)
15' × 8' 4.5 × 2.5 m

'Cupid'

B. R. Cant UK 1915
A lovely single variety. Superbly
formed, large, peachy-pink
flowers with a yellow base and
pronounced golden anthers.
Sometimes rather shy but worth
growing even for one perfect
bloom each year; however, it
occasionally repeats in autumn.
A specimen seen recently in New
Zealand belies its reputation for
shyness.
(S) (P) (N) ● (SF) (AL)
10' × 6' 3 × 1.8 m

'Cupid'

'Eden Rose' Climbing

Bush form F. Meilland FRANCE
1953
'Peace' × 'Signora'
This form F. Meilland FRANCE
1962
The shapely, large, high-centred
bud opens to a blowsy, fully
double bloom of bright pink with
silvery highlights. Very fragrant.
Foliage large, crisp and glossy,
produced on thick, strong steams.
Very vigorous.
(S) (P) (N) ● (MF) (AL)
15' × 10' 4.5 × 3 m

'Ena Harkness' Climbing

Bush form Norman 1946
'Crimson Glory' × 'Southport'
This form Murrell UK 1954
Flowers shapely in the Hybrid
Tea style, with pointed buds of
rich velvety crimson, highly
scented. The weak neck inherited
from its parent 'Crimson Glory'
can be an advantage in the
climber. Wood dark and thorny
with plentiful dark, matt-green
foliage.
(S) (P) ✄ (VF) (AL)
15' × 8' 4.5 × 2.5 m

'Grandmère Jenny' Climbing

'Etoile de Hollande' Climbing

Bush form Verschuren HOLLAND
1919
'General MacArthur' × 'Hadley'
This form Leenders HOLLAND
1931
A red rose, very famous and
popular between the wars.
Superbly fragrant. Rich velvety
red with shapely flowers – turning
purple with age – its only fault.
Shoots plum-coloured and foliage
dull dark green.
(S) M✄ (VF) (AL)
12' × 8' 3.5 × 2.5 m

'Fragrant Cloud' Climbing

Bush form Tantau GERMANY
1963
This form Collin UK 1973
Seedling × 'Prima Ballerina'
Its shapely blooms are coral-red,
though variable. Foliage dark
reddish-green. Growth upright,
sturdy.
(S) (VF) ✄ BS✄ (AL)
12' × 8' 3.5 × 2.5 m

'General MacArthur' Climbing

Bush form E. G. Hill & Co. USA
1905

This form Dickson UK 1923
Large, deep, rosy-red, highly
scented, loosely formed blooms
emerge from pointed buds. Free-
flowering and very vigorous.
Wood maroon with large dark
green leaves.
(S) (P) (VF) (AL)
18' × 10' 5.5 × 3 m

'Golden Dawn' Climbing

Bush form Grant AUSTRALIA
1929
'Elegante' × 'Ethel Somerset'
This form LeGrice UK 1947
Its name is rather misleading in
that its colour is yellow with hints
of pink. Flowers large and globular, with a strong, sweet perfume.
Foliage quite striking, dark green
overlaid with copper. Vigorous
and healthy.
(S) (N) (P) ● (VF) (AL)
12' × 8' 3.5 × 2.5 m

'Grandmère Jenny' Climbing

Bush form Meilland FRANCE
1950
'Peace' × ('Julien Potin' × 'Sensation')
This form Meilland FRANCE 1958
The long pointed buds produce
flowers of considerable size. Their
colour is primrose overlaid with
copper and pink. Sounds vulgar
but the effect is quite refined.
Growth is vigorous, foliage large
and very dark green.
(S) (P) ✄ (MF) (AL)
18' × 10' 5.5 × 3 m

'Guinée'

Mallerin FRANCE 1938
'Souvenir de Claudius Denoyel' ×
'Ami Quinard'
Very dark crimson, the double
flowers emerge from rather tubby
buds to open flat and display

'Guinée'

golden-brown anthers, surrounded by velvety-textured petals. Fragrant. A superb variety with dark wood and dark green foliage. Sometimes produces a second flush in the autumn.
(R) (P) (VF) (AL)
15' × 8'   4.5 × 2.5 m

'Home Sweet Home' Climbing

Bush form Wood & Ingram UK
This form origin unknown
Large, globular flowers of pure rose-pink with a large number of velety-textured petals and considerable scent. Thick, very vigorous stems. Well endowed with large, dark foliage.
(S) (P) (VF) (AL)
15' × 8'   4.5 × 2.5 m

Highly scented. As a climber, it is superior to the bush form. Foliage is plentiful, dull, dark green, and borne on vigorous thorny stems.
(S) (P) (VF) (AL)
15' × 10'   4.5 × 3 m

'Lady Sylvia' Climbing

Bush form Stevens UK 1926
'Mme Butterfly' sport
This form Stevens UK 1933
One of the most popular roses of the 1930s. Shapely buds, opening to full flowers of flesh-pink with deeper undertones, and a fine perfume. Makes an outstanding climber with an upright habit and grey-green foliage. Good for cutting.
(S) (Gh) (P) ✄ (VF) (AL)
15' × 10'   4.5 × 3 m

'Irish Fireflame' Climbing

Bush form Dickson UK 1914
This form Dickson UK 1916
Large, single flowers with pronounced anthers, a mixture of quiet orange, yellow and peach, the name belying its refinement. A healthy shrub, which is not too tall. Ideal for pillar work, especially as it often repeats in the autumn. Foliage dark green.
(R) (AL)   10' × 6'   3 × 1.8 m

'Josephine Bruce' Climbing

Bush form Bees UK 1949
'Crimson Glory × Madge Whipp'
This form Bees UK 1954
Fully double flowers of deep velvety red, at times quite blackish.

'Lady Waterlow'

G. Nabonnand FRANCE 1903
'La France de '89' × 'Mme Marie Lavalley'
Semi-double flowers of soft pink with deeper undertones and veining, particularly at the edges of the petals. A healthy, robust climber, amply foliated and upright in growth. Scented.
(S) (P) (N) ● (MF) (AL)
15' × 8'   4.5 × 2.5 m

'Home Sweet Home' Climbing

'Mme Abel Chatenay' Climbing

Bush form Pernet-Ducher
FRANCE 1895
'Dr Grill' × 'Victor Verdier'
This form Page UK 1917
One of the early climbing Hybrid
Teas and still worth garden space
even at the exclusion of others.
Flowers globular but pointed,
scented, soft silky-pink with a
deeper centre when open. I suspect that over the years, this rose
may have lost some vigour. Foliage small but dense and dark
green. Growth rather angular and
thorny.
(R) (VF) (AL)
10' × 8'   3 × 2.5 m

'Mme Butterfly' Climbing

Bush form Hill & Co. USA 1918
'Ophelia' sport
This form E. P. Smith UK 1926
Shapely scrolled buds open to
full, pale soft pink flowers with a
fine perfume, strong-necked,
good for cutting. Grey-green foliage on an upright vigorous plant.
(S) (Gh) (P) ✂ (VF) (AL)
15' × 10'   4.5 × 3 m

'Mme Caroline Testout' Climbing

Bush form Pernet-Ducher
FRANCE 1890
'Mme de Tartas' × 'Lady Mary
Fitzwilliam'
This form Chauvry FRANCE 1901
A very vigorous climber with lush
grey-green foliage and thick,
upright, thorny shoots. Flowers
large, cabbage-like, deep silvery-
pink, with a strong perfume.
Sometimes remontant.
(R) (P) (N) ● (VF) (AL)
15' × 8'   4.5 × 2.5 m

'Mme Caroline Testout'

'Mme Edouard Herriot', Climbing
'Daily Mail Rose' Climbing

Bush form Pernet-Ducher
FRANCE 1913
'Mme Caroline Testout' × a
Hybrid Tea
This form Ketten Bros
LUXEMBOURG 1921
A vigorous climbing rose, coral
with a faint yellow base. Pointed
buds open loosely to semi-
double, flattish flowers. Growth
upright and thorny with brownish
flecks on the bark. Foliage light
green.
(S) (MF) (AL)
12' × 8'   3.5 × 2.5 m

'Mme Grégoire Staechelin'

'Meg'

'Mme Grégoire Staechelin', 'Spanish Beauty'

P. Dot SPAIN 1927
'Frau Karl Druschki' × 'Château
de Clos Vougeot'
A climbing rose of exceptional
vigour. The large pale-pink
flowers have a deeper pink
reverse and are heavily veined at
the edges. Early-flowering and
very free-blooming. Growth vigorous and foliage dark green. If it
is not dead-headed it produces
superb, large, orange-red hips in
the autumn. A superb variety.
(R) (F) (P) (N) ● (VF)
(AL)   15' × 10'   4.5 × 3 m

'Mme Henri Guillot' Climbing

Bush form Mallerin FRANCE 1938
'Rochefort' × *R. foetida bicolor* seedling
This form Meilland FRANCE 1942
Large, rather loose semi-double flowers of deep, burnt orange. Not much scent. A vigorous grower with plentiful dark green leaves.
(S) (P) (N) ● (SF) (AL)
15′ × 10′   4.5 × 3 m

'Meg'

Gosset UK 1954
Thought to be 'Paul's Lemon Pillar' × 'Mme Butterfly'
An outstandingly beautiful climber. The large, almost single flowers are scented, and have pronounced russet-red stamens and petals of buff-yellow, flushed apricot and peach. The foliage is dark green, glossy and healthy.
(R) (P) (MF) (AL)
8′ × 4′   2.5 × 1.2 m

'Mrs Aaron Ward' Climbing

Bush form Pernet-Ducher FRANCE 1907
Bush form Dickson UK 1922
High-centred buds opening to shapely flowers of creamy yellow flushed pink, occasionally deeper in dull weather, free-flowering, scented. Strong growth with plenty of dark green foliage.
(S) (P) (MF) (AL)
15′ × 8′   4.5 × 2.5 m

'Mrs G. A. van Rossem' Climbing

Bush form Van Rossem HOLLAND 1929

'Mme Edouard Herriot' Climbing'

'Souvenir de Claudius Pernet' × 'Gorgeous'
This form Gaujard FRANCE 1937
Large globular buds opening to flowers of orange and apricot on a yellow backcloth with a much deeper reverse. Growth strong and upright. Foliage highly glossed; rich dark green shoots have only a few thorns.
(S) (P) (SF) (AL)
12′ × 10′   3.5 × 3 m

'Mrs Herbert Stevens' Climbing

Bush form McGredy UK 1910
'Frau Karl Druschki' × 'Niphetos'
This form Pernet-Ducher FRANCE 1922
One of the best white climbers. Shapely flowers produced in quantity, superbly scented. Foliage dark, on vigorous shoots. An old favourite, frequently found in older gardens and often sent to me for identification. Quite happy in difficult situations.
(R) (P) (N) ● ✂ (VF)
(AW)   12′ × 8′   3.5 × 2.5 m

'Mrs Sam McGredy' Climbing

Bush form McGredy IRELAND 1929
('Donald Macdonald' × 'Golden Emblem') × (seedling × 'The Queen Alexandra Rose')
This form Buisman HOLLAND 1937
Very vigorous rose with coppery-red foliage and orange-red young shoots. Flowers shaggy when fully open, fiery copper-orange and scented. Needs plenty of space to develop fully.
(R) (P) (N) ● ✂ (MF)
(AL)   20′ × 15′   6 × 4.5 m

'Ophelia' Climbing

Bush form W. Paul UK 1912
This form Dickson IRELAND 1920
Shapely buds opening soft flesh-pink with deeper shadings and light yellow tints in the centre. Has a strong fragrance. Upright in growth with plenty of foliage.
(R) (P) ✂ (VF) (AL)
15′ × 10′   4.5 × 3 m

'Paul Lédé' Climbing, 'Mons. Paul Lédé'

Bush form Pernet-Ducher FRANCE 1902
This form Lowe UK 1913
Large, shapely flowers of soft pink with peachy shadings in the base, sweetly scented and free-flowering. Foliage plentiful and mid-green. Seldom seen but a sight to remember in full flush.
(R) (P) (VF) (AL)
12′ × 8′   3.5 × 2.5 m

'Paul's Lemon Pillar'

Paul UK 1915
'Frau Karl Druschki' × 'Maréchal Niel'
Massive blooms of creamy-white suffused with lemon; of unusually high quality in most weathers. Scented. A vigorous climber with very thick branches and large, dark green leaves. A deservedly popular old variety.
(S) (P) (N) ● ✂ (VF)
(AL)   15′ × 10′   4.5 × 3 m

'Picture' Climbing

Bush form McGredy UK 1932
This form Swim USA 1942
Flowers not large but shapely, rich clear pink, suffused with many other shades of pink. Scented. An upright grower with plenty of prickles and ample, if somewhat small foliage.
(S) (P) ✂ (VF) (AL)
15′ × 8′   4.5 × 2.5 m

semi-double flowers of vivid orange, red and yellow, slightly fragrant. Prolific light green leaves and very thorny stems.
(R) (P) (N) ● (SF) (AL)
10' × 6'   3 × 1.8 m

'Richmond' Climbing

Bush form E. G. Hill & Co. USA 1905
'Lady Battersea' × 'Liberty'
This form Dickson UK 1912
Variable, from light carmine to scarlet, semi-double, scented blooms cupped initially, opening flattish, freely produced. Foliage dark green with upright growth.
(S) (N) (P) (SF) (AL)
10' × 6'   3 × 1.8 m

'Shot Silk' Climbing

Bush form Dickson UK 1924
'Hugh Dickson' seedling × 'Sunstar'
This form C. Knight
AUSTRALIA 1931
A popular variety, one of the nicest and most reliable. Fully double, cupped flowers, soft cherry-cerise with golden-yellow and lemon base, fragrant, freely produced. Petal texture silky, but stands up to weather very well. Foliage lush dark green and plentiful.
(R) (P) (N) ● ✂ (VF)
(AW)   18' × 10'   5.5 × 3 m

'Paul Lédé' Climbing'

'Reine Marie Henriette'

F. Levet FRANCE 1878
'Mme Bérard' × 'Général Jacqueminot'
Large, loosely double flowers, deep cherry-red, very free-flowering and scented. Foliage large, leathery and dark green. Stems maroon, with few thorns.

Vigorous.
(R) (VF) (AL)
12' × 8'   3.5 × 2.5 m

'Réveil Dijonnais'

Buatois FRANCE 1931
'Eugène Fürst' × 'Constance'
A striking rose. Loosely formed,

'Réveil Dijonnais'

'Souvenir de Claudius Denoyel'

Chambard FRANCE 1920
'Château de Clos Vougeot' ×
'Commandeur Jules Gravereaux'
Shapely, double, cupped flowers
of rich red to scarlet, produced in
loose clusters. Fragrant. Foliage
large and darkish green. Growth
vigorous and rather angular. Not
the easiest to grow.
(R)   (VF)   (AL)
12′ × 8′   3.5 × 2.5 m

'Spek's Yellow' Climbing, 'Golden Sceptre'

Bush form Verschuren-Pechtold
HOLLAND 1950
'Golden Rapture' × unnamed
seedling
This form Walters USA 1956
Double, rich golden-yellow
flowers from pointed, shapely
buds with long stems, ideal for
cutting. Foliage particularly good,
light green and glossy. Growth
upright and vigorous.
(S)   (N)   (P)   (Gh)   ●   ✄
(MF)   (AL)   15′ × 10′   4.5 × 3 m

'Super Star' Climbing, 'Tropicana' (Tangostar)

Bush form Tantau
GERMANY 1960
(Seedling × 'Peace') × (Seedling
× 'Alpine Glow')
This form Blaby UK 1965 and
Boerner USA 1971
The large, full, shapely blooms of
coral-vermilion are high-centred
in bud. Foliage matt and grey-
green. Growth upright and
branching.
(S)   (P)   (MF)   M✿   (AW)
12′ × 8′   3.5 × 2.5 m

'Sutter's Gold' Climbing

Bush form Swim USA 1950
This form Weeks USA 1950
'Charlotte Armstrong' × 'Signora'
Slim buds held on long stems
open loosely to deep yellow
flowers brushed orange and pink.
Foliage mid-green and semi-
glossy. Growth upright.
(S)   (P)   (VF)   (AW)
12′ × 8′   3.5 × 2.5 m

'Talisman' Climbing

Bush form Montgomery & Co.
USA 1929
'Ophelia' × 'Souvenir de Claudius
Pernet'
This form Western Rose Co.
USA 1930
Fully-double flowers, golden-
yellow with orange and copper
highlights. Foliage tough and
leathery on vigorous, upright,
thorny shoots.
(S)   (P)   ✄   (SF)   (AL)
12′ × 8′   3.5 × 2.5 m

'Vicomtesse Pierre du Fou'

Sauvageot FRANCE 1923
'L'Idéal' × 'Joseph Hill'
The luxuriant, glossy foliage of
copper-dark green makes an ideal
foil for the fragrant, double,
loosely-quartered flowers, which
are coppery-pink when fully
open. Vigorous and branching in
habit.
(R)   (P)   (N)   ●   (MF)   (AL)
15′ × 10′   4.5 × 3 m

'Whisky Mac' Climbing (Andmac)

Bush form Tantau
GERMANY 1967
This form Anderson UK 1985
Shapely blooms of rich golden-
amber, with dark green, semi-
glossy foliage on an upright plant.
Needs placing in a sheltered,
warm position to thrive in colder
districts.
(S)   (VF)   ✄   (AL)
12′ × 8′   3.5 × 2.5 m

PART V
The Cultivation of Roses

'Ballerina' growing in a pot

The author's garden in Norfolk

Choosing and Buying Roses

Unless you have a good all-round knowledge of roses to the point where you know the foibles and limitations of the varieties you wish to grow, choosing roses is not a straightforward exercise. It is not like buying a manufactured commodity. A spade is a spade and, as a general rule, will be as good as the price you wish to pay. While the adage 'you get what you pay for' can be applied to roses in the commodity sense, often depending on where you buy them, it does not necessarily follow that a more expensive variety in any one catalogue will be any better than a less expensive one of the same colour. It could be worse, in fact, for the pricing of different varieties is not determined by their size or quality. It is usually calculated by balancing the following factors: the degree of difficulty in producing the rose, the length of time it has been on the market, the royalty the nurseryman has to pay to its raiser, its rarity and the likely demand in comparison to other varieties.

Roses can be purchased in three different ways. By far the most common way and undoubtedly the best is direct from the nursery which has produced them, usually by mail order. Most

such roses are termed 'bare root' or 'open ground' plants. In Britain the rose industry is well served by the BRGA (British Rose Growers Association), an organization which is run by its members and is consumer-orientated, setting standards of quality and service to the public besides attending to the needs of its membership. There is no price fixing within the industry, so prices vary from nursery to nursery and region to region, but by and large a rose purchased from a member of the Association should be at least up to the standard recommended as first-class quality by the British Standards Institute. Other countries have similar guidelines for growers. This does not mean that there are no good growers outside the BRGA, of course, but beware of cheap roses, for inferior stock sometimes finds its way on to the market through dealers who have never grown a rose themselves. Such roses may be sub-standard, wrongly labelled or both – you may be lucky but not often.

The second way to purchase roses is in containers. These are usually obtained from garden centres, although many specialist growers offer a selection. They are seldom, if ever, sent by mail order. Those bought from garden centres will have been acquired

for resale from a wholesale grower. Containerized roses are becoming very popular – though the range of varieties on offer is often limited – because they have the one clear advantage that you can see what you are buying They are usually sold in spring and summer when it is impossible to plant bare-root specimens. It is also possible to buy root-wrapped plants from garden centres, usually in the spring. These are bare-root plants placed in a polythene bag with damp peat to keep them fresh.

The third method of purchase is through a shop or store. Roses sold through these outlets are usually packaged in polythene, often with an exaggerated colour picture of its contents displayed on the bag. If you intend to buy such roses, examine them carefully, and if they are at all dry or have less than two strong shoots at a minimum – think twice

It is important to buy roses only of the highest quality, for if you start with good plants they give far better value for money over the years. There is no doubt, however, that roses are best bought freshly dug from a nurseryman who has grown them himself. He is usually confident of his product and will seldom decline to replace any that fail to grow during the first few weeks of

the growing season after purchase.

As for selecting varieties, again there is no better place than a nursery to see roses growing, either in the fields or in a display garden. Some roses are more photogenic than others and printing processes vary too, so although most catalogues are written in a helpful way, try not to make your choice from pictures alone. Decide on your needs from written descriptions and speak to someone who knows. Most specialist rose growers are too concerned with their reputation to sell you something you don't want or a variety that is not up to your needs.

Flower shows provide good opportunities to see roses, but sometimes those on display have been produced under glass, especially for spring shows, so do not order without first speaking to the grower. Once you have made your choice, order early. Bare-root roses can be safely planted at any time during the dormant season, but if you wish to plant them in November you will need to order by midsummer at the latest. As most nurseries dig up and despatch their orders in rotation as received (and most good growers deal with thousands of orders in the lifting season), it is, therefore, impossible to send

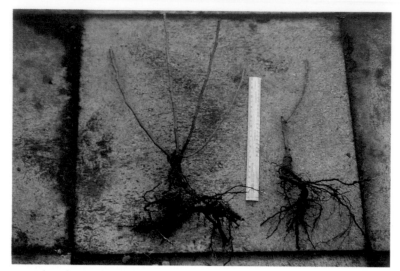

Examples of a good-quality and a poor-quality plant

them all out at the same time. Another good reason for not ordering late is that if a variety is in short supply or in demand, you will be disappointed and it may well be too late to place an order elsewhere. This applies particularly to rare and unusual varieties and to those newly on offer. If you do have to place an order late in the season, prepare a small piece of ground by covering it with frost-proof material in readiness for your roses so that they can be heeled-in whatever the weather. Most nurseries will try to avoid sending roses during severe, frosty spells but sometimes, when the weather changes suddenly after despatch, they are caught out. If the ground is too hard for heeling-in when the roses arrive, plunge their roots (still in their bundle) into a bucket or box of peat or sand and leave them in the garage or a shed until the weather improves. Those that look a little dry on arrival should be completely buried for a couple of weeks; no harm will come to

them and they will be as good as new when dug up.

N.B. An availability rating is given to each rose in the Dictionary section.

A container rose

BUYING CONTAINERIZED ROSES

Roses can be bought, already flowering, in containers. They are naturally more expensive than bare-root stock because of the extra work and material needed to produce them. Many garden centres offer a range of both modern and old-fashioned roses in this form. Some people prefer not to buy such roses and whereas I agree there is no substitute for traditional winter planting, containerized roses are certainly here to stay and will become available in increasing numbers. Provided we learn to adapt to the new techniques of planting and aftercare, buying roses in full flower can be a worthwhile and pleasant experience.

SUCKERS AND UNDERSTOCKS

A rose planted from the nursery actually comprises two different roses, the roots being one species. i.e. the stock, and the shoots another, i.e. the variety chosen. When it is planted the root sometimes decides to become independent and send up a shoot of its own; this is called suckering. Since the roots of the stock are usually more vigorous than their enforced guest, the shoot or shoots, if allowed to grow, will eventually take over and smother the variety being cultivated. Suckers, when they appear, should be removed before they have a chance to grow to any size. Experience will enable a gardener to recognize them as slightly different from the young shoots which sprout to the stems above the ground, for suckers always appear from below ground level and often some little distance

from the plant. It used to be said that shoots from the rootstock had leaves which comprised seven leaflets and that the leaves of the proper rose were made up of five. This has never been a very reliable guide to the recognition of suckers even on modern hybrid roses and should be treated almost as an old wives' tale. It is even less true in the case of the species, old-fashioned shrub roses, climbers and ramblers, since many of them have the same number of leaflets per leaf as those of the rootstock. If doubtful, scrape a little soil away from the rose bush and try to find the original union of stock and scion. If the shoot is coming from below this point, then it is probably a sucker. Remove it at the point where it joins the root; if it is cut higher up, even more suckers will be created in gratitude for pruning. Pulling suckers from the root is more effective than cutting them, especially when they are young. In days now gone, gardeners and rose-growers used a special tool called a 'Spud' for removing suckers. Shaped like a miniature blunt spade, it could be pushed into the soil close to the rose bush in a downward tearing motion, thus eliminating any possibility of secondary growth.

Apart from removing suckers as and when they appear, the best remedy for their prevention is to ensure that the roses are planted sufficiently deep to cover the complete rootstock. Suckers are sometimes encouraged to grow from wounded roots, so avoid inflicting damage when hoeing or digging around roses.

The understocks used in modern rose production are chosen according to the soil and

A badly planted rose with suckers

to the experience of the nurseryman. A selected form of *R. corrifolia froebelii*, commonly known as 'Laxa', a strong-rooted species which produces few suckers, is by far the most widely used in Europe today. In America, Australia and New Zealand *R. multiflora* and 'Dr Huey' are in most widespread use. The common Dog Rose, *R. canina*, has now largely disappeared as an understock; a blessing both to nurserymen and to gardeners, for it was very prone to suckering. Standard roses are usually grown on *R. rugosa* stems, largely because they are the easiest type to grow straight and firm. These can send up both root and stem suckers especially in their early years after transplanting, and a wary eye should be kept open for these as the plants grow. In other countries, where such roses are generally known as 'Tree roses', *R. multiflora* is usually used for this purpose. Until recently, 'Rugosa' stems were grown from cuttings and took three years to develop. Over the last few years, however, stems have been successfully produced in two years by budding specially selected forms of *R. rugosa* on to 'Laxa' stocks. The two varieties currently available in Britain are 'Rocket', developed by Harkness, and 'Chesham's Choice', developed by Paul Chesham.

Planting

HEELING-IN

The term 'heeling-in' simply means the digging of a trench large enough to accommodate the roots of roses so as to hold them temporarily in good condition until they can be planted in their permanent position.

Place the bushes in the trench about 3–6″ (7.5–15 cm) apart and at an angle of 45° to prevent them being blown about in strong wind. Then replace the soil so that it covers the roots, firming with the heel. It is important to ensure that the union, or junction of roots and shoots, is about 2″ (5 cm) below ground level to protect the union from frost. They will keep this way for weeks, even months, until the weather is right for planting.

Roses are very hardy plants and usually quite difficult to kill unless maltreated. The two best ways of killing them before planting are to allow the roots to become frosted while they are out of the ground, or to expose them to drying winds with their roots unprotected.

WINTER PROTECTION

In extreme climates, such as North America and Canada, only the hardiest roses will survive outside during the winter months and it may be necessary to protect them by earthing them up, or insulating the roots.

Malcolm Lowe advises: Use an insulation that doesn't take on moisture – rigid foams for example. Rose cones are also effective; wrapping plants provides more protection than layering – if layering is indicated, pine needles are better than salt marsh hay (the latter retains moisture, thereby attracting field mice that eat the canes). A winter's blanket of snow will protect roses but as a result of the global warming of the past decade, snow is less frequent and melts quickly. A windbreak will also provide protection.

SOILS AND SOIL PREPARATION

Roses prefer soil with a pH of about 6.5, in other words slightly acid or neutral, although they are not too fussy about alkalinity and many will tolerate up to pH 7.5. Should you suspect that the pH of your soil is lower or higher than these tolerance levels, then either have your soil tested or do so yourself with one of the inexpensive soil-testing kits available from most good garden centres.

Good preparation of soils before planting is always rewarded by more contented roses. It is advisable, therefore, to dig over the soil well in advance of planting, incorporating some form of organic material. Well-rotted farmyard manure is undoubtedly the best, but failing this, a mixture of coarse, damp peat* and bonemeal can be used or, better still, well-rotted compost from a compost heap. If the soil is very poor, a balanced fertilizer with added trace elements can be broadcast over the soil ahead of planting. Special rose fertilizer can be bought from most garden centres – a worthwhile investment when you consider that the roses being planted are to last for many years; the same type of fertilizer can be used as top-dressing after the roses are established, preferably before the start of the growing season, usually at the time of pruning. This gives the nutrients the chance of penetrating the soil, prior to the beginning of maximum root activity. On good soils, one top-dressing should be enough to sustain the rose throughout the summer, and no further feeding should be necessary until the following spring. For impoverished soils, however, a second dressing should be applied in early summer, by which time the rose will be seeking further nourishment to provide a second flush of flowers or secondary growth, depending on its habit.

The proprietary brands of fertilizer are specially prepared for roses and will usually contain the proper mix of nutrients in the most beneficial proportions. Should any other type of balanced fertilizer be used – and there is no reason why it should not – it should be low in nitrogen and high in potash, with a good mix of the major trace elements. Iron is particularly important, especially if your soil is alkaline; so is magnesium, which is frequently deficient in many soils. Those who practise organic gardening can supply nutrition by means of liquid seaweed, spent hops, farmyard manure, fish meal, etc., but the levels of potash must be kept up by the use of soot or wood ashes. All soils, of course,

* Peat is a finite resource, and whilst about 8% of the Earth's surface is peatland it is without doubt ecologically harmful to peat bogs for us to continue to use it in the quantities we demand today. So, as and when alternatives to peat become available, these should be used instead. One possible alternative at present is pulverized tree bark. Another, becoming available in increasing quantities, is coconut fibre.

are improved by the incorporation of organic materials, but I do not greatly favour constant mulching of rose beds with farmyard manure. This practice, apart from looking unsightly for much of the year, tends to harbour the spores of diseases by giving them a perfect environment from which to launch themselves at the rose each spring. Mulching, if considered necessary, should be to suppress weeds rather than as a source of nutrition. Bark chippings are ideal, especially if applied to the depth of about 1″ (2.5 cm), to fairly clean ground. Nor do I consider the use of lawn trimmings a good practice; in any event, they should only be applied in moderation. They are best composted and spread at a later date; again, this should be done sparingly, for the high nitrogen content of such compost can lead to abundant growth, fewer flowers and less immunity to disease.

The nutritional requirements of roses growing in containers are the same as for those growing in open ground; remember, however, that nutrients leach from potted soil far more quickly than they do from natural soil, so more frequent applications of fertilizer are necessary. Liquid fertilizer can be applied when watering. Roses also respond to foliar feeding, but this should not be done in hot sunshine.

To sum up, if you love roses, it is worth growing them whatever your soil, provided you do not expect rewards out of proportion to the loving care you give them.

SPECIFIC REPLANT DISEASE

Roses should not be planted in soil where other roses have been grown. This is because of a soil condition known as 'rose sickness'. Soil becomes contaminated by chemical secretions from rose roots, which newly planted bushes find offensive. Such a condition is called 'specific replant disease' and manifests itself in stunted, rather reluctant bushes which never develop satisfactorily, no matter how well they are tended. It is for this reason that commercial rose producers never grow successive crops of roses on the same land without at least a two-year break between each crop. If waiting two years is impossible, the soil should be changed. This is very important and should not present too much of a problem. It is simply a matter of juxtaposing two lots of soil, one, say, from the vegetable garden or from any spot where the soil is good and has not previously grown roses, and the other from the site where the new rose is to be planted. There are no short cuts; soil must be changed even if you are replacing a young bush. If this is not possible, old bushes should be removed and the soil in which they were growing rested for a period of at least two years before new bushes are planted. The vacant plot can, of course, be used for another catch* crop, such as vegetables or bedding plants, whilst resting from roses.

* A Norfolk term for a quick-growing interim crop.

PLANTING BUSH, SHRUB AND OLD-FASHIONED ROSES

Holes should be large enough to take the root of each plant without cramping; about one spade's depth is usually enough. When the hole is dug throw in a handful of bonemeal, then with the spade mix this thoroughly with the soil in the bottom. Scatter another handful of bonemeal on the heap of soil which is to go back into the hole. The rose should then be stood in the centre, ensuring that the roots are well spread out; enough soil is then placed around the roots to hold it in an upright position, thus enabling more soil to be added using both hands on the spade. When half the soil has been replaced, the bush should be given a little shake to ensure that soil falls between the roots, then tread the soil with the feet, firmly enough to hold the rose tight but not so firm as to compact the soil. The lighter the soil the more heavily it will need to be pressed or trodden. With the rose standing upright in the hole, replace the rest of the soil, leaving the last half-spadeful for a tilth around the rose after treading. Having made sure that the label is firmly attached, tidy up any footprints and leave the rose to settle in. If it has been planted in the autumn or winter, it may need a light retreading a few weeks later or in the spring before it starts to grow.

PLANTING CONTAINERIZED ROSES

More often than not containerized roses are purchased during the summer months, but it is quite in order to plant them at any time of the year. When removing the pot, the soil packed around the roots must not be disturbed. Once the plant with its undisturbed ball of soil is in position, refill the hole with care. Since most composts used for container roses are peat-based, which is difficult to moisten, plunge the rose for half an hour or so into a bucket of water before planting out. As with bare-root roses, make sure that the union is 1″ (2.5 cm) below soil level; this is very important as it reduces the possibility of suckers and stabilizes the bush against wind damage.

Standard or tree roses, either bare-root or containerized, require a good stake to support them. This should always be in position before the tree is planted and should be driven at least 18″ (45 cm) into the soil to give adequate support, even deeper if the soil is sandy.

Note: Most roses purchased in containers have not been grown in the pot. They are simply open-ground plants containerized a few months earlier. This is because they are not as amenable to being container-grown as some other plants.

PLANTING SPECIMEN ROSES IN LAWNS

When planting specimen roses in lawns or shrub roses in rough grass, it is important to leave an ample circle of soil around the

Planting Container-grown Roses

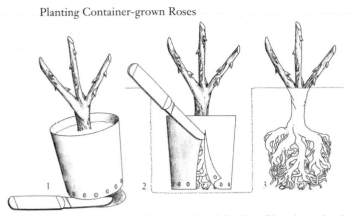

Removing bottom of   Place in hole and slit side   Planted rose showing
polythene pot   of pot - remove polythene   depth of planting

Pruning a newly planted rose

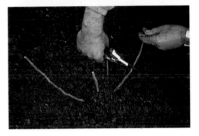

bush. Roses do not like the competition of tall uncut grass, especially in their early years; and apart from looking untidy, it is difficult to remove it from around an established plant and it also makes mowing difficult.

PLANTING CLIMBING ROSES

Adopt the same method for planting climbing roses as with bush roses, but when they are to grow on walls, remember that the soil is often poorer near the house or building and that a little extra organic material will be needed at planting time. Newly planted climbing roses are often the first to suffer from drought, since they have extra foliage to support. Frequently, too, they miss out on some of the rain, especially those on south-facing walls or fences. If planning to plant on pillars or tripods, the structure should be erected in advance of planting.

PLANTING AND STAKING STANDARD ROSES

For standard shrub roses and weepers, stout, tall stakes should

be positioned in advance of planting and inserted at intervals of 18″ (45 cm) into the ground. At least two rose tree ties will be needed to fix the stem to the stake. For weeping standards, which are sometimes 5′ (1.5 m) tall, three ties may be necessary. Stakes usually have a shorter life than the rose itself, so at some point it will need restaking. Provision for this can be made at planting time by placing a metal or plastic tube, of sufficient size to take the stake, vertically into the ground to the correct depth and placing the stake into this before planting the rose. This will enable the replacement of stakes to take place later without too much disturbance to the soil surrounding the roots.

Should a dry or hot spell of weather arrive during the first season, or indeed in succeeding seasons, the rose will need water. The fact that it is deep-rooted and does not show obvious signs of suffering is no reason for neglecting its thirst.

PLANTING ROSES INTO POTS

In an earlier chapter I discussed the growing of roses in pots, tubs and urns; so it is worth describing how these should be planted. Whatever the type of rose, a good, large container is important. Free drainage is essential, so in addition to providing drainage holes, shingle or broken bricks should be placed in the bottom of the container. A thin layer of coarse, damp peat should be placed over the drainage material, followed by John Innes Potting Compost No. 3. If this is dry, dampen it slightly before use, since once *in situ* it is much more difficult to moisten thoroughly. The peat layer over the drainage material is to stop the soil sifting through and blocking the drainage holes. The container should be filled to about 2″ (5 cm) from the top to allow watering without spilling both water and soil over the edge. The

rose should be planted deep enough for the shoots to come from below the soil surface. If a wooden container is used, its life can be prolonged by lining the inside with thick polythene before filling with soil, remembering to allow sufficient drainage holes in the bottom. If the roses are already in containers or pots, these should be removed before planting, taking care not to disturb the ball of soil around the roots. For several weeks after planting they will sustain themselves from the ball of soil in which they have been growing and, until they start making additional roots, will need liberal and frequent watering. Like all pot plants, roses grown in containers will need repotting from time to time. This should be done only in the dormant season, and some of the existing soil should be retained around the roots, especially in the case of older plants.

Pruning

How and when to prune roses usually provokes friendly disagreement among rosarians, and in my experience almost all the arguments in favour of this method or that have some weight to them. In fact, pruning is far less complicated than many books and articles on the subject may suggest. The most important 'tools' a pruner needs are, first, common sense; secondly and most important, a feeling for the plant; thirdly, a strong pair of gloves to give confidence; and fourthly, good, sharp secateurs. Modern secateurs are well-made, precision instruments and it is important to choose only the best. These should have a good, clean cutting edge and a design that provides maximum cutting action with a minimum of effort. For older, more mature shrub roses and climbers, a pair of long-handled pruners, suitable for operating with both hands, will also be needed.

There is one golden rule which applies to all roses, both ancient and modern, be they climbers or shrubs: that no matter what size plants are received from the nursery, they should always be pruned very hard after planting.

The reason for such treatment is to encourage all new shoots to grow from the base, or near to the base of the young bushes. If left unpruned or pruned lightly, the first season's growth will start from the top end of the plant and it will be difficult to induce basal growth in succeeding years.

PRUNING ONCE-FLOWERING ROSES

Pruning can undoubtedly benefit some shrub roses but it must be stressed that others are best left unpruned, except on a general maintenance basis. It is often far more difficult to decide whether or not to prune than how to prune. When in doubt, the best policy to adopt for the vast majority of old-fashioned and shrub roses is, do nothing. I believe that many of the older roses, such as Albas, Centifolias, Damasks and Gallicas, are best pruned in summer after flowering. This enables them to refurbish themselves with flowering wood and give a better display the following year. To prune these roses, remove any dead or diseased wood and any weak shoots that look incapable of supporting flowers the following season. Remove, too, any shoots

Pruning a three-year-old bush; *left:* before, and *right*, after pruning

that are chafing and rubbing against one another, and thin out overcrowded areas likely to give the plant a leggy appearance. Care should be taken, however, not to destroy the general character of the shrubs. Furthermore, try not to overdo the summer pruning, since this will result in much loss of sap, and the plants will not recover in time to make growth for the following year. If severe treatment is necessary, this should be done in the dormant season.

The species roses, Scotch roses and Sweet Briars are, by and large, best left to develop their own personalities until they risk getting out of hand, when it does no harm to prune them fairly hard to keep them within bounds.

PRUNING REPEAT-FLOWERING SHRUB ROSES

The Portlands are usually repeat or continuous flowering, an attribute which in my opinion is positively encouraged if they are pruned whilst dormant each season and dead-headed in summer when necessary.

Except in the largest gardens where they can be given their heads, Hybrid Musks, Bourbons and Hybrid Perpetuals are best pruned every winter. If done sensibly, this will keep them replenished with young shoots and stop them becoming leggy and unkempt. I also believe that intelligent, moderate pruning will help prolong their life. Prune them in February by removing all superfluous shoots, i.e. those too thin to support many flowers. Remove, too, any wood that is overcrowding the shrub, usually from the centre of the bush; and

reduce the length of some of the main shoots by one-third, so as to encourage early flowers. The remaining shoots can be reduced by up to two-thirds or more; these will not only produce flowers but usually provide the foundation for strong growth and replacement wood for future seasons.

Whether grown as a hedge or as individual specimens, Rugosa roses should only be pruned lightly to keep the hedge or shrub in shape. For the first year, of course, they need to be pruned hard. But should they get out of hand in later years they will tolerate harsh pruning and easily recover. The Chinas and older Hybrid Teas should be pruned in the same way as modern roses by removing twiggy, thin or dead wood, and cutting back the stronger shoots to about one-third of their length each year, aiming if possible to encourage basal growth. Tea roses prefer to be treated more sparingly; they need to be pruned, of course, in order to keep them in shape, and to prevent them developing too much old unproductive wood, but not pruned for pruning's sake.

PRUNING CLIMBING ROSES AND RAMBLERS

Climbing roses fall roughly into two categories, those that flower on wood produced in the same year and those that flower on wood produced in the previous year. In the first category are the Noisettes (especially the larger flowering varieties), the Hybrid Teas, the climbing Teas and the Hybrid Perpetuals; these flower on lateral growths and at the same time send up long, strong shoots. They need help and support to be effective as wall plants, especially in their early years. The dual object, therefore, in pruning these types of climbing roses is to encourage ample climbing shoots and to persuade those shoots to produce as many flowers as possible by the development of laterals from the stems. Thus, the method of pruning climbers alters somewhat as the plant ages and settles into its chosen position. Over the first few years, the strong climbing shoots should be trained in as many directions as possible without giving the plant too much of a contrived look. Shoots can be twisted, turned and bent into position by securing them to trellis or wires fixed to the wall. The lateral growths produced by these shoots can then be cut back each year to about one-third of their length. These 'spurs' will then each produce several flowering shoots which, when similarly pruned in their turn the following year, will produce more, and so on. The same treatment applies to climbing roses growing

NORTH AMERICAN PLANTING AND PRUNING SEASONS

The USA is divided into nine climatic zones for pruning and planting (see below). As a general rule 'prune when the forsythia blooms' – a rule which applies wherever forsythia grows.*

ZONE	PLANT	PRUNE
Northeast	March–May, October–November	March–April
Eastern Seaboard	March–May, October–November	March
North Central	April–May, October–November	March
Subtropical	December–January	December–January
Mid-South	February–March and November	December–February
South-Central	December–February	January
Southwest	December–January	December–January
Pacific Seaboard	January–February	December
Pacific Northwest	January–April	January

*Except for climbers and ramblers, which are discussed on pages 426–8

on pillars, pergolas and arches. Species such as *R. bracteata* and *R. laevigata* and their hybrids are likewise best pruned by this method.

In the second category are the ramblers or scramblers, which mostly flower on wood produced the previous season. They can be distinguished from the climbers by their habit of growth, in that they produce shoots which are thinner and more pliable. The types that fall into this bracket are the hybrids of *R. arvensis*, *R. wichuraiana*, *R. sempervirens*, *R. multiflora* and *R. setigera*. To get the best from these roses (unless they are growing up into trees), they should be given their heads for the first few years, with the shoots trained in as many direc-

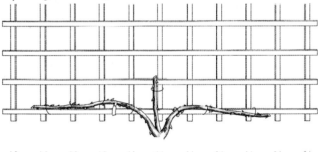

First year climber or rambler before (*above*) and after (*below*) pruning and training to trellis

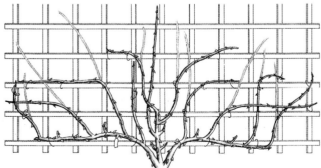

Pruning and training a second-year climber or rambler

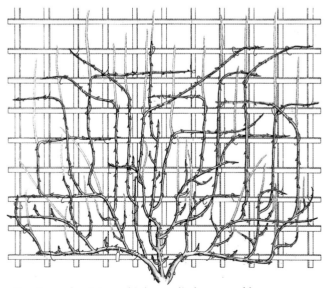

Pruning and training a third-year climber or rambler

tions as possible until they have formed a dense covering over their supports. Where pruning is necessary, it should be done after they have flowered in early summer. Winter pruning is only practical when severe treatment is needed, such as the removal of old wood. Generally speaking, these types of roses are difficult to kill, and if drastic measures are employed, they will usually recover, given time.

Roses of these types that are growing up into trees, covering large buildings or being used as free-growing prostrate plants on banks or in woodlands, are a law unto themselves and best left unpruned, except in necessity. The same advice applies to the specialist tree climbers such as *R. filipes*, *R. moschata* and *R. helenae*. When grown on a sheltered wall *R. banksiae* delights in finding its way into nooks and crannies and twining itself behind guttering; it will even blot out windows if so allowed. To get the best results, let it grow freely without pruning until it becomes a nuisance, then restrain it by pruning in early summer, after it has flowered, removing only the older wood.

PRUNING WEEPING STANDARDS

Weeping standards are varieties of rambling roses, budded by nurserymen on to straight stems. The best weepers are those from the Multiflora and Wichuraiana groups with pliable shoots and a natural tendency to grow towards the ground. These require a combination of winter pruning and summer trimming, by removing any untoward shoots as and when they appear and keeping the dense growth at the top thinned out as necessary.

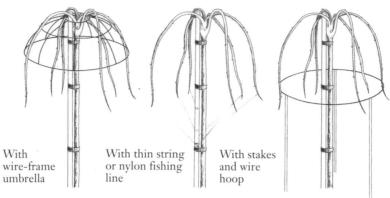

Three ways of training weeping standard roses

With wire-frame umbrella

With thin string or nylon fishing line

With stakes and wire hoop

Reluctant weepers can be trained to 'weep' by three methods. The first is to purchase or make an umbrella-shaped wire frame which can be fixed at the top of the stake supporting the rose, thus enabling the shoots to be trained downward as they grow. The trouble with this method is that the frames are unsightly and will often spoil the appearance of the garden. Far better is the method of attaching nylon fishing-line to the ends of the branches which are not naturally weeping and either pegging these to the ground, thus pulling the shoots downward, or attaching a heavy stone to the nylon line to keep the shoots angled downwards. The third method is to attach a hoop on to three equally spaced stakes around the stems. The hoop should be about 3′ (90 cm) above the ground. The shoots are then tied to the hoop, thus training them downwards to give a good weeping effect.

Old-fashioned roses, species roses or shrub roses growing as standards need the same treatment as afforded to their shrub counterparts, but they will need tidying more frequently to keep them in shape.

DEAD-HEADING

Dead-heading is in many ways far more important to some varieties than pruning, although this can be rather a nuisance where large numbers of old roses are concerned. It is less of a drudge,

however, if the habit of carrying secateurs at all times is adopted whilst walking round the garden, and snipping off any unsightly dead heads as and when they occur. It is best to make the cut at the first proper bud below the flower stalk. Only dead-head those varieties which retain their dead petals and become unsightly. Many others will eventually produce hips – pleasing, not least to the birds.

PRUNING NEGLECTED ROSES

Old, neglected rose specimens pose yet another difficult pruning problem. Breathing new life into old shrub roses and climbers, however, is often impracticable,

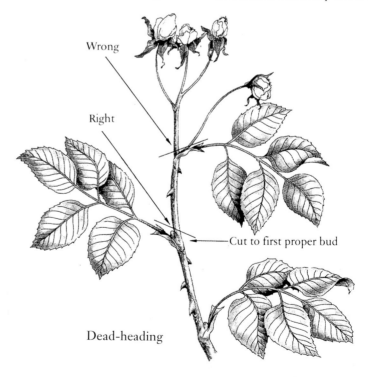

Wrong

Right

Cut to first proper bud

Dead-heading

so it would be misleading to suggest ways of attempting this. Roses do not live for ever and their longevity is often related to the treatment they receive throughout their lives. Broadly speaking, the nearer a rose to a true species, the longer its life. It follows, therefore, that it is easier to rejuvenate an old-fashioned rose than a modern hybrid. Sentiment plays an important part in these decisions but where a rose is obviously approaching its twilight years, it is better to replace it with another. As mentioned earlier, the soil will need changing but provided the variety can still be obtained, this is the most economical procedure. If its name is unknown and identification has proved impossible, some specialist nurseries will produce new plants from stock taken from the old plant. By this means direct offspring can be replanted and an old variety may possibly be saved from extinction.

PRUNING MODERN ROSES

As mentioned in connection with the older roses, the chief and only golden rule that I apply to pruning is the vital one of pruning hard in the first year after planting. Without fail, all newly planted roses should be pruned to approximatly 3″ (7.5 cm) or 3–4 eyes from the bottom of each stem; this applies not only to bush roses but also to climbers, shrub roses and standards. The reason is to encourage all new growth to sprout from as near the base of the plant as possible and so to lay the foundation for well-balanced, sturdy growth in the future. There can be no doubt that timid pruning at this early stage leads to more disappoint-

ment with new roses than any other single malpractice. In the interest of satisfied customers, I would dearly love to send out all our modern roses ready pruned, but when we tried this some years ago, even with a note of explanation, we received too many complaints about quality and size to warrant perseverance.

In subsequent years pruning need not be so severe. It then becomes a question of judgement as to how many shoots to remove and by how much to reduce the length of the remaining ones. Remember, rose bushes will quickly become leggy and bare-bottomed if given half a chance. As a general guide, shoots of Hybrid Teas and Floribundas thinner than a pencil are unlikely to produce flowers of any decent size, so they should be cut back harder than thicker shoots. Bear in mind that all things are comparative, so the thickness of wood will depend upon the overall size of the plant. All dead wood should be removed and the aim should be to keep the centre of the plant as open as possible. I do not place as much importance on a slanting cut as some people do, but where possible the cut should be made just above a bud, preferably a healthy bud, facing outwards from the plant. As time goes on you will learn by your mistakes – but if in doubt, hard pruning is better than no pruning at all. As for timing, there are advocates of autumn pruning, winter pruning and spring pruning, and to some extent the choice is governed by location and the severity of cold weather. Here in Norfolk, late February to early March is about the right time but a few weeks either side might be more appropriate in other tem-

perate climates. Whatever time is chosen for the main pruning, always tidy up the plant by removing a few inches of shoots in late autumn. This will improve the appearance of the garden and help to reduce wind-rock during the winter.

Weed Control

Gardeners fall into two categories where weeds are concerned: those who tolerate weeds and are prepared to live happily with them, and those who insist upon their removal from every nook and cranny. Both schools tend to frown at each other's philosophy. From a nurseryman's point of view wild flowers or wild plants growing rampant among roses are a problem, and they have to be kept under control. However, as I said earlier, I favour leaving weeds until they become a nuisance and start to hamper the performance of the roses.

The most troublesome weeds are the perennial and deep-rooted types, especially couch grass and thistles, which have a habit of taking refuge among the bushes themselves and growing up through the lower branches. If this is permitted the rose definitely suffers and the weeds become almost impossible to eradicate. It is therefore important for roses to start in soil which is as free as possible from perennial weed infestation. Thus in the initial preparation of the ground, make sure that such weeds are dealt with severely. This can be done very successfully with hormone-based herbicides, applied several months in advance of planting and while the weeds are still growing. For those who prefer not to use chemicals,

it is a case of backache and blisters, forking out all the roots and rhizomes from the soil all around the area to be planted. Any small pieces of root left in the ground will rapidly take hold and reinfest the soil with renewed vigour.

Annual weeds, which usually invade in large armies, are not quite such a problem since, apart from reinfestation by seed, they succumb to the hoe pretty quickly on a hot day. There are chemicals that will deal with these both at the pre-emergent stage and whilst they are growing. Such chemicals must be used with great care, not only for the wellbeing of the roses but, more importantly, for the good of the soil, the animal and bird population, and not least ourselves. This is no place to discuss the rights and wrongs of their usage; but before any chemicals are used, read the specific instructions carefully and carry them out to the letter. There are a number of available herbicides, and advice can best be obtained from those experts who supply them.

Another far less obnoxious method of suppressing weeds is to spread a mulch of sterile material to a depth of 2–3″ (5–7.5 cm) over the soil. Bark chippings make by far the best and are obtainable either from garden centres or direct from sawmills, if you are lucky enough to live near to a forest. Sawdust, too, can be used but it will be toxic unless it is from mature wood and, being light, may also blow about in dry weather. No matter what is used as a mulch, it is advantageous to both the roses and the soil to till the ground beneath at least once a year, perhaps at pruning time. One of the disadvantages of chemicals and, to a lesser extent, of mulches is that they prohibit or restrict underplanting of rose beds with companion plants, which is yet another way of hampering weeds, particularly under old-fashioned roses and shrub roses. This subject has been dealt with earlier in the book.

Propagation of Roses

Vegetative propagation as a means of reproducing plants has probably been practised since civilization began. If man had not learned to work with nature and use such means of reproduction, many of our oldest varieties, incapable of self-perpetuation, would have been lost.

Species, of course, can reproduce themselves from seed. So from the beginning they have been relatively independent, needing man's assistance only to develop their hybrids and to help them multiply by producing them from cuttings or by grafting or budding. Although a form of grafting is still practised in the commercial production of roses, this is now done on a limited scale, usually in the form of bench-grafting to propagate difficult subjects such as 'Mermaid', *R. banksiae lutea* and a few other varieties which do not lend themselves readily to the technique of budding.

GRAFTING

Bench-grafting is a fairly sophisticated means of propagation and its success depends mainly on the skill and experience of the nurseryman. Grafting involves placing a branch or shoot from a preselected variety on to the root or shoot of another, thus creating

a union between the two and the eventual growth of a complete plant in its own right. The host plant providing the root is termed the 'stock', and its enforced guest which supplies the branches is called the 'scion'. By careful selection of compatible species and varieties, each will influence the other and so enable hybrids to perpetuate in their exact form. The choice of stocks with specific attributes enables them to influence the scion and, to some extent, vice versa. These reciprocal influences are not so pronounced in roses as they are, for example, in apples, where the ultimate size of the tree is controlled by the stock on which the variety is grafted. Stocks are usually grown from seed by specialist

growers. In recent years, as mentioned earlier, the most commonly used stock has been 'Laxa'.

For bench-grafting roses, suitable stocks are selected each year in early January and plunged, in bundles of fifty or so, into damp sterile peat, under glass. These are forced into early growth for about two to three weeks until root activity is well under way. Scions are then taken from dormant plants of the variety to be propagated, and grafted on to each active stock, the top of the stock having first been removed at a point a few inches above the roots. The scion selected is usually of one-year wood, 3–4″ (6.5– 10 cm) long, with three or four buds. The top end of the scion is usually cut straight across, imme-

diately above a growing point or bud. The bottom is cut into a half-wedge shape and an inverted cut made upwards into the wedge on the exposed-tissue side of the cut. A similar cut is made to match the slant of the scion on one side of the stock, and a reverse cut made, so the two can be joined together in a neat and tidy fashion. Care is taken to ensure that the two cambium layers, which are situated under the bark, are placed together. This done, the joint is bandaged with grafting tape or raffia and waxed watertight, either with grafting wax or petroleum jelly. The top of the scion is also sealed to reduce dehydration.

The stock with scion attached is then potted with enough nutri-

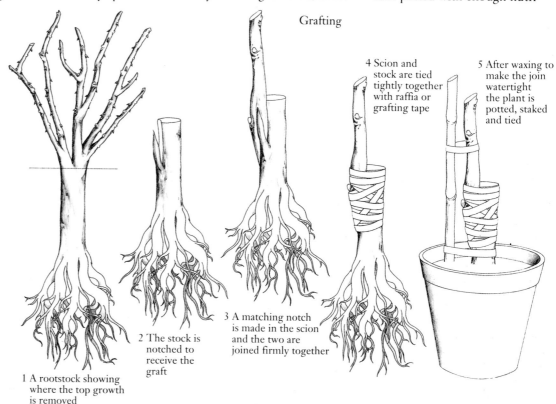

Grafting

1 A rootstock showing where the top growth is removed

2 The stock is notched to receive the graft

3 A matching notch is made in the scion and the two are joined firmly together

4 Scion and stock are tied tightly together with raffia or grafting tape

5 After waxing to make the join watertight the plant is potted, staked and tied

ents in the compost to see it through one season. It is then placed in a heated greenhouse. Within a few weeks the two will fuse together and the scion will begin to grow. Fairly soon, after it becomes obvious that the graft has taken, a 2–3′ (60–90 cm) cane should be placed in the pot with the plant. This should be fixed firmly to both stock and scion by raffia to provide a splint for support during the crucial few weeks whilst complete fusion takes place. By early summer the join should be secure enough to release the grafting-tape or raffia from the union, thus avoiding strangulation as both stock and scion swell with growth. This method of grafting is known as 'whip and tongue', but there are a number of variations on this, such as 'wedge-grafting', 'saddle-grafting', 'chip-grafting' and so on. All rely on the compatibility of stock and scion and the alignment of their respective cambium layers The result should be a sizeable plant by the end of the first growing season.

BUDDING

Budding is by far the most widely used method of producing roses. Success with budding, even on the smallest scale, gives one a very satisfying feeling of achievement and there is no reason why the amateur should not try to produce a few rose bushes by this means. All that is needed is a budding knife with specially shaped blade and handle, available, in various designs, from good gardening shops and ironmongers. Most rose nurserymen will sell a few stocks, knowing that, however successful, no threat is posed to their business.

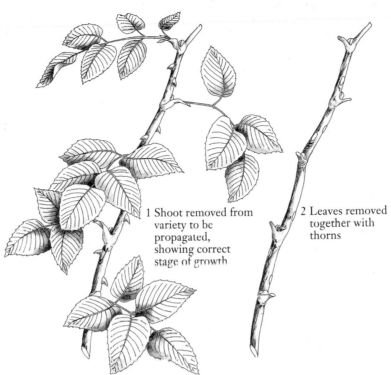

1 Shoot removed from variety to be propagated, showing correct stage of growth

2 Leaves removed together with thorns

Preparation of Wood for Budding

Budding is an acquired technique, and nurseries employ skilled propagators who are capable of working very rapidly, handling up to 400 bushes an hour. Speed is essential since budding is usually done at the peak growing season with both stock and scion in active growth. Stocks for this purpose are normally planted as one-year seedlings in rows during the preceding winter. By mid-June these are ready for budding and will remain in this state of readiness for about two months. The stocks are planted in such a way as to leave 1–2″ (2.5–5 cm) of root protruding above ground level. The scions or buds are selected by taking a ripe flowering-shoot from a ready-made rose bush. The shoot is usually ripe when the flower has started to open. The flower and the top 2″ (5 cm) of the stem are removed together with the leaves, to facilitate handling It is a good idea to leave about ⅓″ (1 cm) of leaf stalk attached to the stem, depending upon the variety. Most rose 'sticks' will have between four and eight buds. At no time must the stick be allowed to become dry. It can be kept fresh for several days if necessary by placing it in damp newspaper and polythene.

To perform the budding operation, first make sure that the stock is clean and free of soil at ground level. Open the bark of the stock with the knife to form a T-shaped cut, taking care not to damage or scrape the tissue inside the bark. A vertical cut about 1″ (2.5 cm) long is enough to tease back the bark at the top of the 'T'. The stock prepared, the scion is then placed in the free hand and held by the index finger and the thumb, palm uppermost, with the thin end or top of the scion pointing towards the wrist. The index finger should be placed directly under the first or top bud on the stick to give support. The first bud is then cut from the stick with one cutting motion of the knife. With the thumb of the knife hand, press the 'sliver' that is being removed firmly on to the knife blade. Having made a clean cut to about ⅓″ (1 cm) above the bud, the bark can then be torn back to remove it completely from the stick, still holding it between knife blade and thumb. Experts retain the stick in their hand as they complete each budding operation but at this point the novice is best advised to place the stick aside and retain only the bud between finger and thumb. The wood from the bud is then separated from the bark, usually in two stages. Holding the blunt end between thumb and finger, with the thumbnail for support, remove half the wood from the top downwards and the other half from the bottom upwards, exposing a plump little bud on the inside of the bark. If there is a hole instead, throw it away and start again.

The next stage calls for dexterity. Hold the top end of the bud with one hand, and use the other to hold open the bark of the stock with the handle of the budding knife; then carefully slide the bud into position under the bark of the stock, finally cutting off any spare bark from the bud at the top of the 'T'. Lastly, the wound has to be bandaged, both to hold it together and to prevent moisture getting in. Nurserymen use special, inexpensive latex patches for this, but if these cannot be obtained, use some thin raffia, winding it around the cut; beneath the bud three times and above the bud four times, and knotting it carefully at the top. After three or four weeks the 'bandage' can be removed; success or failure will be immediately obvious. If the bud has failed to

take and there is still time, another attempt can be made on the other side of the stock. If it has taken it should be left untouched until mid-winter, when the complete top of the stock should be removed at about ⅓″ (1 cm) above the bud. The following summer, lo and behold, a rose! This can either be left where it is for life or transplanted to another position in the following dormant season.

ROSES FROM CUTTINGS
Many gardeners, having had success at rooting roses from cuttings, are mystified by the fact

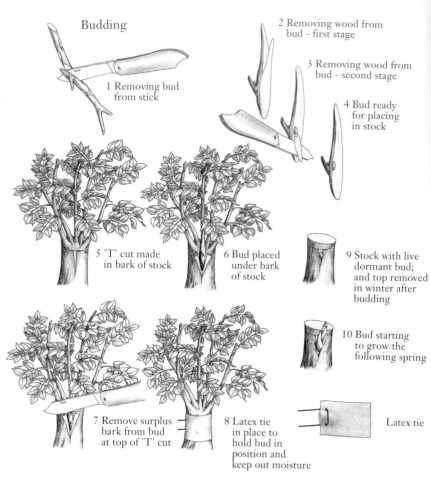

Budding

1 Removing bud from stick

2 Removing wood from bud - first stage

3 Removing wood from bud - second stage

4 Bud ready for placing in stock

5 'T' cut made in bark of stock

6 Bud placed under bark of stock

9 Stock with live dormant bud; and top removed in winter after budding

10 Bud starting to grow the following spring

7 Remove surplus bark from bud at top of 'T' cut

8 Latex tie in place to hold bud in position and keep out moisture

Latex tie

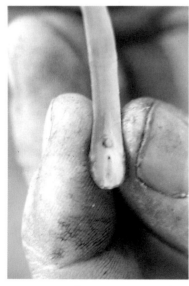

Above left: removing bud from 'stick', and *right*, bud ready for placing in stock
Below left: bud attached to stock, and *right*, latex tie being applied

that this is not done commercially, enabling them to purchase roses which will be free of troublesome suckers. A few types of roses lend themselves readily to this method of propagation, notably *R. rugosa* and its hybrids, and these are sometimes offered commercially on their own roots, as are some of the species and unusual hybrids which have proved resistant to budding or grafting techniques. But most attempts at commercial production over the years have failed. Nowadays, with sophisticated

hormone rooting powders and mist units, getting them to root is not a problem; in fact, many varieties root readily without such aids. The difficulty is growing enough stock plants to provide the cuttings. With the budding method, six buds are the equivalent of only one cutting, so a nurseryman would need six times as many stock plants to produce plants for sale. Although recent developments in tissue culture might provide the answer, I can see no way around the difficulties which arise later when the bush has to be transplanted. Except for some species, the root systems are small when compared with budded roses, and they do not take readily to transplanting. Thus there is a high failure rate for open-ground, bare-root plants produced from cuttings. To counteract this, they have to be grown in pots from an early age, so enabling them to be transplanted complete with soil. This is fine where plants can be sold locally and in garden centres, but it presents a problem for despatch by mail order. Another difficulty is to produce bushes large enough to satisfy the long-established pattern of quality demanded by the public. An own-root rose needs to be at least one year older than its budded counterpart to get anywhere near an equivalent size. I recall vividly an occasion several years ago when a customer asked me to produce for her thirty different roses on their own roots. I explained all the pros and cons

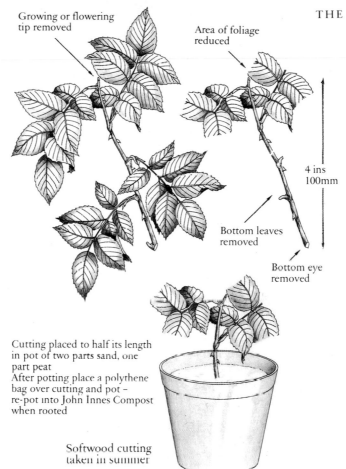

Growing or flowering tip removed

Area of foliage reduced

4 ins 100mm

Bottom leaves removed

Bottom eye removed

Cutting placed to half its length in pot of two parts sand, one part peat
After potting place a polythene bag over cutting and pot – re-pot into John Innes Compost when rooted

Softwood cutting taken in summer

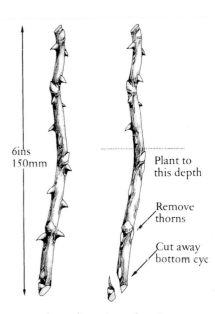

6ins 150mm

Plant to this depth

Remove thorns

Cut away bottom eye

Hardwood cutting taken in autumn

Growing roses from cuttings in Malcolm Lowe's nursery

and she said that she was prepared to wait. In order to be sure of enough plants I produced six of each, which took two years of patient work. When she received them, she promptly returned the lot, saying they were too small! The only consolation, apart from not seeing that lady again, was a lot more experience at growing roses from cuttings.

Despite all this, Malcolm Lowe of Nashua, New Hampshire, USA, has established a system of 'own-root' roses' whereby plants are produced to order. He roots his cuttings under glass in early autumn and plants the rooted

plants straight into the ground the following spring. His success rate is apparently high, but I think the climate of New Hampshire is more conducive to such a method of rose production than ours in the UK. Mike and Jean Shupe of the Antique Rose Emporium, Brenham, Texas, have also evolved methods of successfully producing roses commercially from softwood cuttings. They are particularly efficient with the Old Teas.

The best time to take hardwood cuttings is when the leaves begin to fall and the wood has had all the summer to ripen. For cuttings

of this type, select mature, one-year wood, preferably the thickness of a pencil or more, though this will depend somewhat on the variety. The ideal cutting should be about 6″ (15 cm) long and cut to a growth bud at both the top and bottom. For heel cuttings, the bottom should have a small slice of two-year wood still attached. Leaves, where present, should be removed before placing the cutting straight into the ground to a depth of half its length, preferably in a sheltered, warm part of the garden. If the soil is heavy, a little sand placed in the bottom of the trench before planting will help rooting, having first dipped the bottom ⅓″ (1 cm) or so of the cutting into rooting hormone. Alternatively, the cuttings can be placed directly into a pot containing equal parts of sand and soil, and placed in a cold frame or cold greenhouse.

By early spring these cuttings should start to root and will grow into reasonable small bushes by the following autumn, when they can be transplanted into permanent positions.

If preferred, cuttings can be taken from late June onwards, but these need slightly more coddling. Shoots of the current year's wood should be cut from the bush and cuttings made to a length of about 4″ (10 cm), again cutting to an eye, top and bottom. Remove all leaves except for the top two, which, if need be, should be reduced to just two leaflets to reduce transpiration. The prepared cuttings should then be placed in pots in a mixture of soil and sand, watered, and covered with a polythene bag, held in position with a piece of cane acting as a tent peg and a rubber band to anchor the bag around the top edge of the pot. By this system, cuttings should root quite quickly, especially if the pots are kept in a warm place such as a greenhouse or on a windowsill. During this period very little watering is necessary since moisture builds up within the sealed environment. Placing the pot in a saucer of shingle, into which water can be poured periodically, will ensure that the cutting never dries out before it makes roots. When the cuttings have made some small amount of growth, the polythene can be removed and the plant slowly hardened-off before winter. During the winter, the plant can be repotted into better nourished soil and eventually planted into a permanent situation.

These are just two of the ways of producing roses from cuttings. Remember, however, that not all varieties will root successfully and that others will not make such large plants or grow as quickly as those produced from budding.

MICROPROPAGATION

Amateurs are unlikely to practise this form of propagation, but since more and more of the roses bought in the future will be produced by this means, a few words should be included to give a brief outline of the process. Micropropagation of plants is a form of vegetative propagation carried out in sterile growing rooms or laboratories. Roses produced in this way are grown on their own roots, like cuttings. Before the technique was discovered, biologists and botanists believed that roots and shoots could be formed only from the actual growing parts of plants. Micropropagation is a type of tissue culture and involves the taking of a small piece of tissue, or even a single cell, from a growth point or axillary bud and stimulating this to produce more growth points which, in turn, produce more and so on. At first the shoots are without roots, so these are induced by adding naturally occurring, root-stimulating hormones to the medium in which they are grown. Once roots have formed, the tiny plants are grown on for a time and then carefully weaned into ordinary compost to take their place in the outside world.

There is still some way to go before this form of propagation becomes common practice in the commercial production of roses. The most difficult stage is the weaning of plants into ordinary soil, but research work is going on all the time and there is no doubt that ways and means will be found to make this easier.

Not all types of roses take readily to micropropagation. Hybrid Teas and Floribundas, by and large, do not grow as well on their own roots as they do when budded, and some shrub roses are even more reluctant. Many of the Miniatures and Procumbents seem to thrive, however, and it is these that are mostly produced by micropropagation at present. This is probably because plants formed in this way sprout many more shoots from the base in the first year than those produced by budding or from cuttings. One significant advantage of micropropagation is the speed of rooting; another is the large number of plants produced from just one small piece of tissue. By harnessing this technique, breeders can build up numbers and launch new varieties far more quickly than by conventional means, but this practice is by no means widespread.

LAYERING

Layering is not often practised with roses but, depending upon the variety, it is quite a feasible method of propagation. Although it is not possible with sturdy, upright growers, since they will refuse to bend to the ground, it is however a fairly efficient way of propagating the more flexible old-fashioned roses, climbers and ramblers.

Simply arch a one-year shoot to the ground and place the point of contact – about 12″ (30 cm) from the tip – into a shallow trench, tethering it with a wire pin or similar aid. A knife wound in that part of the bark which is placed underground will sometimes aid rooting; then cover with soil. This can be done at almost any time of the year but rooting is naturally quicker in spring, just before seasonal growth begins.

Once rooting has occurred, the protruding tip will start to grow and the parent shoot can be cut away. The new rose can then be transplanted into a permanent position at any time during the dormant season.

DIVISION

Division as a means of propagation is common practice with many plants, though this is not normally associated with roses; nevertheless, there are some species and varieties where such a method can be adopted quite successfully. The only necessary condition is that candidates for such treatment should actually be growing on their own roots and not grafted or budded on to an understock.

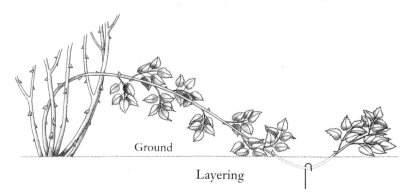

Ground

Layering

Several species of roses and their hybrids are naturally free-suckering plants; if these suckers are removed from the bush with a section of root attached they become new plants in their own right. The Scotch roses are perhaps the best subjects for this form of propagation; indeed it may be their propensity for free-suckering that accounts for their longevity. One frequently comes upon such roses in old gardens, having way outlived their companions from an earlier age and multiplied themselves by suckers several times over and retaining none of their original root systems; in fact, they were probably planted as suckers in the first place. Other types of roses which can be multiplied in this way are R. wichuraiana, R. palustris, R. nitida, R. virginiana, R. eglanteria and, of course, the ubiquitous R. rugosa. Most forms and hybrids of all these species lend themselves to division, provided, as already said, that they are growing on their own roots.

ROSES FROM SEED

All true species will of course grow from seed, but to be sure of identical offspring, parent seed plants need to be grown in isolation in order to avoid becoming 'chance hybridized' with other compatible species or hybrids. Such chance hybrids occur sometimes with only minor differences from their parents, having been fertilized by bees or by some other natural pollen-carrying agent.

Hybrids sometimes pop up in gardens from seeds which have either simply dropped off the plant or have been distributed by birds, R. glauca and R. filipes being just two species which have pro-

duced foundlings in this way. Some hybrids, too, in particular the Rugosas, if growing close to other roses, will sometimes produce interesting if not startling variations from their self-sown seeds.

All rootstocks used in modern rose production in the UK are grown from seed. Parent plants of suitable species such as 'Laxa' and forms of R. multiflora are grown in relative isolation, usually in the warmer parts of the eastern Mediterranean. The seed is collected from parent plants and sold to specialist rose stock growers in Europe, in particular Holland and Germany but lately in the UK as well. Seeds are sown in very early spring and the seedlings are produced, all in one growing season, by the tens of millions. These are then sold to rose nurserymen who produce saleable bushes two growing seasons later by budding. Thus the roots of bought roses are well-travelled; excluding the age of the seed, they are three years old by the time they are planted in the garden.

Economics is not the only reason why rose stocks are grown from seed. Viruses are less likely to be transmitted by this means than by vegetative propagation. Seeds gathered from garden hybrids, even those which have been self pollinated, yield rather different results from those collected from species, in that none will come true and each seedling produced will differ from its parents, only one of which, of course, will always be known. Seed pods from most garden hybrids need a long summer to ripen. Only those from hips provided by the earliest flowers of summer are usually viable in the UK and similar latitudes; this is why hybridizing,

north of about latitude 45°, is carried out in greenhouses.

Growing seed from garden hybrids can be interesting, if not particularly fruitful. An unsophisticated method is to collect ripe hips in early winter and to place them in flower pots full of sharp sand, keeping these outdoors where the greatest fluctuations in temperature can be obtained until about February. Choose a position which can be protected from mice, for these little creatures seem to enjoy the flavour of rose seeds.

The number of seeds in each hip will vary from one or two to as many as fifty in some varieties. Seeds should be taken from the hips in early February, by which time the fleshy part of the pods will have rotted away. They should then be washed and sown about ¼" (0.5 cm) deep in good compost in a seed tray or flower pot; then placed in a warm greenhouse with bottom heat to warm the soil to a temperature of about 45°F (about 6°C). Haphazard germination will start a few weeks later as the days lengthen and may continue spasmodically until early summer. Transplant any seedlings into a good potting compost in 3" (7.5 cm) pots soon after germination and keep them in the greenhouse. Shade them for a few days until they take root. They should flower within a few weeks, depending on the type of rose. Climbers etc. may not flower until the following summer. If budding is not possible, repot them into larger pots and await a second flowering the following year. There is little point in planting them into the garden until they have proved worthwhile. All this has little to do with rose growing, but it is

enjoyable, and no matter how poor the seedlings, at least they will be unique, which may be encouragement to progress to a little real hybridizing.

Pests and Diseases

The belief that shrub and old-fashioned roses are less troubled by pests and diseases than some of their modern cousins may not bear close analysis. The fact that this often appears to be the case is probably due more to their vigour and ability to overcome affliction than to any inherent resistance to contracting disease. This is further borne out by the fact that many have come down to us from the distant past. Frequently, too, the once-flowering varieties will have finished their main flush of flowers before diseases or pests have a chance to affect them seriously, whereas in modern roses, if left unchecked, such afflictions as black spot and rust can cause havoc in late summer and autumn. There is undoubtedly a correlation between the vigour of a rose and its resistance to disease; some of the larger shrub roses, and in particular the vigorous climbers, are usually more healthy than their shorter counterparts.

Good cultivation, adequate feeding and, especially, good drainage and irrigation are the best methods of avoiding problems from diseases. Contented bushes will always give better rewards. Black spot and rust, probably the two worst diseases, have both been given a new lease of life since the late 1950s in the UK when Clean Air legislation was passed – hence less healthy roses – a small price to pay,

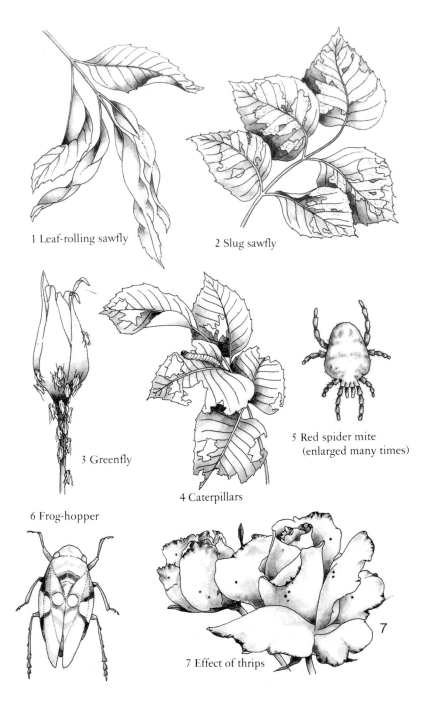

1 Leaf-rolling sawfly

2 Slug sawfly

3 Greenfly

4 Caterpillars

5 Red spider mite
(enlarged many times)

6 Frog-hopper

7 Effect of thrips

admittedly, for the improvement to our own health. Most other countries have similar legislation and their rose growers similar problems. Our best hope in the control of rose diseases comes from the breeders who are becoming ever more conscious of the need to raise healthier stocks. To achieve this they will have to search back among old-fashioned roses and species to find the elusive, disease-resistant genes.

Pests

APHIDS

When conditions are right, aphids of many types attack roses but by far the most common are greenflies and a severe infestation can be very troublesome. Aphids have a number of natural predators, in particular the delightful and harmless ladybird, although it is unlikely that she alone will provide any measure of control. Ants, too, are often seen in company with aphids, but these are attracted to the sticky deposits left behind rather than to the pests themselves. Aphids multiply rapidly if left unchecked. In days gone by gardeners used soapy water to control these pests, and they also sprayed tobacco water on infested shoots. Some even purchased special aphid brushes to remove them, cleverly designed to avoid any damage to the roses. Nowadays we use insecticides, some so sophisticated that they are harmless to birds and predatory insects. The most effective of these are 'systemic', which work from within the plant, thus preventing infestation before it occurs. Such sprays need applying at about 10- to 14-day intervals. Contact insecticides actually kill

aphids after infestation, and such sprays need repeating as and when aphids are seen to be present.

CAPSID BUGS

These are less common than aphids and can be quite elusive little pests, quickly moving on from one bush to another. They damage succulent growing tips, leaving them stunted, withered and peppered with tiny holes. Systemic insecticides are the best preventative measures, although the capsids will often cause some damage before succumbing to their effects.

CATERPILLARS

Various caterpillars occasionally attack the leaves of roses. Evidence of their presence is usually the disappearance of whole sections of leaf or the growing tips of young tender shoots. A search through the foliage usually finds them, for removal and instant disposal.

Caterpillars are the larvae of moths which themselves do not feed on roses, so chemical control is more difficult. Specific chemicals for caterpillar control are nevertheless available. Advice on these should be sought from experts if the infestation is troublesome.

CUCKOOSPIT

The unsightly appearance of this pest is probably more offensive than the pest itself, at least on roses. It is more common on roses with heavy weed infestation or those growing in herbaceous borders than on those in the open. The spittle-like substance surrounding the froghopper nymph can usually be washed away by an extra strong jet from the sprayer, whilst spraying against other pests or diseases.

LEAF-ROLLING SAWFLY

Damage caused by this insect usually manifests itself too late for any remedy. The only answer – and this rather hit-and-miss – is to start spraying with contact insecticides very early in the year to try to catch adult flies whilst they seek out suitable young leaves to infest with their eggs. Not all damaged leaves will have fertile eggs; most, it would seem, are injected by the sawfly with a chemical which causes the leaf to curl, thus protecting the larvae when they hatch. Heavy infestation can be very unsightly in early summer, but the bush, although suffering slightly from the interruption to its natural process, soon recovers. No real harm is done, except perhaps to render it more prone to diseases such as mildew. Spraying with the same chemical as that used for caterpillars will give some measure of control over the developing larvae, but the curled leaves make this extremely difficult.

Another species of sawfly following the same life cycle is known as the slug sawfly. This is less common but can be devastating if an infestation occurs. The larvae feed on the surface tissue of the leaf, leaving just a skeleton structure behind. Control of this is the same as that for the leaf-rolling sawfly.

RED SPIDER

This very difficult little curse is more troublesome on roses under glass than on those outdoors. The mites are almost invisible to the naked eye and live on the undersides of the leaves. They multiply very quickly and often have a severe hold over the roses before an infestation can be diagnosed, causing leaves to lose colour, become limp and eventually fall to the ground; the eggs then lie in the soil throughout the winter. Control is difficult and more effective before severe infestation occurs. Perimiphos-Methyl seems, at present, to be the most effective chemical if applied whilst the mites are active in summer. If the presence of this pest is suspected without actual evidence, give the ground around the bushes a good winter-wash with old-fashioned tar oil while the roses are dormant. This will destroy any eggs before they hatch.

THRIPS

This pest is more troublesome on modern roses than on old-fashioned roses, preferring the tighter buds of the large-flowered roses. It usually occurs in hot, thundery weather and is seldom nuisance enough to warrant spraying, except perhaps on some of the climbing Hybrid Teas and the more doubled Bourbons, Noisettes and Teas. Again prevention is better than cure, and spraying with a systemic or contact insecticide just before the flower buds begin to open will usually stop the tiny little flies from nibbling at the edges of the petals and disfiguring the flowers.

RABBITS AND DEER

Rabbits can be quite a serious pest to roses in country gardens, especially in winter, and particularly in those situated near golf courses and heathland, and open acres of farmland, where they are more numerous. Their activities are unpredictable. In spring baby rabbits, in particular, find the young, succulent tips of roses most acceptable; and in winter rabbits of all ages indulge in what appears to be malicious vandalism, stripping the bark completely off shoots of any age, to tiptoe height. If planting roses in a country garden, take the precaution of fencing it off against rabbit invasion; failing this, encircle each bush, at least during its first years, with small-mesh wire. There are chemicals, offensive to rabbits, which are supposed to keep them off, but these, in my experience, provide only flimsy defence.

Deer, too, enjoy a good meal of roses, especially when hungry in deep mid-winter. They can be a particular problem in the USA; but in Britain, where they are still shy creatures, they should only present a threat to roses growing near woodlands or on parkland. Roses are sometimes grown around paddock fences and the like, and it should be remembered that most grazing animals will sample the taste of any roses they can reach. The most positive precaution here is to plant only the most thorny varieties and species.

Three Persistent North American Pests
By Malcolm Lowe

CANE BORERS

Cane Borers are the larvae of wasps and sawflies which lay their eggs in the ends of freshly cut stems in early summer. Their presence is indicated by sawdust extruding from holes in the stems. Their presence causes canes to die back, often to the bud union. Serious infestations may be fatal.

To prevent cane borer damage, seal all cuts in canes larger in diameter than a pencil with household glue. It is advisable to add a few drops of food colouring to the glue so that the treated canes may be identified.

JAPANESE BEETLES

This half-inch-long metallic green scourge of the American rose-grower emerges from mid-May in the South to early July in New England, after spending ten months underground as a grub. Their period of greatest activity lasts from four to six weeks. Japanese beetles fly only during the day and are most active on sunny days. They congregate and feed on leaves and flowers, eating away large areas of foliage and entire blossoms. Female beetles burrow into turf to lay their eggs, after which they return to the plants to feed again. The most effective controls are those insecticides used for turf and golf courses – 1-Methylethyl-2 (Oftanol) will kill the grubs; Carbaryl is good against adult beetles. To be really effective control procedures should be carried out with near neighbours.

MIDGE

These minute yellow-brown flies lay eggs on leaf and flower buds. The larvae hatch and feed on the leaves causing them to dry up and die, at which time the larvae fall to the ground where they develop into adults. The whole life cycle takes only two weeks. Insecticides sprayed on the foliage and ground in two thorough applications ten days apart will give some control. At one time it was thought that midge had been eradicated by DDT, but it is reappearing exponentially.

Diseases

BLACK SPOT

Of all the diseases to affect roses, with the possible exception of rust, black spot is the most pernicious. Persistent attack on some varieties can leave the shrubs somewhat jaded each year and ultimately reduce them to a fraction of their true selves.

The disease attacks the leaves, usually from mid-summer onwards, often resulting in complete defoliation. Even a partial or mild attack will render bushes unsightly. It can be recognized easily by the black or dark brown patches which spread rapidly over leaves and often extend to the young stems, causing them initially to become mottled and later to die. Each leaf that falls carries with it millions of spores which overwinter in the soil, ready for an attack the following season.

The removal and burning of infected leaves, both from the bush and from the surrounding ground, will therefore help prevent the disease spreading to less susceptible varieties. Black spot is a fact of life in roses and little can be done remedially once the disease has taken hold. A number of chemicals are available which, if sprayed in advance of the infection, will keep the disease at bay, at least until the first flush of the flowers is over. Manufacturers' claims as to the degree of control can only be justified if their instructions are strictly followed and accompanied by good husbandry and cleanliness.

Experience has convinced me that regular overhead irrigation will control black spot, provided it is carried out overnight to avoid scorching the foliage. This should be done, at minimum intervals of

Black spot

ten days, for about five hours on each occasion. From the point of view of cleanliness, a winter wash both of the plant and the surrounding ground with a solution of Jeyes Fluid helps to kill off any spores lurking on decaying leaves or in the soil and helps delay infection from the disease in early summer.

CROWN GALL

This bacterial disease, prevalent throughout the USA and Canada, causes rough irregular galls on stems near the bud union. The only known control is to remove the galls and paint the wounds with a dilute solution of a suitable bleach (take advice at your local garden centre). If this is not effective the bush and the surrounding soil should be dug out, as the bacteria can live in the soil for up to two years after the infected plant is removed.

POWDERY MILDEW

Powdery mildew attacks roses from early summer onwards and, if allowed to flourish, can be quite a serious problem on some varieties. The first signs are small patches of greyish-white powder, usually near the top of the young growing shoots and on the succulent young leaves. If not checked, these patches spread rapidly to cover the entire plant. In severe epidemics it will also extend to

Powdery mildew

the more mature leaves and flower buds. The young leaves curl, distort and fail to develop, thus preventing the plant from functioning satisfactorily. Attacks of mildew on otherwise healthy plants weaken their resistance to other diseases; black spot, in particular, flourishes when mildew has been allowed to take hold. Well-nourished plants, while not rendered immune, will suffer less than undernourished ones. Equally, the 'prevention is better than cure' rule applies to chemical control of the disease. A number of contact fungicides are available, but in order to be effective they should contain a wetting or spreading agent to enable sufficient chemical to adhere to the leaves. Systemic fungicides are the best method of combating mildew. Known susceptible varieties should be sprayed well in advance of the appearance of the disease. Mildew is very persistent and has a very rapid life cycle, enabling spores to develop

resistance to specific chemicals very quickly. For this reason, if the effectiveness of spraying starts to wear off, change to something else for a while. The over-use of nitrogenous fertilizers is often the cause of mildew, especially when mid-summer application leads to excessive growth in the autumn. Mildew may also follow summer drought, so try to keep the roses well watered during such weather.

DOWNY MILDEW

This form of mildew affects roses grown under glass, especially those grown in pots. It takes the form of dull brownish or sometimes bluish patches on the surface of mature leaves, which can also spread to the stems. Infected leaves become limp and fall. Severe attacks may cause the death of whole plants. The disease is usually brought on by extremes of day and night temperatures, especially when linked to bad ventilation in greenhouses

Mildew on a branch

and conservatories. Some control can be achieved by the use of similar fungicides to those used against powdery mildew and black spot. The disease seldom attacks outdoor roses.

RUST

Of all rose diseases, a bad infestation of rust can be the most devastating. If conditions are right – it enjoys moist warm weather – susceptible varieties will deteriorate rapidly and die. Signs of infection are often not noticed until the disease is established but if spotted early enough it can be controlled. Small orange pustules attach themselves to the undersides of leaves and multiply rapidly until they have spread all over the plant including, on occasions, the stems and thorns. As the spores age, they turn to dark brown and eventually to black, killing the leaf in the process. In some extra-susceptible varieties where the stem has also been affected, the lifeless, brown leaves hang on to the plant as it dies. In others, they fall to the ground where the spores overwinter in readiness for the following season.

At the first sign of the disease, all infected foliage should be removed and burned. Chemical control is difficult because spray has to be directed upwards on to the undersides of the leaves. The same fungicides as used for black spot have some preventative qualities but, if an attack is diagnosed at an advanced stage, oxycarboxin, a chemical available under several trade names, is quite effective. Varieties most prone to this disease tend to act as hosts, thus causing the less susceptible ones to become infected. If rust is found to occur repeat-

Rust on leaves in summer

edly on the same plants it is best to remove and burn them 'Conrad F. Meyer' and 'Sarah Van Fleet', both Hybrid Rugosas, are particular culprits and should be kept out of gardens where rust has proved a problem.

STEM CANKER

This is not a serious problem on good, well-nourished bushes. It is more frequently seen on older plants which have been allowed to develop lots of old wood, much of which has outlived its usefulness. It also appears on very old climbers, where constant pruning over the years has permitted the disease to enter the plant through exposed tissue. The disease takes the form of large, irregular-shaped lesions, usually parched brown, sunken near the edges and swollen in the centre. Sometimes the bark is slightly lifted at the edge and rather gnarled in appearance. If infection occurs on expendable branches, these should be

removed and burned; but older plants frequently develop the disease in awkward places. Careful removal of the lesions with a sharp knife and painting the wound with grafting wax or a similar substance will sometimes succeed. Such surgery is only worth trying if the bush or climber has great sentimental value. The best course is to destroy the old badly infected plant and replace it with another.

MINERAL DEFICIENCIES

Iron deficiency is probably the most common nutritional ailment of roses; this manifests itself in a yellowing of the leaves, especially younger leaves either on the margins, or along the veins, or both. The leaves eventually turn completely yellow and drop off. Since the deficiency commonly occurs in calcareous soils, an application of sequestered iron to the soil in early spring should correct it. In the longer term, it is worth applying potash to the soil to help

release locked-up iron.

The other common deficiency is that of magnesium, which, in the case of roses, is probably a major requirement for successful performance. Symptoms of deficiency are not easily recognizable, but the leaves, especially the older ones, show chlorosis and are sometimes badly developed, especially at their apex. Epsom salts, applied to the soil once or twice a season in liquid form, will help rectify this. Where symptoms are markedly obvious, it can be applied as a foliar feed.

MOSAIC VIRUS

My experience of viruses inas much as they infect roses in Britain is limited to observing, from time to time, obvious symptoms of mosaic in one or two varieties. However, if the virus is present in other varieties, and this could well be so, it does not manifest itself in our climate to anywhere near the same extent as it does in the warmer parts of the world, where it can be quite a serious problem in outdoor-grown roses of all types but especially in some of the older varieties. Accepting my limited knowledge therefore and believing that the problem of mosaic virus should be more clearly understood, I am delighted to include the following essay by Malcolm Manners of the Citrus Institute, Florida Southern College, who is not only an authority on this subject but also a devotee of the old garden roses.

Rose Mosaic Virus Disease
By Malcolm M. Manners

The subject of rose mosaic disease has received considerable attention in the popular rose press over the past few years.

Unfortunately, much of the information presented has not been based on demonstrable fact, and some is patently false.

There are many virus diseases of roses, including rose wilt, rose rosette, and rose spring dwarf, but this discussion will be concerned only with rose mosaic disease, which is by far the most commonly encountered viral disease of roses. Rose mosaic is actually a group of diseases having similar leaf symptoms, caused by at least three different viruses. These viruses normally attack fruit trees in the rose family (Rosaceae), such as peach, cherry and apple, and in these trees the disease spreads from tree to tree in the orchard by natural means. In roses, however, the disease apparently is *not* contagious and will not infect healthy bushes adjacent to an infected bush.* Rather, the disease is spread in the nursery, when uninfected roses are grafted or budded on to an infected understock. In areas of the world where understocks are traditionally grown from seed (e.g. the UK and much of Europe), mosaic is not a great problem, since the virus is not transmitted by seed propagation. In areas where understock plants are grown from cuttings (as in the USA), the disease will be present in the newly propagated plants, if the original stock plants were infected. American rose cultivars are therefore very often infected. Once a scion variety is infected, merely bud-

* Arabis mosaic virus, the least common form of mosaic in roses, *is* spread by a nematode through the soil, but the probability of a rose garden being infected with that rare form of mosaic and the correct nematode, simultaneously, is small. M.M.

ding it to virus-free understock will not cure it; all such newly propagated plants will also be infected.

Symptoms of rose mosaic consist of wavy yellow to white lines on the leaves, arranged symmetrically around the veins, or sometimes, irregular yellow to white patches on the leaves. Usually the first growth flush of the spring will show the most obvious symptoms. Most bushes show no obvious symptoms at all, most of the time. Sometimes a plant will remain symptomless for years, and then suddenly show strong symptoms, evidently in response to some aspect of the weather as the leaves developed. This phenomenon has promoted the (false) notion that bushes were 'catching' the disease in the garden, when in reality they were infected all along, and now finally showed some symptoms.

Rose mosaic would be of no great concern if these fleeting leaf symptoms were the only effect of the disease. But tests done on greenhouse roses in Holland, and on outdoor-grown roses in England and California, have shown that an infected plant will produce fewer flowers, poorer quality flowers and shorter stems and show reduced overall growth of the bush, reduced winter hardiness, and a number of other undesirable characteristics. These bushes may be of entirely acceptable quality, but probably could be better if they weren't infected. From the nurseryman's point of view, an uninfected bush would also be superior, in that he could produce plants of higher calibre and more vigorous growth, allowing him to sell a higher quality plant, perhaps in somewhat less time.

Once a plant is infected, there is nothing the gardener can do to cure the plant. Plants can be cured by holding them at precisely 38°C (100°F) for four or more weeks, after which buds are cut and budded to virus-free understocks. Most of the new plants will be free of the disease. But this procedure requires special facilities to keep the plant at the proper temperature without killing it, and only a few institutions actually use the procedure. In the USA, the University of California (at Davis), Florida Southern College (Lakeland, Florida), and Bear Creek Nurseries (who own Jackson & Perkins Roses and Armstrong Roses) are currently doing rose heat-therapy. If there are such programmes in other countries, I am unaware of them.†

Since rose mosaic is not contagious, nor is it deadly or otherwise devastating, there is no great reason to destroy a bush in the garden simply because it shows symptoms. Still, one probably could achieve better vigour and productivity with an uninfected plant of the same variety, so it is worth trying to find mosaic-free plants, when shopping for roses.

† The facility for heat treatment described by Malcolm Manners is available at a number of both educational and private establishments in the UK, but not specifically for roses. – P.B.

Malformation of Flowers

PROLIFERATION

Some of the more double-flowered old-fashioned roses will occasionally sprout a malformed bud from their centre. This is known as proliferation, and is a most unpleasant sight. The phenomenon usually occurs in the early flowers, and in the case of the repeat-flowering shrubs, seldom reappears on autumn flowers. Close inspection of the misshapen flowers reveals that for some reason, probably genetic, the reproductive organs, in particular the pistils, have become fused, and instead of developing normally have changed into another complete flower bud, which grows out of the centre of the bloom.

Although some authorities consider it to be a virus, so far as I know this has not been proved. I know of no other scientific explanation, but since its incidence does not seem to be related to the soil in which a variety is grown, at least out of doors, nor to any noticeable geographical location, we must assume it to be a form of genetic mutation, inherent in particular varieties and pepetuated by careless selection of propagation material. I believe that the severity of the malformation is in some ways influenced either by temperature or sunlight or both. Flowers appear to be more severely affected following a dull, cold spring, and bushes growing in partial shade are invariably worse than those in the open. I have noticed, too that the problem is less severe on plants growing under glass. I find it interesting that 'Mme Isaac Pereire' is more prone to this problem than her sport 'Mme Ernst Calvat'. The same applies to 'Souvenir de la Malmaison', which sometimes suffers, and her sport 'Souvenir de St Anne's', which does not. Apart from those already mentioned, some of the other more double Bourbons are also badly affected, as are one or two Damasks, some of the Centifolias and a few Mosses. The occasional Hybrid Perpetual – closely related to the Bourbons – is also troubled from time to time; likewise the Chinas 'Bloomfield Abundance' and, to a lesser extent, 'Cécile Brünner'. Little can be done by way of prevention or cure beyond the removal of affected blooms as they appear.

BALLING OF FLOWERS

Some old-fashioned roses, in common with some modern roses, do not like wet weather in summer. This is particularly true of the many-petalled, fully-double varieties with tightly folded flowers. They can usually endure it when open, but if prolonged rain occurs during the late bud stage, their outer petals will rot and congeal, thus preventing the flower from opening. Balling can become worse if strong sunshine follows rain, causing the petals to become encased in a crisp cocoon of decay, from which there is no escape. The whole flower then rots and falls off or, worse still, remains on the plant in a ruined, unsightly mess. There is not much to be done about this beyond cursing the weather, although in smaller gardens, where an individual rose is suffering, the outer petals can be teased carefully from the bud with thumb and forefinger before the rot has gone too deep, thus allow-

Above: a balled flower, and *below*, a balled flower after being teased open

ing the flower to unfurl without hindrance. Varieties particularly prone to this are the Bourbons 'Souvenir de la Malmaison' and 'Boule de Neige', and the Hybrid Perpetuals 'Baronne Prévost', 'Georg Arends' and 'Frau Karl Druschki'. Some of the Centifolias and Mosses are also prone

Other Ailments

Other minor ailments can, from time to time, trouble roses. The most common of these stem from our own careless use of chemicals, particularly herbicides. Great care must be taken with these, especially the hormone variety. By far the most common diagnosis I make is that of spray damage. Always use a separate sprayer for weedkillers. No matter how carefully you think you have washed weedkiller from a machine, there could be just enough left inside to kill or disfigure your plants.

Commercial Production

Although no one is certain of the exact figure, between eighteen and twenty-five million rose bushes are produced annually in Great Britain – up to one bush for every three people in the population. Do a similar sum for the rest of the rose-loving world and the answer is – a very large number.

I decided to include a brief word about commercial production after a rather unpleasant experience with a customer who could not understand why it should take us two years to propagate a rare rose for her. Like all businesses, rose nurseries have to run at a profit so methods have changed somewhat since the beginning of this century, but the basic principles have remained unchanged since it was first discovered that two plants could be united by budding. In very recent times, in fact in the last ten years, other methods of production have been tried – micropropagation, for example, though it is by no means certain that the technique will ever become widespread, nor indeed whether all types of roses can be grown by this means. I shall confine my thoughts to a general outline of conventional practice; micropropagation was discussed on page 434.

Commercial rose growers need to own, or have access to, at least four times more land than is needed to grow a single crop. This is because rotation is important and also because roses take two full growing seasons to become saleable, so there will always be two crops of different ages growing at the same time. And, just as

in the garden, roses never like growing on land that has previously grown them without, at least, two years' rest in between.

Growers these days are well mechanized, for good land implements are important. Land is prepared by ploughing and surface cultivation well in advance; rootstocks are ordered from specialist growers many months beforehand, too. Stocks arrive in November and are kept, either heeled-in or in a cold store, until land and weather are suitable for planting. In Britain, this is usually in February or March. Stocks are planted by a tractor-drawn machine with four operators feeding them in. The rows are usually from 30 to 36″ (75–90 cm) wide, with 6″ (15 cm) between the plants in each row. At these planting distances, the density is roughly 25,000 plants per acre. On a good day, a crew can plant about an acre. When planting is finished, the sprayer moves in and sprays the soil with a pre-emergence herbicide. Fertilizers will have been applied well beforehand.

By mid-June the stocks are ready for budding (see page 431). Apart from lifting, this is the most expensive and time-consuming of all the tasks relating to the production of roses. Budding is a skill, the basics of which are not too difficult to learn providing the pupil is reasonably dexterous. Speed is acquired through practice and experience. It is very much a job for the young, for, although it is not physically demanding, it is not easy to work all day with the body bent double. The real secret of good budding is the speed at which it is carried out; the faster the budder works the more likely the buds are to 'take'. Budders usually work in pairs followed by a 'patcher' who places a small latex patch over the wound where the bud has been inserted. A good team of three will put on as many as 6000–7000 buds in a day. Budders are serviced by another team whose job is to cut the budwood from the correct varieties and dethorn them for ease of handling. Weather permitting, budding is usually finished by the end of July. It is never done in the rain. After July the buds will still 'take' but the percentage that live declines as the days get shorter. In peak season budders hope to get at least 90 per cent to take; 100 per cent is not uncommon on some varieties. Anything less than 85 per cent on modern varieties is considered poor, although with old-fashioned roses such a take would be considered good. Throughout the summer the stocks are kept clear of pests and diseases by regular spraying.

After budding, the next stage in the process is 'heading back', as it is known in Norfolk; in other parts of Britain it is called variously 'cutting down', 'heading off' or 'topping'. This takes place in the winter months, usually January or February depending on the weather, and involves the removal of all the top growth from the stock by cutting it off just above the point where the bud was inserted. Secateurs or long-handled pruners are used, though some large nurseries speed up the process with pneumatically operated secateurs. In early spring a balanced fertilizer is applied, together with further applications of pre-emergence herbicide. By May, the buds will have grown to about 3 or 4″ (7.5–

A commercial rose field

10 cm). At this stage, some growers cut the young shoots back to just 1″ (2.5 cm) to encourage several shoots to grow from the union. By early June, the young maiden plants are about 6″ (15 cm) high and it is then that nurserymen pray for calm weather, for the plants are now very vulnerable and easily blown off at the union by wind; invariably there are a few windy days and losses can be heavy. By early July, the roses are in flower and in turn become the source of budding eyes for the next year's crop, and so on. As they grow, a careful watch is kept for suckers which appear from below the bud. These are removed as soon as they are spotted. A regular spraying programme is carried out against aphids, black spot, mildew and rust.

By October, the young plants will have ripened and lifting starts. This is usually done by a special tractor-drawn lifting plough which undercuts the plants, enabling them to be

pulled easily from the ground with a gloved hand. On large, wholesale nurseries part of the crop is lifted and placed in cold stores where the roses come to no harm. On retail nurseries some growers do likewise; others simply lift the roses as they are needed for orders. Grading is important and by the time the roses have become saleable about 75 per cent of most varieties will be first quality; the remainder will have been lost through failure to take, by wind damage or inadequate size. It is impossible to forecast the demand for each variety two years ahead of sales, so few retail growers ever sell completely out of all varieties, although, of course, this is their aim. Roses, like most long-term crops, are both capital- and labour-intensive, and any form of bad husbandry can have dire consequences. Good training and skilled workers are therefore essential.

Breeding New Varieties

Plant breeding and hybridizing is a subject in itself and an elementary knowledge of botany is probably necessary for it to be fully understood.

Of all facets of roses and rose growing, it is probably fair to assume – judging by the questions I am asked – that breeding new varieties holds the most mystery. Many people appear to confuse this process with that of vegetative propagation, which I have already discussed. The breeding of roses is achieved by manual, sexual fertilization and is concerned only with the flowers of the two roses which are being crossed, and the resulting seeds.

Propagation, on the other hand, is achieved by inducing parts of plants to produce roots, as in cuttings; or to join with other plants, as in grafting or budding, thus increasing their numbers by nonsexual means; it therefore concerns only the shoots and roots of plants, not the flowers.

Beauty, fortunately, is in the eye of the beholder, so no one will ever know if the perfect rose is produced; perhaps, if we judge on flowers alone, all roses are perfect; hybridizers, however, seek much more than perfection in flower. They nowadays look for health, vigour, attractive foliage, scent, resistance to weather, and an agreeable habit of growth.

The first step for a hybridizer is to select potential parent roses with care. This choice will depend upon the type of rose he wishes to breed. A professional will give first consideration to parents likely to satisfy public demand. The present vogue for so-called ground-cover roses is the

Breeding new varieties

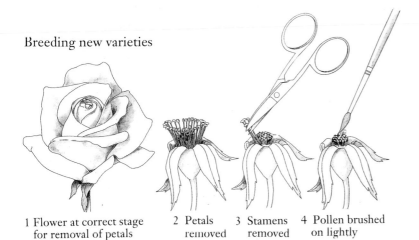

1 Flower at correct stage for removal of petals

2 Petals removed

3 Stamens removed

4 Pollen brushed on lightly

hybridizer's reaction to the modern preference for labour-saving, cost-effective plants. In Victorian times, fashion demanded large, shapely flowers for the show bench, and in the Edwardian era, ramblers and climbers for arches and pergolas. This is not to say, of course, that hybridizers merely follow fashion; they sometimes create it, as, for example, the brightly coloured Floribunda roses of the 1950s and 1960s, and the Miniature roses of the 1970s.

The selected breeding stock will either be planted in cold green-houses or grown in pots. Hybridizing begins as soon as the roses start to flower in late spring or early summer. The first stage is to remove all petals from the selected seed parent. This must be done just before the petals unfold, thus ensuring no previous cross-fertilization. The next stage is to render the seed parent totally female by removing the stamens very carefully, usually with small scissors or tweezers. The stamens can be kept in small containers for use later as a male parent.

Removal of stamens is a delicate operation, and any damage caused to the young seed pod will quickly result in the failure of the cross. The prepared potential mother is then left for about 24 hours, during which time the stigma will be seen to have become 'receptive' by deepening in colour and becoming slightly sticky . It is then ready for fertilization. Ripe pollen (visible as fine powder on the anthers) is then selected from a pre-chosen, compatible variety, and dusted on to the receptive female with a fine, soft brush. It should then be labelled and recorded. If pollen is plentiful, a further application the next day may benefit germination. Particular care must be taken with pollen to ensure that it does not become mixed; and any brushes used should be reserved for each individual batch of pollen and cleaned thoroughly after use. When pollen of selected parents is plentiful, commercial hybridizers often dust it straight on to the stigma from a fully open rose.

After about two weeks, a successful mating will manifest itself in a healthy green hip which will eventually ripen to rich red or orange. If the cross has failed, the pod and stalk will start to wither and eventually turn brown or, in some cases, just drop off. Sometimes, fertile hips which have gone through the ripe stage become brown and rotten, but these are still good and will contain seeds.

The pods should be taken from the plants in late autumn and stored in readiness for sowing in early spring.

When the seedlings come into flower, any that are worth keeping should be either potted on, for another year's growth and testing, or budded in the nursery. If many eventually useless seedlings are kept, it can become a very expensive waste of time; so for commercial purposes only about one in fifty seedlings are taken to a second year of testing. After that time any seedlings with potential can be propagated in larger numbers for further trial. This is never more than one in every 500 or so, and by the third year of trial this could well be reduced to one in 5000. Consequently, unless hybridizing is done on a very large scale, the chances of breeding a top-selling rose are very remote.

APPENDIX A
World Climatic Map

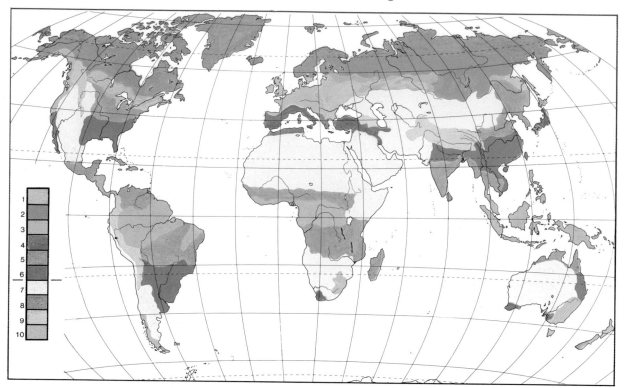

The following are brief notes on the main climatic regions of the world where roses can be grown. Temperature ranges are only an average and from time to time can be far exceeded. Wild, species roses are found widely across Central Asia, but for the main in less arid and less mountainous parts. Areas of desert, arctic waste, high mountains and humid jungle – numbers 7, 8, 9 and 10 respectively on the map colour key – are not conducive to growing roses.

1 Temperature range −3°C (26°F) (winter) to 22°C (72°F) (summer)

Most roses require winter protection, except for *pimpinellifolia* hybrids, *kordesii* hybrids and the very hardy species. Most other types will grow well in summer, but the less hardy ramblers and climbers seldom reach their full potential.

2 Temperature range −25°C (−13°F) (winter) to 16°C (61°F) (summer)

Roses will require winter protection. Avoid all Teas, Chinas, Noisettes and less hardy Hybrid Teas and Floribundas.

3 Temperature range 0°C (32°F) (winter) to 23°C (73°F) (summer)

All roses enjoy such conditions, though Teas, Noisettes, Chinas and some less hardy Hybrid Teas and Floribundas may suffer some frost damage in more severe winters.

4 Temperature range 10°C (50°F) (winter) to 23°C (73°F) (summer)

All roses will flourish in such conditions, except for some hybrid Rugosas, Centifolias, Gallicas and hybrid Pimpinellifolias which will not enjoy the heat of summer and may struggle, especially in areas of low rainfall.

5 Temperature range 10°C (50°F) (winter) to more than 30°C (86°F) (summer)

Almost all roses will grow reasonably well where rainfall is sufficient. In these conditions hybrid Rugosas, Pimpinellifolias and *kordesii* hybrids will suffer in the heat of the summer, as will some Hybrid Perpetuals, Bourbons and older types such as Centifolias and Gallicas.

6 Temperature range 5°C (41°F) (winter) to 25°C (77°F) (summer)

Most roses will grow well, especially Teas, Chinas and Noisettes, Rugosa and Pimpinellifolia hybrids will dislike the heat of summer, as will older roses such as Centifolias, Damasks and Gallicas.

APPENDIX B
Height and Colour Charts
An Introduction and User's Guide

With so many varieties to choose from, designing a completely new rose garden or even just selecting a few varieties for strategic positioning amongst other plants in the garden can be a daunting task, no matter how knowledgeable the gardener.

While other variables such as fragrance, flowering seasons, resistance to disease, autumn colour and availability etc. inevitably come into play, linking colour and ultimate stature is the most important consideration when landscaping with roses. These charts are therefore an attempt to bring together these two criteria and will, I hope, make selection a little easier. Readers should, however, bear in mind that many arbitrary factors prevail and that by their nature such charts can only be a rough guide or, more accurately, a starting point to selection.

HEIGHTS
In all cases heights given are approximate and indicate the probable ultimate size of a species or variety if grown in good, normal soil, in temperate climates and assuming that pruning, feeding and health care are practised along the lines explained in the Cultivation section of this book.

The height differential bands were selected after much careful thought but I am well aware that in some particularly agreeable climates the Teas, Noisettes and Chinas, for example, are very capable of considerably exceeding the heights given.

COLOURS
While it is simple to differentiate between soft yellow and deep yellow or scarlet and crimson, there are many shades in between where the difference is not so clearly defined. The pinks, for example, are particularly difficult. When does a blush become a soft pink, or a bright pink a salmon, or a deep pink a carmine? The orange varieties are not so much difficult as impossible, for many roses of these shades possess just those subtle variations of colour that transpose them from yellowy-orange to reddish-orange or vice versa. In each case the decision to allocate a rose to this rather than that colour band has been a matter of personal opinion based on the predominant colour of the rose at the point when the flower is fully open.

Other more tangible factors also affect colour – climate, soils, aspects and even air pollution are just four examples. The reader is therefore well advised, if colour is a critical factor in any design, not to rely too heavily on these charts but to seek out examples of particular varieties in their own districts before making their choice.

IMPERIAL/METRIC CONVERSION TABLE
20 feet and over = 6m ⟶
15 to 20 feet = 4.5 to 6m
10 to 15 feet = 3 to 4.5 m
7 to 10 feet = 2 to 3 m
4 to 7 feet = 1.2 to 2 m
3 to 4 feet = 90 to 120 cm
2 to 3 feet = 60 to 90 cm
1 to 2 feet = 30 to 60 cm
less than 1 foot = ⟶ 30 cm

Climbers, Ramblers and Scramblers

WHITE AND SOFT CREAMY SHADES

BLUSH

SOFT PINK

BRIGHT PINK AND SALMON

WHITE AND SOFT CREAMY SHADES

20 FEET AND OVER

Bennett's Seedling
Bobbie James
Dundee Rambler
La Mortola
R. arvensis
R. banksiae alba plena
R. banksiae normalis
R. brunonii
R. cymosa
R. foetida
R. gentileana
R. helenae
R. longicuspis
R. moschata floribunda
R. moschata grandiflora
R. mulliganii
R. phoenicia
R. rubus
Rambling Rector
Seagull
Sir Cedric Morris
Wedding Day

15 TO 20 FEET

Astra Desmond
City of York
Cooper's Burmese
Félicité et Perpétue
Frau Karl Druschki
The Garland
Iceberg
Janet B. Wood
Mme Plantier
R. anemoneflora
R. × fortuniana
R. laevigata
R. multiflora
R. multiflora wilsonii
R. sempervirens
Silver Moon

10 TO 15 FEET

Aimée Vibert
Autumnalis
Devoniensis
Ilse Krohn Superior
Lamarque
Long John Silver
Louise d'Arzens
Mrs Herbert Stevens
Niphetos
Purity
R. luciae
R. sinowilsonii
R. soulieana
Sanders White

Snowdrift
Spectabilis
Thalia
White Flight
Wickwar

UP TO 10 FEET

Blanc Pur
Paul's Perpetual White
Princess of Nassau
R. bracteata
R. moschata
Sombreuil
White Cockade

BLUSH

20 FEET AND OVER

Brenda Colvin
Cécile Brünner
Dr Van Fleet
Ethel

15 TO 20 FEET

Champneys' Pink Cluster
Francis E. Lester
Ophelia
Princess Louise
R. multiflora carnea
R. multiflora cathayensis
Venusta Pendula

10 TO 15 FEET

Adélaide d'Orléans
Awakening
Blush Rambler
Flora
Lady Emily Peel
Mme Alfred Carrière
Mme d'Arblay
New Dawn
Souvenir de la Malmaison
Tea Rambler
Wickmoss

UP TO 10 FEET

Eden Rose '88
Swan Lake

SOFT PINK

20 FEET AND OVER

Paul's Himalayan Musk
Ruga
Splendens

15 TO 20 FEET

Baltimore Belle
Breeze Hill
Captain Christy
Evangeline
Lady Waterlow
Mme Butterfly
May Queen
Tea Rambler

10 TO 15 FEET

Alida Lovett
Apple Blossom
Belle Portugaise
Blairii No. 1
Blush Boursault
Cupid
Debutante
Gerbe Rose
Lady Waterlow
Mary Wallace
Paul Lédé

UP TO 10 FEET

Agatha Christie
Anemone Rose
Colcestria
Cupid
Kathleen Harrup
L'Abundance
Martha
Mme Abel Chatenay
Tausendschön

BRIGHT PINK AND SALMON

20 FEET AND OVER

None

15 TO 20 FEET

Albertine
Blessings
Chaplin's Pink
Chaplin's Pink Companion
Constance Spry
Eden Rose
François Juranville
Home Sweet Home
Kew Rambler
Köln am Rhein
Lady Sylvia
Mme Caroline Testout
Mme Edouard Herriot
Mme Grégoire Staechelin
Picture
Queen Elizabeth
Queen of the Prairies
Shot Silk
Vicomtesse Pierre du Fou

10 TO 15 FEET

Alida Lovett
America
Auguste Gervais
Auguste Roussel
Bantry Bay
Blairii No. 2
Coral Dawn
Dorothy Perkins
Fashion
Galway Bay
Gerbe Rose
Handel
Lauré Davoust
Lavinia
Leaping Salmon
Leontine Gervais
Mme Alice Garnier
Mme Sancy de Parabère
Mary Wallace
Minnehaha
Paul Transom
Pinkie
Souvenir de Mme Léonie
  Viennot

UP TO 10 FEET

Aloha
Antique
Clair Matin
Columbian Climber
Lorraine Lee
Mrs F. W. Flight
Norwich Salmon
Rosy Mantle
Sénateur Amic
Zéphirine Drouhin

DEEP PINK	CERISE	VERMILION AND ORANGE	SCARLET	CRIMSON AND DEEP RED

DEEP PINK

20 FEET AND OVER

La Follette

15 TO 20 FEET

American Pillar

10 TO 15 FEET

Jean Lafitte
Leuchstern
Morletti
Morning Jewel
Pink Perpétue
Pompon de Paris
R. × l'heritierana
R. multiflora platyphylla

UP TO 10 FEET

Etude
Karlsruhe
Mme Driot
Malaga
Ramona
Rhonda
Ritter von Barmstede
Summer Wine
Wind Chimes

CERISE

20 FEET AND OVER

None

15 TO 20 FEET

Cerise Bouquet
General MacArthur

10 TO 15 FEET

Parade
Reine Marie Henriette

UP TO 10 FEET

Norwich Pink
Sophie's Perpetual
Captain Hayward

VERMILION AND ORANGE

20 FEET AND OVER

None

15 TO 20 FEET

None

10 TO 15 FEET

Autumn Sunlight
Korona
Superstar

UP TO 10 FEET

Pinata
Warm Welcome

SCARLET

20 FEET AND OVER

None

15 TO 20 FEET

None

10 TO 15 FEET

Allen Chandler
Altissima
Danse de Feu
Danse des Sylphes
Deschamps
Fragrant Cloud
Raymond Chenault
Soldier Boy
Sparkling Scarlet

UP TO 10 FEET

Blaze
Grand Hotel
Paul's Scarlet
Richmond

CRIMSON AND DEEP RED

20 FEET AND OVER

None

15 TO 20 FEET

Château de Clos Vougeot
Crimson Conquest
Crimson Glory
Ena Harkness
Josephine Bruce
Tempo

10 TO 15 FEET

Ards Rover
Chevy Chase
Cramoisi Supérieur
Crimson Rambler
Crimson Showers
Dr Huey
Etoile de Hollande
Excelsa
Guinée
Hiawatha
Parkdirektor Riggers
Reine Olga de Wurtemberg
Souvenir de Claudius Denoyel

UP TO 10 FEET

Cadenza
Don Juan
Dortmund
Dublin Bay
Fountain
Fugue
Hamburger Phoenix
Noella Nabonnand
Souvenir du Docteur Jamain
Surpassing Beauty
Sympathy

Climbers, Ramblers and Scramblers

PURPLE-RED	PURPLE TO VIOLET	LAVENDER AND LILAC	CREAM TO CREAMY-YELLOW	SOFT YELLOW PRIMROSE	BRIGHT YELLOW (LEMON)

PURPLE-RED	PURPLE TO VIOLET	LAVENDER AND LILAC	CREAM TO CREAMY-YELLOW	SOFT YELLOW PRIMROSE	BRIGHT YELLOW (LEMON)
20 FEET AND OVER	**20 FEET AND OVER**	**20 FEET AND OVER**	**20 FEET AND OVER**	**20 FEET AND OVER**	**20 FEET AND OVER**
None	None	None	*R. gigantea*	Mermaid Paul's Lemon Pillar *R. banksiae lutea* *R. banksiae lutescens*	Easlea's Golden Rambler Lawrence Johnston
15 TO 20 FEET	**15 TO 20 FEET**	**15 TO 20 FEET**	**15 TO 20 FEET**	**15 TO 20 FEET**	**15 TO 20 FEET**
None	None	Princess Marie *R. moschata nastarana* Rose Marie Viand	Albéric Barbier Fräulein Octavia Hesse Gardenia Lykkefund Mrs Aaron Ward	Emily Gray Maréchal Niel	Aviateur Blériot La Rêve Spek's Yellow
10 TO 15 FEET	**10 TO 15 FEET**	**10 TO 15 FEET**	**10 TO 15 FEET**	**10 TO 15 FEET**	**10 TO 15 FEET**
Erinnerung an Brod Russelliana	Bleu Magenta De la Grifferie Violette Améthyste	Ash Wednesday Veilchenblau	Belle Lyonnaise Jersey Beauty Louise Darzens Madeleine Selzer	Casino Golden Dawn	Allgold Arthur Bell Christine Golden Glow Golden Showers Leverkusen Ley's Perpetual
UP TO 10 FEET	**UP TO 10 FEET**	**UP TO 10 FEET**	**UP TO 10 FEET**	**UP TO 10 FEET**	**UP TO 10 FEET**
Amadis Souvenir d'Alphonse Lavallée	None	Blush Noisette Narrow Water	Trier	Aglaia Goldfinch Céline Forestier Solfaterre	Night Light Royal Gold Star of Persia

ORANGE-YELLOW

20 FEET AND OVER

None

15 TO 20 FEET

Bettina
Grandmère Jenny

10 TO 15 FEET

Alchemist
Alister Stella Gray
Bouquet d'Or
Butterscotch
Claire Jacquier
Cloth of Gold
Crépuscule
Dreaming Spires
Lady Hillingdon
Maigold
Rêve d'Or
Whisky Mac

UP TO 10 FEET

Ghislaine de Féligonde
Laura Ford
Mme Jules Gravereaux
Norwich Gold

APRICOT AND FLAME

20 FEET AND OVER

None

15 TO 20 FEET

Mrs Sam McGredy

10 TO 15 FEET

Breath of Life
Mme Henri Guillot

UP TO 10 FEET

None

PEACHY BUFF AND COPPER

20 FEET AND OVER

Deprez à Fleurs Jaunes
Treasure Trove

15 TO 20 FEET

None

10 TO 15 FEET

Compassion
Duchesse d'Auerstädt
Gloire de Dijon
Highfield
Schoolgirl
William Allen Richardson

UP TO 10 FEET

Adam
Meg

YELLOW AND RED BICOLOUR

20 FEET AND OVER

None

15 TO 20 FEET

Masquerade
René André

10 TO 15 FEET

Alexander Girault
Mrs G. A. van Rossen
Phyllis Bide
Sutter's Gold
Talisman

UP TO 10 FEET

Irish Fireflame
Joseph's Coat
Réveil Dijonnais

Old Roses, Modern Shrub Roses and Procumbents Spreading varieties indicated by (G)

WHITE TO CREAMY-WHITE

BLUSH

SOFT TO MID-PINK

WHITE TO CREAMY-WHITE

OVER 7 FEET

Frühlingsanfang
Frühlingsschnee
Heather Muir
Mme Legras de St Germain
Mme Plantier
Pleine de Grâce
R. beggeriana
R. × dupontii
R. henryii
R. murielae
R. roxburghii normalis
R. rugosa alba
R. sericea
R. sericea chrysocarpa
R. sericea pteracantha
R. sericea pteracantha atrosanguinea

Merveille de Lyon
The Nun
Pompon Blanc Parfait
Pompon Panachee
Quatre Saisons Blanc
   Mousseux
R. carolina alba
R. × involuta
R. × paulii (G)
R. pyrifera
R. × sabinii
Reine Blanche
Snowflake
Swany (G)
White Bath
White Cécile Brünner
White Grootendorst
White Max Graf (G)
White Provence
White Spray

4 TO 7 FEET

Alba Maxima
Altaica
Blanc Double de Coubert
Blanche de Belgique
Boule de Neige
Frau Karl Druschki
Gloire Lyonnaise
Jeanne d'Arc
Karl Förster
Laxa
Mme Georges Bruant
Mme Hardy
Marguerite Guillard
Marie Bugnet
Nyveldt's White
Pax
Prosperity
R. alba
R. fedtschenkoana
R. maximowicziana
R. × micrugOsa alba
R. wardii
Schneelicht
Schneezwerg
Shailer's White Moss
Sir Thomas Lipton

UNDER 2 FEET

Alba Meidiland (G)
Francine Austin (G)
Katharina Zeimet
Kent (G)
Partridge (G)
Repens Meidiland (G)
Rose de Meaux White
Temple Bells (G)
White Meidiland (G)

2 TO 4 FEET

Anna-Maria de Montravel
Blanc de Vibert
Blanche Moreau
Botzaris
The Bride
Double White Scotch
Mabel Morrison
Mary Manners

BLUSH

OVER 7 FEET

R. corymbifera
R. polliniana
R. stylosa
R. webbiana

4 TO 7 FEET

Blanchefleur
Bloomfield Abundance
City of London
Claire Rose
Coquette de Blanche
Dentelle de Malines
Emanuel
English Elegance
Heinrich Münch
Homère
Hume's Blush
James Bourgault
Janet's Pride
Lucetta
Maiden's Blush Great
Manning's Blush
Marchioness of Londonderry
Mrs Paul
Paul's Early Blush
Penelope
The Prioress
R. × collina
R. multiflora watsoniana
R. × reversa
Shropshire Lass
Souvenir de Philémon Cochet
Stanwell Perpetual
Village Maid (Striped)

2 TO 4 FEET

Alfred de Dalmas
Belle Storey
Butterfly Wings
Cécile Brünner
Country Living
Daphne
Double Pink Scotch
Dove
Giuletta
Hebe's Lip
Juno
Leda
Mme Bravy
Mme de Tartas
Mme Pierre Oger
Mme Zöetmans
Maiden's Blush Small
Pearl Drift
R. koreana

R. macrantha
R. pulverulenta
Rival de Paestum
Sally Holmes
Scintillation
Sharifa Asma
Sidonie
Souvenir de la Malmaison
Souvenir de St Anne's
Triomphe de Laffay
William R. Smith
Yolande d'Aragon

UNDER 2 FEET

Clotilde Soupert
Grouse (G)
Lady Plymouth
Mignonette

SOFT TO MID-PINK

OVER 7 FEET

Carmenetta
Catherine Seyton
Edith Ballenden
Frühlingsduft
Frühlingszauber
Gros Choux d'Hollande
Marguerite Hilling
R. agrestis
R. caudata
R. davidii
R. gymnocarpa
R. inodora
R. roxburghii
R. setipoda
R. tomentosa

4 TO 7 FEET

à longues pédoncules
Antoine d'Ormois
Archiduchesse Elizabeth
   d'Autriche
Catherine de Wurtemberg
Celestial
Celsiana
Charles Lawson
Chloris
Comtesse de Murinais
Coralie
Coup d'Hebe
Cymbeline
Dapple Dawn
Duchesse de Brabant
Fantin Latour
Fritz Nobis
Gloire de Guilan
Honorine de Brabant (Striped)
Ipsilante
Kazanlik
La Noblesse
La Ville de Bruxelles
Mme Ernst Calvat
Maman Cochet
Martin Frobisher
Mary Hayley-Bell
Prairie Princess
R. × dumalis
R. eglanteria
R. glauca
R. hemsleyana
R. macrantha
R. majalis
R. majalis plena
R. marretii
R. × micrugosa
R. multibracteata
R. nanothamnus

R. roxburghii plena
Reine des Centfeuilles
Schoener's Nutkana
Sparrieshoop
York and Lancaster (Striped)

2 TO 4 FEET

Admired Miranda
Agathe Incarnata
Amelia
Anna Olivier
Ballerina
Baronne Henriette de Snoy
Beauty of Rosemawr
Belle Isis
Bibi Maizoon
Brother Cadfael
Camellia Rose
Catherine Mermet
Clio
Cottage Rose
Duchesse d'Angoulême
Duchesse de Montebello
Enfant de France
Falkland
Félicité Parmentier
Fimbriata
Fru Dagmar Hartopp
Gloire de France
Gloire des Mousseux
Her Majesty
Ispahan
Kathryn Morley
Lady Curzon
Le Vésuve
L'Ouche
Mme Antoine Mari
Mme Dubost
Mme Louis Lévêque
The Miller
Mrs B. R. Cant
Omar Khayyam
Potter and Moore
Princesse Adélaide
Quatre Saisons
R. carolina
R. carolina plena
R. davurica
R. melina
R. mohavensis
R. mollis
R. pisocarpa
R. prattii
R. × richardii
R. serafinii
R. sicula
R. suffulta

BRIGHT PINK

DEEP PINK

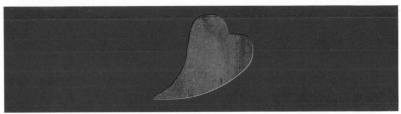

René d'Anjou
Rose d'Hivers
Rosy Cushion (G)
Spencer
Tricolore de Flandre (Striped)

UNDER 2 FEET

Dresden Doll
Fairy Changeling (G)
Fairyland (G)
Northamptonshire (G)
Nozomi (G)
Pink Drift (G)
Pink Wave (G)
Queen Mother
R. orientalis
Rosy Carpet (G)

OVER 7 FEET

Complicata
Conrad F. Meyer
Fred Streeter
Frühlingsmorgen
Jeanne de Montfort
Kathleen
R. bella
R. sweginzowi macrocarpa
Sealing Wax

4 TO 7 FEET

Adam Messerich
Armada
Arrillaga
Belle Amour
Daisy Hill
Duchesse de Verneuil
Felicia
Fred Loads
Georg Arends
Gloire d'un Enfant d'Hiram
Glory of Edzell
Harry Maasz
Julia Mannering
Kathleen Ferrier
Mme Lauriol de Barny
Märchenland
Marie de Blois
Old Blush
Papillon
Poulsen's Park Rose
R. acicularis
R. × hibernica
R. jundzillii
R. woodsii fendleri
Rachel Bowes Lyon
Rose d'Amour
Vanity
Vick's Caprice
Victor Verdier

2 TO 4 FEET

Angelina
Baroness Rothschild
Blush Damask
Bonica '82
Celina
Charles Rennie MacKintosh
Chaucer
Corylus
The Countryman
Duke of York
Félicité Bohain
Ferdy (G)
Flamingo (G)
Gabriel Noyelle

Général Kléber
Heinrich Schultheis
Henri Foucquier
Hermosa
Hero
Hilda Murrell
James Mitchell
John Hopper
Mme Berkeley
Mme Laurette Messimy
Mme Lombard
Mary Rose
Mrs Campbell Hall
Mrs William Paul
Nigel Hawthorne
Papa Hémeray
Petite de Hollande
Pink Grootendorst
Pink La Sevillana
Pink Léda
Pink Prosperity
Queen Mab
R. × paulii rosea
R. ultramontana
R. woodsii
Raubritter
Robert Léopold
Rose d'Orsay
Sarah Van Fleet
Simon Robinson (G)
Sir Clough
Smarty (G)
Spong
St Cecilia
St Nicholas
Triomphe de Luxembourg
Zoe

UNDER 2 FEET

Cameo
Crested Jewel
Dick Costa
Euphrates
Fairy Moss
Margo Costa
Marie-Louise
Pheasant (G)
Pink Bells (G)
Pinky
Rose de Meaux
Rutland (G)
Surrey (G)

OVER 7 FEET

Amy Robsart
Applejack
Eos
Flora McIvor
Greenmantle
Master Hugh
Mechtilde von Neuerburg
R. holodonta
R. kamtchatica
R. moyesii (Pink Form)
R. rugosa
R. villosa
William Baffin
Wintoniensis

4 TO 7 FEET

Agatha
Andrewsii
Baronne Prévost
Belinda
Belle Poitevine
Boule de Nanteuil
Bourbon Queen
Calocarpa
Champion of the World
Chapeau de Napoléon
Comtesse Cécile de
   Chabrillant
Cornelia
Duc de Guiche
Duchesse de Rohan
Elmshorn
Empress Josephine
Erfurt
George Will
Goethe
Hans Mackart
Hon. Lady Lindsay
Königin von Dänemark
La Plus Belle des Ponctuées
Mme Gabriel Luizet
Mme Isaac Pereire
Mme Scipion Cochet
Nymphenburg
Oeillet Parfait (Striped)
Paul Ricault
Paul Verdier
Prolifera de Redouté
R. acicularis nipponensis
R. blanda
R. × centifolia
R. × centifolia bullata
R. × coryana
R. corymbulosa
R. doncasterii

R. forrestiana
R. pendulina
R. setigera
R. sherardii
R. virginiana
R. × waitziana
R. willmottiae
R. yainacensis
The Reeve
Rose Bradwardine
Rose des Peintres
Sadlers Wells
Scabrosa
Thérèse Bugnet
Will Alderman
Wolly Dodd's Rose

2 TO 4 FEET

Anna de Diesbach
Autumn Bouquet
Biddulph Grange
Candy Rose (G)
Canterbury
Charmain
Common Moss
Comte de Chambord
Cramoisi Picote
Delambre
Delicata
Dr Grill
Financial Times Centenary
Gertrude Jekyll
Heritage
Hunslett Moss
Jacques Cartier
   (syn. Marquis Bocella USA)
Jean Rosenkrantz
La Reine
La Reine Victoria
Leweson Gower
Louise Odier
Mme Knorr
Mme Wagram
Magna Carta
Mozart
Mrs John Laing
Nestor
Ombrée Parfaite
Paul Neyron
Petite Orléanaise
Président de Sèze
Pretty Jessica
Queen of Bedders
R. foliolosa
R. gallica
R. × kochiana
R. nitida
R. palustris
R. sertata

R. stellata
R. stellata mirifica
Sale
Sir Walter Raleigh
Soupert et Notting
Souvenir de Pierre Vibert
Striped Moss
Tricolore (Striped)
Ulrich Brunner Fils
Velutinaeflora
Warwick Castle
Wife of Bath

UNDER 2 FEET

Essex (G)
Flower Carpet
Hampshire (G)
Jean Mermoz
Laura Ashley (G)
Max Graf
Pink Chimo (G)
Pink Meidiland

Old Roses, Modern Shrub Roses and Procumbents

SCARLET TO BRIGHT RED

CRIMSON TO DEEP RED

PURPLE-REDS, PURPLES, VIOLETS AND LAVENDER SHADES

CREAMY-YELLOW TO SOFT CLEAR YELLOW

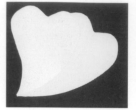

SCARLET TO BRIGHT RED

OVER 7 FEET

Anne of Geierstein
Copenhagen
Geranium
Highdownensis
Scharlachglut

4 TO 7 FEET

Berlin
Bonn
Dorothy Wheatcroft
Général Jacqueminot
Henry Kelsey
Kassel
La Belle Distinguée
Mons Tillier
Papa Gontier
Red Coat
Robusta (Rugosa)
Summer Wind
Will Scarlet

2 TO 4 FEET

Dr Jackson
Eugène E. Marlitt
La Sevillana
Ohio
R. arkansana
Red Max Graf (G)
Red Trail (G)
Robin Hood
Scarlet Meidiland (G)
Single Cherry
Red Blanket (G)

UNDER 2 FEET

Eye Opener
Gloria Mundi
Golden Salmon Supérieur
Hampshire (G)

CRIMSON TO DEEP RED

OVER 7 FEET

Arthur Hillier
Baron de Wassenaer
Dortmund
Eddie's Crimson
Eddie's Jewel
Hillieri
Meg Merrilies
R. moyesii
Till Uhlenspiegel

4 TO 7 FEET

Assemblage des Beautés
Baron de Bonstetten
Baron Girod de l'Ain (Striped)
Capitaine Basroger
Commandant Beaurepaire
 (Striped)
Conditorum
Culverbrae
Ferdinand Pichard (Striped)
Fountain
Gipsy Boy
Grüss an Teplitz
Henri Martin
Henry Nevard
Herbstfeuer
Hugh Dickson
Hunter
James Mason
John Franklin
Jules Margottin
Le Havre
Mme Victor Verdier
Michel Bonnet
Néron
Nur Mahal
Park Jewel
Parkzierde
Prestige
R. amblyotis
R. rugosa rubra
R. rugosa typica
Robusta (Bourbon)
Wilhelm
Xavier Olibo

2 TO 4 FEET

Alfred Colomb
Carmen
Champlain
Cramoisi Supérieur
Crimson Globe
D'Aguesseau
Dark Lady
F. J. Grootendorst

Fabvier
Fiona
Fisher Holmes
Fisherman's Friend
Grootendorst Supreme
Horace Vernet
L. D. Braithwaite
Laneii
Little Gem
Louis Philippe
Malcolm Sargent
Mrs Anthony Waterer
Nanette
Ohl
Pierre Notting
Prince Charles
Robert le Diable
Rose à Parfum de l'Hay
Roundelay
Ruskin
Saint Prist de Breuze
Sir Joseph Paxton
Slater's Crimson China
The Squire
Tuscany
Tuscany Superb
Uncle Walter
Victor Hugo
Wenlock

UNDER 2 FEET

American Beauty
Charles Gater
Charles Lefèbvre
Countess of Oxford
Fairy Damsel (G)
Freiherr von Marschall
Miss Edith Cavell
Suma (G)

PURPLE-REDS, PURPLES, VIOLETS AND LAVENDER SHADES

OVER 7 FEET

R. californica
R. californica plena
R. latibracteata
Tour de Malakoff
William Lobb

4 TO 7 FEET

The Bishop
Capitaine John Ingram
Chianti
Duc de Fitzjames
Duchesse de Buccleugh
Eugène Fürst
Eugénie Guinoisseau
Great Western
Hansa
Hippolyte
Jens Monk
La Belle Sultane
Lavender Lassie
Magnifica
Moja Hammarberg
Orphéline de Juillet
R. farreri persetosa
R. nutkana
Roseraie de l'Hay
Variegata di Bologna (Striped)

2 TO 4 FEET

Alain Blanchard
Arthur de Sansal
Belle de Crécy
Black Prince
Cardinal de Richelieu
Cardinal Hume
Charles de Mills
Cosimo Ridolfi
Crown Prince
Deuil de Paul Fontaine
Ferdinand de Lesseps
Georges Vibert (Striped)
Gloire de Ducher
James Veitch
Louis XIV
Mme de la Roche Lambert
Magenta
Marcel Bourgouin
Maréchal Davoust
Mary Queen of Scots
Mrs Colville
Nuits de Young
Othello
Pélisson
Pergolèse
Pompon de Bourgogne

The Prince
Prince Camille de Rohan
Prospero
Reine des Violettes
Roger Lambelin (Striped)
Rose de Rescht
Rose du Maître d'Ecole
Rose du Roi
Rose du Roi à Fleurs Pourpres
Sissinghurst Castle
William III
William Shakespeare
Wise Portia
Yesterday

UNDER 2 FEET

Baby Faurax

CREAMY-YELLOW TO SOFT CLEAR YELLOW

OVER 7 FEET

Albert Edwards
Cantabrigiensis
Headleyensis
Nevada
R. hugonis

4 TO 7 FEET

Bishop Darlington
Bloomfield Dainty
Callisto
Candeur Lyonnaise
Clytemnestra
Danäe
Daybreak
English Garden
Golden Moss
Jacqueline du Pré
Moonlight
R. pimpinellifolia hispida
R. primula
R. × pteragonis
Red Wing
Thisbe

2 TO 4 FEET

Dunwich Rose
Fair Bianca
Kaiserin Auguste Victoria
Kronprinzessen Viktoria
Mme de Watteville
Mrs Dudley Cross
The Pilgrim
R. pimpinellifolia
Sea Foam (G)
Swan
Symphony
Winchester Cathedral
Windrush
Yellow Button

UNDER 2 FEET

Norfolk (G)
Pearl Meidiland (G)
R. pimpinellifolia 'Nana'
Tall Story (G)

BRIGHT YELLOW AND ORANGE TO YELLOW SHADES

VERMILLIONS, APRICOTS AND FLAMES

PEACHY BUFF AND COPPER

YELLOW-RED BICOLOURS AND MULTICOLOURS

BRIGHT YELLOW AND ORANGE TO YELLOW SHADES

OVER 7 FEET

Canary Bird
Earldomensis
Frühlingsgold
Frühlingstag
Goldbusch
Hidcote Gold
Jayne Austin
R. xanthina
R. foetida

4 TO 7 FEET

Agnes
Francesca
Golden Chersonese
Golden Wings
×*Hulthemosa hardii*
Lady Sonia
Mountbatten
R. foetida persiana
R. × haemispherica
R. × harisonii
Yellow Charles Austin

2 TO 4 FEET

Double Yellow Scotch
Fortune's Double Yellow
Graham Thomas
Isabella Sprunt
Lady Hillingdon
Lichtkönigin Lucia
Ormiston Roy
Park's Yellow
Perle des Jardins
Queen Nefertiti
R. ecae
R. pimpinellifolia lutea
Safrano
Wild Flower

UNDER 2 FEET

Etoile de Lyon
Hulthemia persica

VERMILLIONS, APRICOTS AND FLAMES

OVER 7 FEET

None

4 TO 7 FEET

Abraham Darby
Alexander
Autumn Sunset
Charles Austin
Grandmaster
Heidelberg
Lafter
Leander
L'Oréal Trophy
Perdita

2 TO 4 FEET

Ambridge Rose
Ellen
Evelyn
Lady Roberts
Lilian Austin
Sweet Juliet

UNDER 2 FEET

None

PEACHY BUFF AND COPPER

OVER 7 FEET

Dr Eckener
Lady Penzance
Lord Penzance
Vanguard

4 TO 7 FEET

Buff Beauty
Carefree Beauty (G)
Cressida
Mutabilis

2 TO 4 FEET

Arethusa
Autumn Delight
Bredon
Dean Hole
Général Gallieni
Jean Ducher
Marie Van Houtte
Peach Blossom
Perle d'Or
Souvenir d'Elise Vardon
Troilus
The Yeoman

UNDER 2 FEET

Sussex (G)

YELLOW-RED BICOLOURS AND MULTICOLOURS

OVER 7 FEET

R. foetida bicolour

4 TO 7 FEET

Cocktail
Frank Naylor
Grüss an Coburg
Joseph's Coat
Pike's Peak
Xerxes

2 TO 4 FEET

Clementina Carbonieri
Comtesse du Cayla
Général Schablikine
Juliet
Radway Sunrise
Rosette de Lizy

UNDER 2 FEET

Tigris

Modern Roses – Hybrid Teas, Floribundas, Miniatures and Patios

WHITES AND CREAMY-WHITES

BLUSH

SOFT PINKS TO CLEAR PINKS

BRIGHT PINKS AND SALMONS

WHITES AND CREAMY-WHITES

3 TO 4 FEET

Augustine Guinoisseau (HT)
Iceberg (Flb)
Message (HT)
Sir Frederick Ashton (HT)
White Masterpiece (HT)
White Queen Elizabeth (Flb)
White Wings (HT)

2 TO 3 FEET

Canadian White Star (HT)
Evening Star (Flb)
Grace Abounding (Flb)
Honor (HT)
Horstmann's Rosenresli (Flb)
Irene of Denmark (Flb)
John F. Kennedy (HT)
Margaret Merril (Flb)
Pascali (HT)
Polar Star (HT)
Royal Smile (HT)
Virgo (HT)
Yvonne Rabier (Flb)

1 TO 2 FEET

Bianco (Patio)
Florence Nightingale (Flb)
Ivory Fashion (Flb)
Lady Romsey (Flb)
Pinta (HT)
Snowdrop (Min)
Teardrop (Patio)
White Pet (Flb)
Yorkshire Sunblaze (Patio)

BELOW 1 FOOT

Buttons (Min)
Easter Morning (Min)
Pour Toi (Min)
Snowball (Min)

BLUSH

3 TO 4 FEET

Anna Pavlova (HT)
Marie-Jeanne (Flb)
Pink Pearl (HT)
Pristine (HT)

2 TO 3 FEET

Briarcliff (HT)
French Lace (Flb)
Marie Parvie (Flb)
Nancy Steen (Flb)
Sheer Bliss (HT)

1 TO 2 FEET

Arctic Sunrise (Patio)
Charles Aznavour (Flb)
Grace Darling (HT)
Mme Butterfly (HT)
Ophelia (HT)
Strawberry Ice (Flb)
Yorkshire Bank (HT)

BELOW 1 FOOT

Cinderella (Min)
Peachy White (Min)
Perla de Monserrat (Min)
Phoebe (Min)
Phoenix (Min)

SOFT PINKS TO CLEAR PINKS

3 TO 4 FEET

Congratulations (HT)
Dainty Maid (Flb)
Ellen Willmott (HT)
Gilda (Flb)
Hannah Gordon (Flb)
Lady Diana (HT)
Lakeland (HT)
Louisville Lady (HT)
Perfume Delight (HT)
Promise (HT)
Rosenelfe (Flb)
Royal Highness (HT)
Sea Pearl (Flb)
Sweet Surrender (HT)
Valentine Heart (Flb)

2 TO 3 FEET

Anna Livia (Flb)
Auguste Seebauer (Flb)
Beauty Queen (Flb)
Bonnie Scotland (HT)
Cleo (HT)
The Coxswain (HT)
First Love (HT)
First Prize (HT)
Grace de Monaco (HT)
Lady Beauty (HT)
Lovely Lady (HT)
Marijka Koopman (HT)
Penthouse (HT)
Perfecta (HT)
Savoy Hotel (HT)
Souvenir du Président
  Carnot (HT)
Uncle Bill (HT)

1 TO 2 FEET

Abundance (Flb)
Dreamland (Flb)
Gentle Touch (Patio)
Grüss an Aachen (Flb)
Jean Sisley (HT)
Lady Mary Fitzwilliam (HT)
Los Angeles (HT)
Ma Perkins (Flb)
Petit Four (Patio)
Pink Posy (Patio)
Pink Sunblaze (Patio)
Regensberg (Patio)
Shona (Flb)
Silver Lining (HT)

BELOW 1 FOOT

Air France (Min)
Judy Fischer (Min)
June Time (Min)
Mona Ruth (Min)
Silver Tips (Min)
Stacey Sue (Min)
Sweet Fairy (Min)
Toy Clown (Bicolour Min)

BRIGHT PINKS AND SALMONS

3 TO 4 FEET

Dainty Bess (HT)
Double Delight (Bicolour HT)
Duet (HT)
Everest Double Fragrance
  (Flb)
Liverpool Echo (Flb)
Mischief (HT)
Orient Express (HT)
Pink Parfait (Flb)
Poppy Flash (Flb)
Prima Donna (HT)
Queen Elizabeth (Flb)
Scented Air (Flb)
Sheer Elegance (HT)
Silver Jubilee (HT)
Sunny South (HT)
Touch of Class (HT)

2 TO 3 FEET

Anisley Dickson (Flb)
Anita (Flb)
Betty Uprichard (HT)
Blessings (HT)
Bonsoir (HT)
Cherish (Flb)
City of Leeds (Flb)
Dame Edith Helen (HT)
Dave Hessayon (HT)
Fragrant Delight (Flb)
Gustav Grünerwald (HT)
Joyfulness (Flb)
Mary Donaldson (HT)
Monique (HT)
My Choice (HT)
Nathalie Nypels (Flb)
Paul Sherville (HT)
Plentiful (Flb)
Princess Margaret of England
  (HT)
Scherzo (Flb)
Sonia (HT)
Torvill & Dean (HT)
Troika (HT)
Typhoon (HT)
Wishing (Flb)

1 TO 2 FEET

Coralin (Min)
Dainty Dinah (Patio)
Dearest (Flb)
Deb's Delight (Flb)
Fashion (Flb)
Heaven Scent (Flb)
Irène Watts (Flb)
La France (HT)

Lady (HT)
Lady Alice Stanley (HT)
Lady Barnby (HT)
Lady Sylvia (HT)
Mrs Wakefield Christie-Miller
  (HT)
New Horizon (Flb)
Penelope Plummer (Flb)
Pernille Poulsen (Flb)
Pharisaer (HT)
Picture (HT)
Pinocchio (Flb)
Rosabell (Flb)
Sexy Rexy (Flb)
Shot Silk (HT)
Stella (HT)
Tip Top (Flb)
Violet Carson (Flb)

BELOW 1 FOOT

Angela Rippon (Min)
Coral Reef (Patio)
Cri Cri (Min)
Eleanor (Min)
Joan Ball (Min)

DEEP PINKS AND CERISES

VERMILION AND ORANGE

SCARLET

CARMINE, CRIMSON AND DEEP RED

DEEP PINKS AND CERISES

3 TO 4 FEET

Bobby Charlton (HT)
Centenaire de Lourdes (Flb)
Eden Rose (HT)
Headliner (HT)
Miss All American Beauty (HT)
Pink Peace (HT)
Radox Bouquet (Flb)
Rose Gaujard (HT)
Sweetheart (HT)

2 TO 3 FEET

Abbeyfield Rose (HT)
Curley Pink (HT)
Daily Sketch (Bicolour Flb)
Gail Borden (HT)
Picasso (Bicolour) (Flb)
Pink Favourite (HT)
Prima Ballerina (HT)
Susan Hampshire (HT)

1 TO 2 FEET

Admiral Rodney (HT)
Astrid Späth (Striped Flb)
Augustine Halem (HT)

BELOW 1 FOOT

The Doctor (HT)
Dr McAlpine (HT)
Len Turner (Bicolour Flb)
Little Jewel (Patio)
Mabel Dot (Min)
Magic Carousel (Bicolour Min)
Manuela (HT)
Meilland Jubilee (HT)
Pixie Rose (Min)
Rouletii (Min)
Royal Salute (Min)

VERMILION AND ORANGE

3 TO 4 FEET

Anna Wheatcroft (Flb)
Anne Cocker (Flb)
Dolly Parton (HT)
Julia Cussons (Flb)
Lovers' Meeting (HT)
Korona (Flb)
Montezuma (HT)
Korp (Flb)
Queen Charlotte (HT)
Sue Ryder (Flb)
Super Star (Tropicana) (HT)
Sunfire (Flb)
Texas Centennial (HT)

2 TO 3 FEET

Beautiful Britain (Flb)
Cary Grant (HT)
Cheshire Life (HT)
Clydebank Centenary (Flb)
Duke of Windsor (HT)
Irish Mist (Flb)
Jiminy Cricket (Flb)
Lady Rose (HT)
Liverpool Remembers (HT)
Memento (Flb)
Orange Sensation (Flb)
Orange Silk (Flb)
Orangeade (Flb)
Piccolo (Flb)
Pillarbox (Flb)
Roxburghe Rose (HT)
Violinista Costa (HT)

1 TO 2 FEET

Anna Ford (Patio)
Apricot Sunblaze (Patio)
Can Can (HT)
Chuckles (Flb)
Darling Flame (Min)
Ena Baxter (HT)
Félicité (HT)
Hector Deane (HT)
Little Prince (Patio)
Marina (Flb)
Melody Maker (Flb)
Meteor (Flb)
Mini Metro (Patio)
Princess Michiko (Flb)
St Boniface (Flb)
Stargazer (Flb)
Trumpeter (Flb)

BELOW 1 FOOT

Fashion Flame (Min)
Fire Princess (Min)
Hula Girl (Min)
Little Breeze (Min)
New Penny (Min)
Paint Pot (Min)
Sheri Ann (Min)
Snookie (Min)

SCARLET

3 TO 4 FEET

Cambridge Rose (HT)
Disco Dancer (Flb)
Eyepaint (Flb)
Grand Masterpiece (HT)
Harold Macmillan (Flb)
Highland Laddie (Flb)
Laurence Olivier (Flb)
Marianne Tudor (HT)
Matangi (Flb)
Matthias Meilland (Flb)
Megiddo (Flb)
Mikado (HT)
Milestone (HT)
Olympiad (HT)
Opera (HT)
Orange Triumph (Flb)
Royal Occasion (Flb)
Scarlet Queen Elizabeth (Flb)

2 TO 3 FEET

Ace of Hearts (HT)
Chorus (Flb)
Forgotten Dreams (HT)
Fragrant Cloud (HT)
Irish Elegance (HT)
Mala Rubinstein (HT)
Precious Platinum (HT)
Showbiz (Flb)
Sir Harry Pilkington (HT)
Spirit of Youth (HT)

1 TO 2 FEET

Boys' Brigade (Patio)
City of Birmingham (Flb)
Firecracker (Flb)
Impatient (Flb)
Little Artist (Min)
Little Buckaroo (Min)
Lollipop (Min)
Meillandina (Patio)
Razzle Dazzle (Flb)
Save the Children (Flb)
Topsi (Flb)
Wee Jock (Patio)
Wee Man (Min)

BELOW 1 FOOT

Hotline (Patio)
Scarlet Gem (Min)
Starina (Min)

CARMINE, CRIMSON AND DEEP RED

3 TO 4 FEET

American Pride (Flb)
Arianna (HT)
Baccara (HT)
Big Chief (HT)
Ernest H. Morse (HT)
Frensham (Flb)
John Waterer (HT)
Loving Memory (HT)
Mister Lincoln (HT)
Olala (Flb)
Red Devil (HT)
Red Masterpiece (HT)
Rob Roy (Flb)
Royal Velvet (HT)
Tally Ho (HT)
Viva (Flb)

2 TO 3 FEET

Alec's Red (HT)
Barkarole (HT)
Betty Prior (Flb)
Black Beauty (HT)
Christian Dior (HT)
Chrysler Imperial (HT)
Deep Scarlet (HT)
Ena Harkness (HT)
Eroica (HT)
Etoile de Hollande (HT)
Glad Tidings (Flb)
Inner Wheel (Flb)
Intrigue (Flb)
Invincible (Flb)
Jennifer Hart (HT)
Kan-Pai (HT)
Keepsake (HT)
Lilli Marlene (Flb)
Maestro (HT)
Nina Weibull (Flb)
Old Master (Bicolour Flb)
Pacemaker (HT)
Paddy McGredy (Flb)
Papa Meilland (HT)
Priscilla Burton (Bicolour) (Flb)
Proud Land (HT)
Red Planet (HT)
Rosy Cheeks (HT)
Royal William (HT)
Smoky (HT)
Velvet Hour (HT)
Wendy Cussons (HT)

1 TO 2 FEET

Champs-Elysées (HT)
Crimson Glory (HT)
Dusky Maiden (Flb)

Modern Roses – Hybrid Teas, Floribundas, Miniatures and Patios

CARMINE, CRIMSON AND DEEP RED (contd)	PURPLE-REDS, LAVENDERS AND LILACS (MAGENTA)	CREAMY-YELLOW AND SOFT CLEAR YELLOW	BRIGHT YELLOWS AND GOLDS

CARMINE, CRIMSON AND DEEP RED (contd)

Europeana (Flb)
Evelyn Fison (Flb)
Garnette (Flb)
Hello (Patio)
Ingrid Bergman (HT)
Josephine Bruce (HT)
Mme Louis Laperrière (HT)
Marchioness of Salisbury (HT)
Marlena (Flb)
National Trust (HT)
Peon (Min)
Prince Meillandina (Patio)
Red Rascal (Patio)
Robin Redbreast (Patio)
Ruby Wedding (HT)
Striped Meillandina (Patio)
The Times Rose (Flb)
Warrior (Flb)

BELOW 1 FOOT

Dwarf King (Min)
Gipsy Jewel (Min)
Guernsey Love (Patio)
Guiding Spirit (Patio)
My Valentine (Min)
Perla de Alcañada (Min)
Pot Black (Min)
Red Ace (Min)
Rosemary Rose (Flb)
Stars 'n' Stripes (Striped Min)
Sue Lawley (Bicolour Flb)

PURPLE-REDS, LAVENDERS AND LILACS (MAGENTA)

3 TO 4 FEET

Angel Face (Flb)
Heirloom (HT)
Paradise (HT)

2 TO 3 FEET

Blue Moon (HT)
Blue Parfum (HT)

1 TO 2 FEET

Intermezzo (HT)
Lagoon (Flb)
Lavender Lace (Min)
Lavender Pinocchio (Flb)
Lavender Sweetheart (Min)
Lilac Charm (Flb)
Mr Bluebird (Min)
Plum Pudding (Min)
Ripples (Flb)

BELOW 1 FOOT

Lavender Jewel (Min)
News (Flb)

CREAMY-YELLOW AND SOFT CLEAR YELLOW

3 TO 4 FEET

Dr John Snow (HT)
Honeymoon (Flb)
Peace (Brushed Red HT)
Peaudouce (Syn. Elina) (HT)
Sunsilk (Flb)
Yellow Queen Elizabeth (Flb)

2 TO 3 FEET

Denham (HT)
Garden Party (HT)
Golden Melody (HT)
Golden Times (HT)
Grandpa Dickson (HT)

1 TO 2 FEET

Ards Beauty (Flb)
Champion (HT)
Great Ormond Street (Flb)
Jardins de Bagatelle (HT)
Joanna Hill (HT)
McGredy's Yellow (HT)

BELOW 1 FOOT

Lemon Delight (Min)
Pandora (Min)
Yellow Doll (Min)

BRIGHT YELLOWS AND GOLDS

3 TO 4 FEET

Avignon (Flb)
Buccaneer (HT)
Chinatown (Flb)
Gina Lollobrigida (HT)
Gold Crown (HT)
Miss Hart (HT)
Summer Sunshine (HT)
Sunblest (HT)
Sunbright (HT)

2 TO 3 FEET

Arthur Bell (Flb)
Belle Blonde (HT)
Benson & Hedges Gold (HT)
Broadway (HT)
Cynthia Brooke (HT)
Dr A. J. Verhage (HT)
Dutch Gold (HT)
Fragrant Gold (HT)
Gold Quill (Flb)
Gold Star (HT)
Golden Days (HT)
Golden Jubilee (HT)
Golden Years (HT)
King's Ransom (HT)
Marion Harkness (HT)
Pot o' Gold (HT)
Simba (HT)
Spek's Yellow (HT)
Wisbech Gold (HT)
With Love (HT)
Woburn Abbey (Flb)

1 TO 2 FEET

Allgold (Flb)
Amanda (Flb)
Baby Bio (Flb)
Bright Smile (Flb)
Doreen (HT)
Frenzy (Flb)
Gold Bunny (Flb)
Isobel Harkness (HT)
Mme Pierre S. du Pont (HT)
Norwich Union (Flb)
Penelope Keith (Patio)
Princess Michael of Kent (Flb)
Rev. F. Page-Roberts (HT)
Rise 'n' Shine (Min)
St Bruno (Flb)
Sun Flame (HT)

BELOW 1 FOOT

Baby Gold Star (Min)
Benson & Hedges Special (syn. Dorola) (Min)
Bit o' Sunshine (Min)
Gold Coin (Min)
Golden Angel (Min)
Perestroika (Patio)
Rosina (Min)

ORANGE-YELLOW AND DEEP ORANGE

PEACHY-BUFFS AND COPPER

APRICOT AND FLAME

YELLOW-RED BICOLOURS AND MULTICOLOURS

ORANGE-YELLOW AND DEEP ORANGE	PEACHY-BUFFS AND COPPER	APRICOT AND FLAME	YELLOW-RED BICOLOURS AND MULTICOLOURS
3 TO 4 FEET Amatsu-Otome (HT) Anne Harkness (Flb) Burma Star (Flb) City of Portsmouth (Flb) Corso (HT) Glenfiddich (Flb) Lolita (HT) Norwich Castle (Flb) Southampton (Flb) Sunset Song (HT) Thaïs (HT) Vienna Charm (HT)	**3 TO 4 FEET** By Appointment (Flb) Diamond Jubilee (HT) Iced Ginger (Flb) President Herbert Hoover (HT)	**3 TO 4 FEET** Anne Diamond (HT) Antigua (Flb) Brown Velvet (Flb) Chicago Peace (HT) Helen Traubel (HT) Jema (HT) Johnnie Walker (HT) Medallion (HT) Sandringham Centenary (HT) Seashell (HT) Summer Dream (HT)	**3 TO 4 FEET** Diorama (HT) Kronenbourg (HT) Lloyds of London (Flb) Love (HT) Perfect Moment (HT) Sutter's Gold (HT)
2 TO 3 FEET Adolf Horstmann (HT) Amber Queen (HT) Avocet (Flb) Beauté (HT) Buck's Fizz (Flb) County Lady (HT) Doris Tysterman (HT) Geraldine (Flb) Grandmère Jenny (HT) Harvest Fayre (Flb) Joyce Northfield (HT) Just Joey (HT) The Lady (HT) Las Vegas (HT) Louis Brinas (HT) Moriah (HT) Mrs Oakley Fisher (HT) Rebecca Claire (HT) Remember Me (HT) Soleil d'Or (HT) Super Sun (HT) Whisky Mac (HT) Zambra (Flb)	**2 TO 3 FEET** Alpine Sunset (HT) Amberlight (Flb) Chanelle (Flb) Comtesse Vandal (HT) Elizabeth Harkness (HT) La Paloma '85 (Flb) Royal Romance (HT) Tenerife (HT) Tranquillity (HT)	**2 TO 3 FEET** Ann Aberconway (Flb) Apricot Silk (HT) Brandy (HT) Fragrant Dream (HT) Fulton Mackay (HT) Mojave (HT) Mrs Sam McGredy (HT) Pensioners' Voice (Flb) Royal Volunteer (HT)	**2 TO 3 FEET** Alison Wheatcroft (Flb) Arcadian (Flb) Bonfire Night (Flb) Cairngorm (Flb) Champagne Cocktail (Flb) Charleston (Flb) Circus (Flb) Colorama (HT) Colour Wonder (HT) Dame of Sark (Flb) Harry Wheatcroft (HT) Lincoln Cathedral (HT) Living Fire (Flb) Manx Queen (Flb) Masquerade (Flb) Paint Box (Flb) Painted Moon (HT) Peer Gynt (HT) Piccadilly (HT) Sheila's Perfume (Flb) Summer Fashion (Flb) Talisman (HT) Tango (HT) Tequila Sunrise (HT) Tiffany (HT)
1 TO 2 FEET Angèle Pernet (HT) Bettina (HT) Clarissa (Patio) Gingernut (Patio) Golden Slippers (Flb) Jenny Wren (Flb) Lady Belper (HT) Orange Sunblaze (Patio) Peek a Boo (Patio) Sunblaze (Patio)	**1 TO 2 FEET** Anne Watkins (HT) Apricot Nectar (Flb) Fergie (Flb) Indian Summer (HT) Julias Rose (HT) Langdale Chase (Flb) Michèle Meilland (HT) Peach Sunblaze (Patio)	**1 TO 2 FEET** Baby Darling (Min) Baby Sunrise (Min) Basildon Bond (HT) Cider Cup (Patio) Conversation (Patio) Hombre (Min) Jocelyn (Flb) Lady Cecily Gibson (Flb) Lady Forteviot (HT) Mood Music (Min) Sweet Dream (Patio) Sweet Magic (Patio)	**1 TO 2 FEET** Ambassador (HT) Baby Masquerade (Min) Cilla (HT) Gay Gordons (HT) Honeybunch (Patio) Kim (Flb) Léonie Lamesch (Flb) Lyon Rose (HT) Royal Albert Hall (HT) Rumba (Flb) Vital Spark (Flb)
BELOW 1 FOOT Colibri '79 Jenny Robinson (Min) Party Girl (Min)	**BELOW 1 FOOT** Colibri (Min) Orange Honey (Min)	**BELOW 1 FOOT** None	**BELOW 1 FOOT** Happy Hour (Min) Happy Thought (Min) Little Flirt (Min) Painted Doll (Min)

APPENDIX C
Rose Societies of the World

Rose lovers in many countries can join societies and associations specifically set up to promote and encourage the growing and enjoyment of roses. Most, if not all, of these organizations have display gardens to show large collections of roses at their best and trial grounds to test new varieties. They also issue periodicals, some annually, others quarterly. Almost all organize rose shows at least twice a year and arrange conferences or conventions where rosarians can keep abreast of developments and exchange views on all aspects of the subject.

There are no boundaries or frontiers in the rose world and most of the national societies are affiliated to the World Federation of Rose Societies. This organization operates internationally and among other liaison work arranges conventions in various countries every three years. The last three were held in Canada, Australia and Northern Ireland. India will be the host in 1994.

Rose Societies of the World

ARGENTINA
THE ROSE SOCIETY OF ARGENTINA
Solis, 1348 Hurlingham, Buenos Aires

AUSTRALIA
THE NATIONAL ROSE SOCIETY OF AUSTRALIA
271 Belmore Road, North Balwyn, Victoria 3104

AUSTRALIAN STATE SOCIETIES
NEW SOUTH WALES
279 North Rocks Road, North Rocks, New South Wales 2151
QUEENSLAND
Box 1866, GPO Brisbane, Queensland 4001
SOUTH AUSTRALIA
18 Windybanks Road, Happy Valley, South Australia 5159
TASMANIA
263 Main Road, Austins Ferry, Tasmania 7011
VICTORIA
40 Williams Road, Blackburn, Victoria 3130
WESTERN AUSTRALIA
105 Hemsmans Street, South Perth, Western Australia 6151

AUSTRIA
OSTERREICH GEPRUFTE ROSE
Baden bei Wien, Vienna

BELGIUM
LA SOCIETE ROYALE NATIONALE DES AMIS DE LA ROSE
Vrijheidslaan 28, B-9000 Ghent

BERMUDA
THE BERMUDA ROSE SOCIETY
Box PG162, Paget 6

CANADA
THE CANADIAN ROSE SOCIETY
686 Pharmacy Avenue, Scarborough, Ontario M1L 3H8

CHINA
THE BEIJING ROSE SOCIETY
97 Mu-nan Road, Tianjin, People's Republic of China

CZECHOSLOVAKIA
ROSA KLUB PRAHA
Hradec Kralove

DENMARK
THE VALBY PARK ROSE GARDEN
Copenhagen

EIRE
THE CLONTARF HORTICULTURAL SOCIETY
20 Chapel Street, Dublin 1

FRANCE
LA SOCIETE FRANCAISE DES ROSES
Parc de la Tête d'Or, 69459 Lyon

GERMANY
VEREIN DEUTSCHER ROSENFREUNDE
Mainaustrasse 198A, 775A Konstanz

HOLLAND
NEDERLANDSE ROSENVERENIGING
Mildestraat 47, 2596 SW, S'Gravenhage

INDIA
THE ROSE SOCIETY OF INDIA
1–267 Defence Colony, New Delhi 17

ISRAEL
THE ISRAEL ROSE SOCIETY
Ganot-Hadar, PO Netanya

ITALY
ASSOCIAZIONE ITALIANA DELLA ROSA
Villa Reale, 20052 Monza, Milano

JAPAN
THE JAPANESE ROSE SOCIETY
4–12–6 Todoroki Setabaya-ku, Tokyo

NEW ZEALAND
THE NATIONAL ROSE SOCIETY
PO Box 66, Bunnythorpe
HERITAGE ROSES NEW ZEALAND
91 Richmond Hill Road, Christchurch 8

NORTHERN IRELAND
THE ROSE SOCIETY OF NORTHERN IRELAND
10 Eastleigh Drive, Belfast

NORWAY
THE NORWEGIAN ROSE SOCIETY
c/o Hageselskatet, PB 9008 Vaterland, N-0134, Oslo

SOUTH AFRICA
THE ROSE OF SOUTH AFRICA
PO Box 65217, Bensmore, Transvaal 2010

SWITZERLAND
GESELLSCHAFT SCHWEITZERISCHER ROSENFREUNDE
Haus Engelfried, 8158 Regensberg

UNITED KINGDOM
THE ROYAL NATIONAL ROSE SOCIETY
Chiswell Green, St Albans, Hertfordshire AL2 2NR

UNITED STATES OF AMERICA
THE AMERICAN ROSE SOCIETY
PO Box 30,000, Shreveport, Louisiana 71130
HERITAGE ROSE FOUNDATION
1512 Gorman Street, Raleigh, North Carolina 27606

URUGUAY
THE ROSE ASSOCIATION OF URUGUAY
Blanes Viale 6151, Montevideo

APPENDIX D
Rose Gardens of the World

In addition to the gardens of the various rose societies around the world, many parks, private gardens and commercial nurseries have displays and collections of roses which can be visited by the public either throughout the year or in the flowering season. The following are the most important and well known. Most include both older historical roses and modern varieties.

AUSTRALIA
CANBERRA, The Rose Gardens
NEW SOUTH WALES, The Botanic Gardens, Rumsey Nurseries, Swanes Nurseries, all in Sydney
SOUTH AUSTRALIA, The 'Botanic' Gardens, Adelaide; The Ruston Rose Gardens, Renmark; Carrick Hill Gardens, Springfield; The Duncan's Rose Garden, Watervale; The Ross Rose Gardens and Nursery, Willunga
VICTORIA, The Benalla Rose Gardens, Benalla; The Rose Gardens, Melbourne
WESTERN AUSTRALIA, The Peace Memorial Gardens, Nedlands

AUSTRIA
BADEN, Osterreichisches Rosarium
LINZ, The Rose Garden
VIENNA, Donau Park; Baden bei Wien

BELGIUM
HAINAULT, Rosarium du Roeulx
GENK, Genk Rozentuin, Koningin Astridpark
MELLE, Rosarium de Rijksstation
STEENWEG, International Rozentium

BERMUDA
Camden House; many other small but interesting collections, especially in private gardens occasionally open to the public

CANADA
BRITISH COLUMBIA, Minter Gardens, Rosedale; University of British Columbia, Vancouver
MONTREAL, The Floralies Rose Garden
NIAGARA, The Canadian Horticultural Society Rose Garden
ONTARIO, Hortico, Inc. (Nursery), Waterdown; The Ontario Royal Botanic Gardens, Hamilton; Pickering Nurseries, Pickering
OTTAWA, The Dominion Arboretum and Botanic Gardens

DENMARK
COPENHAGEN, The Valby Park Rose Garden

EIRE
DUBLIN, The Parks Department, St Anne's

FRANCE
ALSACE, Roseraie de Saverne
LYON, Roseraie du Parc de la Tête d'Or
ORLEANS, Roseraie du Park Floréal de la Source
PARIS, Roseraie de l'Hay les-Roses; Roseraie du Parc de Bagatelle
POITIERS, Roseraie de Poitiers Parc Floral

GERMANY
BADEN-BADEN, Gönner Park, Kurgarten, Lichtentaler Allee
DORTMUND, Deutsches Rosarium, Westfalenpark
FRANKFURT AM MAIN, Palmengarten
HAMBURG, Planten und Blumen
KARLSRUHE, Rosengarten
LAUSITZ, The Forest Rose Garden
MAINAU, Rosengarten, Insel Mainau, Lake Konstanz
SAARBRUCKEN, Rosengarten
SANGERHAUSEN, The Rosarium
TAUGAU, The Rose Gardens
UETERSEN, Rosarium
ZWEIBRUCKEN, Rosengarten

UNITED KINGDOM
ENGLAND
BERKSHIRE, Saville Gardens, Windsor
BUCKINGHAMSHIRE, Cliveden (National Trust), Maidenhead
CAMBRIDGESHIRE, Anglesey Abbey Gardens, Lode; The Botanic Gardens, Cambridge
CHESHIRE, C. and K. Jones (Nursery), Chester; Fryer's Nursery, Knutsford
CLEVELAND, Borough Park, Redcar
DEVON, Castle Drogo, Drewsteignton; Rosemore Gardens, Torrington (Royal Horticultural Society Gardens)
GLOUCESTERSHIRE, Hidcote Manor (National Trust), Chipping Camden; Kiftsgate Court, Chipping Camden
HAMPSHIRE, The Sir Harold Hillier Gardens and Arboretum, Ampfield, Romsey; Mottisfont Abbey (National Trust Historic Collection), Romsey
HERTFORDSHIRE, Harkness Rose Gardens, Hitchin, The Gardens of the Royal National Rose Society, Bone Hill, St Albans
KENT, Leeds Castle, near Canterbury; Goodnestone Park, Deal; Sissinghurst Castle, Maidstone
LEICESTERSHIRE, Gandy Roses (Nursery), Lutterworth; Rearsby Roses (Nursery), Rearsby
LONDON, The Queen Mary Rose Gardens, Regents Park, Kew Gardens, Richmond, Surrey
NORFOLK, Heigham Park Rose Gardens, Norwich; LeGrice Roses (Nursery and Display Gardens), North Walsham; Mannington Hall Rose Gardens, Saxthorpe; Peter Beales Roses (Nursery and Display Gardens), Attleborough
NOTTINGHAMSHIRE, Rosemary Roses (Nursery), The Arboretum (Rose Gardens), Wheatcroft Roses (Nursery), all near Nottingham
OXFORDSHIRE, Mattock's (Nursery), Nuncham Courtney; Botanic Gardens, Oxford
SOMERSET, Scotts (Nursery), Merriott; Vivary Park Rose Gardens, Taunton
STAFFORDSHIRE, David Austin Roses (Nursery and Display Gardens), Albrighton; Wolseley Rose Gardens, Rugeley; Roses du Temps Passé, near Stafford
SUFFOLK, Helmingham Hall, near Ipswich; Notcutts' Nurseries, Woodbridge
SURREY, The Gardens of the Royal Horticultural Society, Wisley, near Woking
SUSSEX, Charleston Manor, West Dean; Nyman's Gardens (National Trust), Handcross
WARWICKSHIRE, Warwick Castle Gardens, Warwick
WILTSHIRE, Corsley Mill, Chapmanslade; Sheldon Manor, Chippenham
YORKSHIRE, Castle Howard Gardens, York; Harlow Court Gardens (the Gardens of the Northern Horticultural Society), Harrogate

NORTHERN IRELAND, Dickson Roses (Nursery), Newtownards; Lady Dixon Park, Belfast; Rowallane Gardens, County Down
SCOTLAND, Brodick Castle, Isle of Arran; City of Roses, Aberdeen; Cocker Roses (Nursery and Display Gardens), Aberdeen; Craithes Castle Gardens, Banchory, Grampian; Malleny House, Ballerno, near Edinburgh; The Botanic Gardens, Edinburgh; Mellerstain, Gordon, Berwickshire
WALES, Bodnant Gardens, Gwynedd; Queen Park Gardens, Colwyn Bay; Roath Park Gardens, Cardiff

HOLLAND
AMSTERDAM, Amstelpark Rosarium
THE HAGUE, Westbroekpark Rosarium

INDIA
LUCKNOW, Friends Rosery
NEW DELHI, The Rose Society of India Gardens
PUNJAB, The Zakir Rose Gardens, Chandigarh

ISRAEL
JERUSALEM, The Wohl Rose Park

ITALY
ROME, Municipal Rose Gardens; Cabriglea D'Arezzo – private collection of Professor Fineschi (by appointment only)
GENOA, Municipal Rose Gardens
La Mortola (a Mediterranean garden on the border with France)

JAPAN
CHOFU, The Botanic Gardens
TOKYO, Yatsu-Yuen Rose Gardens

NEW ZEALAND
AUCKLAND, The Parnell Rose Gardens including the Nancy Steen Gardens; Bell's Roses
CHRISTCHURCH, Mona Vale Rose Gardens and Botanic Gardens
HASTINGS, Frimley Rose Gardens
INVERCARGILL, The City Gardens

MOTUEKA, Tasman Bay Roses
NAPIER, The Kennedy Park Rose Gardens
OPOTIKI, The Rose Gardens
PALMERSTON NORTH, The Rose Trial Gardens
ROTORUA, The Murray Linton Rose Gardens
TAUPO, The Rose Gardens
TE AWAMUTU, The Rose Gardens
TIMARU, Trevor Griffiths Roses
WAIKATO, The Rose Gardens
WELLINGTON, The Lady Norwood Rose Gardens

NORWAY
VOLLEBEKK, Agricultural College

PAKISTAN
QUETTA, Department of Agriculture, Baluchistan

SOUTH AFRICA
SWELLENDAM, Western Cape Province
JOHANNESBURG, The Botanical Gardens

SPAIN
MADRID, Parque de Oeste

SWEDEN
NORRKOPING, Horticultural College
GOTEBORG, a recently planted rose garden

SWITZERLAND
GENEVA, Parc de la Grange
ST GALL, Rapperswill Gardens
SCHAFFHAUSEN, Neuhausen am Rheinfall Gardens

UNITED STATES OF AMERICA
CALIFORNIA, The Rose Gardens, Berkeley; The Rose Acres Nursery, Diamond Springs; Descanso Gardens, La Canada; The Exposition Park Rose Gardens, Los Angeles; The Municipal Rose Garden, Oakland; The Tournament House and Wrigley Gardens, Pasadena; Liggett's Rose Nursery, The Municipal Rose Garden, San José; The Huntingdon Botanical Gardens, San Marino; Armstrong's Roses (Nursery), Somis; Moore's Miniature Roses (Nursery), Visalia; Roses of Yesterday and Today, Watsonville; The Pageant of Roses Garden, Whittier
COLORADO, Longmont Memorial Rose Garden, Longmont
CONNECTICUT, The Elizabeth Park Rose Gardens, Hartford; Norwich Memorial Rose Gardens, Norwich
DISTRICT OF COLUMBIA, United States Botanic Garden, Washington DC; Dumbarton Oaks, Washington DC
FLORIDA, Giles Rose Nursery, Okeechobee
GEORGIA, Rose Test Garden, Thomasville
ILLINOIS, Chicago Botanic Gardens; Washington Park Rose Gardens, Springfield
INDIANA, The Lakeside Rose Garden, Fort Wayne; Krider Nurseries Inc., Middlebury; Richmond Rose Gardens, Richmond
IOWA, Vander Veer Park Rose Gardens, Davenport; Greenwood Park Rose Gardens, Des Moines
KANSAS, The Rose and Trial Garden, Topeka
KENTUCKY, The Memorial Rose Garden, Louisville
LOUISIANA, Hodges Gardens, Many; The American Rose Center, Shreveport (headquarters of the American Rose Society)

MAINE, The Rose Circle, Portland
MARYLAND, Rosehill Farm Nursery, Galena
MASSACHUSETTS, The James P. Kelleher Rose Gardens, Boston; The Arnold Arboretum, Jamaica Plain; Nor-East Miniatures (Nursery), Rowley
MICHIGAN, The Frances Park Memorial Rose Garden, Lansing
MINNESOTA, The Lyndale Park Rose Gardens, Minneapolis
MISSOURI, The Capana Park Rose Display Gardens, Cape Girardeau; The Municipal Rose Gardens, Kansas City; The Missouri Botanic Gardens, St Louis
NEBRASKA, The Memorial Park Rose Gardens, Omaha
NEVADA, Municipal Rose Gardens, Reno
NEW HAMPSHIRE, Fuller Gardens Rose Gardens, North Hampton; Lowe's Rose Gardens, Nashua
NEW JERSEY, The Rudolf van der Goot Rose Gardens, Colonial Park Arboretum, East Millstone; The Jack D. Lissemore Rose Gardens, Tenafly
NEW YORK, The Cranford Rose Garden, Brooklyn Botanic Gardens; Kelly Bros. Nurseries, Dansville; The Queens Botanic Gardens, Flushing; The Maplewood Park Rose Gardens, Rochester; Central Park Rose Garden; The Peggy Rockefeller Rose Garden, The Bronx
NORTH CAROLINA, Raleigh Municipal Rose Gardens
OHIO, The Park of Roses, Columbus; The Michael H. Hovath Garden of Legend and Romance, Wooster*
OKLAHOMA, The Municipal Rose Garden, Tulsa; Charles E. Sparks Rose Garden, Oklahoma City
OREGON, Oregon Miniature Roses (Nursery), Beaustrom; Jackson & Perkins (Nursery), Medford; The International Rose Test Garden, Portland; Owen Memorial Rose Garden, Eugene
PENNSYLVANIA, The Rose Gardens, Hershey; The Gardens, Kennett Square, Longwood; The Marion W. Reamus Rose Garden (in the Arboretum), Philadelphia; Robert Pyle Memorial Gardens, West Grove
SOUTH CAROLINA, Wayside Gardens (Nursery), Hodges; Edisto Gardens, Orangeburg
TENNESSEE, The Municipal Rose Gardens, Memphis
TEXAS, The Municipal Rose Garden, Tyler; Antique Rose Emporium, Brenham; Fort Worth Botanic Gardens; Samuell-Grand Municipal Rose Garden, Dallas; Houston Municipal Rose Garden
UTAH, The Municipal Rose Gardens, Salt Lake City
VIRGINIA, Bon Air Memorial Rose Garden, Arlington; The Botanic Garden Rose Garden, Norfolk
WASHINGTON, The Manito Gardens, Spokane; Woodland Park Rose Gardens, Seattle
WEST VIRGINIA, The Ritter Park Gardens, Huntington
WISCONSIN, The Boerner Botanical Gardens, Hales Corner
* A new rose garden is being created as part of the Ameriflora celebrations 1992, commemorating the 500th anniversary of Columbus' discovery of America

APPENDIX E

Rose Producers and Suppliers of the World

Those marked * specialize in old roses.

AUSTRALIA
Rainbow Roses, Ferntree Gulley, Victoria 3156
*Ross Roses, Willunga, South Australia 5172
Swane's Nursery, Dural, New South Wales 2158
Treloar Roses, Pty Ltd, Portland, Victoria 3305
*Walter Duncan Roses, Watervale, South Australia

BELGIUM
Pepinières Louis Lens, Mechelbaan 147 B2860, Onze-Lieve-Vrouw-Waver

BERMUDA
Aberfeldy Nurseries, Box 237, Warwick WK BX

CANADA
Aubin Nurseries Ltd, Carman, Manitoba R0G 090
Carl Pallek & Son, Virgil, Ontario L0S 1T0
Hortico Inc., Waterdown, Ontario L0R 2H0
Morden Nurseries, Manitoba R0G 1J0
*Pickering Nurseries Inc., Pickering, Ontario L1V 1A6
Walter le Mire Roses, Oldcastle, Ontario N0R 1L0

DENMARK
*Lykkes Rosen, Soby, Horslet
Poulsen Roses, Hillderodvej

FRANCE
Bernard Boureau, Grisy, Suyisnes
George Delbard, Paris Cedex
La Vallée Blonde, L'Hotellère, Lisieux
*Les Roses Anciennes de André Eve, Pithiviers
Meilland Richardier, Tassu-la-Demi-Lune, Cedex
Meilland et Cie, 06601 Antibes
Pepinières Rey, Le Pont du Morauce
Roseraie de Berty, Largentière
Roseraie Laperrière, La Verpillière, Cedex
Roseraies Gaujard, Feyzm Isère

GERMANY
W. Kordes Söhne, Sparrieshoop, Holstein
Ingwer Jensen, Flensburg, Herman-Lons-Weg
Tantau Roses, Uetersen, Hamburg

HOLLAND
J. D. Maarse & Zonen, Aalsmeer
Buisman, Heerde
De Ruiter, Hazers Woode
*Rosenkwekerij de Wilde, Bussum

INDIA
Friends Rosery, Mahanaga, Lucknow
K. S. Gopalas Wamiengar Son, Chamarajpet, Bangalore

ISRAEL
Ruben Fischel, Schadmot, Drona

ITALY
Barni Nursery, Pistoria 4
Mini Arboretum Guido Piacenza, Pollone, Biella
Centro Botanico, Via Dell'Orso, Milan

JAPAN
Hirakata Nurseries, Hirakata-shi, Osaka
Itami Rose Nursery Ltd, Itami-shi, Hyogo-Ken
Kersei Rose Nurseries, Yachiyo-shi, Tokyo
Komaba Rose Nursery, Meguroko, Tokyo

NEW ZEALAND
Avenue Roses, Levin
Egmont Roses, New Plymouth
Frank Mason & Sons Ltd, Fielding
Roselyn Nurseries, Whenuapai, Auckland
*Tasman Bay Roses, Motueka, near Nelson
*Trevor Griffith Nurseries, Timaru

SOUTH AFRICA
Ludwigs Roses, Pretoria

SWITZERLAND
Roseraies Hauser Vaumarcus, Neuchâtel

Richard Huber AG, 5605 Dottikon AG

UNITED KINGDOM
Anderson's Rose Nurseries, Aberdeen AB1 9QT
*David Austin Roses, Albrighton, Wolverhampton WV7 3HB
*Peter Beales Roses, Attleborough, Norfolk NR17 1AY
Cants Roses, Colchester, Essex CO4 5FB
James Cocker & Sons, Whitemyres, Aberdeen AB9 2XH
Dickson Nurseries Ltd, Newtownards, Northern Ireland BT23 4SS
Fryer's Nurseries Ltd, Knutsford, Cheshire WA16 0SX
Gandys Roses, Lutterworth, Leicestershire AL3 7PS
Hillier's Nurseries (Winchester) Ltd, Winchester, Hampshire SO51 9PA
R. Harkness and Co., Hitchin, Hertfordshire SG4 0JT
C. & K. Jones, Tarvin, Chester CH3 8JF
LeGrice Roses, North Walsham, Norfolk NR28 0DR
John Mattock Ltd, Nuncham Courtney, Oxfordshire OX9 9PY
Rearsby Roses Ltd, Rearsby, Leicestershire LE7 8YP
*Roses du Temps Passé, Stafford ST19 9LG
Rosemary Roses, Toton, Beeston, Nottinghamshire NG9 5FD
John Sandy (Roses) Ltd, Almondsbury, Bristol BS12 4DA
Wheatcroft Ltd, Edwalton, Nottingham NG12 4DE
Warley Rose Gardens, Brentwood, Essex CM13 3JH

USA
*The Antique Rose Emporium, Brenham, Texas 77833
Armstrong's Roses, Somis, California 93066
Carroll Gardens, Westminster, Maryland 21157
Conrad-Pyle Co., West Grove, Pennsylvania 19390–0904
Donovan's Roses, Shreveport, Louisiana 71133–7800
Farmer Seed and Nursery Co., Fairbault, Minnesota 55021
Fred Edmunds Inc., Wilsonville, Oregon 97070
Gloria Dee Nursery, High Falls, New York 12440
Hastings, Atlanta, Georgia 30302–4274
*Heritage Rose Gardens, Branscomb, California 95417
High Country Rosarium, Denver, Colorado 80218
*Historical Roses Inc., Painsville, Ohio 44077
Interstate Nursery, Hamburg, Iowa 51640-0208
Jackson & Perkins, Medford, Oregon 9751
Justice Miniature Roses, Wilsonville, Oregon 97070
Kelly Brothers Nurseries Inc., Dansville, Kentucky 14437
Lamb Nurseries, Spokane, Washington 99202
Liggett's Rose Nursery, San Jose, California 95125
*Limberlost Roses, Van Nuys, California 91406
*Lowe's Own Root Roses, Nashua, New Hampshire 03062
McDaniel's Miniature Roses, Lemon Grove, California 92045
Mellinger's, North Lima, Ohio 44452–9731
Miller Nurseries, Cananadaigua, New York 14424
Nor-East Miniature Roses, Rowley, Massachusetts 10969
Richard Owen Nurseries, Bloomington, Illinois
Roseway Nurseries Inc., Woodland, Washington Wa 98674
Sequoia Nurseries, Visalia, California 93277
Stocking Rose Nurseries, San José, California 95133
P. O. Tate Nursery, Tyler, Texas 75708
Thomasville Nurseries, Thomasville, Georgia 31799
*Roses of Yesterday and Today, Watsonville, California 95076

Glossary

Throughout this book, rightly or wrongly, I have used the minimum of technical and botanical terms; however, in the interest of accuracy it has been impossible to avoid them altogether.

Anther	That part of the male part of the flower which bears the pollen
Axil	Where a leaf joins the stalk
Bract	A reduced leaf-like structure usually on a flower stalk
Calyx	The leaf-like, outer protective part of a flower
Cambium layer	The growth cells between the bark and the woody part of a stem
Clone	An identical offspring produced vegetatively
Corymb	A group of flowers held on stems of differing lengths
Glabrous	Lacking hairs or glands
Glaucous	Bluish-greyish colour
Hispid	With bristly hairs or thin spines
Inflorescence	Group of flowers forming a cluster on one stem
Lanceolate	(Of leaves.) Long and pointed, but wider towards the base
Lateral	A side branch growing from a main shoot or cane
Node	The point on a stem where a leaf and/or bud can be found
Ovate	(Of leaves.) Oval shaped, usually with the broadest part of the leaf towards the apex
Panicle	Branched inflorescence
Pedicel	The stalk of a flower (also peduncle)
Petiole	The stalk of a leaf
Pinnate	Having leaflets on each side of the axis or midrib
Pistil	The female part of a flower
Procumbent	Naturally growing along the ground
Pubescent	With fine hairs
Receptacle	The part of the flower which holds the seed and later becomes the hip
Recurrent	Flowers produced in succession throughout a flowering season
Reflexed	With petals which curl back as flowers open
Remontant	Of continuous or repeat-flowering habit
Scion	A plant which is grafted on to another
Sepal	The green, individual leaf-like part of the calyx
Spine	A long, thin, sharp thorn
Stamens	The male part of the flower
Stigma	The female part of the flower which receives the pollen on fertilization
Stipule	The small, variously shaped wings at the base of a leaf stalk
Stock	A plant on to which another is grafted
Sucker	A shoot which develops from the root of the stock on a grafted plant
Truss	A group or cluster of flowers forming one head
Umbel	A flat-topped inflorescence
Vegetative propagation	Reproduction other than by seeds, viz. by cuttings, grafting, budding etc.

Further Reading

The following are some recommended books on roses and their cultivation still in print and available from most good bookshops, their authors or libraries; many of them were referred to in the compilation of this book.

Austin, D. *The Heritage of Roses* Antique Collector Club, London 1986, and Antique Collectors' Club, Ithaca, NY 1988

Beales, A. *Old Fashioned Roses* Cassell, London 1990, and Globe Pequot Press, Chester, CT 1990

Beales, P. *Classic Roses* Collins Harvill, London, and Henry Holt & Co., New York 1985

Beales, P. *Twentieth-Century Roses* Collins Harvill, London, and Harper & Row, New York 1988

Dobson, B. R. Combined Rose List. *Hard to Find Roses and Where to Find Them* (published annually) Beverly R. Dobson, Irvington, NY

Fagan, G. *Roses of the Cape of Good Hope* Private publication. Limited edition. 1988

Fearnley-Whittingstall, J. *Rose Gardens* Henry Holt & Co., New York

Find That Rose (published annually) British Rose Growers' Association, Colchester

Fisher, J. *The Companion to Roses* Viking, London 1986

Gault, S. M. and Singe, P. M. *The Dictionary of Roses in Colour* Michael Joseph and Ebury Press, London 1970

Gibson, M. *Growing Roses* Croom Helm, London, 1985, and Timber Press, Portland (USA) 1984

Gibson, M. *The Rose Gardens of England* HarperCollins, London 1988, and Globe Pequot Press, Chester, CT 1988

Griffiths, T. *My World of Old Roses* (Volumes I and II) Whitcoulls, Christchurch 1983 and 1986

Griffiths, T. *The Best of Modern Roses* Pacific, Auckland, NZ 1987

Griffiths, T. *A Celebration of Roses* Viking Pacific, Christchurch, NZ 1988

Haglund, G. *Rosen Blommornas Drotting* Haglund, Göteborg 1986

Harkness, J. *Roses* J. M. Dent & Sons, London 1978

Harkness, J. *The Makers of Heavenly Roses* Souvenir Press, London 1985

Harkness, P. *Modern Roses* Century Hutchinson, London 1987, and in the USA as *Modern Garden Roses* Globe Pequot Press, Chester, CT 1988

Hessayon, D. *The Rose Expert* PBI Publications, London 1981

Krüssman, G. *Roses* Batsford, London 1982, and Timber Press, Portland, OR 1981

LeGrice, E. B. *Rose Growing Complete* (revised edition) Faber & Faber, London 1976

Le Rougetel, H. *A Heritage of Roses* Unwin Hyman, London 1989, and Stemmer House, Owings Mills, MD 1988

McCann, S. *Miniature Roses for Home and Garden* David & Charles, London 1985

Modern Roses 8: The International Checklist of Roses (ed. C. E. Meikle) McFarland, Harrisburg 1980

Modern Roses 9: The International Checklist of Roses (ed. P. A. Haring) The American Rose Society, Shreveport 1986

Money, K. *The Bedside Book of Old-Fashioned Roses* Degamo, London 1986

Nottle, T. *Growing Old-Fashioned Roses in Australia and New Zealand* Kangaroo Press, Kenthurst 1983

Phillips, R. and Rix, M. *Roses* Pan Books, London 1988, and Random House, New York 1988

Rose, G., King, P. and Squire, D. *The Love of Roses* Quiller Press, London 1990
Ross, D. *Rose Growing for Pleasure* Lothian, Adelaide 1985
Ross, D. *A Manual of Roses* Private publication 1989
Scanniello, S. and Bayard, T. *Roses of America* Henry Holt & Co., New York 1990
Swain, V. *The Australian Rose Book* Angus and Robertson, Sydney 1983
Testu, C. *Les Roses Anciennes* Flammarion, Paris 1984
Thomas, A. S. *Growing Roses in Australia* Nelson, Sydney 1983
Thomas, G. S. *An English Rose Garden* Michael Joseph, London 1991, and published in the USA as *The Art of Gardening with Roses* Henry Holt & Co., New York 1991
Thomas, G. S. *Shrub Roses of Today* J. M. Dent & Sons, London 1974
Thomas, G. S. *The Old Shrub Roses* J. M. Dent & Sons, London 1978
Thomas, G. S. *Climbing Roses Old and New* J. M. Dent & Sons, London 1979
Walpole, J. *Roses in a Suffolk Garden* Images, Woolpit, Suffolk 1990
Warner, C. *Climbing Roses* Century Hutchinson, London 1987

GENERAL

Some general botanical or horticultural books containing valuable information on the genus *Rosa*.

Bean, W. J. *Trees and Shrubs Hardy in the British Isles* (8th edition revised) John Murray, London 1980
Hillier's *Manual of Trees and Shrubs* (4th edition) Hillier, Winchester 1974
Keble Martin, W. *The Concise British Flora* Ebury Press and Michael Joseph, London 1965
RHS Dictionary of Gardening Royal Horticultural Society, Wisley 1956
RHS Garden Encyclopaedia of Plants and Flowers Royal Horticultural Society, Wisley 1989

FURTHER READING FOR THE CONNOISSEUR

Some books on roses for the connoisseur – most are available from second-hand booksellers or from specialist gardening libraries.

Anderson, F. J. *An Illustrated Treasury of Redouté Roses* Crown, New York 1979
Beales, P. and Money, K. *Georgian and Regency Roses* Jarrolds, Norwich 1978
Beales, P. and Money, K. *Early Victorian Roses* Jarrolds, Norwich 1978
Beales, P. and Money, K. *Late Victorian Roses* Jarrolds, Norwich 1980
Beales, P. and Money K. *Edwardian Roses* Jarrolds, Norwich 1980
Blunt, W. and Russell, J. *Old Garden Roses. Part II* George Rainbird, London 1957
Buist, Robert *The Rose Manual*, New York 1844. Facsimile reprint, Coleman, New York 1978
Bunyard, E. A. *Old Garden Roses* Collingridge, London 1936. Facsimile reprint, Coleman, New York 1978
Curtis, Henry *Beauties of the Rose*, facsimile edition, Sweetbrier Press, New York 1981
Dodds, F. W. *Practical Rose Growing in all Forms* publisher not known, c. 1908
Fitch, C. M. *The Complete Book of Miniature Roses* Hawthorn, London 1977
Foster, M. A. *The Book of the Rose* Macmillan, London 1864
Genders, R. *The Rose: A Complete Handbook* Robert Hale, London 1965
Gibson, M. *Shrub Roses for Every Garden* William Collins, London 1973

Gibson, M. *The Book of the Rose* Macdonald General Books, London 1980
Goor, A. *The History of the Rose in Holy Lands throughout the Ages* Agricultural Publications Division, State of Israel 1969. English edition 1981
Gore, C. F. *The Book of Roses or The Rose Fancier's Manual*, 1838. Facsimile reprint, Heyden, London 1978, and Coleman, New York 1978
Hellyer, A. G. L. *Simple Rose Growing* W. H. & L. Collingridge Ltd, London c. 1930
Henslow, T. G. W. *The Rose Encyclopaedia* C. Arthur Pearson Ltd, London, c. 1922
Hole, S Reynolds *A Book about Roses* William Blackwood, London 1869
Jäger August *Rosenlexicon* (republished from the 1936 edition) Zentralartigariat, Leipzig 1960
Jekyll, G. and Mawley, E. *Roses for English Gardens* Country Life, London 1902, and Ayar Company Publishers, Salem 1984
Keays, Ethelyn E. *Old Roses*, New York 1935. Facsimile reprint, Coleman, New York 1978
Kingsley, R. G. *Roses and Rose Growing* Whittaker & Co., New York 1908
Kordes, W. *Roses* Studio Vista, London 1964
Macself, A. J. *The Rose Grower's Treasury* Collingridge, London 1934
Mansfield, T. C. *Roses in Colour and Cultivation* William Collins, London 1947
Mayhew, A. & Pollard, M. *The Rose, Myth, Folklore and Legend* New English Library, London 1979
McFarland, J. H. *The Rose in America* Macmillan, New York 1923
McFarland, J. H. *Roses of the World in Colour* Cassell & Co., London 1936
Park, B. *Collins Guide to Roses* Collins, London 1965
Parkman, Francis *The Book of Roses*, J. E. Tilton & Co., Boston, MA 1866
Parsons, S. B. *Parsons on the Rose* Orange Judd Co., New York 1888
Paul, W. *A Shilling Book of Roses* Simpkin, Marshall, Hamilton, Kent & Co., London c. 1880
Paul, W. *The Rose Garden* (10th edition) Simpkin, Marshall, Hamilton, Kent & Co., London 1903. Facsimile reprint of the 1848 edition, Coleman, New York 1978
Poulsen, S. *Poulsen on the Rose* MacGibbon & Kee, London 1955
Redouté, P. J. *Roses, Books One and Two* (facsimile reprint) Ariel Press, London 1954 and 1956
Ridge, A. *For the Love of a Rose* Faber & Faber, London 1965
Rigg, C. H. *Roses of Quality* Ernest Benn Ltd, London 1933
Rivers, T. *The Rose Amateur's Guide* Longman Green, London 1837
Rose Annuals The National Rose Society, St Albans, from 1911 onwards
Rose Annuals American Rose Society, Shreveport, 1917 and others
Ross, D. *Shrub Roses in Australia* Deane Ross, Adelaide 1981
Rossi, B. V. *Modern Roses in Australia* Mitchell & Casey, Sydney 1930
Royal Horticultural Society Journals, numerous and various back issues
Sanders, T. W. *Roses and their Cultivation* W. H. & L. Collingridge, London 1938
Shepherd, R. *History of the Rose* Macmillan, New York 1954. Facsimile reprint, Coleman, New York 1978
Sitwell, S. and Russell, J. *Old Garden Roses, Part I* George Rainbird, London 1955
Steen, N. *The Charm of Old Roses* Herbert Jenkins, Wellington, NZ 1966
'*The Rose*' Magazine, various issues 1950s, and 1960s
Thomas, H. H. *The Rose Book* Cassell, London 1913
Weathers, J. *Beautiful Roses* Simpkin, Marshall, Hamilton, Kent & Co., London 1903
Wright, W. P. *Roses and Rose Gardens* Headley, London 1911

GENERAL INDEX

'A Simplified Rose Classification' (Allen), 113
Albas (forms and hybrids), 175–7; history of, 11
Allen, E. F., *The Rose Annual 1973*, 67, 113
Allison, Sally and Bey, 15
American Rose Annual (Miller, 1907), 6
American Rose Society, 33, 63, 67; Rose classes, 64
American Rose Society Annual, 34
Aphids, 436
Armstrong Nursery, 41
Austin, David, 48–9, 67
Austin, Robert, 20
Ayshires (*R. arvensis*) (forms and hybrids), 216–17; history of, 23

Balling of flowers *see* Malformation of flowers
Banksianae, 125–6
Barbier, 24, 59
Bark chippings *see* Soils and soil preparation
Barton, Marjorie, 89
Bayard, Tania, 20
Beales, Joan, 40
Beales, Peter, 37–8, 42, 46–7, 52–3, 66; *Late Victorian Roses*, 29; *Classic Roses*, 113n.
Bee's, 33
Bennett, Charles, 29
Bennett, Henry, 29, 30, 66
Bentall, J. A., 22
Bermuda Rose Society, 17, 18
Bermuda roses *see* Mystery Roses of Bermuda
Bide, 60
Blackspot, 438
Boerner, Eugene, 34, 41, 42, 50, 58
Borers *see* Cane borers
Bourbons, 329–36; history of, 14
Boursaults (forms and hybrids), 196
Bowditch, James, 51
Bracteatae, 129–32
Bréon, M., 14
British Association of Rose Breeders (BARB), 33, 63, 64, 67, 113n.; *Rose classes*, 65, 67
British National Rose Society, 29
British Rose Growers' Association, 421
British Standards Institution, 421
Brown, Robert, 20

Brownell, 24, 50
Budding, 431–2, 441
Burdett, Ruth, 29
Burnet Roses *see Pimpinellifoliae; R. Pimpinellifolia*

Cambridge University Botanic Gardens, 50
Cane borers, 437
Caninae, 173–84
Cant, B. R., 60
Cants, 33
Capsid bugs, 436
Carolinae, 185–8
Cassiorhodon, 189–214
Castle Howard, Yorkshire, 12
Caterpillars, 436
Centifolias (Provence Roses or Cabbage Roses) (forms and hybrids), 153–6; history of, 8
Champneys, John, 15, 34, 57
Chelsea Flower Show, 53
Chinas, 323–8; history of, 11–13
Chinensis, 321–418
Choosing and buying roses, 421–3; container roses, 422–3
Classification of genus *Rosa*, 113
Classification systems, 63–5; 'Some Thoughts on Rose Classification' (Harkness), 66–8
Climbers, history of, 57; for poorer soils, 73; as standards, 94–5
Climbing Bourbons, 337–8
Climbing Floribundas, 286–7
Climbing Hybrid Teas, 411–18
Climbing Roses Old and New (Thomas), 59
Cocker, Alex, 32, 42
Cocker's, 32, 33
Collier, Lesley, 53
Commercial production of roses, 441–3
Compact Floribundas *see* Patios
Companion plants for modern roses, 102
Companion plants for old roses, 96–100; annuals and biennials, 99; bulbs, corms, etc., 99; fruit and vegetables, 100; herbs, 99–100; wild flowers, 100
Crown gall, 438
Cuckoospit, 436
Cultivation of Roses, 419–43

'Cutting down' *see* 'Heading back'
Cuttings, roses from, 432–4

Daily Mail, 35
Damasks (forms and hybrids), 164–8; history of, 9
De Ruiter, 44, 56
De Vink, 55, 56
Dead-heading, 428
Dickson, Alexander, 30, 66
Dickson, Patrick, 31, 42, 54, 57
Dickson & Brown of Perth, 20
Dickson's, 30, 31, 42
Diseases, 435–6, 438–40
Division, 434
Dog Rose *see Caninae*
Dot, Pedro, 37, 51, 56
Downy mildew, 438–9
Dubreuil, Frances, 35
Duc d'Orleans, 14
Dwarf Polyanthas, 38

East India Company, 16
English Roses, 315–73
Eurosa (*Rosa* subgenus), 125–418
Evergreens *see* Sempervirens Roses

Fa Tee Nurseries, Canton, 16
Farrer, 51
Fertilizers *see* Soils and soil preparation
Festing, Sally, 13n.
Floribundas, 259–86; history of, 38
Flower arranging, old roses for, 89; modern roses for, 106
Foliage, ornamental, 92–3
Fortune, Robert, 16

Gallicanae, 143–72
Gallicas (forms and hybrids), 143–53; history of, 10
Geduldig, 44
Genoa Rose Trails, 38
Grafting, 430
Grandiflora, 41–2, 65
Gregory's, 33
Ground cover roses *see* Procumbents
Guillot, Jean Baptiste, 29, 35, 44

Harkness, Jack, 32, 42, 54, 64; 'Some Thoughts on Rose Classification', 66–8
Harkness & Co., R., 32, 33, 53, 56
'Heading back', 442
'Heading off' *see* 'Heading back'
Heeling-in, 423
Hesperhodos (*Rosa* subgenus), 121–2

Hill, E. Gurney, 34
Hilling's Nurseries, 51
Hips, roses grown for their, 91
Honours and Awards, 114
Hooker, 9
Horticultural Society of Lyon, 66
Howard, F. H., 34
Hulthemia (*Rosa* subgenus), 118–19
×*Hulthemosa* (*Rosa* subgenus), 118–19
Hume, Sir Abraham, 16
Huntington Botanic Garden, USA, 13n.
Hurst, Dr C. V., 8, 8n.
Hybrid Musks, 223–9; history of, 21
Hybrid Perpetuals, 352–65; history of, 18
Hybrid Teas, 373–410; history of, 29–38

Jackson & Perkins, 24, 34, 41
Jacques, M., 14
Japanese beetles, 437
Jekyll, Gertrude, 59, 71
John Innes Institute, 12
Josephine, Empress, Influence of, 25

Kennedy, 25
Kordes, Reimer, 36, 45
Kordes, Wilhelm, 20, 36, 44, 45, 46, 51, 54, 58
Kordes nurseries, 56, 58, 67

Laevigatae, 127–8
Lambert, Peter, 21, 36, 51
Lammerts, Dr E., 41, 58
Landscape, roses in the, 71–109
Late Victorian Roses (Beales and Money), 29
Laver, 56
Lawn trimmings *see* Soils and soil preparation
Layering, 434
Le Rougetel, Hazel, 13, 51
Leaf-rolling sawfly, 437
Lee, Mr, 20
Leenders, 44
LeGrice, Edward Burton ('Father'), 13, 22, 33, 39–40, 41, 42, 46
Lens, Louis, 37
Lindsey, 55
Lowe, Malcolm (Mike), 432

Malcolm, William, 20
Malformation of flowers, 440–41
Mallerin, 58
Malmaison, Château de, rose garden, 25
Manda, 59
Manners, Malcolm, 439; 'Rose Mosaic Virus Disease', 439–40

Manure *see* Soils and soil preparation
Mason, Clarissa, 53, 57
Mason, James, 53
McGredy, Samuel, 31, 33, 42, 44, 56, 57, 58
McGredy's, 33, 42
MacGregor IV, John C., 13n.
Meier, Margaret, 29
Meilland, Alain, 36
Meilland, Antoine, 35
Meilland, Charles, 35
Meilland, Francis, 35, 36
Meilland's, 44, 54, 56, 57, 58, 101
Mercer, Bill, 17
Mercer, Lorna, 17, 17n.
Micropropagation, 434, 441
Midge, 437
Miller, Wilhelm , 6
Mineral deficiencies, 439
Miniatures, 298–310; history of, 55–7
Modern climbing roses, 236–45; uses of, 101–9
Modern roses: as bedding plants and for massed display, 101–2; in containers, 105; for exhibition, 107–8; under glass, 105–6; as hedges, 104–5; for their scent, 108–9; as standards, 108
Modern Roses 9 (American Rose Society), 63, 64, 67
Modern shrub roses, 245–56; history of, 48; in a mixed shrubbery, 74–5
Money, Keith, 29, 37–8
Moore, Ralph, 56
Morey, Dennison, 54
Mosaic virus, 439–40
Mosses (forms and hybrids), 156–64; history of, 9
Mulching *see* Soils and soil preparation
Multiflora Ramblers 230–36; history of, 22–3
Murrell, Hilda, 61
Musks (*R. moschata*), 220–21
Mystery roses of Bermuda, 351–2; history of, 17–18

National Rose Show, 107
National Rose Society, 66; Gold Medal of the, 31
Nicolas, Jean Henri, 34, 66
Noisette, Louis, 15
Noisette, Philippe, 15
Noisettes, 338–42; history of, 15
Norman, Albert, 32, 42
Norwich Union, 47

Old climbing roses: for pergolas, trellises, pillars and arches, 83–5; for trees, 87–8; for walls, fencing panels and northerly aspects, 85–6

Old procumbent and semi-procumbent roses, 88–9
Old roses: for an established garden, 73–4; for formal hedges, 80; informal hedges, 80–81; for mixed shrubberies, 74–5; for Parks and Municipal planting, 75–6; for pots and tubs, 81–2; for terraces and patios, 80–81; for woodland, wild gardens and partial shade, 76–7
Old Shrub Roses, The (Thomas), 8n.
Old shrub roses under glass, 90
Onodera, Toru, 54

Page, Colin, 47
Page, Courtney, 66
Paolino, 56
Parks, John, 16
'Patcher', 441
Patio roses, 298–310; history of, 57
Paul, William, 9, 14, 22, 29, 34, 60, 61
Paul & Son, 66
Peat *see* Soils and soil preparation
Pegging down, 95
Pemberton, Joseph, 21, 22, 48, 60, 66
Penelope Plummer, 46
Penzance, Lord, 21, 48
Penzance Briars, 21; history of, 20; *see also* Shrub roses
Pernet-Ducher, Joseph, 30, 35
Pests, 435–7
Pillars, 73
Pimpinellifoliae (Scotch roses), 133–42; history of, 19–20
Plant Varieties and Seeds Act 1964 (UK), 33
Planting, 423–5; climbing roses, 425; containerized roses, 424; into pots, 425; specimen roses in grass, 424; standard roses, 425
Planting and pruning seasons in the USA, 427
Platyrhodon (*Rosa* subgenus), 123–4
Polyanthas, 257; history of, 38, 44
Polypompons, history of, 38, 44
Portland, 2nd Duchess of, 13n.
Portland, 3rd Duchess of, 13n.
Portlands (forms and hybrids), 169–71; history of, 13
Poulsen, Dines, 38, 39, 44, 46
Poulsen, Niels, 39

INDEX OF ROSES

Poulsen, Svend, 39
Poulsen's, 44, 54, 68
Powdery mildew, 438
Procumbent shrub roses, 288–297
Procumbents, 53–5
Proliferation see Malformation of flowers
Propagation, 430
Provence Roses see Centifolias
Pruning, 425–8; in the USA, 427; bush, shrub and old-fashioned roses, 424; climbing roses and ramblers, 426; modern roses, 429; neglected roses, 428; once-flowering roses, 426; repeat-flowering shrubs, 426; weeping standards, 427, 428
Pyle, Robert, 55, 56

R. agrestis, 173
R. banksiae (forms and hybrids), 126
R. biebersteinii
R. bracteata (and hybrid), 129
R. britzensis, 177
R. brunonii (forms and hybrids), 217
R. canina (forms and hybrids), 177–8
R. carolina (forms and hybrids), 187
R. chinensis see Chinas
R. ecae (forms and hybrids), 133–4
R. eglanteria (forms and hybrids), 179–82
R. filipes (forms and hybrids), 219
R. foetida (forms and hybrids), 134–5
R. gigantea (and hybrids), 321–3
R. glauca (forms and hybrids), 182
R. helenae (forms and hybrids), 219
R. hugonis (forms and hybrids), 136
R. kordesii (forms and hybrids), 193–5
R. laevigata (forms and hybrids), 127
R. macrantha (forms and hybrids), 172
R. macrophylla (forms and hybrids), 197–9
R. moschata see Musks
R. moyesii (forms and hybrids), 199
R. multibracteata (forms and hybrids), 201–2
R. multiflora (forms and hybrids), 222–3
R. nutkana (forms and hybrids), 202–3

R. pimpinellifolia (Scotch Roses) (forms and hybrids), 137–42
R. roxburghii (forms), 123
R. rubrifolia see R. glauca
R. sempervirens (forms and hybrids), 310–11
R. setigera (and hybrids), 311
R. sinowilsonii (and hybrid), 312
R. soulieana (forms and hybrids), 312
R. stellata (forms), 121–2
R. virginiana (forms and hybrids), 188
R. wichuraiana (and hybrids), 313–20; see also Wichuraianas
R. xanthina (forms and hybrids), 142
Ramblers, history of, 59–60
Red spider 437
Redouté, Pierre Joseph, 25
Rehder, 67
Rivers, 9, 30
Robinson, Herbert, 42
Rose Annual 1973, The (Allen), 67, 113n.
Rose Directory of the Royal National Rose Society, 42, 43
Rose Garden, The (Paul, 10th ed., 1903), 9
Roses of America (Scanniello), 20
Roses of Provins see Gallicas
Rose sickness see Specific replant disease
Ross, Deane, 29, 37, 62
Rotation, 441
Roulet, 55
Royal Horticultural Society (RHS), 16, 20
Royal National Rose Society (RNRS), 42, 66, 107, 113
Rugosas (forms and hybrids), 203–13
Russell, James, 12
Rust, 439
Ruston, David, 61
Ruys, 50

Sabine, Joseph, 19
Sadler's Wells ballet company, 53
Saville, 56
Scanniello, Stephen, 20
Scent, older roses grown for their, 93
Schmidt, 60
Schmitt, 59
Scotch or Burnet Roses see R. Pimpinellifolia
Scramblers, history of, 61–63
Seasons in rose cycle, in northern and southern hemispheres, 115
Seed, roses from, 435
Sempervirens Roses (the Evergreens), history of, 23

Shepherd, Roy, 20
Shrub roses, 73–9; for an established garden, 73–4; for poorer soils, 73; as standards, 94–5
Simplicifoliae, 117–20
Soils and soil preparation, 423–4; choosing roses for poorer soils, 72–3
'Some Thoughts on Rose Classification' (Harkness), 66–8
Species roses, 113–14; history of, 1–8
Specific replant disease 424
Spek, Jan, 37
Standard roses, 94–5, 108; for an established garden, 73
Steen, Nancy, 14
Stem canker, 439
Suckers, 422
Sunningdale Nurseries, 61
Sweet, Robert, 55
Sweet Briars, history of, 20–21
Swim, Herbert, 34, 41, 66
Synstylae, 215–320

Tantau Jr, Mathias, 37, 45
Tantau nurseries, 37, 46
Tantau Sr, Mathias, 36, 37, 45, 46
Teas, 342–50; history of, 16
Thomas, Graham Stuart, 8n., 51, 59, 71
Thory, Claude Antoine, 25
Thrips, 437
'Topping' see 'Heading back'
Trellis, 73
Turbat, 44

Understocks, 422

Van Fleet, Dr W., 59
Von Abrams, Gordon, 41

Walkthroughs, 73
Water features, 78–9
Weed control, 429
Wheatcroft, Harry, 37
White Roses see Albas
Wichuraianas, 313–20; history of, 24
Wild roses, distribution of, 4–5; American, 5–6; European, 5; Middle Eastern, 7; Oriental and Asian, 6
Winter protection, 423
Wisley (RHS gardens, Surrey), 50
World Federation of Rose Societies, 63, 67; rose classes, 64

à longues pédoncules, 156
Abbeyfield Rose, 373
Abbotswood, 177, 177
Abraham Darby, 365, 365
Abunancia see Mary Hayley Bell
Abundance, 259
Ace of Hearts, 373
Adam, 342, 344
Adam Messerich, 329, 329
Adélaïde d'Orléans, 23, 224, 310
Adèle Pradel see Mme Bravy
Admiral Rodney, 108, 374
Admired Miranda, 365
Adolf Horstmann, 374
Agatha, 115, 115
Agatha Christie, 236
Agathe Incarnata, 145
Aglaia, 21, 69, 230
Agnes, 50, 204, 204
Agrippina see Cramoisi Supérieur
Aimée Vibert, 15, 338, 338
Air France, 298, 298
Alain Blanchard, 145, 145
Alba Maxima see Maxima
Alba Meidiland, 288
Alba Semi-plena see Semi-plena
Alba Suavolens see Semi-plena
Albéric Barbier, 6, 24, 59, 82, 108, 313, 314
Albert Edwards, 138
Albertine, 6, 24, 24, 25, 59, 92, 313, 313
Alchemist, 111, 236, 236
Alec's Red, 32, 108, 374, 374
Alexander, 32, 33, 245, 246
Alexander Girault, 59, 314
Alfred Colomb, 352
Alfred de Dalmas, 156, 157
Alida Lovett, 314, 314
Alison Wheatcroft, 259, 259
Aloha, 50, 237, 237
Alpine Rose see R. pendulina
Alpine Sunset, 374
Altissimo, 237, 237
Amadis, 196, 196
Amanda, 260
Amanda see Red Ace
Amatsu-Otome, 108, 374
Ambassador, 260
Amber Queen, 42, 105, 260, 260
Amberlight, 260
Ambridge Rose, 365
Amelia, 175
America, 237
American Beauty, 352

American Independence see Air France
American Pillar, 314, 314
American Pride, 260
Améthyste, 314
Amorette see Snowdrop
Amoretta see Snowdrop
Amruda see Red Ace
Amy Robsart, 179, 180, 180
Anaïs Ségalas, 145, 145
Andersonii, 177, 178
André see Calocarpa
Andrewsii, 138
Anemone Rose, 128, 128
Angel Face, 260
Angela Rippon, 298
Angela Pernet, 34, 35, 374
Angels Mateu, 37
Angelina, 245, 245
Angelita see Snowball
Anisley Dickson, 260, 260
Anita, 260
Ann Aberconway, 261
Anna de Diesbach, 352
Anna Ford, 57, 298, 298
Anna Livia, 261, 261
Anna Oliver, 17, 342
Anna Pavlova, 27, 37–8, 93, 109, 374
Anna Wheatcroft, 46, 261
Anna Zinkeisen, 245
Anne-Marie de Montravel, 323
Anne Cocker, 42, 261
Anne Diamond, 374
Anne Harkness, 261, 261
Anne of Geierstein, 180
Anne Watkins, 374
Anneliese Rothenberger see Miss Harp
Antigua, 261
Antike '89 see Antique
Antique, 237
Antoine Ducher, 30
Antoine Rivoire, 29, 31
Antonia d'Ormois, 145
Apothecary's Rose, The see R. gallica officinalis
Apple Blossom, 230, 230
Apple Rose see R. villosa
Applejack, 245, 245
Apricot Nectar, 261
Apricot Silk, 374
Apricot Sunblaze, 298, 298
Arc de Triomphe see Summer Fashion
Arcadian, 261
Archduke Charles, 17, 323, 323
Archiduc Charles see Archduke Charles
Archiduc Joseph, 342, 343
Archiduchesse Elizabeth d'Autriche, 352
Arctic Sunrise, 298
Ardoisée de Lyon, 353, 353

Ards Beauty, 261
Ards Rover, 353
Arethusa, 17, 323, 323
Arianna, 374
Armada, 247, 247
Armosa see Hermosa
Arrillaga, 353
Arthur Bell, 108, 109, 261, 261
Arthur Bell Climbing, 286
Arthur de Sansal, 169, 169
Arthur Hillier, 197
Aschermittwoch see Ash Wednesday
Ash Wednesday, 237, 237
Assemblage des Beautés, 146
Asso di Cuori see Ace of Hearts
Astra Desmond, 230
Astrid Späth Striped, 261, 261
August Seebauer, 261, 262
Auguste Gervais, 314
Auguste Roussel, 197, 197
Augustine Guinnoisseau, 374
Augustine Halem, 374, 375
Austrian Briar see R. foetida
Austrian Copper see R. foetida bicolor
Austrian Yellow see R. foetida
Autumn Bouquet, 247
Autumn Damask see Quatre Saisons
Autumn Delight, 223, 223
Autumn Fire see Herbstfeuer
Autumn Sunlight, 238
Autumn Sunset, 247, 247
Autumnalis, 220
Aviateur Blériot, 314, 315
Avignon, 262
Avocet, 262
Awakening, 315, 315
Ayrshire Queen, 216
Ayrshire Splendens, 23
Azulabria see Blue Peter

Baby Bio, 262
Baby Carnaval see Baby Masquerade
Baby Crimson see Perla de Alcañada
Baby Darling, 56, 298
Baby Faurax, 257
Baby Gold Star, 56, 299
Baby Masquerade, 299
Baby Sunrise, 299
Baccara, 36, 375
Bad Naukeim see National Trust
Ballerina, 22, 22, 94, 105, 108, 223
Baltimore Belle, 6, 311, 311
Bantry Bay, 24, 58, 104, 238, 238
Barbara Richards, 375, 375
Barkarole, 375
Baron de Bonstetten, 353
Baron de Wassenaer, 157
Baron Girod de l'Ain, 353, 353

Baroness Rothschild, 18, 353
Baronne Adolphe de Rothschild *see* Baroness Rothschild
Baronne Henriette de Snoy, 344, **344**
Baronne Prévost, 18, **19**, 353, 355
Basildon Bond, 375
Bassimo *see* Suffolk
Beauté, 375, **375**
Beautiful Britain, 42, **43**, 262, **262**
Beauty of Glazenwood *see* Fortune's Double Yellow
Beauty of Rosemawr, 323
Beauty of the Prairies *see* Queen of the Prairies
Beauty Queen, 262
Belinda, 46, **223**, 224
Belle Amour, 164, **164**
Belle Blonde, 375
Belle de Crécy, 146
Belle des Jardins *see* Village Maid
Belle Isis, 146
Belle Lyonnaise, 344
Belle of Portugal *see* Belle Portugaise
Belle Poitevine, 204, **205**
Belle Portugaise, 322, **322**
Belle Story, 366
Bengal Rose *see* R. *chinensis*
Bengale Pompon *see* Pumila
Bennett's Seedling, 216
Benson & Hedges Gold, **374**, 375
Benson & Hedges Special, 299
Berlin, 247
Bernhard Daneke Rose *see* Showbiz
Bettina, 36, 375
Bettina Climbing, 411
Betty Prior, 262, **262**
Betty Uprichard, 31, 375
Bianco, 299
Bibi Maizoon, 366
Biddulph Grange, 247
Big Chief, 108, 375
Bishop, The, 156, **156**
Bishop Darlington, 224
Bit o' Sunshine, 299
Black Beauty, 376
Black Jack *see* Tour de Malakoff
Black Prince, 353
Blackberry Rose *see* R. *rubus*
Blairii No. 1, 337, **337**
Blairii No. 2, 337, **337**
Blanc de Vibert, 169
Blanc Double de Coubert, 7, 204, **205**
Blanc Pur, 339
Blanche de Belgique, 175
Blanche Moreau, 157, **157**
Blanche Superbe *see* Blanche de Belgique
Blanchefleur, 153, **154**
Blaze, 315
Blessings, 33, 376, **376**
Blessings Climbing, 411

Bleu Magenta, **87**, 230
Bloomfield Abundance, **321**, 323
Bloomfield Courage, 63
Bloomfield Dainty, **62**, 63, 224
Blue Monday *see* Blue Moon
Blue Moon, 37, **37**, 376, **376**
Blue Parfum, 376
Blue Peter, 299
Bluenette *see* Blue Peter
Blush Boursault, 196, **196**
Blush Damask, 164, **164**
Blush Maman Cochet *see* William R. Smith
Blush Noisette, 15, **15**, 339, 339
Blush Rambler, 60, 230, **230**
Bobbie James, 61, **85**, **88**, 230, **230**
Bobby Charlton, 376
Bon Silène, 344, **344**
Bonfire Night, 262, **262**
Bonica '82, 54, 247, **248**
Bonn, 247, **248**
Bonnie Prince Charlie's Rose *see* Maxima
Bonnie Scotland, 376
Bonsoir, 376
Botzaris, **165**, 166
Boule de Nanteuil, 146
Boule de Neige, 329, **329**
Bouquet de la Mariée *see* Aimée Vibert
Bouquet d'Or, 15, 339, **340**
Bourbon Queen, 14, **14**, 329, **329**
Bourbon Rose *see* R. × *borboniana*
Boys' Brigade, 299, **299**
Brandy, 376
Brass Ring *see* Peek a Boo
Breath of Life, 238
Bredon, 366
Breeze, 315
Breeze Hill, 315
Brenda Colvin, 219
Brennus, 324, **324**
Briarcliff, 376, **376**
Bride, The, 350, **350**
Bright Smile, 262
Brightside Cream, 17, **18**, 351
Broadway, 376, **377**
Brother Cadfael, 366, **366**
Brown Velvet, 262
Buccaneer, 377
Buck's Fizz, **262**, 263
Buff Beauty, 22, **28**, **94**, 95, **98**, 224, **224**
Buffalo Bill *see* Regensberg
Bullata, 153
Burgund '81 *see* Loving Memory
Burgundian Rose *see* Pompon de Bourgogne
Burma Star, 263
Burnet Rose *see* R. *pimpinellifolia*
Burning Sky *see* Paradise
Burr Rose *see* R. *roxburghii*
Butterfly Wings, 248

Butterscotch, 238
Buttons, 299
By Appointment, 263, **263**

Cabbage Rose *see* R. × *centifolia*
Cadenza, 315
Cairngorm, 263
Callisto, 224
Calocarpa, 204
Calypso *see* Blush Boursault
Camaieux, 146, **146**
Cambridge Rose, 377
Camellia Rose, 324
Cameo, 257, **257**
Can Can, 377
Canadian White Star, 377
Canary Bird, 74, 108, 142, **142**
Candeur Lyonnaise, 355
Candy Rose, 288, **288**
Canina Abbotswood *see* Abbotswood
Cantab, 202
Cantabrigiensis, 50, **50**, 136, **136**
Canterbury, 248
Capitaine Basroger, 157, **157**
Capitaine John Ingram, 157
Captain Christy Climbing, 411, **412**
Captain Hayward Climbing, 28, 355, **355**
Cardinal de Richelieu, 146, **147**
Cardinal Hume, 54, 248, **248**
Carefree Beauty, 288
Carmen, 205, **205**
Carmenetta, 182
Carnation, 351
Carolin *see* Coralin
Carolyn *see* Coralin
Cary Grant, 377
Casino, 58, 238, **238**
Caterpillar *see* Pink Drift
Catherine de Würtemberg, 157
Catherine Guillot *see* Michel Bonnet
Catherine Mermet, 344, **344**
Catherine Seyton, 180
Cécile Brünner, 56, 324, **324**
Cécile Brünner Climbing, 324, **324**
Cécile Brünner White, 325
Celeste *see* Celestial
Celestial, 92, 175, **175**
Célina, 157
Céline Forestier, 15, **15**, 339
Celsiana, 166
Centenaire de Lourdes, 44, **44**, 263, **263**
Centfeuilles des Peintres *see* Rose des Peintres
Cerise Bouquet, 202, **202**
Champagne Cocktail, 263
Champion, 377
Champion of the World, 355
Champlain, 193

Champneys' Pink Cluster, 15, **34**, 339
Champs-Elysées, 377
Chanelle, 43, 263, **263**
Chapeau de Napoléon, 157, **157**
Chaplin's Pink, **68**, 315, **315**
Chaplin's Pink Climber *see* Chaplin's Pink
Chaplin's Pink Companion, 315
Charles Austin, 49, **49**, 366
Charles Aznavour, 264
Charles de Mills, 146, **146**
Charles Dingee *see* William R. Smith
Charles Gater, 355
Charles Lawson, 329
Charles Lefèbvre, 355, **355**
Charles Mallerin, 36
Charles Rennie Mackintosh, 366
Charleston, 264
Charlotte Armstrong, 63
Charmain, 366
Charme de Vienne *see* Vienna Charm
Charming Vienna *see* Vienna Charm
Château de Clos Vougeot Climbing, 411, **411**
Chaucer, 50, 366
Cherish, 264
Cherokee Rose *see* R. *laevigata*
Chesham's Choice, 423
Cheshire Life, 377
Cheshire Rose *see* Maxima
Chestnut Rose *see* R. *roxburghii*
Chevy Chase, 312, **312**
Chianti, 49, **49**, 172
Chicago Peace, 377, **377**
China Rose *see* R. *chinensis*
Chinatown, 39, **39**, 68, **98**, 264, **264**
Chloris, 175
Chorus, 264
Christian Dior, 377, **378**
Christine Climbing, 411
Chromatella *see* Cloth of Gold
Chrysler Imperial, 378, **378**
Chuckles, 264
Cider Cup, 299
Cilla, 378
Cinderella, 55, 299, **299**
Cinnamon Rose *see* R. *majalis*
Circus, 41, 67, 264
City of Belfast, 264, **264**
City of Birmingham, 264, **265**
City of Leeds, 264
City of London, 248
City of Portsmouth, 264
City of York, 238, **238**
Clair Matin, 58, 238
Claire Jacquier, 339
Claire Rose, 366, **366**
Clarissa, 57, **57**, **298**, 299
Clementina Carbonieri, 344, **344**

Clementine *see* Janet's Pride
Cleo, 378
Clifton Moss *see* White Bath
Clio, 355
Cloth of Gold, 339
Clotilde Soupert, 257
Clydebank Centenary, 264, **264**
Clytemnestra, **78**, 224, **224**
Cocktail, 248, **249**
Coeur d'Amour *see* Red Devil
Colcestria, 239
Colibri, 56, 300
Colibri '79, 300
Colorama, 378
Colorbreak *see* Brown Velvet
Colour Wonder, 36, 378
Columbia Climbing, 239
Commandant Beaurepaire, 330, **330**
Common Monthly *see* Old Blush
Common Moss, **9**, 158
Communis *see* Common Moss
Compassion, 58, 239, **239**
Comte de Chambord, 13, 69, **169**
Comtesse Cécile de Chabrillant, 355, **356**
Comtesse d'Oxford *see* Countess of Oxford
Comtesse de Labarthe *see* Duchesse de Brabant
Comtesse de Murinais, 158
Comtesse de Turin *see* Mme Wagram
Comtesse du Cayla, 325, **325**
Comtesse Ouwaroff *see* Duchesse de Brabant
Comtesse Vandal, 378, **378**
Comtesse Vandal Climbing, 411
Condesa de Sastago, 37
Conditorum, 148
Congratulations, 36, 378, **379**
Conrad Ferdinand Meyer, **204**, 205
Conservation, 300, **300**
Constance Spry, **26**, 48, 49, 239, **239**
Cooper's Burmese, **116**, 128
Copenhagen, 248, **249**
Coquette des Blanches, 330
Coral Dawn, 24, 239, **239**
Coral Reef, 300
Coralie, 166
Coralin, 300
Cornelia, **21**, 22, 225, **225**
Corona de Oro *see* Gold Crown
Corso, 378
Coryana *see* R. × *coryana*
Corylus, 52, 52, 205, **205**
Cosimo Ridolfi, 148, **148**
Cottage Rose, 366
Countess of Oxford, 355
Country Dancer, 248
Country Lady, 378

Country Living, 366, **367**
Countryman, The, **370**, 371
Coupe d'Hébé, 330, **330**
Couronne d'Or *see* Gold Crown
Coxswain, The, 408
Cramoisi Picoté, 148
Cramoisi Supérieur, 12, 17, 325, **325**
Cramoisi Supérieur Climbing, 325
Crépuscule, 339, **339**
Cressida, 366
Crested Jewel, 158
Crested Moss *see* Chapeau de Napoléon
Cricri, 300, **300**
Crimson Boursault *see* Amadis
Crimson Conquest, **85**, 413
Crimson Globe, 158
Crimson Glory, 36, 37, 42, 379
Crimson Glory Climbing, 413
Crimson Rambler, 60, 231
Crimson Showers, 315
Cristata *see* Chapeau de Napoléon
Crown Prince, 355
Cuisse de Nymphe *see* Maiden's Blush Great
Cuisse de Nymphe Emue, 11
Culverbrae, 206, **206**
Cupid, 413, **413**
Curley Pink, 379, **379**
Cymbeline, 249
Cynthia Brooke, 379, **380**

D'Aguesseau, 148, **148**
Daily Mail Rose Climbing *see* Mme Edouard Herriot Climbing
Daily Sketch, 265
Dainty Bess, 379, **381**
Dainty Dinah, 300
Dainty Maid, 39, 265
Daisy Hill, 172
Dame Edith Helen, 31, **31**, 379, 381
Dame of Sark, 265
Dame Wendy, 265, **265**
Danaë, 21, 66, **224**, 225
Danse de Feu, 58, 239, **240**
Danse des Sylphes, 240
Daphne, 225
Dapple Dawn, 249
Dark Lady, 366
Darling Flame, 56, 300
Dave Hessayon, 381
Daybreak, 225
De la Grifferaie, 22, 230, 231
Dean Hole, 344
Dearest, 42, 265, **265**
Deb's Delight, 366
Debutante, 315, **315**
Deep Secret, 381
Delambre, 169
Delge *see* Centenaire de Lourdes

Delicata, 206
Dembrowski, 356
Denham, 381
Dentelle de Malines, 249
Deschamps, 339
Desprez à Fleurs Jaunes, 341, 341
Deuil de Paul Fontaine, 158
Devoniensis, 63, 344, 344
Diamond Jubilee, 34, 381, 381
Dianthiflora see Fimbriata
Dick Koster, 257
Dickson's Jubilee see Lovely Lady
Dickson's Flame, 42
Dicky see Anisley Dickson
Diorama, 381
Direktor Benschop see City of York
Disco Dancer, 265
Doctor, The, 34, 34, 108
Dr A. J. Verhage, 382
Dr Andry, 356, 356
Dr Debat, 63
Dr Eckener, 206, 206
Dr Grill, 344, 345
Dr Huey, 108, 315, 316, 423
Dr Jackson, 249
Dr John Snow, 382
Dr McAlpine, 382
Dr R. Maag see Colorama
Dr W. Van Fleet, 24, 59, 316
Dr Wolfgang Poschl see Canadian White Star
Dog Rose see R. canina
Dolly Parton, 381
Don Juan, 240
Donald Prior, 63
Doncasterii, 67, 197, 197
Doreen, 381
Doris Tysterman, 381, 381
Dorola see Benson & Hedges Special
Dorothy Perkins, 38, 82, 315
Dorothy Wheatcroft, 67, 249, 250
Dortmund, 193
Double Delight, 381, 381
Double French Rose see R. gallica officinalis
Double Marbled Pink see Scotch Double White
Double Pennsylvanian Rose, The see R. carolina plena
Double Pink see Scotch Double White
Double Yellow Forms, 138
Doubloons, 311
Dove, 366
Dreaming Spires, 240
Dreamland, 266
Dresden Doll, 56, 56, 158
Dublin Bay, 240, 240
Duc d'Angoulême see Duchesse d'Angoulême
Duc de Fitzjames, 148
Duc de Guiche, 148, 148
Duc de Rohan see Duchesse de Rohan
Duchess of Portland, 2, 13, 170, 170

Duchesse d'Angoulême, 148, 149
Duchesse d'Auerstädt, 341, 341
Duchesse de Brabant, 345, 345
Duchesse de Buccleugh, 149
Duchesse de Montebello, 149, 149
Duchesse de Rohan, 153
Duchesse de Verneuil, 158
Duchesse d'Istrie see William Lobb
Duet, 382, 382
Duftgold see Fragrant Gold
Duftwolke see Fragrant Cloud
Duftzauber '84 see Royal William
Duke of Edinburgh, 356
Duke of Wellington, 356, 356
Duke of Windsor, 37, 379, 382
Duke of York, 325
Dundee Rambler, 216
Dunwich Rose, 138, 138
Dupontii see R. × dupontii
Dupuy Jamain, 18, 19, 356
Dusky Maiden, 39, 39, 40, 109, 266, 266
Düsterlohe, 216
Dutch Gold, 382
Dwarfking, 300

Earldomensis, 136
Easlea's Golden Rambler, 316
Easter Morn see Easter Morning
Easter Morning, 56, 300
Eclair, 356, 356
Eddie's Crimson, 50, 199
Eddie's Jewel, 50, 50, 199
Eden Rose, 382
Eden Rose Climbing, 413
Eden Rose '88, 240
Edith Bellenden, 180
Edith Holden, 266
Edwardian Lady, The, see Edith Holden
Eglantine Rose see R. eglanteria
Eleanor, 300, 300
Electron see Mullard Jubilee
Elegance, 316
Elina see Peaudouce
Elisa Boelle, 356
Elizabeth Harkness, 32, 382, 382
Elizabeth of Glamis, 42, 43, 43, 266, 266
Ellen, 367
Ellen Poulsen, 38, 39
Ellen Willmott, 382, 383
Elmshorn, 249, 250
Else Poulsen, 39, 44, 66
Emanuel, 367
Emily Gray, 6, 316, 316
Empereur du Maroc, 356
Emperor of Morocco see Empereur du Maroc

Empress Josephine, 25, 149
Ena Baxter, 383
Ena Harkness, 32, 32, 36, 383
Ena Harkness Climbing, 413
Enfant de France, 356, 357
Engineer's Rose see Crimson Rambler
English Elegance, 367
English Garden, 367, 367
English Miss, 42, 43, 266
Eos, 199, 199
Erfurt, 250, 250
Erinnerung an Brod, 311
Ernest H. Morse, 36, 383, 383
Eroica, 383
Erotika see Eroica
Escapade, 42, 43, 266, 266
Esmeralda see Keepsake
Essex, 289, 289
Estrellita de Oro see Baby Gold Star
Ethel, 316, 317
Etoile de Hollande, 37, 37, 46, 383, 383
Etoile de Hollande Climbing, 413
Etoile de Lyon, 345, 345
Etude, 240, 240
Eugène E. Marlitt, 330
Eugène Fürst, 357, 357
Eugénie Guinoisseau, 158, 158
Euphrates, 118, 118
Europeana, 266, 267
Eva, 46, 225
Evangeline, 316, 316
Evelyn, 49, 367, 371
Evelyn Fison, 108, 266, 267
Evening Star, 267
Everest, 357
Everest Double Fragrance, 47, 47, 267, 267
Excelsa, 24, 24, 94, 108, 316
Exception see Märchenland
Eyeopener, 289, 289
Eyepaint, 267

F. J. Grootendorst, 206, 207
Fabvier, 325, 325
Fair Bianca, 367, 367
Fairy, The, 22, 54, 258, 259
Fairy Changeling, 289
Fairy Damsel, 54, 289, 289
Fairy Moss, 158
Fairy Rose see Minima
Fairyland, 54, 105, 289, 290
Falkland, 138
Fantin Latour, 93, 153, 154
Fashion, 41, 41, 63, 267
Fashion Climbing, 286
Fashion Flame, 301
Fée des Neiges see Iceberg
Felicia, 21, 225, 226
Félicité, 383
Félicité Bohain, 159
Félicité et Perpétue, 24, 310, 310
Félicité Parmentier, 175, 175
Fellemberg, 325, 325

Fennica see Invincible
Ferdinand de Lesseps, 357
Ferdinand Pichard, 357, 357
Ferdy, 55, 289
Fergie, 267
Field Rose, The see R. arvensis
Fimbriata, 206, 206
Financial Times Centenary, 367
Finstar see Mini Metro
Fiona, 54, 290, 290
Fire Princess, 301
Firecracker, 267
First Love, 383, 383
First Prize, 383
Fisher and Holmes see Fisher Holmes
Fisher Holmes, 357
Fisherman's Friend, 367
Flaming Peace see Kronenbourg
Flamingo Meidiland, 290
Flora, 311
Flora McIvor, 180, 180
Florence Nightingale, 267
Flower Carpet, 290
Flower Girl see Sea Pearl
For You see Pour Toi
Forgotten Dreams, 384
Fortuné Besson see Georg Arends
Fortune's Double Yellow, 16, 16, 345
Fountain, 67, 250, 250
Fragrant Cloud, 109, 384, 384
Fragrant Cloud Climbing, 413
Fragrant Delight, 109, 267
Fragrant Dream, 384
Fragrant Gold, 384
Francesca, 22, 225, 225
Francine Austin, 290
Francis Dubreuil, 344, 345
Francis E. Lester, 231, 231
François Juranville, 317, 317
Frank Naylor, 250
Frau Astrid Späth Striped see Astrid Späth Striped
Frau Dagmar Hartopp see Fru Dagmar Hartopp
Frau Karl Druschki, 18, 19, 36, 44, 95, 108, 357
Frau Karl Druschki Climbing, 357
Fräulein Octavia Hesse, 317
Fred Loads, 250, 250
Fred Streeter, 200
Freegold see Penelope Keith
Freiherr von Marschall, 345
French Lace, 267, 267
French Rose see R. gallica
Frensham, 42, 42, 267, 268
Frenzy, 44, 268
Frohsinn see Joyfulness
Fru Dagmar Hartopp, 6, 7, 52, 206, 207

Fru Dagmar Hastrup see Fru Dagmar Hartopp
Frühlingsanfang, 138, 139
Frühlingsduft, 138, 138
Frühlingsgold, 20, 74, 138, 138
Frühlingsmorgen, 20, 139, 139
Frühlingsschnee, 139
Frühlingstag, 139
Frühlingszauber, 139
Fugue, 240
Fulgens, 330
Fulton Mackay, 384

Gabriel Noyelle, 159
Gail Borden, 384
Galway Bay, 240
Garden Party, 384
Gardenia, 317, 317
Garland, The, 61, 75, 221, 221
Garnette, 46, 106, 268
Gavolda see Cricri
Gay Gordons, 384, 385
Général Galliéni, 345
General Jack see Général Jacqueminot
Général Jacqueminot, 36, 357, 358
Général Kléber, 159, 159
General MacArthur Climbing, 34, 413
Général Schablikine, 345, 346
Gentle Touch, 42, 56, 57, 105, 301, 301
Georg Arends, 358, 358
George IV see Rivers George IV
George Will, 207
Georges Vibert, 149
Georgie Girl see Wishing
Geraldine, 268, 268
Geranium, 50, 51, 67, 91, 200, 200
Gerbe Rose, 318
Gertrude Jekyll, 368, 368
Ghislaine de Féligonde, 60, 60, 231, 231
Gilda, 268
Gina Lollobrigida, 384
Gingernut, 301
Gioia see Peace
Gipsy Boy, 330, 330
Giulietta, 330
Glad Tidings, 268, 268
Glenfiddich, 42, 268
Gloire de Bruxelles, 358, 358
Gloire de Dijon, 58, 58, 346, 346
Gloire de Ducher, 358, 358
Gloire de France, 149
Gloire de Guilan, 166, 166
Gloire de l'Exposition see Gloire de Bruxelles
Gloire de Paris see Anna de Diesbach
Gloire des Mousseux, 159, 159
Gloire des Rosomanes, 12, 325, 326

Gloire d'un Enfant d'Hiram, 358
Gloire Lyonnaise, 358, 358
Gloria Dei see Peace
Gloria Mundi, 55, 257, 257
Glory of Edzell, 139, 139
Goethe, 159
Gold Badge see Gold Bunny
Gold Bunny, 268, 269
Gold Coin, 301
Gold Crown, 384
Gold of Ophir see Fortune's Double Yellow
Goldbusch, 180, 180
Golden Angel, 301
Golden Chersonese, 50, 134, 134
Golden Dawn Climbing, 413
Golden Days, 384
Golden Glow, 318
Golden Jubilee, 385
Golden Meillandina see Rise 'n' Shine
Golden Melody, 385, 385
Golden Moss, 159
Golden Quill, 268
Golden Rambler see Alister Stella Gray
Golden Rose of China see R. hugonis
Golden Salmon Superior, 257, 257
Golden Sceptre see Spek's Yellow
Golden Sceptre Climbing see Spek's Yellow Climbing
Golden Showers, 58, 58, 240, 240, 241
Golden Slippers, 41, 269
Golden Sunblaze see Rise 'n' Shine
Golden Times, 385
Golden Wave see Dr A. J. Verhage
Golden Wings, 20, 50, 132, 139
Golden Years, 269
Goldfinch, 231, 232
Goldilocks, 41, 63
Goldkrone see Gold Crown
Goldsmith see Simba
Goldstar, 385
Goldstern see Goldstar
Grace Abounding, 67, 269
Grace Darling, 345
Grace de Monaco, 385, 386
Graham Thomas, 50, 368, 368
Grand Hotel, 242
Grand Masterpiece, 386
Grandmaster, 250
Grandmère Jenny, 36, 386
Grandmère Jenny Climbing, 413, 413
Grandpa Dickson, 31, 108, 386, 386
Great Double White see Maxima
Great Ormond Street, 47, 47, 269, 269
Great Western, 331

Green Diamond, 301
Green Rose, The *see* Viridiflora
Greenmantle, 181, **181**
Greensleeves, 269
Grootendorst Supreme, 207
Gros Choux d'Hollande, 331
Grouse, 54, 290, **291**
Grüss an Aachen, 44, **45**, 269
Grüss an Coburg, 346
Grüss an Teplitz, 326
Guernsey Love, **300**, 301
Guiding Spirit, 301
Guinée, 413, **414**
Gustav Grünerwald, 386, **386**
Gypsy Jewel, 301

Hamburger Phoenix, 58, 193
Hampshire, 291
Handel, 58, 242, **242**
Handout *see* Tranquillity
Hannah Gordon, 269
Hans Mackart, 358
Hansa, 52, 207, **207**
Happy Hour, 301
Happy Thought, 301
Harison's Yellow *see* R. × harisonii
Harold Macmillan, 270, **270**
Harry Maasz, 172, **172**
Harry Wheatcroft, 386, **386**
Harvest Fayre, 270, **270**
Headleyensis, 136
Headliner, 386
Heart Throb *see* Paul Shirville
Heather Muir, 142
Heaven Scent, 270
Hebe's Lip, 181
Hector Deane, 386
Heidekönigin *see* Pheasant
Heidelberg, 251
Heinrich Münch, 359
Heinrich Schultheis, 359, **359**
Heirloom, 386, **386**
Helen Knight, 50, 134
Helen Traubel, 34, **34**, 386
Hello, 301
Helmut Schmidt *see* Simba
Henri Foucquier, 149, **150**
Henri Martin, 159, **160**
Henry Kelsey, 193
Henry Nevard, 359
Her Majesty, 359
Herbstfeuer, 181, **181**
Heritage, 368
Hermosa, 326
Hero, 369
Heros, 46
Hertfordshire, 291, **291**
Herzog von Windsor *see* Duke of Windsor
Hiawatha, 60, 231
Hidcote Gold, 142
Hidcote Yellow *see* Lawrence Johnston
Highdownensis, 200, **200**

Highfield, 242
Highland Laddie, 270
Highlight, 42
Hilda Murrell, 369
Hillieri, 200, **200**
Hippolyte, **144**, 149
Holy Rose, The *see* R. × richardii
Hombre, 301
Home Sweet Home Climbing, 414, **414**
Homère, 17, 346, **346**
Hon. Lady Lindsay, 251
Honeybunch, 302
Honeymoon, 45, 270
Honigmond *see* Honeymoon
Honor, 387
Honorine de Brabant, 331
Horace Vernet, 359
Horstmann's Rosenresli, 270, **271**
Hotline, 302, **302**
Hudson Bay Rose *see* R. blanda
Hugh Dickson, 31, 95, **95**, 359
Hula Girl, 302
Hulthemia persica, 118
×*Hulthemosa hardii*, 118
Hume's Blush Tea-scented China, 16, **16**, 346
Humpty Dumpty, 55
Hunslett Moss, 159
Hunter, 207, **209**

Iceberg, 45, **46**, 72, 105, 108, 270, **271**
Iceberg Climbing, 286, **287**
Iced Ginger, 270
Ilse Krohn Superior, 242
Immensee *see* Grouse
Impatient, 270
Incarnata *see* Maiden's Blush Great
Incense Rose *see* R. primula, 141
Independence, 36, 42
Indian Summer, 387
Ingrid Bergman, 387, **387**
Ingrid Weibull *see* Showbiz, 282
Inner Wheel, 271
Intermezzo, 387
Intrigue, 271
Invincible, 271
Ipsilanté, 149
Irene Churruca *see* Golden Melody
Irene of Denmark, 271, **272**
Irene von Dänemark *see* Irène of Denmark
Irène Watts, 44, **44**, 272, **272**
Irish Beauty *see* Elizabeth of Glamis
Irish Elegance, 30, 387
Irish Fireflame Climbing, 414
Irish Gold *see* Grandpa Dickson
Irish Mist, 272

Irish Summer *see* Irish Mist
Irish Wonder *see* Evelyn Fison
Isabella Sprunt, 346
Iskra *see* Sparkling Scarlet
Isle of Man *see* Manx Queen
Isobel Harkness, 387
Ispahan, 166, **166**
Ivory Fashion, 272, **272**

Jack Rose *see* Général Jacqueminot
Jacobite Rose *see* Maxima
Jacqueline du Pré, 251, **251**
Jacques Cartier, 13, 169, **170**
James Bourgault, 359
James Mason, 13, 52-3, **52**, **143**, 149
James Mitchell, 159
James Veitch, 159, **161**
Janet B. Wood, 22, 216
Janet's Pride, 181, **181**
Japonica *see* Mousseux du Japon
Jardins de Bagatelle, 387
Jaune Desprez *see* Desprez à Fleurs Jaunes
Jayne Austin, 251
Jean Ducher, 346
Jean Lafitte, 311
Jean Mermoz, 257
Jean Rosenkrantz, 359
Jean Sisley, 387
Jeanne d'Arc, 175
Jeanne de Montfort, 161
Jeanette Heller *see* William R. Smith
Jema, 387
Jennifer Hart, 387
Jenny Duval, 149
Jenny Robinson, 302, **302**
Jenny Wren, 272
Jens Munk, 207, **208**
Jersey Beauty, 318
Jiminy Cricket, 41, **41**, 272, **272**
Joan Ball, 302, **302**
Joanna Hill, 387, **388**
Jocelyn, 272, 272
John Cabot, **193**, 194
John F. Kennedy, 388
John Franklin, 251
John Hopper, 359, **359**
John Waterer, 388
Johnnie Walker, 388
Josephine Bruce, 33, **33**, 388
Josephine Bruce Climbing, 414
Josephine Wheatcroft *see* Rosina
Joseph's Coat, 251, **251**
Joyce Northfield, 388
Joyfulness, 272
Judy Fischer, 302, **302**
Jules Margottin, 359
Julia Mannering, 181
Julia's Rose, 388
Julie Cussons, 272
Juliet, 359
June Time, 302
Juno, 154, **154**
Just Joey, 33, 388, **388**

Kaiserin Auguste Viktoria, 359, **359**
Kan-pai, 388
Karen Poulsen, 39
Karl Förster, 139, **139**
Karl Herbst, 36
Karlsruhe, 194, **194**
Karolyn *see* Coralin
Kassel, 251, **251**
Katharina Zeimet, 257
Kathleen, 225, **227**
Kathleen Ferrier, 252, **252**
Kathleen Harrop, 336, 337
Kathryn Morley, 369
Kazanlik, **166**, 167
Keepsake, 388
Kent, 54, 291, **291**
Kew Rambler, 312, **312**
Kiftsgate, 61, 79, **218**, 219, **219**
Kiki Rose *see* Pink Drift
Kim, 272
King's Ransom, **388**, 389
Kirsten Poulsen, 39, 66
Köln am Rhein, 242
Königin der Rosen *see* Colour Wonder
Königin von Dänemark, 175, **176**
Königliche Hoheit *see* Royal Highness
Kordes' Perfecta *see* Perfecta
Korona, 45, 273, **273**
Korona Climbing, 286
Korp, 273
Korresia, 273
Korzaun *see* Royal William
Ko-Sai *see* Mikado
Kronenbourg, 389, **390**
Kronprinzessin Viktoria, 331, **331**

L. D. Braithwaite, 369, **369**
La Belle Distinguée, 181, **181**
La Belle Marseillaise *see* Fellemberg
La Belle Sultane, 149, **151**
La Follette, 322
La France, 29, **29**, 389
La Mortola, 92, 217, **217**
La Noblesse, 154
La Paloma '85, 273
La Petite Duchesse *see* La Belle Distinguée
La Plus Belle des Ponctuées, 150
La Reine, 360
La Reine Victoria, **13**, 14, 331, **331**
Le Havre, 360
Le Rêve, 135
Le Vésuve, 326
La Rosière *see* Prince Camille de Rohan
La Royale *see* Maiden's Blush Great
La Rubaneé *see* Village Maid
La Séduisante *see* Maiden's Blush Great
La Sevillana, 252, **252**
La Vésuve, 326, **326**
La Ville de Bruxelles, **166**, 167
La Virginale *see* Maiden's Blush Great

Labrador Rose *see* R. blanda
L'Abundance, 341
Lady, 389
Lady, The, 408
Lady Alice Stanley, 389
Lady Barnby, 389
Lady Beauty, 389
Lady Belper, 389, **389**
Lady Cecily Gibson, 273
Lady Curzon, 209
Lady Diana, 389
Lady Donaldson *see* Mary Donaldson
Lady Elgin *see* Thaïs
Lady Emily Peel, 341
Lady Forteviot, 389
Lady Hillingdon, **90**, 346
Lady Hillingdon Climbing, 346
Lady Mary Fitzwilliam, 29, 30, 389
Lady Penzance, 181, **181**
Lady Plymouth, 347
Lady Roberts, 347
Lady Romsey, 47, **47**, 105, 273, **273**
Lady Rose, 389
Lady Sonia, 252
Lady Sylvia, **106**, 109, 389, **389**
Lady Sylvia Climbing, 414
Lady Waterlow, 414
Lafter, 50, **50**, 252, **252**
Lagoon, 273
Lais *see* Leys Perpetual
Lakeland, 108, 389
Lamarque, 15, 16, **90**, 341
Landora *see* Sunblest
Laneii, **9**, 161
Lane's Moss *see* Laneii
Langdale Chase, 273
Las Vegas, 391
Laura Ashley, 291, **291**
Laura Ford, 242, **242**
Lauré Davoust, 233
Laurence Olivier, 273
Lavaglow *see* Intrigue
Lavaglut *see* Intrigue
Lavender Jewel, 302, **303**
Lavender Lace, 302
Lavender Lassie, 225, **227**
Lavender Pinocchio, 41, 273
Lavender Sweetheart, 302
Lavinia, 242
Lawinia *see* Lavinia
Lawrence Johnston, 135, **135**
Laxa *see* R. coriifolia froebelii
Le Havre, 360
Le Rêve, 135
Le Vésuve, 326
Leander, 369
Leaping Salmon, 242
Leda, 167, **167**
Lee's Crimson Perpetual *see* Rose du Roi
Lemon Delight, 303
Len Turner, 273
Lens Pink *see* Dentelle de Malines
Léonie Lamesch, 273
Léontine Gervais, 318

Lettuce-leaved Rose *see* Bullata
Leuchtstern, 233
Leverkusen, 58, 194, **195**
Lewison Gower, 331
Leys Perpetual, 341
Lichtkönigin Lucia, 252, **252**
Lilac Charm, **39**, 40, 274
Lilian Austin, 369
Lilli Marlene, 45, **46**, **101**, 274, **274**
Lincoln Cathedral, 391, **391**
Liselle *see* Royal Romance
Litakor *see* Lolita
Little Artist, 303
Little Breeze, 303
Little Buckaroo, **302**, 303
Little Flirt, 56, 303, **303**
Little Gem, 161, **161**
Little Jewel, 303
Little Prince, 303, **303**
Little White Pet *see* White Pet
Liverpool Echo, 274
Liverpool Remembers, 391
Living Fire, **268**, 274
Lloyds of London, 274
Lolita, 391
Lollipop, 304
Long John Silver, 311
Lord Penzance, 181
L'Oréal Trophy, 252
Lorraine Lee, 322
Los Angeles, 34, 391
L'Ouche, 326
Louis XIV, 326, **326**
Louis Gimard, 161
Louis Philippe, 326
Louise d'Arzens, 341
Louise Odier, 14, 331, **332**
Louisville Lady, 391
Love, 391, **391**
Lovely Lady, 391
Lovers' Meeting, 391
Loving Memory, 391
Lucetta, 369
Lucy Ashton, 182
Luis Brinas, 391
Lutea *see* R. pimpinellifolia lutea
Lykkefund, 219
Lyon Rose, 391

Ma Perkins, 41, **41**, **274**, 275
Ma Ponctuée, 161
Mabel Dot, 304
Mabel Morrison, 360, **360**
Macartney Rose, The *see* R. bractea
Macrantha Raubritter *see* Raubritter
Mme A. Meilland *see* Peace
Mme Abel Chatenay, 29, 415
Mme Alfred Carrière, 15, **15**, 342
Mme Alice Garnier, 318
Mme Antoine Mari, 347
Mme Berkeley, 347, **347**
Mme Bravy, 347

Mme Butterfly, 34, 109, 393, 393
Mme Butterfly Climbing, 415
Mme Caroline Testout Climbing, 29, 30, 415
Mme d'Arblay, 59, 233
Mme de la Roche-Lambert, 161, 162
Mme de Sancy de Parabère, 86, 196, 196
Mme de Sertot see Mme Bravy
Mme de Tartas, 17, 347, 347
Mme de Watteville, 347
Mme Driout, 342
Mme Dubost, 332
Mme Edouard Herriot, 35, 35
Mme Edouard Herriot Climbing, 415, 416
Mme Eliza de Vilmorin, 393
Mme Ernst Calvat, 332
Mme Eugène Marlitt see Eugène E. Marlitt
Mme Ferdinand Jamin see American Beauty
Mme Georges Bruant, 209, 210
Mme Grégoire Staechelin, 85, 91, 415
Mme Hardy, 72, 167, 167
Mme Hébert see Président de Sèze
Mme Henri Guillot Climbing, 416
Mme Isaac Pereire, 14, 332, 332
Mme Jules Gravereaux, 347, 347
Mme Knorr, 169
Mme Laurette Messimy, 326
Mme Lauriol de Barny, 332, 332
Mme Legras de St Germain, 176
Mme Lombard, 17, 347
Mme Louis Laperrière, 394, 394
Mme Louis Lévêque, 162, 162
Mme Neumann see Hermosa
Mme Norbert Levavasseur, 38
Mme Pierre Oger, 14, 332
Mme Plantier, 176, 176
Mme Scipion Cochet, 360
Mme Victor Verdier, 360, 361
Mme Wagram, 347, 348
Mme Zöetmans, 167, 167
Madeleine Selzer, 233, 233
Maestro, 391
Magenta, 252
Magic Carousel, 304
Magna Carta, 360
Magnifica, Frontispiece, 51, 182
Magnolia Rose, 344
Maiden's Blush Great, 10, 11, 92, 176, 176

Maiden's Blush Small, 176
Maigold, 98, 140
Mainzer Fastnacht see Blue Moon
Maitland White, 351, 351
Maître d'Ecole see Rose du Maître d'Ecole
Major see Rose des Peintres
Mala Rubinstein, 392
Malaga, 242, 242
Malandrone see Don Juan
Malcolm Sargent, 252, 253
Malmaison Rouge see Lewison Gower
Maltese Rose see Cécile Brünner
Malton see Fulgens
Maman Cochet, 17, 63, 347, 347, 348
Manettii, 342
Manning's Blush, 20, 182, 182
Manuela, 392
Manx Queen, 274, 275
Marbrée, 169
Marcel Bourgouin, 150
Märchenland, 252, 253
Marchioness of Londonderry, 360
Marchioness of Salisbury, 392, 392
Maréchal Davoust, 161, 161
Maréchal de Clerc see Touch of Class
Maréchal Niel, 90, 342
Margaret McGredy, 31
Margaret Merril, 42, 109, 275, 275
Margo Koster, 259
Marguerite Guillard, 360, 360
Marguerite Hilling, 51, 52, 67, 200
Maria Callas see Miss All-American Beauty
Marianne Tudor, 392
Marie Bugnet, 209
Marie de Blois, 161
Marie Lambert see Snowflake
Marie Louise, 167, 167
Marie Parvie, 275
Marie van Houtte, 348
Marie-Jeanne, 275
Marijke Koopman, 392
Marina, 275
Marion Harkness, 392
Marjorie Fair, 252, 253
Marjorie W. Lester see Lauré Davoust
Mark One see Apricot Sunblaze
Marlena, 45, 275, 275
Marquise Bocella see Jacques Cartier
Martha, 337
Martin Frobisher, 209, 209
Moje Hammarberg, 209
Mary Donaldson, 392
Mary Hayley Bell, 253, 253
Mary Manners, 209, 209
Mary Queen of Scots, 140
Mary Rose, 50, 369, 369

Mary Wallace, 318
Masquerade, 41, 275
Masquerade Climbing, 286
Master Hugh, 91, 198, 198
Matangi, 275, 275
Matthias Meilland, 275
Max Graf, 51, 51, 209, 209
Maxima, 11, 174, 176
Maurice Bernadin see Ferdinand de Lesseps
May Queen, 59, 59, 318, 318
McGredy's Yellow, 31, 31, 392, 392
Meadow Rose see R. blanda
Mechtilde von Neuerburg, 182
Medallion, 392
Meg, 414, 415
Meg Merrilies, 21, 182
Megiddo, 276
Meillandina, 304
Mélanie Lemaire see Hermosa
Melina see Sir Harry Pilkington
Melody Maker, 276, 276
Memento, 276
Memoria see Cécile Brünner
Merfaid, 61, 61, 63, 67, 86, 131, 131, 430
Merveille de Lyon, 360, 361
Message, 393
Meteor, 105, 276
Mevrouw Nathalie Nypels see Nathalie Nypels
Michel Bonnet, 332
Michèle Meilland, 36, 36, 392, 393
Michèle Torr see Honor
Micrugosa see R. × microgosa
Mignon see Cécile Brünner
Mignonette, 259
Mikado, 393
Mildred Scheel see Deep Secret
Milestone, 393
Miller, The, 393
Mini Metro, 304, 304
Minima, 305
Minnehaha, 108, 318, 318
Minuette see Darling Flame
Minuetto see Darling Flame
Mischief, 392, 393
Miss All-American Beauty, 393
Miss Atwood, 17, 17, 351
Miss Edith Cavell, 259
Miss Harp, 393
Miss Lawrance's Rose see Minima
Miss Lowe's Rose see Sanguinea
Mister Lincoln, 393
Mogador see Rose du Roi à Fleurs Pourpres
Mojave, 34, 394
Moje Hammarberg, 209
Mona Ruth, 304
Monique, 63, 394, 395
Mons. Paul Lédé Climbing see Paul Lédé Climbing
Mons. Tillier, 348, 348

Monsieur Pélisson see Pélisson
Montezuma, 108, 394
Monthly Rose see Old Blush
Mood Music, 304
Moonlight, 21, 66, 227, 227
Moriah, 394
Morletii, 92, 196, 197
Morning Jewel, 242
Mountbatten, 42, 254, 394
Mousseline see Alfred de Dalmas
Mousseux du Japon, 162
Moussu du Japon see Mousseux du Japon
Mozart, 227
Mr Bluebird, 304
Mrs Aaron Ward Climbing, 416
Mrs Anthony Waterer, 210, 210
Mrs B. R. Cant, 348
Mrs Campbell Hall, 348
Mrs Colville, 140
Mrs de Graw see Champion of the World
Mrs Dudley Cross, 348
Mrs F. W. Flight, 233
Mrs G. A. Van Rossem Climbing, 416
Mrs Harkness see Paul's Early Blush
Mrs Henry Morse, 31
Mrs Herbert Stevens Climbing, 31, 416
Mrs John Laing, 29, 361, 361
Mrs Jones see Centenaire de Lourdes
Mrs Oakley Fisher, 394, 394
Mrs Paul, 332
Mrs Pierre S. du Pont, 394
Mrs Sam McGredy, 394
Mrs Sam McGredy Climbing, 416
Mrs W. J. Grant, 30
Mrs Wakefield Christie Miller, 394
Mrs William Paul, 162
Mullard Jubilee, 394, 396
München Kindl see Anisley Dickson
Musk Rose, The see R. moschata
Mutabilis, 62, 326, 327
My Choice, 33, 33, 396, 396
My Valentine, 304
Myrrh-scented Rose, The see Splendens

Nancy Steen, 276, 276
Nanette, 150
Narrow Water, 220, 221
Nathalie Nypels, 44, 276, 276
National Trust, 396, 396
Néron, 150
Nestor, 150, 151
Nevada, 67, 74, 201, 201
New Dawn, 6, 24, 24, 59, 103, 318, 318

New Horizon, 276, 277
New Penny, 304
New Year see Arcadian
News, 40, 40, 277
Nigel Hawthorne, 117, 118
Night Light, 243
Nina Weibull, 277
Niphetos, 348, 348
Nivea see Aimée Vibert
Noella Nabonnand Climber, 348
Noisette, 15
Norfolk, 54, 291, 291
Northamptonshire, 291, 292
Norwich Castle, 47, 277, 277
Norwich Gold, 243
Norwich Pink, 243
Norwich Salmon, 243
Norwich Union, 47, 277, 277
Nova Zembla, 210, 212
Nozomi, 54, 54, 55, 105, 108, 292, 292
Nuage Parfumé see Fragrant Cloud
Nuits de Young, 162, 162
Nun, The, 371
Nur Mahal, 227, 227
Nymphenburg, 253, 254
Nyveldt's White, 81, 210, 211

Ocarina see Angela Rippon
Ocaru see Angela Rippon
Odorata see Hume's Blush Tea-scented China
Oeillet Flamand, 150
Oeillet Parfait, 150
Ohio, 313
Ohl, 150, 151
Ohlala see Olala
Olala, 277
Old Black see Nuits de Young
Old Blush, 12, 12, 14, 15, 57, 327
Old Crimson China see Slater's Crimson China
Old Master, 44, 277, 277
Old Pink Moss see Common Moss
Old Spanish Rose see Russelliana
Old Velvet Moss see William Lobb
Old Velvet Rose see Tuscany
Olympiad, 396, 396
Omar Khayyam, 51, 167, 168
Ombrée Parfaite, 150
Opa Pötschke see Precious Platinum
Opéra, 396
Ophelia, 34, 34, 109, 396
Ophelia Climbing, 416
Orange Honey, 304
Orange Meillandina see Orange Sunblaze
Orange Sensation, 44, 278, 278
Orange Silk, 278

Orange Sunblaze, 110, 304, 304
Orange Triumph, 45, 278, 278
Orangeade, 43, 278
Orangefield Rose, The, see Janet B. Wood
Oregold see Miss Harp
Orient Express, 396
Orléans Rose, 39
Ormiston Roy, 140
Orpheline de Juillet, 151
Othello, 369, 369

Pacemaker, 396
Pacific, 17, 351
Paddy McGredy, 278
Paint Box, 278
Paint-Pot, 305
Painted Damask see Leda
Painted Doll, 305
Painted Moon, 396, 397
Palissade Rose see Pheasant
Pallida see Old Blush
Pandora, 304, 305
Papa Gontier, 348, 349
Papa Hémeray, 327
Papa Meilland, 36, 36, 397
Papillon, 327, 327
Paprika, 46
Para Ti see Pour Toi
Parade, 58, 243, 243
Paradise, 397
Parfum de l'Hay see Rose à Parfum de l'Hay
Parkdirektor Riggers, 58, 58, 194, 194
Parkjewel see Parkjuwel
Parkjuwel, 254
Park's Yellow Tea-scented China, 16, 17, 349
Parkzierde, 332, 333
Parson's Pink see Old Blush
Partridge, 54, 292, 292
Party Girl, 305
Parvifolia see Pompon de Bourgogne
Pascali, 397
Paul Lédé Climbing, 416, 417
Paul Neyron, 18, 19, 361, 361
Paul Ricault, 361, 362
Paul Shirville, 397, 397
Paul Transon, 318
Paul Verdier, 332
Paulii, 292, 292
Paulii Rosea, 88, 292, 293
Paul's Early Blush, 361
Paul's Himalayan Musk, 73, 221
Paul's Lemon Pillar, 86, 416
Paul's Perpetual White, 221
Paul's Scarlet, 233, 233
Paul's Single White see Paul's Perpetual White
Pax, 21, 22, 227, 227
Peace, 31, 34, 35, 35, 397
Peach Blossom, 254
Peach Sunblaze, 305
Peachy White, 305
Pearl Drift, 292, 293

Pearl Meidiland, 293
Pearl of Canada see Perla de Alcañada
Peaudouce, 397, **397**
Peek-a-Boo, 57, 305
Peer Gynt, 397
Pélisson, 163
Penelope, 22, 227, **228**
Penelope Keith, 57, 305, 305
Penelope Plummer, 46, 278, **278**
Pensioners' Voice, 278
Penthouse, 397
Peon, 55, 56, 305
Perdita, 369, **370**
Perestroika, 305, **305**
Perfect Moment, 398
Perfecta, 36, **36**, 108, 397
Perfume Delight, 398, **398**
Pergolèse, 170
Perla Corail see Coralin
Perla de Alcañada, 306
Perla de Montserrat, 56, 360
Perle des Jardins, **16**, 349, **349**
Perle d'Or, **82**, 327, **327**
Pernille Poulsen, 278, **280**
Persian Musk Rose see R. moschata nastarana
Persian Yellow see R. foetida persiana
Petit Four, 306
Petite de Hollande, **112**, 154
Petite Junon de Hollande see Petite de Hollande
Petite Lisette, 154, **154**
Petite Orléanaise, 154, **154**
Pfander, 177
Pfander's Canina see Pfander
Pharisaer, 398
Pheasant, 54, 293
Phoebe, 306, **306**
Phoebe's Frilled Pink see Fimbriata
Phoenix, 306
Phyllis Bide, 60, **60**, 233, **234**
Picasso, 42, 278, **279**
Piccadilly, 31, **31**, 398
Piccolo, 280
Picture, 31, 398, **399**
Picture Climbing, 416
Pierre de Ronsard see Eden Rose
Pierre Notting, 363
Pike's Peak, 254
Pilgrim, The, **49**, 371
Pillarbox, 280
Pinata, 243
Pink Bells, 54, **294**, 293
Pink Chimo, 293
Pink Drift, 293
Pink Favourite, 399, **399**
Pink Form see R. moyesii 'Pink Form'
Pink Grootendorst, 211
Pink La Sevillana, 254
Pink Leda, 168
Pink Meillandina see Pink Sunblaze

Pink Parfait, 41, **42**, 67, 280
Pink Peace, 399
Pink Pearl, 399
Pink Perpétue, 24, 58, 103, 243, **243**
Pink Pixie see Pixie Rose
Pink Posy, 306
Pink Prosperity, 228
Pink Sunblaze, 306
Pink Wave, 293
Pinkie, 259
Pinkie Climber, 243, **243**
Pinocchio, 45, 280, **280**
Pinta, 37, **37**, 399
Pixie Rose, 306
Pleine de Grâce, 254
Plentiful, 280, **280**
Plum Pudding, 306
Poesie see Promise
Point du Jour see Gold Star
Polar Star, 37, 399
Polarstern see Polar Star
Polly, 399
Pompon Blanc Parfait, 176, **176**
Pompon de Bourgogne, 154, **155**
Pompon de Paris Climber, 327
Pompon de Paris Dwarf form, 327
Pompon des Dames see Petite de Hollande
Pompon Panachée, 151
Poppy Flash, 44, 280
Portland Rose see Duchess of Portland
Portland Trailblazer see Big Chief
Pot Black, 307
Pot o' Gold, 399
Potter & Moore, 369
Poulsen's Park Rose, 254
Poulsen's Yellow, 39
Pour Toi, 307
Prairie Belle see Queen of the Prairies
Prairie Princess, 254
Prairie Rose, The see R. setigera
Precious Platinum, 39, 399
Premier Amour see First Love
Première Ballerine see Prima Ballerina
President, The see Adam
Président de Sèze, **151**, 152
President Herbert Hoover, 399
President William Smith see William R. Smith
Prestige, 254
Pretty Jessica, 370
Prima Ballerina, 37, 109, 399, **399**
Prima Donna, 400
Prince, The, 371, **371**
Prince Camille de Rohan, 363
Prince Charles, 332, **334**
Prince Igor see Frenzy
Prince Meillandina, 307

Prince Starblaze see Prince Meillandina
Princess Margaret of England, 400
Princess Michael of Kent, 280
Princess Michiko, 280
Princess of Nassau, 221, **221**
Princesse Adélaide, 163
Princesse de Lamballe, 177
Princesse de Nassau see Princess of Nassau
Princesse Louise, 311
Princesse Marie, 311
Prioress, The, 371
Priscilla Burton, 280
Pristine, 400
Probuzini see Awakening
Prolifera de Redouté, 155
Prominent see Korp
Promise, 400
Prosperity, **21**, 22, 228, **228**
Prospero, 370
Proud Land, 400
Provence Rose see R. × centifolia
Pumila, 327
Purity, 318

Quatre Saisons, 8, 9, **9**, 11, 13, 14, 20, 168
Quatre Saisons Blanc Mousseux, 168
Queen Charlotte, 400, **400**
Queen Elizabeth, 41, **43**, 66, 105, 280, **281**
Queen Elizabeth Climbing, 286
Queen Elizabeth Rose, The see Queen Elizabeth
Queen Mab, 327
Queen Mother, 293, **293**
Queen Mother, The see August Seebauer
Queen Nefertiti, 370
Queen of Bedders, 334, **334**
Queen of Bourbons see Bourbon Queen
Queen of Denmark see Königin von Dänemark
Queen of Roses see Colour Wonder
Queen of the Prairies, 311
Queen of the Violets see Reine des Violettes

R. acicularis, 191
R. acicularis nipponensis, 191, **191**
R. agrestis, 173
R. × alba, 11, 175
R. × alba nivea see Semiplena
R. × alba suavolens see Semiplena
R. alpina see R. pendulina
R. amblyotis, 191
R. anemoneflora, 215

R. anemonoides see Anemone Rose
R. arkansana, 191
R. arvensis, 3, **4**, 5, 23, 61, 216, **216**
R. banksiae alba plena, 6, 92, **124**, 126
R. banksiae banksiae see R. banksiae alba plena
R. banksiae lutea, 7, 106, **125**, 126, 430
R. banksiae lutescens, **125**, 126
R. banksiae normalis, 126
R. banksiopsis, 191
R. beggeriana, 191
R. bella, 191
R. berberifolia see R. × Hulthemia persica
R. biebersteinii, 177
R. blanda, 5, 191
R. × borboniana, 329
R. bracteata, 6, 67, 129, **130**
R. britzensis, 177
R. brunonii, 6, 7, 92, 217, **217**
R. burgundica see Pompon de Bourgogne
R. californica, 191, **192**
R. californica plena, 191, **192**
R. × calocarpa see Calocarpa
R. canina, 3, **3**, 5, 8, 10, 108, **173**, 177, 423
R. canina 'Pfander' see Pfander
R. × cantabrigiensis see Cantabrigiensis
R. carolina, **5**, 187
R. carolina alba, 187
R. carolina plena, 187
R. caudata, 192
R. × centifolia, 8, **8**, 153
R. × centifolia alba see White Provence
R. × centifolia bullata see Lettuce-leaved Rose
R. × centifolia 'Major' see Rose des Peintres
R. × centifolia muscosa, 156
R. × centifolia variegata, 156
R. chinensis, 6, 11, **11**, 12, 16, 38, 55, 57, 62, 323
R. chinensis minima, 55, 326
R. cinnamomea see R. majalis
R. cinnamomea plena see R. majalis plena
R. × collina, 179
R. cooperi see Cooper's Burmese
R. coriifolia froebelii, 192, 423
R. × coryana, 192, **192**
R. corymbifera, 179
R. corymbulosa, 192
R. cymosa, 126
R. × damascena bifera see Quatre Saisons
R. × damascena trigintipetala see Kazanlik
R. × damascena versicolor see York and Lancaster
R. davidii, 192

R. davurica, 192
R. doncasterii see Doncasterii
R. × dumales, 179
R. dumetorum laxa see R. coriifolia froebelii
R. dunwichensis see Dunwich Rose
R. × dupontii, 217, **217**
R. earldomensis see Earldomensis
R. ecae, 134, **134**
R. eglanteria, 5, 20, **21**, **82**, 93, 179, **179**
R. fargesii, 201
R. farreri persetosa, 51, 93, **190**, 192
R. fedtschenkoana, 192
R. filipes, 6, 219, **219**
R. foetida, 7, 7, 20, 134, **135**
R. foetida bicolor, 7, 134, **135**
R. foetida persiana, 7, 30, 134, **135**
R. foliolosa, 5, **186**, 187
R. forrestiana, 192, **192**
R. × fortuniana, 126, **126**
R. × francofurtana see Empress Josephine
R. × francofurtana agatha see Agatha
R. gallica, 5, 8, 143
R. gallica 'Complicata', **79**, **148**, 148
R. gallica officinalis, 10, **10**, 11, 13, 145
R. gallica versicolor, 10, **10**, 145
R. gallica violacea see La Belle Sultane
R. gentiliana, 61, 219
R. gigantea, 6, 16, 57, 322, **322**
R. glauca, **91**, 92, 182, **182**
R. glutinosa see R. pulverulenta
R. gracilis see R. × involuta
R. graveolens see R. inodora
R. gymnocarpa, 5, **5**, 193
R. × hardii see × Hulthemosa hardii
R. × harisonii, 20, **20**, 138
R. headleyensis see Headleyensis
R. helenae, 61, 79, 219, **219**
R. × hemisphaerica, 7, 135
R. hemsleyana, 193
R. henryi, 219
R. × hibernica, 140, **140**
R. holodonta, 201
R. horrida see R. biebersteinii
R. hugonis, 50, 136, **136**
R. indica see R. chinensis
R. indica odorata see Hume's Blush
R. inermis morlettii see Morlettii
R. inodora, 183
R. × involuta, 136
R. jundzillii, 183
R. × kamtchatica, 193
R. × kochiana, 187, **187**
R. × kordesii, 36, 51, 58, 193, **193**

R. koreana, 136
R. laevigata, 6, 127, **127**, **128**
R. latibracteata, 194
R. × l'heritierana, 196
R. longicuspis, 220
R. luciae, 24, 59, 220, **220**
R. lutea see R. foetida
R. lutea punicea see R. foetida bicolor
R. macounii see R. woodsii
R. macrantha, 172, **172**
R. macrophylla, 67, 197
R. macrophylla rubricaulis see Rubricaulis
R. majalis, 198
R. majalis plena, 198
R. marginata see R. jundzillii
R. × mariae-graebnerae, 187
R. marretii, 198
R. maximowicziana, 198
R. melina, **198**, 199
R. micrantha, 183
R. microcarpa see R. cymosa
R. × micrugosa, 52, **198**, 199
R. × micrugosa alba, **198**, 199
R. mohavensis, 199
R. mollis, 183
R. moschata, 5, 8, 15, 22, 38, 57, 61, 220, **221**
R. moschata 'Autumnalis' see Autumnalis
R. moschata floribunda, 220
R. moschata grandiflora, 220
R. moschata nastarana, 220
R. moschata nepalensis see R. brunonii
R. moyesii, **6**, 7, 50, 66, 74, 199
R. moyesii 'Pink Form', 199
R. mulliganii, 222, **222**
R. multibracteata, **201**, 202
R. multiflora, 5, 6, 7, 22, 38, 57, 59, 60, 61, 108, 222, **223**, 423
R. multiflora carnea, 222, **223**
R. multiflora cathayensis, 222
R. multiflora grevillei see R. multiflora platyphylla
R. multiflora platyphylla, 222, **223**
R. multiflora watsoniana, 223
R. multiflora wilsonii, 223
R. murielae, 202
R. myriadenia, 214
R. nankiniensis see R. chinensis
R. nanothamnus, 202
R. nitida, 5, 52, **185**, 187
R. noisettiana manetti see Manetti
R. nutkana, 202, **202**, **203**
R. obtusifolia see R. inodora
R. × odorata see Hume's Blush Tea-scented China
R. × odorata ochroleuca see Park's Yellow Tea-scented China
R. omissa see R. sherardii
R. orientalis, 183
R. palustris, 5, 187

R. × paulii see Paulii
R. × paulii rosea see Paulii Rosea
R. pendulina, 202, 203
R. pendulina plena see Morlettii
R. persica see R. × Hulthemia persica
R. phoenicia, 8, 310
R. pimpinellifolia, 4, 5, 20, 50, 51, 76, 81, 92, 137, 137
R. pimpinellifolia altaica, 137, 137
R. pimpinellifolia andrewsii see Andrewsii
R. pimpinellifolia hispida, 137
R. pimpinellifolia lutea, 137
R. pimpinellifolia 'Nana', 137
R. pimpinellifolia spinosissima 'Altaica' see R. pimpinellifolia altaica
R. × pisocarpa, 203, 203
R. × polliniana, 310
R. polyantha grandiflora see R. gentiliana
R. pomifera see R. villosa
R. pomifera duplex see R. villosa duplex
R. × portlandica see Duchess of Portland
R. prattii, 203
R. primula, 51, 52, 93, 141
R. prubondiciana billieri, 200
R. × pteragonis, 141
R. pteragonis cantabrigiensis see Cantabrigiensis
R. pulverulenta, 183
R. pyrifera, 203
R. reversa, 141
R. × richardii, 172
R. roxburghii, 122, 123
R. roxburghii normalis, 123
R. roxburghii plena, 123, 123
R. rubella see R. × involuta
R. rubiginosa see R. eglanteria
R. rubra see R. gallica
R. rubrifolia see R. glauca
R. rubus, 310
R. × ruga see Ruga
R. rugosa, 6, 7, 51, 52, 76, 108, 204, 423
R. rugosa alba, 203, 204
R. rugosa atropurpurea see R. rugosa rubra
R. rugosa repens alba see Paulii
R. rugosa rubra, 204
R. rugosa rugosa see R. rugosa typica
R. rugosa typica, 204
R. sabinii, 141
R. sancta see R. × richardii
R. semperflorens see Slater's Crimson China
R. sempervirens, 23, 61, 310
R. serafinii, 183
R. sericea, 5
R. sericea pteracantha, 4, 93, 141, 141
R. sericea pteracantha atrosanguinea, 142

R. sertata, 213
R. setigera, 5, 6, 311
R. setipoda, 213, 213
R. sherardii, 183
R. sicula, 183
R. sinica see R. chinensis
R. sinowilsonii, 312
R. sorbiflora see R. cymosa
R. souliana, 312
R. spaldingii, 214, 214
R. spinosissima see R. pimpinellifolia
R. spinosissima nana see R. pimpinellifolia 'Nana'
R. stellata, 121
R. stellata mirifica, 51, 120, 121, 121
R. stylosa, 183
R. suffulta, 190, 214, 214
R. swenginzowii macrocarpa, 92, 214
R. tomentosa, 183
R. triphylla see R. anemoneflora
R. turkistanica see Mutabilis
R. ultramontana, 214
R. ventenatiana see R. × kamtchatica
R. villosa, 5, 5, 184, 184
R. villosa duplex, 184, 184
R. virginiana, 5, 5, 76, 92, 188, 188
R. virginiana alba see R. carolina alba
R. virginiana plena see Rose d'Amour
R. viridiflora see Viridiflora
R. × waitziana, 184
R. wardii, 214
R. webbiana, 214
R. wichuraiana, 6, 6, 24, 51, 54, 57, 59, 76, 77, 313, 313
R. willmottiae, 77, 214, 214
R. wilsonii see R. × involuta
R. woodsii, 77, 214
R. woodsii fendleri, 76, 214, 214
R. xanthina, 142
R. xanthina lindleyii, 142
R. xanthina spontanea see Canary Bird
R. yainacensis, 214
Rachel Bowes Lyon, 254
Radox Bouquet, 280, 281
Radway Sunrise, 254, 254
Ragged Robin see Gloire des Rosomanes
Rambling Rector, 61, 87, 88, 234, 234
Ramira see Agatha Christie
Ramona, 128
Raubritter, 94, 172, 172
Raymond Chenault, 194
Rayon d'Or, 35
Razzle Dazzle, 281
Rebecca Claire, 400
Red Ace, 306, 307
Red Bells, 54, 293
Red Blanket, 53, 54, 295, 295
Red Cedar see Loving Memory

Red Cherokee see Ramona
Red Coat, 254
Red Dandy, 42
Red Devil, 108, 400, 400
Red Dorothy Perkins see Excelsa
Red Druschki see Ruhm von Steinfurth
Red Favourite, 46
Red Masterpiece, 400
Red Max Graf, 295, 295
Red Moss see Henri Martin
Red Planet, 401
Red Rascal, 307
Red Riding Hood, 39
Red Robin see Gloire des Rosomanes
Red Rose of Lancaster see R. gallica officinalis
Red Star see Precious Platinum
Red Trail, 295, 295
Red Wing, 141, 142
Reeve, The, 371
Regensberg, 57, 57, 307, 307
Reine Blanche, 163
Reine Blanche see Hebe's Lip
Reine des Centfeuilles, 155
Reine des Français, 360
Reine des Iles Bourbon see Bourbon Queen
Reine des Neiges see Frau Karl Druschki
Reine des Roses see Colour Wonder
Reine des Violettes, 18, 363, 363
Reine Marguerite see Tricolore
Reine Marie Henriette, 417
Reine Olga de Wurtemberg, 342
Remember Me, 401
René André, 319
René d'Anjou, 163
Repens Meidiland, 295
Rev. F. Page-Roberts, 401
Rêve d'Or, 22, 342, 342
Réveil Dijonnais, 417, 417
Reverend H. d'Ombrain, 334
Rhonda, 243
Richmond, 39
Richmond Climbing, 417
Rimosa '79 see Gold Bunny
Rinakov see Marina, 275
Ripples, 40, 40, 281, 281
Rise 'n' Shine, 56, 307, 307
Ritter von Barmstede, 243, 243
Rival de Paestum, 349
Rivers George IV, 334
Rob Roy, 281, 281
Robert Léopold, 163, 163
Robin Hood, 228, 229
Robin Redbreast, 306, 307
Robert le Diable, 155
Robert le Diable, 155
Robusta (Bourbon), 334, 334

Robusta (Rugosa), 211
Rochester, 66
Rocket, 423
Roddy MacMillan, 401
Roger Lambelin, 363, 363
Roi des Pourpres see Rose du Roi à Fleurs Pourpres
Rosa Mundi see R. gallica versicolor
Rosabell, 281
Rose à Parfum de l'Hay, 210, 211
Rose Baby see Royal Salute
Rose Bradwardine, 182
Rose d'Amour, 188, 188
Rose d'Hivers, 168
Rose d'Isfahan see Ispahan
Rose d'Orsay, 188
Rose de l'Isle see Blush Boursault
Rose de Meaux, 155, 155
Rose de Meaux White, 155
Rose de Rescht, 170, 171
Rose des Maures see Sissinghurst Castle
Rose des Peintres, 155
Rose du Maître d'Ecole, 151, 152
Rose du Roi, 13, 13, 170, 170
Rose du Roi à Fleurs Pourpres, 170
Rose du Saint Sacrement see R. majalis plena
Rose Edouard, 14, 334
Rose Edward see Rose Edouard
Rose Gaujard, 401, 401
Rose Lelieur, 13
Rose Marie Viaud, 234
Rose of Provins see R. gallica officinalis
Rosée du Matin see Chloris
Rosemary Rose, 44, 45, 281, 281
Rosenelfe, 44, 46, 281
Rosenmärchen see Pinocchio
Roseraie de l'Hay, 7, 80, 92, 210, 211
Rosette Delizy, 17, 349
Rosier de Philippe Noisette see Noisette
Rosika see Radox Bouquet
Rosina, 56, 307
Rosy Carpet, 295
Rosy Cheeks, 401
Rosy Cushion, 295, 295
Rosy La Sevillana see Pink La Sevillana
Rosy Mantle, 24, 242, 243
Rosy Meillandia see Air France
Rote Max Graf see Red Max Graf
Rouge Eblouissante see Assemblage des Beautés
Roulettii, 55, 56, 308
Roundelay, 254, 255
Roxburghe Rose, 401
Royal Albert Hall, 401
Royal Dane see Troika
Royal Gold, 244, 244

Royal Highness, 34, 108, 401, 401
Royal Occasion, 281
Royal Romance, 401
Royal Salute, 308
Royal Smile, 37, 38, 402
Royal Velvet, 402
Royal Volunteer, 402
Royal William, 36, 402
Rubricaulis, 198
Rubrotincta see Hebe's Lip
Ruby Wedding, 402
Ruga, 216
Ruhm von Steinfurth, 363, 363
Rumba, 281
Ruskin, 211, 211
Russell's Cottage Rose see Russelliana
Russelliana, 234, 234
Rusticana see Poppy Flash
Rutland, 54, 295

Sacramento Rose, The see R. stellata mirifica
Sadler's Wells, 52, 53, 229, 229
Safrano, 17, 349
St Boniface, 282
St Bruno, 282
St Cecilia, 370
St Davids, 17
St Mark's Rose see Rose d'Amour
St Nicholas, 168, 168
Saint Prist de Breuze, 327
Saler, 163
Sally Holmes, 254, 254
San Rafael Rose see Fortune's Double Yellow
Sanders White, 24, 24, 319, 319
Sanders White Rambler see Sanders White
Sandringham Centenary, 402
Sanguinea, 12, 17, 327
Sarah Van Fleet, 211, 211
Save The Children, 281
Savoy Hotel, 32, 32, 402, 403
Scabrosa, 52, 211, 212
Scarlet Fire see Scharlachglut
Scarlet Gem, 308, 308
Scarlet Grevillei see Russelliana
Scarlet Meidiland, 295
Scarlet Pimpernel see Scarlet Gem
Scarlet Queen Elizabeth, 42, 43, 281
Scarlet Sweetbriar see La Belle Distinguée
Scented Air, 282, 282
Scharlachglut, 13, 51, 91, 152
Scherzo, 282, 282
Schloss Heidegg see Pink Meidiland
Schneelicht, 211
Schneewittchen see Iceberg and Iceberg Climber

Schneezwerg, 51, 91, 212, 213
Schoener's Nutkana, 202
Schoolgirl, 58, 244, 244
Scintillation, 172
Scotch Double Pink, 20, 137
Scotch Double White, 20, 137, 137
Scotch Rose see R. pimpinellifolia
Sea Foam, 296, 296
Sea Pearl, 42, 282
Seagull, 61, 61, 234, 235
Sealing Wax, 201
Seashell, 402
Semi-plena, 177, 177
Semperflorens see Slater's Crimson China
Sénateur Amic, 320, 322
Senator Burda see Spirit of Youth
Seven Sisters Rose see R. multiflora platyphylla
Sexy Rexy, 282, 282
Shafter see Dr Huey
Shailer's White Moss, 163
Sharifa Asma, 370, 370
Sheer Bliss, 402
Sheer Elegance, 402
Sheila's Perfume, 282
Shepherd's Delight, 42
Sheri Anne, 308, 308
Shona, 282
Shot Silk, 31, 403, 403
Shot Silk Climbing, 417
Showbiz, 282
Shropshire Lass, 255
Sidonie, 363, 363
Silhouette see Miss Harp
Silver Jubilee, 33, 33, 108, 403, 403
Silver Lining, 403, 404
Silver Moon, 128, 128
Silver Tips, 308
Silver Wedding, 404
Simba, 404
Simon Robinson, 296, 296
Single Cherry, 140, 140
Sir Basil McFarland, 44
Sir Cedric Morris, 182, 183
Sir Clough, 370
Sir Frederick Ashton, 109, 109, 404
Sir Harry Pilkington, 404
Sir Joseph Paxton, 335
Sir Thomas Lipton, 212
Sir Walter Raleigh, 370
Sissi see Blue Moon
Sissinghurst Castle, 152
Skyrocket see Wilhelm
Slater's Crimson China, 11–12, 13, 17, 328
Smarty, 54, 105, 296
Smith's Parish, 17, 17, 351
Smoky, 404
Smooth Rose see R. blanda
Snookie, 308
Snow Carpet, 54, 105, 296
Snow Dwarf see Schneezwerg
Snow Queen see Frau Karl Druschki

Snowball, 308
Snowdrift, 319
Snowdrop, 308
Snowflake, 349
Soldier Boy, 244
Soleil d'Eté see Summer Sunshine
Soleil d'Or, 30, 35, 404
Solfatare see Solfaterre
Solfaterre, 349
Sombreuil Climbing, 349, 350
Sonia, 36, 404, **404**
Sonia Meilland see Sonia
Sonnenkind see Perestroika
Sophie's Perpetual, 328, **328**
Soupert et Notting, 163
Southampton, 282, **283**
Souvenir d'Alphonse Lavallée, 364
Souvenir de Brod see Erinnerung an Brod
Souvenir de Claudius Denoyel, 418
Souvenir de Jeanne Balandreau, 364
Souvenir de la Malmaison, 14, **14**, 335, **335**
Souvenir de la Malmaison Climbing, 337
Souvenir de la Princesse de Lamballe see Bourbon Queen
Souvenir de Mme Auguste Charles, 335
Souvenir de Mme Léonie Viennot Climbing, 350
Souvenir de Philémon Cochet, 213
Souvenir de Pierre Vibert, 163
Souvenir de St Anne's, 335, 335
Souvenir d'Elise Vardon, 350
Souvenir du Docteur Jamain, 364, **364**
Souvenir du Président Carnot, 404
Souvenir d'un Ami, 350, **350**
Spanish Shawl see Sue Lawley
Sparkling Scarlet, 244
Sparrieshoop, 255
Spectabilis, 311
Spectacular see Danse de Feu
Spek's Yellow, 37, 405
Spek's Yellow Climbing, 418
Spencer, 364
Spice, 351
Spirit of Youth, 405
Splendens, 23, 216, **216**
Spong, 155, **155**

Spray Cécile Brünner see Bloomfield Abundance
Squire, The, 371
Stacey Sue, 308
Stanwell Perpetual, 20, 140, **140**
Star of Persia, 135
Star of Waltham, 364
Stargazer, 282
Starina, 308
Stars 'n' Stripes, 308
Stella, 405
Strawberry Ice, 282
Striped Masquerade, 308
Striped Moss, 163, **163**
Sue Lawley, 44, 284
Sue Ryder, 284
Suffolk, 54, 296, **296**
Sulphur Rose, The see R. hemisphaerica
Suma, 55, 296
Summer Dream, 405
Summer Fashion, 284
Summer Sunshine, 405
Summer Wind, 255
Summer Wine, 244
Summerwind see Surrey
Sun Flare, 405
Sunblaze, 105, 309
Sunblest, 405, **405**
Sunbright, 405
Sunfire, 284
Sunny see Sunblaze
Sunny Meillandina see Sunblaze
Sunny South, 405
Sunset Song, 405
Sunsilk, 284
Sunsprite see Korresia
Super Star, 37, 405, **406**
Super Star Climbing, 418
Super Sun, 406, **407**
Surpasse Tout, 152, **152**
Surpassing Beauty, 364
Surrey, 54, **54**, 296, **296**
Susan Ann see Southampton
Susan Hampshire, 406, **406**
Sussex, 296, **296**
Sutter's Gold, 34, 62, 406, **406**
Sutter's Gold Climbing, 418
Swamp Rose, The see R. palustris
Swan, 370
Swan Lake, **243**, 245
Swany, 54, **81**, 297, **297**
Sweet Briar see R. eglanteria
Sweet Dream, 309, **309**
Sweet Fairy, 309
Sweet Juliet, 370
Sweet Magic, 42, 309
Sweet Promise see Sonia
Sweet Repose, 44
Sweet Surrender, 406
Sweetheart, 406

Sweetheart Rose, The see Cécile Brünner
Sylvia see Congratulations
Sympathie, 245
Symphony, 63, 371

Talisman, 406
Talisman Climbing, 418
Tall Story, 54, 297
Tallyho, 406
Tanamola see La Paloma '85
Tanbakede see Baby Masquerade
Tango, 284, **284**
Taora, 284, **284**
Tapis de Soie see Wee Man
Tapis Persan see Eyepaint
Tausendschön, 235
Tea Rambler, 60, **60**, **234**, 235
Tear Drop, 309
Temple Bells, 54, 297
Tempo, 245
Tenerife, 406
Tequila Sunrise, 406
Texas Centennial, 408
Thaïs, 408
Thalia, 60, 235
Thelma, 319
Thérèse Bugnet, 213, **213**
Thisbe, **228**, 229
Thoresbyana see Bennett's Seedling
Thousand Beauties see Tausendschön
Threepenny Bit Rose see R. farrieri persetosa
Tiffany, 408
Tigris, 118, **119**
Till Uhlenspiegel, 255
Times Rose, The, 45, 284, **284**
Tip Top, 46, 284
Tipo Ideale see Mutabilis
Tipsy Imperial Concubine, 12, 13, 350
Titania see Perla de Alcañada
Tom Thumb see Peon
Top Gear see Little Artist
Topsi, 284
Toque Rouge see Ace of Hearts
Torvill & Dean, 408
Touch of Class, 408
Tour de Malakoff, 156
Toy Clown, 309
Tranquillity, 408
Traumland see Dreamland
Treasure Trove, 219
Tricolore, 152
Tricolore de Flandre, 152
Trier, 41, 235
Trigintipetala see Kazanlik
Trinity, 17, 352, **352**

Triomphe de Laffay, 328
Triomphe de Luxembourg, 350
Troika, 408
Troilus, 371
Tropicana see Super Star
True Love see Yorkshire Bank
Trumpeter, 285
Turner's Crimson see Crimson Rambler
Tuscany, 152
Tuscany Superb, 40, 152, **152**
Typhoon, 408

Uetersen, 255, 256
Ulrich Brunner see Ulrich Brunner Fils
Ulrich Brunner Fils, 18, 364
Uncle Bill, 408, **409**
Uncle Walter, 256, **256**
Unique Blanche see White Provence

Valentine Heart, 285, **285**
Vanguard, 213, **213**
Vanity, 22, 229, **229**
Variegata di Bologna, 335
Veilchenblau, **22**, 60, 95, 235, **235**
Velutinaeflora, 153
Velvet Hour, **408**, 409
Venusta Pendula, 217, **217**
Vick's Caprice, 364, **364**
Vicomtesse Pierre du Fou, 418
Victor Hugo, 364
Victor Hugo see Spirit of Youth
Victor Verdier, 364
Vienna Charm, 409
Vierge de Cléry see White Provence
Village Maid, 156, **156**
Vincent Godsiff, 352, **352**
Violet Carson, 285
Violette, 236, **236**
Violinista Costa, 409, **409**
Virgo, 409
Virgo Liberationem see Virgo
Viridiflora, 328, **328**
Vital Spark, 285
Viva, 285
Vivid, 335, **335**

Wapiti see Laurence Olivier
Warm Welcome, **244**, 245
Warrior, 285
Warwick Castle, **367**, 371
Warwickshire, 297, **297**
Wedding Day, 312

Wee Jock, 309, **309**
Wee Man, 309
Weisse Immensee see Partridge
Weisse Max Graf see White Max Graf
Wendy see Pour Toi
Wendy Cussons, 409, **410**
Wenlock, 371
Westcoast see Penthouse
Westerland, 68
Wheatcroft's Baby Crimson see Perla de Alcañada
Whisky Mac, 37, 409, **410**
Whisky Mac Climbing, 418
White American Beauty see Frau Karl Druschki
White Baby Rambler see Katharina Zeimet
White Bath, 164, **164**
White Bells, 54, 297, **297**
White Cockade, 24, 58, **244**, 245
White Cover see Kent
White Flight, 236
White Grootendorst, 213
White Hermosa see Snowflake
White Knight see Message
White La France see Augustine Guinnoisseau
White Maman Cochet, 17, **347**
White Masterpiece, 410
White Max Graf, 297, **297**
White Meidiland, 297
White Meillandina see Yorkshire Sunblaze
White Moss see White Bath
White Pet, **82**, **94**, 285, **285**
White Provence, 156
White Queen Elizabeth, 285
White Rambler see Thalia
White Rose of York see Maxima
White Rose of York see R. × alba
White Spray, 256
White Wings, 410, **410**
Whitsuntide Rose see R. majalis plena
Wickmoss, 319
Wickwar, 313
Wiener Charme see Vienna Charm
Wife of Bath, **372**, 373
Wild Flower, 256
Wilhelm, 68, 229, **229**
Will Alderman, 213
Will Scarlet, 229, **229**
Willhire Country, 285, **285**
William Allen Richardson, 16, 342
William and Mary, 52, 53, 256, **256**

William Baffin, 194, **194**
William Lobb, **9**, 164, **164**
William R. Smith, 350
William Shakespeare, 373, 373
William III, 140
Winchester Cathedral, 373, 373
Wind Chimes, 236
Windrush, 256
Wintoniensis, 201
Wisbech Gold, 410
Wise Portia, 373
Wishing, 285
With Love, 410
Woburn Abbey, 286
Wolly Dodd's Rose see R. villosa duplex
Woolverstone Church Rose see Surpassing Beauty

Xavier Olibo, 365
Xerxes, 118

Yellow Banksia see R. banksiae lutea
Yellow Button, 373
Yellow Cécile Brünner see Perle d'Or
Yellow Charles Austin, 373
Yellow Doll, 310
Yellow Meillandina see Yellow Sunblaze
Yellow Queen Elizabeth, 286
Yellow Rambler see Aglaia
Yellow Sunblaze, 310
Yellow Sweetheart see Rosina
Yellow Tausendschön see Madeleine Selzer
Yeoman, The, 371
Yesterday, 105, 108, 256, 256
Yolande d'Aragon, 365, **365**
York and Lancaster, 168, **168**
Yorkshire Bank, 410
Yorkshire Sunblaze, 310, **310**
Young Mistress see Regensberg
Yvonne Rabier, 44, **285**, 286

Zambra, 44, 286
Zenobia, 164
Zéphirine Drouhin, 14, 58, 337, 338
Zigeunerknabe see Gipsy Boy
Zoe, 164
Zwergkönig see Dwarfking